The Tapestry of Culture

AN INTRODUCTION TO CULTURAL ANTHROPOLOGY

The Tapestry of Culture

AN INTRODUCTION TO CULTURAL ANTHROPOLOGY

EIGHTH EDITION

Abraham Rosman

Professor Emeritus
Barnard College, Columbia University

Paula G. Rubel

Professor Emerita
Barnard College, Columbia University

Boston   Burr Ridge, IL   Dubuque, IA   Madison, WI   New York
San Francisco   St. Louis   Bangkok   Bogotá   Caracas   Kuala Lumpur
Lisbon   London   Madrid   Mexico City   Milan   Montreal   New Delhi
Santiago   Seoul   Singapore   Sydney   Taipei   Toronto

The *McGraw·Hill* Companies

THE TAPESTRY OF CULTURE: AN INTRODUCTION TO CULTURAL ANTHROPOLOGY

1 2 3 4 5 6 7 8 9 0 FGR/FGR 0 9 8 7 6 5 4 3

ISBN   0-07-283025-5

Publisher: *Phillip A. Butcher*
Sponsoring editor: *Kevin Witt*
Developmental editor: *Pamela Gordon*
Senior marketing manager: *Daniel M. Loch*
Media producer: *Shannon Gattens*
Project manager: *Destiny Rynne*
Production supervisor: *Janean A. Utley*
Design manager: *Laurie Entringer*
Lead supplement producer: *Marc Mattson*
Photo research coordinator: *Nora Agbayani*
Art manager: *Robin Mouat*
Photo researcher: *Inge King*
Art director: *Jeanne M. Schreiber*
Cover design: *Oxygen Design*
Interior design: *Laurie Entringer*
Typeface: *10.5/12 Times New Roman*
Compositor: *Carlisle Communications Ltd.*
Printer: *Quebecor World Fairfield Inc.*

Library of Congress Cataloging-in-Publication Data

Rosman, Abraham,
    The tapestry of culture : an introduction to cultural anthropology / Abraham Rosman and
Paula G. Ruble.--8th ed.
        p. cm.
    ISBN 0-07-283025-5 (softcover : alk. paper)
    1. Ethnology. I. Rubel, Paula G. II. Title.
GN316.R67 2004
306--dc21

                                                                                    2003051236

www.mhhe.com

To the Memory of Daniel

CONTENTS IN BRIEF

CONTENTS

3 Language and Culture   51

4 Learning Language and Culture: Culture and the Individual   73

PREFACE

The Story of the Book

The book had its genesis because we both taught introductory anthropology at Barnard College, Columbia University to several generations of undergraduate students of different ages, as well as those senior citizens who participated in the University's Life Long Learner Program. We both had developed a style of teaching by means of which we wanted to communicate the concepts and theories of anthropology succinctly, then have students read ethnographies, which are the heart of anthropology. We found that the textbooks available were too lengthy or inadequate to the task. Furthermore, at Columbia University a tradition existed in which senior faculty wrote their own texts, emphasizing their own theoretical approaches, when they taught introductory anthropology. So we, too, set about writing our introduction to the subject. The first edition of *The Tapestry of Culture* was issued more than 20 years ago. Since that time, the theoretical framework of anthropology has changed greatly, as has our own theoretical perspective, and the successive editions of the book have reflected these changes.

In the past decade, the lives of people scattered over the world have undergone enormous change. At the same time, American anthropology has also changed drastically, responding to scholarly and political influences as well as changing generations. The influence of postmodernism has created a much more contested and fragmented anthropology than that of 30 years ago. However, in our opinion, it is unfair to introduce students to a field of study like anthropology, which is inherently very appealing, by pointing out its disjointed, fragmented character. It would be equally unfair to imply that a single, unified, agreed-upon point of view exists.

Hallmark Features

The Tapestry of Culture adopts a distinctive approach to anthropology, which attempts to accommodate various viewpoints in anthropology today. It examines cultural differences but also seeks to point out cultural similarities that emerge as a result of comparative study. The approach also emphasizes the interpretation of symbols and the meaning of things. The task of the book is to translate the concepts, ideas, and behavior of other cultures into our culture's terms. Today the trend is to see every ethnography as a description of a unique society, not comparable to any other. However, beyond each society's uniqueness, the presence of cultural similarities is apparent and compelling. From its inception, anthropology has always been comparative, enabling generalizations to be made about human behavior. Formerly, anthropologists generalized about the nature of rules of residence and kinship terminology, but, at present, generalizations may deal, for example, with the nature of ethnic group behavior and the role religion plays in many instances of ethnic conflict. In this edition of *The Tapestry of Culture*, we discuss many different kinds of generalizations.

Postmodernists pay particular attention to the nature of ethnographic texts, and anthropologists today still consider ethnographies, that is, descriptions of unique societies based on field research, the heart of the discipline. One of the best ways for students to be introduced to anthropology is by reading ethnographies so that they can feel the excitement of a first-rate fieldworker engaged in his or her work. Seeing the Trobriand Islands through Bronislaw Malinowski's eyes as he describes them in *Argonauts of the Western Pacific* conveys to the students Malinowski's feeling of being a castaway on a strange shore and his sense of adventure and discovery, in addition to informing them about Trobriand culture, as it was at the turn of the twentieth century. However, students must be provided with the concepts and theories that anthropologists use in order to understand and appreciate such ethnographies and to comprehend the differences between a society like the Trobriands and our own.

Students need a framework for the critical evaluation of ethnographies such as Malinowski's. *The Tapestry of Culture* provides a concise and up-to-date conceptual framework with which to understand not only classic ethnographies but also the ethnographies about complex societies being written today. In teaching introductory anthropology, we ourselves have used studies of groups like the Yanomamo of the South American tropical forest, a small-scale society being forced to adapt to the modern world, as well as those describing aspects of industrialized societies, such as the multiethnic neighborhoods of Philadelphia. *The Tapestry of Culture* is organized so that it can be used with the particular ethnographies that suit the instructor's interests.

The title of our book refers to culture metaphorically as a tapestry, composed of many interconnected threads, in which the whole is more than the sum of its parts. Standing back from the tapestry, one no longer sees the individual threads, but an overall design. The anthropologist does not see "culture," the overall design of the tapestry, while doing fieldwork. Rather, he or she converses with individuals and observes their actions; this is the equivalent of the threads. From this, the anthropologist, collaborating with members of the culture, creates a picture of that culture which results in the ethnography. Therefore, culture is an analytical concept, an abstraction from reality. Like a tapestry, each culture has an overall design, even though we do take it apart and study it, by employing categories such as kinship, economics, and religion, and then examine the interconnections between the parts. However, the fit between the parts, in reality is always far from perfect and there are always disjunctions and contradictions. In today's globally connected world, the disjunctions and contradictions often dominate the picture of a particular culture, including our own.

New to the Eighth Edition

We have passed into a new millennium and are in the twenty-first century. During the past century, the world changed more than it had in the previous 5,000 years. Anthropology, as the study of humans and their ways of life, has the task of understanding the ways in which people bring about changes in their cultures, deal with these changes, and try to understand them. Ethnicity and ethnic identity are crucial issues in the world today. Nation-states and empires have fractured. People of different ethnic groups who lived together in one state and even intermarried are now fiercely at war with one another. Technological advances in many fields have brought about great changes in industrial societies like our own. Automation has made many earlier types of employment obsolete, but not everyone controls the skills to ride the information superhighway. These changes have required the rethinking of the economic organization of modern industrial societies. Technology has even overtaken and transformed human reproduction and required new ways of thinking about motherhood, fatherhood, and parenting. Ideas about gender and gender role are being reformulated, with significant consequences for family organization. Anthropology today has had to come to grips with these various issues, as have we in this eighth edition of *The Tapestry of Culture*.

In the last few years, we have traveled a great deal in distant parts of the globe, which has given us a firsthand look at the momentous changes that are taking place. We have observed how Pushtuns respond to religious fundamentalism in the Swat region of Pakistan. We have watched the way in which many Mongolian families have returned to nomadic pastoralism as their nation detached itself from the former Soviet empire and its industrial collapse. We have seen how globalization affects Burmese (Myanmarese) market towns, where tribal people still maintain their own identities vis-à-vis the majority Burmese. While the technological, economic, and political spheres are undergoing dizzying changes around them, these particular people are clinging to clan and tribal identities.

In this eighth edition, as is our usual practice, we have added a great deal of new material and made discussions and examples in every chapter more current, in accord with present-day thinking in the anthropological literature. In this Preface, we will discuss only the major changes to the text to be found in the eighth edition. Though some issues have been with us since the beginnings of the discipline, contemporary commentators and critics within and outside anthropology have compelled us to confront them anew.

Chapter 1, which deals with the concept of culture, the nature of cultural rules, cultural universals, and contemporary approaches to anthropological theory, has a new section devoted to cooking and its relationship to the evolution of culture. The discovery of fire enabled early hominids to transform raw foods—grasses and tubers—into cooked food, paralleling Lévi-Strauss's discussion of the raw and the cooked. There is a new section in Chapter 3, "Language and Culture," entitled "World Englishes and the Global Spread of English." It describes the way in which English spread as a consequence of colonial expansion, and the later and more recent spread of English as a consequence of globalization and the development of a world market.

Chapter 5 has been retitled as "Symbolic Meanings." We have enlarged the discussion of the relationship between the caste system and food symbolism, including material on the Newar of Nepal. There is a new section entitled "Body Symbolism," which deals with the way in which some societies prefer plumpness in women and other societies, such as our own, prefer women who are thin. The symbolism of organ donation is also considered. "Ties That Connect: Marriage, Family, and Kinship" is the new title of Chapter 6. It includes two new sections. The first, "The Na: A Society without Marriage or Fathers" concerns a matrilineal society in Southwest China, which is under pressure from the Chinese government to conform to the patrilineal descent rules that characterize the Han who are the majority of the Chinese population. The second is entitled, "The Impact of Biological Technologies on Kinship" and deals with the effects of these new technologies and the Human Genome Project on ideas of parenthood and kinship.

Chapter 8 has been retitled, "Production, Distribution, and Consumption: The Economic Organization of Societies." It includes several new sections in the light of the enormous economic changes that have taken place on a global level. It deals with the way in which hunters and gatherers, agriculturalists, and nomadic pastoralists are adapting to these global changes. The new sections are entitled, "How Contemporary Hunters and Gatherers Have Adapted to the Modern World?" "Agriculture in Today's World," "Can Nomadic Pastoralism Be Maintained Today?" "Capitalism and the Market System," and "The Changing Nature of Consumption in Third World Societies." The section, "Barter," now includes a discussion of the increased use of barter in present day Russia, that has replaced, in part, a monetary and banking system that people no longer trust.

We have retitled Chapter 9 as "Politics, Government, Law, and Conflict." The section formerly entitled "Politics in the Contemporary Nation-State" has been broken down into subsections that concern politics in American society, the Mafia, factionalism, empowerment, patron-client relationships, and politics in the postcolonial period. We have included two new sections titled "Warlords" and the "Anthropology of Violence." In Chapter 10, "Religion and the Supernatural," some of the sections have been reworked, and we have added a new section entitled "Cyperspace and Religion: Give Me That Online Religion," which concerns religious practices like the Jewish Seder which have moved "online."

Chapter 11 has been retitled "Myths, Legends, and Folkltales: Past, Present and Future." It includes new sections—"The Sopranos: An American Myth," in which this TV program is analyzed to demonstrate America's love affair with the Mafia, and "Legend Becomes History: King Arthur and the Knights of the Round Table," which illustrates how archeological and manuscript material has been used to show that King Arthur really existed. New sections have been created on "Fairy Tales," "American Films as Legends and Myths," and "Urban Legends".

Chapters 13 and Chapters 14 have been reorganized and there is a new Chapter 15. Chapter 13 is now entitled "The Colonial and Post-Colonial Worlds: Globalization and the Role Anthropologists Have Played in Directed Cultural Change" and it includes sections on "The Historical Background to Globalization: The Colonial Period," "New Ireland: An Example of Increasing Incorporation into the Global System," and "Applied Anthropology: What Is the Anthropologist's Role in Directed Culture Change?" Chapter 14, entitled "Migration, Diasporas, and Cultural Identity Reasserted" contains sections on "Internal Migration," "Transmigration," "Cultural Identity Reasserted and Transformed," "Revitalization Movements," "Cargo Cults," "Rebuilding Cultural Identity," "Ethnogenesis," and "Ethnonationalism." An entirely new section has also been added, "Blood, Culture and Race," which discusses how the Cherokee have used the concept of blood connection to reassert their cultural identity.

Chapter 15 is entitled "Ethnicity, Ethnic Conflict, Race, and Nationalism: Abroad and at Home." It includes sections on "Nation-Building," "Ethnicity and Nationalism after Communism," "Ethnic Processes in Sri Lanka," "From Melting Pot to Multiculturalism in the United States," "The Mexican-American Transformation in Texas," "Culture Unassimilated, Reiterated, and Renewed in America," "African Americans and Their Heritage," and "Hyphenated Cultures." Several sections of this chapter pick up the theme of violence, which was introduced in Chapter 9, and discuss how ethnicity, race, and religion combine to produce ethnic violence in Chechnya, Georgia, and Sri Lanka. New sections, "Ethnic Differences, Ethnic Violence, and the New Nation of Afghanistan" and "African-Americans on the Sea Islands of Georgia: The Gullah" have also been added. The Epilogue reiterates the central themes of the book.

Important new pedagogical and presentation changes have been introduced in the text content and the design of the eighth edition of *The Tapestry of Culture*. They include new end-of-chapter materials—bulleted summaries, increased number of headings, focus on key terms, suggested readings, and websites related to the chapter. The design of the book is intended to make the book aesthetically more attractive and approachable, to help the student focus his or her attention on key ideas and concepts.

Supplements

As a full-service publisher of quality educational products, McGraw-Hill does much more than just sell textbooks. They create and publish an extensive array of supplements for students and instructors. *The Tapestry of Culture* boasts a comprehensive supplements package. Orders of new (versus used) textbooks help to defray the cost of developing such supplements, which is substantial. Please consult your local McGraw-Hill representative for more information on any of supplements.

For the Student

The Student's Website (by Maxine Weisgrau)—This free web-based, student supplement features a large number of helpful tools, interactive exercises, links and useful information at www.mhhe.com/rosman8. Designed specifically to complement the individual chapters of the text, students access material by text chapter.

- Internet Activities—Offer chapter related links to World Wide Web related sites and activities for students to complete based on the sites.
- Chapter learning objectives—Designed to give students signposts for understanding and recognizing key chapter content.
- Multiple choice, matching, true/false and short answer questions—Give students the opportunity to quiz themselves on chapter content.
- Glossary—Illustrates key terms.
- Audio Glossary—Helps students with difficult to pronounce words through audio pronunciation help.
- General Web links—Offer chapter-by-chapter links for further research.
- Career opportunities—Offers students related links to useful information on careers in anthropology.

The McGraw-Hill Anthropology Supersite—Available at *http://www.mhhe.com/ anthrosupersite*, this comprehensive, one-stop supersite provides links to book-specific McGraw-Hill websites, anthropology web links, student tutorials, breaking news in anthropology, and timely, chapter-by-chapter updates of selected McGraw-Hill anthropology textbooks.

For the Instructor

The Instructor's Resource CD-ROM (by Maxine Weisgrau)—This easy-to-use disk provides:

- Chapter highlights—offer comprehensive reviews of chapter material for easy reference.
- Key terms—provide a complete list of important terms in each chapter with definitions.
- Discussion topics/essay questions—provide ideas for classroom discussion sections, lectures and exam questions.

- Films and videos for classroom use—provides an annotated list of useful films.
- A computerized test bank—Offers numerous multiple choice questions and matching exercises in an easy-to-use program that is available for both Windows and Macintosh computers.

The Instructor's Website (by Maxine Weisgrau)—This password-protected site offers access to all of the student online materials plus important instructor support materials and downloadable supplements such as:

- An online versions of the resources available in the Instructor's Resource CD-ROM—Gives professors easy access to these useful aids. Note the computerized test bank is not available online for security reasons.
- Links to professional resources—Provides useful links to professional anthropological sites on the World Wide Web.

PageOut: The Course Website Development Center—All online content for the text is supported by WebCT, Blackboard, eCollege.com, and other course management systems. Additionally, McGraw-Hill's PageOut service is available to get professors and their courses up and running online in a matter of hours, at no cost. PageOut was designed for instructors just beginning to explore web options. Even a novice computer user can create a course website with a template provided by McGraw-Hill (no programming knowledge necessary). To learn more about PageOut, visit *www.mhhe.com/pageout.*

The McGraw-Hill Anthropology Supersite—Available at *http://www.mhhe.com/ anthrosupersite*, this comprehensive, one-stop supersite provides links to book-specific McGraw-Hill web sites, anthropology web links, instructor downloads, breaking news in anthropology, and timely, chapter-by-chapter updates of selected McGraw-Hill anthropology textbooks.

Videotapes—A wide variety of full-length videotapes from the *Films for the Humanities and Sciences* series is available to qualified adopters of the text. Please contact your McGraw-Hill representative for qualifications and conditions.

Acknowledgments

This new edition could not have been written without assistance from many people. First of all, we would like to thank the many students in our introductory anthropology classes who, over the years, have asked us many penetrating questions. We have always learned from our students and have been continuously in their debt. We are especially grateful to the professors who have continued to use *The Tapestry of Culture* in their introductory anthropology courses and who have given us their pithy comments and observations. To these individuals and all the others who have helped us in the past, we owe a debt of gratitude for raising questions that have contributed to a significant improvement in the organization and clarity of this book. We would like to especially thank our friend and fellow anthropologist Aram A. Yengoyan for his thoughtful comments and many suggestions. We must also mention and thank the following reviewers, who offered many valuable comments and suggestions for this eighth edition:

Claire Cesareo Silva, Saddleback College

Margot Nason, Northern Arizona University

Loretta Morris, Loyola Marymount University

Mathea Cremers, University of California, Santa Barbara

Larry Naylor, University of North Texas

We would also like to thank Pamela Gordon and Kevin Witt for their encouragement and help in producing this edition. Finally, our thanks to Phil Butcher for his continuing support of *The Tapestry of Culture* through several editions.

Abraham Rosman

Paula G. Rubel

ABOUT THE AUTHORS

ABRAHAM ROSMAN received a Ph.D. in anthropology from Yale University. His first fieldwork was with the Kanuri of Bornu Province, in northern Nigeria. He has taught at Vassar College, Antioch College, and Barnard College Columbia University, where he taught Introduction to Cultural Anthropology as well as many other courses for many years. He is now professor emeritus.

PAULA G. RUBEL has a Ph.D. in anthropology from Columbia University. She carried out fieldwork on the Kalmyk Mongol refugees who settled in New Jersey and Philadelphia in 1950. Her doctoral dissertation was published as *The Kalmyk Mongols: A Study in Continuity and Change.* She has taught Introduction to Cultural Anthropology as well as many other courses at the undergraduate and the graduate level at Barnard College, Columbia University, where she is now professor emerita.

Abraham Rosman and Paula Rubel began their collaboration in 1971 when they published *Feasting with Mine Enemy,* a comparative study of the potlatch in six Northwest Coast societies. They have done fieldwork together in Iran, Afghanistan, and Papua New Guinea, and in 1978 they published *Your Own Pigs You May Not Eat: A Comparative Study of New Guinea Societies.* They have also published many articles on their fieldwork and comparative research. Their later fieldwork in New Ireland, Papua New Guinea, and their research on the nineteenth-century collecting of ethnographic artifacts have been the basis for several recent articles. They have just edited a volume, *Translating Cultures: Perspectives on Translation and Anthropology,* and are currently working on a volume on the "collecting passion" in America.

1

Anthropological Perspectives

Anthropology informs us about other peoples, and in the process we learn about ourselves. The anthropologist's methods are different from that of other social scientists, and that difference influences the nature of the discipline—its concepts, procedures, and theories. Anthropological research involves a journey—a journey in space, a journey through time, a psychological journey into an alien world. Anthropological investigation of a way of life other than one's own may seem at first like a trip through the looking glass into Alice's wonderland, into another universe where people behave in very different ways, and the rules may be turned on their heads. Though, over the years, novelists and science fiction writers have been drawn to such journeys into different worlds, the anthropologist's journey is different. Fiction writers usually never leave home and merely imagine the far-off place about which they are writing. They have a variety of points of view, which are very personal, but are politically and culturally informed, ranging from the "heart of darkness" to the "noble savage." In contrast, the anthropologist must abandon the prejudices of his or her own society and suspend its cultural rules, learn the way of life of the society being studied, and then return to tell "its story." By doing this, the anthropologist has put himself or herself in the position of being the "authority" about that society. Some have called the gathering, analysis, and publication of information about the society which the anthropologist has studied an "appropriation" of their culture.

Anthropologists refer to the way of life of a people, with all its variation, as their culture. Like the world through the looking glass, each culture has an underlying logic of its own. The behavior of people makes sense once we understand the basic premises by which they live. The anthropologist's task is to translate cultures and their premises to make them understandable in terms of the ideas of our society.

From the beginning, human beings have always moved or traveled beyond the borders of the area they called home. This was the means by which Homo sapiens eventually peopled most of the earth. The process of globalization has brought American culture in the form of Pepsi Cola and McDonald's menus to the most

Among the Tuareg of the central Sahara, it is the men who wear the veil.

remote parts of the world, but a traveler to distant places is still impressed with differences between cultures. Many Chinese people eat dogs and sea cucumbers, but Americans do not consider such creatures to be food. People in every culture think that what they eat is "the right stuff." Veiling is another cultural feature shared by some societies but not our own. In some societies women veil, but in Tuareg society, it is the men who veil. The belief that one's own culture represents the best way to do things is known as **ethnocentrism.** Ethnocentrism emphasizes the pride a group has in its cultural accomplishments, its historical achievements, the supremacy of its religious beliefs, and the god-given virtues of its sexual and culinary practices. Ethnocentrism also includes the idea that other peoples' (often one's closest neighbors') beliefs, customs, and practices are like those of "animals." Ethnocentrism is at the root of ethnic conflict and ethnonationalism, so prevalent in the world today. Ethnocentrism will be explored in Chapter 15.

Anthropology is the study of the world of cultural differences. It examines cultural practices within their own larger cultural contexts. **Cultural relativism** is the idea that each culture is unique and distinctive but that no one culture is superior. This is in sharp contrast to the ethnocentric point of view that one's own culture is superior to all others. Given cultural relativism, how does one deal with the question of morality, that is, good and evil? On the one hand, there are those who believe that killing another human being should be universally condemned.

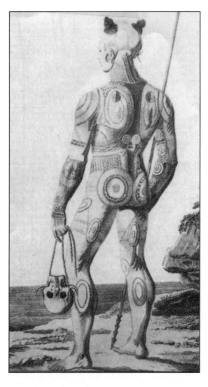

Tattooed Marquesan youth holding a trophy head taken from an enemy, depicted in the account of Langsdorff's voyages published in 1804.

On the other hand, there are cultural relativists who argue that killing within ceremonial or ritual contexts like, head-hunting and cannibalism in the past, was a core feature of societies in which it occurred. For instance, the Marquesans were cannibals and took trophy heads, as described by Melville in *Typee* (see illustration). A doctrine of universal human rights, which emphasizes the rights of the individual over those of the community, would condemn such killings. Those supporting universal human rights say community-supported genital mutilation and arranged marriages, which are found in many parts of the world, are violations of the rights of the individual. Many citizens of the United States feel that the death penalty as practiced here, but renounced by practically all Western countries, is a violation of the universal moral principle that no on has the right to take the life of another human being except God. This conflict over the death penalty becomes an issue when the United States attempts to extradite an alleged criminal to face the death penalty from a foreign country that has renounced it. Today there is an ongoing debate between supporters of a universal morality and supporters of moral relativism. Subjects like the death penalty or abortion are widely discussed in our own society today.

What cultures have in common is frequently revealed when anthropologists focus on cultural differences. In addition, anthropologists can utilize the **comparative approach** to compare cultures, which identifies fundamental similarities of cultural

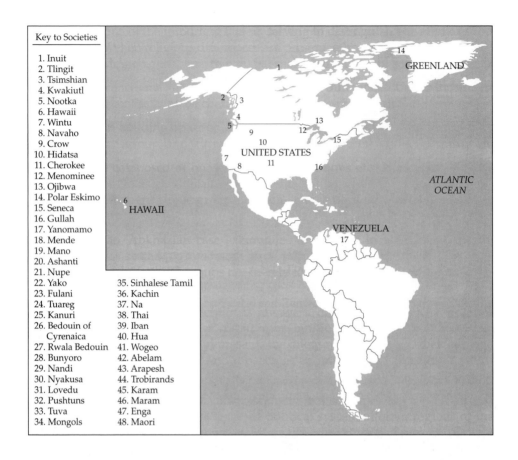

Key to Societies

1. Inuit
2. Tlingit
3. Tsimshian
4. Kwakiutl
5. Nootka
6. Hawaii
7. Wintu
8. Navaho
9. Crow
10. Hidatsa
11. Cherokee
12. Menominee
13. Ojibwa
14. Polar Eskimo
15. Seneca
16. Gullah
17. Yanomamo
18. Mende
19. Mano
20. Ashanti
21. Nupe
22. Yako
23. Fulani
24. Tuareg
25. Kanuri
26. Bedouin of
    Cyrenaica
27. Rwala Bedouin
28. Bunyoro
29. Nandi
30. Nyakusa
31. Lovedu
32. Pushtuns
33. Tuva
34. Mongols

35. Sinhalese Tamil
36. Kachin
37. Na
38. Thai
39. Iban
40. Hua
41. Wogeo
42. Abelam
43. Arapesh
44. Trobirands
45. Karam
46. Maram
47. Enga
48. Maori

patterning as well as differences. For example, until World War II, the Rwala Bedouin of the Saudi Arabian desert depended primarily on their camel herds for subsistence. Until the Russian Revolution, the Kazaks, in what is now Kazakstan, relied on their herds of horses in the grassland steppe environment where they lived. Despite the fact that the environments they inhabited were totally different (desert as compared to grasslands) as well as the animals they herded, the Rwala Bedouin and the Kazaks shared a number of cultural features. They both moved with their animals from place to place over fixed migration routes during the year in order to provide pasture. They lived in similar sorts of communities, nomadic encampments consisting of several groups of people, related by kinship, each with its own tent. They depended on exchanging the products of their herds (such as milk, butter, cheese, and hides) with townspeople for commodities, such as flour and tea, that they could not provide for themselves. Because of the basic similarities in the ways of life of the Rwala Bedouin and the Kazaks, anthropologists characterize them both as a type of society called **nomadic pastoralist.** As nomadic pastoralists, both societies had lifestyles and community structures similarly constructed around a yearly cycle of movement with their herds. But cultural differences existed

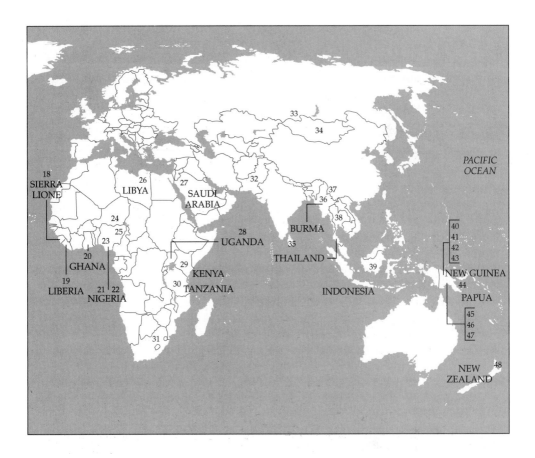

between the Rwala and the Kazak. They spoke totally different languages belonging to unrelated language families and had different beliefs and practices.

CULTURE

The central concept of anthropology is **culture,** which consists of the things people
make, their behavior, their beliefs and ideas. Anthropologists have differing definitions of what constitutes culture. Some have focused upon culture as a set of
ideas and meanings that people use, derived from the past and reshaped in the
present. In this view, historically transmitted patterns of meaning are embodied in
symbols, by means of which humans communicate, perpetuate, and develop their
knowledge about, and attitudes toward, life. The role of the anthropologist, then,
is to grasp, comprehend, and translate those ideas and meanings so people of other
groups may understand them. Other anthropologists, influenced by ideas about
biological evolution, in particular, by evolutionary psychology, see culture as the
means by which human beings adapt to their environment. They argue that the

repertoire of cultural traits of a particular group must have been the result of evolutionary selection. This repertoire of cultural traits is adaptive; otherwise, it would not have been perpetuated. However, not all traits selected for are adaptive. According to evolutionary selection, individuals with adaptive cultural traits are reproductively successful, produce more offspring, and flourish, while those with cultural traits that are not adaptive die out. This perspective emphasizes what humans have in common with other animal species, each of which is adapted to its environment.

Other disciplines, besides anthropology, study the different kinds of human activities in all societies, but each discipline studies a specific sector of this activity. Thus, economists study aspects of the economy like the gross national product or the stock exchange. Political scientists study how laws are enacted. Art historians study the works of Rembrandt. Musicologists study Mozart's symphonies. Religious specialists study Luther's role in the Reformation. Each of these disciplines focuses on particular kinds of activities of humans as if those activities were largely autonomous. Up until recently, the focus of these fields was upon the products of Western industrialized societies. The anthropologist investigates all of these fields, but the emphasis is on their interrelationship. Anthropology's holistic approach uses culture as an organizing concept and stresses the relationship among economics, politics, art, religion, and other activities.

Professionals from other disciplines are now paying attention to the concept of culture. The World Bank employs anthropologists to do research because its leaders recognize that cultural ideas and meanings provide the important context which must be understood in order to solve economic problems (Schweder, 2001: 438). Cultural Studies, which has appeared on the academic stage in recent years, uses a concept of culture that is primarily oriented toward literary concerns and is really remote from the anthropological concept of culture.

Cultures should not be conceived of as separate bounded entities. Many individuals live their lives in a world of overlapping cultures. The Navajo, who have been studied by generations of anthropologists, still retain their Navajo identity even though they are part of a much larger complex culture, American culture, participating in the larger American economy and political system. Most Navajo are bilingual, speaking the Navajo language and English. They retain elements of their Navajo belief system and practice many Navajo rituals. Within the Navajo population, there is considerable cultural variation among individuals, between communities, and between regions. Navajo people have always been very receptive to new cultural ideas. The practice of herding sheep, the weaving of blankets, and the manufacture of silver jewelry, so central to Navajo culture today, were introduced by the Spanish at the time of their conquest of the New World. Though the Navajo adopted these arts from the Spanish, the styles they use are distinctively Navajo. But earlier, the Navajo chose not to adopt the horticulture of their neighbors, the Hopi and Zuni. What emerges from the Navajo experience is an awareness that culture as a concept exists at many levels—the individual, the community, and the larger society or political entity. Cultures do not exist with fixed boundaries; they blend into one another. Changes are constantly taking place in culture. Lastly, individuals are not simply recipients of culture; they are active participants involved in reworking their cultures and their traditions. This is characterized as **agency.**

All cultures have a certain degree of internal consistency. We have called this book *The Tapestry of Culture* because the imagery of a tapestry aptly conveys the integrated nature of culture. Many strands, many colors, many patterns contribute to the overall design of a tapestry, just as many items of behavior and many customs form patterns that, in turn, compose a culture. However, patterns and regularities of culture do not remain eternally the same but, rather, change through time. Every significant new invention—like the electric light bulb, the telephone, the automobile, and the computer—has resulted in major changes in different areas of our American culture. Furthermore, culture is integrated only to a degree. There are frequently internal inconsistencies and contradictions, as will be illustrated in later chapters. Cultures should not be thought of as single, monolithic entities. In most societies like American society, there are subcultures based on regional, class, ethnic, or religious differences, and the like. Feminist studies have made us much more aware that men and women have differing views of their culture. Because of the power differentials between masters and slaves, workers and bosses, or Brahmins and Untouchables, each side will have a differing perspective on the culture that they share. From each of these categories one will get only "partial truths" about the culture. The distinction between what constitutes a subculture, such as a "slave" subculture, and what constitutes a different perspective, a "slave" perspective within a single culture, is not so clear-cut from a definitional point of view.

Culture is learned and acquired by infants through a process referred to by anthropologists as **enculturation.** Mental structures or schema are created in the individual as a result of the process of enculturation. People who share a culture have reoccurring common experiences, which lead them to develop similar mental schema. Individuals are enculturated not as passive recipients, but as active agents. They internalize cultural practices but may change and transform those practices as a result of their experiences. Individuals learn another culture when they migrate to a new country, but the degree to which they learn this new culture may vary, and some may learn very little of the new culture.

Culture is transgenerational; that is, it continues beyond the lifetimes of individuals. There is a stability and consistency of cultural patterning through time, despite the fact that culture is continually being reworked and re-created. Culture is always a dialogue between past and present. As cultures reproduce themselves, changes occur. Some are the result of internal developments, innovations, and inventions, while others represent introductions from outside. Anthropologists study the process of culture change through time by examining historical, archival, and, sometimes, archaeological data deriving from the excavation of prehistoric sites. Tradition can be seen as the "past" as it is recollected in the present. Innovators and rebels, who try to transform their societies, have a view of the society which is different from that of other members. It is a dream of a different future, of a "brave new world," which demands that present ways of doing things be changed.

SOCIETY

Another concept, paralleling culture, is that of **society.** Culture deals with meanings and symbolic patterning, while society deals with the organization of social relationships within groups. Culture is distinctive of humans alone, although there are some primates that have what can be characterized as proto-culture, which will be discussed below. However, all animals that live in groups, humans among them, can be said to have societies. Thus a wolf pack, a deer herd, and a baboon troop all constitute societies. As in a human society, the individual members of a wolf pack are differentiated as males and females, as immature individuals and adults, and as mothers, fathers, and offspring. Individual wolves in each of these social categories behave in particular ways. That there are resemblances between wolf and human societies should not be surprising, since both wolves and humans are social animals. However, human societies are infinitely expandable and much more complex. Human societies have culture, which is transgenerational and based on symbols, and this enables humans to dream and plan for the future.

THE EVOLUTION OF CULTURE: FROM RAW TO COOKED

Human beings are cultural beings. It is the possession of culture that distinguishes humans from all other animal species. In animal species except for primates, social behavior and communication are determined primarily by instinct and are essentially uniform throughout the species.

It was originally thought that only humans possessed culture; however, recent research has revealed that Gombe chimpanzees in Zambia exhibit behavior that resembles culture. Termites are like caviar for these chimps, and during the termite season they carry "termite-fishing wands," which can be grasses, vines, or twigs and which are inserted into the termite mounds to extract the termites. They will spend long lengths of time at the mounds bringing extra "tools" with them (Lieberman, 1998: 24). Chimpanzees in the Tai area of West Africa use stone and wood hammers and anvils to crack open nuts. McGrew earlier had described 34 different populations of chimpanzees that had been observed making and using different tools. They use the same tool to solve different problems, and different tools to solve the same problem; hence, they have what can be described as a tool kit (McGrew, 1993: 158, 159). This would seem to be proto-cultural behavior, since it is transmitted intergenerationally.

Human cultural behavior is not only learned and transmitted from one generation to the next, but is also based on language and the capacity to create symbols, in contrast to what we have described above for other primates. Human cultural behavior is not limited, as is chimpanzee learned behavior, but is infinitely expandable. Ape-human comparisons, as Tattersall notes, only provide a background for understanding the way in which human mental capacities for culture evolved (1998: 49).

A chimpanzee in the Tai Forest, Ivory Coast, uses a stone as a tool to open a nut.

The evolution of the human species from proto-human and early human forms involved a number of significant physical changes, including the development of bipedal erect locomotion and increase in brain size and neurological organization and complexity. It was bipedalism that set the stage for the eventual development of vocal language. Recently a theory has been propounded that views bipedalism as giving rise to body language and visual gesture, which are seen not only as the dominant features of human interaction, but as the primary means of communication for our early hominid ancestors (Turner, 2000). In the Washo Project, several chimpanzees were taught to use American Sign Language. The left side of the brain in chimpanzees, which is involved in the ability of chimps to learn and use American Sign Language, is the same area of the brain used for human language. The asymmetries in the size of the left and right hemispheres of the brain are found in both chimps and humans, but they are more pronounced in humans. With the use of visually based language (gestures), the brain expanded and this resulted in a pre-adaptation for verbal language. Verbal language could only appear after the anatomical features necessary for its production were in place. The vocal tract of Homo erectus, the hominid from which Homo sapiens is descended, was not yet organized in the form necessary for vocal communication. Neanderthals, who are considered different from Homo sapiens, but who were living when Homo sapiens emerged 150,000 years ago, had larger brains and some of the same features that made human language possible. However, since the pharynx was still not in the same place as in Homo sapiens and other parts of the vocal tract were different, they are not considered capable of producing fully human language.

It is clear that language and the use, creation, and manipulation of symbols evolved as did brain size and tool use. However, at this point there is no definitive information about the way in which language evolved, since there are no "linguistic fossils" representing intermediate forms of language, which would be equivalent to the tools from the Paleolithic period. The central role of language in culture will be explored more fully in Chapter 3. Art and music are other systems of human communication that employ symbols. They make their first appearance in the Upper Paleolithic with the people called Cro-Magnon, who were Homo sapiens like us.

The marked development of cerebral asymmetry noted above is connected to right- and left-handedness. The earliest stone tools were made by right-handed individuals (Tattersall, 1998: 76). The use of rudimentary tools by some apes was greatly surpassed even by proto-humans. This was facilitated by the retention of the hand as a generalized organ for grasping, combined with the new characteristic of erect posture. The increase in sophistication of the tools manufactured by early human beings occurred with expansion in brain size and intelligence. The early archaeological record shows the widespread geographical distribution of the same pattern or style of tool type, indicating the presence of the features that characterize culture. Though particular tool types, which would seem to embody common cultural concepts, existed in the minds of individuals living over a wide area, these tools were made for specific and often different purposes.

Recent research has pointed to another significant development in the evolution of the human capacity for culture—cooking (Wrangham et al., 1999). The cooking of food, in particular, vegetable foods, breaks down their molecular structure, bursts cells, and neutralizes toxins, making the food much more digestible. This process transformed vegetation into "food." Later forms of hominids became efficient hunters of large game animals, and meat too is more digestible when cooked. However, these researchers argue that the important transformations that resulted from cooking occurred before the appearance of big game hunters, when the first hominids or humans appeared, some 1.9 million years ago. Australopithecines, who lived 3–4 million years ago and were the ancestors of hominids, were already bipedal and manufactured crude stone tools. The size and shape of their teeth, however, indicates that their diet consisted of raw (uncooked) grasses and vegetable matter—like other nonhuman primates. But it is early humans, like Homo erectus, who show the important fossil changes that one would expect to be associated with cooking. The size of their molars, used to grind food, are much reduced.

Cooking of food, of course, presupposes the control of fire. This is a tricky subject, since the finding of fire in the early fossil record is subject to differing interpretations. It is generally accepted that Homo erectus, especially the form found at Zhoukoudian, in China, is the first fossil type to be associated with fire. The ability to use fire and cooking are universal in human culture, not found

A butcher sells glazed dog meat in the market at Guanzhou (Canton), Peoples' Republic of China.

among any other animal species. As such, they are taken by anthropologists like Claude Lévi-Strauss to be a defining feature of humanity and preserved in human myths throughout the world. Wrangham et al. (1999) focus on vegetable food, particularly on tubers, which they argue were collected and brought back by females. They assume that females did the cooking since cooking is universally a female activity in present-day cultures. Once cooked, such food was converted into a valuable resource, easily subject to marauding and theft. The need to protect this resource fell on the males. This would seem to be the beginning of male-female role differentiation. These features together with the formation of an extended period of female sexual receptivity, led to strong male-female bonds, a pattern not found among nonhuman primates.

Still another feature distinguishes human cultural behavior from animal behavior. Human behavior is governed primarily by cultural rules, not by the need for immediate gratification. The capacity to defer gratification was increasingly built into human physiology as humans evolved. Human beings do not eat the minute they become hungry. Lions or wolves eat immediately after a successful hunt, often gorging themselves. With the introduction of cooking, humans deferred eating until long after the hunt, until cooking was completed. Sex is similarly subject to cultural rules. Unlike other animals, humans do not have a period of estrus during which they need to have sexual intercourse and not during any other time. Instead, human beings usually follow their culture's set of rules as to when and where to have sex and the various positions to use.

CULTURAL UNIVERSALS

The biological nature of the human species requires that all cultures solve the basic problems of human existence such as providing themselves with food and reproducing. As a consequence, though cultural differences do exist, all cultures share certain fundamental similarities, which are referred to as **cultural universals.** All languages are characterized by certain universal features, such as the presence of nouns, possessive forms, and verbs that distinguish between the past, present, and future. Though languages are different from one another, they all have these universal features. Human consumption of food follows cultural rules regarding what is eaten, when and with whom food is eaten, and with which utensils. All cultures have some kind of incest taboo, though the relatives with whom they must not have sexual intercourse vary, as we will describe in Chapter 6. Rites of passage, such as birth, reaching adulthood, marriage, and death, are celebrated ceremonially by societies, though not all of them celebrate each of these rites of passage. Some anthropologists have pointed out that all cultures have law, government, religion, conceptions of self, marriage, family, and kinship (Brown, 1991; Kluckhohn, 1953). These universal cultural categories are present in all human societies since each must deal with the problems and concerns that all humans face (Goodenough, 1970: 120). Ultimately, it is the characteristics of the human species and the human mind that form the basis for cultural universals. Languages and cultures are structured in a particular manner as a consequence of the fact that the mind of Homo sapiens is organized in a certain way.

CULTURAL RULES

Basic biological drives are transformed by cultural rules. What is learned and internalized by human infants during the process of enculturation are **cultural rules.** The enormous variations between cultures are due to differences in cultural rules. Frequently, people from a particular culture can tell the anthropologist what the cultural rules are. At other times, they may behave according to rules that they themselves cannot verbalize. Defining these cultural rules is like trying to identify the rules that govern a language. All languages operate according to sets of rules, and people follow these rules in their speech. It is the linguist's job to determine the rules of grammar that the speakers of languages use automatically and are usually not aware of. The anthropologist's job is to uncover the cultural rules of which people may be unaware. The existence of rules does not imply that speakers of a language or members of a culture are robots who speak and act in identical fashion. Each infant learns cultural rules in a distinctive manner, and every speaker of a language has his or her distinctive pronunciation and linguistic mannerisms. Individual variation is considerable in spoken language, and it is equally present in cultural practice. Rules are meant to be flouted, and some individuals respond to rules that way. Lawyers and accountants in our society advise people on how to get as close as possible to the limit of the law. Sometimes they cross over the line. This was the issue in the recent Enron scandal. When individuals interpret rules, they are acting as agents. As a consequence, there is variation in observing the rules.

Rules govern sexual behavior in terms of with whom it is allowed, as well as when, where, and how. For example, in Lesu, a community in Papua New Guinea, it is acceptable for sexual intercourse to take place before marriage. The marriage relationship is symbolized by eating together. When a couple publicly shares a meal, this signifies that they are married and can henceforth eat only with one another. Even though husband and wife may have sexual relations with other individuals, they may not eat with them. In our society, in contrast, until the beginning of the sexual revolution about 50 years ago, couples engaged to be married could eat together, but sexual intercourse could not take place until after marriage. The act of sexual intercourse symbolized marriage. At that time, if either spouse had intercourse with another individual after marriage, that constituted the criminal act of adultery. However, either spouse could have dinner with someone of the opposite sex. From the perspective of someone in our society, the rules governing marriage in Lesu appear to be like our rules from 50 years ago "stood on their heads."

We noted earlier that workers and bosses have differing cultural perspectives. Their repertoire of cultural rules likewise may vary. Similarly, subcultures also exhibit variability in their cultural rules. This may be referred to as intracultural variation. In our society today, there is cultural variability with regard to sexual behavior. Christian Fundamentalists have beliefs about sex before marriage that are very different from those of members of the entertainment industry, who frequently engage in sex outside of marriage. Many Christian Fundamentalists think that we should return to the cultural rules about sex of 50 years ago—mainly, no sex before marriage—and there are members of Congress who agree with them. Each of these groups, Christian Fundamentalists and the entertainment industry, represents a subculture with different variations of the cultural rules of the society.

On occasion, individuals may violate cultural rules. All cultures have some provision for sanctioning the violation of cultural rules as well as rewards for obeying them. Both rewards and punishments differ from one culture to another, in the same way that the sets of cultural rules differ. Cultural rules also change over time. When many individuals consistently interpret a rule differently than it had been interpreted before, the result will be a change in the rule itself. An example of this sort is the fact that sexual intercourse is no longer solely a symbol of marriage, as we have noted.

SOCIAL STRUCTURE

The particular patterns of social relationships that characterize a society are referred to as its **social structure.** These patterns of social structure are based on cultural rules. Social structure includes the social groupings that a society recognizes, which may be organized on the basis of family, kinship, residential propinquity, common interest, or class. These groupings have continuity through time. Another aspect of social structure is the network of social roles, to be discussed below. The concept of social structure may be distinguished from **social organization** (Firth, 1951). While structure emphasizes continuity and stability, organization refers to the way in which individuals perceive the structure and context of any situation and make decisions and choices from among alternative courses of behavior. Organization refers to variations in individual behavior and emphasizes flux and change. This emphasis on individual choices and decisions is also defined as practice (Bourdieu, 1977). This is referred to as **agency,** from the point of view of the individual making the choices. However, the range of choices which people can choose from is always shaped by the social structure. The action they take as "agents" may serve to reconfigure the social structure (Ahearn, 2001: 115).

In human societies, individuals occupy different positions, or **social statuses.** They usually occupy more than one social status at the same time. An individual may occupy the social statuses of father, chief, and priest at the same time. Societies, of course, vary in the number and kinds of social statuses. The behavior associated with a particular social status in a society is known as the **social role.** Social roles involve behavior toward other people, as a father to his children, a supervisor to her staff, or a headman to his followers. For example, in many societies in Papua New Guinea, a headman will lead his followers to attend a ceremony sponsored by another headman and his followers. When the headman orates on such an occasion, he speaks for his group, and he is carrying out the social role of headman. Interaction of people in their social roles and interaction between groups define social relationships. These social relationships can be analyzed in terms of differentials in power, prestige, and access to resources. The headman has more power, prestige, and resources than his followers.

In anthropology, the terms **structure** and **pattern** refer to and describe form. We may talk about the structure or form of a myth, the various aspects of the structure of a language, or the structure of a political organization. In parallel fashion, that myth or a particular aspect of language—a verb, for instance—has a use or function to perform. This tells what the parts do and how they operate. A linguist will talk about the phonetic structure of a language—a description of formal relationships. This is different from the function of phonemes, the units of sound, which is to differentiate meanings. Cultural anthropologists may talk about political structure, for example, of Trobriand Island society in the South Pacific at the beginning of the twentieth century, which was made up of villages with headmen, formed into a district headed by a chief. The functions of Trobriand political structure were governmental. The village headman organized and directed village ceremonies and collected tribute to be given to the chief of the district. The chief of the entire district maintained order in his district by punishing wrongdoers, and he used his wealth and tribute to reward those who performed services for him. In similar fashion, one can describe the economic structure, the religious structure, and the kinship structure of any society, including one's own.

ANTHROPOLOGICAL THEORIES

The discipline of anthropology has been professionalized for more than a hundred and thirty years. To more clearly understand the work that anthropologists are doing today, as well as the results of their past research, it is necessary to briefly survey the significant theoretical and methodological approaches that have informed, shaped, and focused this research. When anthropology was developing during the nineteenth century, it was envisioned as a science, patterned after the natural sciences. This image was dominant until the early part of the twentieth century. In the decades that followed, anthropology oscillated between humanistic and scientific approaches.

CULTURAL EVOLUTION

The nineteenth century was a period of colonial expansion and the development of great empires by European powers. Darwinian evolutionary theory was dominant. Social Darwinism, which proclaimed the survival of the fittest, was used to justify the domination and suppression of native peoples, as well as the exploitation of the underclass in industrial societies. During this period the discipline of anthropology, which focused on the study of indigenous peoples of the colonies that had been established, came into being. The significant theory of the time was **cultural evolution.** At this point, culture, the central concept of anthropology, was defined by Sir Edward Tylor (1871) in a broad, all-encompassing manner that included language and all the customs one could describe for a social group.

Neither Tylor nor the American Lewis Henry Morgan, the major figures in nineteenth-century evolutionary theory, did the kind of fieldwork with which anthropology was later identified. Morgan did carry out some observations on the Iroquois near his home and on the native peoples of the Plains, and Tylor visited Mexico and wrote about his trip. Generally, the anthropologists of that time remained in their armchairs and utilized the accounts of missionaries; explorers, such as Captain Cook; travelers, such as Prince Maximilian, who explored the area of the Louisiana Purchase; and others who described the native peoples they encountered in their travels. Many of these descriptions were ethnocentric and biased. Tylor and Morgan conceptualized cultural evolution in terms of stages through which all societies had progressed, with the simple societies developing into increasingly more complex forms, culminating in their own Victorian society. According to the theories of these anthropologists, not all societies evolved into complex forms. Some societies, those of the "savages" being encountered by missionaries, travelers, and others, were believed to represent cases of contemporary examples of earlier stages, that is, cases of arrested development or survivals.

The evolutionists organized their data and utilized the comparative approach, which we discussed earlier. They looked for similarities and differences in cultures, classified them into cultural types, and ordered the types from simple to complex. They were ethnocentric in their evaluation of other societies, always making comparisons with Western civilization. Western religion, family life, and so on, were all assumed to be the apogee of evolutionary development. Morgan's emphasis on the economic base of society as the determining factor of stages of cultural evolution caught the attention of Friedrich Engels. Engels's *The Origin of the Family, Private Property and the State* (1884) includes a reinterpretation of Morgan's *Ancient Society* (1877). Both Marx and Engels were very taken with the work of Morgan because, like Morgan, they saw the evolution of culture as determined by the technology and the subsistence base.

At the beginning of the twentieth century, the weaknesses of the nineteenth-century evolutionary approach to culture began to be recognized. The data on which the theories were based were found wanting. The characteristics of Western societies, which were supposed to represent the most highly evolved stage of civilization, like monogamy and monotheism, were arbitrarily selected to represent the highest forms of societal development. As more and more data were collected, based on fieldwork by anthropologists with university training, it was clear that not all societies had passed through the same evolutionary stages. Monogamy and monotheism were found to be characteristic of societies other than the most evolved, and nineteenth-century evolutionary theory based on universal stages was discarded.

In the 1940s, after other theories had been prominent, a new form of evolutionary theory was proposed by Leslie White (1949, 1959). He saw culture as a whole, over the world, evolving and becoming more complex as human beings in different places developed increasingly more efficient ways of capturing energy from the environment. In contrast to White and his universal evolutionary scheme, Julian Steward (1955) was interested in how particular societies evolved. He viewed the relationship among the environment, economic subsistence activities, and associated social and political institutions of particular societies, what he called the cultural core, as the determining factor in their evolutionary transformation. Steward developed a system of cultural types, each of which was seen as having a different line of evolutionary development. In 1960, Marshall Sahlins and Elman Service attempted to reconcile White's and Steward's theories. They proposed a distinction between specific evolution, concerned with the adaptation of specific societies to their environments as they developed through time, and general evolution, concerned with the emergence of more complex forms of culture regardless of historical sequence, which was based upon progress in terms of energy capture. The adaptation of different societies to their environments became the focus of the ecological approach, which saw the society and its environmental setting as a single, interrelated system.

All anthropologists today would agree that complex forms of society have evolved from simpler ones. However, contemporary cultural anthropological theory, by and large, is not concerned with evolutionary questions. Most anthropologists feel that evolutionary theory does not take into account the unique aspects of culture on which they choose to focus. Evolutionary questions remain important to archaeologists. Anthropologists like Ingold, for example, are interested in the role human consciousness plays in cultural evolution and in whether there is a cultural analogue of natural selection (1986). Some anthropologists are interested in the ideas of evolutionary psychology. According to Pinker, an evolutionary psychologist, if people maintain a particular custom over a long period of time, it must have an adaptive value or it would not be continued. This has been challenged by many social scientists as a tautology rather than an explanation.

CULTURAL RELATIVISM

Though Franz Boas started out as a supporter of the evolutionary point of view, his fieldwork with Eskimos of Baffin Island in the late nineteenth century, known today as Inuit, and somewhat later with a variety of Northwest Coast societies, especially the Kwakiutl, soon led him to abandon the evolutionary approach. After learning the Kwakiutl language, he came to respect the significant differences between the way the Kwakiutl viewed the world and the way other people viewed it. He moved away from attempts to range societies from simple to complex, considering all cultures and languages equally distinctive and complex in different ways. This emphasis on uniqueness came to be referred to as cultural relativism or cultural particularism. Boas saw cultures as symbolic systems of ideas. His work stressed the gathering of texts concerning all the aspects of the life of the people, especially art, mythology, and language, in the native language. Boas felt that anthropologists should first concentrate on learning about the history of the development of particular societies, such as the Kwakiutl and other Native American Indian societies, before attempting to theorize about the general process of cultural change and evolution. His emphasis on cultural relativism came to be associated with the humanistic approach, mentioned above, that characterized the work of his students Benedict, Sapir, and Kroeber.

FUNCTIONALISM

The British reaction against nineteenth-century evolutionary theory took a somewhat different form. British anthropologists at the beginning of the twentieth century supplanted evolutionary theory with a model, derived from biology, of society as a living organism. The basic organizing concepts they used were structure and function, discussed earlier. They spurned the speculative nature of nineteenth-century evolutionary stages and substituted for it fieldwork, that is, the empirical field observations of academically trained anthropologists who had spent a year or more in the field learning the language and doing participant observation, which will be discussed in the next chapter.

Bronislaw Malinowski, a major theorist in the development of functionalism, spent an extended period of time doing fieldwork in the Trobriand Islands off New Guinea and is often cited as one of the founders of modern anthropological fieldwork. His method of analysis of field data involved identifying the institutions that made up the "skeleton" of society (i.e., their structure) and then describing in detail how those institutions functioned. In his two-volume work *Coral Gardens and Their Magic* (1935), he described that part of the economic institution of the Trobrianders concerned with horticulture. Not only does he describe the process of planting and cultivating yams, but he also goes into great detail about the magic involved in yam cultivation, the texts of the spells used, and finally, the way the yams are used in the complex exchange system of fulfilling obligations to kin and chiefs. Malinowski saw cultural institutions functioning in response to basic human biological needs, which exist universally for people in all societies, as well as to what he called culturally derived needs. The institutions described in *Coral Gardens and Their Magic* relate to the biological need of providing sustenance.

Though coupled at times with Malinowski as a British functionalist, A. R. Radcliffe-Brown moved in his anthropological theorizing in a somewhat different direction. Using a comparative approach, he tried to develop typologies to sort and categorize different kinds of societies (1952). He was concerned with the "anatomy" of societies, with social structure, not with how institutions functioned to satisfy biological needs. When Radcliffe-Brown talked about the function of a part of the social structure, such as a clan, he used the term *function* to mean the contribution made by the clan to the ongoing life processes of the society. The next generation of British anthropologists became experts in the delineation of different kinds of social structures based on kinship and on related aspects of culture such as law, political organization, land tenure, and religion. The central organizing concept for them was society and its patterns of interrelationship, and culture was merely the medium through which these relations were expressed. Radcliffe-Brown strongly opposed what he referred to as conjectural history, which was characteristic of evolutionary theory. Real history, he argued, existed only where there were written records kept by the people themselves. The effect of Radcliffe-Brown's position was to inhibit all kinds of historical research by British anthropologists for one or two generations.

With the breakdown of colonial empires after World War II and the enormous changes that had been taking place, the functionalist theoretical framework, which emphasized unchanging societies existing in a state of equilibrium, came under attack. British anthropologists, such as A. L. Epstein and Philip Mayer, began to follow the tribal people whom they had studied earlier as they moved into the cities and went to work in the mines. Others, such as E. E. Evans-Pritchard and M. G. Smith, turned to the historical investigation of societies based on archival material, rejecting Radcliffe-Brown's injunctions against the study of what he called conjectural history. A much more processual model, which emphasized not social structure but social organization concepts and the way in which structures change, came into play.

STRUCTURALISM

Structuralism as a theoretical approach is closely associated with the work of the French anthropologist Claude Lévi-Strauss. He took the way in which a linguist analyzes data as a model and applied it to the analysis of culture. Like the sounds in a language, which by themselves have no meaning but are part of a larger structure that conveys meaning, the elements of a culture must be seen in their relationship to one another as they form a structure. Cultural meanings are conveyed through such structures. The structural anthropologist attempts to determine the underlying structure of a culture, which corresponds to the grammar of a language in the linguist's analysis. Lévi-Strauss saw Boas as his intellectual ancestor. It was Boas who first pointed out that the grammar of a language was not part of the consciousness of the speaker and, in a parallel fashion, that culture also had an underlying structure and operated like language. Structuralists analyzed cognitive systems, kinship structure, art, mythology, ritual, and ceremony, among other things. Structural anthropologists were comparative in that they attempted to determine whether there were similarities in underlying structures in different cultures. Thus, this approach may group together societies that seem to be very different at first glance. Poststructuralists and postmodernists have rejected Lévi-Straussian structuralism because its models are too abstract and deal with cultural material in an ahistorical fashion.

HISTORICAL ANTHROPOLOGY

Anthropologists today work with a variety of perspectives. Contemporary approaches are much less unified and do not share a single set of assumptions, as did the theoretical points of view we have discussed up to this point. Most of these approaches do not constitute theories in the formal sense.

Many contemporary anthropologists work within a historical framework. Some ethnohistorians use archaeological, archival, and oral history materials to trace the history of cultures where people left no written records of their own. It is important to understand the local peoples' own narratives of their own history (Donham, 2001: 143). Other ethnohistorians, like Eric Wolf, have examined how European economic and political expansion during the colonial period affected small-scale societies, focusing on the colonial discourse that developed between colonizers and colonized. He was interested in how non-European populations reacted to the introduction of capitalism and how, in turn, these reactions determined the direction of capitalism in Europe (Wolf, 1982). Leland Donald uses colonial eyewitness observations as well as subsequent ethnographic sources to detail how slavery functioned within the economic, social, and belief systems of Northwest Coast societies and how it rapidly changed in the period from 1780 to 1880, when slavery ended (Donald, 1997). Bennetta Jules-Rosette has done a study of three generations of African writers living in France, which discusses the relationship between their writing and French intellectual discourse and culture over this period of time (1998).

Marshall Sahlins advocates a theoretical approach that combines history and structuralism. Sahlins points out that when Captain Cook landed on Hawaii, the Hawaiians, perceiving him in terms of their own cultural categories, saw him as the god Lono. When the Hawaiians killed Captain Cook, because each year they ritually killed the god Lono, his killing not only affected subsequent events involving Hawaiian-European relations (i.e., history) but also resulted in changes in Hawaiian cultural rules (structure). Structure and history are seen as constantly interrelated and influencing one another (Sahlins, 1985). Obeysekere has objected to Sahlins's interpretation, accusing him of adopting an imperialist perspective in which Western white men are always seen as gods by the "natives" (1992).

SYMBOLIC ANTHROPOLOGY

Over the past 20 years or more, symbolic anthropology, which is concerned with determining meaning, has become one of the dominant approaches in anthropology. This emphasis harks back to Boas's interest in meaning as well as to the centrality of meaning in the structuralism of Lévi-Strauss, which are its intellectual antecedents. Culture is seen as a system of symbols, and the task of the anthropologist is to decipher the meanings of the system. In the 1970s, anthropologists such as David Schneider and Clifford Geertz began to focus on the tangle of interrelated meanings that cultures encode. The task of the anthropologist then became one of translating the layers of meaning of a particular cultural phenomenon into our concepts and our language. Clifford Geertz, in his attempt to understand the meaning of the Balinese cockfight, called this type of translation a "thick description." Thick description means that culture is viewed as a text to be read and interpreted. This emphasis on deciphering meaning has been associated in anthropology with particularism and cultural relativism, both of which are basically anticomparative.

Most American anthropologists accept many of the ideas associated with the symbolic approach. If anthropologists, who wrote ethnographies, were collecting texts, then anthropological analysis was the analysis of texts. During the past years, Geertz's approach has increasingly become akin to literary criticism. In the mid-1980s, in *Works and Lives,* Geertz argued that understanding an anthropologist's ethnographic writings is similar to understanding a fictional body of work by Melville or Mark Twain. The meaning of a text is found in the author's voice, and the anthropological material contained therein must be interpreted in that light. In contrast, Schneider continued to view culture as a symbolic system, and each ethnography represented the symbolic system of a particular and uniquely different culture. There was no room for a comparative approach in Schneider's anthropology. As we shall see, postmodernism borrowed heavily from the later writings of both Geertz and Schneider.

An interesting example of the combination of the symbolic and the historical approaches is Raymond Bucko's *The Lakota Ritual of the Sweat Lodge: History and Contemporary Practice* (1998). He shows how symbolic meanings and usages in the contemporary sweat-house ritual of the Lakota draw upon memories and texts from an earlier time when economic and political conditions for the Lakota were very different.

POSTMODERNISM IN ANTHROPOLOGY

Anthropology, along with the other human sciences, has recently been undergoing a reassessment, which has been labeled **postmodernism.** Anthropologists' analyses and translations of the cultures of others and how they operate were deemed insufficient and inadequate to complete understanding. Up to the present, as we have seen, anthropology has straddled both the humanities and the social sciences. In its stance as part of the humanities, anthropology emphasized cultural uniqueness and relativism. As a social science, anthropology emphasized generalization, analysis, and the comparative approach. Postmodernism in anthropology has found fault with generalization and a more scientific approach, arguing that anthropology should totally embrace humanism, striving to capture the uniqueness of each cultural situation, which postmodernists see as lost when one generalizes. Because anthropology depends on the interaction of one human being with others, they argue that a science of anthropology is impossible. The observation of human subjects and their behavior by an anthropologist from another culture is no longer viewed as the foundation upon which to build social science conclusions. Instead, the ethnographer and his or her informants, the people within the culture who provide information, are to be seen as part of the same social time and space, with the ethnographer's task being that of an interpreter or translator. The ethnographer's understanding of the culture is presented in the ethnography along with the understandings of the informants for the reading public to make its own conclusions about the people and their way of life. The focus should be on the life of everyday people to demonstrate that they are not the passive instruments of elite domination but actors making decisions and choices within the structure of constraints, able, if they desire, to modify their behavior and patterns of relationships. The radical political agenda of postmodernism is sometimes more, sometimes less evident as its practitioners focus on how the global affects the local and vice versa.

Some have seen the ethnography, the product of the dialogue between informant and fieldworker, as not sufficiently representative of the variety of points of view or ideas held by individuals in the culture. They have argued that different segments of a society may have contested views regarding cultural meanings. They have advocated representing these different views by including the informants' ideas in their own words in the ethnography itself. In the book by Richard Price, *First Time: The Historical Vision of an Afro-American People,* his picture of the history of the Saramaka is presented alongside the versions of several elders in the culture (1983). In other instances, in order to pay more attention to the views of informants, anthropologists have presented their analyses to their informants for comment, as Steven Feld did to his Kaluli informants to see if they agreed with his conclusions regarding the meanings of sounds in their culture (1987). Some postmodernists prefer that the informants' voices take center stage in telling their story,

utilizing the life history approach, which has traditionally been part of anthropological methodology. This approach is in response to the feeling that in the past the
voices of ethnographic subjects have been marginalized or displaced by the sole
authoritative voice of the ethnographer, the voice which had told "the story." The
role of the native ethnographer, that is, the individual who is a member of the culture who has received training as an anthropologist, is also related to the matter of
representation. Such individuals are seen as having intuitive understanding of the
culture and greater ability to empathize with and interpret their culture than an anthropologist who is a member of another culture. However, there are those who argue that greater empathy comes at the expense of the perspective and
understanding that an outsider can bring. Anthropologists studying their own culture cannot be objective, tend to justify behavior in an ethnocentric way, and often
have their own political agendas. Even outsider anthropologists cannot be completely objective.

When anthropology is seen as a science, observation plays an essential role.
However, to postmodernists who emphasize the humanistic view of anthropology,
observation plays a secondary role to dialogues with informants and the recording
of the information that informants present as an ethnographic text. In the ethnographic accounts postmodernists applaud, analytic conceptual frameworks are
completely absent because it is felt that in each society, which is considered a
unique entity, the categories must be understood in their own terms and cannot be
equated with categories in other societies, as is done in comparative cross-cultural
research.

Postmodernists have forced anthropologists to rethink the nature of fieldwork.
They have put the emphasis in ethnography upon knowing how the ethnographer
felt as a person in the fieldwork situation and was perceived by the community, the
experiential aspects of the field. Postmodernist anthropologists have considered
the writing of ethnographic descriptions to be so central that one of them defines
anthropology as "a discursive category, a type or group of types of writing that
have important filiations to other modern cultural and academic fields" (Manganaro, 1990: 5). They are interested in learning what rhetorical devices are being
used to convince the reader that the fieldworker was "there" and that his or her observations and conclusions are accurate representations of the lives of the "others"
whom anthropologists have traditionally studied. When culture is seen as a text,
as in Geertz's view, and ethnography becomes a type of writing, then anthropology moves much closer to literary theory. Anthropology, in the postmodernist
point of view, becomes part of a new humanistic interdisciplinary approach, which
also includes philosophy, history, art history, and architecture.

At the present time, anthropologists have been forced to rethink the basic concepts and the purpose of the discipline. Not only have basic premises been recon-
sidered, but postmodernist anthropologists have also made central the self-critical
aspects of anthropology, in which readers of ethnographies reflect on their own
culture. In this respect, they are continuing Boas's earlier concern with racism in
the modern world and Mead's discussion of Samoan adolescence in order to illuminate American adolescence. A number of anthropologists have been quite inter-

ested in "subaltern," or underclass, cultures, that is, the way of life of drug dealers in East Harlem, welfare families in Brooklyn, and lower class groups in other societies as well. The postmodern emphasis on uniqueness meant that the comparative aspect of anthropology, which pays attention to what cultures have in common as well as how they differ, was left by the wayside. Further, in this vein, the legitimate anthropological focus on what can be observed and quantified has been played down. The postmodernist argument has been that even the physical world is not characterized by deterministic regularities—so why should we expect such regularities to characterize human social behavior? However, this viewpoint ignores the fact that because of the constraints of culture, there is no absolute freedom of action or complete randomness in human behavior. People do behave in ways that demonstrate cultural regularities, and the concept of culture remains a powerful conceptual tool for organizing anthropological data. An examination of articles in anthropology journals reveals that postmodernism is on the wane. The emphasis now is on substantive ethnographic materials and questions, and the comparative dimension is reemerging as relevant and important in anthropology.

* * *

The journey to another place or another time, which we defined at the beginning of this chapter as the hallmark of anthropology, is recapitulated by each fledgling anthropologist as she or he embarks on fieldwork. Lévi-Strauss, in his personal memoir, *Tristes Tropiques* (1955), saw his own fieldwork in terms of just such a journey. His journey to the field took him from the Old World to the New World, from the cold North to the tropical South, to a world that contrasted in every respect with his own. His goal was to find what he characterized as a simple form of society, since he felt that to understand how societies work, it is best to study one that is elementary in its organization. As in all fieldwork situations, he was first struck by great cultural differences. However, in time, Lévi-Strauss, the sophisticated French student of philosophy, saw behind the painted faces of the Nambikwara a humanity he shared with them. He wrote, "I had been looking for a society reduced to its simplest expression. The society of the Nambikwara had been reduced to the point at which I found nothing but human beings" (Lévi-Strauss, 1961: 310). The pages that follow represent a journey into the world of anthropology.

SUMMARY

- The central concept of anthropology is culture. Culture consists of the things people make, their behavior, their beliefs and ideas.

- The belief that one's own culture represents the best way to do things is known as ethnocentrism.

- Cultural relativism is the idea that each culture is unique and distinctive, but that no one culture is superior.

• Some anthropologists utilize the comparative approach to compare cultures. This method identifies fundamental similarities of cultural patterning as well as differences.

• Anthropology's holistic perspective uses culture as an organizing concept and stresses the relationship among economics, politics, art, religion, and other activities.

• Cultures should not be conceived of as separate, bounded entities. Individuals usually live their lives in a world of overlapping cultures.

• Changes are constantly taking place in culture. Individuals are not simply recipients of culture; they are active participants involved in reworking their cultures. Their activity is referred to as agency.

• Culture is integrated, but only to a degree. Contradictions are frequently found within a culture.

• Culture is learned and acquired by infants through a process referred to by anthropologists as enculturation.

• As cultures reproduce themselves, changes occur.

• Culture deals with meanings and symbolic patterning, while society deals with the organization of social relationships within groups.

• Chimpanzees use tools and this constitutes a type of proto-culture.

• The evolution of culture was dependent on the prior development of bipedalism and increased brain size.

• Verbal language could only appear after the anatomical features necessary for its production were in place.

• The development of cooking some 1.9 million years ago led to changes in the evolution of culture.

• Though cultural differences do exist, all cultures share certain fundamental similarities, which are referred to as cultural universals.

• The variations between cultures are due to differences in cultural rules.

• When individuals interpret cultural rules, they are acting as agents. As a consequence, there is variation within a culture in observing the rules.

• Social structure, which is constituted of particular patterns of social relationship, includes social groupings that may be organized on the basis of family, kinship, residential propinquity, common interest, or class.

• Nineteenth-century anthropology, conceived of as a science, was dominated by evolutionary theory.

• Evolutionary theory then was succeeded by cultural relativism, as propounded by American anthropologists. Each society was seen as unique and different.

• British anthropology rejected evolutionary theory and adopted functionalism, which stressed the concepts of structure and function.

• Structuralism sees the elements of a culture in relationship to one another as they form a structure that conveys cultural meanings.

• Contemporary analytical approaches are much less unified and do not share a single set of assumptions, as did the earlier theoretical points of view. Many contemporary anthropologists work within historical or symbolic frameworks that do not constitute theories in the formal sense.

• Postmodernism in anthropology has found fault with the scientific approach and with generalization, arguing that anthropology should totally embrace humanism and strive to capture the uniqueness of each cultural situation.

 SUGGESTED READINGS

Cerroni-Long, E. L., ed. *Anthropological Theory in North America.* Westport, CT: Bergin & Garvey, 1999; An overview of contemporary anthropological theory at the end of the century.

Erickson, Paul A. and Liam Donat Murphy, eds. *Reading for a History of Anthropological Theory.* Peterbourgh, Ontario: Broadview Press, 2001. A selection of historical readings from Karl Marx and Edward Tylor to Michael Taussig and Marilyn Strathern.

Kuper, Adam. *Culture: The Anthropologists Account.* Cambridge: Harvard University Press, A historical examination of the culture concept, along with an evaluation of its usefulness.

Layton, Robert. *An Introduction to Theory in Anthropology.* New York: Cambridge University Press, 1997. A general introduction to anthropological theory, which takes into consideration the fragmentation of the subject over the last two decades.

Manganaro, Marc, ed. *Modernist Anthropology: From Fieldwork to Text.* Princeton,N.J.: Princeton University Press, 1990. A collection of papers dealing with modernism and postmodernism.

 SUGGESTED WEBSITES

http://www/discoverchimpanzees.org Look at the site to compare chimpanzee behavior and communication with human culture and human language.

http://www.mrs.umn.edu/academic/anthropology/chollett/theory/links.html A list of websites giving biographies and theoretical positions of some fifty eminent anthropologists from the nineteenth century to the present.

http://lilt.ilstu.edu/rtdirks/main_frame.htm A series of sites having to do with the anthropology of food and food habits around the world.

2

The Anthropological Method

Historically, the methodology used by nineteenth-century anthropologists, focusing on the evolution of culture, involved examining the information collected by travelers, explorers, missionaries, and colonial officials who visited or lived for a time in the parts of the world where societies of interest to anthropologists were located. However, as noted in the previous chapter, it was fieldwork by professionally trained anthropologists who lived among the people, observing them firsthand, learning their language, and participating in their ceremonies, that became the defining ethnographic methodology for anthropology after the turn of the century.

Franz Boas was the first person to carry out what we would today call fieldwork. In 1883–1884, he worked with the Eskimos, now called Inuit, of Baffinland in Labrador. Before he embarked on his voyage to Canada, he familiarized himself with all the literature on the area, including accounts of voyages of discovery and missionary descriptions of Inuit ways of life and traditions. He also acquired as much knowledge of the Inuit language as he could from missionaries' word books and grammars. While in Baffinland, he traveled by dogsled from village to village, living with the people in their igloos, or snow houses. He focused his attention on the geography of the region and the way in which the Baffin Islanders exploited it economically and migrated over the terrain. He worked extensively on the language, collecting texts of myths, tales, and sayings. Living with and interacting with the people and learning the language become the hallmarks of anthropological fieldwork.

FIELDWORK

How does one gain perspective on another society? The answer for the anthropologist has always been to step outside the web of his or her own cultural world to closely examine another, often vastly different, way of life. This is what anthropologists do when they carry out fieldwork. Over the years, we have separately carried out fieldwork, Rosman with the Kanuri in northern Nigeria and Rubel with a Kalmyk Mongol emigré community in New Jersey, and we have jointly carried out fieldwork in Iran, Afghanistan, and Papua New Guinea. The heart of fieldwork is **participant observation**—living with other people, learning their language, and coming to understand their behavior and the ideas that are important to them. It usually includes living in their kind of house, be it the black goat-hair tent that we lived in when we did fieldwork in Afghanistan or the mud-brick house used by Rosman in the Nigerian town of Geidam; donning their dress on ceremonial occasions (see Rosman in Kanuri garb in the illustration on page 29); and eating their cuisine—nan, or flat bread, in Iran or the roast pig and taro at a New Ireland funerary celebration. Fieldworkers celebrate the birth rites of the people with whom they live and mourn with them at funerals.

The anthropologist, while learning the language, is also learning the culture of the people. When first immersed in a different culture, the fieldworker experiences **culture shock** on recognizing that his or her own culture is not "natural," that other people do things differently and consider their way as equally natural. This is similar to the experience of plunging into an ice-cold bath. As the anthropologist learns this new culture, he or she is in the position of a child in that culture. American anthropologists, who have learned as children to eat with knives, forks, and spoons, may need to learn to eat with chopsticks or with their fingers from a common bowl, as Rosman did during his fieldwork with the Kanuri. When, because of inexperience, bits of food fell from his hands and soiled his clothing, people discreetly turned away so that their laughter would not embarrass him. It was the fate of Rubel to eat boiled lamb (the Mongolian dish served on festive occasions) and horse meat steaks during her fieldwork with the Kalmyk Mongols in New Jersey. In attempting to present himself or herself in the best possible light to gain rapport and acceptance, the fieldworker engages in what has been called impression management. This means that she or he consciously constructs the persona of someone friendly, helpful, interested, and eager to learn about the culture, suppressing his or her feelings and opinions if they appear to jeopardize developing relationships. Participant observation involves an inherent contradiction. A participant operates inside a culture, while an observer is like a stranger, looking in from outside. As one learns how to participate as a member of a culture, one becomes engaged in that culture and identifies with it. On the other hand, an observer is expected to remain detached and to report objectively what he or she sees and hears. Since the anthropologist is a human being interacting and participating with other human beings, it is impossible for the anthropologist to be completely objective. Because it involves this basic paradox, participant observation is difficult to carry out and remains an ideal that is never completely realized.

Participation in another culture means learning how to view things from the natives' point of view, that is, another culture's point of view. This means investigating the concepts and ideas that order their world. But when anthropologists do

A participant in another culture often will don its clothing while doing fieldwork. This is Abraham Rosman doing research among the Kanuri.

fieldwork, they bring along their own cultural categories, or ways of seeing things, which they try to overcome. This necessitates that fieldworkers be consciously aware of their own cultural categories and make sure not to order their perceptions by them.

In addition to observations, anthropologists gain information by interviewing individuals in the culture, who are referred to as informants. The term does not refer to informing on someone else. To the anthropologist, the informant today is a fieldworker-colleague. In the interaction between informant and anthropologist, the informant increasingly learns what her or his fieldworker-colleague is interested in finding out and also gains a certain amount of knowledge about anthropology. In the process, informants begin to see things about their own culture in a different way. In trying to explain their culture to the questioning anthropologist, informants often start to understand it in a way they did not before. They may become conscious of cultural rules in their own society that they had not previously recognized.

The personal relationship between anthropologist and informant is a complex one. Individuals who become close friends of, as well as mentors to, the anthropologist are referred to as key informants. The key informant for Rosman while he was doing fieldwork among the Kanuri was the District Head, a titled aristocrat (pictured in the illustration on page 29) much older than the fledgling anthropologist, whom he adopted. This relationship was crucial during the fieldwork since many people trusted and were willing to talk to the anthropologist as a consequence of it. However, because of this connection, other sources of information were closed to the anthropologist because they were in opposition to, or belonged to another faction of, the community. Stoller has suggested that the ethnographer should be like the West African *griot*, who narrates the history, myths, tales, and stories of his people so that they can cope with the present. Like the *griot*, the ethnographer should spend long periods of time apprenticed to elders, mastering knowledge in order to respectfully and poetically evoke the tales of a people in his or her ethnography (Stoller, 1994: 354).

Fieldwork involves reciprocity on the part of the anthropologist. However, the nature of what the anthropologist returns to his or her informants is highly varied. In rural as well as urban areas, the anthropologist with a vehicle often reciprocates by becoming chauffeur for the entire community, as Rubel did for the Kalmyk Mongols with whom she worked in New Jersey. Frequently, anthropologists identify with the people among whom they have lived and worked. They become partisans and take on the causes of the community as advocates in the media or become expert witnesses for them in the courts. When legal conflicts between the Hopi and the Navajo arose concerning land ownership, anthropologists who had done research with the Navajo advocated their side of the case, while those who had worked with the Hopi took their part. Anthropologists have shared tobacco as still another way of reciprocating. It is curious that the sharing of tobacco seems to occur in cultures all over the world. In Papua New Guinea, we always presented tobacco to people with whom we talked.

Fieldwork involves the anthropologist in a moral dilemma. It could be said that anthropologists use informants for their own ends, since the anthropologists return to their own societies with the information gathered. The analysis and publication of this information in a dissertation or book helps the career of the anthropologist, but in what way does it help the people whose way of life has been recorded? As indicated above, the anthropologist tries in a variety of ways to make some return for what has been given. Often, research done by anthropologists in the past may be of use to the subjects of that research today. For example, the Kwakiutl as well as other Native American peoples have found that ethnographies written at the turn of the century, like those of Boas, and historical studies of Native American tradition are of value as written records of traditions, the knowledge of which by this time may have been lost. Such information has also proved important for Native Americans in pursuing claims regarding fishing rights and land rights. In a more general way, the product of the anthropologist's work makes a scholarly contribution to the wider understanding of human behavior.

In the field, anthropologists observe and record peoples' actions and with the help of informants seek to understand the meanings of those actions. This is illustrated in the photograph of Rubel collecting information from informants on New Ireland (see page 31). These observations by anthropologists are a very important

Author Paula Rubel recording details of a ceremony in New Ireland.

component of fieldwork, as are discussions with informants. But neither alone is sufficient. When informants attempt to explain their culture to anthropologists, the informants are objectifying their own cultural experiences. In order to understand the informants' experiences and thereby grasp their point of view, anthropologists, as noted above, strive to go beyond their *own* cultural categories. In their interactions, informants and anthropologists are, in a sense, operating in an area between their two cultures. The data are thus produced through the mutual efforts of anthropologist and informant. This process is repeated with other informants, and a pattern begins to emerge. The data are checked against the anthropologists' own observations, as well as with other informants with whom contacts are more limited.

The anthropologist performs two kinds of translation. First, there is the translation from the language of the informants to his or her own native tongue. Problems usually arise because the terms in the indigenous language are never exactly equivalent to the concepts in English. For example, when property passes from one generation to the next before the death of the members of the senior generation, this is sometimes "translated" as inheritance in the ethnographic literature. But the definition of inheritance in English presuppposes the death of the member of the senior generation, so this is not a correct translation. In the Kwakiutl wedding we shall describe below, we will see how Boas carried out this kind of translation. The second kind of translation for the anthropologist is to translate the cultural categories of the society being studied into the language of anthropology, that is, the conceptual framework to be set forth in *The Tapestry of Culture*. The basic assumption of this kind of translation is that cultures have characteristics in common, above and beyond those aspects that are unique, and that this can be revealed through comparative research using anthropological concepts. The final product of fieldwork is an ethnography, which embodies the results of fieldwork and analysis.

In the past, anthropological fieldworkers investigated societies that were small both in scale and in population size, where all the spheres of human activity could be explored by a single investigator. They often selected small islands for study, where the unit of analysis was bounded in a most distinct manner. Other anthropologists went off to study societies in Africa and elsewhere, selecting a village or a camp on which to concentrate and from which they generalized about the culture. This unit, sometimes referred to as a **community,** had a name, and the people within recognized themselves as members. The community was bounded in the sense that its members concentrated their interactions within it, and it had an internal social structure that could be discerned. The interaction of the community with other communities was always of concern to the anthropologist. Today, the community remains the starting point for field research.

FROM SMALL-SCALE TO COMPLEX SOCIETIES

In the study of small-scale societies, the community had been taken to represent the culture as a whole. When anthropologists began to study complex societies in the 1930s, it was clear that a single community could not be considered representative of, for example, India, France, or Japan. Such complex societies could not be encompassed in their totality at the level of detail at which the anthropologist worked. As a result of regional, class, occupational, religious, and ethnic differences, complex societies are very heterogeneous and culturally diverse. Such diverse groups have subcultures of their own that may become units of analysis for the anthropologist, who must keep in mind that what is happening locally must always be related to what is happening on a broader national, international, or even global level. Anthropologists working in complex societies may also focus on particular problems, such as rural-urban migration or the effects of the closing of a mine or factory in a company town. They may even study nuclear weapons scientists at Livermore and Los Alamos National Laboratories (Gusterson, 1996). The unit of analysis here is dictated by the problem. It may be a farming community, a labor union, a corporation, or a social movement. In the United States, for example, an anthropologist might focus on some aspects of American culture—what we have in common—or choose to examine cultural aspects or particular problems among the different racial and ethnic populations that are the subgroupings of our society.

Earlier, anthropologists tended to work in areas where their nations had established colonial empires. American anthropologists worked with American Indians, and British and French anthropologists worked in British and French colonies. Some of the entities that anthropologists in the past assumed were indigenous groupings were, in reality, colonial constructs. After contact with Europeans, these small-scale societies were increasingly brought under the jurisdiction of larger political entities, typically European colonial empires. Colonial administrations imposed a structure consisting of tribes and districts in order to govern more easily. At first, anthropologists paid little attention to the nature of the articulation of these small-scale societies to the colonial empires of which they were a part. Today they are interested in the process of how these societies were incorporated into newly formed nation-states. Often they constitute ethnic groups in conflict with one another and with the nation-state. Modernization, industrialization, and globalization have made small-scale societies part of a world system, and anthropologists now investigate how they have responded to those changes.

In recent years, postmodernist anthropologists have begun to rethink exactly how fieldworkers obtain their data and the way ethnographic texts are produced. They talk about describing the way in which the highly personal experience of fieldwork is reconciled with fieldwork as a method of data collection with specific procedures. As fieldwork procedures were made more explicit, postmodernists began to argue that scientific goals could not be achieved. However, being explicit about one's procedures is also part of the process of being scientific. At first, the concern was with being more reflexive, that is, informing the readers of the ethnography about the experiential aspects of the fieldwork, not just the anthropological conclusions of the field research. Later, the rhetorical devices used by anthropologists in the writing of ethnographies became the subject of concern, with the emphasis on how ethnographers convinced their readers that they were actually "there" in the field and that their ethnographic reports were accurate and truthful.

More recently, some postmodern anthropologists have advocated the production of confessional ethnography. In this new type of ethnography, the fieldworker is at the center of the stage, and the focus is on how he or she came to know a particular social world, not on that world itself—that is, the way of life of the people being studied. These new ideas about the ethnographic enterprise have had an impact on the field, if only to make anthropologists more explicit about what they are doing when they do fieldwork and how the various aspects of fieldwork, and other types of research related to the project at hand, are translated into conclusions, in the form of an ethnography, that accurately reflect the social world that the anthropologist has chosen as a subject of research.

It is typically the case that anthropologists come from powerful industrialized nations to conduct research in Third World countries, and the initial relationship in the field may be perceived in terms of dominance and subordination, or power differentials, between anthropologists and informants. Often, anthropologist and informant use one another. The anthropologist may be at the mercy of the informant's desires, sometimes being used to further his or her political ambitions. Informants may see the anthropologist as exploiting them in that he or she is "taking away" their myths, rituals, and traditions and erroneously representing and portraying them as violent or helpless victims to the outside world. All these factors, which are involved in the interaction, influence the nature of the information that is obtained and must be taken into account when the data are being analyzed.

In addition to fieldwork, anthropologists utilize other techniques to collect data, such as historical and archival information, as well as data from archaeological and linguistic investigations and census materials. Research on a culture's past, the ethnohistorical approach referred to in Chapter 1, has become particularly significant as anthropology has moved to a processual model. As anthropologists study new kinds of problems and the unit of analysis is no longer necessarily a community, many supplement the central methodology of anthropology—participant observation—with a variety of additional techniques, such as questionnaires and statistical analyses. The anthropologist then translates these data into the language of anthropological concepts.

A KWAKIUTL MARRIAGE*

After his work with the Eskimo, Boas shifted his research to the Northwest Coast of Canada and to the Kwakiutl. Their culture was to occupy much of his attention for the rest of his life. Over the decades, Boas accumulated what has been described as the "five-foot shelf" of ethnographic data on the Kwakiutl. In addition to short visits, Boas did three months of participant observation during the Kwakiutl Winter Ceremonial of 1894 to 1895. The rest of this enormous bulk of ethnographic material was collected by means of informant interviews by Boas or more

*This section is based on *Kwakiutl Ethnography* by Franz Boas, edited by Helen Codere, adapted by permission of the University of Chicago Press.

frequently by George Hunt, whom Boas trained to be an ethnographic field re-searcher and to record texts in phonetic transcription in Kwakw'ala, the language of the Kwakiutl. Though Hunt's mother was Tlingit, another tribe on the North-west Coast of North America, and his father was Scottish, he grew up at Fort Ru-pert, British Columbia, the home of a number of Kwakiutl tribes, and was a native speaker of Kwakw'ala. Most of the thousands of pages of Kwakw'ala text, which Boas published in his 1910 volume of texts, were collected by Hunt. As Berman notes, "Hunt was not simply an informant, not simply Boas' guide and interpreter in the field. Although he might not have perceived of his activities in such a light, he was a fieldworker in his own right, an ethnographer and author" (Berman, 1991: 15–16). Hunt was an individual who straddled several cultures, Scottish, Tlingit, and Kwakiutl, not only the culture of the area where he grew up, but also the one into which he married.

Boas began visiting the Kwakiutl in the 1880s and the ethnographic descrip-tion he presents tells very little of the changes that had been taking place. In Boas's time, the aim of the anthropologist was to record as much of the tradi-tional culture as possible before it disappeared. This was referred to as salvage anthropology. As a consequence, his description did not take account of the fact that the Kwakiutl at that time were part of the larger Canadian economic and po-litical systems. The blankets they distribute in the ceremonies described below were purchased from the Hudson Bay Company trade store. (These blankets are still sold by the company today.) The enormous amount of material goods in-volved in the ceremonies were obtained with money earned from working lo-cally in canneries and from employment in Victoria, British Columbia, and elsewhere. This description of a Kwakiutl marriage was based on informants' ac-counts collected primarily by George Hunt as well as some participant observa-tion by Hunt. They were organized into a description of the marriage rite by Boas, which was included in a manuscript that remained unpublished until after his death. It is of marriage rites in the nineteenth century, on the occasion of the marriage of the children of chiefs. It combines a general description of the rites with events from actual marriages. Boas frequently shifted from the generalized account to a specific marriage. To the reader, this may appear to be more a de-scription of several elaborate exchanges of property, primarily the Hudson Bay blankets (as can been seen in the illustration of a distribution), rather than an ac-count of the marriage of two people.

There were three stages to a Kwakiutl marriage. The first stage was the initi-ation of negotiations and agreement on the number of blankets to be included in the bridewealth payment to be made by the family of the groom to the family of the bride. The second stage was the formal "wooing" and the transfer of the bridewealth payment from the groom's family to the bride's family at a **potlatch,** that is, a large-scale ceremonial distribution. The third stage was a "repurchase" of the bride by her family when different kinds of goods, names or titles, and privileges went from the family of the bride to that of the groom, also at a pot-latch. When children of important chiefs married, invariably two different Kwak-iutl tribes were involved. All the property distributed must eventually be reciprocated. Payment was also made for the services performed by various chiefs. The giving away of property enhanced the prestige of the donor. The advance in social rank of the participants that derived from the potlatch aspects of a marriage often entirely overshadowed the marriage's primary purpose—the coming together of a man and a woman to establish a family.

NEGOTIATIONS TOWARD A MARRIAGE

The parents or those responsible for the young people arranged the marriage, sometimes without even the knowledge of the young couple. The first messengers were formally sent by the groom's side to the bride's side. They delivered speeches to her father requesting the bride in marriage, and he rewarded them with a pair of blankets. When they returned to the groom, he too rewarded them with a pair of blankets. Then a second group of messengers was sent, this time, chiefs, to deliver messages to the bride's father concerning the marriage proposal. He gave them each two pairs of blankets in return for the messages. That night, the groom went to eat in the bride's house, sitting next to her. The bride's father talked to the groom about the bride's father's expectation of receiving 500 blankets as the bridewealth payment. Subsequently, the groom's father assembled the 500 blankets, and they were piled in front of the door of the bride's father's house. The groom's father, accompanied by several chiefs, then went to the house of the bride. To one chief he said, "It is your office given to you according to the earliest myths to speak about the blankets given away." As the formal speaker, this chief received two blankets for his service from the father of the groom. The blankets were officially counted by the counter from the groom's side and then were handed over to the bride's father by still another officeholder. On receiving the blankets, the father of the bride expressed his thanks.

"WOOING THE BRIDE" AND TRANSFER OF THE BRIDEWEALTH

Several months later, a second ceremony was held at which 550 additional blankets were handed over, this time to "move" the bride. The men of the groom's **numaym,** the Kwakiut term for group of relatives, and those of other *numaym* blackened their faces and dressed like warriors as they went to the house of the bride with the final payment of blankets, which would move her. Often, the bride's doorway was protected by fire against the "invading warriors" of the groom. They might have had to run a gauntlet of flaming torches held by men of the bride's side or, as in another account by Boas, go through a ring of burning cedar bark soaked in oil. At one wedding, after the groom's men proved they were not afraid of fire and the fire burned down, the bride's father "called forth the Devourer of Tribes [a mythical monster], who had devoured all those who had tried to woo his daughter. It was a large mask of a sea bear attached to a bear skin (worn by a man). Seven skulls and a number of long bones were hidden under the bear skin. As soon as the man wearing this masked dress came forth, the bride's father poked its stomach with a pole and it vomited skulls and bones."

Then the chiefs from the groom's side made their traditional wedding speeches. In these speeches, the chiefs called upon their supernatural powers, which came from ancient mythological times inherited down through their families. These powers were said to be used to "move the bride." At one wedding, Made-to-Be-Tied, chief of the Kwa'wadilikala *numaym,* on being called upon, said, "In the beginning of myth times I was the great supernatural Kwa'wadi-likala, the only owner of the great wolf ceremonial that came down to me from heaven. Now I will go and lift the princess." After going out, he returned to the doorway, wearing the great wolf mask of Walking Body, the chief of the wolves. For this he received five blankets from the official speaker representing the groom's side. At a really great wedding, many chiefs who bore illustrious names made speeches, detailing how their privileges descended to them from ancient times. These privileges included a particular title or name, the animal designs worn on clothing—referred to as crests—or in the shape of masks, the songs they sang, and the dances they were privileged to perform. Each received a payment of blankets for, as the Kwakiutl say, "the weight of his breath," referring to the speech that was delivered at the wedding. Their combined breath acted as a weight upon an imaginary scale used to move the bride. The greater the names of the bride, the more speeches, or "breath," were needed to move her to the groom.

After the last of the chiefs had spoken, the ceremony of giving out the blankets brought by the groom's side for the bride's side took place. Blankets were

A Kwakiutl wedding party stands before the bride's house. The house posts are carved with the crests of her numaym.

counted and ceremonially brought into the bride's house. Then the bride's side piled up 200 blankets with the bride sitting alongside them. A chief from the bride's side said, "Come to your wife and take her into your house with these 200 blankets as her mat." The groom's side sang the traditional song of thanks while the bride walked between two officials to the groom's side. Then the new wife was led to the seat she was to occupy, and the 200 blankets were distributed to the guests from other Kwakiutl tribes on the groom's side, but not to members of the groom's own tribe. In the evening, all the distinguished young men of the Kwakiutl tribes assembled to sing love songs and led the bride and groom back to his father's house. The bride's father brought 50 blankets to exchange for food for the young men, which he gave to them to thank them for bringing the groom. The groom sat alongside his new wife, and this part of the marriage ceremony came to an end.

REPURCHASE OF THE WIFE

Some time later, usually after a child was born to the couple, the wife's side began preparations to make a large return payment of goods to the husband's side, a transfer of property that constituted what Boas refers to as the repurchase of the wife by her own *numaym*. The Kwakiutl term for this payment is translated

The speaker for the chief distributes blankets at a Kwakiutl wedding potlatch held in 1894.

as payment of the marriage debt. Since the wife's group was the "receiver" of the marriage potlatch given by the groom's group, it was under obligation to make a return in kind. The repurchase at another potlatch constituted this return. The return did not consist of Hudson Bay Company blankets, which was what was originally received, but of objects known in Kwakiutl as "trifles, bad things." As we shall see from what the list of items included, trifles and bad things meant just the opposite. The return was far in excess of what the wife's father had received. In one of Boas's examples of a repurchase, the items included the following traditional Kwakiutl valuables—120 box covers set with sea otter teeth, 100 abalone shells, copper bracelets, horn bracelets covered with dentalia shells, miniature coppers, 1,000 strings of dentalia one fathom long, 200 dressed deerskins, 500 cedar bark blankets, 200 mats, an equal number of wooden boxes, two neck rings of twisted copper, and hammered copper objects of great value, "as mast of the marriage debt canoe." A large amount of food was also provided, as well as the horn and wooden spoons with which to eat it. Names or titles and privileges were also given to the son-in-law as part of the repurchase payment.

When everything was ready, the wife's father called together his *numaym* to announce that he was going to hold a potlatch to repay the marriage debt. The song leader of his *numaym* was asked to write a new song to commemorate the occasion, which he did. The song described the privileges and the copper that were to be given to the groom. Coppers were ceremonial objects in the form of a shield, made of beaten local copper, which attained increased value in terms of the number of blankets paid for them as they passed from chief to chief. They had no other function than to be distributed at potlatches. Then father-in-law and son-in-law each invited their respective *numayms* to attend. After breakfast, the men of the father-in-law's *numaym* carried the goods to the son-in-law's house. There they arranged the box covers, which were part of the distribution, in a square or rectangle, which was called the catamaran because it was supposed to represent the boat upon which the father-in-law came to repay the debt. All the other goods were piled on top, and the *numaym* of the father-in-law "went on board," where they then sang the song of repayment of the marriage debt. In keeping with the symbolism of warfare, the younger brother of the son-in-law, his face blackened as a warrior, rushed out and split one of the box covers with an ax, thereby "sinking the catamaran." The box containing the symbols of the privileges to be given to the son-in-law was carried out from the father-in-law's house, and the wife, who was being repurchased, emerged from the house bearing the copper that was to be transferred. The young wife and her father both danced to the accompaniment of the new marriage repayment song. The father-in-law's speaker presented the box of privileges to the son-in-law and then presented the copper. The speaker of the husband's *numaym* expressed his thanks. Then the father-in-law's speaker arose and bestowed names that traditionally belonged to the wife's family upon the husband and his two sisters. These names constituted the final part of the marriage repayment, all the other items having already been transferred. The husband's *numaym* sang songs of gratitude, and this ended the ceremony of marriage repurchase.

ANALYSIS

Marriage for the Kwakiutl was clearly not a single event, but a series of events that extended for years, since the repurchase of a wife was normally not held until after the birth of a child. When the wife had been repurchased by her father and her own *numaym,* she was really free to return to her father unless her husband purchased her for the second time. This was followed by a second repurchase by her own group. These exchanges of property via potlatches could take place up to four times, after which the wife's rank was so high, because of the goods expended in the successive repurchases, that she could "stay for nothing." Since the giver of the potlatch fed the great numbers of guests who came to witness these events and thereby enhanced his prestige with each potlatch, the families of both groom and bride respectively increased their standing with each potlatch and its transfer of goods.

Boas's English translation of the Kwakw'ala texts that describe Kwakiutl marriage includes terms such as property, debt, privileges, inheritance, rank, seats, names, and titles. These English terms do not map onto Kwak'wala terms that have no precise equivalents in English. Boas uses the English term *property* for blankets and valuables, names, rights to songs, dances, and the wearing of "crests"—carved or painted designs. We would not consider rights to use a personal name as "property." Kwakiutl "names" are the "property" of a *numaym*. In our culture, an individual possesses a name. Are these names "inherited" among the Kwakiutl in terms of the English meaning of the word? No, since the meaning of inheritance in English is the passing on of property after death, but among the Kwakiutl property is passed on during the lifetime of the owner, before his or her death. These points all illustrate problems of translation encountered in describing another culture, which we have discussed earlier. The last problem of translation in our description of a Kwakiutl wedding was that Boas never could find a satisfactory English translation for the Kwakiutl term *numaym*, which refers to a kind of kin group. He therefore left the Kwakiutl term, untranslated, in his description. When there are too many such native terms, the reader's ability to comprehend is seriously hindered.

The ritual of marriage among the Kwakiutl embodies many of the central ideas in Kwakiutl culture. The Kwakiutl emphasis on rank was reiterated again and again throughout the course of the marriage potlatch. The high rank of the bride demanded that there be large payments for her. At the same time, such payments enhanced the rank of the giver, the groom. The importance of making a return for what one has received was reflected in the repurchase payment made by the bride's side. Seating of guests at the potlatch and the order in which they received gifts revealed their ranking with respect to one another. The political power and legitimacy of sponsoring chiefs was also demonstrated in the potlatch. The claim to rightfully own a title or name was made by a chief at a potlatch when he recited the line of ancestors through whom the title was passed until it reached him. Lastly, the marriage ceremony was symbolically conceptualized as a form of warfare, in which warriors demonstrated their bravery in capturing the bride and the return purchase was conveyed by a symbolic war canoe.

AN AMERICAN MARRIAGE

As we have noted earlier, when anthropologists began to do fieldwork in complex Western societies in the 1930s, of necessity their fieldwork methods and the nature of their analyses and conclusions changed. This development can be illustrated by an ethnographic example from our own society. As noted in the previous chapter, complex societies such as our own are composed of different social classes and subgroups with differing perspectives. American weddings, for example, are differentiated according to religion, ethnic background, occupation, and social class. The factor of personal preference, absent in the earlier Kwakiutl wedding rituals, plays an important role in the wide range of American weddings that occur each year. Each Sunday, the *New York Times* has a column describing innovative weddings, which illustrates their wide diversity. Weddings are conducted by male and female rabbis, priests, and ministers, Wiccan ritualists, swamis, and so on. They often meld different traditions such, as Jewish and Korean, and Native American, African-American, African, Christian, and Egyptian Kemetic rituals.

Kwakiutl marriage rituals had kinship, economic, religious, political, aesthetic, and performative dimensions, a characteristic that led Marcel Mauss, the French anthropologist of the early twentieth century, to refer to such rituals as "total social phenomena" (1925). In contrast, in complex societies, in addition to the variegated nature of social groupings, there are complex political economies and institutional specialization. As a consequence, when one examines weddings in American, one finds that there is a wedding industry, wedding magazines, wedding boutiques, with wedding planners and individuals who specialize in providing distinctive commodities and specialized services. An American wedding is less than what Mauss referred to as a total social phenomenon. However, just as the Kwakiutl wedding informed us about Kwakiutl culture, an analysis of an American wedding provides insights into the particular American subculture of the individuals who are marrying.

How does one go about doing an anthropological investigation of the pattern of weddings conducted by members of a particular American subculture or class? One could do participant observation at several weddings. This would include observing and recording information about all the preparations of the families of the individuals marrying, as well as interviewing all the various participants to determine the economics of the wedding and to obtain background information on the families for each wedding. What were the considerations that led to the decisions about the date of the wedding, the degree of its elaboration, the kind of wedding dress the bride would wear—her mother's or other relative's dresses, or one purchased in a store specializing in such dresses—and the responsibility for payment of the various expenses of the wedding? One would try to participate in as many events as possible leading up to and including the marriage ceremony. Accurate information on the expenditures for each category as well as the total cost of the wedding might be difficult to obtain because this information is considered private. This is what Rubel did when she studied Kalmyk-Mongol culture in the 1960s, examining which features were from the past, as described in earlier accounts going back to 1776 and which represented successive innovations (Rubel, 1967).

Books on etiquette, such as *Good Housekeeping's Book of Today's Etiquette*, provide guidelines on how to conduct an American wedding. They are statements of the ideal pattern or set of guidelines. We have chosen to describe the wedding of two well-known celebrities in American society because of its similarities to the Kwakiutl marriage of the children of high-ranking chiefs. We will describe the wedding of Maria Shriver and Arnold Schwarzenegger, which was held on April 26, 1986. The authors did not attend this wedding. Therefore, the following description is not based on participant observation and fieldwork. Instead, it is based upon the only public information provided, which was in *Time* magazine, the *New York Times,* and the *Cape Cod Times.*

Just as the daughter of a Kwakiutl chief belongs to the highest ranks of her society, Maria Shriver, a member of the Kennedy clan, belongs to the moneyed American elite. Her mother, Eunice, is a sister of the late president John F. Kennedy. Her father, Sargent Shriver, was the first director of the Peace Corps, a former ambassador to France, and the Democratic nominee for vice president in 1972. The bride is a television celebrity, who, at the time of her marriage, was co-anchor of the *CBS Morning News.* The Austrian-born Schwarzenegger, originally a bodybuilder and now a film superstar, is the son of a local Austrian police chief, now deceased. The two first met eight years earlier, a year after her graduation from Georgetown University, at a tennis tournament sponsored by the Kennedy family and named for Maria's late uncle, Robert F. Kennedy. At that time she was working for a small television station. She interrupted her own career to work on her Uncle Ted's presidential bid in 1980. In 1981, breaking with the East Coast family tradition, she moved to Los Angeles to continue her career on her own and to be near her boyfriend, Arnold. She worked as a magazine reporter for two years and then returned to television as a reporter for CBS. Schwarzenegger, who has a degree in business and marketing from the University of Wisconsin, became famous as a bodybuilder. He subsequently became a movie star after starring in the movie *Pumping Iron.*

Arnold proposed to Maria during a trip to Austria in August 1985, and they then purchased a $3 million house in Pacific Palisades. After their decision to marry, Maria was offered the anchor position at *CBS Morning News,* which required her to move to New York and be apart from her future husband. The couple did not marry until she was 30 and he was 38, eight years after they first met. This may have been due to the demands of their two careers. Women with careers now tend to marry when they are in their thirties, though this was not the case in American society at an earlier time.

The wedding was held at the summer residence of the Kennedys in Hyannis, Massachusetts. At the rehearsal dinner, which was held at the Hyannisport Country Club, Arnold's mother hosted an "Austrian clambake" and served lobster and wiener schnitzel, and Arnold dressed in traditional Tyrolean lederhosen, a bit of an ethnic touch. A bachelor party for Arnold had been held a month earlier in Santa Monica. The Roman Catholic wedding mass, performed by the Reverend John Baptist Riordan, was held at St. Francis Xavier Roman Catholic Church, the Kennedy family's parish church in Hyannis. Since the couple wanted their wedding to be a "private" affair, details of the wedding were kept from the media, except for information provided by a publicist hired to handle wedding press coverage. Kennedy influence was used to maintain tight security and keep gossip columnists and journalists away from the wedding party. Provincetown-Boston Airline, which flies to Hyannis, was "persuaded" to lock up its computer a day before the wedding so that the guest list would not be revealed. The bride, ever career-oriented, told her viewers she would be off for several days, without mentioning her forthcoming wedding, and the groom arrived the day before the wedding from Puerta Vallarta, where he had been filming a new movie, *Predator*, the film that subsequently launched him as a superstar.

The bride wore a white muslin, silk, and lace gown with an 11-foot train. The gown was made by Christian Dior, who had designed the wedding dress of the bride's mother in 1953. The groom wore a classic gray cutaway coat, pleated white shirt, gray vest, and gray-striped ascot, what Emily Post deems appropriate for afternoon weddings. A fellow bodybuilder, Franco Columbu, served as his best man. The 13 ushers included the bride's four brothers, the bridegroom's cousin and nephew, and bodybuilder friends of the groom. The maid of honor was the bride's cousin Caroline Bouvier Kennedy, daughter of the late President Kennedy. Among the bridesmaids were several other Kennedy cousins. Some 60 women, guests and members of the bridal party, had their hair coiffed at the local beauty salon on the morning of the wedding, but the bride's hair was done by her own hairdresser, who came from Los Angeles specifically for this purpose. Besides members of the Kennedy family, the more than 450 guests included television celebrities Diane Sawyer, Tom Brokaw, and Barbara Walters; advice columnist Abigail Van Buren; pop artist Andy Warhol (wearing a black leather jacket over a black tuxedo, and black Reebok sneakers); and singer/actress Grace Jones. Proclaiming the most recent fashions of that time, female guests wore dresses sporting geometric designs from the art deco period and from pop art. Since reporters were barred from the church itself, a viewing stand was erected across the street for them.

The bride and her father walked up the aisle to the familiar wedding march, Wagner's "Bridal March" from the opera *Lohengrin* ("Here comes the bride . . ."). The details of the religious ceremony had been planned by the bride and groom themselves. The couple exchanged traditional Roman Catholic vows, which had been rewritten to remove sexist language, replacing "man and wife" with "husband and wife." Short selections from the New Testament were then read by Senator Ted Kennedy and by a friend of Schwarzenegger. Intercessions, which are included in a Roman Catholic wedding, written by the wedding couple and read by the bride's parents and brother called for an end to terrorism and war, proclaimed the bride and groom as a model couple, honored deceased Kennedys, and discussed the meaning of Passover. These topics were a reflection of themes important in America at the time. Discussing the meaning of Passover, which was taking place that month, demonstrated the ecumenical feelings of the bride and groom. Oprah Winfrey, the television host, then read Elizabeth Barrett Browning's poem "How Do I Love Thee?"—a choice of the bride. After a series of musical selections, the ceremony concluded with the bridal couple's walking together down the aisle to Rodgers and Hammerstein's "Bridal March" from *The Sound of Music*.

After the ceremony, limousines and buses took the guests to the Kennedy compound for the reception. All air traffic within a two-mile radius of the compound was prohibited from cruising below 2,000 feet for the entire day. The reception was held in two huge white tents, with heaters to keep out the chill winds. Fruit trees in pink and white blossoms decorated the tents. The guests danced to music played

Maria Shriver and Arnold Schwarzenegger exiting the church after their marriage.

by Peter Duchin's band, which often plays at society occasions. An elaborate lunch (including cold lobster in the shell and chicken breast with champagne sauce) was concluded with the cutting of an eight-tier, 425-pound wedding cake, topped by traditional figures of a bride and groom, baked by the Shriver family chef and modeled after Maria Shriver's parents' wedding cake. The couple took a brief honeymoon before returning to work, he to his filming in Puerta Vallarta, she to her anchor position at CBS in New York. Today, Maria Shriver is a contributor editor for *Dateline NBC* and an author of several books. Arnold continues to make movies and even has his own website. The couple have four children, two boys and two girls.

This account is a description of a single wedding taken from the published sources. Many events occurred that were not reported by the press. When the families of the bride and groom are strangers to one another, there is usually a formal meeting of the two sets of parents before the wedding. There is no information on whether or how the Shrivers met Mrs. Schwarzenegger. Often, the bride receives an engagement ring, and an engagement party is held. Wedding gifts may be publicly displayed at the bride's home. According to *Good Housekeeping's Book of Today's Etiquette,* "The expenses of the wedding are divided in a time-honored way." The bride's family pays for the following: invitations; reception cards and announcements; rental of the place where the ceremony is to be held; fee for the organist, choir, and sexton; transportation of the bridal party from house to church or temple and from there to the reception; bridesmaids' bouquets; the bride's gifts to the bridesmaids; the bride's wedding dress and trousseau; and all the expenses of the reception. The groom pays for the engagement and wedding rings, marriage license, contribution to the clergyman, flowers for the bride's mother and groom's mother, and the bachelor dinner. No information was provided regarding the financial arrangements of the Shriver-Schwarzenegger wedding and who paid for which expenses. The financial status of the parties involved is not the sole factor in determining which of these features of an American wedding will be present or absent. Today, couples often live together, sometimes for several years, before getting married. Despite this, they may elect to go through some or all of the ceremonies associated with an American wedding. The bride wears a white gown, a symbol of virginity, even though the couple may have lived together for several years.

Just as a Kwakiutl wedding reveals themes and patterns central to Kwakiutl culture, so does an American wedding illuminate symbolic themes in American culture. The bride in her white gown symbolizes purity and virginity, though given today's sexual mores, she in fact may not possess these attributes. Nevertheless, the bride is not likely to wear a purple gown. The hall bedecked with blossoms and the wedding march with its all-too-familiar lyrics echo the same themes. In American society, the powerful, moneyed elite frequently reiterate their familial connections at ritual occasions. Thus we are reminded in various ways of Maria Shriver's connection to her mother, Joseph Kennedy's daughter, and to the rest of the Kennedy clan. Like her mother's gown, her gown was designed by Dior; and her wedding cake was a replica of her mother's. This extravagant wedding with 450 guests was characterized by the couple as a "private" affair. However, though they called it a private affair, Maria and Arnold meant just the opposite, just as in a Kwakiutl wedding reference to "trifles" meant just the opposite. The fact that there was a publicist controlling information dispensed about the wedding attests to its public nature. At the Kwakiutl wedding, marriage is symbolized in a very different way, with an enormous audience witnessing the capture of the bride by warriors of one *numaym* and her movement to her husband's *numaym.*

 ## THE COMPARATIVE APPROACH— EXAMINING SIMILARITIES AND DIFFERENCES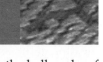

Earlier we noted that fieldwork and participant observation were the hallmarks of anthropological methodology. In the same manner, the comparative approach is central to the discipline. A comparison of Kwakiutl and American weddings reveals that in an American wedding, even that of a member of an important family, the focus is almost exclusively on the bride and groom. The Shriver-Schwarzenegger wedding more or less conformed to the ideal pattern of an American wedding, though much grander in scale. American weddings are less a matter of two kin groups establishing a relationship, as was the case in a Kwakiutl wedding, and more a matter of bringing together and displaying the groom's and bride's personal network of friends and colleagues. Because, in the wedding just described, both bride and groom had established careers and were such well-known celebrities, their personal network was large and studded with famous personalities, making this wedding different from other American weddings. Celebrities like Oprah Winfrey and Andy Warhol used the occasion of the wedding to draw attention to themselves. The bride and groom planned the wedding themselves. They acted as the centers of all activity, though other individuals from their respective families as well as friends and relatives played some part. This emphasis on the couple themselves demonstrates the importance in American culture of the newly formed family as autonomous and separate from other families. The Kwakiutl wedding, on the other hand, was a total social phenomenon in which the entire community was involved and in which elements of economics, politics, and political maneuvering concerning transfer of a whole series of privileges as well as property were at issue. In fact, Boas, the observer, noted that these things overshadowed the purpose of the wedding—to establish a new family. In the American wedding, economics were involved, in that goods were purchased and there were many expenditures. But the Kwakiutl marriage itself was an institution for transfers of large amounts of property. Religion was involved in the American wedding, in that a priest officiated and Roman Catholic vows were exchanged. Similarly, in the Kwakiutl marriage the rights and privileges exhibited demanded the recitation of myths linking people to their ancestors, a cornerstone of Kwakiutl religious belief. In a Kwakiutl marriage the whole underlying structure of Kwakiutl society is played out. In contrast, in America, where there has been more institutional separation, an entire wedding industry exists. A wedding really focuses on the couple who are establishing the new family, and other aspects are only tangentially related.

In addition to the differences, there are some interesting similarities that should not go unnoticed. In both Kwakiutl and American societies, all weddings are public ceremonies witnessed by guests. In both instances, the guests who attend the ceremony and communally eat the food perform the function of publicly witnessing a rite of passage. In the American wedding described, an attempt was made to keep it "a private affair," limited to just 450 witnesses. However, as celebrities, the bride and groom also wanted the entire society to witness their wedding, but they wanted to control the information that was made available. In both societies, prestige is determined by the size of the outlay, which, in turn, relates to the social status of the families involved. The more lavish the display, the greater the standing and renown of the participants and their families. In these respects, the display exhibited at the Shriver-Schwartzenegger wedding—the lavish hair-dressing activities, the art deco costuming of the guests, for example—resembled that of a potlatch, at which prestige derives from conspicuous extravagance.

SUMMARY

- The defining methodology of anthropology is fieldwork. This involves living with and interacting with the people and learning their language.

- Cultural shock is the realization that other people do things differently and one's own culture is not "natural."

- The heart of fieldwork is participant observation, which involves an inherent contradiction in that one is at the same time an observer outside the culture as well as a participant inside the culture.

- The fieldworker must learn how to view things from the native's point of view, that is, according to the concepts and ideas which order their world.

- The anthropologist gains information from people who are referred to as informants. They eventually become fieldworker-colleagues.

- Fieldwork involves reciprocity in the sense that informants provide information and the anthropologist gives various forms of assistance, including acting as a partisan for the group in legal matters.

- The anthropologist not only talks to informants about a variety of matters, but also makes his or her own observations.

- The anthropologist does two kinds of translations. The first is from the indigenous language to the anthropologist's own language and the second is into the analytical concepts of anthropology.

- The unit of analysis for anthropology in small-scale societies was the community. As anthropology has shifted to complex societies, the unit of analysis is now dictated by the particular problem selected.

- Small-scale societies have now become part of the world system and are now affected by modernization, industrialization, and globalization. Anthropologists examine how they have responded to these changes.

- Postmodernists have forced us to make our fieldwork procedures more explicit, including informing readers about the experiential aspects of fieldwork and how the data are translated into conclusions in the form of ethnography.

- In addition to fieldwork, anthropologists utilize other techniques to collect data, such as historical and archival information, as well as data from archaeological and linguistic investigations and census materials.

- The description of the Kwakiutl wedding is based on informant interviews conducted by Boas and Hunt in Kwak'wala language and recorded in the form of Kwak'wala texts that were then translated into English.

- The description of the American wedding is based on public documents.

• Rich, detailed ethnographic descriptions, applied in the comparative approach, reveal certain basic similarities between American and Kwakiutl weddings, along with the differences in symbolic meanings. The Kwakiutl marriage ceremonies emphasize central themes in Kwakiutl culture such as exchange of property at potlaches and relations between kin groups and rank. The American wedding symbolizes different themes: the kinship networks of the bride and groom and their wealth and status in American societies. The similarities in both examples are conspicuous consumption and display, making the American wedding look like a potlatch, and the public witnessing of the ceremony.

 SUGGESTED READINGS

Bradburd, Daniel. *Being There: The Necessity of Fieldwork.* Washington, D.C.: Smithsonian Institution, 1998. An account of fieldwork with the Komache nomads of southern Iran, which shows how direct interaction with another culture is essential for anthropological understanding, and documents the author's progress towards understanding another culture.

Codere, Helen. "Kwakiutl" in *Perspectives in American Indian Culture Change,* edited By Edward Spicer. Chicago: University of Chicago Press, 1961. An account of Kwakiutl culture change from the time of the Indians' original initial contact with white society to the contemporary period.

DeWalt, Billy R. *Participant Observation: A Guide for Fieldworkers.* Walnut Creek, CA: Altamira Press, 2002. A detailed account of how to do participant observation, a central aspect of anthropological fieldwork.

Dresch, Paul, Wendy James, and David J. Parkin (eds.). *Anthropologists in a Wider World: Essays on Field Research.* New York: Berghahan Books, 2002. A group of anthropologists who have worked in many parts of the world explore the transformation in their worldview and approach necessitated by their shift from village studies to the study of large-scale or dispersed communities.

Sanjek, Roger (ed.). *Fieldnotes: The Making of Anthropology.* Ithaca, N.Y. Cornell University Press, 1990. Selections of articles by anthropologists on the problems of analyzing their Fieldnotes.

Wolf, Diane L. (ed.) *Feminist Dilemmas in Fieldwork.* Boulder: Westview Press, 1996. A collection of essays that focus on the way in which gender, as well as ethnic identity, influence the data collected as a consequence of the ethnographic encounter.

 SUGGESTED WEBSITES

http://coombs.anu.edu.au/Biblio/biblio_fieldwok7.html A bibliography containing numerous personal accounts of anthropological fieldwork.

http://www.temple.edu/anthro/ruby/boas.html Analysis of a film Boas made of the Kwakiutl in 1930, when Boas was 70 years old. It depicts the movements involved in Kwakiutl dance, basketry and woodworking.

http://www.schwarzenegger.com/en/index.asp For more on Arnold Schwarzenegger see his personal website.

3

Language and Culture

Language is a part of culture, and yet it is more than that. It is central to culture since it is the means through which most of culture is learned and communicated. As we shall see below, when a group begins to lose its language, its cultural tapestry starts to unravel. Infants learn the language and simultaneously acquire the culture of the society into which they are born, and we will discuss the processes by which these take place in Chapter 4. In our discussion of fieldwork in Chapter 2, we described the way in which anthropologists carrying out field research learn the language as they study the culture, just as a child does in that culture. Only humans have the capacity for language, grammar, syntax, and speech. In any language, a limitless number of possible sentences can be constructed and used to convey an infinite number of cultural ideas. This allows humans to communicate cultural ideas and symbolic meanings from one generation to the next in a cumulative fashion and to constantly create new cultural ideas. Because of this, human language is significantly different from any other system of animal communication.

THE STRUCTURE OF LANGUAGE

Like culture, language is patterned. As the Swiss linguist Ferdinand de Saussure (1915) pointed out, the units of language that carry meaning are two-sided. One side is the physical characteristics that make up the word. These characteristics consist of sounds, or vibrations of the vocal chords, transmitted through the air, which emanate from one person and are received by the ear of another. The other side consists of the word's meaning or what it stands for. For example, the word *tree* is made up of a particular series of sounds—t/r/e—and it stands for:

The same object is referred to as *arbre* in French and *Baum* in German. Thus the connection between any combination of sounds that make up a word and its meaning is mostly arbitrary—that is, there is no intrinsic and natural connection between the sounds of a word and its meaning. The same meaning—tree—is conveyed by a different combination of sounds in each language. Occasionally, there is some natural connection between sound and meaning, as occurs in words that imitate natural phenomena, such as *buzz* and *hiss*. Language is therefore not completely arbitrary.

PHONEMIC STRUCTURE

We have mentioned that language is patterned. Let us begin at the level of sound, the building blocks of language. Every language has a small number of basic sounds, usually between 20 and 40, which are used in various combinations to make up the units of meaning. These basic sound units are called **phonemes.** All languages are constructed in the same way. From a small number of phonemes, arranged in different ways, an infinite number of words can be produced. For example, the English word *pin* differs in meaning from *pan* since /i/ is a different phoneme from /a/. Add /s/ to *pin* and you get the plural form of *pin,* that is, *pins.* But if the /s/ is added to the beginning of the word, rather than the end, the result is *spin,* a word with a totally different meaning. Thus, the same phonemes in a different order produce a word with a different meaning.

If the reader has been paying close attention, he or she will have noted that the /p/ in *pin* is different from the /p/ in *spin*. If you hold a sheet of paper in front of your mouth and pronounce *pin* loudly, the paper will flutter because the /p/ in *pin* is aspirated (air blows out of the mouth). Pronounce *spin* and the sheet of paper remains still, because the /p/ in *spin* is not aspirated. The two /p/'s are said to be **allophones** of the same phoneme. They are variant forms of the single English phoneme /p/. They vary because of their environments, that is, the contexts in which they are found.

The phonemes of a language form a structure or system. The phonemes of English can be divided into vowels and consonants. For a native speaker, English consonants seem independent and unrelated to one another. However, let us examine the following list of some English consonants:

t   d

p   b

$$f \qquad v$$

$$s \qquad z$$

$$k \qquad g$$

When one makes the sounds /t/ and /d/, the tongue, teeth, and lips, which are called the points of articulation, are in the same position for both. This is also true for the other paired sounds on the two lists—/p/ and /b/, /f/ and /v/, /s/ and /z/, and /k/ and /g/. There is a relationship between the group of consonants in the left-hand column and the group of consonants in the right-hand column. The consonants in the column on the left are all pronounced without vibrations of the vocal cords. They are voiceless consonants. The vocal cords vibrate when those in the right-hand column are pronounced. These are called voiced consonants. The distinction between voiced and voiceless consonants is one of the several kinds of distinctions characterizing English phonemes. All these features organize the set of English phonemes into a structure and serve to differentiate each phoneme from every other. If the phonemes of a language are structured, then what is their function? Phonemes serve to differentiate words like *pin* and *pan.* Though phonemes themselves do not carry meaning, their function is to differentiate words in terms of their meanings.

MORPHEMIC STRUCTURE

The units of language that carry meaning are called **morphemes.** Morphemes are not equivalent to words, because some words may be broken into smaller units that themselves carry meaning. For example, the word *shoemaker* may be subdivided into three separate morphemes: *shoe, make,* and *-er,* each with its own meaning. Each of these morphemes is in turn made up of phonemes. Some morphemes, like *shoe,* can stand independently. These are called free morphemes. Others, like *-er,* meaning "one who has to do with," are always found bound to other morphemes (as in *speaker, singer,* and *leader*) and are referred to as bound morphemes. Sometimes two or more forms, that is, combinations of phonemes, have the same meaning. The form *-er* has the same meaning in English as *-ist* in the word *pianist.* These two forms, *-er* and *-ist,* are known as **allomorphs** of the same morpheme. Every language has its own morphemic structure.

SYNTAX AND GRAMMAR

The rules by which larger speech units, such as phrases and sentences, are formed compose the **syntax** of a language. English, like all other languages, has rules about the order of words in a sentence. Word order conveys meaning. Thus, "man bites dog" has a meaning different from "dog bites man." In the film *E.T. The Extra-Terrestrial,* E.T.'s sentence "Home phone" is undecipherable; when he says "Phone home," however, his hearers understand him. The ways in which a language indicates singular and plural are also part of its syntax.

The complete description of a language is known as its **grammar.** This would include the phonology (a description of its phonemic system), the morphology (a description of its morphemic system), and the syntax. In addition, a complete description of a language would also include a lexicon, or dictionary, that lists all the morphemes and their meanings.

LINGUISTIC RELATIVITY

Early in the nineteenth century, European philologists made the discovery that ancient Sanskrit, Latin, Greek, and most of the languages of modern Europe belong to a single language family—Indo-European—meaning that all these languages had evolved from a single ancestral language and are basically similar to one another. When linguists began to encounter the languages spoken by native North Americans, languages unrelated to Indo-European, they assumed (incorrectly) that these languages could be analyzed in terms of Latin grammatical categories. These linguists were ethnocentric in their approach and ranked languages as more or less advanced. They termed languages "advanced" if they were spoken by people who were "civilized." Hunters and gatherers, who were considered at a lower cultural level, were said to speak "primitive" languages. The intensive study of American Indian languages, spearheaded by Franz Boas at the beginning of the twentieth century, demonstrated the fallacious reasoning behind this nineteenth-century evolutionary approach to language. Boas's own work concentrated on the Kwakiutl, as we noted in Chapters 1 and 2. He encouraged his students to go out and study other American Indian languages. It became evident to Boas, and later to others, that languages could not be rated on a scale from simple to complex and that there is no one-to-one relationship between technological complexity or cultural complexity, and linguistic complexity. All languages known to linguists, regardless of whether the society had writing, are equally complex. This is known as **linguistic relativity.** It parallels the concept of cultural relativity. Furthermore, Boas convincingly demonstrated that it was necessary to analyze each language in terms of its own structure. This is not to say that there are no universals in language and that languages are not related to one another. All languages have a phonemic system, a morphology, and syntax. The American linguist Noam Chomsky has taken a position against linguistic relativity. He argues that there are a great many other shared characteristics in all languages. These, he claims, are due to the underlying structure of the human brain.

HISTORICAL LINGUISTICS
AND LANGUAGE CHANGE

As noted in Chapter 1, cultures are continually undergoing some degree of change. Since language is a part of culture, it too is always changing. Of course, during one's lifetime, one is not aware of linguistic change, except for changes in vocabulary, particularly slang words and expressions. (How many Americans under age 70 would understand the meaning of "The Flat Foot Floogie with the Floy Floy," the title of a popular song of 1940?) If we compare our language usage today with that of the language of Shakespeare's plays, the extent to which English has changed over the past centuries is obvious.

It is apparent that present-day dialect differences represent developments from a single earlier form of the language. How do such dialect differences arise in the first place? Speech communities are made up of members of a group within a society who interact and speak frequently with one another. One speech community that is very similar to a neighboring speech community will develop slight differences in pronunciation or vocabulary, differentiating it from its neighbor. As these differences increase, they become the basis for greater dialect differentiation. Dialect differentiation, over time, leads to further divergence and eventually to the development of two separate languages.

If one examines French, Spanish, Portuguese, and Italian, one can immediately recognize many similarities. Some languages, such as Spanish and Portuguese, are more closely related than others, such as French and Portuguese. Because of the high degree of mutual intelligibility between Spanish and Portuguese, one could argue that these two languages are more like different dialects of a single language. All these languages, along with other languages, such as Rumanian, are daughter languages, descendants of the vernacular Latin spoken during the time of Julius Caesar. Vernacular Latin was the language spoken by the common people, and it differs from the literary Latin familiar to us from the scholarly works of that time. Dialects of the Latin language spread over large parts of Europe and the Mediterranean world as a result of Roman conquest. These dialects of Latin later developed into separate languages. The vernacular Latin of the Roman period is referred to as the **proto-language,** and the present-day daughter languages descended from it are known as Romance languages. In parallel fashion, English, Dutch, German, and the Scandinavian languages compose the Germanic language family—all descended from a common proto-language called Proto-Germanic. Similarly, all the Slavic languages (Russian, Polish, Czech, Serbo-Croatian, for example) are descended from Proto-Slavic. The European languages we have just mentioned, along with other European and Asian languages, such as Persian, Hindi, and Bengali, form a large family of related languages called the Indo-European language family. All these languages are descended from a common ancestor, Proto-Indo-European.

Recent research on the identity of the language community of Proto-Indo-European speakers, and where and when they lived, demonstrates how useful a convergence of linguists and archaeology can be (Anthony, 1996). Since the Proto-Indo-European speakers had words for beaver, otter, birch, and aspen, and used euphemisms for the ritually important bear, they must have lived in a temperate climate—now thought to be the Ukraine and western Russia. Archaeologists identify them with the Yamna people who lived in this area about 3500 B.C. and who were among the earliest to domesticate and ride horses, and to use wheeled vehicles. The latter enabled some Yamna people to migrate into western Europe, while others moved south into Iran and southeast into India, resulting in the diversification that produced the various branches of Indo-European.

Not all languages spoken in Europe are part of this family. Finnish and Hungarian belong to the Finno-Ugric family, while Basque, which is completely unrelated to any other language, is called a language isolate.

For the languages of Europe, where written records have existed for millennia, the historical sequence of language development is known. The written record going back to Latin enables us to know what Proto-Romance was like. Languages thought to be related are systematically studied, using the **comparative method.** This can be illustrated with a simple example from the Germanic languages. The English word *dance* has as its equivalent the German word *Tanz,* and the English word *door* has as its equivalent the German *Tür.* These forms have the same meaning, and their phonemic structures are similar but not identical. These pairs are referred to as **cognates.** The initial *d* in English regularly corresponds to the initial *t* in German. These two forms represent modern divergences from the original phoneme in Proto-Germanic. This correspondence operates throughout the two languages, so that everywhere one finds an initial *d* in English, one would expect to find an initial *t* in German. This is just a single example of the many sound correspondences to be found between German and English.

As a result of their traditional association with small-scale societies, anthropologists studied the languages of the indigenous people of North and South America, Africa, and Oceania. Until studied by anthropologists, these languages had not been recorded in written form. In the same fashion as the European languages discussed above, these languages are organized in terms of language families. Some of these language families are very large, encompassing many languages, whereas others may be very small or may even be isolates, like Basque.

If one systematically compares cognates in two unwritten languages, such as Navajo and Apache, and finds similar sound correspondences, this demonstrates that the two languages were genetically related to one another and belonged to the same language family, Athapaskan. It also enables one to reconstruct a tentative picture of the phonemic and morphemic structure of the proto-language from which these present-day languages have descended. This provides information about what the culture of the speakers of this proto-language was like. Words in the proto-language for plants, trees, and animals are used to pinpoint the possible location of the speakers' original homeland before they dispersed. This type of research enables us to say that the original homeland of the Navajo and the Apache was in the forest area of northwestern Canada where many speakers of other Athapaskan languages still live. The Navajo and Apache migrated from this area to their present home in the Southwest more than a thousand years ago. Recently linguists have shown the relationship between language families like Indo-European and Uralic, Altaic, Eskimo-Aleut, and Chukchi-Kamchatka, placing them in a single super-family, Eurasitic. The objective of this research is to try to show the hierarchical relationship between language families and the way in which different language groups developed as *Homo sapiens* spread out from Africa. The aim is to create a model of the Proto-Language from which all other languages developed (Cavalli-Sforza, 2000: 169). These people are "lumpers," in contrast to those who see each language as different and unique.

Languages also change as a result of diffusion, or borrowing from speakers of one language by speakers of another language. This may be the borrowing of words, sounds, or grammatical forms. Contact and borrowing come about in a number of different ways, some of them peaceful, others not. An excellent example of language change as a consequence of military conquest occurred after the Norman conquest of England (A.D. 1066). The Norman invaders, the conquering class, were speakers of an earlier version of French, while the subjugated English spoke Anglo-Saxon, a Germanic language. The effects of that invasion are present today in our own language. The French, famous for their cuisine, introduced a series of terms referring to different kinds of cooked meat into the Anglo-Saxon language. The *cow* (Saxon), when cooked, became *beef* (*boeuf* in French); *calf* (Saxon) became *veal* (*veau* in French); sheep (Saxon) became mutton (*mouton* in French); and *swine* (Saxon) became *pork* (*porc* in French). (See the following chart.)

Raw Meat (Saxon)	Converted into Food (French)
Cow	Beef (boeuf)
Calf	Veal (veau)
Sheep	Mutton (mouton)
Swine	Pork (porc)

CONTACT LANGUAGES—PIDGINS AND CREOLES

One consequence of the European exploration and colonization of many parts of the world was to bring indigenous languages into contact with European ones. The result was the development of new languages known as contact languages, or pidgins and creoles. **Pidgins** are created by social conditions, like trade, that require communication between two or more language communities. The most important characteristic of pidgins is that they have no native speakers. For all speakers, they are second languages. Governed by rules, they have vocabularies and grammars that are simpler than their source languages. They are sufficiently different from their source languages so as not to be mutually intelligible with them (Sebba, 1997: 15).

Pidgin English, widely used in the Far East and the Pacific, developed out of a nautical jargon during the nineteenth century. As a consequence of historical circumstances, several varieties of this pidgin developed, which have since become national languages. Bislama, the official language of the Republic of Vanauatu (formerly the New Hebrides, ruled jointly by the French and the English), developed during the period of trade in bêche-de-mer, edible sea slugs. It originally was known as Bêche-de-Mer English. Solomon Islands Pijin, or Neo-Solomonic, is an important lingua franca in the Solomon Islands, where there are 80 local languages. Tok Pisin is the Melanesian variety of pidgin in this area. It originated among workers in the German colony of New Guinea, especially from the islands of New Ireland and New Britain, who were recruited to work on German-owned plantations in Samoa. They brought the pidgin back with them on their return. Fifteen percent of the vocabulary of Tok Pisin derives from Tolai, spoken in the area around Rabaul, on New Britain, the early headquarters of the German colonial government (Lynch, 1998: 223–224).

When a pidgin language is the native language for the next generation and no longer a second language, then it becomes a **creole.** For over 100 years, Tok Pisin remained a second language for its speakers. However, in the twentieth century, during the postwar period, Tok Pisin began to become the primary language for families in the urban areas of Papua New Guinea, where the adults came from different language areas, as a consequence of increasing rural-urban migration and social mobility (Sebba, 1997: 107). Tok Pisin is in the process of becoming a creole. Since independence in 1975 it has been the official language of the nation of Papua New Guinea. Harrison notes that upon revisiting the village of Avatip, on the Sepik River, where he had done fieldwork in the late 1970s, the children no longer spoke their vernacular languaage, but "Papua New Guinea Pidgin" (Tok Pisin) was their first language (Harrison 2001: 4).

LANGUAGE IMPERIALISM VERSUS LANGUAGE RENEWAL

One type of linguistic change is what Muhlhausler has called **linguistic imperialism** (1996). Before the arrival of Europeans in the late fifteenth century, the Pacific area was one of marked linguistic diversity. Up to 4,000 languages were spoken there, most of them in Melanesia, where 2 million people speak (or spoke) one-quarter of the world's languages (Muhlhausler, 1996: 10). This intensive language diversity existed side by side with bi- and multilingualism. As a consequence of European colonization and language imperialism, English, French, or German, or one of the pidgins we have discussed earlier became the dominant language in the respective colonial areas, and a trend from linguistic diversity to monolingualism and language death began. There were many changes in the indigenous languages that persisted, including losses of lexical items and changes in grammatical forms. The question of indigenous language maintenance in a new nation-state like Papua New Guinea pits multilingualism against the need of the nation-state to build a national culture and to have a single national language, in this case, Tok Pisin (or Neo-Melanesian, its more formal name). In urban areas of Papua New Guinea intermarriage is more common, and Tok Pisin is the language of the household as well as of the public arena. In rural areas, however, older people often speak only the indigenous language, while others are bilingual, speaking the indigenous language and Tok Pisin.

In some states in the United States, there have been attempts at legislation to make English, and only English, the official language. The argument advanced for doing so is, as in the case of Papua New Guinea, that the use of English alone would reinforce the notion of a single American culture and nation and have a unifying effect. This represents a kind of linguistic imperialism in the face of the current multilingual nature of education in our school system and the use of a multiplicity of languages in the courtrooms and the voting booths of the United States.

A large erosion of indigenous languages took place after the conquest of North America by the English, French, and Spanish. The recent response of some groups, like the Navajo, was to attempt to maintain and rejuvenate their language by developing Navajo language materials using the phonetic alphabet to teach the language to their children in a school setting. There is even a college at Rimrock in New Mexico that provides Navajo language instruction.

When a language dies, does that mean that the culture has died along with it? Language is often used as an important marker of cultural or ethnic identity. But it is not the only such marker. When a community is bilingual, and members speak their indigenous language along with the dominant language spoken by the much larger language community of the nation-state, we find that each language may have its own functions and that switching from one language to another follows predictable patterns. Even when the trend toward monolingualism progresses, and only the grandparental generation speaks the indigenous language fluently, underlying patterns may be perpetuated in the manner in which the dominant language is employed. Woodbury cites a fascinating example of this in an Alaskan community. College students from Inupiaq and Yupik (Eskimo) communities use a variety of devices as qualifiers in written English essays to avoid sounding assertive, since such circumspection is part of the way an individual in their native culture should properly behave (Kwachka and Basham, 1990, cited in Woodbury, 1996). This way of nativizing a replacement language is fragile and tentative since it is likely to disappear under pressure from the mainstream community. Woodbury concludes that while we cannot assume that a culture has died when a language dies, a fundamental way of organizing the surrounding world eventually disappears when a language dies, because it simply cannot be translated into the words and phrases of the dominant language, which through linguistic imperialism, has replaced it. According to Woodbury, "Loss of a language leads to an unraveling, or restructuring, or reevaluation of cultural tradition" (1996: 14).

The language endangerment crisis has recently been recognized and linked to the environmental crisis. Threatened languages are like endangered species—both are irreplaceable once they are gone. To solve the environmental crises, we must preserve local eco-systems "through the empowerment of indigenous peoples who live there. Preserving and creating small-scale community habitats in turn support languages and cultures" (Nettle and Romaine, 2000: 24).

WORLD ENGLISHES AND THE SPREAD OF ENGLISH

The English language was spread over the world in two waves. It was first carried by English speaking immigrants to what are today the United States, Canada, Australia, and New Zealand. Different versions of the English language are spoken in all of these countries. These differences were brought about through the process of dialect formation. The second spread of English was the consequence of England's colonial expansion to parts of Africa and South and Southeast Asia. English is spoken today in countries such as Nigeria, Ghana, Kenya, Tanzania, South Africa,

India, Pakistan, Bangladesh, Malaysia, and Singapore. According to Bhatt, English is so widespread that it has far exceeded the spread of Latin during the expansion of the Roman Empire, as cited earlier in this chapter (Bhatt, 2001: 529).

Linguists, who have described the spread of English, have emphasized two somewhat contradictory processes. On the one hand, in the context of Britain's colonial empire, it is an example of linguistic imperialism, which produces a hierarchical ordering of the speech of colonial "masters" and that of indigenous speakers. As Pennycook points out, "There are . . . continuing relations of global inequality . . .—of economic, political, military, communicative (communication and transport), cultural and social imperialism—and the global spread of English" (2001: 61). The second process stresses English as the language of a world market, that is, the language of global commerce. Peoples in the new nations, which emerged in the postcolonial period, learned the language for practical economic reasons, rather than having been forced to learn English by their colonial masters. For example, in postcolonial South Asia, learning English served different functions. The knowledge of English has enabled Indians to be in the forefront in writing software programs for the computer industry, which is closely tied to the United States as a consequence of outsourcing. English was also useful in other areas. Like pidgin, English served as a medium of communication when people spoke mutually unintelligible indigenous languages; it was a method of gaining further education; it helped in legal and administrative areas; it enabled entry into English literary genres such as English literary journals, newspapers, and political journals (Bhatt, 2001: 531–532). The last point, however, is a source of controversy. Is it better for writers from what formerly were colonial areas to write in the colonial language (English or French) or in their indigenous language or dialect? Writers like Chinua Achebe or V. S. Naipul have chosen English as their medium of expression.

Many linguists have adopted a point of view that stresses that the context in which English is learned and spoken, in each particular colonial setting, is uniquely different. The context in which English is learned in India is different from that of Nigeria or South Africa, so that in each of these areas a different variant of English is spoken. Instead of speaking about the spread of the same form of English throughout the world, linguists speak about many world Englishes. Bhatt states that "nonnative English speakers thus created new, culture-sensitive and socially appropriate meanings—expressions of the bilingual's creativity—by altering and manipulating the structure and function of English in its new ecology" (2001: 534). He provides an interesting example from the English that is spoken in India. In English, there is a device known as "the tag question" to turn a statement into a question, such as: "He said he would come home early, didn't he?" In Indian English, such tag questions are transformed into: "You are going home soon, isn't it?" Politeness in verbal expression demands that the "you" and "he" forms be replaced by what is called an undifferentiated tag—"isn't it?" We will see how language expresses forms of respect and even subservience in accordance with the social structure, as when Samoan children simultaneously learn the Samoan language and social structure or the way in which female speech in Japan reflects so-

English is widely understood in Malaysia, so advertisements in Kuala Lumpur, the capital, can be in three languages.

cial structure in Chapter 4. In the tag question example above, the way in which English is used by Indians is shaped and modified by Indian social structure.

Linguists who have adopted a world English perspective—meaning that there are many forms of English, not a single correct one with incorrect subservient variants—are aware that their view carries a political agenda with it. The approach that says that each variety of English is one of many world Englishes argues for "pluricentricity." The external threat to indigenous languages that is posed by the spread of English and world Englishes is countered by the idea of "language rights," that is, "the right to identify with, to maintain and to fully develop one's mother tongue(s)" (Pennycook, 2001: 63). This linguistic right is seen as a fundamental human right.

The *New York Times* of August 26, 2002, announced that at a new university which is being formed with branches in several Central Asian countries—Tajikistan, Kyrgyzstan, and Kazakhstan—students must learn computer science and English before they are able to begin their matriculation toward their bachelors' degrees. The *Times* notes that English is "the language that people in the region believe will best connect them to the outside world." They will be learning standard English. Whether it will be modified in the manner we have described above is an interesting question.

LANGUAGE AND COGNITION

There is a close and intimate relationship between language and experience. Boas's study of the Kwakiutl language, which led him to his concept of linguistic relativity, includes a discussion of how, in Kwakiutl, the speaker must indicate how she or he knows about an action other individuals are performing. For example, in the sentence:

The lady was washing clothes.

it is necessary in Kwakiutl to make the following distinctions: Did the speaker actually see the lady washing clothes? Did the speaker infer that she was washing clothes from the sound that was heard? Did a third party tell the speaker that she was washing clothes? In the Kwakiutl language, these distinctions must be made as part of the grammar of the language. In some languages the grammar includes forms by means of which speakers must specify how they acquired the information they are imparting. English does not have this feature as part of its grammar, though the information can be provided by the speakers, if they wish to give it, with additional words. Boas made the general point that in all languages, grammatical rules, such as the one in this example, are obligatory. Just as Kwakiutl speakers are obliged to use a grammatical category that specifies how they know what they know, English speakers must use one or another tense form to indicate whether they are speaking about the past, the present, or the future. The speakers of a language are not usually aware of these grammatical rules, though they guide all utterances. Boas pointed out that such grammatical rules remain unconscious.

People speaking different languages have a different way of organizing what they experience. Thus a Kwakiutl person always attends to how he or she receives information, because this is necessary in conveying information to others. Since a vital issue is how you know what you know, one can imagine the comparison between the precision of a Kwakiutl speaker as a witness at a court trial and the lack of specificity of the equivalent English-speaking witness at the same trial. The relationship between language and how society organizes experience was also explored by Boas's student Edward Sapir. He argued that language was a guide to social reality. Conceptualizations of the real world are seen, to a great extent, to be based unconsciously upon the language usage of a society. This line of argument was carried to what many people considered an extreme position by Benjamin Lee Whorf. He proposed that the conception of the world by a member of a particular society was determined by the language or "fashion of speaking" of that society.

ETHNOSEMANTICS

There is a close connection between the way language is organized and the way culture is organized. This can be seen most clearly by examination of a specific cultural domain, such as the organization and classification of the world of animals, the world of plants, or the system of colors.

In all languages, there is a set of terms used to refer to animals. The world of animals is separable from other domains in the world. It is distinct from the domain of plants, though they both are alive in contrast to the inanimate world of rocks and soils. People using different languages will sort the world of animals in ways different from our own. For example, the Linnaean system of classification, which we use, groups human beings, bats, and whales as mammals on the basis of such criteria as being warm-blooded, suckling their young, and having hair. Whether these animals fly, live on the land, or swim in the sea is not important. Other peoples use different criteria for their animal classifications. For example, the Karam of Papua New Guinea, studied by Ralph Bulmer, distinguish birds from other animals in their language. However, the cassowary, a flightless bird like an ostrich, which stands over five feet tall, is not placed in the category of birds (where we place it). Rather, the Karam place it in an anomalous category. Unlike birds, it does not fly. It walks on two legs and is seen as related to humans. We have noted above that our category of mammals is distinguished by a series of criteria, distinctive features or components, which differentiate this category from that of reptiles. The categories are hierarchically organized into successively more inclusive groupings, from species to genus to class. When anthropologists like Bulmer study Karam language and Karam culture, they not only collect the meanings of all animal terms and the categories in which the Karam place them but must then determine the reasons why the Karam sort and classify animals in this way. They ascertain the distinctive features the Karam employ when they classify forms such as the cassowary. Each language employs its own cultural logic in making classifications. The anthropological investigation of this topic is known as **ethnosemantics.**

Another cultural domain that has been studied in this manner is the set of linguistic terms used for colors. Every language has a set of terms for colors, though the number of these terms varies from one language to another. Viewers looking at a rainbow see an undivided series of colors, one color grading into another, while as speakers of different languages they will divide this spectrum differently. Brent Berlin and Paul Kay did a comparative study of basic color categories in many different languages throughout the world that shows that the classification of colors in different languages is not completely arbitrary (1969). In some languages, there are only two basic color terms, bright and dark (which can be equated to white and black). More common are languages with three terms, and those terms will always be red, bright (white), and dark (black). Still other languages, with four color categories, add either yellow or green. Other groups of languages through time will successively add blue, brown, purple, pink, orange, and gray. What Berlin and Kay have demonstrated is that the color spectrum is not randomly divided. There is order and regularity in the way in which languages add to the number of color terms. In recent research, color categories have been further divided into the dimensions of brightness and hue in order to explain the findings of Berlin and Kay in terms of cognitive processes.

This does not mean that people over the world, who lack terms for particular colors, cannot in a descriptive fashion express in their language the colors they see (without a term for blue they might say "it is the color of a robin's egg"). What it does mean is that the color categories their language possesses will organize their experience in a particular way.

In this general discussion of ethnosemantics, we have shown the way in which the concept of distinctive features is used. A common way of distinguishing two categories from one another is for one of the categories to possess an attribute that the other category lacks. In the Linnaean classification, mammals are warm-blooded animals while reptiles are not. Thus, one might say that the category of mammals is the "plus" category. This is a distinction biologists make. The linguist Roman Jakobson makes a similar classificatory distinction which he called **markedness.** The category in which the attribute was present he called the marked category, and the category in which it was absent, the unmarked category. Jakobson pointed out that in linguistics, the unmarked category is the more general and inclusive of the two. For example, in English, we have the words *lion* and *lioness.* The marked category is the word *lioness* (*-ess* is added to *lion*—thus marking it). *Lion* includes *lioness,* as in the sentence "Christians were thrown to the lions." The presence of marked and unmarked categories is found in all languages (Greenberg, 1966).

SOCIOLINGUISTICS

Saussure made a distinction between **langue** and **parole,** that is, between language and speech. To obtain information about a language, the fieldworker observes and records many examples of speech. These examples are analyzed in order to obtain a picture of the grammar, or underlying structure, of that language. **Sociolinguistics** deals with the analysis of parole, or speech, and its social functions. Recently, anthropological linguists have been interested in a more integrative way of understanding how language organizes social life. Language is an integral part of the construction of social life; it also provides a window on the social process. Language forges shared cultural understandings and acts as a medium of social exchange and connection between people (Mertz, 1994: 441). In Chapter 1, we discussed the concepts of social structure, social organization, and the concept of agency. Agency emphasizes individual choices and parallels *parole* (or speech) in that each individual uses his or her own idiosyncratic speech patterns. Nevertheless, just as the behavioral choices (or agency) of each individual are constrained by the rules of his or her social structure, so too speech patterns selected are constrained by the grammar of the language (Ahearn, 2001). The speech patterns selected for use by individuals provides the force for language change.

MALE AND FEMALE SPEECH

In many societies, there are distinctions between male and female speech, though, of course, men and women speak to one another as members of the same speech community. As infants and young children learn their language and their culture, they are simultaneously learning female-specific and male-specific be-havior, as well as appropriate gender-related forms of speech. In a survey of dif-ferences between male and female speech in Great Britain, Coates noted that men and women have different interactive styles (1993). In mixed-sex conversations, men dominate the conversation by interrupting women, by controlling the top-ics of the conversation, and by becoming silent. Men talk more, swear more, and use imperative forms to get things done. In contrast, women use more tentative speech, use more linguistic forms associated with politeness, and make greater use of minimal responses (like "uh-huh") to indicate support for the speaker. In single-sex conversations, a different pattern emerges. Whereas men disagree with or ignore each other's utterances, women, in conversations with other women, meld or blend their talk, arriving at a collaborative account satisfactory to all participants. In this way, men pursue a style of individual assertion and power, while women's style is based on solidarity and support (Coates, 1993, 1996: 64). These different styles sometimes result in miscommunication between the sexes.

Investigations of male and female speech in American society reveal the same hierarchical pattern of dominance and subordination. While women will talk on topics raised by men, men may and do reject women's topics in mixed conversa-tions. When men make commands, they use the imperative form. Women tend to use interrogatives ("Would you mind closing the window?") and declarative forms ("I wonder if you would be so kind as to shut the door"). Poynton argues that men and women use different forms of a common language, which encodes an ideo-logical opposition between the sexes (1989). That ideology maintains that males and their activities are of great importance and value, while females and their ac-tivities are of less importance and value.

Gender differences in speech are found in other cultures in the world, but sometimes the forms contrast with what we have described for Great Britain and the United States. In a study of a Malagasy-speaking community of Madagascar, Keenan (1974) has observed that men tend not to express their sentiments openly, are not confrontational, do not show anger, and behave with discretion. This is re-flected in men's speech. They favor subtlety in speech and more indirect and cir-cumspect forms of expression, especially on ceremonial occasions. In contrast, women tend to speak in a straightforward manner, directly expressing anger and criticism that may insult the person being addressed. Women do much of the bar-gaining, buying, and selling in this society and, therefore, direct speech is charac-teristic of the marketplace. Men usually sell goods that are more or less fixed in price. When they do bargain, it is an elaborate and circumspect procedure in which confrontation is to be avoided. In Japanese the marked differences between male and female speech are so strong that some observers talk about a "true" women's language. In contrast to Malagasy, in Japanese, it is the women's speech that is said to be characterized by the more frequent use of polite forms. Japanese women's speech is also distinguished from men's speech by the presence of dif-ferent sets of first- and second-person pronouns and special terms of self-reference and address. However, Ogawa, in a study using ratings of politeness, masculinity and femininity from a wide range of Japanese speakers, shows that in Japan, politeness is Japanese and is not correlated with femininity. Males are associated with rudeness, but they can use polite forms as well, since they are Japanese (Ogawa, 2000).

Backchanneling is the use of a verbal signal like "yeah" or nonverbal signals like head nods, which are inserted by the listener when the speaker pauses. In Japanese, this is called *aizuchi*. Ashwell has discussed the differences between Japanese speakers and English speakers in the use of backchanneling. Women use this form more often than men because they frequently play a supportive role. In English, the use of such forms is associated with powerlessness, while in Japanese it does not have such an association. In Japanese such forms are used more frequently with superiors from outside one's group, such as employers, to smooth relations. English speakers find the Japanese use of this form excessive and completely misunderstand its function, making translation more difficult (Ashwell, 2000).

LANGUAGE AND POWER

Language is always politically important. The way in which speech is used to express power varies from culture to culture. As Gal notes, "Extensive ethnographic case studies have demonstrated that in some societies, it is the holders of greatest power who must restrain themselves physically, linguistically, and often in the expression of emotion exactly because it is superior restraint that culturally and ideologically defines their power, enabling them to properly exercise it" (1995: 413). For example, among the Kanuri, speaking in a low and unexcited tone demonstrates control and exercise of power. In contrast, in Western cultures, demonstration of power is often achieved by cursing, screaming, and ignoring the personhood of others present, as was characteristic of the speech of Hitler and former president Nixon.

People in the underclass and in positions of powerlessness may express their opposition and resistance by means of different linguistic styles or languages. In a bilingual community in Hungary, Gal has found that "any single villager expresses many and often conflicting opinions about the value of the two languages he or she speaks, including opinions that show evidence of resistance to official languages and ideologies" (1995: 412–413). Abu-Lughod's discussion of Bedouin love poetry, examined in detail in Chapter 5, demonstrates how this form of expression is associated with women and young men expressing defiance and rebellion toward male tribal hierarchy.

Other kinds of variations in speech within a language correspond to class differences—that is, to vertical differences that structure a society. Such class-correlated linguistic differences are found in the United States. In the film *Working Girl*, popular some years ago, the heroine learns an American dialect, that of her upper-class business superiors, in order to further her career, differentiating herself from her friend who speaks a lower-class Staten Island dialect.

REGIONAL DIFFERENCES AND DIALECTS

In contrast to speech differences based on class, differences in speech due to geography and region may be conceptualized as horizontal differences. Speakers in different geographical areas speaking different versions of a language are said to speak different **dialects.** Different regions of the United States are characterized by different patterns of speech, including differences in pronunciation, vocabulary, and syntax. One can immediately recognize a Boston accent, a Midwestern accent, or a Southern accent. Some of these differences are a consequence of the immigrant populations from different countries who settled in these areas. In the film *Fargo,* the local population in Minnesota and adjoining South Dakota employed an excessive number of "you betchas" and substituted "yah" for "yeah" (or "yes") in their American English. These usages are markers of their ethnic identity as Scandinavian Americans.

AFRICAN-AMERICAN SPEECH

Differences in language usage in the United States also parallel racial differences. The speech of the African-American community, referred to in the past as Black English but now referred to as African-American Vernacular English (AAVE), in contrast to Standard English (SE), is the subject of much scholarly research and debate (Morgan, 1994; Mufwene et al., 1998). AAVE was originally viewed by some as a collection of mistakes and deviations from Standard English, which reflected deficits in the cultural behavior of its speakers. However, Labov, in his several decades of work, and others have demonstrated that AAVE should be viewed as a system, with an invariant core, that should be analyzed without reference to other dialects (Labov, 1972, 1998). Labov's findings marked the beginning of serious consideration of the linguistic attributes of African-American Vernacular English, the range of its usage, and its origins. There are phonological, syntactic, and lexical features that mark African-American English as different from American English, though some of these differences are also present in other American English dialects.

Most recently, Labov has proposed that AAVE represents the coexistence of two distinct components, General English (GE), which is similar to the grammar of Other American Dialects (OAD), and the African-American (AA) component (1998: 117 ff.). The General English component, consisting of a fairly complete set of syntactical, morphological, and phonological structures, provides speakers with the same grammatical and lexical machinery as Other American Dialects. The African-American component is a subset of grammatical and lexical forms that are combined with part of the grammatical inventory of GE, permitting the development of a specialized semantics and the construction of sentence types not available to OAD. The main grammatical work is done by the General English system of AAVE, permitting a semantic efflorescence in the AA component. One of the most important points made by Labov in his recent work regards the continuing divergence of AAVE from OAD and the fact that "many important features of the modern dialect are creations of the twentieth century and not an inheritance of the nineteenth" (Labov, 1998: 119). Though AAVE is also seen as having creole affinities and creole roots, it is not viewed as a full-fledged creole such as Gullah, the language spoken on the Sea Islands, off the coast of Georgia. In its early form Gullah was structurally related to the creole languages that developed on the islands in the Caribbean where English was the colonial language (Rickford, 1998: 191).

Originally, it was believed that African languages and cultures were completely destroyed by the experience of slavery. However, today scholars have challenged this opinion and have come to the conclusion that the African heritage continues to exist in both African-American language and culture. According to Smitherman, the uniqueness of AAVE is to be found in the following three areas: "(1) patterns of grammar and pronunciation; (2) verbal rituals from the oral tradition and the continued importance of the word as in African cultures; and (3) the lexicon, developed by giving special meaning to English words, a practice that goes back to enslavement and to the need for a system of communication that only those in the slave community could understand" (1998: 207). Many studies have analyzed the African-American male style of speech referred to as signifying, sounding, or playing the dozens. This kind of verbal skill, which is an echo of the verbal rituals of the African language tradition, is most frequently associated with adolescent males and involves taking a serious topic that is culturally significant and playing with it in an ironic, sarcastic, and humorous fashion (Morgan, 1994: 333).

Language is an important aspect of the construction of cultural identity. African-American Vernacular English is seen by some as a symbol of slave mentality, in particular by members of the Nation of Islam, but by others as a symbol of resistance to slavery and oppression (Morgan, 1994: 338–339). More significantly, today African-American Vernacular English plays a role in the construction of African-American identity in a multicultural America. However, as Mitchell-Kernan points out, both African-American Vernacular English and Standard English are necessary to improve one's life chances, since lack of Standard English harms one in school and in the workplace while absence of African-American Vernacular English deprives one of status within one's ethnic group (Mitchell-Kernan, 1972, cited in Morgan, 1994). In recent years, there has been an increase in the size of the African-American middle class. Studies have noted that for African Americans, the higher the class, the greater the consciousness of racial identity (Morgan, 1994: 337–338). This is illustrated by African-American students in elite college campuses who employ African-American lexical, phonological, and grammatical features of African-American Vernacular English in both formal and informal contexts in order to reinforce their ethnic identity (Baugh, 1987, 1992, cited in Morgan, 1994: 338). During the last decade of the twentieth century, the curious spectacle of crossover, in which white people have begun to use aspects of African-American Vernacular English lexicon in their own speech, has been observed. As Smitherman notes, "This is a historical moment in which Rap and other forms of Black language and culture are used to sell everything from Coca-Cola and Gatorade to snow blowers and shampoo for White people's hair" (1998: 223). Of course, sounding "hip" is not a new phenomenon, as Norman Mailer observed in 1957.

SUMMARY

• Language allows humans to communicate cultural ideas and symbolic meanings from one generation to the next in a cumulative fashion and to constantly create new cultural ideas.

• The units of language are two-sided. One side is the sound and the other is the meaning. There is no intrinsic and natural connection between the sounds of a word and its meaning.

• Every language has a small number of basic sounds, called phonemes, usually between 20 and 40, which are used in various combinations to make up the units of meaning. The phonemes of a language form a structure or system.

• Phonemes themselves do not carry meaning; their function is to differentiate words in terms of their meanings.

• The units of language that carry meaning are called morphemes.

• The rules by which larger speech units, such as phrases and sentences, are formed compose the *syntax* of a language.

• Languages can not be rated on a scale from simple to complex. There is no one-to-one relationship between technological complexity and linguistic complexity. All languages are equally complex.

• Dialect differentiation, over time, leads to further divergence and eventually to the development of two separate languages.

• Languages thought to be related are studied, using the comparative method, in order to derive the proto-language from which they are descended.

• Words in the proto-language for plants, trees, and animals are used to pinpoint the ecology and thence possible location of the speakers' original homeland before they dispersed.

• Aspects of language are borrowed by speakers of one language from another language through a process of diffusion.

• European exploration and colonization of many parts of the world brought indigenous languages into contact with European ones, resulting in the development of new languages known as pidgins and creoles.

• As a consequence of European colonization and language imperialism, English, French, German, or one of the pidgins became the dominant language in the colonial areas, and a trend from linguistic diversity to monolingualism and language death began.

• The question has been raised regarding whether when a language dies, a culture dies.

• English has spread over the world as a result of emigration, conquest, and the dominance of the language in world commerce.

• Linguists, who have adopted a world English perspective—meaning that there are many forms of English, not a single correct one with incorrect subservient variants—are aware that their view carries a political agenda with it.

• People speaking different languages organize what they experience differently.

• There is a close connection between the way language is organized and the way culture is organized, as seen in the classification of the world of animals, the world of plants, or the system of colors.

• Men and women play different though usually complementary gender roles in society, and differences in male and female speech reflect this.

• Class differences in speech are vertical differences; regional dialect differences are horizontal differences.

• The speech of African Americans, referred to as African American Vernacular English (AAVE), has its own distinct phonology, morphology, and syntax and is not an incorrect, incomplete version of English. It constitutes an important marker of ethnic identity.

 SUGGESTED READINGS

Chomsky, Noam. *New Horizons in the Study of Language and Mind.* Cambridge, MA: Cambridge University Press, 2000, The brilliant and provocative linguistic philosopher's most recent statement of his position on the relationship between language and mind.

Duranti, Alessandro, (ed.). *Linguistic Anthropology: A Reader.* Malden, MA: Blackwell Publishers, 2001. A comprehensive reader that covers a wide diversity of contemporary topics in linguistic anthropology. The major contemporary anthropological linguists discuss their current research.

Fishman, Joshua (ed.). *Handbook of Language and Ethnic Identity.* Oxford: Oxford University Press, 1999. A compilation of scholarly articles on the relationship between language and ethnicity, given the ethnic revival of the last 20 years.

Hardin, C. L. and Luisa Maffi (eds.). *Color Categories in Thought and Language.* Cambridge: Cambridge University Press, 1997. A reexamination of the theories about basic color terminology of Berlin and Kay.

Kuipers, Joel C. *Language, Identity and Marginality in Indonesia: The Changing Nature Of Ritual Speech on the Island of Sumba.* Cambridge: Cambridge University Press, 1998. An analysis of the changes that have taken place in the tradition of ritual poetic speech in the Sumba language as a consequence of the rapid spread of Indonesian, the national language. The book also analyzes the new and hybrid forms of poetic expression that have developed, as well as the linguistic consequences of marginality.

Skutnabb-Kangas, Tove. *Linguistic Genocide in Education—or Worldwide Diversity and Human Rights*. Mahwah, N.J.: Erlbaum Associates, 2000. This book deals with topics such as linguistic and cultural diversity, linguistic genocide, threatened languages, and government policies promoting linguistic hegemony and linguistic imperialism. The author shows how minority and multilingual education can contribute to linguistic genocide.

 ## SUGGESTED WEBSITES

http://www.sil.org A list of the known languages of the world, the locations of the speakers of these languages, and their groupings into language families. Also includes information on language isolates like Burushaski and Basque.

http://cognet.mit.edu/MITECS/Entry/bloom Deals with a variety of factors (use of the hand, gestures, etc.) involved in the evolution of language through natural selection.

http://jom-emit.cfpm.org/1998/vol2/vaneschoutte_m&skoyles_jr.html In contrast to most discussions of the origins of language, these theorists argue that the origin of language is related to musicality.

http://eleaston.com/world-eng.html Lists of varieties of English spoken around the world which, taken together, form World English.

4

Learning Language and Culture
Culture and the Individual

It is now appropriate to pause and consider the ways in which individuals born into a particular society learn its language and its culture and the behaviors which individuals in that culture consider appropriate. In the course of this discussion, we will also be talking about the relationship of the individual to his or her culture, the range of personality variation within cultures, and the ways of dealing with individuals whose behavior is outside the norms of their culture. This will take us into a consideration of how mental illness is defined in particular cultures, and how innovators and rebels, whose societies sometimes consider them mentally ill, are viewed.

HOW CHILDREN LEARN LANGUAGE

To be able to acquire language, "human children must be equipped with a general primate auditory apparatus and a specialized human speech mechanism . . . which work in concert with one another . . . to produce native-like speech" (Tomasello and Bates, 2001: 3). Recent advances in research techniques have shown that the fetus can hear and differentiate its mother's conversation from other sounds, like music or white noise as they are filtered through the amniotic fluid, as early as the last trimester before birth. Auditory stimuli elicit changes in fetal heart rate and in motor responses like kicking. Since it has been shown that the newborn immediately identifies his or her mother's voice, it is clear that this recognition is learned prenatally, when the fetus learns to recognize the intonation and stress patterns of its mother's voice (Karmiloff and Karmiloff-Smith, 2001: 43–44). Studies of speech perception of infants have shown that "infants are born to perceive most if not all of the speech contrasts used by natural languages . . . [and are] able to . . . learn any natural language" (Tomasello and Bates, 2001: 16). At four days or earlier, newborns can discriminate phonemes and perceive well-formed syllables as units. They can distinguish the difference between the rhythmic characteristics of mother's language and other languages and show that they would rather hear their "mother tongue" than other languages. French babies suck harder when they hear French and less hard when they hear Russian (Karmiloff and Karmiloff-Smith, 2001: 44, 45). Between six and twelve months, infants lose the ability to perceive nonnative speech contrasts as they move to master the sound structure of their own speech community.

"Motherese" is the special language in our society, which mothers use in their interactions with their infants. Stress patterns within words and sentences are exaggerated, and repetitions and vocatives to attract the infant's attention and questions with rising intonation are used. It is the rhythm pattern, not word meaning, that attracts the attention of the infant. In other cultures, mothers may speak to the fetus. This serves to demonstrate "that the dynamics of social interaction play a role in encouraging the infant's attention to language" (Karmiloff and Karmiloff-Smith, 2001: 47). However, Schiefflin has shown that in some cultures parents barely speak to their infants until the latter produce speech. At that point they converse with the child in adult language.

The infant gradually learns which sound combinations most frequently occur in its mother tongue, and which are correct and which incorrect. This is in turn related to speech segmentation and word boundaries. The infant also becomes familiar with word pattern and stress pattern, often through motherese, which exaggerates rhythm and intonation. Where motherese is absent, information on segmentation comes from adult speech where it may not be so easy to detect.

So far, we have been concerned with the infant's perception of speech, but what about speech production by infants? Between two and three months of age, during which time the baby is learning to create sounds, the infant produces cooing sounds that are nonlinguistic; between four and six months, its marginal babbling consists of vowel- and consonant-like sounds (these sounds may go beyond his or her native language, but when not heard often, they are dropped); from seven months onward, other vowel and consonant transitions like da-da are produced; by ten months the infant's native tongue begins to affect the types of sounds produced; just past the first year word production usually begins (Karmiloff and Karmiloff-Smith, 2001: 56, 57). The building of infant vocabulary relates to external factors such as sex—girls tend to produce language earlier than boys because girls' brains mature somewhat faster. Mother's linguistic competence, mother's intelligence, maternal socioeconomic status, parental education, social competence, and attitude toward child-rearing are also factors that relate to the way parents interact with the child (Karmiloff and Karmiloff-Smith, 2001: 60). Though infants do not produce comprehensible words until between 12 and 20 months, they can understand words before that point. By 24 months, toddlers can produce 50 different words. At first single words are used to designate whole concepts and categories—overgeneralization. This refers to the use of the word "dog" for all four-legged animals.

Learning the meanings of words does not occur in a vacuum. Cognitive development and social constraints (i.e., aspects of the child's social environment) all play a role in language learning. Beginning in the second year, the toddler be-

A five-month-old infant responds to her father's use of "motherese," or "baby-talk".

gins to learn the morphemic structure and the syntax of his or her language. The onset varies with the language. For English, where there are more unbound morphemes, 24 months is the age at which the child begins to pay attention to how morphemes function. For Turkish, where many morphemes are bound together, this learning begins at 18 months (Karmiloff and Karmiloff-Smith, 2001: 88). Though sentence production at two years is rudimentary, the child has already begun to become sensitive to complex grammatical forms and the nature of word order. It is clear, however, that sensitivity to grammar is greater than production of grammatical form. Grammatical speech, in the form of word combination, can begin with as few as 50 to 150 words. English-speaking children soon learn the importance of word order in their language. Some studies have revealed cross-linguistic differences in the development of the use of nouns and verbs. Children usually learn nouns first, except when learning non-Western languages like Chinese, Korean, Tzotzil, and Tzeltzal, where verbs are more salient (Tomasello and Bates, 2001: 59).

Dialogue of infant with mother occurs long before knowledge of words and syntax are acquired by the child. This discourse is a crucial factor in language learning, but it is also the basis for the discourse skills used in later language exchanges between parent and child and between child and child. Children learn the meaning of symbols in discourse with adults, symbols being the association between words and other things (Nelson and Shaw, 2002: 32).

Derek Bickerton has worked on the problem of the development of pidgins and creoles and the evolution of languages. He has suggested that the child until the age of two utilizes a kind of proto-language that is primarily devoid of syntax. Phylogenetically, it resembles an earlier stage of language evolution; it also has the properties of pidgin, which develops when direct linguistic communication between speakers of different languages is not possible. Around the age of two, a developmental explosion occurs in the quantity and quality of the child's utterances. This is a consequence of an innate "language biogram," hypothesizes Bickerton, that specifies an increase in language complexity at that point of maturation. When children of speakers of pidgin acquire pidgin as a first language, this innate mechanism creates creole language. In Bickerton's provocative hypothesis, language ontogeny recapitulates phylogeny.

LEARNING ONE'S CULTURE

Scholars like Schiefflin and Ochs see language acquisition and its cultural context as being inextricably tied together, with learning of linguistic forms closely interrelated to the cultural setting within which learning takes place (1986). Sociocultural information is encoded in the organization of conversation, and from earliest infancy, children acquire knowledge as they are involved in such interactions.

At the same time that children acquire language, they are also acquiring knowledge of the statuses and roles that constitute the social order of their society. In Samoa, children use the word for "give" earlier and more frequently than the word for "come," though the former is semantically more complex. The use of "give" is more appropriate for small children in directing older siblings and adults, while "come" is used solely for animals and younger siblings (Ochs, 1986). Clearly these usages relate to the hierarchical nature of Samoan social structure. The child is learning correct use of language at the same time as it is learning how to behave properly within the social structure.

The learning of the attitudes, feelings, and emotions characteristic of a culture is connected to language acquisition and varies from culture to culture. Schiefflin has investigated the range of linguistic forms that Kaluli children can use to perform the act of requesting. It is necessary for children to learn the appropriate request forms in order to operate successfully in the all-important reciprocity and exchange activities that organize Kaluli society (Schiefflin and Ochs, 1996: 255, 256). Kaluli adults tease and shame children, using name-calling, formulaic expressions, rhetorical questions, and what the Kaluli refer to as "turned-over words," to teach children how to become adult Kaluli who are individually autonomous, assertive, and direct (Schiefflin, 1986). In contrast, the Japanese communicative style, which relates to the nature of Japanese culture and is somewhat depersonalized, is inculcated in children by Japanese mothers by using indirect forms of communicating and correcting children's use of direct utterances, which

A Navajo girl learns to weave from her mother.

are considered improper. Children learn a variety of greetings and polite expressions, as well as other linguistic forms of politeness used to indicate particular roles and situations (Nakamura, 1996: 248).

As children learn language from those surrounding them, those who care for them, and those with whom they interact, at the same time, they learn social roles, politeness and deference toward elders, autonomy, assertiveness, and initiative. They are learning cultural values and what is appropriate behavior for a child in their culture. While Kaluli children learn that autonomy and assertiveness are valued in their culture, Samoan children learn that assertiveness toward elders is bad, and Japanese children learn that indirectness and circumscribed behavior are valued over directness. Particular forms of language as they relate to correct forms of behavior in each society are taught to children.

Self-reliance is a characteristic that is more valued in some societies than in others. It is inculcated in the young infant through the process of enculturation. Before World War II, self-reliance was encouraged and fostered in both American infants and German infants, but after World War II, in America, an ideology of love and trust replaced this. American mothers never leave infants alone and rush to pick them up when they cry, believing that if they were to do otherwise, the child would not develop a secure sense of attachment and would feel abandoned. In contrast, German mothers may leave an infant alone while they go out shopping, and will pick up a crying child only if they think he or she is hurting. They want the infant to be enculturated into a sense of independent self-reliance and are concerned lest the child become "spoiled." At 10 months of age, German infants expect less attention from their mothers than do American infants. According to LeVine and Norman, these differences in child-rearing practices between Germans and Americans begin during the first year of life and are part of each culture's concepts of moral virtue (2001: 91). German moral concepts of "love of order" and "self reliance" differ from the American moral precept of parental love freely given.

Brown has described the way in which Tzeltal-speaking Mayan farmers in southern Mexico have socialized their children from babyhood to "lie" in culturally appropriate ways (2002: 243). Since lying is routine in Tzeltal, it is a cultural phenomenon that children must begin to learn early in life in order to become effective in their lying. Children learn to manage social lies "with fair competence by the age of five or so, when they are called to perform them as they are sent around to different households on errands" (Brown, 2002: 268–269). By the age of four or even earlier Tzeltal children become aware that people can hold false beliefs and lie. They learn how to tell when others are lying to them as well as how to lie themselves. Lying threats are a means of social control, and children who assume child care responsibilities for younger children at an early age acquire this skill (Brown, 2002: 243). It is interesting to compare American culture to Tzeltal culture with regard to lying. American values denigrate lying, especially to one's young children. But in today's American corporate culture, we have seen many instances where lying frequently occurs.

Shweder, Mahapatra, and Miller (1990), in a study that focuses on inculcation of moral rules among Brahman and Untouchable families in Orissa, India, and Judeo-Christian families in Chicago, Illinois, illustrate how the Indian child is socialized regarding moral understandings relating to pollution and purity. Menstruating women must remove themselves from physical contact with other people. A menstruating mother exclaims, "I am polluted (*mara*). Don't touch me!" when her young child tries to sit on her lap. She will get up and walk away if the child comes closer. These women explain that their state of menstrual pollution is due to their having stepped in dog excrement. Children soon learn that when their mothers are *mara*, they will avoid others, sleep alone on a mat on the floor, stay out of the kitchen, eat alone, and not groom themselves. According to the authors, "Most six-year-olds think it is wrong for a 'polluted' (*ëmaraí*) woman to cook food or sleep in the same bed with her husband; most nine-year-olds think that *ëmaraí* is an objective force of nature and that all women in the world have a moral obligation not to touch other people or cook food while they are *ëmaraí*" (Shweder, Mahapatra, and Miller, 1990: 196). In the social interaction and communication between the young child and his or her cultural world, the child learns about the moral tenet of pollution experientially.

LEARNING GENDER ROLES

Gender roles and the kinds of persons men and women are expected to be are also acquired during the socialization and language acquisition processes. If boys are expected to be more assertive than girls in a particular culture, they are taught by the individuals around them to be that way. Their assertive use of language reflects this gender difference. The people who inhabit the Kerkennah Islands, 12 miles off Tunisia, think of males and females as having sharply different ideas of self, which are basically different by nature (Platt, 1988). They think that a female fetus rides "in the lap" and a male fetus "astride the hips" during the mother's pregnancy. After birth, babies of both sexes are swaddled to avoid any external influences or dangerous forces. Beyond two months of birth, Kerkenni males are treated differently from females, based on the belief that they are different by nature. The mother behaves toward the male child as if he were an adult male, playfully referring to him as "oh, Daddy" or "oh, Sir." This results in an earlier and fuller development of a sense of self on the part of male infants as compared with female infants. The female infant instead is treated as an extension of the mother herself. Male infants are seen as more demanding and requiring more attention. They are the focus of much more ritual activity. After circumcision, between the ages of three and four, the male child moves beyond the sphere of the mother and into the world of male peers. There is no equivalent sharp break for the female child, who remains close to her mother. Older boys are expected to express aggression outwardly, and they are teased to foster this, while girls turn their anger inward upon themselves. Two different kinds of selves, one for males and another for females, are characteristic of this society. However, as noted earlier, the Kerkenni themselves see these differences in the expression of self as attributable entirely to nature, not to cultural learning.

In the United States and Australia, studies of the interaction of parents and children and of children themselves demonstrate that gender is a social construct that is constantly being modified as a consequence of the interactions in which children and their parents and teachers engage. In a study of Australian parents and children, male and female gender roles are presented as mutually exclusive and are seen in that manner by most children. It was clear that the chores that mothers and fathers, and girls and boys, performed at home were primarily complementary, with fathers and boys concerned with tidying the yard, washing the car, and working on the periphery of meal preparation, and mothers and girls concerned with domestic tasks. The study further showed that in play situations at school "girls felt at home in home corner setting, where they were familiar with the rituals and positions involved. The boys, on the other hand, were more comfortable exploring the boundaries of socially acceptable behavior and developing the skills they felt they would need as adults to work outdoors and outside the home" (Lowe, 1998: 209). It is apparent that children enter school with gender roles already clearly defined. Not only are they aware of the complementarity of roles, but observation of the interaction of children in play settings in school reveals that in their behavior, they also enact male domination of space and language and female submissiveness (Lowe, 1998: 214). It is interesting to conjecture what such a parallel study in the United States would reveal, given the movement to make gender roles more similar, rather than complementary. Some educators in the United States and Australia have made deliberate efforts, in their organization of the classroom and class activities, to make children aware of the possibility of roles that are more egalitarian in nature, rather than those roles that suggest male dominance and female subordination.

Studies of socialization in different types of societies indicate that, while teaching is the predominant method for learning economic and social roles in urban-industrial societies, societies dependent on horticulture, and on hunting and foraging, rely much more on children's observing and imitating elders, and on honing such skills by playing games. Such devices for socializing the child do not seem to be used as much in industrial societies (Munroe and Munroe, 1996).

CULTURE AND PERSONALITY

Not only do individuals in a society learn a language and a culture; the personality structure, as well the idea of personhood and self that is characteristic of their culture, is also inculcated in them. As we have shown above, some societies stress self-reliance and assertiveness, while other societies stress respect and subordination. In all societies, people exhibit individual personality differences as a result of genetic differences, upbringing, and particular life experiences. Each individual has a certain personality, a certain character, which is more or less stable over his or her lifetime. This is not to say that individuals never change. An individual's personality can change, sometimes through his or her own efforts and sometimes with the assistance of a therapist. But most frequently, individuals demonstrate stability of personality. They act consistently in different kinds of situations. The stability of individual personality is the result of the interaction of genetic, biological predispositions and the individual's life experience from birth on. A range of personality types exists in our society, as well as in every other society in the world.

PERSONALITY TYPES THAT CHARACTERIZE CULTURES

Though there is a range of personality types in every society, in any one society there is a preponderance of individuals with a particular kind of personality. This range of personality types differs from one society to the next. The attempt to characterize the personality types that are dominant in different societies and tribes goes back to ancient times. Tacitus, the Roman historian, of the first century A.D., in his work *Germania: On the Origin, Geography, Institutions, and Tribes of the Germans,* characterized the Germans as "a race without either natural or acquired cunning, they disclose their hidden thoughts in the freedom of the festivity." He also noted that they represent a strange combination of idleness and sloth and readiness to go to war. Tacitus tried to capture what was distinctive about the personality characteristics of the Germans as a people. Throughout history, such characterizations of different peoples have been made. One must always be wary of stereotypes based on prejudice, as distinguished from accurate characterizations based on data and observations.

In the 1930s and 1940s, anthropological studies of the relationship between personality and culture focused on personality differences between various cultures, the measures for determining and verifying these differences, the investigation of the cultural institutions that bring about the development of these particular personality types through time, and the other aspects of culture to which these personality differences are related. In American anthropology during this time, investigations of the relationship between personality and culture were strongly influenced by the ideas and concepts of Sigmund Freud, especially those concerned with child-rearing techniques, and the way in which these affected the development of the adult personality. Margaret Mead and Ruth Benedict, both students of Franz Boas, took Freud's emphasis on early childhood experiences and combined it with Boas's ideas of cultural relativism. In separate works written in the 1930s, Mead and Benedict applied this point of view to personality, maintaining that cultures varied in terms of patterns of child-rearing, personality development, sex-role behavior, and types of mental disorder. In her first important work on Samoa, Mead demonstrated that while adolescence in America involves a period of crisis and search for identity, in Samoa there is no equivalent period of crisis. In her subsequent fieldwork in the Admiralty Islands off New Guinea, she focused upon the specific ways in which children were reared, weaned, and toilet trained; how and when they learned to walk and to swim; how infants were handled; and how children were taught and encouraged to become adults and develop the kind of personality valued by the Admiralty Islanders. In *Sex and Temperament,* published in 1935, Mead demonstrated how male and female roles, and the personality characteristics associated with them, were culturally determined in three New Guinea societies. Mead claimed that in Tchambuli society, the females were assertive, usually a male characteristic, and in Arapesh, the males were passive, gentle, and sensitive, characteristics usually associated with female roles. Mead and Bateson subsequently studied the relationship between child-rearing and personality in Bali.

CHILD-REARING AND PERSONALITY

We have discussed how children acquire language and learn the rules of their own culture. In the process, the particular personality characteristics favored in that culture are also inculcated in them. Through the process of enculturation, children learn not only the rules of their culture, but also, as noted earlier, the values of their society. In addition, they increasingly become motivated to act according to those values. The motivations that have been built in during the enculturation process are what lead most people to conform to those rules. To act otherwise—to violate rules—produces guilt in the individual. As the psychoanalyst Erich Fromm (1944) long ago noted, stable individuals in a well-integrated culture will want to do the things that they have to do. This applies not only to cultural behavior, but to emotion as well, which is also culturally determined. Though the form in which emotion is expressed varies from one culture to another, there are certain aspects of emotional states, like happiness and grief, that are universal. The psychoanalytic approach conceived of personality development as proceeding through a series of developmental stages, such as weaning and toilet training.

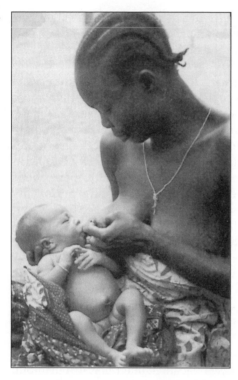

A Fulani mother from northern
Nigeria nurses her infant daughter.

Erik Erikson (1963), a psychoanalyst strongly influenced by anthropologists, broadened Freud's stages of psychosexual development in order to make them applicable to non-Western cultures. He was impressed by the cultural differences among the Yurok, the Sioux, and the American patients whom he was treating, and he saw these differences in culture and in child-rearing as being related to differences in the adult personality. Among the Sioux of South Dakota, children were freely breast-fed up to age three, and there was no systematic weaning. The Sioux child was toilet trained by imitating older children, and the matter of toilet training was treated in a very relaxed fashion. Erikson saw a clear relationship between the way in which the Sioux handled these two developmental stages and the value that the Sioux placed on the generous adult individual, as expressed, for example, in the economic institution of the "giveaway." In contrast, among the Yurok of California, a child was breast-fed for only six months, and weaning, which was called "forgetting the mother," could be brought about by the mother's leaving the house for a few days. Autonomy was encouraged very early. With respect to toilet training, the Yurok were particularly concerned that the child not urinate into the Klamath River, which each year brought them salmon on which they depended. In Erikson's view, these aspects of child-rearing were tied to an adult Yurok personality characterized by retentive hoarding, suspicious miserliness, and compulsive ritualization. It was Erikson's interpretation that the Yurok, who had their own kind of money in the form of shells, adapted well to American economic institutions since their personalities and their own economic system were already very similar to those of American culture. Sioux culture and Sioux personality were quite different; thus the Sioux did not adapt well to American culture.

THE RELATIONSHIP OF SOCIAL STRUCTURE TO PERSONALITY

Individuals who make up a society occupy different social positions, different statuses in the society. In all societies, people are minimally differentiated according to age and sex. Beyond this, there are many other bases for differentiation. Individuals who occupy different statuses within the same society are likely to have different personality characteristics. For example, shamans in a society will have somewhat different personalities from nonshamans in the same society. The Big Man, a type of political leader, which we discuss in Chapter 9, will have a somewhat different personality from his followers. There are two ways to view this relationship between social status and personality. In the first view, individuals with certain kinds of personality characteristics will gravitate toward those social roles or occupations that suit their personalities. These differences in personality characteristics result from individual differences in socialization. For example, in our own society, individuals who are self-confident, assertive, and willing to take risks often gravitate toward entrepreneurial positions in the business world. Others, with personality traits such as a tendency to intellectualize and a curiosity about the world but a sense of uneasiness in dealing with other people, are more likely to become scientists and to do research.

In the second view, people moving into particular social roles will undergo personality changes brought about by the demands of the role. A classic example of this is Thomas à Becket, who, as chancellor of the exchequer in the twelfth century, was a free spirit and caroused with King Henry II. When Becket was appointed archbishop of Canterbury, he proceeded to behave according to that role. He changed from a frivolous, pleasure-seeking individual to the committed defender of a moral cause who chose martyrdom at the command of his former friend, the king, rather than surrender his principles.

CULTURE AND MENTAL ILLNESS

If, in our society, a man said one day that a guardian spirit had come to him and told him that it would protect and watch over him throughout his life as long as he followed certain commands and obeyed certain taboos, we would consider him mentally ill. If he reported that he had actually seen and spoken to the spirit, we would say that he was having hallucinations. However, adolescent boys among the Crow of the Plains were expected to go on a vision quest to seek such a spirit. Seeing visions was very common among the Crow, as well as among many other Native American societies who also had the vision quest. What is regarded as a symptom of mental illness in one society may be merely one aspect of normal, healthy life in another.

The anthropological definition of *mental illness* takes the normal, expected, and acceptable behavior in a culture as a baseline and views deviance from this baseline as abnormal behavior or mental illness. Seeking a vision was normal and expected behavior for Crow boys, and they might torture themselves and undergo deprivation until the vision came to them. But visions of spirits are not considered normal behavior in our society. Someone who sees them and hears them is exhibiting abnormal behavior. Another instance of exhibiting signs of abnormal behavior is the belief in witchcraft. Among the Navajo and the Basseri, individuals who believed that someone was practicing witchcraft on them would not be considered abnormal. However, in most segments of our society, individuals who came into the emergency room of a hospital complaining of internal pains because they had been bewitched would be considered mentally ill.

This approach to abnormal behavior and mental illness is essentially a relativistic one. Nevertheless, anthropologists who study forms of mental illness cross-culturally use certain general categories. They distinguish between disorders caused by brain damage and behavioral disorders, where there is no apparent brain damage. The latter category is subdivided into psychoses, such as schizophrenia, depression, and paranoia, and neuroses of a variety of types. Recently, depressive illness has been examined cross-culturally (Kleinman and Good, 1985). Grief is the emotion that accompanies bereavement, which is experienced in all societies. The relationship between the normal experience of grief and pathological grieving or depression has yet to be investigated. In many different cultures, depression as an emotion or affect seems to be experienced in a similar fashion. However, the boundary line between a depressed state as normal behavior and abnormal depressive disorder has not yet been established. Depressive illness has a psychophysiological syndrome of behaviors that can be recognized by clinicians cross-culturally. At the same time, the cultural meanings of depressive illness and the cultural expression of the symptoms differ from one culture to another. Universal aspects of other mental illnesses, such as schizophrenia, neuroses, and personality disturbances, have also been recognized (Draguns, 1980). However, these illnesses are also culturally shaped. Variations in their manifestations are related to social, economic, technological, religious, and other features of the societies in which they are found.

Some kinds of symptoms seem to be specific to a particular culture. These symptoms have been viewed in two quite different ways. One view is that there are universal psychopathological disease categories (such as schizophrenia and depression) that are manifested in different kinds of behavior from one culture to another. The opposing view is that universally stressful situations produce different kinds of diseases in different cultures.

The Windigo psychosis, which occurred among Algonquian Native Americans in the Northeast, was characterized by feeling persecuted by supernatural spirits and having cannibalistic fantasies. Though its symptoms were specific to Algonquian culture, Windigo psychosis is much like paranoid schizophrenia. In Western society, the symptoms of paranoid schizophrenia include ideas of persecution by others, such as people in the government, people in the telephone company, or men from Mars, as well as anxiety over homosexual impulses.

Amok is another mental illness, found in Malaysia and Indonesia, that has a specific set of symptoms. The central feature of *amok* is that the victim kills people while in a temporarily deranged state, experiencing complete amnesia of the attack afterward. Some researchers consider *amok* a disease specific to these particular cultures, while others consider it a form of depression psychosis produced by extreme stress, which is culturally determined. We get our expression "to run amok" from this mental illness of Southeast Asia. It has been pointed out that *amok* occurs in societies where individuals also may go into trance. While in trance they perform "stereotyped behavior which allows the release of repressed feelings" (Azhar and Varma, 2000: 171–172). Symptoms similar to *amok* have also been reported in the United States (Azhar and Varma, 2000: 173). A suggested explanation for *amok* in Malaysia is that it may be an extreme expression of aggression in a society which strictly prohibits such expression. The same explanation may also account for students "running amok" and slaughtering classmates and teachers in American schools and then killing themselves.

Latah is another disease found in Malaysia. Found predominately in females, its symptoms are a startle reaction, after which the individual falls to the ground, and compulsive imitation of words, gestures, and acts. The person may also utter obsenities. In a recent survey of *latah,* Winzeler indicates that it occurs in association with societies where there is familiarity with trance states and which practice shamanism. *Amok* also is associated with trance states. Both *latah* and *amok* were much more common in the past then they are today. They have been replaced by depression, hypochondriasis, and anxiety, which are now treated with therapies that include the use of the Qur'an (Azhar and Varma, 2000: 184).

Winzeler also notes the similarities of *latah* to certain symptoms in Western illnesses, namely, startle reactions and imitative behavior. Winzeler is unable to conclude whether it is a specific form of illness related to Malay culture or a symptom of a universal category of illness. These forms of behavior are recognized as abnormal by the peoples of the cultures themselves, and the terms *amok* and *latah* are the native terms used to describe these behaviors. Good has pointed out the profound role that culture plays not only in the expression of symptoms but also in the course the illness takes (1992).

As we have pointed out above, the belief in witchcraft and sorcery in some societies is not an indication of mental illness, as would be the case in our own society. However, in Algeria, a sick person is believed to be possessed by *jinn* (spirits), and this is considered to be a form of "madness" (Al-Issa, 2000: 103). This condition is often considered to be the result of sorcery. People believe that someone else, motivated by envy, will use the "evil eye," so that the victim's behavior and desires come under the control of supernatural beings. The *marabout* is one type of traditional therapist who treats such patients. According to Al-Issa, "Exorcism consists of conversing with the evil spirit through the patient" to convince him to leave (2000: 104). The *marabout* is regarded as a saint and healer, and his burial place often becomes a shrine. The use of traditional therapists like the *marabout* are not only legal but on the increase in Algeria. In countries like Iraq, Kuwait, and Tunisia, such therapies are illegal because they are associated with underdevelopment and backwardness in contrast to modernization (Al-Issa, 2000: 104).

Mental illness has been defined as abnormal behavior, that is, behavior that is different from the cultural norm in a particular society. It is important to differentiate deviant behavior that represents mental illness from deviant behavior that does not. Not all those who violate the rules of a society are, by definition, mentally ill. Some are criminals; some are rebels; some are innovators.

REBELS AND INNOVATORS

From time to time, individuals appear who renounce important aspects of their own culture and propose that a radically different way of doing things be substituted for the old way. They are frequently considered mentally ill by the members of their society, but when they are successful in attracting followers and in overthrowing the old order, they are called innovators and revolutionaries. These individuals are often central in bringing about changes that result in significant transformations in the design of the tapestry of culture for their society. Their conceptualization, which may come to them in the form of a vision or a dream, is often a new organization for society.

The typical personality type of the well-adjusted individual in all cultures incorporates the motivations and values of the culture. Such an individual will want to do the things considered desirable in the society and will not think of changing them. The well-adjusted individual is very different from the rebel and innovator. The rebel, therefore, should differ in personality in some significant way from the typical person. The difference in personality between the rebel and the typical person reflects a difference in early life experience on the part of the rebel. Erik Erikson (1969) explored the relationship between successful rebels, their early life experiences, and their cultures in a series of biographical case studies of individuals such as Martin Luther and Gandhi. Erikson has stressed the significance of these individuals to the historical process of cultural change. His emphasis is on the psychological characteristics of innovators as these relate to the cultural setting within which these individuals lived and their effect on history. This approach might be seen as ancestral to psychohistories being done by some historians today.

CULTURE AND THE STRUCTURE OF EMOTION

The emotional endowment of humans is universal and largely innate. However, the way in which emotion is expressed and interpreted is culturally determined (Wierzbicka, 1999: 249). Emotion is expressed through gestures such as facial expressions and bodily movements. It is also asserted through various levels of language (i.e., intonation, nouns, and phrases).

Wierzbicka presents an interesting series of contrasts between Anglo-American and Polish attitudes toward emotions and their expression (1999: 240 ff.). For example, Polish culture values the expression of one's feelings truthfully, saying and showing what one really feels, in contrast to Anglo-American culture, where a display of good feelings is valued even if one does not necessarily feel that way. For Americans, this is coupled with the suppression of bad feelings, which may damage one's image and be unpleasant for other people. Americans are seen as smiling all the time even if that is not how they feel. Wierzbicka is arguing that Americans are being deceptive when they hide their true feelings behind polite language ("Have a nice day"), while Poles are simply honest. Among the Swat Pushtuns (and also the Mafia), to allow one's enemies to know one's true feelings is to show one's weakness, so one must therefore always hide feelings and emotions and present oneself as even-tempered and not show anger. These examples raise the question of whether there is a universal recognition of what constitutes lying. From the evidence on the Poles, Americans, and Swat Pathans, it is clear that there is cultural variability regarding whether or not lying is culturally valued. Earlier we saw that lying was a cultural requirement for the Tzeltzal Mayans, which they inculcated in their children during child-rearing.

In the Faeroe Islands, men in particular must control their anger, since expression of anger is considered harmful to ongoing social relationships. The Faeroe Islanders live on some 20 islands in the North Atlantic and until recently preserved much of their distinctive cultural identity as a consequence of limited trade and contact with the outside world. Faeroe women, whose lives are confined to the domestic sphere, can express their anger, and it is not thought to be threatening since their activities are limited to the domestic sphere. On the other hand, Faeroe men should be unemotional or, at least, less expressive of anger. A strong value is placed on male emotional control because men work outside their homes, often in cooperative endeavors in close quarters, and under such circumstances the expression of anger is socially destructive (Gaffin, 1995: 161).

The structure of emotion that characterizes Faeroe Island society is a dynamic creation that sometimes involves the "intentional production of emotional states in others" (Gaffin, 1995), which develop as a result of taunting and teasing. These are deemed undesirable and are negatively sanctioned, but they occur to test an individual's emotional mettle, as well as to demonstrate that anger must be controlled. Particular men seem more susceptible to taunting and teasing. The teasing of these men not only is an emotional sport but also channels community ideas about male behavior. The provoking behavior, by eliciting undesirable and negatively sanctioned behavior, not only tests the taunted individual's self-control but, at the same time, serves as a form of social control. If the victim controls his anger and can tolerate the teasing, he is viewed in a positive manner. If he loses his temper, then he is the target of ridicule. The lesson to be learned is that a man must maintain an even temperament because loss of control damages the man's ability to be an effective member of the community.

THE PERSON AND THE SELF

The socially constituted person, as distinguished from the individual self, is a concept with a long history in anthropology. Individuals learn to perform a repertoire of social roles, and those roles constitute a major component of the social person.

The notion of the self is a human universal, though the conception of the person varies from one society to the next. Each society has its own conception of what emotions persons can appropriately express and when they can be expressed, as well as its own ideas about what is right and wrong and what characterizes the good person and the bad person. A distinction can be made between the "poles of biological and existential universals on the one hand and cultural particulars [regarding the nature of the self] on the other" (Sax, 2002: 7). While the person may be conceived of in different ways in various cultures, there are certain universal characteristics of the person. These universal features are present in the early stages of the process of development of the person. Developmental psychologists are of the opinion that the boundedness of self and self-motivation are found in children in all societies. During the enculturation process in some societies, such as Java and Bali, a different notion of self is inculcated. All infants share boundedness and act as autonomous entities who are in contrast with others. However, as the child develops in some non-Western cultures, he or she learns to suppress this autonomous self.

Clifford Geertz (1974) examined differences in personhood in Java, Bali, and Western societies. Geertz, whose theoretical approaches are discussed in Chapter 1, was concerned with the methodology used by the anthropologist to see things from the native's point of view. Rather than putting himself in the place of the other or conducting psychological tests, as did earlier psychological anthropologists, Geertz preferred to analyze the series of symbolic forms that people in a culture use to represent themselves to themselves and to others. Like Margaret Mead, he began his analysis with the Western conception of the person, which he described as "a bounded, unique, more or less integrated motivational and cognitive universe, a dynamic center of awareness, emotion, judgment, and action organized into a distinctive whole and set contrastively both against other such wholes and against its social and natural background" (1984: 126).

The sense of personhood in Java, according to Geertz, is different from the Western conception of the person. It is based on two sets of contrasts: inside/outside and refined/vulgar. The ideal for a person is, through religious discipline, to achieve a state of stilled emotion in the inner realm (he "thins out his emotional life to a constant hum"), while in the outer realm, the same kind of purity and refinement is achieved through elaborate etiquette. Refinement is desired both inside and outside, and vulgarity is to be avoided. The Javanese concept of person is a bifurcated one, in contrast to the Western concept, which emphasizes the integration of the person.

The Balinese view of the person is as an appropriate representative of a category, rather than a unique individual. People attempt to mute individual personal characteristics and to emphasize, in contrast, features of status. Geertz, who frequently used the dramatic or theatrical metaphor to describe Balinese culture, likened Balinese persons to a cast of characters. In Bali, the face itself is considered a mask. Geertz's point is that the Western concept of the person as an autonomous, bounded entity operating in his or her own way vis-à-vis other like entities is not shared by other cultures. Since Geertz is a cultural relativist, who emphasizes the unique features that differentiate cultures, he also views personhood as being distinctive for each culture.

The Hindu vision of the self is that there is an eternal self and an ephemeral self whose caste, class, gender, personality, and subjectivity are transient. The conception of the self in Western cultures, where the self is seen the locus of creativity and moral value, is viewed very negatively among Hindus (Sax, 2002: 10–11). Marriot, in his model of the Hindu self, sees it as an entity composed of shifting and inherently unstable substance. Interestingly, this seems to parallel the postmodern view of the deconstruction of the self/person in which the self/person has no status except as the transient effect of a variety of causes. Sax examines a series of public ritual performances, which he sees as "an especially powerful means for creating (and sometimes undermining) selves, relationships, and communities, because they inscribe cultural concepts on the whole person, the body as well as the mind" (Sax, 2002: 14).What he demonstrates through his analysis of the series of *Pandav lila* public rituals, which are part of the village tradition of the Garhwalis of North India, is that the "empirical 'selves' of Garhwalis are multiple" (Sax, 2002: 161). The public performance and all that it entails plays out the nature of the multiple selves of this population.

Conceptualization of the self in Western cultures like that of the United States differs from conceptualization of the self in Eastern cultures like those of India, Java, Bali, Japan, and China. This difference is expressed in language. In order to use the proper linguistic forms in Javanese or in Japanese, the speaker must know his or her relationship to the listener (or receiver). Misperceiving the relationship and using the wrong or impolite form is a disgraceful act. Thus, the speaker must know certain information—for example, whether the person being addressed is a professor, is of a higher social class, or is older than the speaker. Relative age is always a factor—one is either a younger brother or an older brother. One must always use the appropriate form of address. In discussing the Japanese concept of the self, Brown suggests that it is basically relational—the self constantly viewed in relation to others (higher or lower, more respectful or less respectful, older or younger). In contrast, the American self is bounded (rather than relational), autonomous, and individualistic (Brown, 1996: 47–48). As the anthropologist Dorinne Kondo observed, when she conducted her research in Japan, "I was always defined by my obligations and links to others" (Kondo, cited in Brown, 1996: 47). The self only exists in relation to others. Because it is necessary for the Japanese child to learn the complexities of the social structure and his or her place in relation to all others within that structure, learning the proper forms of linguistic expression may take hard work and years of training.

Ewing deals with how the self is constructed in a transnational situation. A Turkish woman, though born in the Netherlands, moves between the culture of her Turkish homeland and the culture of the Netherlands. She is the daughter of a Turkish guest-worker whose family has established permanent residence in the Netherlands, yet maintains close ties with Turkey. As Ewing notes, "In Turkish guest-worker communities in northern Europe, young women often find themselves caught between two worlds, negotiating identities which are radically disjunctive" (2002: 97). It is no longer a matter of giving up "old ways" and an old identity and becoming modern, but something more complicated. Even though young people born in the

Netherlands, where their parents are guest-workers, live in encapsulated communities and go to schools that exclusively serve immigrant populations, these young people are nevertheless influenced by Dutch and European media and a very different vision of the self and gender relations than is operative in the communities of their homeland, Turkey. Ewing describes, in particular, the situation of a young Turkish woman, a professional with a business school education and a career, who had been in an arranged marriage with her mother's sister's son who was an uneducated assembly line worker in a pillow factory. She had lived a compartmentalized existence, part of a professional cosmopolitan world, on the one hand, while on the other hand she had been engaged at the age of 11 and married at 18 within her Turkish world, which she had visited every summer as a child. Her self in these two worlds was significantly different, though as she got older she resisted the arranged marriage and being more and more engulfed in Turkish culture and identity, where girls and women are subservient to the will of their parents and the dictates of Turkish culture. Though she resisted marriage with her cousin, her parents eventually won out, though a factor was her desire to be identified as a "good girl" within Turkish culture (Ewing, 2002: 107). The life trajectory of this individual reveals the way in which her view of herself, her self-representation, is as a strategizer, moving, at first, between Turkish and educated professional identities. Eventually, however, she runs away from her husband and is finally able to get a divorce and makes a settlement with him and her parents, which gives her the independence and professional identity she so vigorously sought (Ewing, 2002).

The concept of the individual "caught between two worlds" and properly belonging to neither is an old one in anthropology. It has also often been explored in novels. Dr. Aziz, in *Passage to India*, memorably captures the dilemma of the educated Indian who is unable to cross the cultural boundary of colonialism and establish a friendship with Mr. Fielding. Dr. Aziz finds that he cannot change his Indian identity to assume another identity that will allow him to establish a true friendship. In *The Death of Jim Loney*, James Welch portrays the predicament and tragic consequences of the "half breed" who has neither the self which would place him in the world of his father or that of his mother. He commits suicide as a result of this conflict. Individuals often feel that they cannot simultaneously live in two worlds. Novelists frequently succeed in capturing this dilemma more effectively than social scientists.

SUMMARY

- At birth, the infant can already distinguish the sounds of his mother's language from those of other languages.

- The infant gradually learns which sound combinations most frequently occur in its mother tongue, which are correct and which incorrect, as these are related to speech segmentation and word boundaries.

• By 24 months, toddlers can produce 50 different words.

• At the age of two, grammatical speech, in the form of word combination can begin with as few as 50 to 150 words.

• Sociocultural information is encoded in the organization of conversation, and from earliest infancy, children acquire knowledge as they are involved in such interactions.

• Self-reliance, a characteristic that is valued more in some societies than in others, is inculcated in the young infant through the process of enculturation.

• Gender roles and the kinds of persons men and women are expected to be are also acquired during the socialization and language acquisition processes.

• Not only do individuals in a society learn a language and a culture; the personality structure, and the idea of personhood and self, which is characteristic of their culture, is also inculcated in them.

• In the process of acquiring language and learning the rules of their culture, the particular personality characteristics favored in that culture are also inculcated.

• What is regarded as a symptom of mental illness in one society may be merely one aspect of normal, healthy life in another.

• One view is that there are universal psychopathological disease categories (such as schizophrenia and depression) that are manifested in different kinds of behavior from one culture to another. The opposing view is that universally stressful situations produce different kinds of diseases in different cultures.

• The emotional endowment of humans is universal and largely innate. However, the way in which emotion is expressed and interpreted is culturally determined.

• The notion of the self is a human universal, though the conception of the person varies from one society to the next.

SUGGESTED READINGS

Bock, Philip. *Rethinking Psychological Anthropology: Continuity and Change in the Study of Human Action.* New York: W. H. Freeman, 1988. An excellent introduction to the history of psychological anthroplogy.

Hirschfeld, Lawrence A. *Race in the Making: Cognition, Culture, and the Child's Construction of Human Kinds.* Boston: MIT Press, 1996. Explores the development of the child's notion of race and demonstrates the way race is dependent upon the human capacity for classification, rather than being the product of the observation of physical differences.

Lindholm, Charles. *Culture and Identity: The History, Theory and Practice of Psychological Anthropology.* Boston: McGraw-Hill, 2001. Overall coverage of psychological anthropology and the dialectic between the self and the other.

Mageo, Jeannette Marie. *Theorizing Self in Samoa: Emotions, Genders, and Sexualities.* Ann Arbor: University of Michigan Press, 1998. A psychological and historical ethnography of Samoa, which demonstrates the way in which Samoan understandings of the self are more sociocentric—accentuating the social roles that people play—than egocentric—emphasizing individual, interior feelings and perceptions.

Mead, Margaret. *Growing up in New Guinea.* 1930. Reprint. New York: Mentor Books, 1960. One of the earliest anthropological studies of how a child was socialized into a non-Western society.

Ochs, Elinor. *Culture and Language Development: Language Acquisition and Language Socialization in a Samoan Village.* New York: Cambridge University Press, 1988. How Samoan children are enculturated and learn the Samoan language.

Packer, Martin J., and Mark B. Tappan (eds.). *Cultural and Critical Perspectives on Human Development.* Albany: State University of New York Press, 2001. A series of articles on the cultural and social aspects of human psychological development.

 SUGGESTED WEBSITES

http://www.chinasprout.com/html/column3.html A bilingual speech therapist points out the universals in the process of language acquisition.

http://www.as.ua.edu/ant/Faculty/murphy/cult&per.htm A historical survey of the culture-and-personality school in anthroplogy, presenting its basic premises, information about key figures, and recent critiques of this approach.

http://www.age-thnomedizin.de/e_Selbstdarstellung.htm Surveys the relationship between medicine and culture, including mental illness, ethnopharmacology, and ethnobotany.

5

Symbolic Meanings

In the first scene of *Citizen Kane,* one of the most famous films ever made, a powerful old man who is dying utters the mysterious word "Rosebud." The symbolic meaning of this word is an important clue to his character and to the unfolding narrative of the film. "Rosebud," whose meaning is not revealed until the conclusion of the film; is an important personal symbol to Kane. The behavior of people in a culture is framed according to a set of symbols or cultural ideas that constitute the overall design of the tapestry of their culture. To understand people's economic behavior, political behavior, and social behavior, one must understand the system of cultural meanings that permeate these institutions. People in their day-to-day actions thereby create and convey cultural meaning as they re-create their culture. How they walk, how they dress, how they talk—all convey cultural meaning. Sometimes people change their behavior, and then its meaning also changes. To understand the meaning of cultural behavior, one must "read" culture like a text. In their fieldwork, anthropologists observe and record what people say and do. The next step is to understand and interpret the meanings of these words and actions, by discussing the material with informants and examining the actions, words, and their symbolic meanings in a number of other cultural contexts.

The analysis of symbols deals with the meanings of words, the meanings of actions, and the meanings of objects in a culture. In addition to involving meaning, symbols are also expressive and convey emotion. This is especially true with regard to symbols in art and in religion. As noted in Chapter 3, language itself is a system made up entirely of symbols. All symbols, like the morphemes of language, operate as if they are two-sided coins. On one side are the physical characteristics, and on the other side are the meanings, or what the symbols stand for. Symbols are manifested in behavior as well as in ideas. Symbols and their meanings guide people's actions and also motivate such actions. Further, people's behavior itself has symbolic meaning to those who observe it.

Metaphor, a kind of symbol, is an important analytical concept used by anthropologists in the study of symbolic systems. A metaphor is an idea that people use to stand for another set of ideas. The meaning of the metaphor is the recognition of the connection between the metaphor itself and the "something else" it represents. In the Kwakiutl marriage ceremony, discussed in Chapter 2, many of the activities described were also characteristic of warfare, such as blackening the faces, dressing like warriors, and running through a gauntlet of fire in order to demonstrate courage. Among the Kwakiutl, marriage is metaphorically a form of warfare. Warfare is apt as a metaphor to symbolize marriage among the Kwakiutl because both involve competition. The competitive aspect in the marriage ceremony is also seen in the potlatch, which pits one side against the other.

In our society, games are often used as metaphors for life. Games involve struggle and competition. Sometimes you win and sometimes you lose, but games must be played according to a set of rules. Games demand from the players strategic ability, risk taking, stamina, and courage—virtues in our culture. During Nixon's presidency, White House officials talked about "playing hardball" and used the expression from baseball, "When the going gets tough, the tough get going." Baseball was being used to stand for something else—politics—because both include competition, struggle, and some element of danger, though they may differ in many other respects.

Competition or struggle can be physical or mental. The chessboard is a miniature world peopled with a feudal society. In the classic movie *The Seventh Seal*, the White Knight plays against death, represented by the black pieces. The White Knight plays for his life against death, which represents the Black Death—the plague sweeping Europe. The moviemaker, Ingmar Bergman, talks about life and death using the chess game as a metaphor.

Another type of symbol is a **metonym.** Like a metaphor, a metonym is also based upon a substitution of one thing for another, but in this case the symbol standing for the something else is one of the several things that constitute the something else. Thus the monarch can be referred to as the head of state, and the crown or throne can stand as a symbol for the monarchy. The capital of any type of government can be referred to as the seat of government. In each case, a part has been taken and used to stand as a symbol for the whole.

One category of symbols, **public symbols,** constitutes the cultural system for a society. Much of that body of cultural symbols is known, understood, and shared by all the members of the society. However, some symbols, often the most important ones, are more esoteric and may be known only by religious practitioners. Individuals also create symbols out of their own experiences, which are not commonly shared by others. These are known as **private symbols** and are the symbols of our dream life and fantasies. In the creative process, the artist, novelist, or filmmaker uses private symbols. The process of interpretation of artistic works by the public and the critic involves trying to decipher what the private symbols of the artist mean. We will discuss how the creative artist uses private and public symbols in Chapter 12.

At the beginning of this chapter we referred to the two-sidedness of symbols and the arbitrary relationship between the two sides, as occurs in language. For public symbols, the connection between the two is culturally, not individually, determined. The symbols and the meanings, which are connected, differ from culture to culture, as words do from language to language. Thus there are two ways in which the study of symbolism can be approached. The first is to examine a particular symbol and the different meanings that are attached to it in various cultures. The second is to begin with the other side of the coin—to study the thing symbolized and the different symbols used for it.

THE SYMBOLISM OF FOOD

As an example of how a symbol may have various meanings attached to it in different cultures, we will examine the symbolism of food. From the utilitarian or materialist perspective, food is ingested by humans to sustain life. It is made up of calories, protein, fats, minerals, and carbohydrates and is introduced into the human animal by eating. This aspect of food is equivalent to the physical manifestations or sounds that make up a word. Not to go beyond this aspect of food in terms of one's investigation would be like analyzing words without considering their meanings.

Eating is a metaphor for sexual intercourse in a great many societies, including our own. Why is one a metaphor for the other? What do the two actions have in common? These two acts are completely different physiologically; nevertheless, they are tied together in their symbolic significance. In many societies "eating" can be used figuratively for sexual intercourse. "To hunger for" is a metaphor for sexual desire. Among the Mehinaku, of the Amazon region, having sex is defined as "to eat to the fullest extent. . . . The essential idea is that the genitals of one sex are the 'food' of the others" (Gregor, 1985: 70). In a different part of the world, among the Lardil of Mornington Island, Australia, "there is a strong identification between food and sex, sexual intercourse and eating" (McKnight, 1999: 23). In discussing eating practices among Americans, Lukanuski has pointed out the same equation and intertwining of eating and sex (1998: 114).

Eating is a metaphor that is sometimes used to signify marriage. In many New Guinea societies, like that of the Lesu on the island of New Ireland in the Pacific and that of the Trobriand Islanders, marriage is symbolized by the couple's eating together for the first time. Adolescent boys and girls freely engage in sexual intercourse without commitment to marriage and without any gossip or criticism from the community. But eating together constitutes a public announcement that they are now married. Eating symbolizes their new status as a married couple. In our society, it is just the reverse. One can take a date to dinner, but engaging in sexual intercourse used to be and frequently still is a sign of marriage.

In other New Guinea societies, such as Wogeo, if a man eats with a woman, then she is like his sister and he can't marry her. Here, eating is equally symbolic but has the reverse meaning. Instead of marriage, eating symbolizes a brother-sister relationship—those who cannot marry. Among the Na of China, sexual intercourse is forbidden among close consanguineal relatives. The Na say, "Those who eat from the same bowl and the same plate must not mate" (Cai Hua, 2001: 125).

In Jordan, eating reveals the social structure. Bedouin men eat with other men, and women eat with women.

In some New Guinea societies the nuclear family is not the unit that eats to-gether, as is the case in American society. The men take their meals in the men's house, separately from their wives and children. Women prepare and eat their food in their own houses, and take the husbands' portions of food to the men's house. This pattern is also widespread among Near Eastern societies, where men usually eat with other men and women with other women, and husbands and wives do not eat together. This is the case among the Marri Baluch of west-ern Pakistan, where the family arranges marriage between close relatives, and husbands never eat with their wives. But in adulterous relationships between a man and a woman, illicit eating together symbolizes their love for one another. In Lesu, the symbolic meaning of eating is exactly opposite from its meaning among the Marri Baluch. In Lesu, betrothal and marriage are symbolized by a man and woman sitting down and eating together, but a woman never eats with her lover.

Recognition of the metaphoric connection between eating and sexual inter-course can also help to explain some other cultural rules that have to do with taboos against eating certain things. In some societies, members of a clan, a type of kin group, are not allowed to eat the animal or bird that is their totemic ancestor. Since they believe themselves to be descended from that ancestor, it would be like eating that ancestor or eating themselves. This would be equivalent to sexual intercourse within the group, which is incest. For the Siuai of Bougainville in the Solomon Islands, eating the totemic animal is seen as a form of incest, having intercourse with a person from one's own clan. There is another incestlike prohibition involving food among the Abelam and the Arapesh of Papua New Guinea. The Arapesh express it in the form of an aphorism:

Other people's mothers

Other people's sisters

Other people's pigs

Other people's yams which they have piled up

You may eat,

Your own mother

Your own sister

Your own pigs

Your own yams which you have piled up

You may not eat.

The pigs that a person raises are considered his children, and the owner of a pig is referred to as its father. The Arapesh explicitly recognize the symbolic connection between eating and sexual intercourse, as evidenced in the prohibition against eating one's own pigs and yams and the prohibition against incest with one's sister and mother. In Abelam and Arapesh, the taboo against eating one's own pigs and yams compels social groups to exchange their pigs and yams with other groups, resulting in ongoing exchange relationships with those groups.

It would be unthinkable to eat with one's enemies. Even in our own society, one may be compelled to say a polite good morning to one's enemy, but the line is drawn at breaking bread together. This is generally true in societies around the world. Eating together, or commensality, symbolizes goodwill and peaceful relations. What happens when enemies accidentally find themselves together for one reason or another? The Pathans of Swat, Pakistan, place great stress on hospitality, which is symbolized by giving food. Even if the host learns his guests are enemies, with whom he would normally not share food, the rules of hospitality dictate that as guests they must be fed. When the guests are ready to leave, the host escorts them to the border of his territory where his obligations of hospitality end, and he is free to treat them like enemies and kill them.

The association between food prohibitions and rank is found in its most extreme form in the caste system of India. A caste system consists of ranked groups, each with a different economic specialization. In India there is an association between caste and the idea of pollution. Members of highly ranked groups can be polluted by coming into contact with the bodily secretions, particularly saliva, of individuals of lower-ranked castes. Because of the fear of pollution, Brahmans and other high-ranked individuals will not share food with, not eat from the same plate as, nor even accept food from an individual from a low-ranking caste.

Among the Newars of Nepal, the giving and receiving of food serves to express caste as well as kinship "positions" within the society (Lowdin, 1998: 174). The Newar have a complex caste system with some 26 castes. Members of higher castes cannot accept water from individuals belonging to the lower castes. The ritual food par excellence of the Newar is boiled rice. When a child eats boiled rice for the first time, this symbolizes that he is now a member of his caste and a member of Newari society. Lowdin notes that "the general rule here is that accepting [boiled] rice implies that one, in terms of caste, is of equal or possibly lower status than the giver" (1998: 59). If one wants to eat with people of the same, lower, or higher caste, the only food that can be eaten together is *baji*, that is, beaten or flattened rice. If a high-caste individual eats boiled rice with a lower-caste person, he becomes polluted and must subsequently purify himself or become an outcaste. If he remains polluted, other members of his caste also become polluted as a consequence of his act. Brahmans, the priestly caste, may be given gifts of unhusked and uncooked rice by members of any caste since, unhusked, uncooked rice is not pollutable. In the Newari view, the reason that one caste is lower or higher is a consequence of the rules about giving and taking food.

Food is also used to express kinship symbolically among the Newar. Relatives are all in the same caste, since one must marry within the same caste. The food items that signify kinship are of a different sort than those signifying caste relationships. The Newar trace descent through their fathers, but the mother's brother is of particular ritual and emotional importance. When a sister's son is initiated, the mother's brother provides buffalo for the sacrifice. After the animals are cooked, highly prized parts of the buffalo are given to him. Before he returns home the next day, he is given a variety of specific food stuffs, including one leg of the sacrificial animal, in return.

The relationship between eating and sexual intercourse may be carried one step further in that men may be prohibited from eating foods that have metaphoric associations with women's reproductive functions. Meigs (1992), writing about the Hua of Papua New Guinea, relates the series of prohibitions to which men are subject. These include foods that are red, identified with menstrual blood; foods associated with holes, such as birds and possums that live in holes in trees; foods that are hairy, like furbearing animals and birds with facial plumage; and foods that smell like a menstruating woman, such as certain species of possum and two species of yam. Among the Hua, sexual intercourse, though initiated by men, is thought to be debilitating for males whereas it increases the vitality of females because of what is viewed as a transfer of *nu*, or grease. Feeding, its metaphorical opposite, is the quintessential female activity. Women feed others, including men, and by this transfer of *nu* to those who eat, produce strength and vitality in the eaters.

Cultural rules determine every aspect of food consumption. Who eats together defines social units. As noted above, in our society, the nuclear family is the unit that regularly eats together. The anthropologist Mary Douglas (1972) has pointed out that for the English, the kind of meal and the kind of food that is served relate to the kinds of social links between the people who are eating together. She distinguishes between regular meals; Sunday meals, when relatives may come; and such occasions as when guests come for drinks or acquaintances are invited to a cocktail party. The food served symbolizes the occasion and reflects who is present. For example, only tidbits and snacks—finger foods—are served at a cocktail party. It would be inappropriate to serve a steak or hamburgers. The distinctions among cocktail parties, regular meals, and special dinners mark degrees of social distance and the social boundaries between those guests who are invited for drinks, those who are invited to dinner, and those who come to a family meal. In this example, the type of food symbolizes the category of guest with whom it is eaten.

A similar analysis would apply to American society. As previously noted, individualism is prized in American society; nevertheless, when Americans eat alone, they feel uncomfortable. Eating is primarily a group activity. "Eating alone is a stigmatized behavior because it defies the expectations we have of eating. It will probably continue to be thought of as an unfortunate activity of the social outcast" (Lukanski, 1998: 119).

Food has a great many meanings in present-day American society. For example, regions are symbolized by different foods. Grits, fried chicken, barbecue, black-eyed peas, collards, and mustard greens represent the South. Shore dinners, clam chowder, and lobster immediately symbolize New England. Some American foods, like the Big Mac and Classic Coke, have become international and can be found in almost every part of the globe. On the other hand, ethnic foods and ingredients, such as bagels, pita bread, and oriental condiments, today are on the shelves of supermarkets in small towns and large cities across America. This reflects the fact that ethnic identity has become increasingly important as a component of American identity. Particular dishes distinctive of a national cuisine are used to create an ethnic identity; but beyond that, members of other ethnic groups have become familiar with such foods. For example, the principal characters in *The Godfather* films are constantly signaling their Italian-American identities by what they cook and eat ("Take the cannoli; leave the gun"). Americans of other ethnicities also eat cannolis.

SOCIAL GROUPS, SOCIAL CATEGORIES, AND THEIR SYMBOLS

In the previous section, we selected something tangible, food, and then discussed the various meanings attached to it in different cultures. Group identity may be symbolized in a number of other ways in addition to cuisine. For example, a social group such as a clan may be represented by a totemic animal, with pictorial representations of the animal being used to signify that clan. The Kwakiutl, whose wedding ceremony is discussed in Chapter 2, as well as other tribes of the Pacific coast of Canada, painted the specific totemic animals of the group on the facade of the house and carved these animals on the totem pole standing before the house. These tribes were like many other societies of the world in that personal names given to

A tsimshian mortuary totem pole, still stands today at Git Winkul, British Columbia erected by a family of the Wolf phratry which depicts crests from its origin myth.

members of the group were the property of the entire group. When a person died, his or her name returned to the pool of names, to be used again when a child was born. There was also the belief that a name carried an identity, and that identity was perpetuated through the names handed down from generation to generation. In this way, individual identity was linked to clan identity, since, to the outside world, the name symbolized membership in the group.

In general, the clan as a social group may be associated with particular spirits, including spirits of the clan ancestors, who are said to dwell in specific locations in the clan territory. The spirits and the territory represent the clan. Strangers crossing the territory or hunting in it are in danger from the spirits that protect it. In such a situation, where the land symbolizes the continuity of the social group (the clan) from mythical times to the present, the land could not be sold for money without destroying the identity of the group itself. Thus, as food stands as a symbol for the group, so too can an animal, a painting, a carving, a name, or a territory.

Fairly common forms used to symbolize social groups are birds, fish, and animals. One may ask why it is that animals are used to stand for people. Though the animal world exists apart from the human world, people use the animal world to talk metaphorically about the human world. The world is seen as a jungle or referred to as an animal farm. Though the world of animals and the world of people are very different, there are links between them. The world of animals is divided into species; the world of people, into social groups. Some animal species are more like others and share a certain number of characteristics: There are those that fly, those that swim, and those that walk or crawl. Societies use these different characteristics to make systems of classification of animals, like those discussed in Chapter 3. This classification will differ from one society to the next, because each society may single out a different series of characteristics upon which its classification is based. In a society with clans, each clan is different from the others, just as the animal species differ from one another. This is why differences among animal species are used to express differences among groups of people.

Sometimes society is conceptualized as being divided into halves, which may be symbolically represented as higher and lower, sun and moon, or right side and left side. The Yafar of New Guinea think of the two parts as male and female. Each village is divided into two sides, one side referred to as "male" and made up of several clans, and the other side referred to as "female" and also comprising several clans. In rituals, men of the male half of the village use objects conceptualized as male and associated with plants designated male, while men of the female half of the village use ritual objects that are female and connected to female plants (Juillerat, 1996: 48, 49, 71). The symbols of male and female are used by the Yafar to designate the halves, each with its own distinctive character, which are nevertheless complementary.

The animal world may be ordered in still another way. Some animals live very close to humans, even under the same roof; others live under human protection in the barn; still others live in the forest, where humans hunt them; and finally, certain exotic, inedible animals live in the zoo. Edmund Leach (1964) has pointed out that this particular series of animal categories corresponds to categories of social distance in English society. Sisters make up the closest category. Next come first cousins. The third category is neighbors who are not kin, and the fourth category is complete strangers with whom one has no social relationship. The significant aspect of Leach's analysis of these corresponding categories is the connection between edibility and permissible sexual relationships. The first category of animals—pets—is equivalent to the first category of females—sisters. Pets may not be eaten, and sisters are not permissible as sex partners. Farm animals make up the second animal category, and these are eaten only if they have been castrated or have not reached physical maturity. The corresponding category of women is cousins, with whom one might have sexual relations but whom one cannot marry. The third category is made up of game animals, which are edible; they correspond to neighbors, who are very marriageable. The fourth category is composed of exotic animals, which are not edible, and, correspondingly, exotic women, who are not marriageable. Leach's analysis demonstrates that the cultural domains of animal classification and of degrees of social distance of females are organized in the same way; at the same time, the parallel between edibility and permissible sexual relations becomes apparent.

Another common way to symbolize social groupings and social relationships is to use the human body. Among the Teutonic tribes at the dawn of history, close and distant relatives were symbolized by close and more distant parts of the body, reckoned from the head. The father and mother were symbolized by the head; brothers and sisters were at the neck; first cousins at the shoulders; second cousins at the elbows; third cousins at the wrists; and fourth, fifth, and sixth cousins at the knuckles and finger joints. At the cutoff point of kin were seventh cousins, who were called nail relatives. Individuals beyond seven degrees of relationship were not considered kinsmen.

The internal skeletal structure of the body is also used as a metaphor for the internal structure of society. The word *bone* was used for clan among the Mongols, and the aristocracy were referred to as *White Bone* to distinguish them from commoners, who were referred to as *Black Bone*. A slightly different metaphor is used by the Riff of Morocco, who refer to their clan as a *vein*. Just as the Mongols used a skeletal metaphor, the Riff use the metaphor of blood vessels to represent the interconnection between the parts of their society.

Americans use the metaphor of blood to represent kinship. In thinking about the biological facts of conception, we can see that the sperm from the father and the egg from the mother, which unite to form the new individual, have nothing to do with blood. Yet Americans say that the blood of their fathers and mothers flows in their veins. This is our symbolic way of talking about kinship.

THE SYMBOLIC MEANINGS OF SPACE

Arrangements of space also make important symbolic statements about social groupings and social relationships. Among the Nuchanulth (Nootka) of the Pacific coast of Canada, each of the large plank houses in the winter villages in which they lived in the nineteenth century represented a social group. The floor plan of the house was divided into spaces that were ranked with respect to one another (see Figure 5-1). The place of honor, the left corner of the rear of the house, was occupied by the owner, who was the highest-ranking person in the house and held the highest title, and his family. The next most important man and his family occupied the right rear corner of the house; the third most important man and his family occupied the left front corner of the house; the fourth most important man and his family were in the right front corner; the least important titled man lived with his family on the left-hand side of the house. Untitled commoners and their families lived in the remaining spaces along the sides of the house. Each location had its own hearth. Each nuclear family in the Nuchanulth house was ranked with respect to the others, and this rank was symbolized by the location of each family's hearth and its living space in relation to the others. The house floor plan was like a seating plan according to seniority. There is archeological evidence of this type of house with its status divisions that goes back at least 2,000 years. However, with demographic decline and the incursion of the cash economy in the late nineteenth century, a new pattern developed in which related nuclear families lived in single-family dwellings clustered behind the large houses that were now used for "sociopolitical rituals . . . [and were] transformed into potlatch houses" (Marshall, 2000: 102).

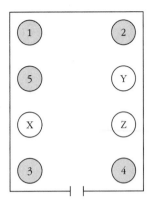

FIGURE 5-1
Nuchanulth house floor plan.

1, 2 . . . . 5 = ranked title holders
X, Y, and Z = commoners

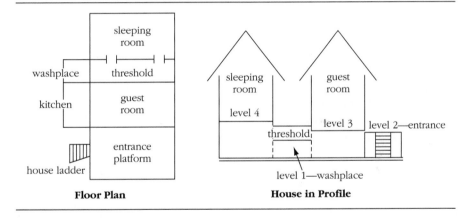

FIGURE 5-2 Thai house floor plan.

In a peasant village in northeastern Thailand, space in a house is divided to symbolize not rank, but rules about marriage and sex (see Figure 5-2). The sleeping room is the most sacred part of the house. First cousins, with whom sexual relations and marriage are not permitted, may enter that room but may not sleep there. More distant relatives, whom one may marry, are not allowed to enter the sleeping room and must remain in the guest room. S. J. Tambiah (1969), who has analyzed the Thai material, also relates categories of animals and their edibility to relatives whom you may and may not marry. First cousins, whom you cannot marry, are equivalent to your own buffalo, oxen, and pigs, who live under the house. You may not eat them and must give them to other people. More distant relatives, whom you can marry, are equivalent to other people's domestic animals, which you can eat. The same logic that connects edible and inedible animals with marriageable and unmarriageable relatives (as pointed out in English society by Leach) is also found in Thai society. Since social space symbolizes degree of social relationship, and edibility also signifies social relationships, then the meaning of social space is also related to edibility.

Gender differences are also symbolized in the use of space. As noted earlier, husbands and wives in Papua New Guinea not only do not eat together but also live in separate houses. Women will take their husband's food to the door of the men's house but will not enter it. Space is also gendered in the Middle East, where men who are not members of the family may not enter the women's quarters.

The way in which people use social space can also reflect social relationships and ethnic identity. Early immigrants to America from Europe brought with them a communal style of living, which they retained until late in the eighteenth century. Historical records and archaeological findings document a group-oriented existence, in which one room was used for eating, entertaining guests, and sleeping (Dietz, 1977, cited in Pader, 1993: 18). People ate stews from a communal pot, shared drinking cups, and used a common pit toilet. With the development of ideas about individualism, people soon began to shift to the use of individual cups and plates; the eating of meals, which included meat, starch, and vegetables, served on separate plates; and the use of individual chamber pots. They began to build their houses with separate rooms to entertain guests (living rooms), separate bedrooms for sleeping, separate work areas (kitchen, laundry room), and separate bathrooms.

In Mexico, the meaning and organization of domestic space is strikingly different. Houses are organized around a patio, or courtyard. Rooms for sleeping, dressing, talking when the weather is inclement, cooking, and storage open onto the patio, where all kinds of domestic activities, such as socializing, child play, bathing, and doing laundry, take place. Individuals do not have separate bedrooms. Children often sleep with parents, and same-sex siblings share a bed, emphasizing familial interdependence. Rooms in Mexican houses are locations for multiple activities that, in contrast, are rigidly separated in the United States.

The households of Mexican Americans in Los Angeles represent a transition between Mexican and American usages. According to Pader, they "blur the lines between the U.S. coding system, with its emphasis on greater bodily privacy and the individual, and the Mexican system, with its emphasis on sharing and close daily interconnection" (Pader, 1993: 130–131). As Mexican-American children mature, they change their ideas about family, become more individuated, and desire their own beds and bedrooms.

Gypsies, who are found in every major American city, have retained important elements of their own culture, including extended families, which form households, and their ideas about pollution and space utilization. When the

Gypsies of Richmond, California, move into a house previously occupied by non-Gypsies (*gaje*), the house must first be ritually cleansed of the polluting effects of *gaje* by a thorough cleaning with disinfectants and the burning of incense. Then the inner walls are torn down and the doors removed to create communal living space, which is divided by hanging drapes. One space is devoted to palm reading, the major source of income; the other space is used as a living area for the extended family who will live there. The head of one Gypsy family moved into what had formerly been a bar and dance club in order to house the 28 members of his family and the many guests the family entertained (Sutherland, 1986).

In many societies like our own, individuals have their own private spaces, reflecting the premium placed upon privacy. People feel that others should not intrude into one's own space. When a teenager closes the door to her or his room, this is a sign that parents should not enter. This is in contrast to other societies, in which space is communal and has a different meaning. When space is communally shared by a group, that group may have shared responsibilities, such as collective group responsibility when a member commits a crime or shared responsibilities for payment of a bride price.

Space may also be symbolically conquered and inscribed with new meanings. In recent decades, many Muslims, members of Sufi regional cults centered in the North-West Frontier Province of Pakistan, have migrated to England, extending and expanding cult influence (Werbner, 1996). At first, Muslim religious and ritual observances were conducted in mosques and in the home, where immigrants' religious observances were protected from external hostility. Expansion and conquest of new space is a significant aspect of Sufi cult organization. As Werbner notes, "The moral conquest of alien space is a test of the charismatic authenticity that legitimizes the rise of new 'living saints' " (1996: 310). Muslim men march and chant twice a year in the *julus* ceremonial procession through the Manchester, Birmingham, or London Pakistani immigrant neighborhoods, "sacralizing and 'Islamazicizing' the very earth, the buildings, the streets and the neighborhoods through which they march" (Werbner, 1996: 312). The "new order" with its own "living saints" is established in a foreign place, but these diasporas are still connected to home, creating a transnational network encompassing the East and the West. The march is also "an expression of the rights of minorities to celebrate their culture and religion in the public domain within a multicultural, multifaith, multiracial society" (Werbner, 1996: 333).

SYMBOLS, POLITICS, AND AUTHORITY

Just as clans can be represented by such things as totems, houses, space, and personal names, so too may an entire nation be represented by an array of symbols. The combat between symbolic animals—the eagle and the bear—was used by political cartoonists to portray the conflict between the United States and the former Soviet Union. In the same way, two buildings represent the United States and Russia. News reports often indicate that the White House says this and the Kremlin says that. National flags, anthems, and food also symbolize nations. The act of desecrating the flag by burning it makes a negative statement about the country the flag represents. Trees sometimes are used to symbolize the nation-state, as exemplified by the cedar, which symbolizes Lebanon.

Individuals in positions of authority are associated with particular objects that become symbols of the office they hold. Sometimes the object is something, such as a crown or imperial regalia or insignia, that the officeholder alone may wear. The installation ceremony for a successor usually involves putting on the garments or insignia of office. Sometimes the officeholder carries a staff, wand, umbrella, or fly whisk. In our definition of *metonym*, we pointed out how the crown or the throne could alternatively stand for the monarchy. A parallel is found in the term referring to the leader of an academic department at a college or university. He or she is re-ferred to as either the chair or the head. These symbols of authority are metonyms. Use of the term *head* draws attention to one end of the human anatomy, while use of the term *chair* draws attention to the opposite end.

In a number of African societies, the ruler or paramount chief represents the entire society. Thus the health of its members, as well as their fertility and the fer-tility of their crops, is dependent on the ruler and his health. Among the Aluund of southwestern Zaire, the paramount chief is linked metaphorically not only to the entire body politic of Aluund society but also to the kapwiip tree (De Boek, 1994). Trees in general serve as Aluund metaphors for the sexual joining of male and female, and, therefore, trees serve a unifying and purifying function. Just as the chief is the elder at the center of the community around whom the populace gathers, the kapwiip tree is the elder among trees. The chief is perceived as the trunk, and the people are the fruit surrounding the trunk. The chief rarely leaves his compound; instead, he listens (a mark of wisdom) to the people who come to him there, like the wise kapwiip tree, which remains in one place and "listens." By listening well, the chief mediates and resolves disputes. He is seen as asexual, with both powerful masculine and nurturant feminine characteristics, and is por-trayed as Janus-like in carvings—one face male, and the other female. The staff he holds, made from the wood of the kapwiip tree, is carved to represent three levels—a bird (usually the fish eagle) symbolizing heaven, a female human sym-bolizing earth, and a snake and crocodile symbolizing the underworld. The chief is seen as mediating between these three worlds. He is "lord of the soil," respon-sible for all regenerative aspects of Luunda culture (De Boek, 1994: 457). Since fertility and reproduction depend on the state of the paramount chief, he must not show signs of disease, decay, or old age. The Aluund have a complex sym-bolic system in which metaphors are simultaneously extended in many different directions.

If authority is represented by a series of symbols, opposition to that authority is symbolically represented by an inversion of those symbols. In the 1960s in the United States, all men in authority had short hair. Young men created a symbol of opposition when they allowed their hair to grow long. If authorities have short hair, then long hair is a symbol of opposition to that authority. However, today,

The Cavaliers of seventeenth-century England wore their hair long, while their Puritan opposition wore their hair short. In this cartoon of the period, both men and their dogs are characterized by their respective hairstyles.

wearing one's hair long is acceptable. Long hair is no longer considered a symbol of opposition to society, but dyeing one's hair fuchsia, blue, or orange is. During the seventeenth century, the Cavaliers of Charles I of England wore their hair long, while those who opposed them, the Puritans led by Oliver Cromwell, wore short hair. The Puritans' hairstyle became the focal symbol of their opposition, and so they were called Roundheads (as depicted above in a cartoon of the period). These examples relate to the general principle that those who oppose the established authority will select as their symbol something that is the reverse of the symbol of those in authority. Political symbols may seem trivial, but, in reality, people will die rather than deny them or give them up. People's identity or concept of self as members of a group is powerfully bound up with such symbols. To deny or reject them is to deny one's identity and worth.

BODY SYMBOLISM

Societies have different cultural conceptions about the human body. Similar standards of body morphology usually apply both to men and to women. In most societies plumpness is considered desirable, particularly for women, due to its association with love, nurturance, power, hardiness, and fertility. Fijians prefer plumpness because it symbolizes generosity, care, and social cohesion. Jamaicans find a fat body sexy, emitting fertility. In the United States, however, thinness is desirable for women, though it is less important for men. According to Counihan, "Americans cultivate their bodies as reflections of individuality and focus on thinness as [a] symbol of self control and power" (1999: 11). Many American women have an obsessive fear of getting fat and, as a consequence, limit the amount of food they eat. An enormous amount of energy and effort is expended by American women in their attempt to remain thin. Is there a connection between depriving oneself of food and the "prodigious fasting of Western women over 800 years" (Counihan 1999: 111)? Over the world, women are identified with food; it can be said to be a symbol of the female self. Denial of food denies the self. For medieval women it was a pathway to piety and holiness. Victorian women denied themselves food to seek a "sublime femininity." For modern anorexics the earlier meanings no longer apply. Food denial now represents striving toward thinness and perfection (Counihan, 1999).

Sharp illustrates some of the ways in which "the human body is a symbolically charged landscape" in her analysis of organ transplantion (2001: 112). Organ donation and procurement, an emotionally charged area, have generated a complex set of "symbolic renderings of the body, death and mourning." Once it has been determined that brain death, the point considered to be the death of the self or the individual, has taken place, "harvesting" of the viable organs from a body still otherwise functioning can take place if the donor's kin have given their approval. To the transplant specialists, the donor has become dehumanized, and his or her organs have become "sophisticated, replaceable mechanical parts" completely separated from the identity of the donor (Sharp, 2001: 115). Donated organs are not paid for at present; however, because of the shortage of such organs the suggestion has been made that such a system of payment be instituted. Even now organs are treated as if they were commodities, like other commercial medical goods that are bought and sold today (such as blood, sperm, and ova). In an effort to mask this commercialization, the donor kin are encouraged to see the transplanted organs of their loved ones as continuing to live in the bodies of unknown recipients, a life after death, so to speak. The donated organs are seen as a "gift of life," and transplant personnel use various strategies to accomplish the "veiling of procurement" (Sharp, 2001: 118). The identity and life history of the donor are always kept secret, as well as the circumstances of his or her death, violent or otherwise. The message of the transplant professionals is "a *greening of the body,* a form of 'semantic message' that foregrounds the goodness associated with donation while simultaneously denying transplantation's more disturbing reliance on death and organ retrieval" (Sharp, 2001: 120). Using logos associated with ecology, such as butterflies, trees, and foliage, on stationary, pamphlets, label pins, rings, T-shirts, posters, and bumper stickers shifts the emphasis from death to life. The use of agricultural metaphors is pervasive (e.g., organs are said to be harvested or transplanted through grafting). Some hospitals and organ procurement organizations have gone so far as to establish "donor gardens" and "donor trees" which are decorated by recipients of donated organs at ceremonies (Sharp, 2001: 125). Interestingly, the kin of the donors reject such symbolism and imagery, since it dehumanizes and depersonalizes their deceased loved ones, and have begun to make donor memorial quilts, which are like the AIDS memorial quilts, in which each panel commemorates a loved one who had given the "gift of life."

THE SYMBOLISM OF SPORTS

As noted earlier, games in a culture are often metaphors for life. Sports in American society are children's games played by adults, but they are much more than just games. They make symbolic statements about the society, which explains their enormous popularity. Individual sports, such as tennis, pool, and even chess, whether they are physical or intellectual activities, have certain aspects in common that relate them to American culture. They involve situations of head-to-head competition in which each person relies only on himself or herself to win. This is the rugged individualism of American society. In such one-on-one sports, it is important to establish a reputation, which is often not an accurate reflection of the individual's true abilities, but rather an attempt to create the impression that the individual is much better or much worse than he or she really is. This is done either to frighten an opponent or to create overconfidence in the opponent. In pool, this is referred to as one's speed, and one should never let an opponent know one's true speed. In many Western films of the past, these same features of individualism and reputation characterized the gunfighter. These same symbols, rugged individualism and a reputation that will create fear in others, are also operative in American business, where the people at the top are perceived as having gotten there on their own by beating out their opponents in head-to-head competition.

In American team sports, such as football, individual achievement is subordinated to team effort. Here, the symbolism is different. Football is an exclusively male activity in which male bonding ties individuals together in a collective effort. In this aspect, it is similar to male initiations in other societies, in which a ritual separates men from women and binds them together into a male peer group. As in such male initiation rites, in professional and college football during the training period and before games, male players are separated from women. In his analysis of American football, entitled "Into the Endzone for a Touchdown," Alan Dundes examines the folk speech involved in football and observes "that American football could be a ritual combat between groups of males attempting to assert their masculinity by penetrating the endzones of their rivals" (1978: 86). He likens football, which he sees as a form of symbolic homosexual behavior, to the initiation rites of aboriginal Australia, which also have a homosexual aspect. The male bonding of American football sets males, the participants, against females, the outsiders. This would also explain why the New England Patriots had strong feelings that the presence of a female reporter in their dressing room was completely inappropriate. In their eyes, she was intruding into a male ritual. The team aspect of football is also a recapitulation of the value of teamwork, pulling together for a common goal, in American society.

When a sport that originated in one culture spreads to another culture, it may take on a completely different set of symbolic meanings. With the expansion of the British Empire, cricket moved into the colonial areas that the British conquered, and today it is enthusiastically played from the Caribbean to the Pacific, especially on the Indian subcontinent. During the colonial period, it personified the quintessence of British colonialism. In fact, the expression *not cricket* means not acting like a proper Englishman and refers to stretching the rules. Nowhere is cricket played in a more spirited fashion than in the Trobriand Islands, where it was introduced by English missionaries at the beginning of the twentieth century. Over the years, the Trobrianders transformed the English version of the game, which represented colonial domination, into a cultural creation that has a multiplicity of meanings in their own Trobriand culture. In contrast to English cricket, where all the players wear white, in Trobriand cricket the players dress in the traditional regalia for warfare, and each team may have up to 40 players. The cricket game is usually part of the competition when one village challenges another to a *kayasa*, a competitive period of feasting and exchange of yams. Magic that was used in warfare, which was outlawed by the colonial authorities, is used during the cricket game, since the game of cricket is symbolically like warfare as well as like competitive exchange. When the bowler pitches the ball, he recites the magic formula that was formerly used to make a spear hit its target. In Trobriand cricket, the home team always wins; this is not supposed to happen in Western sports. The symbolism of Trobriand cricket may be seen as more like that of competitive exchange—first you "win," then I "win"—than the way sports are played in the United States, that is, to decide the "ultimate" winners. The symbolism of warfare characterizes other aspects of culture in other societies. In Chapter 2, we saw such symbolism being used in the Kwakiutl marriage ritual. Other usages include competitive exchange, religious crusades, and the "war against drugs."

UNIVERSAL SYMBOLS

It can be argued that certain symbols are found universally and carry similar meanings in all cultures. Colors are frequently associated with emotional states and sometimes with other meaningful messages as well. Some have argued that red brings about emotional arousal on the part of the viewer. In American society red means danger and is used for stop signs in traffic control. Green is the complementary color to red and is used to symbolize the opposite of red. Since traffic lights, like all symbols, are arbitrary, the question of whether they might have originally been put forth in reversed fashion, so that red meant go and green meant stop, could be asked. Because these symbols are part of the larger category of color symbolism in our society, in which a red dress symbolizes a prostitute, the red-light district signifies a den of iniquity, and red hair means a fiery temper, it seems likely that the colors could not have been reversed. The question of whether red has the same meaning in other cultures remains to be systematically explored. In our society, black is the color of mourning; at a funeral, people wear black clothing. In contrast, white, the color of Maria Shriver's wedding gown, represents purity and virginity. A bride wears white when the relationship is established and black if the relationship is terminated by the death of her husband. In China the color symbolism for death and mourning is exactly the opposite; there, white is the color of death and mourning, so mourners wear white clothing. It is clear that the meanings of colors vary from one culture to another.

Other symbols have been suggested as ones that have universal meaning. Hair is one of these. As noted earlier, long hair can be a symbol of rebellion when everyone else is wearing short hair. However, Edmund Leach (1958) has pointed out that, in a number of widely separate cultures, long hair, especially unkempt long hair, is a symbol of sexuality. Short hair symbolizes restraint, while a shaved head often indicates celibacy, although today it has other meanings as well. Rituals that involve the cutting of hair are seen as symbolic forms of castration. The symbolism of hair is quite overt. We are not dealing here with private symbols of the type referred to earlier in this chapter, but rather with a culturally accepted and widely understood symbol. It is not a symbol whose meaning is unconscious.

 SUMMARY

- Symbols and their meanings are crucial to understanding what a culture is all about.

- The term *metaphor* refers to the relationship in which one thing stands for something else, as eating is a metaphor for sexual activity.

- *Metonym* refers to a part of something standing for the whole, such as the crown that stands for the political authority of the Queen of England.

- Symbols are two-sided—the physical properties of the symbol as distinct from what the symbol stands for.

- Food has many different meanings in different cultures.

- Group identity may be symbolized in a number of other ways in addition to cuisine.

- Arrangements of space also make important symbolic statements about social groupings and social relationships.

- The shape of the human body has different meanings in different cultures.

- Organ transplantation uses a series of agricultural metaphors to mask the goriness of the process.

• Sports activities resonate symbolic meanings, which are often unconscious.

• Different cultural domains, such as kinship, economics, political organization, and religion, are all imbued with symbolic meaning. To understand how these institutions work, one must understand the symbols and the cultural meanings through which they are organized.

SUGGESTED READINGS

Cieraad, Irene (ed.). *At Home: An Anthropology of Domestic Space.* Syracuse: Syracuse University Press, 1999. A series of articles about how domestic space in different cultures is organized in terms of domestic relations.

Counihan, Carol. *The Anthropology of Food and Body: Gender, Meaning and Power.* New York: Routledge, 1999. Discusses the relationship between food, culture, gender, and food symbolism. Articles examine the meanings of food and eating across cultures, paying particular attention to the way in which men and women define themselves differently through their food ways.

Geetz, Clifford. *The Interpretation of Culture.* New York: Basic Books, 1973. A influential collection of essays by the leading proponent of culture-as-symbols school.

Guttmann, Allen. *A Whole New Ball Game: An Interpretation of American Sports.* Chapel Hill: University of North Carolina Press, 1988. A historical and sociological study that relates American sports to its cultural context.

Low, Setha. *On the Plaza: Politics of Public Space and Culture.* Austin: University of Texas Press, 2000. Deals with how public space is organized in various countries in Latin America.

O'Neill, Barry. *Honor, Symbols and War.* Ann Arbor: University of Michigan Press, 1999. Examines the role that symbolism plays in international relations and conflict resolution. The importance of national honor is also considered.

Rubenstein, Ruth P. *Dress Codes: Meanings and Messages in American Culture.* Boulder, CO: Westview Press, 2001. Discussion of how power, authority, and gender are symbolized by the way in which people dress.

Turner, Victor. *The Ritual Process: Structure and Anti-structure.* Chicago: Aldine, 1969. A series of lectures by a leading proponent of symbolic analysis.

SUGGESTED WEBSITES

http://cognet.mit.edu/MITEC/Entry/glucksberg A website that discusses metaphor as a "figure of speech" that is used universally in all cultures to convey meanings.

http://www.anthro.washington.edu/Faculty/Faculty %20 Syllabi/anth 570/18.htm A website that argues that meaning is encoded in landscapes and therefore that landscapes can be "read" for their meanings.

http://www.dickwalla.com/article.php.com/article.php?cid=1148&aid+1127 This site explains the meanings of symbols that are part of the Sikh religion, such as the iron bracelet that men wear and the custom of men never cutting their hair.

6

Ties That Connect

Marriage, Family, and Kinship

In a "free" society like our own, one should have the right to have sexual relations with anyone one chooses, isn't that so? Why does the government have to tell us who we may or may not marry? By what right does the United States government tell us that we may have one, and only one, spouse? We open a newspaper and read that in Pakistan, in the year 2002, a woman was gang raped because her *brother* had a sexual affair with a woman of a higher caste. Barbaric! Sexual affairs should be no one else's business. Why should the sister be held responsible for her brother's actions? In the case just cited, the Pakistani caste groups are endogamous, and this sexual affair violated the rules of endogamy. Families and clans are frequently held collectively responsible when a member violates the rules, and a sister was punished for her brother's transgressions. There are strict rules about sex, even in free societies like our own. If you live in Massachusetts, you can marry your first cousin. In Pennsylvania or Oregon, you cannot. Though polygamy, marriage with more than one wife, was practiced among the ancient Isrealites, as described in the Bible, it is not permitted among Orthodox Jews today. Mormons had to give up polygamy so that Utah could become a state.

As we will see, kinship plays a fundamental role in weaving the tapestry of culture. In the societies anthropologists studied earlier, most of daily life was organized on the basis of kinship relationships. In these small-scale societies, all religious, economic, and political behavior took place within the context of the social structure. This social structure was organized on the basis of kinship, which is why the study of kinship was so important in anthropology. Even with increasing industrialization and globalization in so many parts of the world today, kinship continues to be important. As Parkin notes, "Many societies still think in terms of lineages, affinal alliance systems, residence rules and marriage payments, while virtually all are still organized in families of some sort and use kin terms to idenitity and classify relatives" (1997: ix–x). One of the striking features an examination of kinship reveals is the limited number of possibilities of rules regarding whom one can marry—that is, marriage rules, family organization, residence patterns after marriage, forms of descent and descent groups, and other aspects of kinship. We must also remember that these are the rules for societies and that people's actual practices may vary from these rules, as is always the case for all rules, even rules about an explosive topic like incest.

In Chapter 2, when we described weddings in two different societies, kinship played a role in the proceedings. In each case, groupings of kin played significant roles in the course of the event. The Kwakiutl have groups based on kinship that they refer to as *numayms.* How does one become a member of a *numaym?* What are one's responsibilities toward other members of the *numaym?* What are one's rights and privileges as a member of a *numaym?* What is one's relationship with people in different *numayms?* Are all one's kin in one's own *numaym?*

In contrast to the Kwakiutl wedding is the American wedding described in Chapter 2. Once again, groupings of people based on kinship participated—the bride's side and the groom's side, immediate relatives and distant relatives. In addition, there were those who were not relatives at all but who attended as friends, neighbors, and fellow workers. What are the differences between the ways relatives are grouped in Kwakiutl society and the ways they are grouped in our own society? What do these differences mean? This chapter presents concepts that anthropologists have developed to answer these questions.

In Chapter 2, we point out that a Kwakiutl wedding is an example of what are called **total social phenomena.** This means that political, economic, religious, and aesthetic aspects of the society, as well as kinship, are brought into play simultaneously. Despite the interwoven nature of all these aspects of culture in a Kwakiutl wedding, kinship can be disentangled for the purposes of analysis. The discussion of marriage, family, and kinship that follows will deal with the cultural rules to be found in a variety of societies. It is important to note that in every society, there will always be variations in behavior and deviations from these cultural rules. Through time, these cultural rules may be transformed. In the succeeding chapters on religion, politics, economics, and art, we will see that kinship plays a crucial role in these various cultural domains of small-scale societies.

Such societies were shaken to their roots as they were incorporated into colonial empires and then into new nations. However, kinship and kin groups have continued to be very significant in people's lives, whether they remained in their rural villages or migrated to look for work in expanding cities like Lagos in Nigeria, or Port Moresby in Papua New Guinea. Until recently, it was widely believed by anthropologists that kinship relations withered in modern industrial societies. The sociologist Lewis Wirth had hypothesized that with the growth of urbanism, kinship bonds would weaken and decline in importance. As we shall see later, research on kinship in America has revealed just the opposite. New forms like the transnational families in parts of Europe, Asia, and the Americas have been created. Though relatives may not be living in the same town or city, they maintain contact by letter, phone, and e-mail.

MARRIAGE

Almost all known societies recognize marriage. The ritual of marriage marks a change in status for a man and a woman and the acceptance by society of the new family that is formed. However, the Na, which we describe later in this chapter, do not have marriage or marriage rituals. Marriage, like all other things cultural, is governed by rules. Just as the rules vary from one society to another, so does the ritual by which society recognizes and celebrates the marriage. In the American wedding, the bridegroom places a ring on the third finger, left hand, of the bride and repeats the ritual formula, "With this ring, I thee wed." In the Kwakiutl wedding, the bridegroom comes as a member of a feigned war party to capture the bride and "move" her from her father's house with the payment of many blankets. These represent just two of the many ways that societies recognize and accept marriage and the formation of a new family. At both Kwakiutl and American weddings, large numbers of guests are present who represent society, serving as witnesses to the marriage signifying that marriage is more than a private affair and is recognized publicly by society. Sometimes, the ritual may be as minimal as in the Trobriand case mentioned in the previous chapter, where marriage is symbolized merely by the couple's publicly eating together.

MARRIAGE PROHIBITIONS

Societies also have rules that state whom one can and cannot marry. Rules about whom one cannot marry are directly related to the **incest taboo.** Like marriage, the incest taboo is found in all societies and is therefore a cultural universal. The incest taboo forbids sexual relations between certain categories of close relatives. Almost universally, forbidden categories include mother and son, father and daughter, and brother and sister. Since sexual partners cannot be sought within the immediate family because of the incest taboo, they must be sought elsewhere. The incest taboo that forbids sexual relations also necessarily forbids marriage, since marriage almost always includes sexual access. In many societies, there are people with whom one can have sexual intercourse but whom one cannot marry. Marriage prohibitions, therefore, are wider in scope than the prohibitions against sexual intercourse. Both the incest taboo and prohibitions against marrying certain close relatives have the effect of compelling individuals to seek sexual partners and mates outside their own group. Beyond the immediate family, there is great variation from one society to another in the rules regarding which categories of relatives one is forbidden to marry. Even within the United States, there is variation among the states in the laws regarding which relatives one may not marry. Some states permit marriage between first cousins while others prohibit it; still others prohibit marriage between second cousins. For example, the Office of Human Services of the Commonwealth of Massachusetts decrees: "No man may marry his . . . stepmother, grandson's wife, wife's mother, wife's daughter, brother's daughter, sister's daughter, father's sister or mother's sister" in addition to other relatives (Registrar of Vital Records and Statistics, Commonwealth of Massachusetts, courtesy of Ron Palazzo). However, first cousins are absent from this list.

There are a few striking examples of marriage between members of the immediate family that seem to violate the universality of the incest taboo. Among the pharaohs of ancient Egypt, such as Tutankhamen, the boy king, as well as among the royal lineages of Hawaii and the Incas in Peru, brother and sister married. In each instance, the ruler had to marry someone equal in rank, and who could be better qualified than one's own brother or sister?

ENDOGAMY AND EXOGAMY

In anthropological terms, marriage within the group is called **endogamy** and marriage outside the group is called **exogamy.** A rule of exogamy, like the incest taboo, requires that members of the group seek spouses outside their own group. A rule of exogamy is frequently conceptualized as an extension of the incest taboo in that the same term is used for both. For example, among the Trobriand Islanders, the term **suvasova** is used for the incest taboo and is also extended to forbid sexual relations and marriage with women of one's own larger kin group, or **dala,** all of whom are called sisters. A rule of endogamy requires individuals to marry within their own group and forbids them to marry outside of it. Religious groups such as the Amish, Mormons, Catholics, and Jews have rules of endogamy, though these are often violated when marriages take place outside the group. As noted in Chapter 5, castes in India and the castes of the Newari of Nepal are also endogamous. Rules of endogamy preserve separateness and exclusivity, and are a means of maintaining boundaries between one group and other groups. In this sense, the brother-sister marriages referred to above reach the absolute limit of endogamy in order to preserve sanctity and power within the ruling families of those societies. More typical are those cases where the immediate family is exogamous, while the larger group, frequently an ethnic group or religious sect, is endogamous.

SISTER EXCHANGE

Since a rule of exogamy demands that spouses come from outside one's group, relationships are created through marriage with other groups. If a man cannot marry his own sister, he gives his sister to someone in another group. According to the basic principle of exchange, something given, if accepted by the receiver, must be returned with its equivalent. If a man accepts another man's sister, he must therefore return his own sister as the equivalent. After all, the receiver, too, may not marry his own sister. In fact, in a number of societies over the world, there is a rule requiring that two men exchange sisters; anthropologists refer to this as **sister exchange.** If a man does not have a biological sister, he returns a woman for whom he uses the same kinship term that he uses for his sister. Recently, feminist anthropologists have argued that this form of marriage could just as easily be conceptualized as brother exchange. However, where men are dominant in a society, this is seen as sister exchange "from the native point of view." When Margaret Mead went to study the Mountain Arapesh in New Guinea, she asked them why they didn't marry their own sisters, expecting a response indicating revulsion at the very thought. Instead, Mead's informant stated, "What is the matter with you anyway? Don't you want a brother-in-law?" (Mead, 1935: 68). This is because one hunts, gardens, and travels with one's brother-in-law among the Arapesh. Thus a marriage creates a link not only between husband and wife but also, through the wife, between two men who are brothers-in-law to each other.

Marriage Payments

In many societies marriage involves a transfer or exchange of property. Sometimes, payments are made by the groom and his family to the family of the bride, as occurs among the Kwakiutl. This payment is known as **bridewealth.** In other instances, the bride brings property with her at the marriage. This is known as **dowry.** When dowry is paid, goods move in the opposite direction from bridewealth payments. In societies that practice sister exchange, there may be an option to give bridewealth if one does not have a sister to exchange. However, it is also common to find sister exchange accompanied by the payment of bridewealth, so that groups are exchanging both women and bridewealth payments. In China, both bridewealth and dowry were paid.

Bride Service

Sometimes the groom exchanges labor for his bride, in lieu of the payment of bridewealth. When the groom works for his wife's family, this is known as bride service. It may be recalled that in the Old Testament Jacob labored for seven years in order to marry Leah and then another seven years to marry Rachel, Leah's younger sister, thus performing fourteen years of bride service for his father-in-law. Bride service is also practiced by the Yanomamo, a people living in the lowlands of Venezuela. During this time, the groom lives with the bride's parents and hunts for them. Since the Yanomamo also have sister exchange, one might say that during this period of bride service, when men live with the bride's parents, they really are practicing brother exchange. However, since men determine whom women will marry, the Yanomamo do not conceptualize this as two women exchanging their brothers. After the period of bride service is over, the husband takes his wife back to his group. Yanomamo women prefer to marry within the same village rather than into some distant village; that way they can remain close to their families after marriage so that their brothers can offer them a degree of protection from husbandly abuse.

Number of Spouses

Another set of rules concerning marriage is exemplified by the biblical case of Jacob—rules regarding number of spouses. Some societies, like our own, practice **monogamy;** that is, only one spouse at a time is permitted. However, according to the Bible, husbands could have more than one wife. This is known

Shell rings are presented as bridewealth at an Abelam marriage.

as **polygyny** and is still permitted in many societies in the world, particularly Islamic societies. Jews living in Muslim countries continued to practice polygyny,
as occurred in the Bible, up until recently but not in Christian countries. Jews
coming to Israel from Muslim countries were allowed to bring several wives,
but they were forbidden to marry more than one wife in Israel itself. Sometimes,
as in the case of Jacob, a man marries several sisters. This practice is known as
sororal polygyny. In the societies in which it occurs, it is usually explained by
saying that sisters have a good relationship with one another, and this will help
overcome the inevitable jealousy that arises between co-wives. On the other
hand, many people, such as the Trobriand Islanders and the Kanuri of Nigeria,
explicitly forbid sororal polygyny. The Kanuri explanation for this prohibition
is that the good relationship between two sisters should not be undermined by
the unavoidable friction that arises between two co-wives. This simply demonstrates that whatever rules are in effect, the people will offer an explanation for
their existence that is perfectly rational in their eyes. An alternative form of marriage, known as **polyandry,** in which one woman may have several husbands,
occurs but is rather rare. In almost all cases, a woman marries several brothers;
this is known as **fraternal polyandry.** Today, among ethnic Tibetans in northwest Nepal, the ideal form of marriage is fraternal polyandry, in which the eldest brother is the primary husband and nominally the father of all the children,
whether or not he is the biological father (Levine, 1987). Sometimes, anthropol-

A Tibetan polyandrous family—the twelve-year old bride with 3 of her 5 husbands.

ogists wish to refer to plural spouses in general, either husbands or wives. In that case, they use the term **polygamy,** in contrast to the term *monogamy.* Because of the frequency of divorce and subsequent remarriage in the United States, it is sometimes said that Americans practice **serial monogamy.** We may not have more than one spouse at a time, but some people have numerous spouses, one after the other. Some of the Mormons in the southern part of Utah still practice polygamy, usually sororal polygamy, and the law looks the other way unless the bride-to-be is under the legal age for marriage. The rest of the Mormons formally gave up polygamy in order to be able to form the state of Utah.

LEVIRATE AND SORORATE

The exchange of a woman for another woman or the exchange of a woman for bridewealth is an indication that more than the bride and groom are involved in a marriage. Marriage is a significant concern of the kin groups of the marrying couple. A further demonstration of this is found in the customs of the **levirate** and the **sororate.** Under the levirate, if a man dies, his widow then marries one of his brothers. The brother of the dead man steps into the deceased's place, thereby continuing the relationship between the two kin groups established by the first marriage. In the levirate, a woman marries one brother after the death of another brother; in fraternal polyandry she can be married to two brothers simultaneously. Orthodox Jews today still practice the levirate if the brother of the deceased husband is unmarried. When a deceased wife is replaced in the marriage by her sister, usually an unmarried younger sister, this is known as the sororate. It is like sororal polygyny, but in the sororate a man marries two sisters, the second after the death of the first. The levirate and sororate illustrate what the British anthropologist Radcliffe-Brown referred to as the equivalence of siblings (1952), where one same-sex sibling can be substituted for another.

DISSOLUTION OF MARRIAGE

Stability of marriage varies from one society to another. Almost all societies provide a means for divorce or the dissolution of a marriage; however, this may be very difficult in some societies. Divorce is invariably more difficult after children have been born to the couple. Where bridewealth has been paid, it would have to be returned if the wife leaves her husband. This may be difficult to achieve if the bridewealth, paid several years before, has been spent, dispersed, or consumed. Some anthropologists have argued that the higher the bridewealth payment, the more stable the marriage and less likely a divorce, since it would require the return of bridewealth, which is so difficult in such societies. Others have said that frequency of divorce and stability of marriage are related not to the amount of bridewealth but to the degree of incorporation of a wife into her husband's family or kin group. Among the Manchus of Manchuria, who conquered China in the seventeenth century, the wife went through a fire ceremony in front of the hearth in her husband's house. This ritual served to conceptually incorporate her permanently into his kin group. In contrast, as noted in Chapter 2, at marriage, the Kwakiutl paid bridewealth to the bride's family. At a subsequent ceremony, the bride's family paid a large amount of goods to "repurchase" her, thereby reiterating her membership in the kin group of her birth. The husband must make a new bridewealth payment if he wishes her to continue to be his wife. The bridewealth and repurchase payments of the Kwakiutl, which were integral parts of Kwakiutl marriage, symbolize how two people may be joined in marriage and yet retain an identity in their own kin groups. The difference in these ceremonies indicates that divorce was more difficult among the Manchus than among the Kwakiutl.

POSTMARITAL RESIDENCE

Where the newly married couple live after the marriage ritual is performed is also governed by cultural rules, which are referred to as **rules of postmarital residence.** In the North American wedding described in Chapter 2, the newly married couple set up their own household. In the case of a couple with two careers in two different cities, two households are often created, though it would appear that the primary residence of the Schwarzeneggers was their Pacific Palisades home. The postmarital residence rule in American society is that the new couple form an independent household. This is referred to as **neolocal residence** (see Figure 6-1). It is clear that this is a rule in American society, since breaching it brings sanctions. If the newly married couple live for an extended period with the family of either the husband or the wife, this move is typically explained in terms of economic hardship or the couple's student status. Gossips will make snide comments about the lack of independence of the couple, since they continue to live as though they were children, and gossip is a strong sanction. If the newly married couple move in with the husband's parents, comments are

FIGURE 6-1 Rules of residence.

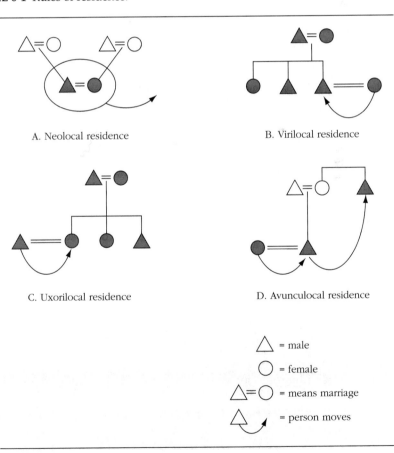

A. Neolocal residence

B. Virilocal residence

C. Uxorilocal residence

D. Avunculocal residence

△ = male

○ = female

△=○ = means marriage

△ = person moves

made about two women in the same kitchen and the mother-in-law problem; if they move in with the wife's parents, the result is inevitable difficulties between father-in-law and son-in-law. Neolocal residence not only characterizes our society but is found in other societies as well.

Probably the most common form of postmarital residence is the situation in which the newly married couple live in the household of the groom's parents. This is known as **virilocal residence** (also referred to as patrilocal residence). With a rule of virilocal residence, the wife is incorporated, to a greater or lesser extent, into the household of her husband's kin, since it is she (the bride) who must leave her own family. The groom merely remains in his household.

Less frequent is the case in which the newly married couple live in the household of the bride's parents. This is called **uxorilocal residence** (also referred to as matrilocal residence). In this instance it is the husband who must be incorporated into his wife's family. In the past, in some Pueblo societies of Arizona and New Mexico that had a rule of uxorilocal residence, the degree of incorporation of the husband into his wife's family was so slight that the wife could divorce him simply by leaving his belongings on the doorstep. Today in the Pueblo area, neolocal residence prevails, reflecting the influence of the larger American society. When a groom performs bride service for his wife's father, as Jacob did for Laban in the Bible, he lives uxorilocally for the period of the bride service. Then, like Jacob, he usually returns with his wife to live virilocally, with his own family.

Still another rule of postmarital residence is the arrangement in which, after marriage, the wife joins her new husband, who is living with his mother's brother rather than with his own father. This is called **avunculocal residence.** This rule of residence involves two separate and distinct moves. The earlier move occurs when a man, as an adolescent, leaves his father's house to go to live with his mother's brother, from whom he will inherit later in life. The incorporation of the young man into the household of his mother's brother is associated with matrilineal descent, discussed below. After the marriage, the wife joins her husband at his maternal uncle's house. The Trobriand Islanders have an avunculocal rule of postmarital residence.

Sometimes a society will have a rule of residence stating that after marriage, the couple can live either with the bride's family or with the groom's family. In contrast to our own society, they cannot establish an independent household. This is called **bilocal residence.** On Dobu, an island near the Trobriands, the married couple spend one year in the bride's village and the following year in the groom's village, alternating in this manner between the two villages every year. Among the Iban of Borneo, however, a choice must be made at some point after marriage between affiliation with one side or the other, and this choice becomes permanent.

Lastly, there is a postmarital residence rule in which husband and wife live with their respective kin, apart from one another. This is known as **duolocal residence.** The Ashanti of Ghana, who traditionally lived in large towns, have this form of postmarital residence. Husbands and wives live in the same town, but not in the same household. At dusk, one could see young children carrying the evening meal from their mother's house to their father's house for their father to eat.

FAMILY TYPES AND HOUSEHOLDS

The rules stating where a couple should live after marriage result in different types of families. People who are related to one another by some form of kinship constitute a family, while people who live together under one roof form a household. The members of a household may not necessarily all be related by kinship to one another. Family and household units, therefore, may not coincide. In the Ashanti example just discussed, the family unit of husband, wife, and children live in two separate households. With neolocal postmarital residence, as exists in America, the family that is formed is the **nuclear family** (see Figure 6-2). It consists of the husband, the wife, and children until they marry, at which point those children will establish their own nuclear families. The nuclear family is an independent household that operates autonomously in economic affairs, in the rearing of children, and in other phases of life.

What happens when there are plural spouses, as in societies that practice polygyny or polyandry? Among the Kanuri, where polygyny is practiced, only a small proportion of men actually have more than one wife. However, in polygynous families, each wife must have her own house and hearth. This is typical of a number of African societies. The husband must visit each wife in turn, at which time she cooks for him, and he must stay the night with her. Though he may favor one wife over another, he should treat them equally. A man's house and those of his wives form a single walled compound or household. Even though they have separate hearths and separate houses, they are all under the authority of the husband, who is the head of the household. Such a household might also include slaves belonging to the head of the household. In polyandrous societies, like Tibet, a woman and her several husbands, usually brothers, live in the same house and form a single household.

When several related nuclear families live together in the same household, they form an **extended family.** When there is a rule of virilocal residence, the household consists of an older married couple, their married sons and wives, and the unmarried children of both the older couple and their married sons. These all form one extended family. Their married daughters will have left the household to join the households of their husbands. The center of this type of extended family is a core of related men. Their in-marrying wives come from many different places and are not related to each other. Uxorilocal postmarital residence results in extended families of a very different sort. In this case, a core of related women remain together, and their husbands marry into the extended family. With avunculocal residence there is once again a core of men forming the basis of the extended family, but this core of men is linked through women. Avunculocal residence occurs when a young man moves to his mother's brother's house during adolescence. The wives in this case also marry into the family.

FIGURE 6-2 Family types.

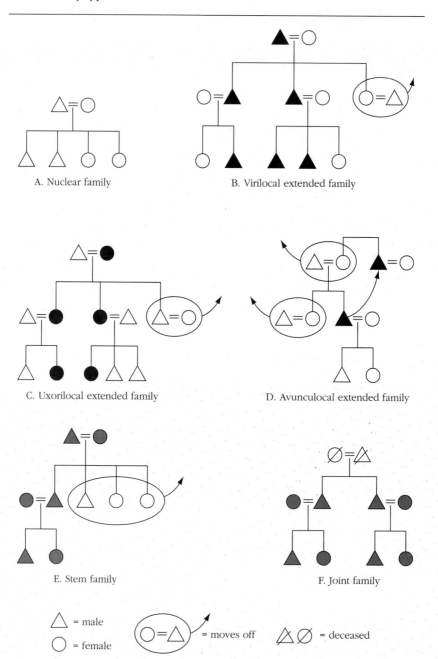

A. Nuclear family

B. Virilocal extended family

C. Uxorilocal extended family

D. Avunculocal extended family

E. Stem family

F. Joint family

△ = male
○ = female
(○=△)→ = moves off
△ ∅ = deceased

A Kirghiz extended family from the Pamir Mountains posing in front of their yurt.

Extended families also vary in their extent. The most extensive extended family is the one that consists of parents and married children of one sex, their spouses, and their own children. Some extended families consist only of parents and one married son and his family. Such a family is known as a **stem family** and occurs in parts of rural Ireland. Since the amount of land inherited is small and cannot be profitably subdivided, only one son, typically the youngest one, inherits the land, while his older brothers go off to the cities, become priests, or emigrate to Boston or Hong Kong. Another type of extended family is the **joint family,** which includes brothers and their wives and children who stay together as a single family after the parents have died. In most of the examples discussed above, family type and household coincide and perform a variety of functions, including the socialization of children, cooperation in economic activities, and political decision making.

DESCENT

The kinds of family groups that we have just described are based on both kinship and common residence. Beyond the family, there are groups based upon shared kinship or descent where the members need not live in the same place. Descent groups are those whose memberships are descended from a common ancestor. These groups are usually called **clans** by anthropologists. We have previously discussed exogamy, that is, the rule that one must marry outside one's group. In most societies that have clans, though certainly not in all, clans are exogamous, and one must marry outside one's own clan.

PATRILINEAL DESCENT AND MATRILINEAL DESCENT

Societies have rules that state that the child belongs either to the mother's clan or to the father's clan. A rule that states that a child belongs to his or her father's clan is called a **patrilineal rule of descent.** This means that children belong to their father's clan, the father belongs to his father's clan, and so forth, as illustrated in the diagram (see Figure 6-3). A daughter belongs to her father's clan, but her children do not. Children share common clanship with only one of their four grandparents; however, the other three grandparents are still their relatives and kinsmen. As one goes back through the generations, ties of kin relationships form a web of kinship. A rule of descent carves out of this web of kinship a much smaller segment, which comprises the members of one's own clan. Clans continue to exist through time, beyond the lifespan of individual members, as new generations continue to be born into the clan.

A **matrilineal rule of descent** states that a child belongs to the clan of his or her mother, not that of the father. The Trobriand Islanders have such a rule of descent. Among the Trobrianders, as in all matrilineal societies, the continuity of the clan is not through a man's own children but through those of his sister.

In societies where either matrilineal or patrilineal clans are present, the clans have certain functions; that is, they carry out certain activities. Some of the activities of clans concern rituals. For example, the matrilineal clan of the Trobrianders serves as host at the ceremonial distribution (*sagali*) accompanying a funeral when a member of their clan dies. Ritual objects and spells are owned by clans. Clans also have political functions and may compete with one another for power and political positions and may even fight with one another. Each clan has some kind of leadership, almost always male, to organize these political activities. The chief (the leader) of a Trobriand clan directs the accumulation of large amounts of food to be given away at a Trobriand *sagali*. Finally, what has frequently been seen as the most important function of the clan is its ownership of land. Members of a clan have the right to use its land by virtue of the fact that they are born into the clan. Clan members may work together at tasks, such as building a communal house or canoe, that benefit the clan as a whole. The common ancestor from whom all the members of a clan believe that they are descended is sometimes conceived of as an ancestral or clan spirit. This ancestral spirit may be thought of as having a nonhuman form, perhaps that of an animal. In that case all members of the clan are thought of as having a special relationship to that animal, and they may be forbidden to eat it. Such an animal is called the **clan totem,** and, as noted in Chapter 5, it is a symbol that represents the clan and could be graphically represented, as depicted in the totem pole on page 100.

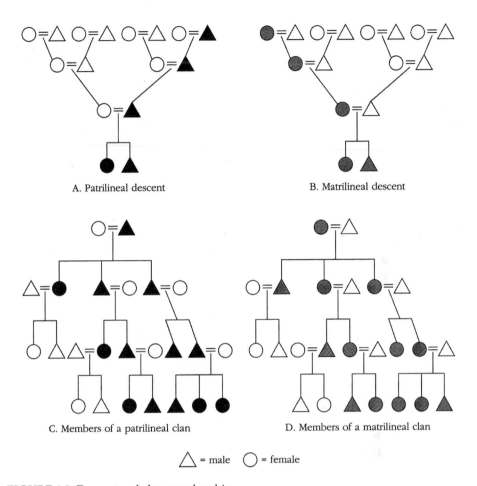

A. Patrilineal descent

B. Matrilineal descent

C. Members of a patrilineal clan

D. Members of a matrilineal clan

△ = male   ○ = female

FIGURE 6-3 Descent and clan membership.

The clan is frequently referred to by anthropologists as a **corporate descent group,** because it has many of the characteristics of a modern corporation. Like a corporation, it has an existence independent of its individual members. Old clan members die and new ones are born, while the clan continues to operate through time. The corporation owns property, and so does the clan. However, anybody can buy stock in a corporation and become an owner, but membership in a clan is restricted to certain kinds of kin, as defined by the rule of descent.

In Chapter 5 we noted the way in which elements of the human body can be used metaphorically to discuss kinship. They can also be used to contrast relationships through the mother and relationships through the father. The way in which the contrast is symbolized differs in patrilineal and matrilineal societies. In many patrilineal societies, the connection between the child and the mother is seen in terms of mother's milk and menstrual blood. In these societies, milk or blood symbolizes the maternal relationship. Connection to the father is seen in terms of se-men or bone. The Arapesh of New Guinea believe that a child is created through the semen contributed by the father and the blood of the mother. The Arapesh are patrilineal; the child belongs to the father's clan. The child is seen as linked to the mother's clan through the blood she provided. The mother's clan continues to "own" the blood, and whenever the child's blood is shed through injury or cutting initiation scars, the child's mother's clan must be paid.

Since the Trobrianders have matrilineal descent, one would expect them to conceive of their kinship system in a different way than the Arapesh do. Among the Trobrianders, children belong to the clan of their mother, sharing common substance with their mother and other clan mates. The father is considered an affine, a relative by marriage only, in contrast to a consanguine, a blood relative. When a child is conceived in the mother's womb, the Trobrianders believe that an ancestral spirit from the mother's clan has entered her womb. The creation of a child is not seen as the result of the merging of substance from mother and fa-ther, and therefore they do not believe that sexual intercourse has anything to do with the conception of a child. The father, by repeated acts of intercourse, not only makes the child grow, but molds the child so that the child resembles him in appearance. The child is like a piece of clay pressed between two palms that takes on the shape of the hands that mold it. But this has nothing to do with the conception of the child in the first place, which is all the doing of the maternal ancestral spirit of the mother's clan. The child cannot be claimed by the father's clan, which had nothing to do with its creation. Though the Trobriand father is a very important relative, he is still an affine, as are all the members of his mater-nal clan.

COGNATIC DESCENT

Up to now, we have discussed clans based upon either a patrilineal or a matri-lineal rule of descent. Anthropologists refer to these as **unilineal descent groups.** There are also societies that have groups based upon descent from a common ancestor, where individuals belong to the group because either their fa-ther or their mother was a member of that group. This is called a **cognatic rule of descent.** Individuals have the choice of belonging to either their father's or their mother's group, or they may have rights in both groups, though there is usually active membership in only one since a person can live in only one place at a time. Individuals may even have rights in all four kin groups of their grand-parents. Although the kin group created by a cognatic rule of descent is based upon descent from a common ancestor, the links through which individuals trace their descent are through either males or females. The kin group that the Kwakiutl refer to as a *numaym* is a cognatic descent group. A Kwakiutl boy could claim membership in both his mother's and his father's group. He usually be-came a member of the *numaym* of the parent of higher rank, from whom he hoped to inherit the highest titles and the most property. In addition, he inher-ited rights in the *numaym* of the other parent. Cognatic descent groups have the same functions as unilineal descent groups (patrilineal and matrilineal clans), though their structures are different. For example, the Kwakiutl *numaym* owned houses, fishing sites, berry-picking grounds, and hunting territories. The chiefs of a *numaym* acted as political leaders in potlatching and in warfare. The *numaym* acted as a unit on ceremonial occasions, such as the marriage and repurchase of the bride, which is described in Chapter 2. Kwakiutl myths tell how the supernatural ancestors of present-day *numayms* acquired magical powers that were transmitted down the generations to their descendants.

Double Descent

In some societies in the world, each person belongs to two descent groups, one patrilineal, where descent is traced through the father and father's father, and the other matrilineal, where descent is traced through the mother and mother's mother. Anthropologists call this **double descent** (see Figure 6-4). The two groups to which an individual belongs do not conflict with one another, since each group has its own distinct functions. For example, the Yako of southeast Nigeria had patrilineal clans called *yepun*, which owned land in common and possessed a single shrine and an assembly house, and whose men and their families resided together and farmed together. At the same time, each Yako individual also belonged to the matrilineal clan, or *lejima*, of his or her mother. The matrilineal clans carried out ritual and religious activities, such as funerals and periodic rites during the year aimed at maintaining fertility and harmony. While land is inherited patrilineally, movable wealth, such as valuables and household goods, is inherited through the matrilineal line. Thus, the two types of kin groups, patrilineal and matrilineal, serve different functions.

DESCENT GROUPS AND
THEIR STRUCTURES

Though patrilineal clans, matrilineal clans, and cognatic descent groups have the same kinds of functions, they are structured very differently. Because of the rule of descent, the structure of the patrilineal clan is that of men linked through their fathers, along with their sisters who marry into other clans. The patrilineal clan is almost always associated with virilocal postmarital residence. Sisters who marry out and wives who marry in are incorporated in varying degrees into the patrilineal clans of their husbands. In the discussion of marriage and the family in the earlier part of this chapter, we pointed out the variations in the degree of incorporation of the wife into her husband's clan. Matrilineal clans are composed of women related through their mothers and the brothers of these women. The brothers remain members of the clan into which they were born throughout their entire lives. Though they marry into other clans, in matrilineal societies, men are never incorporated into the clans of their wives. When they die, their bodies are usually brought back to be buried in their own clan land. Matrilineal clans are usu-

FIGURE 6-4 Double descent.

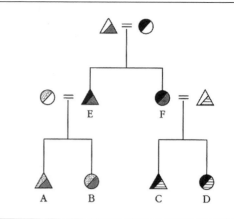

A and B are brother and sister and belong to the same two descent groups, gray from their father and stippled from their mother. Similarly, C and D belong to the same two descent groups, striped from their father and black from their mother. E and F are also brother and sister and share the two descent groups that they get from their two parents, gray from their father and black from their mother. But their respective children, A and B, and C and D, do not have any descent groups in common.

ally associated with avunculocal or uxorilocal postmarital residence. With a rule of cognatic descent, both men and women have membership in several cognatic descent groups, since they can trace multiple lines of descent. In this situation, husbands and wives, regardless of where they reside, are never incorporated into the descent groups of their spouses; this is the case among the Kwakiutl. As can be seen, the different kinds of descent structures are associated with particular rules of postmarital residence and have consequences for the degree of incorporation of one spouse into the other spouse's kin group.

One can see the different ways in which descent groups are structured when one looks at the way in which political leadership operates. The political functions of descent groups are carried out under the direction of leaders. In patrilineal societies like that of the Mongols, inherited leadership is usually structured in the following manner: It passes from father to son and from brother to brother (see Figure 6-5). Leadership in matrilineal societies, like that of the Trobrianders, is handed down from mother's brother to sister's son or from brother to brother. In a matrilineal society, a son can never directly inherit a position of leadership from his father. In such societies, though the line of descent goes through women, the women themselves are rarely the heads of their clans. One may contrast the nature of the relationship of a man to his father in patrilineal societies and to his mother's brother in matrilineal societies. In patrilineal societies, a son will replace his father in the position of leadership and is often perceived of as a competitor and antagonist of his own father. His mother's brother, who is not in his clan, is a source of support. In contrast, in matrilineal societies, a sister's son will succeed to the position of lead-

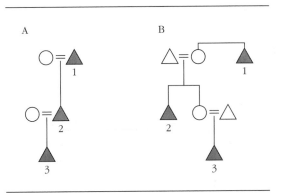

A   B

FIGURE 6-5 Passage of political leadership.

In a partilineal society (A) and in a matrilineal society (B).

ership held by his mother's brother. The relationship between these two parallels that of the father-son relationship in a patrilineal society. In the relationship between father and son in a matrilineal society, all the elements of antagonism and potential conflict between them are removed. In societies with cognatic descent groups, like that of the Kwakiutl, a man can succeed to political leadership by virtue of descent through his mother or through his father; thus he can be the heir of either his father or of his mother's brother. The contrast between the father-son relationship and the mother's brother–sister's son relationship is therefore of no importance in societies with cognatic descent. An important structural feature of cognatic societies is that brothers are not equivalent. The optional nature of the descent rule permits the possibility that brothers may be in different descent groups. Among the Kwakiutl, it frequently happens that two brothers are in different *numayms,* which can even fight each other. In patrilineal and in matrilineal societies, which are unilineal, this can never happen, since brothers are always in the same clan.

CLANS

Clans come in many shapes and forms. In some societies, you belong to a clan simply because your father or your mother belonged to that clan. Other people with whom you cannot trace a relationship of kinship also belong to your clan. Anthropologists say that descent is *stipulated* in such a clan system. Where **stipulated descent** is found, there are no lengthy genealogies, and people usually remember back only to their grandfathers. Where long genealogies are kept, written or oral, each member of a clan can trace his or her kinship back to the founding ancestor of the clan and in this way to every other member of the clan. Anthropologists call this **demonstrated descent.** In societies where clans include large numbers of people living dispersed over a wide area, each clan may in turn be divided into smaller units. These are referred to as **subclans.**

Clans based on unilineal descent continued to exist, assuming a variety of roles, even long after the emergence of complex societies and states. Patrilineal clans in twentieth-century prerevolutionary China carried out religious functions in connection with ancestor worship, maintaining ancestral shrines and cemeteries. They also had some economic functions and assisted clan members in obtaining education and other such endeavors. These patrilineal clans continue to function in the form of clan associations among overseas Chinese in San Francisco and New York within an urbanized, industrialized society moving into the second millennium.

When peasant societies were incorporated into nation-states, even Communist states, larger-scale kin units continued to exist. As recently as 1987, ethnic Albanian clans in Kosovo continued to feud with one another, answering one murder with another. As is the case in clan-based societies, when ongoing feuds are involved, all clan members are held responsible for the actions of a single member. The progress of this feud was reported on Yugoslavian television. After the Turkish earthquake, which occurred in the summer of 1999, the *New York Times* reported that forty members of a clan had traveled 600 miles from their home to try to rescue five trapped relatives. They brought their own equipment, including jackhammers, drills, electrical equipment, generators, and lights. This illustrates that members of a clan feel it absolutely necessary to come to the aid of fellow clan members in distress (*New York Times*, August 22, 1999: 12). In South Korea today, individuals still cannot marry if they have the same family name, and marriages within the same clan are legally banned, despite the fact that the Korean Civil Code on kinship was amended in 1990 to reflect a more bilateral system (Lee, 1999).

LINEAGES

Within clans with demonstrated descent, there are smaller units referred to as **lineages.** Sometimes all the people in the society believe themselves to be descended from a single ancestor. This founding ancestor may be historical or mythical, or a little of both. The kin groups of various sizes are related to one another in an extensive genealogy. The Bedouin Arabs of Cyrenaica in eastern Libya, studied by Emrys Peters (1960), provide us with an example of such a society. They are nomadic pastoralists who keep herds of camels and sheep in the desert areas of their territory and cows and goats in the wooded plateau areas. All the Cyrenaican Bedouin alive today consider themselves descended from the single ancestor Sa'ada, who heads the genealogy (see Figure 6-6). Sa'ada was the mother of the two sons, who are said to be the founding ancestors of the two largest groups of tribes—Baraghith and 'Aqqara. The genealogy in the diagram provides a set of ideas that the Cyrenaican Bedouin use to talk about how they are related to one another and how their group is related to all other groups. The genealogy is like a branching tree, extending out to its many twigs. Several twigs, or lineages, are part of a branch, and several branches, or groupings of lineages, are part of a larger limb. The larger limb represents a still larger grouping of lineages. This kind of descent system is called a **segmentary lineage system.** Groups at all the levels of segmentation are referred to as lineages. This kind of system is found in societies with patrilineal descent such as the Cyrenaican Bedouin. The constant branching out represents levels of segmentation. The branching out of the genealogy also has a close relationship to the occupation of geographical areas. The two groups of tribes, descended from each of the sons of Sa'ada, occupy the eastern and western halves of Cyrenaica. Lineages de-

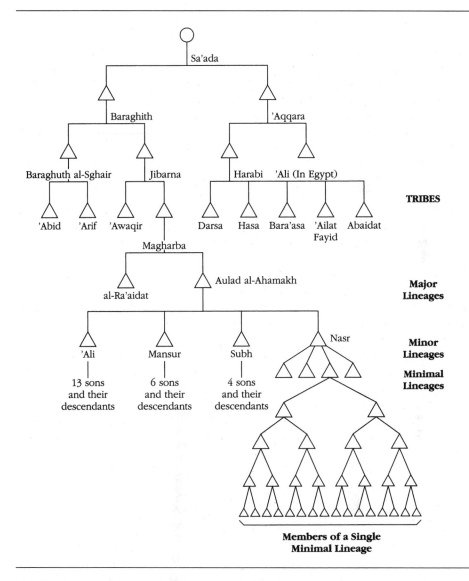

FIGURE 6-6 Genealogy of the Cyrenaican Bedouin.

scended from brothers a few generations back graze their herds on lands adjacent to one another. Lineages that are further away genealogically occupy lands farther apart. In political action, lineages closely related to one another unite to oppose a threat from a more distantly related lineage. The Pushtuns who straddle the border between Afghanistan and northwestern Pakistan also have a segmentary lineage system. We will be discussing their current situation in Chapter 14. In Chapter 9 we examine how segmentary lineage systems operate politically.

MOIETIES

Another kind of grouping based on descent is one in which the entire society is divided into two halves, which are referred to as **moieties**. Moieties may be based upon a patrilineal or a matrilineal rule of descent. Sometimes in societies with moieties, a village site was divided in half, each half being occupied by the members of one moiety. As noted in Chapter 5, the two parts of a moiety are often referred to in oppositional terms, such as *left* and *right*. The Abelam of the Sepik River area of New Guinea have patrilineal moieties referred to simply as "us" and "them." Among the Tlingit of the Pacific coast of northern Canada and Alaska, the two moieties are known as Raven and Wolf and are based on matrilineal descent. Moieties are usually composed of several clans.

THE NA: A SOCIETY WITHOUT MARRIAGE OR FATHERS

The Na live in Yunnan Province, China, not far from the Chinese border with Myanmar. Recently, a Chinese ethnographer has described their society as one in which marriage is absent. Consequently families have neither husbands or fathers (Cai, 2001). Is this believable? Didn't we say that marriage is almost a human universal? Don't the Na believe that males are involved in procreation? Don't individuals know their biological fathers? When we look at other societies comparatively, the answers fall into place. The Na are not that different from other matrilineal societies we have looked at, such as Lesu and the Trobrianders. They are only more extreme in their practices.

The Na believe that sexual intercourse is necessary for procreation to occur. They say, "If the rain does not fall from the sky, the grass will not grow on the ground." But they consider that the substance of which the child is made comes solely from its mother, as the Na are strongly matrilineal. "The man is merely a waterer" (Cai, 2001: 119). If the child resembles its father, they will guess who the father is (2001: 20) These beliefs are very similar to those of the Trobriand Islanders, who don't even believe that a male is required for a female to become pregnant.

A Na child belongs to its mother's lineage, and kinsmen are counted solely through its mother. Each lineage has two heads. One, the child's mother, who is concerned with the internal affairs of the lineage; the other, its mother's brother, who is the authority figure concerned with external affairs. Several lineages comprise a matrilineal clan, the members of which are collectively responsible for payment of blood money when someone from their lineage kills an individual from another group. The father has no social role since he is not considered a relative. There is no kinship term for him or for any members of his matrilineage. The mother's brother plays the role that the father has in patrilineal societies (2001: 145).

The Na procreate through the practice of visits at night, in which men, unrelated to the women, visit them furtively, and leave at dawn, when the first rooster crows. Pleasure rather than procreation is the purpose of these visits. When a woman becomes pregnant, the child will belong to her lineage. The "biological" fa-

 *A Na mother and child, from Yunan Province, China. The Na are a matrilineal society in predominantly patrilineal China.*

ther considers her impregnation to be an act of charity on his part. The taking of "lovers" is very reminicent of Lesu and the Trobrianders. In Lesu, all women take male lovers, who visit them like Na "lovers." In matrilineal societies, offspring clearly belong to the mother, and "marriage," if it occurs, may not restrict sexual partners to one's spouse.

Na rules about incest are very strict. No woman may have sexual intercourse with a relative, that is, with anyone matrilineally related to her (Cai, 2001: 125). The strongest incest taboo concerns brother and sister. Na brothers and sisters "work, eat, and raise the children born to the sisters together" (Cai, 2001: 121). Furthermore, they cannot speak about sex or make any allusions to sex (Cai, 2001: 127). Today, only one sex at a time can watch TV in the village, because if that sexual flirtation should occur on the TV, both sexes should not be watching it together. Brother and sister cannot sit in the same row at the movies. Since it is not always known who one's father is, it may happen that sexual relations take place between a father and his daughter (Cai, 2001: 460). For the Trobrianders, father-daughter sexual relations are not absolutely forbidden.

Today, the Na, a minority group, are under strong political and legal pressure to be more like the Han Chinese, the majority population, who are patrilineal, and to practice marriage like them. But the Na try to cling to their own cultural ways.

Cai Hua, the ethnographer, who is Han Chinese, questioned them closely about such matters as "jealousy between lovers," adultery and illigitimacy, and the Na told him that these things do not exist in their culture. These subjects are the characteristic "problems" of patrilineal societies, such as the Han Chinese, since such societies are obssessed with doubts about who the father is. However, these issues are absent in matrilineal societies like the Na.

KINDREDS

The descent groups examined above are all based on a rule of descent from a single common ancestor and are said to be **ancestor-oriented. Kindreds,** on the other hand, are reckoned in an entirely different way. Earlier, we described kinship as a web. Like a spider's web, it extends out from the center. Each person is at the center of his or her web of kinship. Anthropologists refer to the individual at the center as the ego, and the relatives who make up that web of kinship constitute ego's kindred. The kindred includes relatives on both ego's mother's and father's sides. Individuals who are descendants of ego, as well as ego's ancestors and everyone descended from those ancestors, are included in ego's kindred. The kindred is **ego-oriented.** The kindred as a unit does not own land or any other property; it only has coherence as a group around the ego at its center (see Figure 6-7). Societies like our own, which do not have unilineal descent groups but do have kindreds, are known as **bilateral societies.** On an occasion such as the American wedding described in Chapter 2, the kindreds of the bride and groom attend. If any of the first cousins of the groom, for instance, his father's brother's son, get married, a different set of relatives will be present, though there will be an overlap with his kindred. This overlap occurs since the two egos share a certain set of relatives. Kindreds do not have continuity through the generations as do corporate kin groups based on a rule of descent.

RELATIONS BETWEEN GROUPS THROUGH MARRIAGE

A rule of exogamy compels one group to give its women to another group in marriage, receiving the women of the other group in return. This is called sister exchange. Arapesh men state that they marry their sisters outside the group in order to obtain brothers-in-law. In general, marriages not only create links between brothers-in-law but also serve to create linkages between their respective kin groups. Groups that give women to and receive women from one another also exchange goods and services such as bridewealth, bride service, and other kinds of services at rites of passage after children are born from the marriage. These links between kin groups established by marriage are called **affinal links.** During warfare, kin groups frequently use these affinal ties and turn to their in-laws for assistance. For this reason, marriage is the basis for what is referred to as **alliance.** Although affines may be in opposition to one another and may even fight one an-

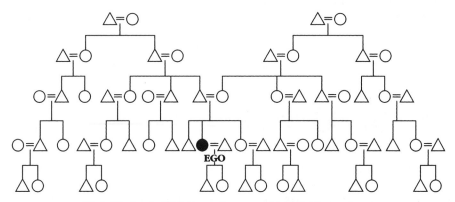

Ego's Kindred With Ego at the center, the kindred extends out
to include Ego's siblings, his first cousins, his second cousins, and
even more distant relatives not included in the above diagram.

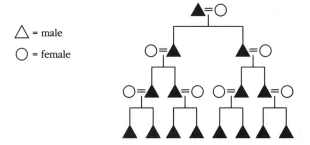

$\triangle$ = male

$\bigcirc$ = female

The Patrilineal Descent Group In contrast to the kindred,
the clan is ancestor-oriented.

FIGURE 6-7 The kindred.

other, the concept of alliance is nevertheless used by anthropologists to refer to
linkages between kin groups established by marriage.

In our society, marriage is based upon the decision by the bride and groom
to get married. Parents and other individuals are rarely involved. As we shall see
below, today families from India play a more important role in the marriage
choices of their American-born children. However, in other societies there are
rules stating that one should marry a certain category of relative. These rules
have the effect of continuing alliance over time between the groups. When
groups continue to exchange sisters over generations, then women of one's own
group are always marrying into the group from which wives come. This marriage pattern, which we have called sister exchange earlier, is also referred to as
a system of **reciprocal exchange** (see Figure 6-8). In such a system, the prospective husband and the prospective wife will already be related to one another.

FIGURE 6-8 Sister exchange, or reciprocal exchange.

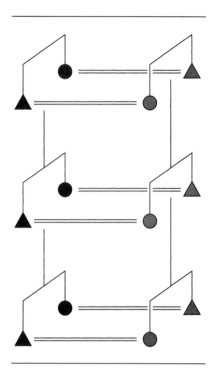

Since their parents are brother and sister, they will be first cousins. Anthropologists refer to two kinds of cousins: **parallel cousins,** who are the children of the mother's sister or father's brother, and **cross cousins,** who are the children of the mother's brother or father's sister (see Figure 6-9). In a system with reciprocal exchange, parallel cousins, who are members of one's own group, are frequently referred to as siblings. Therefore they cannot marry. Cross cousins are never in one's own group but rather are members of the other group with which one has been intermarrying. These cross cousins are known as **bilateral cross cousins,** since they are simultaneously mother's brother's children and father's sister's children. Sister exchange continued over the generations has the same effect as marrying one's bilateral cross cousin. The Yanomamo of southern Venezuela have such a marriage system of direct reciprocal exchange. Every Yanomamo man must marry a woman whom he calls by the kinship term for female cross cousin (the Yanomamo term is *suaboya*), and this term is at the same time the term for wife. Among the Yanomamo, the terms for female cross cousin and wife are identical, as are those for husband and male cross cousin. Female parallel cousins, among the Yanomamo, are called by the same term as sisters. If a Yanomamo man has no biological sister to return to the man who gave him his wife, as we noted earlier, he returns a sister who is really his parallel cousin.

FIGURE 6-9 Types of cousins.

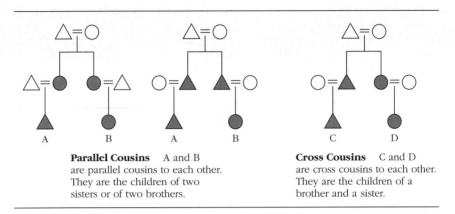

Parallel Cousins   A and B
are parallel cousins to each other.
They are the children of two
sisters or of two brothers.

Cross Cousins   C and D
are cross cousins to each other.
They are the children of a
brother and a sister.

FIGURE 6-10 Mother's
brother's daughter marriage,
or generalized exchange.

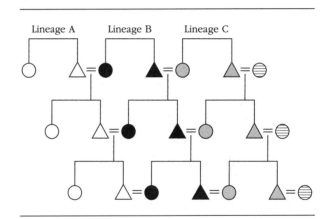

There are societies where the two kinds of cross cousins, mother's brother's children and father's sister's children, are referred to by different terms. These two types of cross cousins are not equally marriageable, as is the case for the Yanomamo. Some societies have a rule that a man ought to marry the daughter of his mother's brother, but he may not marry the daughter of his father's sister. Ideally, if every man married his mother's brother's daughter, in every generation, the result would be a picture like that in Figure 6-10. In Figure 6-10, the groups labeled A, B, and C, linked by the marriages, are patrilineages. This marriage rule occurs much more frequently in societies with a patrilineal rule of descent, though it also occurs in societies with matrilineal descent. If a man does not have a real mother's brother's daughter to marry, he may marry a classificatory mother's brother's daughter. A classificatory mother's brother's daughter is a woman whom a man calls by the same kinship term as his real mother's brother's daughter, and she is a member of the mother's brother's daughter's patrilineage. As one can see from the figure, lineage B gives its sisters to lineage A, and lineage C gives its sisters to lineage B, in every generation. From the perspective of lineage B, lineage A is always wife-taker and lineage C is always wife-giver. This system is very different from sister exchange in that you never return a woman to the lineage that gave you a woman. Since wife-giving lineage and wife-taking lineage are always different, a minimum of three groups is required. (However, it is usually the case that more than three groups are tied together in this kind of marriage alliance.) If there are three groups, then they can marry in a circle, with lineage A giving its women to lineage C. If, for example, the royal family of Great Britain gave its daughters in marriage to the royal family of Denmark in every generation, and the royal family of Denmark gave its daughters in marriage to the royal family of Sweden in every generation, and the royal family of Sweden gave its daughters in marriage back to the royal family of Great Britain in every generation, all intermarrying in a circle, then they would have this kind of marriage system. The Kachin of Myanmar (Burma), whose political organization will be discussed in Chapter 9, actually did have this kind of marriage system. It produces a structure of alliance between groups that anthropologists refer to as **generalized exchange.**

In the village of Lamalera in East Timor, this type of marriage system involving generalized exchange continues to be practiced, despite the adoption of Catholicism and substantial transformations of village economy (Barnes, 1998: 106). Though there is considerable variation in practice, 52 percent of marriages are with a man's mother's brother's daughter, and the hierarchical distinction between wife-givers and wife-takers remains significant today. Although the village of Lamalera is involved in the Indonesian national economy, economic cooperation in whale hunting, ownership of fishing and whaling boats, and the organization of fishing crews are still based on clan membership.

Some societies have the opposite form of the preferential rule of marriage with mother's brother's daughter. In those societies, a man cannot marry his mother's brother's daughter but *should* marry his father's sister's daughter. If every man married in this fashion, the result would be what is pictured in Figure 6-11. In the figure, groups A, B, C, and D are matrilineal lineages. This kind of marriage rule always occurs in societies with matrilineal descent. A man marries either his real or his classificatory father's sister's daughter. This marriage rule involves the return of a wife one generation after a wife has been given. In the first generation, D gives a woman to C, C gives to B, B gives to A, and A gives to D (if the lineages are marrying in a circle). In the next generation, the flow of women is reversed. Now D gives to A, A gives to B, B gives to C, and C gives to D. In the third generation, the flow is reversed once again. Every generation, women move in the direction opposite from the way they did in the previous generation. This resembles sister exchange in that a woman is returned to the group that originally gave a woman, but the return is made a generation later. Because the return is delayed one generation, there must be more than two groups operating in the system. A minimum of four groups is required. The Trobrianders

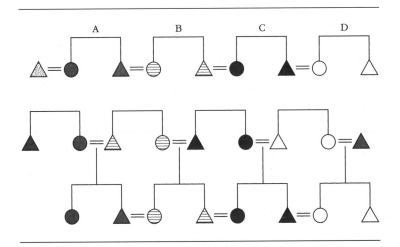

FIGURE 6-11
Father's sister's daughter marriage.

are an example of a society with a rule for marriage with father's sister's daughter and have this form of **delayed exchange.**

Each of these two marriage rules produces a different structure of alliances among groups, and both are different from the kind of alliance produced by bilateral cross-cousin marriage. Marrying one's cross cousins, either mother's brother's daughter or father's sister's daughter, begins with a rule of exogamy stating that one must take a wife from outside one's group. By specifying which relatives one should marry, different patterns of alliance among groups are created. Figures 6-8, 6-10, and 6-11 represent models of these different patterns and particular societies represent variations on these models.

Some societies, particularly in the Middle East, have a preferential marriage rule that is structurally opposite to this rule of exogamy. The rule states that a man should marry his parallel cousin, in this case, his father's brother's daughter. Since the societies of this area, like the Bedouin of Cyrenaica discussed above, are all patrilineal in descent, this marriage rule results in endogamous marriages. The Riff of Morocco, who have this marriage rule, say that they prefer to hold on to their daughters and marry them within their own group to avoid becoming entangled in alliances with other groups. This is not an explanation of what they do but rather their rationalization.

When one views marriage as an alliance, marriages may be contracted in which the procreative and sexual functions are not relevant. The Lovedu, a Bantu-speaking people of southern Africa, had a queen to whom women were given in marriage. The purpose of such marriages was to create political alliances, and sexual intercourse and procreation did not occur. Among the Kwakiutl, where privileges were transferred as a result of marriage, one man could "marry" the foot of another, become son-in-law to the man whose foot he married, and obtain privileges through this fictive marriage at the repurchase ceremony described in Chapter 2.

KINSHIP TERMINOLOGY

Each society in the world has a set of words used to refer to relatives. This set of words or terms is called **kinship terminology.** Of course, the terms differ from one society to another, since all their languages are different. However, anthropologists have been able to sort the terms used in all societies into a few basic types. Americans accept their own kin terminology as being the "natural" way of classifying relatives as do members of all other societies. Both your father's brother and your mother's brother are referred to as *uncle* in American usage. *Uncle* is also used to refer to your mother's sister's husband and father's sister's husband. Though the term *uncle* is used for these four relatives, two of them are blood relatives on different sides of the family, while two are relatives by marriage. Each of these four relatives is related to you in a different way, but our kinship terminology ignores these differences and groups them under one term. Anthropologists diagram kinship terminologies such as our own in the method depicted in Figure 6-12.

The Yanomamo of Venezuela have a very different way of sorting their relatives. They use the same term for both father's brother and mother's sister's husband, while they use a different term for mother's brother and father's sister's husband. The Yanomamo kinship terminology is pictured in Figure 6-13.

You can see that the two societies sort the terms for kin in different ways. For the parental generation, both the Yanomamo and Americans have four terms. The Americans use *father, mother, aunt,* and *uncle*; the Yanomamo use *haya, naya, yaya,* and *shoaiya.* In the Yanomamo system, father's brother and mother's brother have different terms, whereas in our society the same term, *uncle,* is used for both. Conversely, the Yanomamo class father and father's brother together, while we use different terms. In your own generation, we have a single term, *cousin,* for all the children of uncles and aunts. This term is unusual in that it is used for males and females. The Yanomamo are also consistent in their usage. The children of all relatives called by the same term as father and mother are referred to by the term for brother and sister. This means that parallel cousins are grouped with siblings. In contrast, the children of *shoaiya,* who are one's cross cousins, are referred to by terms different from brother and sister, *suaboya* and *heriya.* Which is more complicated? Neither. Which is more natural? Neither. These kinship terminologies are different because each is related to a different type of social structure. The terms in a kinship terminological system group some relatives and set apart other relatives in a way that reflects the relation of these relatives according to the rules of residence, marriage, and descent.

The American and Yanomamo kinship terminologies conform to two of these basic types of kinship terminology. Strange as it may seem, American kinship terminology is classified as *Eskimo* since it is identical to that of the Eskimos—or Inuit, as they

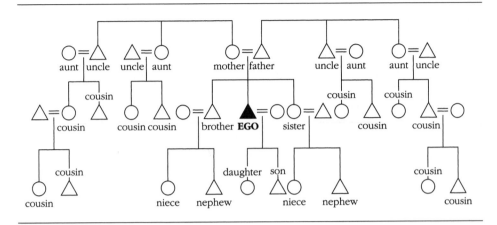

FIGURE 6-12 American kinship terminology.

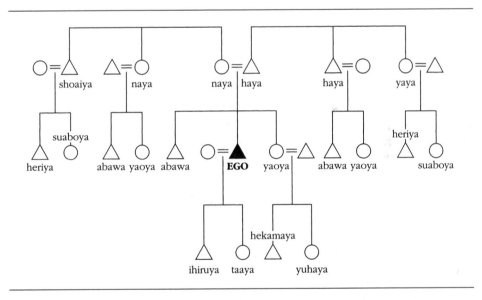

FIGURE 6-13 Yanomamo kinship terminology.

now prefer to be called—not in the words for the terms but in the pattern of organization. Its major characteristics are that it distinguishes between the generations and it distinguishes **lineal relatives** from **collateral relatives** (see Figure 6-14). Lineal relatives are those in the direct line of descent, that is, grandfather, father, son, grandson, grandmother, mother, daughter, granddaughter. The rest of the relatives are referred to as collateral and can be distinguished in terms of **degree of collaterality,** meaning

FIGURE 6-14 Degree of collaterality.

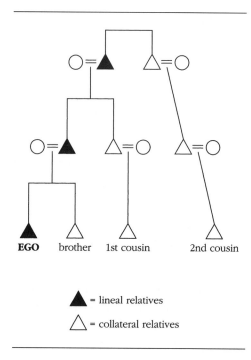

that second cousins are more remote than first cousins, and first cousins are more remote than siblings. The Eskimo type of terminology emphasizes individual nuclear
families, and it is found in societies with a particular cluster of characteristics, such as
neolocal rules of residence, kindreds, bilateral descent, and the absence of descent
groups. Though Inuit society and our own differed in degree of complexity, subsistence pattern, and environmental setting, the pattern of organization of kinship terms
and other kinship features was the same.

The kinship terminology of the Yanomamo is classified as *Iroquois.* The Iroquois type of terminology distinguishes between father's side and mother's side.
However, the difference between lineal and collateral relatives is ignored; father
and father's brother are classed together, as are mother and mother's sister. Generational differences are always recognized, as in Eskimo terminology. The social
structure with which this terminology is usually associated is one in which one's
own kin group is distinct from the kin group from which one's mother came. The
group from which one's mother came is the same group into which one's father's
sister marries. In other words, the Iroquois terminology goes with sister exchange,
which is the type of marriage pattern the Yanomamo have. This is why, in
Yanomamo, the term for father's sister's husband is the same as that for mother's
brother, and the term for mother's sister's husband is the same as that for father's
brother. Female cross cousin is classed with wife and male cross cousin with
brother-in-law. In every generation, "sisters" are exchanged between the two
groups, and the kinship terminology reflects this. Iroquois terminology is associ-

ated with virilocal or uxorilocal residence, but not with neolocal residence. Instead of independent nuclear families, extended families are present. This type of terminology is also generally associated with unilineal descent, but not with cognatic descent or bilateral kinship reckoning. Iroquois is by far the most common type of kinship terminology found in the world. It should be noted that societies that have Iroquois kinship terminology may not have all these social structural features, but only some of them. The Iroquois themselves did not have sister exchange.

Besides Eskimo and Iroquois terminologies, four other major types of terminologies are distinguished by anthropologists. The *Crow* type, found, for example, among the Trobriand Islanders, is almost always associated with matrilineal descent groups, avunculocal residence, and extended families. Unlike Eskimo and Iroquois terminologies, the same term may be used for members of different generations. *Omaha* kinship terminology is the mirror image of Crow. It is associated with patrilineal descent groups and, like Crow, ignores generational differences in some terms. The simplest terminology, the one having the fewest terms, is the *Hawaiian* type, in which only generation and male-female distinctions are made. It is usually associated with cognatic descent groups. Despite its simplicity, it has been found in association with some societies, like the Hawaiian, that have complex political economies. In the last type of kinship terminology, *Sudanese*, every category of relative is distinguished by a different term. It is frequently associated with patrilineal descent and economically independent nuclear families, such as those found among certain nomadic pastoral societies of the Middle East.

Kinship terminology is a subject that has a long history in anthropology, and the regularity of its patterning was first noticed by Lewis Henry Morgan (1877). Studying kinship terminology is vital to the anthropologist in gaining insights into how societies operate. The anthropological data that have been accumulated have revealed that there is a general association of types of terminology with particular kinds of social structure, as pointed out above. However, some terminologies correspond only in part to the types of social structure described above, and sometimes particular terminologies are associated with different social structural features. For example, Iroquois kinship terminology may be found in association with kinship systems that have patrilineal descent but do not have sister exchange, such as the Enga in Papua New Guinea.

Some anthropologists, for example, David Schneider (1984), have been critical of the use of the anthropological concepts for analyzing kinship presented in this chapter. They see the use of this set of analytic concepts as the imposition of Western social science categories on indigenous ideas. Instead, they prefer to utilize only the native categories that the people in each society use to conceptualize kin relationships. In our view, the analysis must always begin with indigenous categories. These can and must be translated into anthropological concepts. These concepts have made possible the cross-cultural comparisons that have revealed the same regularities or patterns in social structural features in societies in many parts of the worlds. The kinship variables discussed so far in this chapter, including number of spouses, degree of incorporation of spouse, type of descent rule, and structure of descent group, do not operate independently. They fit together into the particular patterns that have been revealed cross-culturally.

FICTIVE KINSHIP

People also rely on social relationships established by means of ritual observances, which are known as **godparenthood,** or *compadrazgo.* Godparenthood creates a set of relationships that, though nonkin in their derivation, utilize a set of terms based on kinship. The English labels for these relationships use kinship terms such as *father, mother, daughter,* and *son,* plus the prefix—*god*—differentiating them from real kinship. This is not simply an extension of kinship, but a different kind of relationship, which uses kinship as a metaphor. This kind of relationship is found in many parts of Mediterranean Europe and in Latin America. It also occurs among Hispanic populations in the United States. The ritual occasions upon which godparenthood is established are baptism, confirmation, and marriage, at which the godparent serves as a kind of sponsor. Real parents never carry out the role of godparents. Sometimes more-distant relatives may serve as godparents, while in other cases they may not. The *compadrazgo* relationship is frequently established between individuals of different classes for social, political, and economic reasons. In peasant communities, for example, a patron who is a wealthy or powerful member of the community and probably the landlord may serve as godparent to the children of clients who are economically and politically dependent upon him. In the relationship between godparent and godchild, the godparent is expected to protect and assist the godchild, while the godchild honors the godparent, just as the patron receives support from the client when it is needed and the client receives favors from the patron. Among the Quichua-speaking Otavaleno of the Ecuadorian Andes, *compadrazgo* has not been squeezed out by the expansion of capitalism, as some anthropologists in the 1960s had predicted (Colloredo-Mansfeld, 1998: 50). These indigenous people have become prosperous weavers and traders, and they now select *compadres* as they extend their handicraft business. When their children are confirmed or marry, they select *compadres* on the basis of their need to connect with sweater-factory owners, transport operators, and shopkeepers with whom they do business (Colloredo-Mansfeld, 1998: 52).

In Serbia, godparenthood, or *kumstvo,* described by anthropologist Eugene Hammel (1968), which could only be established between nonkin, was continued from one generation to the next. The word *kum* can be translated as "sponsor." Members of one group (A) stood as godparents to another group (B), and the children of those godparents in A served as godparents to the next generation of godchildren in B. Godparenthood was not reciprocal, since the group of godchildren in B did not return the favor and act as godparents to A, but instead, acted as godparents to children in still another group (C). This created a structure of alliances between groups by means of godparenthood, which is the same as the structure of alliances created by marriage with mother's brother's daughter, which we referred to as the structure of generalized exchange.

KINSHIP IN AMERICA TODAY

The symbolic meanings that Americans attach to kinship were investigated by David Schneider (1980). He pointed out that Americans conceive of two kinds of relatives, blood relatives and relatives by marriage. Americans think that a child receives half of its blood from the mother and half from the father, while more distant relatives have smaller shares of that blood, depending on the degree of distance. People think that such relationships can never be terminated because blood—the symbolic carrier of the relationship—is always present. On the other hand, relatives through marriage are different from blood relatives in every respect. The relationships are established by people making choices rather than as the result of a natural process. Such kin are termed relatives-in-law. Relationships that are made by people can also be terminated by people, through divorce. When this happens, the in-law is no longer considered a relative.

THE IMPACT OF BIOLOGICAL TECHNOLOGIES ON KINSHIP

As a result of what have come to be known as **reproductive technologies,** Americans recently have begun to rethink the meaning of kinship in their own culture (see Strathern, 1992). The meanings of motherhood and fatherhood have been called into question by these new reproductive technologies. When an egg in a surrogate mother is fertilized with sperm from a man who, with his wife, have contracted to be the child's parents, there may be conflict over the child between the couple and the surrogate mother. Motherhood has also been called into question when test-tube fertilization of an egg takes place. An egg from the would-be mother and sperm from the would-be father are brought together and the developing embryo is then implanted in a surrogate mother. If the sperm comes from an unknown donor, who is the real father—the man who has provided the sperm or the man who has acted as father in raising the child? Children conceived by artificial insemination are now seeking the identity of their donor fathers, who are often medical students who had donated their semen merely to help infertile parents have children. What formerly had been seen as a natural tie of kinship between father, mother, and child is clearly much more complicated by these new technologies.

The advent of the Human Genome Project and the "current comprehensions that diseases are genetically transmitted from generation to generation . . . [has led to] the medicalization of kinship" (Finkler, 2000: 3). Just as reproductive technologies have made us rethink definitions of family and kinship, so has the emphasis on the genetic transmission of disease resulted in a rethinking of kinship by many Americans. This is particularly true of those afflicted with diseases, which have been determined to be genetically inherited, as well as those with the potentiality of being afflicted. There has been an astronomical increase in the numbers of diseases that are now attributed to genetic inheritance, and consequently there is increased emphasis on family medical histories (Finkler, 2000: 15). Kinship is now being thought of in terms of shared DNA. Finkler studied breast cancer patients with a family medical history of the disease as well as women with no symptoms, but with a similar genetic history. All of them, whether they had already contracted the disease or not, saw family and kinship and the genetic distribution of the disease in their families as the cause of their breast cancers or the likely possibility that they might contract the disease. She also worked with a group of adoptees. They also shared the same "ideology of genetic inheritance [which] motivated them to seek their birth parents to discover their *real* being and to learn about their medical histories" (Finkler, 2000: 121). This emphasis on genetic inheritance in contemporary American society is in effect a focus on the faulty genes, which one may have inherited from one's ancestors, and which might cause one to become ill and even die. It has therefore become important to individuals to know their biological parents as well as the extended network of other biological relatives. Interestingly, "the medicalization of kinship creates a tension between the stress on individualism and choice in a democratic society [America], and an orientation to family and kin" (Finkler, 2000: 185).

Twenty years ago, when children were adopted, the adoption papers were sealed by the court and knowledge of their biological parentage was kept from adopted children. If Schneider's principle—that biological blood ties to parents can never be severed—is valid, then one can readily understand the need that such children, now adults, often feel to know who their biological parents are. This desire frequently invades the privacy that these biological parents sought. At present, many adopted children have gone to court to have the sealed adoption papers opened. Today, adoption has become such an open process that the adoptive parents may establish a relationship with the biological parents even before the child is born. A *New York Times* article revealed the way in which a prospective adopting mother moved in with the biological mother weeks before the child arrived and was fully involved in all the activities leading up to the birth (October 25, 1998). The adoptive parents indicated that they intended to continue to involve the biological parents in raising the child.

One might argue that this represents a greater emphasis on the biological and genetic aspects of kinship, a reinforcement of the idea of blood and consanguineal relationships in the minds of Americans. The physical process of procreation is very significant, since birth creates a social identity. For Americans, kinship represents ties of substance. When there is a question of where the substance is coming from, questions about kinship and identity are also raised. In recent years, what social scientists have come to call a new biologism has been added to biological conceptualization of family for Americans. Primordial conceptualizations of gender, race, ethnicity, and genes as representing the "true essence of a person" have become important in shaping the identity of Americans (Skolnick, 1998: 240).

Two highly publicized court cases, both settled in 1993 after extensive litigation, highlight these issues. In Florida, two female babies were switched at birth. One of them died in early childhood, and genetic tests then revealed that she was not the biological offspring of the parents who raised her. They sued for custody of their living biological daughter, and a settlement was reached giving them visitation rights. The girl herself, who felt a strong tie to the father who had raised her, sued some time later and was permitted by the court to terminate her relationship with her biological parents, to "divorce" her parents. A biological or blood relationship, which theoretically can never be severed, was treated as if it were equivalent to an in-law relationship. In another case, in Michigan, a baby was given up for adoption by her mother soon after birth. Then the mother, who later married the child's biological father, regretted the decision and sued for custody. After a two-year court battle, the biological parents won out over the adoptive parents, who were forced to relinquish the little girl. These two cases reveal the extent to which parentage and kinship have become contested. Biological relationship in one case has been reinforced, and the other case hinges on whether one can divorce one's parents. As Skolnick notes, "In some states today, unless a parent is found to be unfit or to have abandoned the child, the rights of biological parents are all but inviolate" (1998: 239).

DIFFERENT TYPES OF AMERICAN FAMILIES

Until the mid-twentieth century, the usual family type for Americans was the nuclear family that lived neolocally after marriage. Immigrant families, which included three generations, were an exception. As the age at which Americans married became later and later, the single-individual household became more frequent. A variant on this form is the household consisting of several unrelated young people, both men and women, who live together for financial reasons. The TV show *Will and Grace* portrays this form. Another household form consists of one or both grandparents and grandchildren. This occurs when the parents of the children are unable to care for them. Grandparents assume custody and responsibility instead of the state. There are now several websites which provide information about where grandparents raising grandchildren can receive help and support.

THE STEPFAMILY

The high rate of divorce and the subsequent remarriage of the divorced spouses has created a new type of family—the stepfamily. Thirty-five percent of children born now can expect to live with stepparents (Erera, 2002: 137). The stepfather is more likely to be living with and raising young children than the biological father, though the latter may continue to be involved in child-rearing and child support. Stepmothers rarely live with their stepchildren, unless the mother of the children has died or left the family. The stepfamily may also include nonresident children, in addition to nonresident parents. The modern stepfamily includes a variety of sibling relationships, such as full siblings, half-siblings, and stepsiblings. Half-siblings are considered blood relatives, while stepsiblings are not. Relations with in-laws and grandparents of the step family are highly varied. It may take from two to seven years for the stepfamily to "develop a sense of family with their [sic] own customs, rituals and history . . . [despite the absence of] clear behavior guides, norms or models" (Erera, 2002: 143–144). Mason notes that, in contrast to the Cinderella story, adolescent stepchildren experience less conflict with residential stepmothers than do adolescent children with their own mothers in nondivorced families (1998: 98).

GAY AND LESBIAN FAMILIES

The increasingly public lifestyles of gays and lesbians today have also challenged American views on the definition of marriage and the family, as well as contributing to the debate on biological versus other forms of parentage. Sexual relations between two men and between two women are still outlawed by statute in many states, although some states like Vermont have adopted a Civil Union Law, which provides a legal framework parallel to marriage (Erera, 2002: 164). Gay couples and lesbian couples, who see themselves as equivalent to heterosexual couples, may go through a ritual they refer to as a marriage or commitment ceremony. A New York Times op-ed column on August 11, 1993, dealt with the publication of an announcement of the wedding of two men in the Salina Journal, published in Salina, Kansas. The wedding ceremony had been performed by a Presbyterian minister. While gays and lesbians from all over the country wrote the newspaper, congratulating it, 112 subscribers canceled their newspaper subscriptions in protest, and some advertisers grumbled. The story gained a nationwide audience when the couple and the writer of the Salina Journal story were flown to New York to appear on a nationwide TV program.

In some places, homosexual couples can legalize their relationship by registering—as, for example, at City Hall, in New York City. Lesbian and gay couples have used various kinds of public ceremonies to make a public commitment to one another. These included a Jewish religious ceremony in which rings were exchanged and a *ketubah* (traditional wedding document) was signed, followed by a formal catered affair and wedding cake. Other examples included an elaborate "wedding" on a yacht beyond the three-mile limit, and a *Wiccan* ("early female spiritual tradition, or witchcraft") "handfasting," or betrothal ceremony (Sherman, 1992). Another gay couple described their ceremony as a "theme wedding" combining Jewish liturgical elements and a country-and-western theme (Lewin, 2001: 47).

Homosexual couples demand legal status as married couples, but much of American society does not yet seem to have accepted the validity of their claim. In California, which has a large homosexual community, the surviving member of a couple can inherit the deceased member's pension. Mention of the surviving member of a homosexual couple in an obituary is often contested by the biological family of the deceased. Recently, in Hawaii, there has been discussion about the passage of legislation that would permit gays and lesbians to legally marry, but the Hawaii Supreme Court upheld an amendment to the state constitution forbidding gay and lesbian marriage (Erera, 2002: 164). There has been much consternation about this issue throughout the country, since laws about marriage and divorce passed by one state must be recognized by all other states. The backlash to this proposed legislation was the passage, in 1996, of the Defense of Marriage Act, signed by President Clinton, though he supported the rights of gays in the military. The campaign for the legalization of gay and lesbian marriage continues nevertheless.

Homosexuals not only "marry," but also create three-generation families in a variety of ways. Lesbians previously in heterosexual marriages often try to bring their biological children into the new family, creating a stepfamily that resembles a heterosexual family in many ways (Erera, 2002: 168). In such a situation, the mother must also deal with the children's father (Lewin, 1993). Though some

At a lesbian marriage ceremony in San Fransisco, both parties
chose to dress as brides.

states prohibit lesbians and gays from adopting children, independent adoption
was often a route followed if possible, particularly by gay couples. Some married
lesbian couples have used artificial insemination to have children. They prefer to
call it alternative insemination to emphasize that it is as natural as insemination
through sexual intercourse (Weston, 1991: 171). Stacey notes, "Numerous lesbian
couples solicit sperm from a brother or male relative of one woman to impregnate
her partner, hoping to buttress their tenuous legal, symbolic, and social claims for
shared parental status of the 'turkey-baster babies' " (Stacey, 1998: 120–121). Gay
men may create families by using a surrogate mother, who is impregnated with
the sperm of one of the gay partners, or they may adopt or foster a child (Erera,
2002: 169).

The issue then is: What will be the relationship of the other woman in the couple to such children, who are the results of artificial insemination? That woman
may attempt to adopt the children of her "spouse." In several states, including California, New Jersey, and New York, this kind of adoption by lesbians has been approved by the courts. Other states, such as Florida and New Hampshire, have
statutes prohibiting adoptions by a second female parent, under the reasoning that
a second female could not adopt a child until the natural mother surrendered her

rights to that child. Sometimes, each woman will have a child to produce a more equally balanced family. When gays and lesbians terminate their familial relationships, they sometimes end up in court arguing over the custody of the children and challenging the court system, since there are no precedents for such situations. As one might expect, biological claims of relationship are usually those that are recognized. The court has favored "the parental claims of donors who had contributed nothing more than sperm to their offspring over those of lesbians who had co-parented from the outset, even when these men [the sperm donors] had expressly agreed to abdicate paternal rights or responsibilities" (Stacey, 1998: 122).

Recently, several studies have focused on the distinctions between heterosexual and homosexual families. In terms of compatibility, same-sex couples seem to get along better than heterosexual couples. They share more interests and spend more time with one another. Heterosexual couples have the least egalitarian relationships, and lesbian couples, the most. These studies find that child-rearing is more nurturant, children more affectionate, parental relationships more cooperative and egalitarian among gay parents than among heterosexual parents. Gay parents prefer to live in communities that support the diversity of family life. As Stacey concludes, "Perhaps what is truly distinctive about lesbian and gay families is how unambiguously the substance of their relationships takes precedence over their form, emotional and social commitments over genetic claims" (1998: 138). Same-sex families are deemed to have a higher level of cohesion and be more flexible than heterosexual families (Erera, 2002: 173).

In American kinship, the term *family* refers to an infinitely extendable unit. It can be used to refer to the family group living together as a single household or, in its widest sense, to all the descendants of a single couple who gather at a family reunion. The anthropologist Kath Weston has studied the formation of lesbian and gay families in the San Francisco area (1991). When homosexuals "come out" to their biological families, they are often rejected and left to feel that they have no families. In response, a gay kinship ideology has emerged, which proclaims that "love makes a family." These are families that people create by choosing one another, providing a great contrast with their own biological families. For homosexual kinship, choosing is valued over biology. These are extended families of choice and mutual agreement, which perform many of the functions of extended families based on kinship and marriage (Erera, 2002: 175). Schneider's conclusions about American kinship were the reverse of this formulation. The composition of gay and lesbian families is highly varied, and the only consistent kinship terminology in use is in reference to generational peers as *sister* and *brother*. These "sisters" and "brothers" become "aunts" and "uncles" when their "siblings" have children. Within the lesbian family, kin terms used by children for their parents are still highly varied.

KINSHIP AND CLASS

David Schneider's work on American kinship was conducted among middle-class Americans, and he assumed that their value system was the ideal for the entire society, including the lower class. Lower-class kinship was seen as an adaptation to the world of racism and poverty. Carol Stack (1974) has described a kinship system among poor black people in a small midwestern city that is quite different from the one described by Schneider. In this situation, relatives form a wide support network within which there is reciprocation, which Stack calls "swapping," of money, child care, food, clothing, shelter, and emotional support. Those biological relatives who choose not to be involved in a support network thereby renounce their status as kin. The core of this network is a cluster of linked households, usually two or even three generations of women. Relatives such as aunts and grandmothers may carry out the role of mother for children. Males are present, but they are usually boyfriends and mothers' brothers, rarely husbands or fathers. If a young couple should marry, the newly formed nuclear family draws the individuals away from their kin and out of their support networks. Should the young husband lose his job, the marriage has little chance to survive, since the couple always fall back on the resources of their respective kin networks, destroying the marriage. In this situation, ties between brother and sister are stronger than those between husband and wife. In the film *Do the Right Thing*, Spike Lee captures this contradiction when he contrasts the close emotional ties between the hero and his sister with the hero's antagonism toward his girlfriend, the mother of his child. In the kinship system described by Stack, mother's brothers more frequently serve as role models for young male children than fathers, giving the system a matrilineal cast. In writing about the way in which the criminal justice system should deal with juvenile offenders from the kinds of families Stack describes, Lund proposes that mother's brothers rather than fathers be made responsible for the supervision of such young offenders (1995).

More recent research in a small African-American low-income suburb near a once-booming industrial region in the Midwest presents the same picture of interdependance of kin for financial support, and an array of essential services (Hicks-Bartlett, 2000: 35). Even after employment is obtained, in the need for child care, funds for clothing for the new position, and money for transportation to the new job, individuals rely on their families and a network of relatives. Life in Chicago is the same where extended kin constitute a significant support group for girls in female headed households (O'Connor, 2000: 112). In a study of young low-income African-American men from the West Side of Chicago, out of 26, 14 lived with their mothers or grandmothers while 9 others regarded mother's address as their permanent address (Young, 2000: 146). Only four grew up with their fathers in the home, but only intermittently. Twenty-one of the 26 were fathers themselves, but only three lived with their children. On the basis of the information provided by Stack, above, one might hypothesize that the fathers who did not live with their own children were closer to their sisters than to the mothers of their children. They serve as mother's brothers, if their sisters have children. In contrast, in Skylan, a housing project in a major midwestern city, there were resident fathers (Barclay-McLaughlin, 2000: 60). Groveland, an African-American neighborhood in Chicago where 70 percent of the residents in single-family brick houses are homeowners, is characterized as lower middle class; however, some families had incomes below the poverty line. Though there are some intact families with resident fathers, in other families the father is absent (Pattillo-McCoy, 2000: 95). The perilous economic situation of the African-American middle class in Groveland "often renders stability and mobility an extended family [concern], and sometimes even a community effort" (Barclay-McLaughlin, 2000: 99).

NEW FORMS OF THE FAMILY

The migration of men and women from the Caribbean to the United States within recent decades has created the phenomenon of the international family (Ho, 1993). Ho's study of Afro-Trinidadians living in Los Angeles reveals the way in which the households of women who migrate from Trinidad may include kin, fictive kin, friends, and the children of kin and friends. Family and the network of kinship are dispersed internationally. For individuals living in Los Angeles, the family includes people in such far-flung places as Trinidad, Tobago, Jamaica, Barbados, St. Vincent, the United States Virgin Islands, New York, and cities in Connecticut and Canada. Such networks of kin and family, out of which households potentially may be formed, include up to four generations of kin and fictive kin. These individuals constitute a network of support and exchange like the network described by Carol Stack. They may own property in common and provide child support, "childminding," and informal adoption. Ties are maintained by telephone contact, letter writing, visits during vacation, and even family newsletters and e-mail. The international family represents a globalization process, the result of migration for economic reasons, but a process with cultural outcomes, specifically, the "Caribbeanization" of America and the "Americanization" of the Caribbean (Ho, 1993: 39). The advent of the Internet has enabled such families, with members scattered across the globe, to keep in close touch with one another. In the summer of 1999, the *New York Times* reported that such a family, scattered over five continents, went online to hold a wake. One member delivered a eulogy online while the rest of the family watched it on their computer screens.

KINSHIP AND FAMILY REUNIONS

The family reunion in the United States, which involves kin relations beyond the nuclear family, has also been the subject of anthropological research. Neville (1987) recounts how every summer many southern Protestant families attend such gatherings. The descendants of a male ancestor, who are now living dispersed over the United States, come together at the same time and place each year (like the Worthy family, which meets at an old camp meeting ground in north Georgia on the third Sunday in July). The descendants of the common ancestor, both male and female, constitute a constantly expanding group of descendants, which doubles with each generation. However, not all these descendants choose to come to the reunion. Such reunions include a shared meal cooked and contributed by the women of each family as well as visiting and telling of stories about the common ancestor and the kinship connections that bind them all together. They may also include church services, introduction of members, business matters, and the election of officers. When the descendants come together at the reunion, they are reenacting the

Protestant biblical ideal of family and kinship. Exchanging food and partaking of a meal together once a year symbolize the solidarity of the kin group. Neville also points out a tendency to emphasize connections through women over those through men in the southern Protestant families. A nuclear family is more likely to attend the reunions of the mother's family than the father's. Such family reunions have become common among various ethnic and racial groups such as African Americans in the United States. In sharp contrast to the Afro-Trinidadian and African-American kin networks described above, the family unit that comes together at family reunions has only expressive and symbolic functions.

SUMMARY

- This chapter presents the basic concepts of kinship that anthropologists have used to analyze the small-scale societies that were the focus of their attention when anthropology first developed as a discipline. These include descent, family, postmarital residence, and marriage.

- The incest taboo and marriage prohibitions compel individuals to marry outside of the family.

- Societies have rules regarding number of spouses and postmarital residence rules, which result in the creation of a variety of types of families.

- Societies also have rules regarding how marriage is contracted. Bridewealth, dowry, and bride service are the alternatives.

- Kinship rules of descent create different kinds of kin groups or clans.

- Though their structures may differ, the functions of such groups—land ownership, economic and ceremonial functions—remain the same.

- Different types of marriage rules result in different structures of relationship or alliance between descent groups.

- Kinship terminology in different societies reflects the pattern of descent, family type, and marriage found in those societies.

- Some societies use kinship as a metaphor to create the important relationships of godparenthood.

- Americans have their own cultural ideas about kinship, which are currently being rethought in light of reproductive technologies, surrogate parenting, artificial insemination, the emphasis on genetic inheritance of disease, stepparenthood, and adoption by gay and lesbian couples.

- Kinship continues to be important not only in our own complex industrial society but also in other societies all over the world.

SUGGESTED READINGS

Collier, Jane Fishburn, and Sylvia Junko Yanagisako (ed.). *Gender and Kinship: Essays toward a Unified Analysis.* Stanford, CA: Stanford University Press, 1987. Gender viewed from the perspective of a redefined approach to kinship. Articles from a conference.

Edwards, Jeanette, Sarah Franklin, Eric Hirsch, Francis Price, and Marilyn Strathern. *Technologies of Procreation: Kinship in the Age of Assisted Conception.* 2nd ed. New York: Routledge, 1999. An analysis of the social and cultural implications of assisted conception, and the potential these create for parenthood, procreation, and kinship.

Faubion, James D. (ed.). *The Ethics of Kinship: Ethnographic Inquiries.* Lanham, MD: Rowman & Littlefield, 2001. A series of articles concerning the relationship between ethics and kinship and the ways in which individuals are involved with families of choice rather than families of kinship.

Fox, Robin. *Kinship and Marriage: An Anthropological Perspective.* Cambridge: Cambridge University Press, 1983. A clear and wittily written introduction to the field of kinship, social structure, and marriage.

Godelier, Maurice, Thomas R. Trautmann, and Franklin E. Tjon Sie Fat (eds.). *Transformations of Kinship.* Washington D.C.: Smithsonian Institution, 1998. Essays demonstrating that the great variety of kinship systems in the world are variants of a limited number of classic types.

Mackey, Richard A., Bernard A. O'Brien, and Eileen F. Mackey. *Gay and Lesbian Couples: Voices from Lasting Relationships.* Westport, CT: Greenwood Publishers Group, 1997. A well-documented study of the relationships between members of same-sex couples, focusing on what is actually involved in such relationships.

  ## SUGGESTED WEBSITES

http://www.era.anthropology.ac.uk/Era_Resources/Era/kinship A website that teaches the reader how to calculate his or her own genealogy.

http://emuseum.mnsu.edu/prehistory/egypt/dailylife//kinship_marriage.html Incest, kinship, and marriage among ancient Egyptians.

http://www.umanitoba.ca/faculties/arts/anthropology/tutor/kinterms.html Compares kinship terminology in English and in Dani (Papua New Guinea). French and Spanish kinship terminologies are also considered.

7

Gender and Age

In American society, justice is personified as female and death as male. In German culture, death is also male, but so is one's homeland—fatherland. However, for Russians, the homeland is one's motherland. A child with a German mother and a Russian father has no "homeland." A priest is called "Father" and pope is another term for father. These are statements in which male and female are used in a symbolical fashion. Women veil in some societies but men veil in others (see photo of Tuareg man in Chapter 1). Men may herd cattle and women milk cows in some societies, while in other societies like ours, men and women both work as computer technicians. Senior citizens in our society may sometimes live in communities where children are not allowed to live, while in other societies, aged parents are revered members of the family and accorded the best living arrangements in the household. These are examples of how age and sex distinctions form the basis for social roles. Every society makes social distinctions of some sort based on sex and age. As we noted in Chapter 1, they also form the basis for role differentiation in animal societies like the baboon troop and the wolf pack. Relations between the sexes in human societies are always culturally patterned. The nature of their patterning forms a powerful motif in the tapestry of culture.

MALE AND FEMALE

In the last two decades, the relationship between males and females and the way in which male and female roles are culturally construed have received a good deal of attention. Before that time, anthropologists, male and female, focused primarily on male roles in their field research. In doing so, they were unconsciously reflecting the cultural bias of their own society, which emphasized the significance of male roles and projected its gender ideology onto the society they were studying. Sometimes this focus on the primacy of male roles reflected the male bias of the society being studied. The work of Margaret Mead and one or two other female anthropologists were exceptions to this male bias. With the growth of the feminist movement within the past 30 years, many anthropologists of both sexes began to pay attention to female as well as male roles and to the female as well as the male point of view of society. They focused attention on the cultural construction of gender roles and how these related to other patterns in the culture. The cultural constructions of what is male and what is female are much more than natural categories based on biological differences. As Errington puts it, "Culture does not lie on the surface of the anatomical and physiological base as decoration, the way icing lies on a cake. If human social life were compared to a cake, we would better say that 'biological givens' are analogous to flour, eggs, and sugar, and the socializing process of human interaction 'cooks' them into their final form: cake" (Errington, 1990: 14).

While all societies construct female roles as different from male roles, the nature of the contrast differs from one society to another. In Wogeo, an island off New Guinea, the difference is based on the belief that men and women live separately in two different worlds. But realistically, men and women must come together to reproduce the society as well as to carry out the usually complementary social and economic roles upon which their society depends. Politics and power are controlled by men. Associated with these ideas about the separateness of the sexes is the belief that sexual intercourse is polluting to both sexes and that menstrual blood is harmful to men. While women menstruate naturally, in Wogeo the men incise their penises to rid themselves of the bad "menstrual" blood (Hogbin, 1970).

In contrast to Wogeo, other societies play down the differences. The Wana on the island of Sulawesi, in Indonesia, conceptualize gender relationships very differently from the people of Wogeo. They minimize the differences between male and female, seeing male and female as almost identical anatomically. Husband and wife are equally involved in procreation. The Wana say that the man carries the child for the first seven days of gestation and then puts the child into a woman. It is believed that in the past men menstruated. Men's menstrual blood is said to be "white blood" and to contain the essence of humanity, which solidifies in the womb as a fetus (Atkinson, 1990: 75, 76). Both the national state organization and the wilderness surrounding the village lie outside the Wana communities. These areas are dangerous, but they are also the source of spiritual knowledge and power. The Wana believe that men are braver than women. This is one area in which there are gender differences. Men obtain knowledge from the spirits of the forest and become shamans. The overwhelming majority of Wana shamans are men. Even in a society where men and women are seen as fundamentally the same, gender does make a difference when it comes to the public realm of politics. Atkinson also reports several cases of gender shifting. In one of them, a woman, who had borne and lost a child, lived like a man "married" to another woman and performed as a shaman (Atkinson, 1990). Among the Wana, even though most shamans are men, both men and women may become shamans, while among the Yanomamo only men may become shamans. On the other hand, in Korea most shamans are female (see Kendall, 1996).

The discussion above of the island of Wogeo made note of the fact that menstrual blood and sexual intercourse are seen as harmful to men. Menstrual blood is

Signs in Indonesian and English at the entrance to a Balinese temple ask menstruating women not to enter.

a substance that, perhaps more than any other, is associated with femaleness and also with pollution. We saw this in Chapter 4, where young children from India had to keep their distance from their menstruating mothers. In the course of interaction between male and female in Wogeo, as in some other societies, men may perceive women as dangerous, and this danger is often projected onto menstrual blood. Among the Mae Enga, a highland New Guinea society, men always take wives from enemy groups, and consequently, wives are seen as dangerous. They believe that a man can be harmed if he has sexual intercourse with a menstruating woman or when menstrual blood is introduced into food. The Mansi are a hunting and gathering society on the eastern slopes of the Ural Mountains in Siberia today. Like the Mae Enga, Mansi married women belong to a "'strange' clan different to that of her husband" (Fedorova, 2001: 227). Women in that society are subject to a series of complex taboos that "stem from beliefs regarding the allegedly harmful essence of women related to their 'impurity'" (Fedorova, 2001: 227). These taboos include moving to a special dwelling during menstruation and immediately before childbirth. After the birth, the woman stayed in the menstrual house for two or three months. The wife could not expose her face to her husband's male kin . She could not touch the "idols" in her husband's home, though after her marriage and move to the husband's house she was supposed to be protected by "his domestic

gods" (Fedorova, 2001: 233). During the Soviet period, education and modernization brought about a weakening of these taboos. Since the collapse of the Soviet
system, many Mansi are said to be returning to "their old ways." The belief that
menstrual blood is a dangerous substance is also found in other societies in the
world where wives do not come from enemy groups.

A comparative study of beliefs about menstruation points out that the idea
about the polluting effect of menstrual blood on men tends to be part of a male vision of society (Buckley and Gottlieb, 1988: 35). There are few studies of how females in particular societies view menstruation. Menstrual blood can be used
symbolically in harmful ways in witchcraft and in a positive fashion in the manufacture of love charms.

In all societies, economic roles are based on cultural constructions of gender. In
the past this was referred to as the sexual division of labor. The difference in economic roles between men and women is not an outgrowth of their biological differences. A specific task may be associated with men in one society and with
women in another. As we have noted above, milking herd animals (cows, goats,
sheep), for example, may be a female task in some societies and a male task in others, as is also the case with making pottery and weaving cloth. Men's economic
tasks invariably have greater prestige, even though women's tasks, such as horticulture and collecting plant foods, may provide the bulk of subsistence. This is an
example of gender stratification. Whatever the economic role of the man, it is that
role which the culture values. In America and in other industrialized countries,
women have become lawyers, stockbrokers, and judges, economic roles formerly
reserved for men, and men have taken over some female roles, like nurses and airline attendants, which were formerly exclusively female roles.

Earlier, we discussed the ways in which space takes on different symbolic
meanings. Particular spatial areas may be associated respectively with males and
females. Because women are identified with mothering, the hearth, and the home,
women are associated with the domestic realm. Men in contrast, are identified with
the public realm. This distinction between domestic and public is an analytical tool
that aids us in comparing male and female roles in different societies. The association of males with the public sphere and females with the domestic was widespread in the past; today this distinction is not always the case, particularly in
many Western societies.

In a number of New Guinea societies, the men's house and the ceremonial
plaza are male turf, while women are associated with their own dwelling houses.
Women in many Middle Eastern societies are restricted to certain parts of the house
and may only come into contact with males who are members of their own family.
When they leave the house, they must veil their faces. In such societies, the coffee-
house and the market are defined as male domains.

However, markets are not universally male domains. As mentioned in Chapter 3, Malagasy women conduct the haggling that takes place in the market, while
in some West African societies, women actually control the marketplace. A recent
comparative study gives a number of examples of women traders in markets in
Java, South India, Ghana, Morocco, and the Philippines (Seligman, 2001).

A veiled woman walks past a walled mosque in Herat, Afghanistan.

Middle Eastern women's clothing is characterized by the use of the veil or scarf to hide one's hair. For Western feminists, the veil has become the object of attack because it is seen as an infringement upon women's human rights. This position is seen by others as ethnocentric, since it ignores the particular cultural meanings of veiling. It is "a language which communicates social and cultural messages, a practice which has been present in tangible form since ancient times" (El Guindi, 1999: xii-xiii). Veiling is part of a set of related practices, including the presence of a harem, polygamy, female seclusion, and eunuchs, said to have originated "millennia" ago and to have spread widely over the whole area of the Middle East. However, as El Guindi notes, "there is sufficient evidence to indicate that we are dealing with multiple phenomena, layers of meaning, and diverse contexts" (1999: 4). If one looks as veiling as an aspect of clothing, it is said to also be an aspect of clothing for men in Arab society. For example, there is evidence that for several centuries before Islam, Arab men veiled, and it is even reported that the Prophet Mohammed veiled on certain occasions (El Guindi, 1999: 117). The best-known case of male veiling are the Tuareg, a Berber people living in the Sahara desert. They are matrilineal and organized into three endogamous classes—nobles, vassals, and slaves. Their blue veils and headdresses, the most distinguishing feature of their dress, are worn continually during the day and evening; at home while eating, smoking, and sleeping; while travelling; and even, according to some, during sexual intercourse (El Guindi, 1999: 124). Murphy notes that "among all segments of the Tuareg population, the veil is worn higher when confronting a person of power and influence" (1964: 1267). Those of the vassal or slave classes were most lax about veiling. The reason for Tuareg male veiling is unrelated to why Moslem women veil. Masking, and men wearing veils, is related to the desire, in some cultures, not to let others know how one feels, which would give an advantage to one's enemies. The Javanese say that the face itself is a mask.

In Egypt today, some young Egyptian women have taken up veiling as an aspect of their support of Islamic militancy. It replaces the secular dress that many of their mothers and even grandmothers wore. In Turkey, which has been secularized since the revolution of Kamal Ataturk after World War I, some young women Muslim advocates have recently begun to wear long coats and head scarves (El Guindi, 1999: 129ff.).

Americans perceive differences between males and females as natural differences. They consider the differences in genitalia to be signs of differences in fluids and substances that naturally divide the population into two different, mutually exclusive, categories (Errington, 1990). Behavior, dress, and demeanor are viewed by Americans as determining membership in one of these two categories. Clearly, this idea of what is considered natural by Americans is a culturally constructed category that is continually expressed and enacted, as we shall describe below.

SHIFTING GENDER CATEGORIES

Masculinity and femininity are culturally construed concepts. We have pointed out that gender shifting occurs among the Wana. As in the Wana case, women in Western society who carried out masculine roles, such as the author George Sand and Joan of Arc, usually dressed and acted like men.

In Native American Plains societies, the term *berdache,* a term of French derivation, was originally used to refer to men who dressed like women and sometimes lived in homosexual relationships with other men, a kind of "third gender." We now recognize that there were also women in these societies who dressed like men and assumed male roles, who constituted a "fourth gender" (Roscoe, 1998). Perhaps the most famous *berdache* in American Indian history was We'wha, a Zuni *berdache* who was accepted as a woman during his trip to Washington, D.C., in 1886, where he met many dignitaries, including President Grover Cleveland. He lived as a woman and was skilled at women's crafts. When he died, he was dressed in a dress, with a pair of pants beneath the dress, the pants symbolizing his "raw state," as a biological man, and the dress his "cooked state," that of a woman (Roscoe, 1998: 145). It would appear that the Zuni used the same metaphor employed by Errington above, that the biological state is the raw state and the cultural construction is the cooked state. *Berdaches,* who were known as *nadleehi,* were also to be found among the Navajo. Roscoe notes that the *nadleehi* tradition still continues in parts of the Navajo Reservation (1998: 65).

Roscoe gives a number of examples of female *berdaches* who were warriors. He notes that Cheyenne female warrior chiefs "dressed like the male members of

 *The* berdache *We'wha, wearing the ceremonial costume of a Zuni woman.*

the Hohnuka, or Contrary society, who fought wearing only their breachcloths" (Roscoe, 1998: 75). Some of these Cheyenne female warriors sat with the Chief Council and their opinions had weight. Similar cases occurred among the Pend d'Oreille and Flathead Indians, both from Montana, as well as the Crow and the Blackfoot. Running Eagle, a female warrior of the Blackfoot in the early nineteenth century, became a legendary subject. Her story was reprinted and given new meaning in 1984 as a positive image for young women today. The Navajo also had female *nadleehi*, masculine females or female *berdaches*, giving them four culturally identified genders. Today some male *nadleehi* may use that label to identify themselves, being Navajo traditionalists in their belief. Younger acculturated and assimilated Navajo homosexuals use the Western categories gay and homosexual and may be completely unfamiliar with the *nadleehi* tradition (Thomas, 1998: 162, 169).

A form of male transvestism occurs today among Samoans (Mageo, 1992). In the past, it was part of the sexual ribaldry and buffoonery that took place during ceremonial competition between kin groups, when both men and women performed sexually provocative dances. If a girl referred to as "sister" (in the real or extended sense) was present, no one was allowed to use coarse and sexually suggestive language in joking. Therefore, girls of one village needed to perform their suggestive dances before boys of another village to ensure that brothers were not present. As a result of the introduction of Christianity, women in general had to cease such ribald sexual banter and dancing and become modest and circumspect in their behavior. Only old women are still involved in teasing, sexual banter, and sometimes lewd dancing. The behavior of male transvestites, or *fa'afafine*, as performers and the objects of sexual joking has replaced the sexually suggestive talk and performances of young women. Many *fa'afafine* are to be found in bars in urban areas today, and there are at least one or two in each rural village. When male transvestites perform at a beauty contest for *fa'afafine*, sexual ribaldry can occur because they are not really women. In the role of *fa'afafine*, there is a complete reversal of the normal male role. The sexually expressive *fa'afafine* is also the virginal sister turned on her head. We therefore see in Samoa the construction of a gender that is different from the present constitution of male or chaste female roles and patterned upon a ribald version of a female role from the past. This is, of course, a completely cultural construction made up of inversions of other gender roles in the culture.

Within recent years, people have begun to think beyond the division between heterosexual and homosexual and talk about queer theory. Queer theory prides itself on going against the grain and taking an antinormative position against the usual sexual categorizations. Though associated primarily with lesbians and gays, it also includes cross-dressing, hermaphroditism, gender corrective surgery, and gender ambiguity. It is an outgrowth of postmodernism and associated with postcolonialism (Hawley, 2001).

CHANGING GENDER ROLES

In our own and other industrial societies, economic, spatial, and behavioral separation of the sexes was present until the beginning of the twentieth century. Ginsburg (1989) points out that in preindustrial America, the home was basically the workplace for both men and women. With increasing industrialization during the nineteenth century, men were drawn into the factories and businesses, while women remained in the home, an essentially female domain. Women were identified with an ideology of nurturance and domesticity, despite the fact that some women worked in stores and factories for wages. Politics, the courts, businesses, banks, pubs, and so forth, were male bastions; so too were the social clubs, where real business was carried out.

THE FEMINIST MOVEMENT AND THE FEMALE ROLE

At the beginning of the twentieth century, women who questioned the assignment of the male and female roles of this time formed the suffragist movement and began to agitate for the right to vote, which had been denied them heretofore. Men perceived the pioneers in this movement as very masculine women. World War II brought many women into the workforce, and since that time, ever-increasing numbers of women have become part of the American labor force. It took the feminist movement of the 1970s and affirmative action legislation to begin to raise both female and male consciousness and bring about the transformations that we see today. As women have moved into occupations like law and medicine, formerly occupied almost exclusively by men, the society at large has come to accept women as well as men in those roles. In this way, women in American society have invaded the public realm of men, and as this has occurred, men have increasingly had more to do in the domestic realm, taking on cooking and child care.

Another example of how gender roles have changed in America concerns childbirth. In the nineteenth century, American women gave birth in the home, which, as we noted, was identified as a female sphere. At the beginning of the twentieth century, with the increasing professionalization of medicine and the growth of hospitals, the medical profession, then male-dominated, took control over the process of giving birth, and by the 1930s more births occurred in hospitals than at home. Under these conditions, birth was defined as a medical procedure, and the female reproductive process was taken over and placed in the hands of male physicians.

With the significant changes in gender roles in our society, this process is being reversed. There are more female physicians now. Interest in natural childbirth has brought about changes, and home birth is a possibility that some feminists advocate. Other aspects of the new reproductive technology, such as amniocentesis, genetic counseling, and the use of various birth control techniques, for example, intrauterine devices and birth control pills, have also been seen as giving women more choices and greater control over their lives in regard to reproductive functions. However, the introduction of these procedures does not really empower women but, rather, increases the control of technology and technologists over women and their reproductive processes (Rapp, 1993).

The change in gender roles just described is in no way an inevitable progression through which all modernizing societies will pass. Anthropologists have described all sorts of changes affecting gender roles in different parts of the world in recent decades. Many women in parts of the Middle East and Asia have left their traditional domestic domains to go to work outside the home with varying consequences. For example, in Hong Kong in the 1970s, in families where fathers were unemployed or underemployed, daughters went to work, becoming semiskilled factory workers (Salaff, 1995). Their incomes played a prominent role in the household economy, though their personal gain was limited. There was some loosening of family ties, and they were freed from household duties and received small amounts of spending money. Their marriages were no longer arranged and they could choose their own spouses. However, core family values of paternal rule and filial obedience were still maintained.

The constitution of gender roles often swings back and forth like a pendulum in response to political changes. In Iran, Riza Shah Pahlevi, who ruled for several decades during the mid–twentieth century, tried to modernize and industrialize the country on a grand scale. He invited foreigners, particularly businessmen, to come and set up factories and transform Iran into a Western-oriented country. He introduced universal education, and women were encouraged to seek occupations outside the home. The wearing of veils was outlawed and Family Protection Laws were passed stipulating that wives had to give their consent to all the aspects of the marriage contract, including the taking of another wife by the husband. When the

Shah was overthrown, the new regime, led by the Ayatollah Khomenei, turned the society 180 degrees, replacing the Shah's Westernization efforts with strict Islamic social norms and morality, especially with regard to the position of women. The sexes were viewed as having very different roles, with men being seen as more rational, brave, conquering, and aggressive in sexual urges. Women were viewed as emotional and sexually conniving (Nakanishi, 1998: 88). The Family Protection Laws were abolished, giving men the primary role in the stipulation of the conditions of the marriage. Women were required to wear the *hijab*, a scarf covering the head and shoulders, to enable men to control their own sexuality.

Women have reacted to these new edicts in several ways. A moderate position has been proposed by the Women's Society of the Islamic Revolution of Iran, which sees itself as reformist but not feminist. The political writings of the group describe and critique the two extreme responses. Those still favoring the Western orientation introduced by the Shah are characterized as the "west-toxicated" women who "blindly" accept Westernization and modernization, who do not wear the *hijab* and who have lost their "true" Muslim identity (Nakanishi, 1998: 87). Traditional women, who blindly accept what the religious leaders promulgate about their inferiority, who do not take the initiative about their own lives, and who wear the *chadar*, a black garment that covers them from head to foot, are also criticized. The proper path, advocated by the society, is that of "ideal Muslim women" who accept their identity as Muslims, demonstrated by the wearing of the *hijab*, but who are independent, participate in politics, and are not passive and subordinate to men (Nakanishi, 1998). Though the government has established councils on women's affairs in 1987 and 1992, little legislation has been passed to ensure women's rights within the context of the Islamic tradition.

Another Muslim society, the Minangkabau, who live on the island of Sumatra and are part of the Indonesian nation-state, provide us with an interesting example of the way in which the contemporary women's role is sensitive to political currents. The Minangkabau have a matrilineal rule of descent and the wife's relatives play a significant role in social and economic affairs. *Adat,* the unique body of traditions related to this social system, has melded with the Qur'an since Islam was introduced in 1600. The laws of the Qur'an were developed in the context of patrilineal societies. Since the Minangkabau are matrilineal, this necessitated making compromises between *adat* and the Qur'an. These traditions have survived more than 300 years of Dutch colonial rule, as well as the development of the Indonesian nation-state after the country won independence in the mid-1950s (Whalley, 1998: 229).

The Minangkabau began to move to the urban areas of Sumatra and to educate girls as part of the modernization and transformation of Indonesia that took place under the aegis of President Suharto. This presented many challenges to both Islam and *adat*. The response, in the 1980s, was an Islamic renaissance parallel to that occurring in other Islamic countries. The government itself then began to fund the building of mosques. Soon major religious events and family celebrations were emphasized, and girls began to wear Muslim dress to school. In terms of *adat* tradition, as early as the beginning of the twentieth century, there had been a shift from uxorilocal residence, when the husband moved to live with the wife's relatives, to nuclear family households, though the families still lived on her lineage land and in close proximity to the wife's female relatives (Whalley, 1998: 233). Despite the continuation of the matrilineal tradition, husbands began to invest more time and interest in their wives and children and less on their own matrilineage, as had been the case in the past. The growing importance of the nuclear family household has resulted in the husband's providing more subsistence for his family, as well as providing for the education of his children, allocating inheritance of personal property to them, and having more of a voice in whom his daughters marry. However, mother's brother and matrilineage relatives, especially older women, still play a significant role in deciding schools to attend, professions to pursue, and marriages to be arranged. With the growing importance of Islam in the 1980s combined with the efforts at modernization, young women had to tread a narrow line to resolve the dilemma of career and family (an issue not unfamiliar to young American women). However, in contrast to traditional Islamic thinking in Iran, for example, Minangkabau women are seen as being of equal moral worth with men. Islamic scholars proclaimed women to be the pillars of society given their critical roles as mothers and wives. Women's education was encouraged, in order to enable them to better raise and educate their children. The educational choices of young women today may necessitate making decisions that do not always fit with the cultural traditions of the senior generation. Young Minangkabau women have continued to wear more modest Western-style dress, though they wear traditional Muslim Minangkabau dress for ritual occasions. Islamic traditions were being aggressively taught in contrast to the Western-style education of the 1960s and 1970s. Islam was being promoted as an answer to reestablishing order in a country threatened by Westernization. Recently, however, as a counter to the threats to the traditional *adat*, children in school are being exposed to programs emphasizing this tradition. In addition, urban middle-class Minangkabau are hosting large-scale marriage festivals that mix rock music with "all the intricate observances of high *adat*" (Whalley, 1998: 245).

We have just considered the changing position of women in America and in a number of non-Western societies. It is clear that feminist achievements in many Western societies are not paralleled by similar attainments elsewhere. Women in lower social classes in the West as well as women of color feel that the feminist movements and its achievements have not included them. The question also arises regarding which direction the women in that society wish to go, modernization or a more traditional role or some combination of the two. Our discussion of veiling below will show that some women in Egypt wish to return to a position much like that of their grandmothers.

MASCULINITY AND MASCULINIST STUDIES

In parallel fashion to the examination of the feminist role, it is necessary to understand the nature of masculinity. Masculinity, like feminity, is a series of cultural constructions "whose basis is not biological—even though the cultural construction is based on biological differences—but constructed, designed, agreed to, and upheld by a system of beliefs, attributes, and expectations" (Ramirez, 1999: 28). To Foucault and others, sexualities are constantly being made and modified. Foucault demonstrates this in his depiction of how the modern Western idea of sexuality arose in a specific historical and social context (1990; Whitehead and Barrett, 2001; Brittan, 2001: 53). What constitutes masculinity changes through historic time for all societies. We also need to recognize that "masculinities" is a contested term, and there is considerable variation in what constitutes masculinity within as well as between societies (Morgan, 2001: 223–224). However, in an interesting cross-cultural study done more than a decade ago, Gilmore found in an overwhelming number of the societies he studied that masculine ideologies were dominant, as is the case among non-Western societies like the Mae Enga and Wogeo, discussed above.

One must consider not only the nature of the male role but also, at this point in time, what effect the women's movement and the fight for "equality" have had on the position of males in different societies. As we have noted above, gender roles must be viewed in relation to each other since no society consists solely of males or females. With respect to the great changes in women's role, "as feminists have long argued, men retain a capacity to resist and threaten this challenge . . . [and] many men are now actively resisting women's burgeoning demands for equal rights, and doing so increasingly through recourse to discourses of religious fundamentalism, not only Islamic but also Christian and Jewish" (Whitehead and Barrett, 2001: 7). Religious fundamentalism means a return to religious ideas of an earlier time, and these involve a restricted female role, particularly with regard to power relations and decision making within the family. An examination of the Hasidic Jewish family today, in New York, for example, reveals that the power to make important financial and life decisions is always in the hands of the man. One could characterize family relations as "patriarchial." The idea of women's rights has not penetrated this subculture. Women who wish education and a career must leave the group.

In the past it was suggested that while women controlled the domestic domain, which revolves around cooking and child-rearing, men controlled the public domain of ritual and politics. This was equally true of Western societies, with their early patriarchal history, as well as small-scale societies. The priests, the rabbis, and the Imams of Catholicism, Judaism, and Islam are men, and religious fundamentalists give historical reasons for why these offices must remain in male hands. (The Apostles at the Last Supper were all males). Feminist pressure has been directed against such male domination of religious offices. Some Jewish groups, Reform and Conservative, have accepted female rabbis, and Episcopalians have ordained female priests. But neither the Catholic religious hierarchy nor Orthodox Jews have as yet accepted the idea of female priests and rabbis.

Guttmann, in his study of the working-class neighborhood of Santo Domingo, a *colonia* founded on the outskirts of Mexico City by "land invasion," focused on the dramatic transformation of what it means today to be male and female (2000). The following demonstrates the changes that are taking place in gender roles. It is common to hear women and men say that there used to be a lot of macho men but they are not so common today. Older men still divide the world of men into *machos*,

Hispanic father performs the non-macho role of feeding the baby.

meaning men of honor who responsibly provide for their families, financially and otherwise, and *mandilones*, meaning female-dominated men (Guttmann, 2000: 162). The latter are seen as being bossed around by women and undependable. The term *machismo* is also associated with wife beatings, sexual episodes of infidelity, consumption of alcohol, gambling, abandonment of children, defiance of death, and bullying behavior in general (Guttmann, 2000: 164). Younger married men see themselves in a new category, "non-macho." The macho label may be rejected by the man who helps his wife and does not beat her, the latter (i.e., beating one's wife) being a characteristic of the macho man. This is clearly a divergent "cultural trajectory." The terms *macho mexicano* and *la mujer abnegada*, the self-sacrificing woman, are now regarded by many working-class men as "pejorative and not worthy of emulation." The title of *macho*, the model of aggressive masculinity, is rarely claimed by younger men, since *machos* do not spend time with their children, cook, or wash dishes (Guttmann, 2000: 172). However, sometimes the role of "the macho" is a playful one, which is performed "on demand," and there are still depictions of macho men in dramas in places like Santo Domingo. Beyond these categories is "the broad category of men who have sex with other men . . . [including] male prostitutes who have sex for money with other men and always play the active role, and the *homosexuales*. . . . Men who have sex with other men are by some people's definition outside the bounds of masculinity altogether" (Guttmann, 2000: 174). But in the final analysis, "no man in Santo Domingo neatly fits into any of the four categories, either at specific moments or throughout the course of his life "(Guttmann, 2000: 174). The main point here being that for Mexicans in this *colonia* today, masculinity has shifting meanings and this has been the case historically as well.

Ramirez deconstructs the concept of "machismo" as it is used in Puerto Rico and explores the construction of masculinity by analyzing slang used in a wide variety of everyday contacts between people. He shows how the expressions that people use not only reflect but also enact power relations between Puerto Rican men and women. In Puerto Rico as elsewhere, masculine ideology stresses sexuality, which men should declare and boast about, delighting in women as objects of pleasure (Ramirez, 1999: 44). The genitals, particularly the erect phallus, symbolizes male power in Puerto Rico, as in all of Latin America and the Mediterranean world, while the female genitals are devalued (Ramirez, 1999: 49, 52). One of the demands of masculinity, which continues to be part of the dominant ideology of Puerto Rico, is that the man continue to be the breadwinner for the family. Though women are entering the labor force in greater numbers, even into those positions that were "male strongholds," most women are in fields like teaching and nursing, considered feminine. The continued dominance of men is demonstrated by the fact that their occupations are accorded greater prestige, decision-making power, and financial rewards (Ramirez, 1999: 62). Whatever men do is always accorded greater prestige. Puerto Rican men must constantly demonstrate that they possess the attributes of masculinity and are not *mongo,* that is, weak men who are at the mercy of others. To continue to have the respect of others, which is very important to them, men should make sure that their women are not unfaithful to them. *Maricon*—the nonman or the homosexual—is seen as the total negation of masculinity, "an individual who is devalued and despised" (Ramirez, 1999: 200).

Masculinity in American society has been examined in a variety of institutional contexts, including various industries, the military, and sports. The military is still largely male. It also "plays a primary role in shaping images of masculinity in the larger society" (Barrett, 2001: 77). However, even within one of the services—the navy—for example, there are a number of different "masculinities," different strands of "hegemonic masculinity" that naval officers call upon to "secure" different forms of masculine identity (Barrett, 2001: 95). For example, risk is an important value for aviators since they have more opportunities to display such behavior, while "surface warfare officers have opportunities to demonstrate physical hardships and grueling work schedules, and supply officers frequently have more opportunity to display . . . responsibility for resources" (Barrett, 2001: 95). These characterizations are always seen in contrast to military men's definitions of women as emotionally unstable and less capable of enduring the physical challenges and harsh conditions of life aboard a ship.

Variations in the nature of manhood in other American settings are revealed in an examination of masculinity in various types of workplaces. Meyer, in a consideration of masculine culture on the automotive work floor during the three decades from 1930 to 1960, sees two polar forms, or ideal types, as operative during that time, which were a continuation from the nineteenth century (2001: 15). "Respectable manhood," which was related to the craft tradition, was characterized by a tempered and channeled masculinity in which mental and physical skills were used in a evenhanded fashion. In contrast, "rough manhood" related to the tradition of unskilled labor characterized by risk taking, physical strength, and disorderly behavior. Others have also associated this rough masculine culture with construction workers and steelworkers. In the Northeastern part of the United States and Canada, many of these steelworkers were Iroquois who transferred the masculine warrior ethic into the daring required to walk the steel beams as skyscrapers were being constructed. As Meyer points out, under industrialization and semiskilled mass production, workers blended and merged elements of these two types, the respectable elements being fed by high wages and economic stability, while in auto plants "boylike playfulness on the shop floor . . . [and] drinking, fighting and gambling" retained aspects of the rough male identity (Meyer, 2001: 19).

Majors argues that the "cool pose" that black men in sports express is a means of countering social oppression and racism and a way of expressing their own creativity (2001: 215). Their expression of pride and respect for themselves in the "cool pose" expresses their masculinity as dominant and hegemonic, and ultimately it is about "men's domination of women." In general, according to Kimmel, our culture's definition of manhood includes a repudiation of the feminine; the necessary acquisition of power, success, wealth, and status; being strong and reliable in a crisis; never showing your emotions; exuding manliness and aggression (2001: 278). The quest to prove one's manhood is a lifelong endeavor.

Many have equated male dominance with male sexuality. This is true not only on the symbolic level of meaning, as we have seen in the Mexican and Puerto Rican examples. Others have argued that male and female sexuality is more complex, and that feminists must work to transform the ideology away from that of male dominance toward a more egalitarian relationship between men and women.

CATEGORIES BASED ON AGE

Aging is a continuous process, from birth to death. However, the way in which this continuum is divided varies from society to society, as well as over time within a single society. Every society has terms for different age groups, but the number of terms varies. In our own society, for example, we use such terms as *infant, child, adolescent, adult,* and *senior citizen*. Therefore, senior citizens is a social category.

AGE GRADES

When the age categories are formally named and recognized and crosscut the entire society, they are referred to as **age grades**. In a number of primarily herding societies in East Africa, from Ethiopia in the north to Tanzania in the south, formalized male age grades play an important role in the social structure. In many of these societies these have continued to be important, while in others there have been changes as a consequence of the pressure of economic transformation. The Nandi of Kenya, studied by Huntingford (1953), have a system of seven age grades that correspond to divisions of a man's life cycle. Every 15 years or so, men move from one age grade to the next, more senior, age grade. This change takes place at a ceremony that is held simultaneously at several places throughout Nandi territory. All the boys born between one ceremony and the next form a single **age set,** which is given a permanent name. Since there is a 15-year period between one change in grade and the next, there is a 15-year range in the ages of members of a single set. When the last man of the oldest set dies, the name that was assigned to that age set is free to be used for the age set of male infants being born. There is thus a set of seven names, each of which is recycled every 105 years (7 grades × 15 years, the period of time between changes of grade).

The most junior of the age grades consists of young boys. The second grade consists of initiates, averaging 15 years in age, who will be circumcised at some point while they are in this grade. Boys, during their time in this grade, learn the role of warriors, which they will take over when they move into the next grade. The third age grade is that of the warriors, the "set in power," who carry out all military actions in Nandi society, including raids against neighboring peoples. The warriors live in special bachelor houses and are allowed free sexual access to uninitiated girls. They have primary responsibility for organizing the circumcision of the younger age grade of initiates and for testing the younger grade for bravery and valor. Before the official movement into the next grade, the oldest group of warriors take wives and retire from active participation as warriors. On leaving the grade of warrior, a man and his set pass into the first of the four grades of elders. At the ceremony that marks the change from warrior to the first grade of elder, the retiring warriors remove their clothes and put on old men's fur cloaks.

There is no elaborate system of age grades, nor age sets, for women. Instead, they are divided into two categories—girls and married women. A rite, corresponding to male circumcision, is performed upon older girls, which involves an operation on the clitoris. This elaborate system of age grades among the Nandi coexists with other kinds of social groupings based on family, lineage, and clan. The age grade system divides the society like a seven-layer cake, and assigns particular functions to each of the grades.

The Nyakyusa of Tanzania, who were studied by Monica Wilson (1951, 1977), use divisions according to age as the basis for a different kind of age grade system. Age mates, as they mature, join to form a new village. When they are 10 or 11 years old, boys build huts and establish a village at the edge of their fathers' village. They sleep and spend time in their fledgling village but return to their mothers' huts for meals and assist their fathers in agriculture. The Nyakyusa emphasize that boys at this age should move out because they should not be aware of the sexual activities of their parents. Where other societies, such as the Trobriand Islanders, have the institution of the bachelor house to which adolescent boys must move, the Nyakyusa have extended the idea of the bachelor house to the formation of an entirely new village. When the original founders of the village reach the age of 15, the village becomes closed to new members. At about the age of 25, the boys, now young men, marry and bring their brides to live with them virilocally in the new village, and now each wife cooks for her husband. Once in a generation a great ritual is held, at which time administrative power and military leadership are handed over by the older generation to the younger. The men of the retiring generation move to one side, and the new villages of young men are formally established on their own lands. At this ritual the old chief retires, and his sons are recognized as chiefs of the small chiefdoms into which the Nyakyusa are divided. The retiring old chief reallocates all the land and selects a headman for each new village.

All over Nyakyusaland, at any time, there are three kinds of age grade villages. There are the villages of the grandfathers, who have retired from leadership positions but who still perform certain ritual functions. There are the villages of the fathers, who rule and are responsible for defense and administration. Finally, there are the villages of the sons, who have not yet "come out" but when necessary, fight under the leadership of men of their fathers' generation. The Nyakyusa have an intense fear of sexual relations between a young man and his father's co-wives, who are his stepmothers. Similarly, possible sexual relations between father-in-law and daughter-in-law are dreaded. The age villages are a way of keeping the generations apart and thus avoiding intimate contact between these categories of people. On the positive side, the Nyakyusa stress the friendship and fellowship within one's peer group, which promotes the solidarity of the village. Though the Nyakyusa have a rule of patrilineal descent and patrilineages, the members of a lineage are dispersed over a number of villages. In contrast to the Nyakyusa, most societies with patrilineal descent have villages based on lineage and clan organization, where the lineage or clan owns the land. However, in these societies the tension between the generations may undermine the solidarity of the clan. The Nyakyusa say that they prefer to live with people of their own generation with whom they can have easy communication, since relations between members of the same lineage but of different generations are governed by the formal respect required of juniors for their seniors. Retirement communities in the United States recapitulate this pattern of solidarity within an age group.

Under the recent pressure of economic change, the Nyakyusa have been moving away from their traditional age villages. When men migrate from their homes for wage labor, they leave their wives with their mothers, thereby negating the traditional value of separating a daughter-in-law from her father-in-law. Furthermore, individuals seeking economic advancement for themselves create a conflict with the traditional value of sharing between members of an age village (Wilson, 1977). This situation is in contrast to that of the Samburu, a pastoral society in nearby Kenya that also has an age grade system. Though some Samburu have moved to town, many of them still retain their herds. Their age grade system is still intact (Bilinda-Straight, 1997: 68).

RETIREMENT COMMUNITIES

We pointed out earlier how the cultural construction of gender has been changing in North America. A significant change has also taken place in the construction of the category of senior citizen. The existence of Social Security and pensions has made retirement a twenty-first-century institution. By law, there is no longer a retirement age and therefore no longer a clearly defined point at which an American moves into the category of senior citizen. However, the fact that the law has changed does not necessarily mean that people's attitudes and behavior have also changed. A person need not retire at any particular age, but individuals may begin to consider themselves senior citizens, join the American Association of Retired Persons, and retire from their employment as early as age 55. However, the movement toward early retirement, which characterized the 1980s and 1990s, seems to be passing. The trend now is for people to continue to do some type of work.

Some people "age in place" while others, upon their retirement, migrate elsewhere, usually to a retirement community in the Sun Belt. Pensions and Social Security allow them to move to another place and live independently. This is in contrast to the elderly in nonindustrialized societies. These people are financially dependent on their children who are, in a sense, their "Social Security." However, in countries like China or India that have patrilineal descent and patrilocal or virilocal postmarital residence, it is sons, not daughters, who care for their elderly parents. As a consequence, sons are greatly preferred over daughters at birth.

Those Americans who are retiring in the South are usually younger, more affluent, and healthier than older people in general. Many retirement communities are self-contained and focus on leisure activities (Riekse and Holstege, 1996: 252). These communities, whose residents must be over 55 years of age and which do not allow children to live there, resemble a Nyakyusa village of grandfathers. As a consequence, they have no schools and therefore pay no school taxes. Retirement communities are sometimes built around religious affiliation or ethnic identity. They may also be constructed on the basis of social class. Some of them consist of mobile homes, while others contain condominiums or private homes. As a result of chain migration, when earlier migrants attract later ones from the same community, clusters of individuals having long-term relations develop. A Finnish-American retirement community of this sort exists in southeast Florida, though very few other Finns live and work in this area (Stoller, 1998). The community began to develop in 1940 when Finnish Americans living in New England and the Midwest, particularly Minnesota, first came to this area to retire. Some members of the community are second-generation Finnish Americans, while others were born in Finland and came to the United States after World War II. This is not a planned retirement community, like the ones described; rather, it consists of residents scattered through a large metropolitan area and linked through informal networks and organizations. The ethnic identity manifested by the Finnish Americans in this community is the basis for informal ties and the development of solidarity and support among these older people (Stoller, 1998: 289). The community contains two "Finn Halls," which sponsor cultural and social programs. Other Finnish institutions include two churches that conduct weekly services in Finnish, a Finnish-language newspaper, and a Finnish-American rest home. In the community, 123 merchants and service providers identify themselves as Finnish.

Retirement communities are not exclusive to the United States. They have begun to be established in Japan. Traditionally, elderly parents lived with the family of one of their children in the extended family form known as *dokyo.* In the rural areas, 62 percent of senior citizens still live this way while in the urban areas only 33 percent do so. A recent ethnography describes Fuji-No-Sato, an example of a community or "life-care" facility, located near a small fishing and farming village, which is also an upper-class summer resort area (Kinoshita and Kiefer, 1992). Those desiring to live there purchase a right to live in the community rather than an apartment. They must be 60 years of age, live independently, pay an endowment fee when they move in and then a monthly operating fee. This community, located a day trip away from Tokyo, includes primarily individuals who remain there full-time, though a quarter of the individuals use their apartments as second homes. The well-educated inhabitants are from the middle or upper-middle class. The community is self-contained, consisting of two-story buildings in a wooded environment with a shuttle bus to the village, because most of the residents do not have cars. There is a residents' association, which all must join, and a wide variety of hobby groups; Christian groups, which hold prayer meetings; and volunteer groups. Gardening is a very important activity. Since the community is an unfamiliar, unstructured, newly constituted social situation with few guidelines for behavior, people's relationships are primarily formal in nature, which characterize Japanese behavior in such unstructured situations. Japan is relatively homogeneous compared with the United States; therefore, ethnicity cannot serve as a basis for Japanese retirement communities. Only social class can function in this way.

Societies may have important rituals that move individuals from one culturally construed age category to another. These are called **rites of passage** and they will be discussed in Chapter 10.

SUMMARY

- Age and sex are the most common bases for distinction between social roles in every society.

- Categories based on age and sex do not simply build upon biological differences, but are defined by culture.

- With the growth of the feminist movement within the past 30 years, many anthropologists of both sexes began to pay attention to female as well as male roles and to the female as well as the male point of view of society, though before they concentrated upon the role of males in a society.

• Females are always defined in terms of their relationship to males and vice versa.

• The cultural expressions of gender vary from society to society. For example, the Wogeo believe that men and women are very different and live separate and complimentary lives though they come together to reproduce. In contrast, the Wana see men and women as more alike.

• In many societies like the Wogeo menstrual blood is believed to be polluting to males. Among the Wogeo, since reproduction is polluting, men remove the bad blood from menstration by incising their penises.

• Particular spatial areas may be associated respectively with males and females.

• For Western feminists, the veil has become the object of attack because it is seen as an infringement upon women's human rights. This position is seen by others as ethnocentric, since it ignores the particular cultural meanings of veiling.

• In Native American Plains societies, the term *berdache,* a term of French derivation, was originally used to refer to men who dressed like women and sometimes lived in homosexual relationships with other men, a kind of "third gender." Women who dress and act as men constitute a kind of "fourth gender."

• The feminist movement of the 1970s and affirmative action legislation raised both female and male consciousness and bought about the transformations that we see today.

• The change in gender roles described for industrialized societies is in no way an inevitable progression through which all modernizing societies will pass.

• Masculinity, like feminity, is a series of cultural constructions that are not based simply on biological differences. It is constructed, designed, and upheld by a system of beliefs and attitudes.

• The *macho* man as a symbol of masculinity is beginning to be rejected by a younger generation of Hispanic men.

• Every society has terms for different age groups, but the number of terms varies. In our own society, we use such terms as *infant, child, adolescent, adult,* and *senior citizen.*

• These categories, young and old, and their relationships change over time.

• When the age categories are formally named and recognized and crosscut the entire society, they are referred to as age grades.

• Retirement communities are not exclusive to the United States; they have begun to be established in Japan.

SUGGESTED READINGS

di Leonardo, Micaela (ed.). *Gender at the Crossroads of Knowledge: Feminist Anthropology in the Postmodern Era.* Berkeley: Calif: University of California Press, 1991. Essays dealing with feminist research on biological anthropology, primate studies, global economy, new reproductive technologies, ethnolinguistics, race, gender, etc

Ginsberg, Faye, and Anna Lowenhaupt Tsing (eds.). *Uncertain Terms: Negotiating Gender in American Culture.* Boston: Beacon Press, 1990. A series of articles concerning the different domains of American life in which definitions of gender are being contested and renegotiated, such as the family, the workplace, the clinic, the hospital, and the school.

Jacobs, Sue-Ellen, Wesley Thomas, and Sabine Lang (eds.). *Two-Spirit People: Native American Gender Identity, Sexuality and Spirituality.* Champaign: University of Illinois Press, 1997. Empirical and theoretical essays revisiting the concept of the "North American Berdache."

Kapchan, Deborah. *Gender on the Market: Moroccan Women and the Revoicing of Tradition.* Berkeley: University of California Press, 1999. Describes the way in which Moroccan women challenge some of the most basic cultural assumptions of their society about honor and shame, privacy and modesty, obligation and hospitality, and particularly about power and authority.

Lamphere, Louise, Helena Ragone, and Patricia Zavella (eds.). *Situated Lives: Gender and Culture in Everyday Life.* New York: Routledge, 1997. A series of articles regarding gender and its construction in a range of cultures throughout the world.

Lugo, Alejandro, and Bill Maurer (eds). *Gender Matters: Rereading Michele Z. Rosaldo.* Ann Arbor, MI: University of Michigan Press, 2000. A number of younger anthropologists reevaluate the ideas of Michelle Rosaldo concerning gender, feminism, and masculinity.

Schreck, Harley. *Community and Caring: Older Persons, Intergenerational Relations, and Change in an Urban Community.* Lanham, MD: University Press of America, 2000. Deals with the care of the aged in Minneapolis, Minnesota.

SUGGESTED WEBSITES

http://www.globaled.org/nyworld/materials/african4.html A discussion of age grades and age set in Mali, West Africa.

http://www.retirement-living.com This website is a guide to retirement living in the United States, presenting all of the possibilities that are available.

http://hermaphrodite.arriba.net An individual who characterizes himself as an "intersexual," deals with sexual indentities that differ from the usual male/female distinction.

http://www.radford.edu/~gstudies/sources/gsources.htm A site that provides Internet sources and links to other sites that concern a whole range of topics relating to women, men, masculine studies, and gender expectations.

8

Production, Distribution, and Consumption

The Economic Organization of Societies

The socialist British author George Orwell characterized capitalist industrial society as one in which the economy dominated all other aspects of life. Paraphrasing Paul the Apostle, Orwell mocked our contemporary life, stating, "Though I speak with the tongues of men and angels and have not money . . . I am nothing. . . . And now abideth faith, hope, and money, these three; but the greatest of these is money." The point that Orwell was making is that money has become the medium by which all things—labor, land, services, sex, time, art, votes, and even love—have come to be measured, bought, and sold in Western society. This increasingly has come to be the case, as the cultural principle referred to as market mentality has spread through every aspect of modern and postmodern society. This means that in capitalist society, where a market mentality predominates, a person has absolutely no worth other than his or her monetary worth. This is true even more today than it was in Orwell's time. For example, Senator Mitch McConnell argued that money equals free speech, and that when one restricts campaign distributions, one is restricting freedom of speech. In the film *Wall Street*, the villain, Gordon Gecko, orates, "Greed is good." What Gecko is saying is that greed motivates people to work very hard in order to get ahead in the business world. Today's corporate executives, like Jack Welch, formerly CEO of General Electric, are seen as operating unscrupulously, lying, cheating, and deceiving because greed guides their behavior. Congress is now investigating this kind of behavior. It may be immoral, but not necessarily illegal. As Western ideas and industrialization have spread to other parts of the world, so has the Western idea of market mentality. As we shall see later, market mentality was not characteristic of the societies that anthropologists used to study, nor of Western society at a much earlier time.

In this chapter, we will discuss production, that is, how societies produce the goods necessary for maintenance as ongoing entities. We will describe how kinship groups and societies are linked to one another by systems of exchange and distribution, like the potlatch, the *kula*, and the market. Kinship groups and societies can never be examined as isolates except for purposes of analysis. The societies we will be discussing in this chapter have become part of the world system, in one way or another, as we will describe later and then in more detail in Chapter 13. Economic organization is also concerned with consumption.

The economic organization of a society is how that society, in a regularized fashion, goes about providing the material goods and services it needs to reproduce itself. Economic organization is a cultural construction that operates according to sets of cultural rules. Human and animal labor, man-made technology, and natural resources are brought together for the provisioning of society. Rules relating to economic organization are similar to rules that govern the other aspects of culture. Individuals may interpret the rules to their own advantage. In economic terms, this is known as *maximizing*. In small-scale societies economic behavior operated to a large extent within the context of the kinship structure. In such situations, rules governing who owns the resources, how work is organized, who uses or eats the product, and so forth, were governed by kinship rules. As societies expanded in scale, economic behavior was separated from the realm of kinship, and economic institutions became more and more delimited as separate systems. Though we deal with economic organization, in this chapter, separately from our discussion of political organization, the subject of the next chapter, the two topics are intertwined. Economic decisions always have political implications, and political decisions likewise have economic implications, as reflected in the term **political economy.**

For purposes of analysis, we will consider economic organization in terms of production, distribution or exchange, and consumption.

PRODUCTION

Production is the process whereby a society uses the tools and energy sources at its disposal and the labor of its people and domesticated animals to create the goods necessary for supplying society as an ongoing entity.

Technology is that part of culture by means of which people directly exploit their environment. Technology encompasses the manufacture and use of tools according to a set of cultural rules. Tools are "embedded" in culture so that they relate to and impact on other aspects of culture. Hence, the symbolic meanings of the artifacts are important. The elaborate yam house and canoes in the Trobriand Island are significant symbols of chiefly power. This is true not only for the finished object, but the process of manufacture also has religious and symbolic meaning.

Today, the anthropology of technology includes the study of tool manufacturing and use not only in small-scale and in prehistoric societies but also in modern industrial societies, despite the differences in the types of tools. Hence, production design and development has recently become a subject of anthropological research (see Suchman, 2001: 163–178; Aronson, Bell, and Vermeer, 2001: 179, 193).

Hunting and Gathering

For the greatest time of their existence on earth, some 5 million years, human beings subsisted by means of a combination of hunting wild animals; gathering roots, seeds, and plants; and fishing and collecting sea life along the shores. This mode of exploitation of the natural environment is referred to by anthropologists as *hunting and gathering*.

It represents "a mode of existence characterized by the *absence of direct human control* over the reproduction of exploited species and little or no control of . . . the behavior . . . of food resources" (Panter-Brick et al., 2001: 2). There are some investigators who suggest that hunting-and-gathering societies represent an amalgam of traits that were associated with this particular type of subsistence base. These include individual autonomy regardless of gender and age, extreme eqalitarianism, relatively loose attachment to the group as a result of the pattern of mobility, and a set of beliefs that are fluid and dynamic. This enables them to readily adapt and alter ways under changing circumstances (Kent, 1996: 13–14). Obviously this circumscribes a category or a type, which applied to actual hunter-gather societies to a greater or lesser extent.

Conway makes a distinction between foragers, who move relatively often and return to their residential base daily and consume what they have found, and collectors, who move less often. Collectors are to be found in environments where resource availability varies in space and time. They practice resource storage and sometimes process resources at a special-purpose field camp from which the processed resources are transported back to the base camp (Conway, 2000: 40). Another variation was in the diet of hunter-gatherers. Humans have explored an enormous range of wild foods. In terms of nutritional value, meat—in particular, large game animals—provided the greatest food value per weight and, not surprisingly, tubers, seeds, and nuts the lowest (Kuhn and Steiner, 2001: 101ff.). Variation in diet also follows latitude, which clearly relates to climate. The degree of dependence on vegetable food declines as one moves farther from the equator. There is more diversity nearer the equator where birds, small mammals, and reptiles complemented the vegetable diet. As one goes north, the percentage of meat rises until one gets to the far north where meat comprises almost 100 percent of the diet (Kuhn and Steiner, 2001: 103–104; see also Jenike, 2001).

By the early twentieth century, when anthropologists began to do fieldwork, they discovered that societies dependent primarily on hunting and gathering were found only in a range of marginal environments. The Inuit (or Eskimo) of the Arctic region, the Pygmies of the Ituri Forest in Zaire in Central Africa, the San (or Bushmen) of the Kalahari Desert in southern Africa, and the Washo of the Great Basin on the California-Nevada border are examples of societies that formerly depended exclusively on hunting and gathering for their subsistence. These hunting and gathering societies occupied very different kinds of environments with very different flora and fauna. Nevertheless, several generalizations can be made about their mode of subsistence. All of these societies had sparse populations with very low population densities. The plants and animals they depended on were scarce or abundant

Buffalo hunters, disguised as wolves, stalk their prey on the Great Plains. The "hunter" on the right is actually the artist George Catlin, sketching the scene in 1832.

according to the seasons. Migratory animal species were absent for much of the year and then present for a short time in superabundance. Similarly, nuts, fruits, tubers, and seeds ripened during a particular time of the year, at which point they needed to be harvested. Hunters and gatherers typically had to exploit all the resources present in their environments in order to deal with variations in availability.

As a consequence, these societies followed a migratory cycle because it was necessary to be in particular areas to harvest what had become available in those areas at that time. While there were regular sites to which they returned every year, they did not have year-round, permanent village settlements. Larger agglomerations of individuals came together when greater amounts of food were available in one locale. This was usually the case when some single food resource was abundant (migratory caribou, spawning salmon, ripening pine nuts, and the like). Religious festivals were frequently held at such times. At other times of the year, small dispersed groups of one or more nuclear families migrated as a unit.

The technology of hunting-and-gathering people was simple in that natural materials taken directly from the environment, such as stone, bone, wood, and sinew, were used; additionally, the manufacturing techniques were relatively simple, involving only a few kinds of operations. Hunters and gatherers had an intimate knowledge of the environment, including animal behavior and the growing patterns of plants. For example, the Inuit hunted seal in many different ways, depending upon climatic conditions, seasons, and seal species. Hunters put to use every part of the animals they captured for food and for the manufacture of a whole variety of goods. In hunting-and-gathering societies, there were no specialists whose only occupation was to make tools. Everyone made his or her own tools. Children were taught how to manufacture tools as part of their education.

Task differentiation was primarily between males and females, with men hunting and fishing while women gathered plants, collected shellfish, and took care of the domestic tasks, such as clothing manufacture, food preparation, and child care. Children began to learn tasks at a young age and at puberty assumed adult economic roles. Individuals who excelled at their tasks (successful hunters or fishers) were accorded respect and prestige, and their advice was often sought. Hunting-and-gathering societies tended not to have social class divisions. Nor did they usually rank individuals as higher or lower in social status.

The environment itself changes as a result of human exploitation. Ecological balance is altered as people harvest those species they utilize. In some societies, an effort was made to limit exploitation of the environment by imposing some controls on the hunting of certain species or animals of young ages. In other cases, the environment became permanently degraded. For example, centuries ago in New Guinea, fire was used as an aid in hunting, and as a consequence the primary forests were destroyed and replaced by grassland, totally altering the ecosystem and the fauna of the area. Today, in the United States, we are suffering the consequences of having overfished halibut and cod on the Grand Banks off Nova Scotia and on the New England seacoast.

Hunting-and-gathering populations were never isolates; they have always had long-term exchange relationships with agriculturalists and pastoralists of the same or different ethnic groups once these other modes of production developed (Headland and Reid, 1989; Bird-David, 1992; Shott, 1992). Before the present upheavals, the Twa of Ruanda were hunters who were part of a hierarchical, castelike structure. They exchanged the products of the hunt with Hutu agriculturalists and Tutsi pastoralists. Archeological evidence supports the antiquity of this kind of interaction. Sites on the edge of the Kalahari Desert show remains of ceramics, iron, and cattle in Dobe San sites from the eighth to the eleventh century (Layton, 2001: 297).

The Kwakiutl of British Columbia, discussed in Chapter 2, are an exception to other hunting-and-gathering societies because of the presence of ranked differences. Their environmental resources were so rich, particularly in sea life, that they were able to support a much denser population than is usual in hunting-and-gathering societies. They had permanent winter villages with wooden plank houses, though they migrated from these villages at other times of the year to exploit particular resources in other areas. They had full-time craft specialization. Their political system was more complex and they had inherited titles and chiefly positions. There are several reasons for this series of differences between the

Kwakiutl, along with other Northwest Coast societies, and hunting-and-gathering societies in other parts of the world. The rich environment of the Northwest Coast provided both mammals and birds; many species of edible plants; numerous varieties of fish, shellfish, and sea mammals; and lastly, but importantly, the several species of salmon that annually spawned in the rivers. The Kwakiutl had highly developed techniques for the preservation and storage of the wide range of products they obtained. This enabled them to produce surpluses; maintain large, permanent village communities; and support a more complex culture. How they utilized the surplus produced for social purposes will be discussed below. Another technological factor important in enabling Northwest Coast societies to reach a level of complexity that included ranking and chiefs was the development of large, oceangoing plank canoes (Arnold, 1995). For example, these canoes, among the Nuchanulth (Nootka), who live on the west coast of Vancouver Island, enabled social interchanges and exchange of goods to take place over wide areas. They were also extremely useful in raiding and warfare, they facilitated hunting of sea mammals and fishing for various kinds of ocean fish, and they permitted the ease of movement of household goods and house planks from one village site to another.

How Contemporary Hunters and Gatherers Have Adapted to the Modern World

Hunting and gathering as an economic endeavor and a way of life still continues today. The environment is still an important source of subsistence for people in Alaska, northern Canada, and Siberia. But even in these areas, it is always combined with other kinds of economic activities, in mixed economies (Hitchcock and Biesele, 2000: 6). Foraging provides subsistence as well as market-oriented items to be sold for cash, which is used to purchase manufactured items. Foragers depend on human labor, are closely attached to the land, have common property resource management systems, and have a world view that combines nature with spiritual phenomena (Hitchcock and Biesele, 2000: 7). People who still pursue a hunting-and-gathering mode of subsistence as a part-time endeavor use such modern tools as rifles, steel traps, and snowmobiles. Since mineral and petroleum deposits have been found in some areas where foragers traditionally lived, they have had to cope with the problem of whether and to what degree they will accept commercial development of these resources, while promoting conservation and the survival of their ecosystem. This modified mode of subsistence is always integrated, to a greater or lesser degress, into national and international economies. Though the Kwakiutl and Nuchanulth still fish, their catch of halibut or salmon goes to the cannery or fish market. Then it can be sold locally, or it is sent to other parts of the world since they are now an integral part of the Canadian economy and beyond that, the world economy. Most of the food they eat is purchased at the store with money they have earned.

The Mbuti of the Ituri forest of Zaire have begun a commercial meat trade whereby they sell meat to town dwellers. The meat not only provides animal protein but is valued by the town people because it seen as a source of "wild power" not obtained from fish or domestic animals (Ichikawa, 2000: 269). The Misstassini Cree of eastern Canada still spend part of the winter season in multifamily communal dwellings in the forest, trapping animals with modern steel traps. The skins of the marten, lynx, mink, and weasel they trap end up in the fur markets of New York. When protesters demonstrate against the wearing of fur coats because it represents what they see as the needless killing of furbearing animals, this directly affects the livelihood of Cree families.

This controversy is similar to the Inuit problem with animal rights groups who are against the "large-scale industrial" harvesting of seals, particularly harp seal and hooded seal pups in the North Atlantic. These groups argue that the Inuit should use traditional technology and should restrict use of the products of the hunt to subsistence only. The Inuit argue that their tradition centers on maintaining a way of life in the same environment as in the past. To be Inuit today means to maintain traditions, such as sharing the products of the hunt within kinship networks. Traditional religious beliefs can be practiced within an economic system that includes modern hunting equipment as well as other products of modern technology. They sell part of their harvest to purchase store-bought items (Hovelsrud-Broda, 1997). In an even further extension of globalization into the Inuit hunting-and-gathering economy, Inuit sell the right to hunt walruses to white trophy hunters at $6,000 a piece. Inuit guides lead the trophy hunter up to the walrus, who dispatches it with one well-placed shot, carefully avoiding the tusks and the head, which the white hunter takes. The Inuit crew butchers the carcass in the traditional manner, intestines and all, to be stored and eaten throughout the winter by the entire Inuit community (*New York Times Magazine*, August 25, 2002). The Inuit contrast with the Amish, who reject the products of modern technology, such as automobiles, electricity, and even zippers.

Subsistence use and marketing of "wild foods" is primarily a concomitant of rice production in parts of Southeast Asia (Price, 2000: 191–207). These wild foods are harvested and marketed, for the most part, by women. In northeast Thailand, where production of glutinous rice ("sticky rice") is subsistence oriented, wild foods are not only central to the family diet, but are also marketed locally. These foods include insects, wild plants, frogs, paddy field crabs, and fish. Besides rice fields, these foods are also gathered in house areas, public and private swamps, ponds, canals, and forests. The women marketers of wild foods decide, themselves, how to spend the money they earn from marketing, though they sometimes consult other family members on these purchases. In central Thailand, where a new method of rice production has been introduced, wet direct-seeded rice with the use of herbicides, the number of wild food plants has been reduced from twenty to two. Wild vegtables are now grown in gardens.

In northern Thailand, women's income from selling wild foods is as significant as the amount of money earned from producing rice; hence, northeast Thai women who market wild foods are more independent than those who do not and depend on the income of their husbands. However, because of the use of pesticides in high-productivity rice areas, women can no longer earn such substantial incomes, and this has served to marginalize their position in the production of food for market.

There is no indigenous society in the world that has not been affected by the domination of colonialism and neocolonialism. Yet they seem to have a "dynamic adaptive potential," enabling them to resist the economic predations of the world system (von Bremen, 2000: 275). The Ayoreode of the northern Gran Cacao near the border between Paraguay and Bolivia were hunter-gathers up until the late 1950s, resisting sustained contact with the outside world as long as possible. Today, with the exception of one small group, all have become wage laborers in the mission stations or in the cattle and agricultural businesses of nonindigenous people, participating in the market economy of the area. Their adjustment to modern conditions is within the context of their existing explanatory system of beliefs. The new phenomena with which they are confronted, like new material goods and the Christian belief system, are reformed within the context of their mythic belief system. The new environment is a given to which they have to adapt. Formerly it was a matter of "finding" food by hunting and gathering, while today one must "find" the means and goods to satisfy basic needs (von Bremen, 2000: 280). The Ayoreode recognize the need to deal with the changes forced by colonization and participate as social actors, rather than becoming objects of external manipulation by development workers. By begging, agriculture, and wage labor, they acquire or "gather" resources necessary for life.

Ecotourism and the development of national parks have also impinged upon the lives of hunters and gatherers. In the nineteenth century, Miwok inhabitants had been killed or driven out of the Yosemite area, which made it appear as "virgin territory" and suitable for the establishment of a national park. The indigenous inhabitants were driven out to enable the establishment of Yellowstone National Park. In Australia, the traditional practice of controlled burning has been incorporated into the management of Kakadu and Uluru National Parks, and the park rangers have reached a degree of cross-cultural understanding that enables them to accept the fact that "traditional owners had retained the necessary skills . . . , [and] applied them systematically" (Layton, 2001: 311).

AGRICULTURE

The domestication of plants and their use for subsistence, beginning some 8,000 to 10,000 years ago, represented a significant transformation of human society. This change depended upon the development of a new corpus of information by which human beings acquired much greater control of the environment and, in turn, transformed it in a much more significant way than had been done by hunters and gatherers. Social groups were tied to territories differently than they had been with hunting and gathering. With a shift to dependence for subsistence upon domesticated plants, social groups utilized a smaller area—population was more dense and was concentrated in hamlets and villages. Agriculturalists are much more in control of the productive process than are hunters-and-gatherers. We have noted that the exploitation pattern of hunting-and-gathering societies was seasonal. Agriculturalists also operate on the basis of a seasonal cycle, especially where there is a marked climatic difference between winter and summer or rainy and dry seasons. The year is usually divided into planting time, growing time, and harvest. Audrey Richards (1961), the British social anthropologist, pointed out that the several months before harvest are known as the "hungry months" for the Bemba of Central Africa, who depend primarily upon their crop of millet. Even when they are under the threat of starvation, agricultural people must restrain themselves from eating their seed or they will have no crop during the following year. Agriculture includes horticulture, which deals with root crops, and grain agriculture. The factors to be considered in an examination of different economic systems based on agriculture include how people utilize their labor, how they work the land, how they use water resources, which crops they grow, and whether they grow crops for their own subsistence or for sale in the market.

Horticulture   Throughout lowland South America and Melanesia, the mode of production is based upon crops that are grown through vegetative propagation, using a part of the plant itself, rather than through the planting of seeds. These crops are grown in gardens, and this form of cultivation is known as **horticulture.** Systems of production based upon horticulture vary in terms of the number of crops grown in a garden, the length of the fallow period, and whether the water necessary for plant growth is controlled. A continuum of New Guinea societies reflects greater and greater complexity of horticultural techniques for cultivating gardens and achieving higher crop yields and more permanent gardens. The simplest form of horticulture, known as the **swidden** type, or **shifting cultivation**, involves making gardens by burning down the forest and planting the garden in the ashes, which act as a fertilizer. No other means of fertilizing is used. Because the soil is rapidly exhausted, a new garden in a new location must be planted every few years—hence the name shifting cultivation. Gardens contain many kinds of plants on a single plot, and a digging stick was often the only tool used for cultivation. This kind of horticulture is supplemented by both hunting and the collection of wild plants. In lowland New Guinea, the sago palm, a wild plant whose pith is used for food, is an important supplement to what is produced in the gardens. For example, as much as 90 percent of the diet of the Tor in western New Guinea may come from wild sago. Their sparse population makes them like the hunting-and-gathering societies, though they live in villages surrounded by their yam gardens.

The Abelam of New Guinea illustrate an intermediate type of horticulture. Many varieties of short yams, taro, sweet potatoes, and a range of other plants are grown in gardens that are used several times and then allowed to remain fallow and uncultivated. The Abelam also grow a special species of long yam, which may be eight to ten feet long and is used in ceremonial exchange, described later in this chapter. Its cultivation involves special techniques, such as mounding the soil to create a plant bed and erecting trellises for vines. Soil around the growing point may be carefully loosened to allow the tuber to grow. Abelam villages are much larger and more permanent than those of the Tor.

The most complex forms of horticulture in New Guinea are found in the mountains of the central highlands. There, people like the Enga use a variety of labor-intensive techniques. The gardens may be used for a generation or more. Each garden is made of a regular series of mounds separated by ditches. The mounds are formed from soil and mulch and are used only for sweet potato cultivation. These single-crop gardens are separated from mixed gardens in which most other crops are grown. The yields from the mounded gardens of the Enga are considerably greater than the yields from the two types of horticulture described earlier. Enga society numbers over 150,000, so there is considerable pressure for land, and Enga clans may fight one another for land. The complex exchange system of the Enga, which will be described below, is linked to their great productivity. The horticultural systems just described depend upon rainfall for water. However, root crop cultivation can involve water control. The Dani of the Grand Valley in western New Guinea have used dams, ditches, and drainage systems to turn a natural swamp into a productive cultivation area.

Just as hunting-and-gathering peoples have intimate knowledge of the plant and animal species that they exploit, horticulturalists display an extensive knowledge of soils, food plants, and cultivation techniques. This practical know-how is frequently combined with magical practices performed during the process of production.

The simplest kind of swidden horticulture is practiced by sparse populations that live in widely separated villages and control access to land. As horticultural techniques become more intensified, gardens become more permanent and population density increases. There is increased competition for good land, and warfare is frequently waged by one clan to drive another from its land. Today, in Papua New Guinea, these subsistence horticultural practices are supplemented by the extensive cash-crop production of coffee in the New Guinea highlands and by coconut production for oil to manufacture soap in the lowlands and the Bismarck Archipelago.

Grain Agriculture   In the more temperate areas of several continents of the world, grain is the focus of swidden agriculture—maize in the New World, millet and sorghum in Africa, and rice in Asia. In preparing fields for growing grain, the same technique of cutting down trees and burning off brush is used as in swidden horticulture. There is also a long fallow period after several plantings. The only source of water is rainfall.

Agricultural societies in much of Europe and Asia depend on a technology that involves crop rotation and the use of the plow drawn by draft animals and of animal manure as fertilizer. Wheat, rye, and barley are the predominant crops. A system may be employed whereby fields are divided, so that some are used while others lie fallow for a year. The use of draft animals requires raising crops such as hay to feed those animals. Grain agriculture dependent on the use of elaborate irrigation systems, developed millennia ago, is much more extensive than the type of water control practiced by the Dani, which we have mentioned above. An enormous input of labor is required to create the necessary artificial environment of lakes, ponds, dikes, and terraces that comprise the irrigation sys-

Drying coffee, grown for export, in the New Guinea highlands.

tem. The advent of irrigation systems was associated with urban civilizations and the development of states. Increased productivity per acre of land, the basis for increasing cultural complexity, depends on several factors. Establishing elaborate irrigation systems initially requires great outputs of labor; maintaining them also requires a certain amount of labor. The crops on which people subsist also vary in terms of their storage potential, which affects how crop surplus will be utilized for social purposes (which we will discuss more fully in the section on distribution later in this chapter). The nature of the technology utilized is also an important factor. Steel axes and machetes are more efficient than stone axes. Animal labor is more efficient than human labor, except in places of high population density, like China. Machines and the mechanization of agriculture, as has occurred in the United States, represent a quantum jump in efficiency and therefore in productivity.

Each technological advance produced its own set of problems. Mechanized agriculture, for example, has resulted in overproduction and the need to store vast agricultural surpluses; the use of chemical pesticides has led to widespread pollution of soil and water. In the United States, fewer farmers grow more and more food, and the family farm has become a corporation and may even be listed on the stock exchange.

AGRICULTURE IN TODAY'S WORLD

Today, "globalization and the new international division of labor" have resulted in the penetration of the outside world into the lives of people in rural areas throughout the world (Barlett, 1999: 5–6). There is an international flow of goods and of technological information and new political forms that serve as challenges to local ways of life. The effects of globalization may include changes in local political structures and in gender relations, sometimes resulting in more economic power for women, as well as changes in economic formations. But local people have responded in a variety of ways and such connections do not always mean a loss of local power.

Among the Asante, an ethnic group with matrilineal descent dominating the forest area of Ghana in West Africa, both men and women actively farm. Men grow coca, which is exported, and both men and women participate in commercial food production for Ghanaian cities and to provide food, including tomatoes, cassava, eggplant, plantains, and yams, for those farmers who specialize in coca and other cash-crop production (Clark, 2000: 253–270). The expansion and diversification of the food-crop marketing network provided centers where food crops, locally produced, are marketed. Traders of food are predominantly women, and they control the marketplaces. In addition, women dominate food farming. The flexible market system with its many marketplaces not only supplies food stuffs, but also provides a market for secondary crops and craft products that are "fall-back" options for the periods when crop production suffers in bad years. Women farmers, suffering from gender disparities in resource allocation, restricted from the planting of cocoa, and discouraged from expanding their farm, have diversified into food processing and trading (Clark, 2000: 259–260). Female farmers and traders gain income from trading and are able to demonstrate their personal autonomy in the agricultural and commercial sectors.

Throughout Java, the colonial system emphasized the production of products for export even within the sector of peasant subsistence agriculture. In the postcolonial period, this involved engagement with the "development" plans of whatever political regime was in power. As a consequence of this process, the To Pamona of Central Sulawesi were forced by the Dutch colonial government to move from their hilltop hamlets, where they practiced swidden cultivation, to narrow valleys to develop *sawah,* irrigated or wet rice agriculture. Despite their engagement in a market economy, they maintained their earlier multifamily households, feasting pattern, and gift exchange (Schrauwers, 1999: 105). This limited capital accumulation and resulted in a "Janus-faced" economy, which is seen by the Indonesian state as hindering development.

The major thrust of the Indonesian government has been to move subsistence agriculturalists, many swidden agriculturalists, down to the plains where they can practice wet-rice agriculture. There they are to use the products and techniques introduced by the "green revolution" to produce a market crop—rice—which can be exported. For those remaining in the uplands, development was introduced in the form of fruit tree farming to serve the new wants of the increasingly affluent urban population. This shift, as well as the investment of capital for seed stock and the like, served to introduce social differentiation among the producers (Suryana, 1999: 257–278).

ANIMAL DOMESTICATION

In most areas, the domestication of animals followed soon after the domestication of plants. In the Old World, a wide variety of animal species were domesticated, most of which furnished meat and milk. Some animals, such as the horse, donkey, bullock, and buffalo, were also used for transportation. The hair of others, such as sheep and goats, was woven into cloth. In the New World the only significant animal domesticates were the camelids, such as the llama and alpaca. The process of domestication involved a shift in the biological characteristics of the animal species, since the animals were selectively bred to enhance those characteristics that make the animal more controllable and more useful to humans and to eliminate characteristics such as intractability. In a sense, humans have shaped these animals through the process of domestication. At the same time, pastoral societies adapted to the needs of their animals, particularly in the migration cycle followed.

Societies that are completely dependent upon their domesticated animals are known as **nomadic pastoral societies.** Only rarely do they cultivate. This is a specialized mode of subsistence that developed from an earlier economy that included domesticated plants and animals. Nomadic pastoral societies, with one or two exceptions, were found in Old World, particularly in arid zones. Sheep, goats, camels, horses, cattle, yaks, water buffalo, and reindeer constituted the basic herd animals for these societies. All these animals are social, not solitary, in their habits. In most cases one or two types of animals formed the basis for herds. This is a way of life, much more widely practiced in the past than in the present. However, as we shall see below, when governments try to end this way of life they face opposition. Nomadic pastoralists depended upon their herd animals for a range of products. Daily yields of milk and the products made from milk were central to the diet. The wool and hair were also important for making cloth. Nomadic pastoralists were never solely dependent on their pastoral products. From earliest times, live animals, wool, and milk products were exchanged by the pastoralists for essentials, such as tea, sugar, and flour, with sedentary people. Since wealth was measured in numbers of animals in the herd, pastoralists were loath to kill animals for their meat alone; therefore, this was done only on special occasions.

The nature of animal care varied. Some domesticated animals foraged in the bush for their food but returned to places of human settlement at night; other domesticated animals were kept in pens and depended on humans for their entire care and feeding. The mithan, a type of domesticated ox found in Southeast Asia among the Nagas and Chin of Myanmar, was allowed to roam freely, depending completely upon forage for food. Only its meat was used, and then only on ceremonial occasions. In contrast, in Europe, the dairy cow, a relative of the mithan, was kept in a stall and fed with fodder, or on ranges in an enclosed pasture, and was milked daily. The dairy cow and the ox were part of the mixed farming complex in Europe and North America. In the American west, cattle were allowed to range freely, being rounded up once or twice a year and moved to market to be sold and used for meat.

The animal species upon which particular nomadic pastoral societies depend is related to the nature of the environment that is exploited. Some species, such as camels, are best adapted to arid desert areas, and others, such as horses, to well-watered grassy plains. Some can withstand extremes of temperature, while others cannot. Some, such as goats, do best in steeper mountain environments, while others, such as water buffalo, can live only on flat, swampy lowlands. The way of life of nomadic pastoralists involves seasonal movement or migration in a regular pattern from one place to another. The community and its herds may move from summer to winter pasturage or from wet to dry locations. In their seasonal movements, pastoral nomads resemble hunters and gatherers, particularly those who hunt large herds of migratory animals, such as the caribou. However, there is a crucial difference in that hunters followed the migratory herd wherever the herd went in its natural migration, whereas the herds that belong to the nomadic pastoralists follow the people who herd them.

Nomadic pastoralists herd different species utilizing a range of environments. The most widespread form of pastoral nomadism involves the herding of sheep and goats. Excellent examples are the Basseri, Bakhtiari, and Qashqai, pastoral nomads in Iran. Their migration cycle takes them from winter pasturage in the southern lowlands, roughly at sea level, to summer pasturage in the Zagros Mountains, at an altitude of 10,000 feet. The sheep herded by the Basseri are so adapted to the migratory cycle that they can survive neither the cold winters of the mountains nor the torrid summers of the lowlands. In addition to sheep and goats, the Bakhtiari have in their herds a species of cow that is small and agile and can make the arduous migration. Though most societies have nomadic pastoralism as their dominant mode of production, combinations are frequently found. For example, the Bakhtiari practice some agriculture and hunting and gathering in addition to nomadic pastoralism.

The Marsh Arabs of Iraq, who inhabit the swampy area at the confluence of the Tigris and Euphrates rivers, rely completely on their herds of water buffalo. Since they depend solely on the buffalo, they must trade the dairy products produced from the milk of their buffalo for grain and other foodstuffs from sedentary peoples, who are culturally the same except for mode of subsistence. The watery environment of the Marsh Arabs is a sharp contrast to the desert zone of the Arabian plateau inhabited by another Arabic-speaking group, the Rwala Bedouin. In the past, they were mainly herders of camels, but they also had some sheep, goats, and horses. The camels were herded by men and boys, often at some distance from the nomadic camp. The products of the camel included milk and hair, but even more important, the animal was a mode of transportation. The Rwala bred camels for sale to sedentary oasis dwellers and to transporters who needed the animals for long-distance caravan trade. The seasonal cycle of the Rwala involved moving into the desert in the spring, when available water has allowed grass cover to grow. As the year progressed, the climate became drier, and the Rwala moved closer to the desert oasis sources of water. Since goats and sheep as well as camels were herded, the Rwala needed to be mindful of the water requirements of all these animal species.

In the savanna grasslands of West Africa, between the Sahara and the tropical forest area to the south, the Fulani practice still another form of nomadic pastoralism, one that is dependent solely on herds of cattle. The cattle are a long-horned variety of zebu with a humped back. The migration pattern is from the northern desert fringes in the wet season to the well-watered borders of the tropical forest of the south in the dry season. The availability of grassland is not the only determining factor in the migratory pattern; another consideration is the distribution of the tsetse fly, which is a carrier of sleeping sickness and whose territory they try to avoid. The Fulani are dependent primarily upon the milk from their herds and milk products such as clarified butter. They migrate within an area containing villages of sedentary grain-growing agriculturalists with whom they trade their milk products for grain in the marketplace.

From the seventeenth until the twentieth century, Mongolia was ruled by the Manchu dynasty of China. In 1911, the Mongolian nobility declared independence and Bogd Khan, who was both a political leader and head of the Tibetan Buddhist Church, became the new head of state. In 1921, the Mongolian Revolutionary Party seized control of the state with the support of Soviet troops. Monastery herds, which were huge, were distributed to families. However, collectivization of the pastoral sector did not occur until the 1950s (Humphrey and Sneath, 1999). Collectivization involved the detailed establishment of joint work teams, the organization of herd movement, the introduction of new breeds of sheep, and the production of hay in some areas for use as fodder (Humphrey and Sneath, 1999: 110). Pastoralism also became more mechanized.

Pastoralism in Mongolia depended on a mix of horses, sheep, goats, camels, and sometimes cattle. Before the revolution, pasture land was held in common, though its use was sometimes controlled by lords or monastic leaders. Later, pasture land was controlled by the collectives and the state planning bureaus, which also owned herds, machinery, and the like. Herders have always dwelt in yurts or *gers*, using dried dung for fuel. All of the different animals herded are milked, with the milk being used to make an alcoholic drink, *kumis*, and a great variety of cheeses. Flour, tea, tobacco, and other products came from the outside as a consequence of trade in pastoral products. During the period of the collectives, control of animals, herd movements, and pasture use as well as marketing was done by the collective, and people received wages and then pensions.

CAN NOMADIC PASTORALISM BE MAINTAINED TODAY?

A series of economic factors have brought about significant transformations in the way of life of nomadic pastoralists. Sheep and goat herders in Iran and in Syria no longer migrate with their herds. Instead, they move their animals and their belongings from one pasture site to another by truck, rather than using traditional draft animals like camels or donkeys. They need not even set up camp near a water

Milking a mare outside a Mongol encampment.

source, since tank trucks bring water to wherever they set up camp, which may even be next to a highway. The Rwala no longer raise camels, since trucks have replaced the camel as the principal means of transportation in the desert.

Most nomadic pastoral societies have undergone great changes under political pressure from the governments of their nations and as a result of wars, revolutions, and famines; thus their way of life is no longer as we have described it above. The homeland of the Marsh Arabs became a major battleground of the Iran–Iraq war in the 1980s and was a center of military activity during the Gulf War. The long period of drought in the Sahel seriously affected the economy of the Fulani and has forced them to sell their herds. The nomadic groups of Iran were forcibly sedentarized by Reza Shah in the 1920s in order to exercise political control over them, resulting in the loss of their herds and livelihood. Migration was resumed after the abdication of Reza Shah in 1941. Sedentarization was attempted again by Mohammad Shah, Reza's son, in the 1960s, with the same disastrous results. There is no information on how the nomadic tribes of Iran have fared since the Khomeini revolution. Since nomadic pastoral peoples usually occupy marginal lands that are not suitable for agriculture, when they are forced to sedentarize, usually for political reasons, we often find them returning to nomadic pastoralism when political pressure is relaxed.

This has been the case in Mongolia. After the Soviet state fell, Mongolia held elections in 1992 and the communists lost. However, many of the elected leaders are from the families of former leaders. Privatization of the herds had begun in

1990 with the adoption of the Mongolian privatization law. The number of herders has increased since that time, though the quality of livestock has fallen as a result of climatic disasters over the past few years. As a consequence, many Mongolian pastoralists have returned to a subsistence economy. District heads try to control the "adminstration of pastoralism" but with little success. There are companies from which individuals receive wages for caring for some of the company-owned flock and as advances for products produced, but many herders belong to no organization. Because of the extensive availability of pasture and the low rate of stock per pasture, Mongolians have been able to avoid degradation of the environment, which remains relatively unpolluted. They still keep large herds of horses. There is no market for horses; they represent prestige items. There has also been a reduction in the use of fodder since the end of collectivization. Herders today are better able to plan their migrations because of their knowledge of how different grass species grow and the behavior of animals. There is now much more economic diversity in Mongolia, including the multimillionaire who has made his money from entrepenurial activity and who lives next to a very poor household (Humphrey and Sneath 1999: 110, 114, 132–133).

Sometimes, people pursue a mix of different forms of production. The Dolgan and Ngansan, two indigenous groups who live in the northcentral forest tundra area of Siberia east of the Yenesei River in the former Soviet Union, had a prerevolutionary economy that was an interesting mix of reindeer herding, hunting, fur trapping, subsistence hunting and gathering, and trade (Zicker, 1998). After the revolution, they were gradually collectivized, forming fewer, larger reindeer collectives over time. In 1970, the two groups were sedentarized into the community of Ust Avam, as reindeer herding had become less viable as a way of life. Men still hunted caribou, fished in the lakes and rivers, and trapped animals for their pelts, primarily for subsistence. There were still 50 to 60 professional hunters who lived in state housing and maintained a high standard of living. The state provided them with the necessary tools, and each hunter had to provide the state with a certain number of caribou, Arctic fox pelts, and fish each season, which was destined for a larger market; the hunters received a salary in exchange (Zicker, 1998: 196).

During the present transitional period, there is uncertainty as to what will eventually happen to this state enterprise. Severe budget cuts, nonreplacement of tools, and gasoline shortages, as well as the cessation of many rural enterprises, have resulted in a much heavier reliance on the products of local subsistence—hunting and fishing. Meat and fish beyond subsistence needs are shared with consanguineal and affinal relatives, since many in the community are related to one another. Friends, neighbors, and those who may be in need may also receive meat. In 1992, then President Yeltsin signed a decree that enabled the establishment of family/clan holdings for the "aboriginal people of Siberia." Only a few families have legal control of their ancestral lands. These individuals, interestingly, had holdings near industrial cities, enabling them to become involved "with external sources of capital and energy in recent years" (Zicker, 1998: 230). Even these families, though they have become oriented toward money making, still participate in the sharing of the products of the hunt with the other members of the community.

The Organization of Work

The productive tasks performed by men and women are culturally determined in all societies, as noted earlier. In hunting-and-gathering societies, there was a sexual division between the female domain of gathering and collecting and the male domain of hunting. Often the gathering activities of women provided the bulk of the food on which the group subsisted. Nevertheless, the products of the hunt brought back by the men represented the most desirable food, and hunting was a more prestigious activity than gathering, reflecting the relative valuation of male and female roles in the society. As we observed in the chapter on gender, the productive tasks assigned to men in one society may be assigned to women in another. In some New Guinea societies, such as the Tor, women cut down the sago palm to get its pith, while in other societies, such as the Abelam, men do this. In our own society today there are many tasks that men formerly performed that are now performed by women.

In both male and female domains, some work tasks are done individually and others in cooperative groups. The hunting of herd animals, such as caribou by the Nunamiut Eskimo and wild peccary by the Mundurucu of Brazil, was carried out communally. However, for species in which the animals tend to move individually, hunting was done on an individual basis. Gathering and collecting by women also tended to be done on an individual basis. It would seem that working communally is more pleasurable than when each person goes off to work by himself or herself. Myanmar (Burmese) women who work together at the different tasks involved in the manufacture of silk sing as they work. Volga boatmen sang as they pulled the ropes that moved the boats up the river. In our own society today many people have left their offices where they worked on particular tasks, usually as part of a large, multinational company. They now work as freelancers or consultants out of offices set up in their homes. The invention of computers, e-mail, and FedEx has made this possible. This goes against the pattern of communal work. Will it last?

In societies whose mode of subsistence involves the cultivation of crops, men tend to be concerned with the preparation of the garden plot or field, and also with water-control systems if these are present. Both men and women may be involved in planting, weeding, and harvesting. In New Guinea societies a clear distinction is made between certain crops, such as bananas and sugarcane, which are referred to as male crops, and other crops, such as sweet potatoes, grown by women, referred to as women's crops. When plows and mechanized agricultural implements are introduced, the whole range of agricultural tasks usually becomes the province of men, and women, if they are involved in agricultural tasks at all, are limited to growing vegetables in gardens. As we have noted earlier, men tend to be involved with cash crops and women with subsistence crops. In nomadic pastoral societies, the task of herding and moving the camp is in the male realm, while women milk the animals and manufacture milk products.

The organization of work in a society relates to the nature of postmarital residence and the formation of kinship groups in that society. Cooperative endeavors in which people work communally serve to reinforce the social solidarity of the group. When the most important subsistence tasks for a society are performed by men acting cooperatively, the residence pattern after marriage tends to be virilocal, whereas when the tasks are performed by women working together, the postmarital residence pattern tends to be uxorilocal. As we shall see in Chapter 9, on political organization, the way that work is organized is often also part of the political system. Chiefs, in societies where they were found, were frequently instrumental in organizing certain kinds of production. For example, Trobriand chiefs organized the activities of their clan members in building a canoe, and Kwakiutl chiefs organized the members of their *numaym* when they build a new house.

THE ORGANIZATION OF WORK IN CONTEMPORARY SOCIETIES

The organization of work in contemporary societies has also become the subject of investigation. In many societies over the world today, more and more women are leaving their homes for full- or part-time work. In our discussion of gender we saw the way in which Yoruba and Asante women dominated the marketplace; this is also true in other parts of the world. Javanese market culture, for example, seems to be gendered in that women play a substantial role in the more localized small-scale trading that occurs, while men are more frequently the "wholesalers" (Alexander, 1998).

Women have, over the past few decades, become more and more significant in the labor force of various countries in Latin America. In these countries, as working women increased in number, their participation in decision making within the family became more and more significant. However, in a study of decision making of working wives versus nonworking wives in Mexico, it was found that "working wives do not have more power within the household than non-working wives" (Casique, 2001: 154). If the husband or wife are better educated or if the couple live in an urban environment, the wife will have more power and more of a role in making familial decisions. Age is also a factor in increasing autonomy for women in both urban and rural areas. Responsibilities for housework are the wife's regardless of whether she is working or not. Though working contributed to an increase in autonomy for wives, because of the maintenance of the traditional "patriarchal values," there was a maintenance of unequal relationships between husbands and wives, and women were not "empowered" (Casique, 2001: 158).

DISTRIBUTION

Distribution is the manner in which cultural products circulate through societies. What is of concern in discussing systems of distribution or exchange is who gives what to whom, when, where, and how. As we shall see below, the structure of the distribution of material goods is sometimes identical to the structure of relationships between groups established by marriage, which we described in Chapter 6. In every society, the system of distribution is determined by the operation of cultural rules and the way in which individuals in the system interpret them. Even where distribution of goods is carried out in markets, such as in our own society, supply and demand are culturally construed.

Market exchange is different from other forms of exchange, and it operates according to its own principles. All of the exchange systems we will discuss below have been penetrated to a greater or lesser degree by market exchange and globalization. Certain general principles apply universally to the other systems of exchange we will describe below. Exchange may be broken down into three components: giving, receiving, and returning. When an object is offered, the process of exchange begins. It may be accepted or declined. If the object is accepted, then its equivalent must at some point be returned. The acceptance creates a relationship through time, until the return is made. The refusal to accept creates a relationship of a negative sort, diametrically opposite to the relationship created by acceptance. Giving, receiving, and returning constitute a process over time. From the initial offer until the return, two individuals or two groups are linked to each other in a relationship. The acceptance of something offered constitutes the assumption of an obligation to return—recipients place themselves in debt to the givers. If such indebtedness continues for a long period of time or if goods go repeatedly in the same direction and are not returned, the recipients become inferior in their own eyes, as well as others, and the givers superior. Giving, receiving, and returning create links, since exchange may be the basis for seeking assistance, recruiting allies, and creating alliances. But there is also an aggressive component since the process usually involve competition. Recipients who are in an inferior position and cannot return may even perceive the initial offer as an aggressive act designed to shame them in the eyes of others. Some analysts see *"deception as an integral part of exchange"* (Gerschlager, 2001: 8). In fact the word for exchange in German, *tauschen,* is similar to the word for deceiving, *täuschen.* One might add that deception is present, in particular, in market exchange. An old expression, going back to Roman times, says *caveat emptor*—let the buyer beware! Though exchange may be perceived primarily as an economic phenomenon, in fact, it is frequently linked to the political structure and differences in rank, hence the utility of viewing these conjointly as political economy.

Earlier in the last century—before globalization, development, and all the things that contact with Western societies and subsequently colonialism wrought—societies in many parts of the world had very distinctive ways of organizing their social life, as well as their exchanges, ritual and otherwise, which occupied varying amounts of their time. We have pointed out several examples, like the To Pamona of Indonesia and the Dolgan and Ngansan of Siberia, who have been drawn into the global market and at the same time retain traditional exchanges and ritual obligations of gift-giving to their affines.

After ethnographic information was gathered about many of these societies by anthropologists' fieldwork, comparative research—that is, comparing and contrasting different aspects of these societies—revealed that there were many similarities. This enabled anthropologists to recognize a limited range of structures or forms, which were to be found in very different places. Below, we will describe these structures of exchange and provide examples of how they operated in different societies.

DISTRIBUTION IN EGALITARIAN SOCIETIES

Several types of exchange systems characterized egalitarian societies, societies in which rank differences were absent. The simplest type of exchange system involves two sides, of equal status, in continuing exchange with each other. The two sides can be two parts of a village, two clans, or two moieties. This type is referred to as **reciprocal exchange** (see Figure 8-1). It is identical to the exchange of women in marriage referred to as direct reciprocal exchange (see pages 137–138).

Reciprocal exchange characterizes the exchange system of the Abelam of New Guinea, whose mode of production has already been described in this chapter (Kaberry, 1940). Their reciprocal exchange system involves only the exchange of goods between moieties, since they do not have direct sister exchange or bilateral cross-cousin marriage. The moieties are not named, but are referred to as "us" and "them." The Abelam live in patrilineal clan-hamlets that are paired with one another. Men in one clan-hamlet have *tshambura,* or partners, in another clan-hamlet, with whom they exchange. Earlier, we talked about the special gardens in which men alone grow long yams solely for purposes of exchange. These yams are of a different species than the subsistence yams grown by the women and are selected and bred for their great length. The head of the clan uses his special magical knowledge to make the yams grow very long. He himself must abstain from sexual intercourse for the whole growing period of the yams, since sexual contact with women will prevent the yams from growing long. The strength, prowess, and magical power of the group is measured by the length of their yams. Under the supervision of the leader of the group, the yams are carefully harvested and individually decorated with flowers, feathers, and masks. They are then displayed at the ceremony, from which all women are barred, where they will be distributed to the exchange partners of the group. All the important men from surrounding hamlets are present as witnesses to the exchange, and they partake of the feast that accompanies it. The giver of the yam keeps a record of the length

FIGURE 8-1

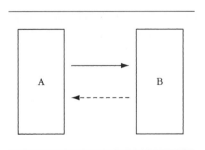

Decorated long yams, wearing masks, are displayed before exchange by the Abelam.

and circumference of that yam. The yam given in return must be the equivalent of what has been given. The return is not immediate. It is delayed until the group that has received is ready to give. Exchange partners also exchange pigs and perform important services for one another in connection with the initiation of their respective sons (Rubel and Rosman, 1978). Reciprocal exchange systems such as that of the Abelam exhibit the following characteristics: They involve two sides that are equal in status. Though they may compete to outdo one another in their continuing exchanges, the rule of equivalence in exchange keeps that sort of competition in check. Each side needs the other, since they perform important services for each other at boys' initiation.

More complex systems of economic distribution develop when changes occur in the rules of exchange. When more than two groups are involved in exchange, the pattern becomes significantly different from that of reciprocal exchange. Delays in the exchange also operate in these kinds of systems. The Maring of the New Guinea highlands have a system of economic distribution or exchange that involves one host group distributing simultaneously to a number of other groups (Rappaport, 1984). These groups are equal in status. The distributive system is part of a religious ceremony referred to as the *kaiko,* which extends over many months. A group of closely related patrilineal clans serves as hosts of the *kaiko.* The guests

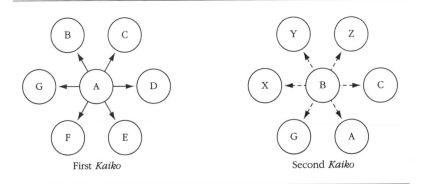

First *Kaiko*   Second *Kaiko*

FIGURE 8-2 *Kaiko* exchange

at the *kaiko* come in groups from the surrounding territories (see Figure 8-2). The host group intermarries with these neighboring groups and is allied with them in times of war. Guests come brandishing their weapons and singing war songs. The dancing performed by both guests and hosts involves an aggressive display. The aggressiveness occurs despite the fact that guests and hosts intermarry, are allied to one another, and distribute food and valuable goods to one another. A great number of pigs are killed by the hosts, and cooked pork is distributed at the final *kaiko* event. Production is directed toward amassing pigs for the *kaiko* distribution. Each of the guest groups, who come from a wide area, will in the future hold its own *kaiko*, at which it will fulfill its obligations to make a return. The Maring distribution system involves not two groups, as in reciprocal exchange, but rather one group giving to many groups at the same time. All groups are relatively equal in status. The host group is invited in turn to the *kaiko* that each guest group will hold in the future. Despite the fact that the Maring are involved in plantation wage labor and grow some coffee for sale, they continue to hold the *kaiko* up to the present (LiPuma, 2000: 197ff., 202)

More complex systems of exchange link groups in chains so that goods move from group to group and serve to tie together an entire region. This is an example of **generalized exchange,** and it is identical to the structure of generalized exchange created by marriage with mother's brother's daughter. The *Te* distribution system of the Enga, whose production we have already described, is of this type (Meggitt, 1974). Enga patrilineal clans, occupying contiguous areas, fight with their neighbors but also exchange women and goods with them. People who are affines may also become exchange partners, or *Te* partners, to one another. Instead of giving to all one's *Te* partners in many clans at the same ceremony, as is the case for the Maring, an Enga man will have two groups of *Te* partners, one set in clans to the east of his clan and a second in clans to the west of his clan. He transmits goods he has received from his eastern partners at their *Te* ceremonies to his western partners at the *Te* ceremony that his clan hosts, and vice versa (see Figure 8-3).

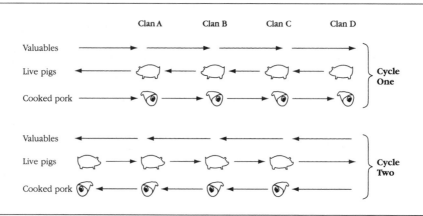

FIGURE 8-3 Enga *te* exchange

The Enga have a system of delayed exchange in which goods move from one group to the next until they reach the end of the chain, when they must reverse and go down the line in the opposite direction. People who were givers of valuables such as stone axes, shells, plumes, and small pigs in the first stage become receivers of live pigs in the second stage. Live pigs move down the chain as they are distributed at successive *Te* distributions held in turn by each clan. At the end of the chain, there is a second reversal, when the last receiver of live pigs becomes the first distributor of cooked pork. The distribution of cooked pork completes one cycle of the *Te* (see photograph). It will begin again when initiatory gifts go in the direction opposite to the pork. Built into the rules of the *Te* is the delay in the return, since goods must go down the entire length of the chain through successive *Te* ceremonies before the *Te* partner to whom clan A has given live pigs gives cooked pork back to clan A.

Giving and receiving in the *Te* exemplifies the ambivalence seen in exchange in general. Clans who are neighbors, though potential enemies to one another, are dependent upon one another to pass on the objects of the *Te*. If warfare does break out in the middle of a *Te* cycle, the *Te* is disrupted. It is in the interest of *Te* partners in other clans to make peace between the combatants so that goods can continue to move along the *Te* chains. The Enga production system, as has been shown above, is based upon the intensive cultivation of sweet potatoes, used to feed the large numbers of pigs in the *Te* as well as people. The Enga value their pigs greatly; yet their distribution system sends out the pigs that they raise along a line of exchange partners until the pigs eventually come back as roast pork (Rubel and Rosman, 1978). The value they place on their pigs is what the pigs in size and number will bring in renown when they are distributed to one's exchange partners. It seems that the Enga no longer hold the *Te*.

Sides of cooked pork are displayed on an enormous platform, 90 feet long, before they are distributed at an Enga Te ceremony held in the summer of 1974.

SYSTEMS OF EXCHANGE IN SOCIETIES WITH FLEXIBLE RANK

In our general discussion of the principles of exchange, we noted that continued indebtedness on the part of the receiver could lead to status differences, with the giver becoming superior and the receiver, who is unable to repay the debt, placed in an inferior position. The kinds of exchange systems in the societies we have discussed so far stressed the equivalence in status of groups that constitute givers and receivers. There are, however, societies in which rank differences, which are an integral part of the political structure, played a significant role in the exchanges. Here we will be dealing with societies in which the rank of individuals and groups is constantly subject to modification.

The Kwakiutl wedding potlatch, described in Chapter 2, was a kind of distribution in which rank and rank differences were central to the exchanges. Theoretically, every person in Kwakiutl society holds an inherited rank position, associated with a name owned by his or her *numaym*, or cognatic descent group. However, rank can be raised through potlatching, or lowered by the absence of potlatching. The Kwakiutl used a number of rite-of-passage events as occasions for potlatches, ceremonies at which large amounts of food and property were distributed to assembled guests. Great quantities of food and goods must be accumulated in preparation for a potlatch. One hundred years ago, this meant gathering and storing smoked salmon, olachen grease (oil from the candlefish), berries, and other food, and accumulating blankets and other valuables such as jewelry, masks, and even canoes, referred to as "trifles," as described in Chapter 2. Potlatches may be hosted by one *numaym* or by a group of *numayms*, or tribes. At each potlatch, the person whose rite of passage is being celebrated receives a new name. A succession of potlatches was held for a great chief's son as he grew older; at each one he got increasingly more important titles until at the most important potlatch he assumed the name that entitled him to the position of chief.

The guests who come to a potlatch serve as witnesses to the event, for example, the succession to chiefly power, and receive goods for this service. The guests, affines of the hosts, are seated according to their rank and receive goods in that order. The guest *numayms* must at some future time reciprocate by making a return potlatch. Kwakiutl potlatches were sometimes described as if the motivation for them was competition and the desire to shame one's rivals. But all exchange involves some form of competition, as well as deceit. Since guests at a Kwakiutl potlatch are also affines, the Kwakiutl potlatch is no more competitive than some other examples of affinal exchanges. The exchanges at a Maring *kaiko* and an Enga *Te* are also between affines, like the Kwakiutl potlatch, and they also exhibit aggressiveness. Even when valuable coppers were "destroyed" by being cut by the giver who is the host, as described in Chapter 2, the receiving chief, who is challenged by this act, thanks his host for doing this. One must hold a potlatch in order to raise one's rank, but one needs equally high-ranking competitors to challenge. Once again, as in all exchange systems, the givers and receivers are dependent upon and need one another, while they are competing with one another. In addition, the potlatch provides a mechanism for redistributing the productive resources of Kwakiutl society.

By the end of the nineteenth century, the time period for the wedding potlatch described in Chapter 2, the Kwakiutl were involved in the Canadian cash economy. The goods distributed at potlatch ceremonies came to include, in addition to Hudson Bay blankets, power boats, sewing machines, tea cups and saucers, and other goods from the Euro-Canadian economy purchased with wages from work in fish canneries, logging, and other kinds of employment. During this period, the potlatch was outlawed by the Canadian government because such large-scale distributions and the destruction of property that sometimes occurred were seen as going against the Protestant ethic, which supported the modern Canadian capitalist economy and which missionaries and government officials thought the native population should emulate. However, potlatches continued to be held in secret. The prohibition against holding the potlatch ceremony ended in Canada in 1951, and since then, large-scale potlatches have been held on occasion by many Kwakiutl groups.

The potlatch as a form of ceremonial exchange was found in other Native American societies on the Pacific coast of Canada and Alaska, like the Tlingit, but took a somewhat different form depending on the nature of the kinship system of the society. While the Kwakiutl have cognatic descent and *numayms*, the Tlingit have a social structure based on matrilineal descent, matrimoieties, matrilineal clans, avunculocal residence, and a preference for marriage with father's sister's daughter. This means that each Tlingit clan intermarries with two other matrilineal clans, both of them in the opposite moiety (see Chapter 6, Figure 6-11).

Chiefs in ceremonial garb wearing their crests at a Tlingit potlatch in Sitka, Alaska, held at the turn of the twentieth century.

While the Kwakiutl held potlaches on the numerous occasions marking the growth and increased achievement of a person, the Tlingit had basically only one occasion for a potlatch. When a chief died, his heir, his sister's son, sponsored a potlatch, which included the various rites of the funeral, and assumed the title, name, and political position of his mother's brother. He also had a mortuary totem pole erected (see the totem pole pictured in Chapter 5). The two other matrilineal clans who intermarried with the host clan came as guests to the potlatch since they had performed important services for the host clan. One clan built a new house for the heir, and the other clan buried the dead chief and erected the totem pole in his honor.

The Tlingit and Kwakiutl potlatches are both systems in which large amounts of goods are accumulated by chiefs with the help of their kin groups specifically for the purposes of ceremonial distribution to other groups. However, potlatches take place on occasions that relate to the differences in social structure and marriage rules in cognatic and matrilineal societies. The potlatch system of economic distribution operates through the kinship system, which provides the links through which the flow of goods is channeled.

The Trobriand Islanders, whose system of production is very different from that of the Tlingit, hold *sagali,* or large-scale ceremonial distributions of yams and other foodstuffs. The distributions are structurally identical to the potlatches of the

Tlingit, though they take place on two occasions, not one. Like the Tlingit, the Trobrianders have matrilineal clans, avunculocal residence, and father's sister's daughter marriage (see Chapter 6, Figure 6-11). Trobriand funerary rites include the mortuary *sagali*, a distribution to the clan of the wife of the dead chief in exchange for all the funerary services provided by clan members. This is the same pattern as the Tlingit potlatch. Contenders for the chiefly position compete to be the organizer of the funerary *sagali*. The Trobrianders also hold a *sagali* when the chief's sister becomes pregnant. It is her son who will succeed to the position of chief in this matrilineal society. The guests at a pregnancy *sagali* are the father's lineage of the chief and his sister, who have performed various services for the chief's sister during her pregnancy and are receiving the ceremonial distribution of food, yams, areca nuts, and bananas in exchange. Among the Trobrianders, the two clans that intermarry with the host clan are guests at two separate *sagali*, a funeral *sagali* and a pregnancy *sagali*, whereas in the Tlingit potlatch these two groups of guests are present at the same time but are seated on opposite sides of the house (see Chapter 6, Figure 6-11).

As is the case for most societies, the Trobrianders had several types of exchanges. In addition to *sagali*, there is a distribution of yams called **urigubu,** which occurs after every harvest. Marriage initiated this annual payment of yams, the *urigubu*, by a man to his sister's husband (see Figure 8-4). The *urigubu* yams are displayed in a yam house that is built by a man's brother-in-law, who will be giving him the yams. The Trobrianders have the mixed garden and the taro garden for their own subsistence, and the main yam garden to produce the *urigubu* that goes to the sister's husband. At harvest time, the accumulating piles of yams are displayed and then ceremonially carried to the house of the sister's husband in another village and presented to him to be stored in his yam house. Meanwhile, the giver of yams will in return be receiving yams from his wife's brother. Great care and productive effort are given to these particular yams, which will eventually be given away. Yams for *urigubu* represent the prestige of the giver as a gardener and as a kinsman fulfilling an obligation. Yet these yams are consumed by households other than that of the producer. To market economists, the most rational, economically efficient system would be for everyone to grow and then eat his own yams. The *urigubu* distribution system of the Trobrianders makes sense only in terms of their social system. The *urigubu* is paid to the husbands and fathers of the matrilineal lineage for carrying out the important social role, not the biological role, of father, since in the past Trobrianders did not believe that fathers

FIGURE 8-4 Urigubu payments

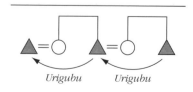

played a role in conception. Malinowski referred to *urigubu* as economic tribute for chiefs since they take many wives, up to 20 or more, given to them by village headmen in their districts. The chief uses the yams to make *sagali*. With so many brothers-in-law, the chief accumulates many yams after each harvest, which he then redistributes as rewards to his followers on the various occasions for feasts (Malinowski, 1935).

In addition, at harvest time, there are competitive yam feasts, called **kayasa,** between villages. The game of cricket played by the Trobrianders, discussed in Chapter 5, is part of the competitive *kayasa* being held between villages.

Kula exchange is still another important form of Trobriand exchange. The *kula* exchange system links the Trobriand Islands with a circle of other islands that are different culturally and linguistically and that the Trobrianders considered dangerous places because warfare and cannibalism were endemic in precolonial times (see Figure 8-5). The goods exchanged in the *kula* are two kinds of shell valuables—red shell necklaces, which are exchanged from island to island so that they move clockwise around the circle, and white armshells, which move counterclockwise. Men sailed their small native crafts to the islands of their *kula* partner, but nowadays use motorboats. According to the rules of the *kula,* those who are to receive in the exchange always undertake the voyage to the givers' island. To receive armshells, the Trobrianders would sail east in a clockwise direction to the island of Kitava. To receive red shell necklaces, they would sail south in a counterclockwise direction to the island of Dobu. Thus, *kula* partners are always exchanging red shell necklaces for armshells, and vice versa, but never armshells for armshells or necklaces for necklaces. *Kula* exchange is identical in structure to generalized exchange, that is, the structure of matrilateral cross-cousin marriage described in Chapter 6.

The exchange of shell valuables in the *kula* created alliances between groups living in potentially hostile areas. While the *kula* exchange, with its elaborate ceremony, is being carried out, direct barter of food, pottery, and other manufactured utilitarian objects is also taking place between the *kula* visitors and their hosts. Barter, as noted earlier in this chapter, involves the exchange of items that are scarce or absent in one place but not another. For example, when the Trobrianders go for *kula* objects to the Amphlett Islands, they bring food, plentiful on their island, to exchange for the pottery made there. The rules of *kula* exchange require a great deal of ceremonial behavior, while the accompanying barter is just the opposite. *Kula* exchange is delayed, and barter is immediate; *kula* does not involve bargaining, while barter involves trying to get the best deal for oneself, as occurs in market exchanges. Barter is never conducted with one's *kula* partners but, rather, with others on the island that one visits.

Over the past decade the results of ethnographic field research with the Trobrianders and others in the *kula* area, as well as ethnohistorical research, seem to point to the following conclusion: Since the Massim area before extensive contact with Europeans was an area of chronic warfare, the precontact *kula* exchange system alternated with warfare, and the *kula* system described by Malinowski operated as it did because of European pacification (Keesing, 1990: 152). This

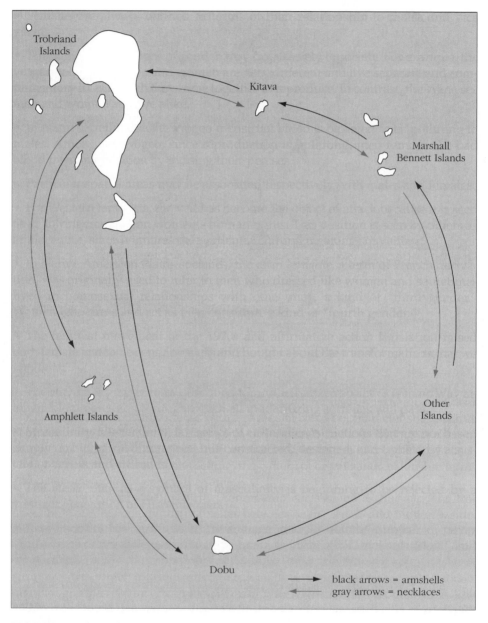

FIGURE 8-5 The Kula ring

 *Armshell valuables, which have been brought from the island of Kitava, are to be given to* kula *exchange partners on Trobriand Island. Photographed by Malinowski during his 1914–1918 fieldwork.*

relationship between *kula* exchange and warfare appears to parallel that between warfare and the Enga *Te* exchange described earlier.

These exchange systems, though somewhat modified, continue to operate among the Trobrianders today, though they are now citizens of Papua New Guinea (Schiefenhovel and Bell-Krannhals, 1996). A recent description of *kayasa* on Kaileuna (not the island where Malinowski or Weiner did fieldwork) indicates that it is now a contest among men of a village to see who can grow the most yams (Schiefenhovel and Bell-Krannhals, 1996). One man will offer prizes for the winners. The *kayasa* organizer uses this as a means of increasing his prestige. Chiefdomship is still a matter of ascribed status, but success in competitive events like the *kayasa* is also an important element (Schiefenhovel and Bell-Krannhals, 1996: 249). Visitors come to the final stages of the ceremony as witnesses. *Urigubu* is also a matter of competition, since men gain prestige from giving large amounts of *urigubu*. Two men may also compete in the growing of special long yams called *kuvi*, whose tubers have enormous dimensions. This kind of competition in the growing of *kuvi* may also be the means of settling quarrels. Though Trobrianders today travel in fiberglass boats and are Christians, "in many respects the Trobrianders of today seem to have stepped from the pages of their famous ethnography" (Schiefenhovel and Bell-Krannhals, 1996: 236).

Though the horticultural mode of production of the Trobrianders is markedly different from the fishing, hunting, and gathering mode of the Tlingit and Kwaki-utl, all three have flexible rank systems. All three societies produced economic surpluses, despite the differences in mode of production. In these societies, distribution of goods at potlatches and at *sagali* serves to enhance one's rank and prestige. Goods are given to chiefs by their followers in their kin groups as a kind of tribute which is redistributed on ceremonial occasions. When the chief serves as a host at such a ceremonial redistribution, he validates his claim to high rank. The acceptance of the redistributed goods by the guests means they recognize this claim. Rank in these societies is flexible, in that the more one distributes, the higher one's rank becomes.

Systems of Exchange with Fixed Rank

When rank differences are permanent the nature of exchanges is significantly altered. In such systems, aristocrats are separate from commoners, lords from vassals, patrons from clients, and high castes from low castes, as occurs in India. The groups in particular systems differ not only in rank and prestige but also in the economic resources that they control. Societies with fixed rank systems also have economic specialization and a permanent division of labor. The systems of economic distribution always emphasize the inferiority of vassal, client, commoner, and low-caste individual, and the superiority of aristocrat, lord, patron, and high-caste individual. When superiors give to inferiors, the act is seen as generosity or largess. When inferiors give to superiors, it is considered tribute. No matter how much tribute the inferiors give, it does not raise their status; it merely further enhances the prestige of their superiors. At the same time, the greater generosity and continual distributions of the superiors enhance their status, not that of the inferiors. These cultural formulations are not contrary to the principle of exchange in which the person who receives more than he returns becomes lower in status. Rather, it is a demonstration of the way in which the social structure and political organization determine the meanings of the exchanges. If the lord is defined as superior, his superiority is demonstrated both when he gives and when he receives. Objects given by inferiors as tribute and objects that are the largesse of aristocrats are usually different types of objects. They derive their cultural meanings solely from the status of the giver, whether the goods move up to a higher-ranked individual or down to a lower-ranked individual.

In precolonial times, the Bunyoro of western Uganda had a fixed system of rank with its concomitant system of economic distribution. Among the Bunyoro, the king granted rights over land and over those who cultivated it to chiefs as a reward for service (Beattie, 1960). Chiefs visited the king to give him tribute, which consisted of cattle, beer, and grain. The king, on his part, gave frequent feasts. For special services, the king might also give cattle to particular individuals. The chiefs stood in the same relationship to their commoners as the king stood to the chiefs. Commoners brought tribute to the chief, and the chief gave feasts. The Bunyoro also illustrate a point made in Chapter 5 about the symbolism of food. Tribute always seemed to be paid in the form of food in its uncooked form, raw or on the hoof, while the generosity of superiors took the form of feasts or cooked food.

In India, castes are endogamous, highly specialized occupational groups. In any particular place, all the castes form a system in which members of the various castes perform their services for one another under the supervision and control of the landholders. The castes are hierarchically ordered, from the Brahmans, who are priests, at the top, to the untouchables, who are tanners, washers, and sweepers who carry away human excrement. Though Indian castes are relatively fixed in rank, individual castes may disagree on their placement within the system. Today they quite frequently attempt to change their position with respect to other groups. As we noted earlier in Chapter 5, caste members may start to eat food formerly forbidden to them.

Where rank differences in the social system are fixed, we find economically specialized occupational groups that are tied together in an interdependent system of economic exchanges. Economic subsistence in these societies is completely dependent upon exchange. Distributions in egalitarian societies serve to create and maintain ongoing social relations between groups that are equal in status. In societies with flexible rank, distributions allow different groups to improve their rank. Distributions in societies with fixed rank maintain the status of some groups over others.

The different types of exchange systems we have discussed are all related to particular types of political organization. This is why many anthropologists prefer to talk about political economy, reflecting the interrelationship between the two.

BARTER

Barter is a type of distribution that conforms in part to principles of exchange. It involves direct, immediate exchange, always of different objects. As a consequence, barter does not create ongoing relationships. It usually involves goods and commodities that each party does not have in its own environment. Occurring within a context governed by cultural rules, it includes haggling and bargaining (Humphrey and Hugh-Jones, 1992). These characteristics make barter much more like monetary exchange.

Since barter usually does not create or lead to continuing social relationships, it is often seen as the most simple and direct type of exchange. However, in recent years barter has appeared in the collapsed ruins of former communist economies in Eastern Europe. It is particularly important in Russia and the other republics that have replaced the Soviet Union. In these areas, barter is currently employed in what formerly were planned socialist economies that used money and credit. In Russia, barter increased from 5 percent of GDP in 1994 to 60 percent in 1998 (Marin and Schnitzer, 2002: 2). According to Marin and Schnitzer, "Barter trade has become a dominant phenomenon in the domestic economies of the former Soviet Union" (2002: 103).

Why has this transformation from money to barter occurred? The most common reason given for using barter, rather than cash, is that the buyer simply doesn't have cash. Money is in short supply. However, this appears to be a common excuse offered, and it may not be true. Other common reasons are that people have no trust in the value of money, and that payments in goods are faster than payments in cash (Marin and Schnitzer, 2002: 123). Banks today are mistrusted and avoided. "It is feared that they may crash or arbitrarily freeze personal accounts" (Humphrey, 2002: 77). Finally, many contemporary economic transactions are of a shadowy, criminal character. Barter helps in evading taxes, circumvents customs procedures when importing goods, allows for the use of fake documents and fake contracts, and for payment of "presents" for the service of solving problems (Seabright, 2000: 310).

How does this system of widespread use of barter work? A business will pay its electric bill with young fruit trees (or other produce that it obtains). Since farm produce is raised on a yearly cycle, the "seller" may have to wait till harvest time to receive the goods. Even if manufactured goods are involved, the "seller" of some products may still have to wait until they are available to receive his or her return. The result is that this type of barter is a form of delayed exchange (Humphrey, 2002: 78). One side is in debt until the goods become available. Unlike the simple form of barter in which exchange is immediate—like the yams exchanged for pots, which occurs alongside *kula* exchange—Russian barter depends on trust, since the return isn't made until sometime in the future. It is more like the potlatch, *Te,* or *kula,* all of which also depend on some degree of trust. This requires working and exchanging within a community (called a "suzerainty" by Humphrey) and having a powerful and successful boss who can protect you from the authorities (Humphrey, 2002: 18). This is particularly important when most of this economic activity is marginally criminal.

For the tribal people of Siberia, like the Evenki (formerly called Tungus), present-day barter has some of the characteristics of their exchange system of sharing and gift-giving to one's affines. Under the Soviet system, the Evenki, who are reindeer herders and hunters and gatherers in the Siberian taiga forest, were collectivized. Before that, under the Czar, taxes were collected from the Evenki, who were reduced to a form of serfdom (Ssorin-Chaikov, 2000: 358). In their traditional system, the hunter cannot eat game that he has killed. Today, their furs are given to intermediaries in a form of gift-exchange. The Evenki hunter gives it to a nonrelative, or trader. The same term for affine is also used for trader. The hunter receives a countergift of flour and other food supplies, which the community shares. What one side (the trader) perceives as barter, the other side perceives as gift-exchange with one's "affine" (Ssorin-Chaikov, 2000: 359). It is not uncommon for two sides in a relationship to perceive that relationship differently.

THE MARKET SYSTEM

The term *market* has two meanings. The first refers to the location, or site, where food commodities and craft items are bought and sold. The second meaning characterizes an entire economic system based upon the determination of prices by the market, that is, in terms of supply and demand. This is the only exchange system with which Americans are familiar. Its characteristics are different in many respects from those of the exchange systems we have discussed so far. Perhaps the most distinctive feature of market exchange is that the buyer need have no other social relationship with the seller. While one may deal with the same grocer, butcher, supermarket, or stockbroker over many years, one may shift overnight and carry out the same transactions with another store or stockbroker. The relationship between buyer and seller is not dependent upon any other relationship but has its basis solely in the fact that the seller has something that the buyer wants or needs and is willing to pay for. The relationship can even consist of a single purchase, never to be repeated. The basic premise of a market system is to make a profit, and the essence of profit is to buy cheap and sell for more than you have paid. Transactions in a market system are governed by bargaining, or haggling over price, rather than determined by social relationships. In haggling, a buyer tries to buy something as cheaply as possible. This is in contrast to a Kwakiutl potlatch, where the more that is given, the greater the prestige of the giver. In the market system, the buyer gives as little as the seller will accept.

A market system depends on the presence of money. Societies that did not have market systems did not have money in the usual sense of that term. Money serves a number of purposes. It can be used as a standard of value, because any commodity, service, or labor can be expressed in terms of its monetary worth. Money can be used as a store of value, because it can be hoarded and used later to obtain commodities or services. But most important, money can serve as a medium of exchange, whereby one commodity can be converted into money and then that money can be used to exchange for any other kind of goods or services. The money used in our society is considered all-purpose money, because it can be exchanged for anything in the society, as noted at the beginning of this chapter, and serves all the above uses and others as well. The valuables discussed in connection with ceremonial distribution, like the armshells and necklaces in the *kula*, are objects that have value but can be used only for particular ceremonies, such as the *kula*. The restricted uses to which such valuables are put is in sharp contrast to the many purposes that money serves.

Markets served to articulate peasant communities with the economy of the city, when cities first arose some 5,000 years ago. There are different kinds of market structures. One kind of market structure links a number of different peasant communities to a central market town. In addition to its subsistence activities, each of these communities may specialize in a different craft activity, such as weaving, manufacture of pottery, or manufacture of tiles. People from each of these communities come into the market, often once a week, to sell their wares and to buy the goods, frequently of Western manufacture, which they require but do not make for themselves. In some places markets are held in different villages and towns on successive days of the week. In places like the Golden Triangle area of Myanmar (Burma) the Five Day market moves between five different villages

Tribal women coming into the five-day market in the Golden Triangle region of Myanmar (Burma).

during the week. The sellers are primarily women from tribal villages, who come to the market in their tribal dress to sell garden crops and food (see photograph). Western products like sneakers, shoes, shirts, jackets, and baby clothing are also sold. The same items are sold in all the villages that make up the Five Day market. The buyers are from surrounding villages. These kinds of marketing structures define a region.

CAPITALISM AND THE MARKET ECONOMY

Capitalism and what is characterized as the market economy have been around for many centuries. As Collins notes, "It is a dynamic economic system that is accumulative and expansive. Once established, its tentacles spread and envelop peripheral societies both in industrial nations and in those at the margins" (2000: 1). This spread of capitalism is referred to today as **globalization.** It means not only the penetration of entrepreneurship, technology, technological knowledge, and modes of production, but most recently, also the development of multinational corporations and the movement of capital to most places in the world without concern for national boundaries or different currencies. The establishment of global institutions like the World Trade Organization, the World Bank, and the International Monetary Fund has had an impact in many parts of the world. Not only do the tentacles of capitalism spread from the Western world to other societies, but they also spread from economic institutions to other institutions like religion, politics, and the art world.

Even a fishing community in Malaysia can be effected by the expanding global economy (Kedia, 2000: 40–51). The ethnic Malay fisherman have large families that they must support from the sale of fish harvested under recently instituted fishing licenses for fish and gear. This restricts the amount of fish caught in order "to balance sustainability with the fishermen's needs" (Kedia, 2000: 50). However, the establishment of factories in the area has brought about inflation in the price of basic food items. The desire for piped water, electricity, and telephones, and the costs for children's education, which is now deemed desirable, and other items formerly considered luxuries have placed strain on family income because of the need for more cash. The inflation in bridewealth (the exchanges accompanying engagement and marriage), the "new consumerism" (meaning the inclusion of nontraditional Western items as part of such exchanges), and the greater elaborateness of marriage feasts have also increased the need for money (Kedia, 2000: 48). Notions of whether fishing is a desirable occupation are also being questioned as the need for increased income rises. A study of fishermen in a community like New Bedford, Massachusetts, would reveal many of the same economic factors, such as declining fish yields, declining income, and increased costs for family maintenance and college education for children. People feel that they should remain in the community where they grew up and not move to where jobs are, despite a worsening economic situation.

In a market economy under capitalism, all economic behavior is evaluated in market terms, with individuals making decisions in order to cut the best deal for themselves. Anthropologists have been interested in the factors that determine how decisions are made and whether these decisions are based exclusively on expectations of economic gain or loss. Such studies often assume that individuals make rational choices for themselves and that their purpose is always to maximize their own position. In a market economy, labor also operates according to the laws of supply and demand. Workers go to places where employment is available. If a factory closes, its workers are expected to move freely to other places where work is to be found. In Europe, this sometimes means moving to another country. If an industry like that of manufacturing TV sets in the United States loses out to foreign competition, the workers in that industry are expected to retrain themselves for positions in other industries. Much of the world today operates as a single market. However, what is good for workers manufacturing sewing machines in the modernized economies of Taipei or Hong Kong creates hardships for workers who have lost their jobs as a result of the closing of a plant manufacturing sewing machines in Elizabeth, New Jersey.

Whereas in nonmarket economic systems, the economy is embedded in a larger cultural matrix, the growth of a market economy in an industrialized capitalist society marks the development of an economic institution that is separate from other institutions. Nevertheless, capitalism and the market system must be seen and understood in terms of the cultural matrix with which it is associated. The Japanese and Americans both manufacture cars within capitalist market systems, but there are differences in these two cultures in factors such as the social organization of factories and the relationships between managers and workers. In our country, the capitalist mode of the economy sets the tone and the values for other institutions. The economy influences morality. The axiom "What's good for business is good for the country" illustrates this point. Some people even believe that if a few bribes or kickbacks are necessary to conduct business, then bribery is not immoral, especially if the bribes are given to individuals outside the United States. At first, social scientists assumed that market economies operated rationally and were not influenced by cultural factors. However, now they recognize that the economy is "embedded" and "Japanese capitalism may be quite different from Chinese, and both in turn from American" (Hefner, 1998: 11). Business as it is conducted by overseas Chinese in Southeast Asia, for example, is based on particularistic relationships in which family as well as reciprocal relationships known as *guanxi* are significant in the conduct of business. The traditional family firm as a basis for conducting business has given the Chinese in Southeast Asia the edge over the less commercially oriented Thai, Javanese, Malay, Burmese, or Vietnamese (Mackie, 1998: 129). The small- and medium-sized Chinese family businesses in Taiwan underlie Taiwan's dynamic form of capitalism (Hamilton, 1998). With the development of the global system, these differences in the cultural settings of capitalism and market economies in different countries sometimes causes miscommunication and misunderstanding.

The world system of money and markets has penetrated even the most remote societies. In places such as Papua New Guinea, and other places in the Pacific, it coexists with reciprocal and generalized exchange. The Western economic aspect is called *bisnis* and continuing traditional systems are referred to as *kastom*. The market principle, which is based upon the law of supply and demand, assumes that nothing exists within our society that cannot be purchased with money. However, in our society other kinds of exchanges continue to coexist alongside the market system. We have cultural rules about reciprocal gift exchange. People who give gifts expect to be reciprocated with gifts that are roughly equivalent. Our rules do not require the recipient to return like for like, as the Abelam do. People often bring gifts when invited for dinner. It is appropriate to bring wine or flowers but not considered appropriate to bring a pound of ground sirloin or to give the hostess a $10 bill. This kind of gift exchange is exchange between equals.

Capitalism and market economy also involve other kinds of "gifts." Gift exchange as we have just described it is different from the case of the congressmen who receive gifts from constituents or lobbyists and who are exchanging these "gifts" for influence. The givers of these gifts will have influence in the setting of rules and the passage of legislation favorable to their businesses. Under capitalism, the giving of large monetary gifts can thereby serve to undermine government regulations. Gift giving may also be involved in competition. In the dress industry, gifts may be given by dress manufacturers to the buyers of dresses of a department store chain in order to have the chain buy dresses from that company and not another. The line between giving gifts to lobbyists, which is legal, and gifts to "facilitators" who help in the avoidance of true tax assessment of property, which is not, is a fine one. What one person may call a gift, another will call a bribe.

CONSUMPTION

In its most general sense, consumption means the way in which people use goods that they have obtained. As with other aspects of culture, consumption is determined by cultural rules. There is a relationship between the consumption of goods and the nature of the social system as well as the system of cultural meanings. In the small-scale societies anthropologists used to study, food and other material goods were consumed in relation to subsistence and in the context of ritual. In many instances these goods were grown or manufactured within the local community, but we also saw how yams as *urigubu* were ceremonially moved from one Trobriand community to another. In this example, goods manufactured in one place were ceremonially distributed and then taken to be utilized someplace else. Hence, the aim of production was distribution or exchange. In complex societies, as we shall see below, consumption often stimulates production of more of the same; that is, people's demands for a product stimulate production.

With the development of complex modern industrial society came the notion of the consumer and a narrower definition of consumption. Consumers used goods manufactured by someone else, which are referred to as commodities. Commodities were sometimes further subdivided into goods required for subsistence and luxury items whose acquisition was usually related to high rank or elite status. The anthropological focus shifted to the way such commodity consumption was mediated by global capitalism that had produced the commodities in various places all over the world and how such objects become incorporated into the local scene. Consumption communicates social differentiation. The material goods one possesses or wears mark one's identity (Miles et al., 2002: 3). These material goods define a consumer lifestyle.

Sometimes religious beliefs dictate the nature of product consumption. A visit to Lancaster, Pennsylvania, or Shipshewana, Indiana, the location of Amish communities, will immediately demonstrate the way in which their religious beliefs have dictated the use of horse and buggy rather than car and pickup truck, and the wearing of very modest clothing, blue or black in color, rather than the latest fashion. They still farm and depend on the products of their fields and herds and carefully control the commodities that enter their world. Their religious beliefs dictate what enters and is incorporated into their community. Their sphere of social relations has resisted "commodification." One can find examples of this process in many other parts of the world.

THE CHANGING NATURE OF CONSUMPTION IN THIRD WORLD SOCIETIES

Consumption and consumerism in the Third and Fourth Worlds are sometimes directly related to consumption in the industrialized world. We know what a significant role clothing plays as a consumer item in the West. Styles both for women and men change if not seasonally then yearly. What is in fashion one year is discarded the next. Though clothing is a commodity, its purchase represents an expression of the self. What happens to this clothing when it is discarded? In the United States, some of it ends up in Salvation Army stores to be reused by members of the underclass, who usually cannot afford what is in fashion. Other items may end up in "resale stores" to be purchased by frugal members of the middle class. However, much of it is sold in 100-pound lots by dealers and shipped overseas as part of a global trade to countries in Africa and Asia. One might say that the clothing is sold as a commodity to be "consumed" in the United States. After being used, it is discarded and usually donated to a charitable organization. As part of an international trade, these same items are sent overseas, to Africa and parts of Asia, not only from the United States but from Canada and Europe. Clothing, shoes, hats, belts, and the like, for men, women, and children, as well as linens and towels, may end up as far away as the bazaar in Chakhcharan in the middle of Afghanistan or in markets in Zambia, in Africa. They are recommodified and reconceptualized in their new context. In Zambia, this clothing, discarded by Westerners, is referred to as *salaula* and perceived as a very desirable commodity. *Salaula* means "rummaging," which describes the process whereby buyers select the garments they want to purchase from the opened bales of secondhand clothing that came to Zambia as a consequence of the large international secondhand clothing trade. In Zambia as elsewhere, this clothing also represents self-identity, as well as well-being (Hansen, 2002: 225). It is interesting to note that there have been complaints that this secondhand clothing industry has had a negative affect on the domestic clothing industry and thus on textile production in Zambia. In part, this trade in secondhand clothing marks the impoverishment of Third World peoples from the Western point of view since they are wearing "our" discarded clothing. Yet, at the same time, from the Zambian point of view it represents new styles in the from of the introduction of Western fashion.

The sale of religious objects in Cairo, Egypt, represents the reverse process to what occurs among the Amish, the manner in which "sacred" objects have been turned into commodities (Starrett, 1995). Religious objects are mass-produced in factories, sometimes even in other countries, like Japan, for sale to devout Muslims. Such objects include a wide variety of items, such as copies of the Qur'an in velvet boxes, which are commonly displayed in the back windows of automobiles or taxis. These objects are displayed in order to obtain God's blessing and protection, to ward off the evil eye, and to signal the owner's Muslim identity. There are differences of opinion about such objects, and their religious meanings are contested. Educated Muslims feel that employing such manufactured commodities in this way reduces religion itself to the level of mass consumption. This use of sacred objects, which is very widespread, has produced a backlash among more scholarly Egyptian Muslims, who claim such a use of sacred objects is really resorting to magical charms and is counter to Islamic values.

Sometimes commodification of a particular product for sale in an international market can result in significant changes in a people's way of life. The lives of the Otavalo, indigenous Quecha-speaking people with their distinctive dress and customs, have been significantly transformed as a consequence of their success in the weaving trade (Meisch, 1998). They were weavers and traveling merchants even before the Inca of Peru incorporated the area of Ecuador into their empire. The Spanish created *encomendias*, estates of land and inhabitants granted to Spanish colonists, and made traditional textiles part of the tribute owed to them. In the midtwentieth century the Spanish loom was brought in and the weaving of casimir or woolen tweeds was introduced; the latter became a significant Otavalo product. When mass tourism worldwide began in the 1960s and the extension of the Pan-American Highway to Quito made Otavalo accessible, Indian products, such as scarves, ponchos, shawls, belts, and other clothing (and, later, daypacks and duffel bags), became popular tourist items. Population growth and land shortages in the 1970s and 1980s sent many Otavalos to towns and cities in other parts of Latin America, Spain, and the United States. Weaving workshops and stores were set up, ties being maintained with the home community. All Otavalos are textile producers, though many still plant crops for their own consumption. To the town, tourism meant expansion not only of the marketplace but of restaurants, folk music clubs, and other businesses, from which the indigenous people profited sufficiently to buy property in increasing numbers. Besides sales to tourists "and other Ecuadorians at local markets and in stores throughout the country . . . sales to foreign exporters constitute another large market" (Meisch, 1998: 20).

As a consequence of this prosperity, the indigenous population, now half the population of the town, has transformed the ethnic and power relations in the valley. Wealth always gives the possessor power in a capitalist society, and the financial success of the Otavalos has significantly altered their position in society. They buy the goods of a capitalist society—refrigerators, cars, trucks, stereos—and send their children to universities to be lawyers and doctors (Meisch, 1998: 24–25). Another consequence of this now transnational textile industry has been the increase in the elaborateness of *compadrazgo* fiestas, including the introduction of new dishes and an increase in the number of *compadres* honored (Colloredo-Mansfield, 1998: 57).

In Western capitalist society, consumption has often been associated with gender; the useful and important activities were conducted outside the home by men, while the home was seen as a place of leisure and consumption rather than of productive activities. Income creation is accorded higher value than the transformation of that income into goods and services important to the maintenance of elite status in society; the realm of production is valorized and the realm of consumption denigrated (Beal, 1998: 158–160). Women and their world are devalued and the activity of shopping is seen as an insignificant female endeavor. Among Jordanian elites, shopping is seen as a critical aspect of the female gender role by both men and women; it is associated with women and is essentially women's work. Even though it is evident from their homes that possession of consumer goods in great number is a significant aspect of social life, the activity of shopping is nevertheless seen as essentially trivial by both men and women. Even the shopping activities of professional women who earn their own income is denigrated, while the hunting, yachting, and drinking activities of men, though income-depleting, are not. Since shopping alone, seen as a leisure activity for women, and not the leisure activities of men, is disparaged, it would seem that it is the gendered identity of the shopper rather than the shopping per se that is *the* factor for Jordanian elites (Beal, 1998: 160). Professional women who work in the business world outside the home may denigrate shopping because they are expected to conform to the male idea of what constitutes proper behavior. Jordanian men, though they talk disparagingly about shopping, are consumers themselves, often insisting on choosing the furniture that will decorate the formal, public rooms of the house. The cultural valuation of shopping depends upon the gender of the shopper. Shopping is clearly part of the construction of gender idealogy among the Jordanian elites, and it becomes a means by which female activity and agency can be subordinated and denigrated in contrast to the valorized sphere of male activity (Beal, 1998: 160). This relationship between consumerism, shopping, and gender ideology is interesting to explore cross-culturally. Among Americans, all sectors of society, male and female, seem to engage in shopping and there would no longer seem to be a specific connection with gender ideology.

Earlier studies of modernization and modernity assumed that when Third and Fourth World people adopted the use of money and began to purchase jeans, transistor radios, canned food, and other items of Western manufacture, the result would be either incorporation and a global homogenization of material culture or some form of mass resistance to Western culture. These goods often came to stand for becoming modern, and people could, by the use or nonuse of such objects, signify Americanization and Westernization, or a conscious rejection of such an identification. Sometimes, as on the island of Tanga in Papua New Guinea, modernization and its attendant goods become a separate category, *bisnis,* as we noted above for a wider area, in opposition to *kastom,* that is, those practices continued from the past (Foster, 1992). Frequently, what has happened has been an acceptance and recontextualization of material items. Sometimes objects used in the past have come to stand for a nostalgia for that past and a continuity of identity. The Japanese tea ceremony performs that function for modern Japanese today. The passion many Americans have for collecting toy trains, metal lunch boxes from the 1950s, and antique baseball cards derives from that same sense of nostalgia for the past, loss of youth, and remembrance of a more tranquil period in the nation's history. There is a market for such items, and they have become commodities.

SUMMARY

- The economic organization of a society is how that society, in a regularized fashion, goes about providing the material goods and services it needs to reproduce itself. Economic organization is a cultural construction that operates according to sets of cultural rules.

- In small-scale societies economic behavior operated to a large extent within the context of the kinship structure and its rules that governed who owns the resources, how work is organized, and who uses or eats the product. As societies expanded in scale, economic behavior was separated from the realm of kinship, and economic institutions became more and more delimited as separate systems.

- Economic decisions always have political implications, and political decisions likewise have economic implications, as reflected in the term *political economy*.

- Technology plays an important role in all productive modes.

- For the greatest time of their existence on earth, some 5 million years, human beings subsisted by means of a combination of hunting wild animals; gathering roots, seeds, and plants; and fishing and collecting sea life along the shores, using a mode of exploitation referred to as hunting and gathering.

- Hunting and gathering as an economic endeavor and a way of life still continues today, as an important source of subsistence, but always combined with other kinds of economic activities.

- Agriculture, the domestication of plants and their use for subsistence, beginning some 8,000 to 10,000 years ago, represented a significant transformation in human society.

- Throughout lowland South America and Melanesia, the mode of production is based upon crops that are grown through vegetative propagation, using a part of the plant itself, and this form of cultivation is known as horticulture.

- In the more temperate areas of several continents of the world, grain is the focus of swidden agriculture—maize in the New World, millet and sorghum in Africa, and rice in Asia. In Europe and in parts of Asia, agriculture is practiced with a plow and the use of animal fertilizer.

- More complex modes of production produce storable surpluses, which are used to support full-time specialists and social hierarchies.

• In most areas, the domestication of animals followed soon after the domestication of plants. Humans have shaped these animal domesticates through the process of domestication.

• Societies that are completely dependent upon their domesticated animals are known as nomadic pastoral societies.

• A series of economic factors have brought about significant transformations in the way of life of nomadic pastoralists. Many pastoralists now move their animals and belongings by truck from one pasture site to another.

• In every society there is a division of labor based on gender and age.

• Several types of exchange systems characterize societies in which rank differences are absent. The simplest type of exchange system, reciprocal exchange, like that of the Abelam, involves two sides, of equal status, in continuing exchange with each other.

• More complex systems of economic distribution develop when there are delays in the exchange. Among the Maring of the New Guinea highlands, one host group distributes simultaneously to a number of other groups, which are hosts later, at their *kaiko* ceremony.

• More complex systems of exchange link groups when goods move from group to group in a chain identical to generalized exchange created by marriage with mother's brother's daughter. The Enga system involves moving goods from one group to the next until the end of the chain is reached, when gifts reverse and travel in the opposite direction.

• In societies with flexible rank, distributions are the means by which the ranking of groups is raised or lowered.

• When rank differences are permanent, the nature of exchanges is significantly altered. In such systems, aristocrats are separate from commoners, lords from vassals, patrons from clients, and high castes from low castes, as occurs in India. Groups differ in rank and prestige and in the economic resources that they control, and they have economic specialization and a permanent division of labor.

• When superiors give to inferiors, the act is seen as generosity or largess. When inferiors give to superiors, it is considered tribute.

• The term *market* has two meanings. The first refers to the location, or site, where food commodities and craft items are bought and sold. The second meaning characterizes an entire economic system based upon the determination of prices by the market, that is, in terms of supply and demand.

• The relationship between buyer and seller is not dependent upon any other relationship but has its basis solely in the fact that the seller has something that the buyer wants or needs and is willing to pay for.

• Globalization means not only the penetration of entrepreneurship, technology, and technological knowledge, but most recently, also the development of multinational corporations and the movement of capital to most places in the world without concern for national boundaries or different currencies.

• Whereas in nonmarket economic systems, the economy is embedded in a larger cultural matrix, the growth of a market economy in an industrialized capitalist society marks the development of an economic institution that is separate from other institutions.

• Nevertheless, capitalism and the market system must be seen and understood in terms of the cultural matrix with which it is associated.

• The world system of money and markets has penetrated even the most remote societies. In places such as Papua New Guinea and other parts of the Pacific, the Western economic aspect is called *bisnis* and continuing traditional systems are referred to as *kastom.*

• In its most general sense, consumption means the way in which people use goods which they have obtained. As with other aspects of culture, consumption is determined by cultural rules.

• With the development of complex modern industrial society came the notion of the consumer and a narrower definition of consumption. Consumers used goods manufactured by someone else, which are referred to as commodities.

• Sometimes religious beliefs dictate the nature of product consumption. In Western capitalist society, consumption has often been associated with gender.

• Consumption and consumerism in the Third and Fourth Worlds are sometimes directly related to consumption in the industrialized world.

 SUGGESTED READINGS

Cohen, Jeffrey H., and Nobert Dannhaeuser (eds.). *Economic Development: An Anthropological Approach.* Walnut Creek, CA: Rowman and Littlefield, 2002. A collection of essays dealing with current economic developments in various parts of the world. Topics include effects of tourism as a resource and the effects of globalization in the Philippines.

Ensminger, Jean (ed.). *Theory in Economic Anthropology.* Walnut Creek, CA: Altmira Press, 2002. A series of articles dealing with new theoretical ideas in economic theory.

Gudeman, Stephen. *The Anthropology of Economy: Community, Market, and Culture.* Malden, MA: Blackwell, 2001. An approach that emphasizes the community as the core of the economy.

Hann, C. M. (ed.). *Property Relations: Renewing the Anthropological Tradition.* New York: Cambridge University Press, 1998. A series of essays considering the cultural, social, and symbolic aspects of property, as well as its material component in a number of different societies.

Haugerud, Angelique, Margaret Priscilla Stone, and Peter D. Little (eds.). *Commodities and Globalization: Anthropological Perspectives.* Lanham, MD: Rowman and Littlefield, 2000. Articles dealing with the role of commodities in an increasing globalized marketplace.

Humphrey, Caroline, and David Sneath. *The End of Nomadism? Society, State, and the Environment in Inner Asia.* Durham, NC: Duke University Press, 1999. Deals with the ways in which nomadic pastoral societies in inner Asia are changing and the question of whether societies of this type will survive in this modern world of increasing globalization.

Schweitzer, Peter, Megan Biesele, and Robert Hitchcock. *Hunters and Gathers in the Modern world: Conflict, Resistance, and Self-Determination.* New York: Berghahn Books, 2000. Discusses the current status of hunters and gatherers and the adaptations in their lives, which have been made as a consequence of the penetration of the global system.

 SUGGESTED WEBSITES

http://www.yale.edu/environment/publications/bulletin/103pdfs/103bekk/pdf A discussion of land use by nomadic pastoralists in Iran and the way in which they changed their use of the physical environment. These changes also related to their economic practices.

http://www.openair.org/cyjour/bib.html A bibliography of articles and books about open-air markets.

9

Politics, Government, Law, and Conflict

What is politics? Does politics always involve the use of power? What does it mean "to get an offer you can't refuse"? In American society, that phrase represents the exercise of power in a variety of contexts. It may be a way of forcing someone to do something he or she doesn't want to do, or getting a competitor to remove himself or herself from competition. How do power and politics operate in different societies? A Trobriand man aspiring to chiefly office might seize the opportunity of his mother's brother's death to organize the latter's funeral *sagali* to give him an advantage in inheriting the chieftainship. Thus, a Trobriand funeral *sagali* is a political, as well as a social, religious and kinship event. So too are the funeral of a Mafia boss and the funeral of a dictator in a totalitarian state. In these examples, though the successor comes from a small circle of eligible individuals, there is no fixed rule regarding succession. Questions about politics and power may be illuminated first by comparing the processes of political organization in two contrasting small-scale societies. Durkheim long ago pointed out that one or two detailed examples were useful explanatory devices. Trobriand political organization involved the division of the main island of Kiriwina into a number of districts, each of which contained several villages. Members of the four matrilineal clans were dispersed throughout the districts, though subclans were localized. Within a particular district, one subclan would rank higher than all the others, and its chief would be the paramount chief of the district. The other villages in the district had headmen who were subordinate to the chief and gave their sisters to him as wives, as pointed out in the previous chapter. Each year they furnished him with yams—*urigubu*—as tribute. Since there was no rule of succession like primogeniture, in which the first-born succeeds to the position, when a chief died, his real or classificatory sisters' sons competed with one another to succeed to the position. Before the man who succeeded to the position could make the funerary *sagali* for his predecessor he had to demonstrate that he had many followers who would support him as the new chief and assist him at the *sagali*. The chief controlled resources as well as labor and was the titular owner of all the land in the district, although the garden magician and actual users of the land also had some rights to it. The chief decided when the time was propitious to declare a *kayasa*, a period of feasting and competitive games, such as cricket, between his own village and another to be held at harvest time. As a result of the chief's decision, all the people of the village were bound to work their hardest so the *kayasa* would be a success.

Malinowski mentions that the chief had "special henchmen" to punish people who did not obey him. They might even inflict capital punishment. Frequently, people obeyed the chief because they were afraid that he might command that evil magic be used against them. Several political symbols were associated with Trobriand chieftainship. Special signs of deference were shown to the chief. No man's head might be higher than that of the chief, so either the chief sat on a high platform or people bent when they walked past him. The chief's large, elaborately decorated yam house, displaying the *urigubu* yams given him as tribute, was another symbol of his political authority. Only the members of the chief's subclan could wear a certain kind of ornament, red spondylus shell disks, on their foreheads. The food taboos that had to be observed by people of rank were also symbols of political authority.

Yanomamo political organization provides a clear contrast (Chagnon, 1997). Every Yanomamo man is his own boss; no other Yanomamo can give him orders. Each Yanomamo village is a completely independent unit. One village will entertain and feast another village in order to win its support as an ally. Villages that are enemies of one another will raid each other to capture women. Every Yanomamo village has a headman, an individual who has demonstrated leadership qualities. These include fearlessness in war, as well as wisdom and judgment in planning the course of action for the village—in making alliances with other villages, in planning attacks on other villages, and in moving the village to another area when gardens are depleted. The position of headman is not hereditary. The headman of the village must obtain the agreement of all the men of the village when a decision about any course of action must be made. The headman does not direct individuals to do things; first he does them himself, setting an example for the others to follow. Headmen are constantly challenged by others who aspire to the position. A man is headman only as long as the villagers have confidence in his judgment. Another individual with supporters can begin to oppose the headman in his decisions. As this opposition grows, the headman, if the people lose confidence in him, may be supplanted by his rival, or the headman may inspire his villagers to use force to drive out the opposing leader and his followers to form their own village. Since there is no fixed rule of succession, the younger brother or son of a headman is no more likely to succeed as headman than any other adult man in the village. No one performs labor for the headman; he works his own garden. The headman has no special magical knowledge. Since there are no rank differences among the Yanomamo—all adult males are equal—there are no outward signs of rank, no special deference, and no special food customs to differentiate the headman from other villagers, or those with power from those without it. The equal status of all adult Yanomamo males is consonant with the egalitarian relationship they have in exchange (see Chapters 6 and 8). Today, the Trobriand and Yanomamo political structures that we have just described are both encompassed within nation-states, and how much of these structures have persisted is not clear.

CONCEPTS IN POLITICAL ANTHROPOLOGY

These examples provide us with a framework within which to examine the concepts that are employed to analyze political systems found in different societies, including our own. Power is the key concept used in defining political organization. **Power** is the ability to command others to do certain things and to get compliance from them. One can immediately see the contrast between the Yanomamo and Trobrianders. The Yanomamo headman does not have the power to compel villagers to act in a particular way, whereas the Trobriand chief demonstrates his power in a whole range of activities. Power must be distinguished from **authority.** When power becomes institutionalized, we say it has been transformed into authority. This means that there is a recognized position, or **office,** the occupant of which can issue commands that must be obeyed. It is apparent that the Trobriand chief has authority as well as power, which derives from his chiefly office, and his commands are always obeyed. Does the Yanomamo headman have any authority? He holds a recognized position (office), but since the headman has no power to compel people to obey him, he has no authority. Nevertheless, he is a leader, since others will follow him if he has influence with them. **Influence** is the ability to persuade others to follow one's lead. They will continue to follow him and he will have influence over them as long as they have confidence in his leadership ability. Some form of leadership is found in all human groups. When leadership is not vested in a formal institutionalized position and is based solely on influence, as is the case of the Yanomamo headman, loss of confidence means loss of followers and loss of leadership position. Influence represents informal power, in contrast to the power vested in formal political positions.

A distinction is also made between government and politics. **Government** refers to the decisions made by those in office on behalf of the entire group in carrying out common goals. This may involve going to war to maintain the defense of the group, a decision President Bush must make. It also involves dealing with the day-to-day matters of law and order. Thus, the Trobriand chief carries out important governmental functions. For example, when he decides to hold a competitive *kayasa* with another village, as we have described in Chapter 8, he organizes the production of those under him. The chief initiates the overseas *kula* exchange we have described previously and is the owner of the canoe used. *Kula* deals with overseas relations between Trobrianders and other peoples, in effect, foreign affairs. Today, Trobriand chiefs are sometimes members of the Papua New Guinea Parliament, continuing this chiefly control over external affairs. In contrast, among the Yanomamo, the consensus of the whole group is what is important, even though they have a headman as their leader.

Politics is concerned with an entirely different aspect of political organization. Whereas government involves the carrying out of shared goals, politics involves people's competing for power. **Politics** concentrates on the manipulation of people and resources, the maneuvers intended to enhance power, the rise of factions that compete for power, and the development of political parties with differing points of view. Politics emphasizes opposing points of view and conflict, divergent rather than common goals. Of course, in our own society as well as others, those vying for power in the political arena usually claim that they are operating for the common good and not just for their own personal aggrandizement. They may actually believe this to be true.

Politics operates among both the Trobriand Islanders and the Yanomamo. When a Trobriand chief dies, the choice of a new chief is open to political maneuvering and competition among the individuals in the group of people eligible to succeed. These candidates must demonstrate their political abilities to followers who are their fellow subclansmen. At this point, potential claimants to the chiefly office make promises and point to their demonstrated skills in organizational leadership and their wealth. The man who is recognized as the new chief now has the authority to govern and assumes the appropriate Trobriand symbols of political authority.

Politics is constantly present among the Yanomamo, since Yanomamo headmen regularly face the potential opposition of those who also aspire to leadership in their village. Even the decision to hold a feast may be the basis for political maneuvering. A rival for the position of headman may himself try to organize a feast. He tries to convince others in the village that this is a wise decision politically. If he succeeds in enlisting the support of the majority of the villagers, then he has in effect become the new headman. If he can mobilize only partial support, he will come to lead his own faction in the village, and he may try again in the future. He may also fail to get any support, in which case he retires to the sidelines and sulks.

Anthropologists refer to a position that depends on personal qualifications and individual ability as an **achieved status,** in contrast to an **ascribed status,** which one inherits.

FORMS OF POLITICAL ORGANIZATION

Some form of authority and leadership has always existed in all human societies. Though the forms of political organization that we will describe characterize societies that are all now parts of nation-states, such descriptions will provide us with a picture of how successively more complex political structures developed. This process of greater and greater political complexity involved increasingly more sharply defined positions of leadership.

INFORMAL LEADERSHIP

In the simplest form of political organization, leadership was manifested intermittently. This type of organization may be called **informal leadership.** The Iglulingmiut, an Inuit (Eskimo) group of eastern Canada, formerly had this form of political organization. The name given to the group means the people *(miut)* of Iglulik, who were all those living in that area. There were no fixed political offices, and a number of men, but never women, exerted leadership in certain situations. There were winter villages along the coast where a number of families related through various kinds of kin ties, though not the same families every year, came together to spend the winter, exploiting the resources of the ocean. The men of influence who exercised leadership in the winter village were the "boat owners," the senior males of the kin units that owned the boats, which were used to hunt seals. Leadership was also exhibited in connection with the inland summer hunting of caribou, at which time numbers of families came together. The hunting of caribou was conducted under the leadership of a man with hunting expertise. At the end of the hunt, the families scattered, and the leader was no longer a leader. Leadership operated only through influence, and different men exercised their influence in those areas where they had special knowledge or ability. These temporary leaders, which Kurtz calls episodic leaders, did not have the power to compel people to obey them (2001: 460). Generally people who were respected made decisions, adjudicated disputes, and represented the community in discussions with outsiders (Hitchcock and Biesele, 2000: 19). This kind of political organization was found only among peoples whose subsistence was based exclusively upon hunting and gathering.

BAND ORGANIZATION

Some hunting-and-gathering societies had a more complex form of political organization known as **band organization.** Bands had a more fixed membership that came together annually to carry out joint ritual and economic activities. The Ojibwa—hunters and gatherers in the forests of the eastern Canadian subarctic— had this type of political organization. During most of the year, small groups of related families moved from one hunting area to another. In the summertime, the whole band frequently came together on the shores of a lake and remained as a unit for the summer. The men with influence were leaders of the group.

The Yanomamo structurally have band organization, though dependent on horticulture, a completely different mode of subsistence. Each village has a delimited membership and a headman, who has influence over his fellow villagers. Though fluid in its membership, the band had more cohesiveness than societies with only informal leadership. The band acts as a unit under recognized leadership, though that leadership is based on influence, not on authority.

BIG MAN STRUCTURE

A still more complex political organization is the **Big Man structure.** There is usually a term for the Big Man position, and frequently, it literally means "big man." The Big Man structure represents a greater delineation of the leadership position, in comparison with that of band organization. As leadership becomes more clearly defined, so does the group of followers (see also Kurtz, 2000: 47–48). In Melanesia,

An Abelam political leader sits before his men's house, wearing emblems and ornaments signifying that he is a Big Man.

the Big Man takes the initiative in exchanges with other groups. In contrast, ordinary men fulfill their obligations in exchanges with affines and kin and contribute to what is accumulated by the Big Man of their group, as described in the depiction of Abelam and Enga exchange ceremonies in Chapter 8. The followers of a Big Man also include rubbish men, unmarried men who do not fulfill any of their obligations with regard to exchange. The Big Men organize their group's production and are the nodes in the exchange system. The Big Man derives his power from his direction of the ceremonial distribution of the goods accumulated by his group and the decisions he makes in the redistribution of goods within his own group. The Abelam Big Man depicted above wears the emblem of his office around his neck.

The Big Man also directs a range of other activities. As noted in the previous chapter, not only does the Abelam Big Man organize the labor involved in the production of long yams, but he also acts as the ritual expert, since he alone knows the magical spells that make the yams grow so long. On behalf of his entire group, he maintains sexual abstinence for the whole growing period. Artistic ability as a carver or painter of designs is also a desirable characteristic in an Abelam Big Man, but the most important characteristic is his ability to produce the long yams on which the prestige of the entire group depends. Throughout New Guinea, the oratorical skills of the Big Man are essential, since he must deliver speeches at ceremonial distributions as the representative of his group. The Big Man should also show prowess in warfare, though his involvement is usually in the organizational area. Since women cannot be near any phase of the growing or exchange of long yams among the Abelam, they cannot be Big Men.

The position of Big Man is an achieved status, dependent on personal qualifications and individual ability. As he ages, a Big Man may no longer be able to carry out all the activities necessary to maintain his influence in his group. In that case, his leadership position may be challenged by other aspiring Big Men. Competition between challengers involves political skills and maneuvering. Though in a patrilineal society the Big Man's son may have an initial advantage, he will not be able to become a Big Man himself if he lacks the necessary abilities. A man who has leadership qualities, although he may be from another family in the clan, may surpass the Big Man's son in gaining followers and, in time, be recognized as the new Big Man.

Though women have influence and play an important role in exchange in many societies of Melanesia, they rarely occupy the Big Man position. The women of the island of Vanatinai in the Coral Sea, one of the islands in the *kula* ring, are an exception. The term *giagia*, which literally means "giver," is a gender-neutral term that refers to Big Men and Big Women (Lepowsky, 1990). These Big Women are central nodes in the exchange of goods and valuables. They lead *kula* expeditions, organize mortuary feasts, and orate at ceremonies, just like Big Men do.

Big Man political structure is associated with distribution in egalitarian societies, as we have described in Chapter 8. In reciprocal exchange systems, like that of the Abelam, they organize the ceremonial distribution of yams. With more complex exchange systems, like the *Te* of the Enga, the Big Man, as pictured in Chapter 8, stands on a platform distributing side of cooked pork to other Enga Big Men, who then redistribute the meat to their followers.

CHIEFTAINSHIP

The introduction of fixed positions of rank and some method of succession leads to a fourth type of political organization—**chieftainship**—in which individuals as well as kin groups of the descent system are ranked with respect to one another. The Trobriand case, with which we began this chapter, exemplifies this type of organization. As shown earlier, the chief does not merely exert influence over others but has real authority, which means that he has the power to enforce his decisions. Power and authority are vested in the office, and whoever occupies that office exercises authority and has power. In the Big Man structure, any man can become a Big Man if he has the ability and works hard. In chiefdoms, which are ranked societies, the chiefly position is restricted to certain high-ranking individuals. Among the Kwakiutl, who have chiefs, the oldest child, regardless of sex, inherits the chiefly position through primogeniture. This position is represented by the highest-ranking name in the *numaym*, or kin group. Though a Kwakiutl female may inherit the name, a male kinsman usually carries out the duties of the office. In chieftainships, there is a hierarchy of other political positions. These are ranked with regard to one another. Whereas the Big Man has influence over a group of people—his followers, who are members of his kin group or clan or even others not of that clan—in the chieftainship, the chief exercises control over an area and the kin groups contained within that area. For example, the Trobriand chief heads a district with villages whose headmen give their sisters to the chief as wives, and therefore pay *urigubu* to the chief. Malinowski called this tribute. These village headmen are not of the chiefly subclan but of other subclans lower in rank than the chief's, though they are the chief's affines.

The political economy of chieftainships is a more complex redistributive system than that associated with the Big Man structure. In a chieftainship, because there are more levels of political organization, villagers give to their village headmen, who in turn give to the chief. This is exactly what happens at a Trobriand *kayasa*, when two villages compete with one another. Yams are presented to the chief by the heads of the two villages. The chief later redistributes what he has received in feasts to reward the villages in his district for various services. Chieftainship is also associated with potlatch exchange systems like those of the Kwakiutl and Tlingit. While some chiefdomships are associated with flexible rank, others are associated with systems of fixed rank.

Another type of political organization, tribe, is frequently referred to in the anthropological literature. Since "tribe" is a postcontact formation, we will discuss it in Chapter 13.

TRANSFORMATION FROM BIG MAN TO CHIEFTAINSHIP AND BACK AGAIN

The Kachin, a hill people of Kachin Province, northern Myanmar (Burma), provide an example of how Big Man structure can be transformed into chieftainship. Segmentary lineage structures, such as those described in Chapter 6, could be found in combination with either the Big Man type of political organization or with chieftainship. Big Men operated at each of the levels of the segmentary lineage structure. Minor Big Men headed lineages, and important Big Men headed clans composed of several lineages, all equal in rank. Edmund Leach, in his analysis of the political system, a patrilineal lineage structure, as it operated in the 1940s, provides us with a unique example which shows how the Kachin Big Man structure could develop into chieftainship and how chieftainship could collapse into the Big Man structure. In its Big Man form, which the Kachin called *gumlao*, a number of Kachin villages, all equal in rank, were tied together by a patrilineal genealogy. Each village had a headman, who could come from any lineage in the village. Each lineage was headed by its eldest male, and there was a council of elders (from each lineage) for every village. At village ceremonies and festivals, the heads of lineages sacrificed separately to a variety of spirits. The Kachin marriage rule favoring marriage with mother's brother's daughter separates lineages who take women (wife-takers) and those who give women (-wife-givers) (Chapter 6, Figure 6-10). Among those Kachin with the *gumlao* structure, there were no differences in rank between wife-givers and wife-takers, bridewealth payments were low, and a number of lineages in the same village married in a circle in such a way that lineage A gave wives to lineage B, which gave wives to lineage C, which returned wives to lineage A. If one lineage in a village grew wealthier or stronger than the others, it might try to raise its status by offering to pay a higher bridewealth and by seeking wives from high-ranking lineages in other villages. If successful, it could transform itself into a chiefly lineage that dominated the other lineages in its own village, sponsoring village feasts, which would further raise its prestige. The head of this lineage became the village headman, since his lineage was deemed to be the highest-ranking lineage of the village. Succession to this position became ascribed rather than achieved. The rule of succession was **ultimogeniture,** which meant that the new chief was the youngest son. His line was superior to the line of descendants of other sons. If the aristocratic lineage of a village succeeded in gaining control of other villages, inhabitants of the newly formed domain were subordinate to the chiefly lineage. At this point, the Kachin would say that the political form was of the *gumsa* type. It had become a chieftainship.

In the *gumsa* form, the chief, called *duwa*, held both a political and ritual position. Though there was still a council of lineage heads, only the chief made sacrifices on behalf of the domain to his ancestral lineage spirit, which was now taken to represent the ancestral spirit of all the lineages in the domain. Since the chief was entitled to receive a hind leg of all animals killed either in hunting or for sacrifice from everyone in his domain except his own lineage, he was referred to as the "thigh-eating chief." This right to the hind leg was one of several symbolic manifestations of chiefly authority, including the erection of a special kind of house post. The chief also had the right to have the people in his domain build his house and work on his agricultural land. In addition, in some cases, he exacted a portion of the rice harvest from each household in his domain every year as tribute. Whereas under the *gumlao* system, all lineages were equal in rank and married in a circle, in the *gumsa* form, there was a ranked series of lineages, and a lineage that gave women to another lineage was superior to it. There were also gradations in bridewealth to match the ranking of lineages. Since women moved down the ranking order, the men of the chiefly lineage had to get their wives from the aristocratic lineages of other domains.

Among the Kachin, not only could the unranked *gumlao* turn into the *gumsa* chieftainship, but the reverse process could also occur. When the *gumsa* structure placed great economic strains upon the people, there was a revolt and the egalitarian *gumlao* system was reestablished. Thus the process could go in either direction, from *gumlao* to *gumsa* and back again to *gumlao*. It appears that the Kachin marriage pattern has the potential for the development of rank differences from a state in which all lineage groupings exchanging women are equal.

All of the societies we have described here are encompassed within the boundaries of modern-day states, as we have noted above. The Trobrianders, Abelam, Maring, and Enga are all part of the nation-state of Papua New Guinea, where today both Big Men and chiefs run for the office of representative in the New Guinea parliament or for the position of Councilor in the local District Council (on the Maring, see LiPuma, 2000: 83). In the Trobriands, in particular, despite involvement in national politics, Trobriand chiefs are still strong and "hold the reins in their hands, much to the dismay of the national administration and missions" (Schiefenhovel and Bell-Krannhals, 1996: 236). But Schiefenhovel and Bell-Krannhals also note that "the Trobrianders thus have an interesting mix of ascribed chieftainship and men who achieve their rank and influence by merit. The latter position, as a rule, can not be transferred to the first position" (1996: 249). Those who run for office often act like Big Men in their political activities. Today the Yanomamo live in both Venezuela and Brazil. Only a few villages remain in remote areas, away from "civilization," while many have moved to mission stations, where the power is in the hands of the missionaries. In Brazil, the army, with assistance in the form of $1.5 billion, have begun to construct new military bases and expand old ones in territories set aside for the Yanomamo and other "tribes," and have also begun to recruit Yanomamo young men for the army. The so-called "tribal leaders" have protested and with the help of Indian advocates have instituted legal action to stop this intrusion, which has resulted in the introduction of venereal diseases and the birth of mixed-race children who will no longer have rights as Yanomamo (*New York Times,* October 1, 2002). The Iglulingmiut, Ojibwa, Kwakiutl, and Tlingit are part of Canada, although Tlingit also live in Alaska, and some Ojibwa live in Wisconsin. Politically, they operate as tribes within the nation-state. Many Inuit have moved from nomadic camps into multiethnic settlements run according to community bylaws, and with a Community Council and settlement officers. In these settlements, the social order needs to be " 'renegotiated' on a new basis and new modes of communication appropriate to life in a large diverse community have to be found" (Briggs, 2000: 116–117). The Kachin live under a military government in which the *duwa,* or chief, has no political power, and ceremonials are organized and controlled by the provincial government.

THE STATE

The last type of political organization that we will discuss is that of the **state.** Archaeologists have been interested in the conditions that produced the earliest states in Egypt, Mesopotamia, the Indus Valley, China, Mexico, and Peru. Cultural anthropologists focused upon still-functioning indigenous states that existed as a consequence of the colonial policy of indirect rule. Many of the well-studied examples are to be found in Africa and Southeast Asia.

The state differs from the other types of political organization in a number of significant ways, the most important of which is a difference in scale. Though some states may be quite small, the state has the potential for encompassing within its orbit millions of people. It is organized on a territorial basis, made up of villages and districts, rather than on the basis of kinship and clanship. Though in the chieftainship there was a differentiation between the chiefly lineage, which controlled power and wealth, and other lineages made up of commoners, the system was still tied together by kinship and affinity. In contrast, in the state we find social stratification—rulers, aristocrats, commoners, and various low-status groups. These strata may be endogamous and are never tied together by kinship. All those under the control of the state are its citizens or its subjects. Frequently today, states contain not only small-scale societies like the Yanomamo but also multiethnic populations, who speak different languages and are culturally different from one another.

The state is governed by a ruler whose legitimate right to govern and command others is acknowledged by those in the state. Many of the early states were theocracies; that is, the ruler was head of both the religious hierarchy and the state at the same time. The same symbols were used for the merged religious and political structure. In many indigenous states, the ruler was not only the political symbol but also the religious symbol of the whole society. This was particularly true in East African states. As was the case among the Aluund of southwestern Zaire, whom we discussed in Chapter 5, the ruler's state of health and ritual purity affected the welfare of the entire kingdom. In the symbolism of the Aluund, the paramount chief is the lord of the soil and must not show disease, decay, or old age, since the productivity of crops depends on the state of his health.

The administrative functions of the state are carried out by a bureaucracy, which is delegated authority by the ruler and which grows in size and complexity as the state expands. Customary law becomes formalized into a legal code. The adjudication of disputes by the leader grows into a court system, which enforces its decisions through the police. The tribute given to the chief is transformed into taxes paid to the state, which support the growing bureaucracy. The state expands by conquering neighboring peoples, who become culturally distinct subject peoples, and whose territories are incorporated within the state. The ruler maintains a police force and an army, mobilized from the subjects to protect the state from attack by external invaders as well as to expand it by conquest. States also include law-making bodies, whose power depends on whether the state is a democracy, a kingdom, or a dictatorship.

The way in which an indigenous state functioned in the twentieth century can be seen from a description of the empire of Bornu, the Kanuri state on the borders of Lake Chad in northern Nigeria. This state was studied in 1956 when it was still under British colonial rule, by Abraham Roseman, one of the authors of this book. When the British entered the area at the turn of the century, they resurrected the partially collapsed indigenous state and governed through the Shehu of Bornu, the head of state. This highly stratified society included the royal family, aristocratic families, and commoners, including village farmers. There were also different kinds of traders and crafters, and lastly slaves. Only the Shehu could grant aristocrats titles, which sometimes came with land, including entire villages. The slaves were war captives and their descendants, who became the personal property of the Shehu. They could become titled aristocrats, though they remained the Shehu's slaves.

Prior to the arrival of the British, there was an empire of Bornu, which was located at the southern end of a strategic caravan route that led from the Mediterranean Sea across the Sahara to the populous states of West Africa. Caravans brought manufactured goods from Libya and returned there with slaves, ivory, and other raw materials. The government of Bornu used Maria Theresa silver dollars from Austria, brought in by the caravan trade, as the medium of exchange. Muskets, introduced through the caravan trade, were monopolized by the state.

Mounted retainers of a Kanuri district head in northern Nigeria demonstrate their allegiance to their leader. This photo was taken in 1956, when Nigeria was a British colony.

The army of Bornu was completely controlled by the Shehu. Its generals, who bore high titles, were slaves of the Shehu. Besides conquest and the raiding of neighboring tribes for slaves, the army also defended the borders of Bornu from incursions by other states, particularly Bornu's enemies, the Hausa states to the west. As a result of conquest, non-Kanuri people, such as the Babur and some Bagirmi, permanently became part of the empire of Bornu.

In the fourteenth century, Islam spread to Bornu, following the same path as the caravan routes, and as happened, for example, with Christianity and the Roman Empire, Islam was adopted by the entire population when the ruler of Bornu converted. The Islamic legal code, as practiced in North Africa, was adopted, and judges trained in the Qur'an and in Islamic law were appointed by the Shehu to hear criminal cases. The Shehu and his appointed district heads heard and arbitrated civil cases involving personal and family disputes. The Kanuri believed that persons in authority at every administrative level up to the Shehu must be available every day to hear the disputes and complaints of their people.

The administrative structure of the state was centered in the capital city, from which the Shehu and his personal court governed. There were also districts, with their capitals, in which district heads, who were titled aristocrats, resided. Titles, positions, and their associated districts tended to be inherited along family lines, but these appointments were ultimately at the discretion of the Shehu, who could

also depose the titleholders. Districts included many villages, with village headmen appointed by the district head. Though the village headship tended to be inherited along family lines, the officeholder had to demonstrate loyalty to the
district head, who could appoint or depose him. Members of the district head's ret-
inue, freemen or slaves, were assigned to collect taxes from villages and nomadic
pastoral peoples, the Fulani, who paid their taxes by patrilineage, according to the
number of cattle that they owned.

Though the Bornu government was a hierarchical structure with the Shehu at
the apex, politics operated with regard to succession to that position. Only the son
of a man who had been Shehu could himself become Shehu. But the Shehu had
many wives, including slave wives, so there were always many contenders. After
the death of a Shehu, the eligible contenders vied for support among the members
of the council of aristocrats, who made the final decision. Politics was rife until a
successor was chosen. When a new Shehu came to power, the district heads had to
shift their loyalty to him or else lose their positions. On the other hand, the new
Shehu would appoint as many of his own supporters to district head positions as
he wished. In the same way, a reshuffling of power at the district level led to the
appointment of new village heads.

Under British colonial rule, Kanuri officials of the indigenous state structure,
including the Shehu, carried out the actual administration of districts, applied native law, and collected the taxes. They were supervised by British officials under a
lieutenant governor who resided in the capital of Bornu Province. Real authority
was in the hands of the colonial masters. Under British pacification, the Kanuri
army had been disbanded. After gaining independence in 1960, Bornu became a
province within the new state of Nigeria. It had a democratic government for a
brief time. It was ruled by military governments, until several years ago, when
democratic elections were held. A civilian government is currently in control,
though the head of state is a general.

States in Africa, Asia, and Latin America that were organized and fashioned at
independence after the colonial period were organized on a Western model. The
Western European idea of state development had global influence, but not everywhere. For example, in the Islamic Republic of Pakistan, "Islam constitutes the
moral-symbolic language of Muslim politics" (Verkaaik, 2001: 347). But there are
varieties in Islamic interpretation, which range from the strict fundamentalism of
the Wahabi regime in Saudi Arabia to the more modernist interpretation that in-
spired the founders of Pakistan. In the twentieth century, the equation of the state,
the economy, the society, and the nation was predominant. However, in today's
postcolonial world there is a challenge to the state, and state power as a locus of
territorial sovereignty and cultural legitimacy, by ethnic separatism, the globalization of trade and capital movement, and the migration of immigrants and refugees
(Hansen and Stepputat, 2001: 1–2). Demands upon the state by ethnic groups for
autonomy, and often independence, on the one hand, are countered by the need for
the state to be a part of supranational organizations like the UN and the proliferation of treaty arrangements relating to trade, like the World Bank, and security, like
NATO. For example, the collapse of the Soviet Union was soon followed by the

requests from the now independent countries like Latvia and Lithuania to join NATO for the advantages thereby bestowed.

WAR AND PEACE

Decisions about going to war are among the most important decisions made by those in positions of authority. Warfare, feuds, and revenge seeking between social groups are resorted to when no lawful, mutually acceptable means of peaceful resolution of conflicts exists. Under such conditions, one group will make the decision to take hostile action against the other group to force it to submit. Anthropologists have defined *feuding* as hostile action between members of the same group and *warfare* as hostile action between different groups. Feuds, conducted according to rules, involve collective, not personal, responsibility, so revenge can be taken against any member of the group. In a segmentary lineage system, such as that found among the Enga, discussed earlier, it is hard to tell the difference between feuding and warfare, because subclans within the same clan may fight each other on one occasion but come together as a single clan when fighting another clan. It is then hard to say which is feud and which is war.

The question of how to define warfare has been raised again recently, particularly with reference to whether there were ever social groups whom one could define as "peaceful" in contrast to groups considered "warlike." This is a definitional question similar to the one we will encounter when we discuss law and social control, below; nevertheless, it is an interesting and important question. The "omnibus" definition, held by the "hawks" sees war as "nearly ubiquitous, or very nearly so," and this ties in with a view held by some sociobiologists that humans are basically, even "genetically," aggressive (Sponsel, 2000: 838; see also Otterbein, 1999). The contrary view, held by the "doves," is that humans are basically peaceful beings with an occasional homicide here and there. Clearly if one defines warfare and human aggression more narrowly, then it would not be considered a human universal. For example, " 'Bushman,' 'Pygmies,' and 'Semai' [are seen as] . . . 'ethnographic classics' of peaceful societies" . . . [while] warlike societies [are the] Yanomami, Maring, and Dani" (Sponsel, 2000: 8328–8329). The definitional matter again arises when one considers that there has been a spread of the Western idea of warfare throughout the world, of total victory, its forms and rituals (Whitehead, 2000: 835). Dani warfare, which we would consider more ritual, involves the killing of one or two individuals, after which both sides retreat, a very different kind of "aggression." We must remember the fact that warfare is "embedded" in culture, and the cultural meanings of warfare differ from society to society. Head-hunting, cannibalism, torture, and mutilation are clearly aggressive acts that could be considered warfare. Anthropological accounts are all postcontact and often reflect the efflorescence of warfare that was a response to conquest. The Yanomamo and the people of New Ireland are excellent examples of these phenomena.

Kelly has recently written on the origins of warfare in human societies, based on a comparative study (2000). He argues that we first see clear evidence of warfare in the Upper Paleolithic, about 12,000 years ago. It is neither common nor frequent, but it is definitely present. Evidence for warfare in the archeological record is found "in the form of skeletal evidence of violent death, the relocation of habitations to defensive sites, changes in weapons technology and the like" (Kelly, 2000: 148). Since this precedes the inventions of animal and plant domestication, this type of warfare was present among hunting-and-foraging societies (we have used the term *hunting and gathering* for this type of society; see Chapter 8). A number of comparative studies reveal that hunters and foragers tend to be relatively peaceful. Like the Hadza, they resolve disputes by the disputants going their separate ways and getting out of one another's way. However, Kelly observes that some societies based on hunting and gathering do, in fact, practice warfare. Warfare must first be distinguished from a murder or the killing of a murderer as punishment. Kelly states that warfare involves collective responsibility. When a wrongdoer is punished and a murderer is killed, the perpetrator is held responsible for his on her actions. In cases of collective responsibility, all members of the murderer's lineage, clan, or tribe are held equally responsible. Earlier, we have called this type of collective responsibility feuding when it takes place within a group, such as subclans within a clan. When warfare exists, collective responsibility means that any member of the offending group may be killed. Kelly argues that warfare evolves side by side with increasing complexity of political organization (2000). As societies become more complex, warfare become more frequent and is carried out for a variety of reasons.

What do we know about warfare among contemporary hunters and foragers? Kelly distinguishes between two types of hunters and foragers. The first type are "unsegmented foraging societies" that consist solely of families in a local community. These societies, such as the Mbuti ("Pygmies"), Semang (Semai), and !Kung ("Bushman"), do not have warfare. It is in the second type, hunters and foragers with segmental organization and a hierarchy of kin groups, that warfare occurs. It is Kelly's position that since there is evidence of warfare beginning 12,000 years ago, this demonstrates that more complex social forms were developing, and that this was a consequence of conflict over resources. Collective assignment of responsibility for transgressions led to both feuding and war, where any member of the offending group was attacked on sight.

Contrary to the belief that warfare is a no-holds-barred action aimed at exterminating one's foe, it operates according to cultural rules, like all other forms of cultural behavior. Peacemaking, the opposite of warfare, is also governed by cultural rules, as we shall see below. Anthropologists have attempted to comprehend warfare as it operated in small-scale societies in order to try to understand it in today's complex societies. Unfortunately, by the time anthropologists went to do field research, those small-scale societies that they studied had been conquered and pacified and were under colonial rule or were parts of nation-states. It is only from field descriptions of societies in Amazonia and New Guinea, where warfare continued despite contact with Europeans and colonial rule, that we have some understanding of indigenous ideas about warfare, its causes, and how it was conducted. There is also ethnohistorical data on how warfare was conducted by Native Americans during the early period of European colonization.

One of the fullest accounts of warfare practiced by a small-scale society is that of the Yanomamo in Amazonia (Chagnon, 1997). However, this account is now contested. There are several levels of hostility among the Yanomamo, each of them representing a distinct phase in the escalation of conflict, but hostilities can terminate at any level. The chest-pounding duel, halfway between a sporting contest and a fight, can take place between two individuals of the same village or, at a feast, between the men of two different villages. Chest-pounding duels arise from accusations of cowardice, stinginess with food, or gossip. The next, more-intensive level is the side-slapping contest. The provocations are the same as for the chest-pounding duel. The third level is the club fight, which can also take place within or between villages. Two men attack one another with wooden clubs eight to ten feet long and attempt to hit each other on the skull. Such fights typically arise as a result of arguments over women. These contests end when one opponent withdraws. The most intensive kind of hostility is the raid, conducted by one village against another, which one could define as warfare. Villages that have a history of being enemies raid one another to take revenge for past killings. Hostile relations can also build from a club fight to raiding if one or another individual has been seriously injured or killed. Women are frequently captured in the course of a raid, and this becomes another reason to continue to raid. Preemptive first strikes may take place even after a feast because the Yanomamo say that you can never trust another Yanomamo.

Periods of warfare alternate with periods of peace for the Yanomamo as for all other peoples and "peacemaking often requires the threat or actual use of force" (Chagnon, 1997: 7). The Yanomamo ceremonial dialogue, or *wayamou*, is a ritual that takes place as a way of making peace when relations between villages that normally have close ties are deteriorating or when people from more distant, potentially hostile villages come to visit. The venting of grievances prevents violence from breaking out, and the ceremonial dialogue, consisting of a reciprocal exchange of words, strengthens existing connections. Stylized body movements, rapid speech, and particular rhetorical features, such as metaphors, metonyms, repetition, and incomplete sentences, are utilized. Goods are often requested, which will be returned when the present hosts of the feast are invited to a feast at some future time.

Taking a more ethnohistorical view, Ferguson sees the accessibility of steel goods as central to Yanomami warfare in the postcontact period, though Peters, the ethnographer of the Xilixana Yanomami of Brazil, sees an abundance of steel goods in their area and considers the reasons for warfare to rest with avenging sorcery and revenge in general (Ferguson, 1995; Peters, 1998: 216–217). Once gold was discovered in the Yanamamo area of northwest Brazil, the Yanomamo became the victims of raids by gun-toting Brazilian gold miners, who successfully took over their land. In this conflict, Yanomamo rules of warfare and peacemaking no longer applied.

Anthropologists have been very concerned with offering explanations for warfare. Most find unsatisfactory the frequently offered explanation that warfare is due to instinctive human aggressiveness. Warfare is prevalent at certain times and not others, and under certain conditions and not others. The task of the anthropologist is to explain why warfare occurs when and where it does. Proposing a universal human aggressive instinct cannot explain this variability. Anthropological explanations for warfare must be distinguished from those of the combatants. The Yanomamo themselves say that they go to war to avenge a previous killing and as a result of conflicts over women. Lizot (1994), who has also done fieldwork with the Yanomamo, likewise sees warfare and peace as related to, or as transformations of one another that relate to, the social structure of reciprocity in which sisters are exchanged, as well as goods at feasts (see Chapter 6). When a killing occurs, it must be avenged by a return killing. Lizot's explanation of Yanomamo warfare is a structural one—warfare is the exchange of blow for blow and blood for blood, while peace is the exchange of sister for sister, feast for feast, and goods for goods.

Earlier, Chagnon argued that the Yanomamo went to war in order to maintain their political autonomy (1983). More recently, he has adopted a sociobiological approach, noting that successful warriors known as *unokais* (men who have killed) have more wives and over three times as many children than do other men (Chagnon, 1997: 205). He concludes that the cause of warfare is ultimately biological or reproductive success. In a recent reanalysis of all the historical and ethnographic data on the different Yanomamo groups in both Venezuela and in Brazil, Ferguson argues "that the actual practice of war among the Yanomami is explainable largely as a result of antagonisms related to scarce, coveted and unequally distributed Western manufactured goods" (1995: 8). He claims that before Western contact, warfare was limited or absent among the Yanomamo (Ferguson, 1995: 75). When Western goods were introduced, access was unequal, leading to conflict between Yanomamo groups and increased warfare. Koch offers another kind of explanation for warfare as it occurred in small-scale societies based on his research among the Jale in New Guinea. He claims that warfare breaks out when no third party exists to settle disputes. In his view, war is just another means of dispute settlement.

Many of the points made about warfare in small-scale societies are also applicable to complex societies. The motives of those who carry out the war, both the soldiers and the planners, are different from the causes of war as seen by analysts. For example, the United States declared war on Japan after Pearl Harbor was bombed. We, as natives, explain the war as a result of Japan's aggressive act. A disinterested analyst might explain the war as a result of the fact that Japan, an increasingly more powerful and industrializing state, needed to expand its sphere of influence to obtain more raw materials, such as oil from Indonesia (then the Dutch East Indies). They thereby impinged on the U.S. sphere of influence in the Pacific.

Like the wars fought by the Yanomamo, our wars are also conducted according to rules. After World War I, the use of poison gas in warfare was outlawed by international agreement. The Korean War was conducted as a limited war—limited in that nuclear weapons were not used. When certain unspoken agreements about the geographical extent of the war were violated and the United States moved its troops north of the Yalu River, the People's Republic of China entered the war and the level of conflict escalated. Materialist or ecological explanations of warfare seem to be as applicable to modern complex societies as they are to small-scale societies. The desire to obtain more land or other important strategic resources, such as mineral wealth or oil, has often caused warfare in modern times. Sometimes modern states carry out preemptive strikes, that is, attacks on the enemy when they believe that the enemy is about to launch an attack. The United States, at present, is contemplating a preemptive strike against Iraq. This parallels Chagnon's explanation of Yanomamo warfare as being conducted to maintain the political autonomy of a group. In a sense, this same explanation operates for ethnic groups today who are trying to maintain their autonomy within a larger nation-state. Sometimes, as in the Kosovo crisis, Albanians used warfare to try to gain their independence from Yugoslavia.

THE ANTHROPOLOGY OF VIOLENCE

The focus on what has come to be known as the "anthropology of violence" began with the shift, under the influence of postmodernism, to a consideration of cultural life from the subjective point of view. The anthropology of violence also includes a concern with the "culture of terror," "torture," and how these are used to establish "hegemony," or the domination of one group by another (Taussig, 2002: 172–173). The focus has been upon the way in which narratives "are in themselves evidence of the process whereby a culture of terror was created and sustained" (Taussig, 2002: 179). The presentation of the indigenous population of Latin America as "Wild Men" and Savages in the colonial imagination was seen as the way in which to justify the cruelty imposed upon this subordinate population.

There are those who link conflict to violence, seeing violence as "an assertion of power or a physical hurt deemed legitimate by the performer and some witnesses" (Schroeder and Schmidt, 2001: 3). This is a broader conceptualization, which includes what we have subsumed under warfare, above, but this newer perspective on the larger category of violence also focuses on the subjective aspect and on the role played by memory, as for example the connection between wars and prior conflicts (Schroeder and Schmidt, 2001: 3, 9). For example, President Bush makes connections between our need to make a preemptive strike on Iraq and the Desert Storm war in 1991 and September 11. Recourse is even made to the December 7 attack on Pearl Harbor and the need for us to protect our country against preemptive strikes. Narratives keep alive the memory of former wars and conflicts. Since, by and large, anthropologists do not observe violent events directly, the anthropologist deals with the participants' narratives after the event (Schroeder and Schmidt, 2001: 11).

Collective large-scale violence is also seen as connected to "massive trauma" (Suarez-Orozco and Robben, 2000: 1). Large-scale violence is connected to the reshaping of cultural identity. The post-9/11 period in our country was marked by a rethinking of how Americans thought of themselves and their relations with other peoples in the world. One can seen how these are encoded into cultural narratives in the proliferation of different kinds of stories, books, television programs, documentaries, and the like. The violence of 9/11 served to reshape the world not only of the inhabitants of New York City, but of the rest of the population throughout the country. Adults and children were both affected. It was an example of how violence "penetrates people's psychic constitution" (Gampel, 2000: 59). We saw ourselves as the victims of a dastardly act, the first "invasion of our country" since the War of 1812.

LAW AND SOCIAL CONTROL

At various points in this chapter, we have touched upon the subject of law. Anthropologists have been interested in the way disputes have been settled in the societies they have studied. In the absence of any written legal codes or formal courts before which lawyers argued cases, anthropologists in the field would listen to and record the manner in which disputes were aired and conflicts resolved. By doing this, they tried to get at the rules, what constitutes proper behavior in light of those rules, what is the acceptable range of deviation from the rules, what is unacceptable behavior, and how it is dealt with and punished. The legal principles or bases upon which disputes are resolved were frequently not explicitly verbalized by the people. They emerge only through the analysis of specific cases, from which anthropologists have abstracted the legal principles that are the basis for decision making. As with other aspects of culture, law is a cultural system of meanings that the anthropologist must interpret (Fuller, 1994: 11).

Anthropologists have come to realize that "classic" studies in legal anthropology, written in the decades between the 1930s and the 1960s, were studies of legal systems that had already been transformed as a consequence of European contact and encapsulation within colonial empires. As Fuller notes about one of the South African societies whose legal system had been intensively studied, "Tswana 'law and custom,' in other words, became more law-like as the indigenous normative order was reconstituted within the new colonial environment, in which Christianity and trade were at least as crucial as the colonial legal system itself" (1994: 10).

Societies without written legal codes had a variety of ways to settle conflicts or disputes. Sometimes the two parties thrashed it out themselves; the solution might be a fair one, or the stronger party would force the weaker to capitulate. Sometimes each side mobilized support from people with whom they had economic relationships (as among the Ndendeuli of southern Tanzania). Song contests might be held in which an audience decided the winner (as among both the Inuit and the Tiv of Nigeria), or the disputants might simply disperse (which is what the Hadza of Tanzania did). Interestingly, today, since the Inuit have moved into permanent settlements, personal communications broadcast over the radio, received by a large audience, has some of the same characteristics of the song duel (Briggs, 2000: 120)

Some societies have an authority who, as a third party, acts to resolve disputes and either decides the case on its merits or plays the role of a mediator. Such authorities may be political leaders or judges who have the power or influence to force the disputants to accept their decisions or recommendations. The legal principle applied in a particular case becomes the legal principle for future cases. This idea of universal application is what makes it a principle of law, rather than simply the political decision of someone in authority. When a legal decision is made after a violation of the law, some sort of sanction must be applied, possibly the use of force. A punishment just as severe may result if the community avoids someone or shames a person by public flogging. Other methods of social control in addition to the law include gossip and accusations of witchcraft, a topic to be discussed in greater detail in Chapter 10.

In complex societies, a distinction is made between civil, or private, law and criminal, or public, law. Civil law deals with private disputes between individuals, in which society acts as an arbitrator. For example, if a car stops short on a highway and your car plows into it, the owner of the car will take you to civil court and sue you for damages to his or her car. Criminal law deals with crimes, such as theft, assault, and murder, that are considered offenses against society as a whole. The wronged party against whom a crime has been committed is not allowed to punish the offender himself; the accused perpetrator is tried in criminal court. Private disputes in small-scale societies rend the fabric of the social structure and they are dealt with as actions against society as a whole. No distinction is made between civil and criminal law.

Law is also associated with morality and value systems. When viewed as a series of statements of what constitutes proper behavior, the law differentiates right from wrong, good from bad. In our own legal system, some of our laws represent, in effect, the continuation of ancient religious commandments, such as "Thou shall not steal." For most individuals, laws of this sort have been internalized. That is, most people do not break such laws, not because they are afraid of being punished but because if they did break such laws, they would feel guilty. The enforcer of the law is the person's own conscience.

LAW IN THE POSTCOLONIAL PERIOD

Postcolonial nation-states, like the Sudan and Papua New Guinea, have been very interested in anthropological studies of customary law. They have sought to take into account the various forms of customary law found within their borders in creating legal codes for their nations, rather than simply adopting Western-oriented legal systems. The concept of legal pluralism, which refers to the relationship between indigenous forms of law and the originally foreign (European or American) law that developed in colonial and postcolonial societies, may also be used to describe the situation that develops when people migrate from postcolonial states to European countries. This has occurred in France when Muslim people from Algeria and other parts of North Africa migrated there with their Islamic culture and Islamic legal ideas (Botiveau, 1992–1993). There are two possibilities—either the Islamic migrants submit completely to the hegemony of the French legal system (as Muslims migrating to the United States submit to the U.S. legal system), or the French legal system takes into account the Islamic legal system. During the colonial period, Islamic law had already been codified in accordance with the French legal system in both Egypt and Algeria, so migrants were familiar with more modern procedures. For example, the modern legal systems in Arab states such as Syria, Jordan, and Morocco require that civil marriages or the civil registration of a marriage takes place before the Muslim religious ceremony.

At present, with regard to matrimonial matters, foreign Muslims in France to some extent may choose the law that they wish to be applied. French mayors cannot celebrate polygamous marriages, but a Muslim man can choose to have a consular marriage, though this marriage has no legal status in France. When polygamous marriages have taken place prior to emigration, the French courts have recognized the husband's obligation to support each wife. Nor could the second wife of a polygamous North African migrant be denied entry into France. However, if a North African man first marries a French woman and then a North African woman, the latter's right to inherit is barred by the French courts. Islamic revivalism has developed today in France, and Islamic law is accepted by the French if there is no contradiction "with public order." When Muslims become French citizens, the definition of equality of rights is at stake and "Islamic positive law" is becoming a part of French legal culture (Botiveau, 1992–1993: 96).

In recent years, Native Americans have more and more frequently been engaged in legal battles with federal and state governments as well as with non-Native Americans. They assert their hunting and fishing rights, or their rights over land promised them in treaties, or the freedom to pursue their own religious practices, or their rights to tribal cultural objects now in the hands of various museums. These cases represent an affirmation of Native American sovereignty clashing with the sovereignty of the United States. This confrontation can be seen, for example, in cases involving the use of Native American sacred sites. In the past, tribal people have been discouraged from using the courts to protect their freedom of religious expression because legal doctrines often equate such customary religious expression with fringe nonindigenous religions, which mainstream Americans regard with great skepticism (Carillo, 1998: 277). In 1978, Congress passed the American Indian Religious Freedom Act, which was supposed to protect Native American religious expression. Though this act was supported in principle, only sometimes did the courts uphold Native American claims. In others, such as *Lyng v. Northwest Indian Cemetery Protective Association*, in which a road construction project was to invade sacred sites that were significant in the belief systems of native people of Northwest California, the Native American litigants lost their case (Carillo, 1998: 7). In another case, Earl Platt was unsuccessful when he tried to prevent the Zuni from crossing his land when they made their regular quadrennial summer solstice pilgrimage from their reservation to the mountain area they called Kohlu/wala:wa in northeastern Arizona (*U.S. on Behalf of the Zuni Tribe v. Platt*, 7300 F. Supp. 318 1990, in Carillo, 1998). In this case, the United States government acted on behalf of the Zuni when in 1985, Platt, one of the largest landowners in Arizona, challenged the right of the Zuni to cross his land and sought to interfere with their pilgrimage. Evidence was presented indicating that the pilgrimage had been taking place at the time of the Spanish conquest of the area and until recently had been largely uncontested. The area is believed by the Zuni to be their place of origin and the home of their dead. The trek, which takes four days and is 110 miles long, has been consistently the same. The Zuni had lost control over the ancestral land, which the pilgrimage traversed, after 1876. To the Zuni, the pilgrimage was the fulfillment of a religious obligation (Meshorer, 1998: 318). One of the problems encountered during the trial, which has characterized other court cases regarding Native American religious practice, was the need to present evidence to support the case while at the same time trying to avoid revealing ritual place-names and esoteric information that normally remains secret. Since Zuni witnesses were reluctant to testify, archaeological, ethnohistorical, and contemporary information from non-Indian local inhabitants was provided to demonstrate that the Zuni pilgrimage continued to be held. In its decision, the court deemed that the defendant, Platt, was aware that the pilgrimage had been taking place and went across his property, that such usage was "actual, open and notorious, continuous and uninterrupted," that "such use was known to the surrounding community," and that the Zuni believed that their crossing was a matter of right (*Zuni Tribe* v. *Platt,* in Carillo, 1998: 318). The court then ordered that the Zuni be granted an easement over Earl Platt's land for 25 feet in either direction of the route of their pilgrimage for a two-day period every four years during the summer solstice, without rights to use Platt's water or light fires on this pathway, and with the necessity to notify Platt at least 14 days before the pilgrimage.

Not only Native American religious practices, but the religious practices of ethnic minorities are also challenged in the courts despite the fact that the United States has had a long tradition of accommodating cultural differences. Especially in the area of religious practices, one would expect a wide degree of tolerance in a nation whose earliest settlers came here seeking freedom from religious persecution. However, the Supreme Court case *Church of the Lukumi* v. *City of Hialeah, South Florida* (Palmie, 1996) reminds us that the American majority, if permitted, will suppress religious practices that it finds offensive. Hialeah is part of greater Miami, and its politics are dominated by Cuban Americans who escaped from Cuba during the Cuban Revolution. These Cuban-American political leaders are successful middle-class people who, though proud of their Cuban heritage, seek to distance themselves from the waves of lower-class Cubans who came here during the Mariel "invasion" when Castro permitted convicts, petty criminals, and lower-class people to emigrate. The Church of the Lukumi Babalu Aye, of the Afro-Cuban religion known as Santeria, which had its origins in Cuba in the 1930s, moved into Hialeah in 1987. One of its religious rituals is the sacrifice of live animals to "feed the gods." This brought about an impassioned debate within the Hialeah City Council. Anglos saw sacrifice as a form of devil worship, and even the Cuban Americans on the city council sought to distance themselves from Santeria. As the Hispanic chaplain to the police department testified, "Nations that are controlled by this system of religion are in darkness, and the Bible says that these things are an abomination to the Lord" (Palmie, 1996: 188–189). In 1987, the mayor of Hialeah approved a bill outlawing the sacrifice, and the possession for sacrificial purposes of animals, in the city of Hialeah (Palmie, 1996: 193). Within two weeks, Ernesto

Prichard, a Santeria practitioner and leader of the Lukumi Church, filed suit against the mayor and the city council. Though two lower courts upheld the ordinances, in June 1993 the United States Supreme Court ruled that these ordinances unlawfully suppressed rights guaranteed by the First Amendment. Justice Kennedy, in his opinion, wrote: "Although the practice of animal sacrifice may seem abhorrent to some, religious beliefs need not be acceptable, logical or comprehensible to others in order to merit First Amendment protection" (Palmie, 1996: 185). As we will see in our discussion of American multiculturalism in a later chapter, tension continually exists in American society between the desires of the (white Christian) majority to assert themselves and the rights of minorities to express religious beliefs that differ from those of the majority.

Native Americans like the Zuni are a people engaged with the legal system of those who have conquered them. Their assertion of sovereignty represents their claim of independence. On the other hand, Cubans in Hialeah City are voluntary immigrants who have adapted to the legal system of the country they have entered. Though one is an immigrant group and the other is not, both groups are protected by our legal system, specifically by the First Amendment to the Constitution.

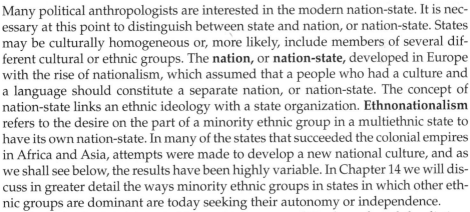

POLITICS IN THE CONTEMPORARY NATION-STATE

Many political anthropologists are interested in the modern nation-state. It is necessary at this point to distinguish between state and nation, or nation-state. States may be culturally homogeneous or, more likely, include members of several different cultural or ethnic groups. The **nation,** or **nation-state,** developed in Europe with the rise of nationalism, which assumed that a people who had a culture and a language should constitute a separate nation, or nation-state. The concept of nation-state links an ethnic ideology with a state organization. **Ethnonationalism** refers to the desire on the part of a minority ethnic group in a multiethnic state to have its own nation-state. In many of the states that succeeded the colonial empires in Africa and Asia, attempts were made to develop a new national culture, and as we shall see below, the results have been highly variable. In Chapter 14 we will discuss in greater detail the ways minority ethnic groups in states in which other ethnic groups are dominant are today seeking their autonomy or independence.

Anthropologists interested in contemporary politics have found the distinction between social structure and social organization, referred to in Chapter 1, particularly useful. Though they agree that political structure is important, they have focused primarily upon the organizational dimension—how individuals go about making choices and decisions in the political arena and the factors involved in such choices. Choosing to support one leader over another or one faction over another is a decision that will determine who will have power. The person who gains power makes administrative decisions, rewards supporters, and punishes the opposition.

The Sultan of the Afar tribe, surrounded by supporters and retainers, in present-day Ethiopia.

FACTIONALISM

One of the recurring themes in the study of local-level politics has been factionalism. Many of the earlier studies of peasant communities in the Old and New Worlds explored the operation of political factionalism as it related to the way national politics was played out on the local level. Leaders of factions vying for power may build their followings in a number of different ways, depending upon the structure of the village community. The faction consisting of the leader and his followers resembles the Big Man and his followers. Like the Big Man, the leader of a faction is in opposition to other faction leaders. The faction leader vies with other leaders to attract followers, as does the Big Man. There is an exchange relationship between the faction leader and his followers, as there is between the Big Man and his followers, and both types of leaders need to continue supporting and rewarding followers in order to hold onto them. When the leader in either case loses power or dies, the faction or group of followers dissolves. In this aspect, factions contrast with political parties, which continue to exist though individual leaders may come and go. However, within political parties in the United States, factions may be found on a local level as party leaders and their supporters compete for

Uzbek Warlord Rashid Dostum of Afghanistan, greeted by residents of
the northern town of Shibergan.

control of the party apparatus at that level. In nation-states, factionalism may be
based on differences in ethnic background. In such situations factionalism is transformed into ethnic conflict.

WARLORDS

Today, the term *warlord* is frequently used with reference to Afghanistan, Somalia,
and Myanmar (Burma). A warlord and his followers are structurally similar to a
faction and its leaders. A warlord is like a militarized Big Man. There is a continuum from the warlord who is a military commander with an extensive regional following and the ability to use his personal prestige to secure benefits for his
followers, like General Dostum (see photo above) and the late General Massoud,
in Afghanistan, to a more limited militarized ethnic or clan formation mobilized
behind a local strongman such as is found in Somalia (Rich, 1999b: 4–5; for Somalia, see below). Warlordism has become a growing phenomenon in contemporary

international politics as can be seen from reading the daily newspaper. It is a result of what have come to be known as "failed states," states that frequently were the aftermath of colonial departure and were based upon the political units that had been cobbled together from various disparate tribal groups by the colonial powers. The boundary separating Pakistan from Afghanistan today, the Durand line, was drawn to separate the lands held by czarist Russia and the British Empire.

Some warlords and their groups are the consequence of the post–cold war disappearance of "superpower hegemony" subsequent to which multiplicities of ethnic and other loyalties emerged to become the basis for these new groupings of warlords and followers. It is like a "barbarians at the gates" phenomenon that occurs at the end of imperial eras (Rich, 1999a: xi–xii). Warlordism is confined, primarily, to what one might consider to be peripheral, more undeveloped areas. These are the areas in which anthropologists have frequently done their research. Warlords are often involved in the illicit trade of opium and other narcotics, as well as in the arms trade, all of which have become completely globalized. The emergence of mercenary armies, a new kind of "warrior class," is also associated with warlordism, which serves to undermine "the authority of conventional governments" (O'Brien, 2000). In Afghanistan, some of the warlords and their followers are of a different ethnicity from the Pushtuns, who presently lead the central government. Thus their opposition constitutes ethnic conflict.

In Somalia, the population of nomadic pastoralists was culturally and linguistically homogeneous, subsumed under a single overarching segmentary lineage system. Under colonialism, titular clan leaders were officially recognized by the colonial government. The postcolonial democracy elections pitted 65 parties, which represented important lineages and sublineages, against one another. After the assassination of the president of the country in 1969, clans and clan families became the basis for militias, with modern weaponry introduced by the United States and the Soviet Union. These militias were run by warlords. The warlords and their groups in opposition to one another, in effect, represented different parts of the segmentary lineage system (Roseman and Rubel, 1999).

PATRON-CLIENT RELATIONSHIPS

The patron-client relationship discussed in connection with *compadrazgo* in Chapter 6 also has important political dimensions. In the past, patrons, frequently landowners, played roles as intermediaries between the peasants of a village and the provincial or national government. Problems with tax collectors and the court system brought clients to their patrons, who were always of a higher class, for assistance. The patrons could help clients because of their wide social contacts with their social equals in the towns and cities. The social contacts of clients, in contrast, were usually entirely within their own villages. Though there were no links of actual kinship between patrons and clients, the *compadrazgo* ties between the families of patron and clients were perpetuated over generations. Patrons as landlords and clients as tenants were distinguished by their differential access to land and by their class differences as gentry and peasants. These social and economic differences were the basis for a difference in political power. Patron-client relationships are usually superseded when opposition between socioeconomic classes serves to separate and oppose them.

Today, a form of patron-client relationship continues to be important in the political economy of Bangladesh. At first a homeland for Bengali Muslims and a province of the Islamic republic of Pakistan, Bangladesh became an independent nation in 1971 after a bloody civil war. An earlier class structure of commoners and nobility has been replaced by a system based on landownership, wealth, education, and power, in which a hierarchical network of interpersonal patron-client relationships dominates (Kochanek, 1993: 44). In the countryside, this system is reinforced by economic forces, such as scarcity of credit, land, tenancy contracts, and employment opportunities, along with political factors, such as the need for protection. The concept of *daya*, meaning "grace" or "blessing," constitutes the intellectual underpinning of the reciprocal patron-client relationship. Individuals feel that they have the moral right to demand food and subsistence from those "well placed," and the well-placed individuals, who acquire their prosperity from a higher moral authority, are expected to give generously to their clients. The patrons who distribute are expected to be authoritarian and to be feared and obeyed (Kochanek, 1993: 45).

This pattern of patron-client relationship has extended beyond the rural area and has come to dominate not only the whole of the Bangladesh political process but the business community as well. Though Bangladesh has formal legal, constitutional, and administrative governmental structures, these have come to be monopolized by a "traditional pattern of patron-client relationships based on *tadbir*, a process of personal lobbying" (Kochanek, 1993: 251). Policymaking and implementation always require personal connections. For example, the entire governmental structure of General Erhsad from 1982, when he came to power as a result of a military coup, to 1990 was based on the patron-client pattern. He traveled through the countryside "like a ward boss distributing benefits in exchange for support" (Kochanek, 1993: 265). The business community, which is in its early stages of development and modernization, is characterized by the same pattern, with primary emphasis on personal relationships. Businessmen often obtain exemptions from rules and other kinds of business benefits by manipulating the regulatory system and the administration of policy, using their personal connections. Patron-client relationships, from the countryside to the capital, are a way of life in Bangladesh.

POSTCOLONIAL POLITICS

Colonialism and the emergence of new nation-states in Africa and Asia have brought about great political changes. These nation-states tried to develop a national culture to unify the new nation. Traditional forms of leadership and politics were transformed as they were integrated into the state systems of these new nations. Modern methods of social control were also introduced to deal with detection and prevention of crime. However, as has happened in many parts of the world, the modern Western forms that were introduced did not completely replace the older indigenous forms, but existed side by side with them. In Ghana, a police force was established soon after conquest by the British (Abotchie, 1997). The British colonial government curtailed the authority and jurisdiction of the indigenous political leadership. Jurisdiction over all criminal and civil cases was vested in a Supreme Court, with colonial district commissioners dealing with lesser offenses. Postindependence governments modernized the police force and expanded the court system to include magistrate's, district, and circuit courts when the level of crime rose.

Abotchie describes in detail the way in which, despite "the prohibition under the Criminal Code of some of the traditional modes of crime control such as trial by ordeal, the 'patronage' of these techniques has persisted side by side with modern methods of crime control" (1997: 7). Many people, though nominally Christian (Abotchie calls them "Christians of little faith"), still believe in the traditional deities and express fear of them. As a consequence, traditional forces serve as a greater deterrent to criminal activity than do modern police methods and the fear of imprisonment (Abotchie, 1997: 116–119). The Ghanaian police are seen as corruptible. They are easily bought, and one may escape from them. Prison is not viewed as a reforming experience, and police activity is seen as retarding justice. Supernatural forces, however, are inescapable, and their penalties are more severe. Those who accept bribes will suffer the wrath of the deities, or instant death. Though lineage leaders and chiefs have lost their politico-legal authority, their "religious functions, and [the] sanctions of the lineage head and the chief, however, remain effective . . . ; besides, both rulers still hold themselves accountable to the supernatural forces" (Abotchie, 1997: 128). Ceremonies and rituals serve to reinforce the traditional system of values and norms. Though female puberty rites and marriage rituals have been transformed, the "outdooring" of the newborn—during which the child is named and is symbolically socialized into society and introduced to the notion of good and evil—and mortuary rites are still performed. It is evident that earlier forms of social control have continued despite the introduction of modern political and legal forms and police practices.

Today's nation-states contain culturally diverse populations. The newly emerged states of Africa and Asia were successors to colonies that were arbitrarily carved out by the colonial powers. These colonies brought together as a single political entity tribal groups that often were very diverse culturally. Lewis has recently made the point that precolonial states in Africa, such as the kingdom of Ethiopia and Zulu, Bemba, and Ganda states, were also multiethnic in their composition (1999: 58ff.). This was also true of other conquest states, like the empire of Bornu, described earlier in this chapter, which included non-Kanuri peoples like the Bagirmi. After independence was gained, in many countries, tribalism was seen as a problem to be overcome in forging a new national identity. However, tribalism does not die; rather, it is transformed and then maintained as ethnic difference. Though the ideology of ethnicity is new, the members of an ethnic group have returned to a conceptualization of themselves as all related by bonds of kinship. When the state developed, the kinship links tying a community together disappeared, only to return as an ideology when ethnicity has become important. Ethnic differences become the basis of political competition in the new nation-states. The drive to establish a national culture may be (or is often seen as) an attempt by the dominant and most powerful group or the numerically superior ethnic group to establish its culture as the national culture. This was the case with the Javanese, who dominate Indonesia. In the former Soviet Union there had been efforts to develop a "communist" culture, but this became, by and large, an attempt to Russify the distinctly different Central Asian and Caucasian peoples. This policy was met with opposition but little overt conflict because of Soviet suppression. Under the policy of *glasnost,* which opened up Soviet society, ethnicity and nationalism reasserted themselves, and many republics, such as the Baltic states, Moldavia, the Ukraine, Tadjikistan, Kazakstan, Kyrgyzstan, and Uzbekistan, became politically independent. For the non-Russian republics, this meant moving out from under the domination of Russian culture. These independent states now have the problems of defining themselves as nations and dealing with their own internal ethnic minorities. In Sri Lanka, ethnic conflict, which we will discuss in more detail later, has exploded into prolonged warfare between the dominant Sinhalese and the Tamil ethnic minority, which is demanding independence, or at least cultural autonomy. The attempt on the part of the Indian government to submerge the Sikh ethnic and religious minority has resulted in guerrilla warfare and a demand for Sikh autonomy. The Kurdish ethnic minority, which straddles the borders between Turkey, Syria, Iran, and Iraq, has been fighting an unending war of independence in order to establish its own state.

Though this is the postcolonial period, nation-states in Europe which have been in existence for hundreds of years may still exhibit tribalism, meaning identity with a particular group likened to a tribe, and exhibit ethnic differences in ways similar to postcolonial nations in Africa and Asia. The southern area of Belgium, Walloonia, where French is spoken, has been in conflict with the northern area, where Flemish, a Dutch dialect, is spoken. If this is the result of postcolonialism, then the colonialism that it involves is that of the ancient Romans, whose colony extended up to the Flemish-speaking border, but not beyond it (see Chapter 4). The conflict concerns not only language but also control over economic resources. Each of these areas of Belgium now has its own legislature and regional executives, and the central government includes a fixed proportion of ministers from each group. This is an example of ethnic conflict. Why and when it arises, and its relationship to class conflict will be considered in greater detail in Chapter 14.

EMPOWERMENT

At the beginning of this chapter we talked about power as the ability to command others and authority as the institutionalization of power. Over the past decade, a new term, *empowerment,* has become a buzzword in many political contexts. It has been used variously to refer to actions by the people to get what they want, populist action, revolt from below to subvert those in authority, and the devolution of power to place it in the hands of the have-nots, the subalterns. Using the ideas of Foucault about the way in which power is vested in discourse, one can say that with empowerment, the have-nots gain a voice. When successive African states gained their independence, empowerment of the African populace was a primary policy.

In Zimbabwe, for example, when independence was gained in 1980, there was a presidential directive on Africanization of the Zimbabwean civil service. Its goal was the indigenization of the civil service and the empowerment of the African population. Though the public sector and various types of funds are now managed by indigenous Zimbabweans, most Zimbabweans continue to participate in the economy as unskilled, seasonal, and unpaid domestic and agricultural laborers. The policy of indigenization and empowerment of the black population has been articulated by the male, black, self-employed business lobby. The rest of the black population, however, was convinced that black politicians and leading bureaucrats were interested only in empowering themselves (Gaidzanwa, 1999: 118–119). Those Zimbabwean groups lobbying for empowerment, such as the Indigenous Business Development Council, a black business lobby; the Affirmative Action Group, which included the War Veterans' Association; and the Indigenous Businesswomen's Organization, themselves were still involved in patronage politics, by and large. Even the businesswomen's group, which was organized to combat the problems women encountered in venturing into business in a male-dominated world, and which explicitly supported the economic empowerment of black women, supported Robert Mugabe in the 1996 election and they have continued to rely on the patronage of his ruling party. There have been no plans for the democratization of landholding, from which women are barred, though they are the sources of labor and management. The emphasis has been on acquiring land from white farmers. More recently, the political situation has changed and President Mugabe has assumed dictatorial power and ordered the confiscation of land belonging to white farmers. The War Veterans Association is the group taking over the land. It is clear that the term *empowerment* serves as an effective political slogan; in Zimbabwe the policy of indigenization and empowerment, in practical terms, has meant the empowerment of a limited, predominantly male, political circle.

POLITICS IN AMERICAN SOCIETY

The concepts we have discussed in this chapter can be applied to our own society. The operation of leadership in terms of power and exchange, the politics of empowerment, bureaucracy and administration, the emergence of leaders through political maneuvering, factionalism, police corruption, and patron-client relationships are as relevant to political situations in our own society as they have been in the situations described thus far in this chapter. If Ghanaian citizens are afraid that the police can be bought off, many segments of American society feel the same way. Just as Bangaladeshi businessmen manipulate the regulatory system of the government, so do businessmen in our country. In the past, the ward boss in big American cities was like a New Guinea Big Man in redistributing patronage in the form of material benefits among the "ward heelers." Factions representing different political positions and coalitions operate at every level of our political system. They may coalesce around individuals or around an issue, such as abortion, equal rights for women, or affirmative action for minorities. Ethnic politics are as active today in American cities as they are in any nation-state in Asia or Africa. Elections pit Poles against African Americans in Chicago, Hispanics against Anglos in Texas and California, and Cubans against African Americans in Miami.

THE MAFIA

Patron-client relations also operate in the United States. They have been seen as characterizing the Mafia in the United States, having been imported from Sicily. The patron-client relationship is characteristic of the Sicilian rural scene from which the men in the American Mafia emigrated. As we all know, the American Mafia don serves as godfather to the children of his followers. A study of the Mafia in Sicily and in Detroit explicitly likens the don to a Big Man (Louwe, 1986). The Big Man in the Mafia family provides a source of income for his "family" and protection against the risks of making money illegally; in return, family members pay him respect, grant him complete obedience, and give him a share of their profits from the criminal enterprise. His status is achieved through the demonstration of his ability. The don maintains his influence by manipulating his connections with the police, politicians, and judges. Loyalty of followers to him is paramount. The greatest threat to the family is the member who is turned into an informer by the police. A son may succeed his father as don and continue as patron to his father's clients. However, more in keeping with the Big Man structure, the clients whose patron has died may move to become followers of another don. The TV program *The Sopranos* presents a very sympathetic portrait of a Mafia family, which we will discuss in Chapter 11.

Within the past decade, the media have been referring to the Russian Mafia in the United States. The twilight period of the Soviet Union was marked by the "efflorescence of ethnic mafias," Chechens, Azerbijanis, Armenians, Georgians, and Dagestanis (Salter, 2002: 4; McCauley, 2001: 74–75). Most of these groups are non-Russian and from the Caucasus and they have been the subject of prejudice. Not much is known about the organization of crime among the Russians, many of them Jewish, who began to emigrate in large numbers in the late 1970s and who settled in that part of Brooklyn known as Brighton Beach, now often referred to as "Odessa by the Sea." (McCauley, 2001: 72; Friedman, 2000: 13) In a recent study, *Russian Mafia in America,* there was disagreement regarding whether Soviet émigré criminal groups operated like La Cosa Nostra or were less organizationally complex and hierarchical. However, particular leaders have been identified as "capo di tutti capi" (Finckenhauer and Waring, 1998: 164). Many Brighton Beach residents, in discussing crime in their area, used the term *Russian Mafia* and saw the Italian Mafia and Soviet émigré crime groups as being very similar in their mode of organization. Others saw Russian crime groups as less well organized, resembling, perhaps, the first stage of the development of the Italian Mafia, with leadership and followership not yet fully distinct (Finckenhauer and Waring, 1998: 224–226). Ethnic Mafias, internationally, are seen as emphasizing ties resembling kinship, in which blood was associated with solidarity, and blood symbolism reinforced family ties. Salter argues that because they engage in "risky business" there is a great need for trust, and therefore Mafias rely on kin and ethnic ties in the conduct of their business (2000: 5). Blok also emphasizes that agnatic ties and marriage alliances were operative in reinforcing bonds within Mafia families, describing how this functioned in the Gambino families that operated in both Sicily and the United States (2000: 111, 113). Structurally, this made Mafia families resemble the royal families of Europe who were linked to one another by marriage alliances.

POLITICAL ECONOMY

At the beginning of this chapter we again noted that political organization and economics are intimately interwoven and that this interrelationship is referred to as political economy. What are the ways in which the forces of production shape the culture and social organization? As shown throughout this chapter, the various types of political organization are associated with different forms of distribution and often different forms of production. For example, chieftainship is interwoven with a redistributive system, as described in Chapter 8, where surplus goods funnel into the central political position, that of the chief, and are distributed on ceremonial occasions to other chiefs, who in turn redistribute to their followers. The chief maintains political authority by controlling and disbursing economic goods, while the economic system is dependent upon the establishment of fixed positions of authority. Markets are always associated with state structures. The state as a political system, as we have pointed out, operates on a territorial basis beyond the level of kinship and clanship. The less personal relationships of a market are in accord with this type of system.

Ortner's landmark discussion of political economy as a framework of analysis points out its advantages (1984). She notes that an approach in terms of political economy is very open to symbolic analysis. Throughout this chapter, we have indicated how symbols are used to express rank and authority—as, for example, among the Trobrianders. Among the Kachin, who oscillate between two forms of political structure, the Big Man of the *gumlao* type and the chieftainship of the *gumsa*, symbols are used in different ways to express these opposing structures. In the context of the modern nation-state, symbols become a powerful means of constructing ethnic identity, and they are employed to express ethnic conflicts as well as class struggles.

As opposed to an emphasis on particular societies as isolates, political economy promotes a regional perspective. As we pointed out, systems of ceremonial exchange such as the *kula* demonstrate how societies with differing political systems were joined in a regional system of ceremonial exchange and barter. Cultural

Marxism, focusing in particular on Latin America, points out how capitalist forces of production have shaped the way of life of oppressed people. An emphasis on political economy can show how societies have been drawn into a world system, a topic to be explored in greater detail in Chapter 13.

SUMMARY

- Power, the key concept in defining political organization, is the ability to command others to do certain things and to get compliance from them.

- When power becomes institutionalized, it has been transformed into authority. This means that there is a recognized position, or office, the occupant of which can issue commands that must be obeyed.

- Influence is the ability to persuade others to follow one's lead.

- Government refers to the decisions made by those in office on behalf of the entire group in carrying out common goals.

- Politics concentrates on the manipulation of people and resources, the maneuvers intended to enhance power, the rise of factions that compete for power, and the development of political parties with differing points of view.

- Anthropologists refer to a position that depends on personal qualifications and individual ability as an achieved status, in contrast to an ascribed status, which one inherits.

- In the simplest form of political organization, leadership was manifested intermittently. This type of organization is referred to as informal leadership.

- Some hunting-and-gathering societies had band organization, with a more fixed membership that came together annually to carry out joint ritual and economic activities.

- A still more complex political organization is the Big Man structure, which represents a greater delineation of the leadership position. As leadership becomes more clearly defined, so does the group of followers.

- The position of Big Man is dependent on personal qualifications and individual ability.

- The introduction of fixed positions of rank and some method of succession leads to a fourth type of political organization—chieftainship, in which individuals as well as kin groups are ranked with respect to one another.

• The political economy of chieftainships is a more complex redistributive system than that associated with the Big Man structure. In a chieftainship, because there are more levels of political organization, villagers give to their village headmen, who in turn give to the chief.

• The Kachin, a hill people of Kachin Province, northern Myanmar (Burma), provide an example of how Big Man structure could be transformed into chieftainship and back again into Big Man structure.

• The state differs from the other types of political organization in scale. It is organized on a territorial basis, rather than on the basis of kinship and clanship. In the state we find social stratification—rulers, aristocrats, commoners, and various low-status groups.

• Those under the control of the state are its citizens or its subjects, including multiethnic populations, who speak different languages and are culturally different from one another.

• Warfare, feuds, and revenge seeking between social groups are resorted to when no lawful, mutually acceptable means of peaceful resolution of conflicts exists.

• Feuds, conducted according to rules, involve collective, not personal, responsibility, so revenge can be taken against any member of the group. Warfare is hostile action between different groups.

• Warfare is prevalent at certain times and not others, and under certain conditions and not others. The task of the anthropologist is to explain why warfare occurs when and where it does.

• The anthropology of violence also is concerned with the "culture of terror," "torture," and how these are used to establish "hegemony," or the domination of one group by another. It emphasizes the subjective point of view, in keeping with its postmodern origins.

• The legal principles or bases upon which disputes are resolved emerge only through the analysis of specific cases. Law is a cultural system of meanings that the anthropologist must interpret.

• The broadest anthropological approach to law considers that whenever conflicts or disputes arise and a cultural mechanism for resolving them exists, we are dealing with law. There are also anthropologists who argue that law should be more strictly defined and recognize it as being present only when it exists as a codified system with courts, judges, and a penal system.

• In complex societies, a distinction is made between civil law, which deals with private disputes between individuals, in which society acts as an arbitrator, and criminal law, which deals with crimes, such as theft, assault, and murder, that are considered offenses against society as a whole.

• The faction consisting of the leader and his followers resembles the Big Man and his followers.

• Today's nation-states contain culturally diverse populations. Ethnic differences become the basis of political competition in the new nation-states.

• After independence was gained, in many countries, tribalism was seen as a problem to be overcome in forging a new national identity. However, tribalism does not die; rather, it is transformed and then maintained as ethnic difference.

• Empowerment, has been used variously to refer to actions by the people to get what they want, populist action, revolt from below to subvert those in authority, and the devolution of power to place it in the hands of the have-nots, the subalterns.

• The concepts discussed earlier—the operation of leadership in terms of power and exchange, the politics of empowerment, bureaucracy and administration, the emergence of leaders through political maneuvering, factionalism, police corruption, and patron-client relationships—are all relevant to political situations in our own society.

• Patron-client relations characterize the Mafia, having been imported from Sicily to the United States.

 SUGGESTED READINGS

Kurtz, Donald. *Political Anthropology: Power and Paradigms.* Boulder, CO: Westview Press, 2001. A recent introductory text on the subject of political anthropology.

Rich, Paul B. *Warlords in International Relations.* New York: St. Martin's Press, 1999. A survey and analysis of the role that warlords play in contemporary world politics.

Schroeder, Ingo W., and Bettina E. Schmidt (eds.). *Anthropology of Violence and Conflict.* New York: Routledge, 2001. A series of articles concerning the role that violence and conflict play in contemporary world politics.

Sponsel, Leslie E., and Thomas Gregor (eds.). *The Anthropology of Peace and Nonviolence.* Boulder, CO: Lynne Riener, 1994. A series of essays about peacemaking in small-scale and complex societies. The authors examine nonviolent direct action, political action, and economic sanctions, which have been used as remedies to confront political and economic injustices.

Vincent, Joan (ed.). *The Anthropology of Politics: A Reader in Ethnography, Theory, and Critique.* Malden, MA: Blackwell Publishers, 2002. An excellent survey of both historic and contemporary theoretical ideas that deal with political anthropology

White, Geoffrey, and Lamont Linstrom (eds.). *Chiefs Today: Traditional Pacific Leadership and the Postcolonial State.* Palo Alto, CA: Stanford University Press, 1998. Discussions of the ways in which the role of chiefs has been transformed within modern Pacific states. The articles also illuminate ways in which chiefs operate in fashioning national identities and managing the direction of political and economic development in 13 contemporary Pacific societies.

SUGGESTED WEBSITES

http://www.d.umn.edu/cla/faculty/trou/s/anth1604/copolitical-systems.html Different tribes and peoples are identified in terms of their political type.

http://www.simians.co.uk/drc/working/WP6.pdf An anthropologist's account of fieldwork with an urban Nicaraguan criminal youth gang and how this relates to the anthropology of violence.

http://www.hrw.org/press/2002/06/warlordsogo5.htm A discussion and related websites dealing with warlords in Afghanistan.

10

Religion and the Supernatural

Many people in the world believe in an order of existence beyond the observable universe, that is, in what we call the supernatural. For example, the Trobriand Islanders believe that when a person dies, his or her spirit splits in two. One part goes to live on the island of Tuma in the village of the dead, to remain there until it is reincarnated in the spirit of a newborn child. The other part of the spirit haunts the favorite places of the deceased, and its presence is frightening to the villagers still alive. They are even more afraid of sorcerers, especially flying witches, who are thought to have caused the death in the first place.

Beliefs in sorcery, spirits, and witchcraft are not limited to societies like that of the Trobriand Islanders. One can ride along a country road in England and see a billboard announcing an impending meeting of a local witches' coven to be held the following week. Meetings of American witches' covens are also announced in the newspaper. There are people in England and America today who believe in witchcraft as a religion. To them, the witchcraft trials in seventeenth-century Salem, Massachusetts, were an example of religious persecution. Can witchcraft and Christianity coexist as sets of religious beliefs in a society like our own? Believers in witchcraft, like the believers of many other faiths in America today, are protected by the fundamental right to religious freedom. Is the modern belief in witches, or Wicca, the same as the belief in witchcraft described in classic ethnographies?

Although our country is founded on freedom of worship and belief, one periodically finds accounts of religious communities that run afoul of the law in the practice of their religious rites. In the course of their religious rituals, Snake Handlers in Appalachia hold up venomous snakes. Believers, while in an ecstatic state, pick up large rattlesnakes, a practice based on the belief that if they are free of sin, worshipers will not be bitten by the snakes. This belief derives from the Scriptures, in which it is stated that "they shall speak with new tongues; they shall take up serpents" (the Bible). Members of this religious com-

A contemporary witches' coven in Salem, Massachusetts, site of the seventeenth-century witch trials.

munity, like many other fundamentalist Christian groups, take the Bible literally. Some people who are bitten during the ritual subsequently die. The worshipers believe that those who die in this way are being punished for their sins. The snake, in this instance, is seen as acting as an agent of God. Whether a person is pure or sinful determines if the snake will bite that individual. This is a matter of belief, not an empirical explanation of why rattlesnakes bite. The cause of this phenomenon is understood to be supernatural. Though their beliefs may be considered extreme by some Americans, the Snake Handlers are part of the larger Christian community. Despite beliefs that seem aberrant to some, the sect is a historical offshoot of the Christian tradition, in which one aspect has been developed to an extreme.

The Trobriand belief in the power of sorcerers and the Snake Handlers' belief that, because of the purity of their character, God will protect them from the snake's bite go beyond what one can observe. Such explanations rely on phenomena that fall into the domain of the supernatural. From the Western point of view, empirical explanations of the observable world are scientific. Further, explanations that do not depend on empirical evidence, but instead rely on strongly held beliefs in nonempirical or supernatural forces, are categorized as religious. However, people in other societies, like the Trobrianders, consider their spiritual culture heroes and the ghosts of their ancestors absolutely real, no less real than the physical world around them. Culture heroes and ghosts are as real and natural as wind, rain, and thunder. In our society, scientific explanations that involve the forces of nature are distinct from religious beliefs and ideas about the supernatural. How

A member of the congregation of The Church of the Lord Jesus in West Virginia handling a rattler. He will not be bitten by the rattler, which represents the Devil, if he is "fully right with Jesus."

can we distinguish between religion as a belief in the supernatural and the other parts of culture is a question also encountered in the discussion of economics and political organization. Religious phenomena involve the use of symbols that evoke powerful emotional responses. One has merely to consider the difference between water and holy water and the emotional response evoked only by the latter to realize this. Water is transformed into holy water by the blessing of a priest. However, symbols that evoke strong feelings are to be found in parts of culture not labeled religious. Political symbols, such as the flag and the national anthem, produce emotions. Sometimes the emotion evoked by secular symbols and secular rituals is as strong as a religious response.

Religion is defined as the cultural means by which humans deal with the supernatural, but many humans also believe that the reverse is true—that the supernatural deals with humans. In this interaction, the supernatural is usually seen as powerful and human beings as weak. Another definition of religion has recently been proposed. Saler (1993) defines religion in terms of a pool of elements that tend to cluster together. They include a belief in God, gods, or "spiritual beings" with whom humans can have spiritual contact; a moral code believed to emanate from extrahuman sources; belief in a human ability to go beyond human suffering; and rituals that involve humans with the extrahuman (Saler, 1993: 219). The "spiritual beings" and the extrahuman of Saler's definition can be equated with what we call "the supernatural."

If religion involves the interaction of humans with the supernatural, then it is necessary to pose the question, Why do human beings believe in the existence of the supernatural in the first place? What is it about human life and the world in which that life is lived that seems to compel human beings to propose that the world is governed by forces beyond their empirical observations? Many theorists over the years have attempted to answer this question. Max Weber (1930) argued that since life is made up of pain and suffering, human beings developed religion to explain why they were put on earth to suffer. St. Paul constantly asked God why he was afflicted with a "thorn in the flesh," without ever receiving an answer. Sigmund Freud (1928) proposed that religious institutions represented society's way of dealing with childish needs of dependency on the part of individuals. What would otherwise be a neurotic trait thereby finds expression in the form of all-powerful gods and deities who control an individual's destiny. Melford Spiro (1966) attempted to deal with the issue of religion by suggesting three kinds of needs that religion fulfills. The first is called the cognitive need, that is, the need to understand. This is the need for explanations, the need for meanings. The second is the substantive need—to bring about specific goals, such as rain, good crops, and health, by carrying out religious acts. The third is the psychological need to reduce fear and anxiety in situations in which these are provoked. Émile Durkheim (1915) and others who have followed Durkheim's approach saw religion as the means by which society inculcated values and sentiments necessary for the promotion of social solidarity and the society's ultimate survival.

Recent explanations have involved what is referred to as the cognitive science of religion. It examines religious phenomena, such as ritual and belief, in an attempt to reach a cognitive understanding of these phenomena. Boyer claims that religious symbolism and representations are constrained cognitively by the universal properties of the mind-brain (cited in Andresen, 2001: 19). Nevertheless, he is defining religious expressions as "counter-intuitive ontologies." For example, holy water is physically no different from H_2O; however, it is seen as different by believers and this is counterintuitive. Rituals represent behaviors that are separate from everyday life, and religious representations "violate" what people consider to be natural phenomena according to Boyer. On the other hand he believes that "the vague notion of supernatural entities and agency is the only substantive universal we find in religious ideology" (cited in Andresen, 2001: 21). One of the areas of research that has been pursued involves the neurophysiological and neurobiological investigation of religious phenomena such as trance and meditation and the role played by the temporal lobe of the brain in the expression of religious ideas, emotions, and ritual behavior.

From these different considerations of why religion exists and what explanations have been offered for religious phenomena, we can suggest some tentative answers to the questions we have posed. Human beings are part of a social world as well as a natural world. They are dependent upon the actions of other humans, as well as upon the forces of nature. Some of these actions and forces can be controlled through their own behavior. However, they are helpless in the face of other actions and forces. Humans attempt to understand and at least influence or control through a belief in the supernatural what is otherwise uncontrollable and unexplainable. As Spiro (1966) suggests, by doing this, they alleviate their anxieties about their helplessness in the situation. The organization of the supernatural world that is constructed by human beings reflects the society in which they live (Durkheim, 1915). The sentiments and emotions generated by the supernatural are an important force in the enhancement of social solidarity.

RELIGION, SCIENCE, AND MAGIC

There is a distinction between the explainable parts of the universe and those aspects that are unexplainable. Today, we would say that many aspects of the natural world, which were formerly explained by religion, are now explained by means of science. In the seventeenth century, the Catholic Church insisted that the Earth was at the center of the solar system, and persecuted Galileo for his scientific research, which demonstrated that Copernicus' earlier research was correct and that the Sun, not the Earth, was at the center of our solar system. Despite conclusive evidence supporting this scientific view of the solar system, it took the Catholic Church hundreds of years to accept the scientific explanation and admit its error. The theory of evolution is another example of the shift from a religious explanation to a scientific explanation. Judeo-Christian belief states that humans, along with all the other species, were created by God. The seventeenth-century clergyman Bishop Ussher determined for Christians that creation occurred in the year 4004 B.C. Until the late nineteenth century, this was the accepted belief about creation in the Western world. Darwin proposed his theory of evolution based upon scientific evidence from comparative anatomy, geology, and paleontology in the mid-nineteenth century. This scientific theory proposed an alternative explanation for the development of all the species in the world and the appearance of human life. For a time, both religious and scientific explanations of creation competed with one another.

Today, many people accept the scientific theory of evolution. Some see it as incorporated into a divine plan. However, in America many people (perhaps 48 percent of the population) believe in what is called creationism. This belief that each of the species on Earth was created and placed here by God is spelled out in the Bible. Some religious groups, such as the Jewish Hasidim, even deny that dinosaurs existed 60 million years ago. Fundamentalists in the United States have attempted to transform creationism into a scientific theory, which they argue should be given equal status with evolutionism in school curricula. United States courts have ruled that creationism is a religious belief, while evolutionism is qualitatively different and, as a field of study, open to question and thus teachable in U.S. public schools. Recently, however, creationists gained the upper hand in Kansas when the Kansas Board of Education voted in August 1999 to delete any mention of evolution from the science curriculum of the state's schools. Though teachers are not forbidden to teach about evolution, the examination of students will no longer include evolution, discouraging school districts from spending students' time on evolution (*New York Times*, August 12, 1999). For those who accept Darwin's theory of evolution, religion has not ceased to be important. However, religion is no longer used to explain how humans came to be on Earth, because the creation of humans is no longer in the realm of the unexplainable.

Observations of the world are the basis for scientific knowledge for people in less complex societies as well as for those in the Western world. The Trobrianders used their empirical knowledge, about the displacement of objects in the water and about wind currents, when they constructed outrigger canoes. Since they had no scientific explanation based on empirical evidence for why the wind blows or why storms come up, they resorted to supernatural explanations. They tried to control the wind through the use of wind magic. In our own society, some people also resort to nonscientific explanations. Scientific knowledge cannot at present determine why some children contract leukemia while others do not. If such a disease strikes a child in a family, the family may search for nonscientific cures such as faith healing or the "laying on of hands."

Science and religion, which includes magic, are all ways of understanding and influencing the natural world. Magic and religion differ from science in that what is unexplained by science in the natural world is explained in magic and religion by recourse to the concept of the supernatural. Magic and science are similar in that the aims of both are specific, and both are based upon the belief that if one performs a set of specific actions, one will achieve the desired result. Magic and science differ in that they are based on different theories of knowledge—*magic* (which is part of religion) is based on the belief that if spells or rituals are performed correctly, the supernatural will act in such a way that the desired end within the natural world will result. Magic is based on the idea that there is a link between the supernatural and the natural world such that the natural world can be compelled to act in the desired way if the spell is performed as it should be. *Science*, on the other hand, is based on empirically determined logical connections between aspects of the natural world. Its hypotheses concerning these logical connections are subject to change if new empirical data suggest better hypotheses. Science is based on empirical knowledge obtained through the five senses, whereas the defining feature of religion is the supernatural, a belief in a reality that "transcends the reality amenable to the five senses" (Lett, 1997: 104). The competition between religious explanations and scientific explanations that we described above continues to be present today.

Magic differs from other aspects of religion in that people attempt to manipulate the supernatural through magic. If the right magical formula is used, success is inevitable because magic is seen as being able to bend the supernatural to the will of the practitioner. Other religious practices, on the other hand, are not as specific in their aims. Religious rites emphasize the degree of human beings' powerlessness and do not compel direct results in the way that magic does. Religious rites involve people making appeals to the gods, which the all-powerful gods may or may not choose to grant. Magic is therefore manipulative and religion is supplicative. Magical knowledge manipulates on behalf of individuals, whereas religion is the belief system and ritual practice of a community.

CONCEPTIONS OF THE SUPERNATURAL

People who believe in any religion see the supernatural world as inhabited by a variety of superhuman creatures, agents, and forces whose actions will bring about good fortune or misfortune, rain or drought, famine or fertility, health or disease, and so forth. Since these superhuman creatures are the cultural creation of human minds, the real world serves as a model, though not an exact one, for people's conceptualizations of the supernatural. It would be too simplistic to say that the supernatural world is simply a mirror image of people's life on earth. Nevertheless, there is a relationship between the social structure of a society and the way in which its supernatural world is organized. Similarly, the power relationships in the supernatural world are related to the kind of political organization found in the society.

The kinds of spirits that populate the supernatural realm may be grouped into types using the English terms that analysts have developed to describe them. This use of English terms is seen as the imposition of Western or English concepts on indigenous categories. Translation into these terms represents the best equivalent that can be made, although it is usually not an exact equivalent. Several different categories of spirits of the dead may be recognized. These usually include the ghosts of the recent dead; the ghosts of the more remote dead of previous generations, who are considered ancestor spirits; and the ancestral spirits of the ancient past, who were founders of the group in mythological times. In societies with totemic clans, such as the Kwakiutl, which we described in Chapter 5, founding ancestors may be represented as animal spirits, not human spirits. This belief in totemic animal spirits as ancestors of human groups links humans with the natural animal world.

In addition to totemic animal ancestor spirits, some people believe that all animal and plant species have both physical and spiritual components. The natural world is then seen as having its spiritual counterpart. Inanimate forces such as rain, thunder, lightning, wind, and tide may also be seen as spirits themselves, or as motivated by spiritual beings, or controlled by deities or gods. If the spirit is directly perceived as having human characteristics as well as supernatural power, then it is referred to as a god or deity and not a spirit. The population of gods and deities recognized by a society is referred to as a *pantheon*. The relationships between the gods of a pantheon are frequently conceived of in human terms. The gods show jealousy, have sexual intercourse, fight, and live much like human beings. Human characteristics of this sort are also attributed to ghosts and ancestral spirits in many societies. The origins and activities of supernatural beings are depicted in myths, a topic we will discuss in the next chapter.

In some societies, like the American Indians who lived on the Plains, individuals go out alone to seek a vision of an animal spirit, who then becomes their protector and **guardian spirit** throughout life. There is also a widespread notion that particular individuals acquire special supernatural powers that enable them to perform evil deeds. Finally, there is the belief in an impersonal supernatural force or power that is inherent in people or things, to which the Polynesian term *mana* is applied.

Ideas about ghosts and spirits are part of a larger category of beliefs about the spiritual or noncorporeal counterparts of human beings. Tylor (1871), the nineteenth-century evolutionist, termed this **animism.** He saw this idea as the seed from which all other forms of religion grew. He hypothesized that primitive people saw all living things, including the forces of nature, as composed of a corporeal, or bodily, form and a spiritual aspect. This was an extension of the idea that each person has a body and a separable other self or soul. This other self was seen in the person's shadow, or in the reflection in a pool, and it traveled far and wide in the person's dreams. Tylor saw this belief in a separable spirit projected onto the natural world. Tylor's ideas about animism were the cornerstone for the development of his evolutionary theory of religion, in which animism evolved into a pantheon of deities and finally into monotheism.

Any particular combination of different kinds of spiritual entities may be found in a given society. The supernatural world conforms to its own logic. This will become apparent as we examine the supernatural worlds of several different societies. Often people believe in a monotheistic religion such as Judaism, Christianity, and Islam, and still maintain beliefs in ghosts, witches, and spirits of nature as parallel systems. Indeed, as we have observed, this occurs in our own society.

Christianity, in its Roman Catholic form, was introduced to the people of Wogeo in 1934. By and large, the traditional belief system continues, in a synthesis with the belief system of Christianity and the Roman Catholic church structure. The belief system of the people of Wogeo, an island off New Guinea, represents a particular combination of spiritual entities (Hogbin, 1996). To the Wogeo, the supernatural world is just as real as the natural and cultural world around them. Their traditional supernatural world is made up of three kinds of beings. The first is called *nanarang,* or culture heroes. These culture heroes are the founders of the Wogeo natural world and the givers of all cultural inventions. The Wogeo believe that the earth is a huge platter under an upturned bowl, which is the sky. The island of Wogeo, seen as the home of humankind as well as of the culture heroes, is at the center, and radiating out are other islands, the moon, and the stars. Myths provide the stories of how the culture heroes formulated all the customs of Wogeo society. Those culture heroes who disappeared left behind black basalt columns as reminders of their deeds, while the remaining culture heroes still dwell in certain sacred places, which they guard against intruders. Present-day magic rites are directed toward them to bring about what is desired.

A second category of supernatural beings is the ghosts of the dead. Only the spirits of men killed in a raid or women who have died in childbirth are harmful. They may try to steal the spirit of a living person. Persons who have lost part of their spirit become unconscious or delirious. They are deemed to be in a cold state and are fed hot curry so their spirit will return. When the soul of a dead person appears in a dream, it may try to take the soul of that person to the land of the dead.

In addition, there are two types of spirit monsters: one represented by flutes, called **nibek**, and the other by masks, called **lewa**. Prior to ceremonial distributions, people are not allowed to collect certain crops so that large quantities will grow, and they are not allowed to kill pigs so that a sufficient number of them will mature. Men put on masks to impersonate the *lewa* spirit and blow the flute to impersonate the *nibek* spirit. As a consequence, men are in a dangerous ritual state. The *lewa* are said to be cold and are offered hot curry to warm themselves. The *nibek* spirits are said to have "eaten" the pigs distributed at the ceremony before they are sent back to the spirit world.

These three kinds of Wogeo spirits do different kinds of things and deal with different kinds of problems. Accounts of culture heroes, who are the creators of the natural and cultural world, form the basis for mythologies, as do such supernatural individuals found in other societies. The spirit monsters are that part of the supernatural and the sacred which is involved in large-scale ceremonial distributions that have political and economic aims. These monsters are called forth to lend their sacred presence to the ceremonial to promote the well-being of the society and are given offerings of food and pigs. Lastly, there are the Wogeo ghosts, who connect people to their ancestors.

A somewhat different conceptualization of the supernatural was found among the Kachin, discussed in both Chapters 6 and 9. However, the Kachin have become Christians. Since Myanmar (Burma) is a Buddhist country, Kachin Christianity is something of an anomaly. Whether the system of belief we will describe has disappeared or is now in a synthesis with Christianity, is not known. Kachin social organization consists of a patrilineal segmentary lineage structure with mother's brother's daughter's marriage, so there is a division between wife-givers and wife-takers (Chapter 6). The Kachin supernatural world is made up of spirits called **nats**, who are hierarchically ordered like the hierarchical *gumsa* world of Kachin political organization. Shadip, the chief of the *nats* and the reincarnation of the creator of everything, is responsible for good fortune and fertility. Beneath him are his children, the sky spirits. Since the Kachin have a rule of succession of ultimogeniture, the senior-most sky spirit is Madai, the youngest of the sky spirits. *Nats,* like people, belong to lineages. Madai's daughter is said to have married a human being who was the first ancestor of all Kachin chiefs. The Madai *nat* gave a woman to the first Kachin chief and is therefore wife-giver to the most senior Kachin line of chiefs. This links the world of the supernatural to human beings through marriage alliance. The sky spirits are superior to humans because they are wife-givers to humans. Below the sky spirits are the ancestor *nats,* the spirits of the ancestors of the various Kachin lineages. The sky *nats* are approached by making offerings to one's ancestor *nat,* who acts as an intermediary. Only the senior chief can make offerings to Madai directly, because his ancestor was wife-taker to Madai.

Another category of *nats* is seen as inferior to humans because they are the offspring of a human girl and an animal. These inferior spirits are said to cause all kinds of misfortunes to humans, such as death in childbirth and fatal accidents. Witches, who are human beings, also have a relationship to the supernatural. Witchcraft is inherited in a particular lineage, and the people in the lineage themselves are unaware that they possess this attribute. They unknowingly cause misfortune and illness to people who are their affines, those to whom they give wives.

It is apparent that the Kachin picture of the supernatural world is an extension of and directly correlated with their own social organization. The relationships among the spirits and between the spirits and human beings are the same as the relationships between individuals and social groups on the human level. Like human beings, the spirits are also organized into lineages, with wife-takers always lower in rank than wife-givers. The Kachin example supports Durkheim's idea that the supernatural world mirrors the organization of human society and that human propitiation of the supernatural world through prayers and sacrifices has the function of reinforcing human society and reinforcing social solidarity. Human worship of the supernatural was, in effect, the worship of a projection of society. The relationship between the social structure and the organization of the world of the supernatural is often not such a simple one-to-one relationship. For example, the Kaguru of East Africa believe that witches, unlike humans, walk upside down, on their hands. In this case, the supernatural world is an inversion of the real world.

RITUAL—APPROACHING THE SUPERNATURAL

Generally speaking, human beings approach the supernatural by carrying out ritual acts, usually involving a combination of speech and patterned behavior that alters the emotional state of the participants. **Hortatory rituals** consist of exhortations to the supernatural to perform some act (Firth, 1951). Just before a shipwreck, the captain of a Trobriand canoe would exhort the supernatural powers to send the marvelous fish to guide the drowning victims to a friendly shore. The Trobrianders have a native term for this category of exhortation. The term means "by the mouth only." *Prayer*, involving words only, differs from hortatory ritual in its method of approach and intent. Prayer emphasizes people's inferior position to all kinds of gods since they beseech the gods to act on their behalf.

Sometimes, the gods can be approached only by going into a self-induced or drug-induced trance. The Yanomamo blow the hallucinogenic substance *ebene* up their noses to induce a trance and enable contact with the spirit world. In the trancelike state produced by the drug, individuals may hallucinate that they are flying to the spirit world. Sometimes trances may be induced without the use of any drugs. Many North American Indian societies had the **vision quest,** in which a man, through starvation, deprivation, and sometimes even bodily mutilation, attempted to induce a trance in which a supernatural being will visit him and thenceforth become his guardian spirit and protector. Among the Crow of Montana, an adolescent boy would go out into the wilderness and fast and thirst for days in order to induce a vision. He might even mutilate himself by cutting off a joint of a finger on his left hand if the vision was not forthcoming. The vision usually came on the fourth night, since for the Crow the number four had magical significance. Supernatural visitors came most frequently in the form of animals, sometimes powerful ones like buffalo and eagles, at other times animals like dogs or rabbits. The Crow believed that the supernatural spirit adopted the individual who saw him, and thereafter the spirit acted as a protector, teaching its protégé a sacred song, instructing him in special medicines, and imposing special dietary restrictions. The man wore tokens of his vision and accumulated a medicine bundle consisting of sacred objects connected to the first and subsequent visions of his spirit protector. Part of the man's power could be used to protect others whom he adopted for this purpose, as his spirit protector had adopted him.

Still another way of approaching the supernatural is by making sacrifices. The Kachin attempt to intercede with the *nats,* or spirits, when they cause sickness or misfortune by making sacrificial offerings. There is a relationship between the size and value of the sacrificial offering and the importance of the spirit to which it is offered. The inferior *nats* are offered rats, dogs, pigs, and chickens, but never cattle. Household ancestral spirits are offered only chickens. The village headman's ancestral *nats* are given offerings of pigs. Sky *nats* are given offerings of pigs and buffalo. Shadip, the creator, is given a sacrifice of a whole pig, which is not eaten but is buried. In all other cases, the essence of the sacrificial animals is given to the *nats,* while the meat is consumed by the human participants. Sacrifices are made on ritual occasions to ensure the supernatural protection of crops and their fertility. The *nats* must be remembered or they will cause misfortunes. The sacrifice consists of giving up something of value in an exchange with the spirits. Eating the meat from sacrificial animals is eating sacred food, which brings humans into contact with the gods. Today, these ceremonies have become a single large ceremony held in a stadium, in which a single mithan is sacrificed. As a consequence of the advent of Christianity, this sacrifice seems to be a cultural rather than a religious ceremony.

W. Robertson Smith (1889), another nineteenth-century theorist on religion, saw the sacrifice as the eating together of god and man, which signified the bond of kinship between them, just as eating together among men symbolically signifies kinship, as noted in Chapter 5. The widespread sacrifices and offerings of live animals, food, vegetables, incense, and even money are a way of approaching the supernatural by bearing gifts. Since the relationship between humans and the supernatural emphasizes the subordination of the humans, people can only hope for supernatural support in fighting wars; in warding off misfortune, sickness, and death; and in providing fertility in exchange for their gift. The sacrifice of live animals is the sacrifice of life itself. In ancient Israel, lambs were sacrificed, but this practice stopped before the diaspora.

RITES OF PASSAGE

Two broad categories of ritual have been identified by anthropologists: rites of passage and rites of intensification. **Rites of passage** are communal ceremonies held to publicly mark the changes in status an individual goes through as he or she progresses through the life cycle. The beginning of life—birth—and the end of life—death—are always marked by some kind of ritual. In addition, one or more points between life and death at which one's status changes, such as a girl's first menstruation or marriage, as described in Chapter 2, may be marked with a ceremony. In Chapter 7 we discussed the cultural construction of gender as expressed in such rituals. Cultures may emphasize a biological change in their rites of passage, or the changes may be culturally determined, such as the first catch of a fish or a child's first haircut. The cultural determination of such rites is demonstrated in the variation in the age at which a male child is circumcised in societies over the world.

Van Gennep (1960), in his analysis of rites of passage, pointed out that all such rites involve three stages. The first stage marks the separation of the individual from the category or status previously occupied. Next is a period of transition in which the individual is in a kind of limbo. During this period, the individual is frequently secluded from the rest of the society. Victor Turner (1967) has characterized this period as a particularly sacred one, a **liminal period** in which the individual is literally "in between," no longer in one status and not yet in another. The last stage is one of reincorporation, in which the individual is ceremonially reintegrated into society, but this time in the new status. Frequently, this three-stage process is represented by means of the metaphor of death and rebirth. The individual in the former category "dies" and is "reborn" into the new category. In the third stage of the ceremony, the person is often given a new name and puts on a different type of clothing, marking the birth of a new person.

The Arapesh of New Guinea celebrate several different kinds of rites of passage. Though the Arapesh have a patrilineal rule of descent, as noted in Chapter 5, they believe their blood comes from the mother while the father contributes the semen. When one's blood is spilled, the mother's group must be recompensed by the payment of shell valuables. This principle underlies all rites-of-passage ceremonies, as well as other aspects of Arapesh culture. After the birth of a child, the child's father "pays for the blood" by giving shell rings to the child's mother's brother. Through this act the child now belongs to the father's group, though the mother's lineage is still said to "own" the child's blood.

At puberty, several boys are initiated at the same time to make them into men. The rites involve isolation from females, with whom the boy has spent most of his time, the observance of a series of taboos, and the incision of the boy's penis. He is also introduced to the secret male Tamberan Cult, where he learns that the Tamberan spirit is the sounds of the drums and the flute secretly played by the men. This information is kept from women and children. During initiation, the boy is beaten by his mother's brother and his penis is incised by a man designated the Cassowary, who removes the "female" blood from the initiate. The initiate then drinks blood that has been contributed by all the old men of the group and is thereby reborn as a man. At the end, he is reincorporated into society as a man at a feast made by his father to honor the boy's mother's brother, who must be paid for the shedding of the boy's blood. Finally, the boy, now a man, goes on a trip and meets all his father's trading partners, signifying his new status.

Contemporary mortuary rite of passage in New Ireland involves payments to members of the opposite moiety of the deceased who erected the cement grave marker.

The Arapesh have child betrothal, after which a girl frequently goes to live with the parents of her future husband. Her first menstruation is marked by a rite of passage, during which she is secluded and does not eat. She is then scarified on the shoulder and buttocks by her mother's brother, and becomes an adult woman. She is ceremonially fed by her new husband. He then hunts for meat, which is used to make a feast for the girl's mother's brother, since her blood was shed by the scarification process.

The final Arapesh rite of passage occurs at death, at which the deceased's mother's lineage is paid in shell rings in compensation for the death. The ceremonial payment of shell rings that marked all the other Arapesh rites of passage marks the death.

Male and female initiatory rites are found in societies with matrilineal as well as patrilineal descent rules; however, there is a difference at boys' initiation between patrilineal and matrilineal societies. Lesu, in New Ireland, is a matrilineal society. Before the colonial period and missionary activity, boys were initiated and circumcised. But even in this matrilineal society, boys were forcibly removed from their protesting mothers and turned into men. This initiatory rite, as well as girls' initiation, was performed in conjunction with mortuary rites. Young girls were secluded, fed special foods, and tattooed during this period of seclusion. Both boys and girls emerged as men and women during the final stages of the mortuary ceremony.

Rites of Passage in American Culture   Different kinds of rites of passage characterize American culture, with its multiethnic complexity and religious diversity. These include the Jewish circumcision rite, Christian baptism, bar mitzvah, confirmation, different types of wedding (described in Chapter 2), (in a sense), the retirement party, and various types of funeral. The same stages of separation, transition, and reincorporation can be seen in these rites of passage as in those of other cultures. Jewish male circumcision and Christian christening, or baptism, are both similar in that they perform the same function. When a child is born, he or she is not a member of society at that point. Just as the Arapesh payment of shell rings marks the entry of the child into his or her father's patrilineal group, circumcision and baptism perform the same function. At birth the child moves from being a neonate into a liminal state, not yet part of society. On the occasion of the Jewish circumcision, the cutting of the foreskin by the *mohel* marks the male child as a Jewish male. The recently introduced naming ceremony for Jewish girls soon after birth performs the same function. At the christening, the priest or minister dabs the child's forehead with water and names the child, thereby marking its entry into Christian society. Having been born, some Americans, like President George W. Bush, are "born again" into Fundamentalist Christian groups. This rebirth involves the three stages Van Gennup described.

RITES OF INTENSIFICATION

The other major category of ritual—**rites of intensification**—is celebrated communally either at various points in the yearly cycle, such as spring, fall, or the winter and summer solstices, or at times when the society is exposed to some kind of threat, like the threat that terrorists pose to the United States today. Societies may hold rites of intensification to mark planting, in hope for a good crop, or to mark the harvest, in thanks for what has been given. The Kachin ceremonial sacrifices known as *manau*, carried out by the chief on behalf of the whole community, were rites of intensification that served to reiterate the social structure and reinforce the solidarity of the group.

When an event of importance to the whole community on Wogeo takes place, such as appointing the official heir to the chief, a rite of intensification, known as a *warabwa*, is held. The *nibek* spirit monsters are summoned. The community as a whole sponsors the *warabwa* and is host to many other villages. The climax of the ceremony is a great distribution of food and pork. One of the occurrences at a Wogeo *warabwa* takes place the day before. At this time, there is a free-for-all at which the rules regarding the respect relationship between certain categories of relatives are suspended, and they may insult and humiliate each other. The suspension of rules in this case serves, in a negative fashion, to emphasize the rules of the group. The rites allow the expression or release of tension in a ritual context that could not be permitted in the everyday course of events. A similar reversal of everyday behavior occurs at Mardi Gras, just before Ash Wednesday, which marks the beginning of the 40-day period of penance leading to Easter. Mardi Gras rites, marked by great exuberance and extravagant behavior, contrast with the restraint and somberness of Lent that follows.

Thanksgiving, the "giving of thanks," is an American rite of intensification. It has a historical basis in the Pilgrims' celebration, when they gave thanks to God for their survival during their first year in the New World. Today, most Americans participate in a Thanksgiving meal and, by their participation, give thanks in a way that is completely secular. The religious aspect, if present, involves saying grace at the start of the meal. This rite of intensification demands that particular foods be eaten to symbolize Thanksgiving. It is turkey, not lamb chops or meatballs, that symbolizes this celebration. Though Native Americans, who were conquered by European immigrants, are said to have contributed to the first Thanksgiving, today most do not celebrate Thanksgiving as a rite of intensification. They feel they have no reason to do so.

Ritual does not simply mirror society and culture, but helps shape its defining features. Ritual can also challenge the existing order, as Gluckman pointed out in his work on rituals of rebellion in Africa. Today, rituals are seen as dynamic and flowing, ever responsive to the changing aspects of modern and postmodern life. Experimentation and the development of new rituals, such as the Wiccan rituals we will discuss below, or commitment ceremonies have become important foci of anthropological research. Anthropologists study the performative aspects of ritual and are interested in how participants "constitute themselves through their actions." However, there is a tension or dialectic between the traditional rules of ritual and innovation or experimentation in actual performances. The meaning of the ritual for the participants, its subjective aspects as encompassed in the "native point of view," is in line with the postmodern perspective.

RELIGIOUS SPECIALISTS

The supernatural is often approached indirectly, through intermediaries, who have access to it because they possess some special gift. Many have been through extensive training, or have inherited esoteric knowledge or ability. Religious specialization is found in small-scale societies as well as in complex, hierarchically organized societies. Religious specialists often have a primary function, such as curing illness or predicting the future. The English labels for these specialists—diviner, oracle, magician—usually refer to that function, though the translation of the indigenous terms for these specialists may not be exact. Religious specialists operate on a full- or part-time basis.

SHAMANS

In small-scale societies, the **shaman** was usually the only religious specialist. These part-time specialists used their powers primarily to diagnose illness, cure illness, and sometimes cause illness as well. They also had other functions, such as divining the future. Early travelers referred to these individuals as "witch doctors" to highlight their curing functions. This was a particularly unfortunate translation. The term *shaman* comes from the Tungus of Siberia. Shamans were found throughout Asia and among a great many indigenous societies of North and South America.

The practices and functions of the Kwakiutl shaman typify shamanic activities elsewhere. Kwakiutl shamans were classified on the basis of the level of their expertise or power. The least powerful were those who were able only to diagnose and locate the disease, that is, determine the place in the body where the object causing the disease was lodged. But the most powerful could not only cure diseases but could also cause illness in others. Both Kwakiutl men and women could become shamans. One became a shaman as a result of an initiation by a supernatural spirit that came to the person while he or she was sick. The most common spirits were wolf, killer whale, and toad. The spirit taught the novice songs and dances and gave the shaman a new name, which was always used by the shaman when acting in that capacity. The shaman wore certain paraphernalia—a neck ring of shredded red cedar bark to which was attached a pouch bearing small objects, which represented the diseases the shaman could cause—and used a special rattle and a ring of hemlock branches for purifying patients.

The curing of a patient took place at a public ceremony. Diagnosis was made by the shaman through contact with the supernatural spirit by going into an altered state of consciousness. If the cause of the disease was loss of the soul, the shaman used the purification ring to call back the soul. If the cause was the intrusion of some foreign object, the supposition was that it had entered by accident or been "thrown" by another shaman acting on behalf of an enemy of the patient. The shaman removed it by sucking or squeezing it out of the patient's body. The shaman resorted to a variety of tricks to produce the removed object. He could conceal bird down (tiny bird feathers) in his upper lip and then bite his lip and spit out the bloodied bird down as if it were some wormlike object. In keeping with the ranked social structure of the Kwakiutl, great chiefs "owned their shamans," who protected them by throwing disease into their enemies. The Kwakiutl are now Christians and there is no information as to whether there are any practicing shamans and whether they are still curing people today. In other parts of the world, shamanism is practiced today alongside other religions.

In a nonranked society like the Inuit, shamanistic activity was not limited to curing or causing disease. The Inuit shaman intervened with the supernatural in attempting to control the forces of the environment. When game was unavailable, shamans were asked to call on their spirits to divine where animals were located. Shamans were also said to control thunder and stop snowstorms and the cracking of the ice. The Inuit believed that sickness was caused by the sufferer's loss of his or her soul or by evil ghosts and spirits who were usually angered by the breach of some taboo. An Inuit boy became a shaman by joining the household of an elderly shaman as a novice, where he observed special taboos, had visions, and was taught special shamanistic techniques. The novice also had to refrain from sexual relations.

Shamanism was widespread in Siberia. It was and is still found among the Buddhists of the Buryat Republic, and in Tuva, an autonomous, Turkic-speaking republic in the geographical center of Asia, both of which are part of the Russian

An early twentieth-century Tlingit shaman wearing ritual paraphernalia, including a horn crown, shakes his shaman's oyster-catcher rattle while dealing with a witch.

federation. Tuvan shamans are healers dealing with various diseases and with the loss of the soul. They treat the sick by holding seances, which begin at nightfall and last until dawn, during which time the shaman contacts the spirits and "voyages" to the three worlds—the subterranean, the celestial, and the middle world of humans (Kenin-Lopsan, 1997: 110). The shaman employs spirit-helpers, animals ranging in size and power from bears to moths, and these spirit-helpers are artistically portrayed on wands, which the shaman employs in the ceremony. In addition, the Tuvan shaman wears a decorated coat and boots, and uses a drum and a rattle.

The Tuvan shaman may also be called in to divine the location of game for a hunter. A childless couple may seek help from the shaman to "summon the soul" of an unborn infant to their home, a felt yurt (Kenin-Lopsan, 1997: 127). Kenin-Lopsan, a Tuvan ethnographer who collected many poetic chants, or songs, performed by Tuvan shamans, pointed out that these songs were a major form of Tuvan artistic expression and served to keep the Tuvan language alive. Tuvan shamans in their shamanic performance employed the "throat singing" for which Tuva is famous. In this special kind of singing, they imitated the languages of their animal spirit-helpers (Kenin-Lopsan, 1997: 132–133). Tuvan shamans may be female or male. Kenin-Lopsan's maternal grandmother was a famous shaman imprisoned several times by Stalin. She died in prison in the mid-1940s. The renewal of Tuvan shamanism in the post-Soviet era is demonstrated by the fact that in 1992

A contemporary Tuvan shaman wearing special shaman's garb, lays out his paraphernalia before a curing performance.

a Society of Tuva Shamans was formed and was subsequently recognized by the Tuvan Ministry of Justice (Kenin-Lopsan 1997b: 132). Tuvan shamanism continues to be an integral part of Tuvan culture, and today, in particular, is part of their eth-nic identity.

Along the Amur River, in far eastern Siberia, the songs and stories of female shamans from several Siberian peoples have also been recorded (Van Deussen, 2001). Bears and Siberian tigers frequently appear as shamanic spirit-helpers, and humans frequently intermarry with them in these tales. The Ul'chi and Nivkh peoples kept bears, which were ritually sacrificed at a ceremony. At one time, throughout the Cir-cumpolar region, the bear was commonly venerated as a religious symbol.

These examples of shamanic practice reveal some of the basic characteristics of shamanism. Shamans deal with two dilemmas: One of them is the loss of self, and the other is that something, perhaps a tumor or cancer cells, is growing in a person's body. These concerns are universal, found in all societies. The shamanic solution to travel to the spirit world for the answer is but one of the solutions. Through a variety of means shamans go into an altered state of con-sciousness, or a trance, during which they have direct contact with the spirit world. They use spirit-helpers and can call spirits to be present during their seances (Townsend, 1997: 431–432).

Several recent analysts of shamanism have pointed out that since it began in the Paleolithic period, and has persisted for thousands of years, it must fulfill biological and psychological functions. Instead of being replaced by scientific theories of curing, shamanism has actually undergone a present-day revival, as we shall discuss below (Winkelman, 2000; McClenon, 2002). Shamanism, for both of these writers, has to involve "soul flight" and "ecstatic communication with the spirit world" (Winkelman, 1992: 48; McClenon, 2002: 157). Winkelman argues that shamanism "manipulates self-identity and social identity" (2000: xiii) by emphasizing "integrative brain functions." In his view, the soul journey, which the shaman helps the patient to undergo, and the search for a guardian spirit constitute forms of self-objectification. They are a form of role-playing that serves to expand human sociocognitive dynamics (Winkelman, 2000: xiv). Shamanism provides a mechanism for stepping outside of one's self, to take a journey to another land, to return in a reborn form, and thereby to acquire a new understanding of one self.

DIVINERS

Diviners are part-time religious specialists who use the supernatural to enable people to make decisions concerning how they should act in order to have success. The Chinese, in general, have always placed great emphasis upon omens. Archaeological information has revealed that the Chinese many millennia ago interpreted the cracks in tortoise shells to foretell the future. They also used geomancy—the interpretations of the future from cracks in dried mud—and fortune-telling. Diviners use other methods to gain their information. Sometimes chickens or other animals are killed and their entrails inspected to determine what action to take in the future. Roman diviners, or augurs, inspected the entrails of sacrificial animals for good or bad omens. Julius Caesar was advised not to venture forth on the Ides of March because the animal sacrificed had no heart. Calendrical divination was used in Mesoamerica before the arrival of Columbus.

In our own society, many people seek help to divine what their future holds for them. Gypsy fortune-tellers in storefronts in many cities, large and small, as well as at rural country fairs are paid to read palms, tea leaves, and Tarot cards, and to look into crystal balls to foretell the future. The services of astrologers, who foretell the future from the positions of the stars, were even sought by a president to help him make decisions affecting the entire nation.

As part of his functions, in addition to curing, the Inuit shaman would also tell hunters where they would find animals. They took the shoulder blade, or scapula, of an animal such as a reindeer, a moose, an elk, an otter, or a seal and placed it on a fire until cracks appeared, which formed a pattern. This practice is called *scapulimancy*. The pattern of cracks was then interpreted to locate the place where animals were to be found. Scapulimancy is similar to the Chinese use of tortoise shells, just described.

Divination ceremonies, which vary in form enormously from ethnic group to ethnic group, are still an essential part of life in Sub-Saharan Africa (Pemberton III, 2000: 10). The 16-signs divination still practiced among the Yoruba people of southwestern Nigeria and the Fon of the Republic of Benin was also brought to America during slave trade days and "the casting of sixteen palm nuts or cowrie shells continues to be widely practiced today by Caribbean and Brazilian people of West Africa descent in New York and other metropolitan centers in the United States" (Pemberton III, 2000: 11). Mouse divination, used by the Baule of the Ivory, involves the interpretation of the random movements of a mouse over bats' or birds' bones or sticks by a diviner who can interpret the signs thought to be controlled by spiritual powers. Royal Luba mediums of today use sculptures consisting of figures holding bowls to advise Luba political leaders about governmental problems and medical and judicial matters. The diviner speaks to the figure in the sculpture, which then becomes an oracle and mouthpiece for the spirit's response to the questions posed (Pemberton III, 2000: 14, 34–35). People at all levels of life still feel that divination is an important mode of communication with the spirit world that enables them to find answers to life's problems.

SORCERERS AND WITCHES

Sorcerers and witches, as religious specialists, concentrate upon doing evil things, causing illness and death rather than curing. *Sorcerers* and *witches* are the English terms into which indigenous terms are translated, and they may be inexact. Since there is a logical connection between curing illness and causing it, in many societies the same specialist, the shaman, sometimes performs both functions. **Sorcery** is defined by anthropology as something that is learned, whereas people are born with a propensity toward **witchcraft.** As pointed out in the discussion of the Kachin, Kachin witches were unaware that they had this power. Witchcraft and sorcery involve the use of supernatural means to cause bad things to happen to one's enemies, or to the enemies of individuals who engage the services of a sorcerer. These enemies may be persons outside one's own group or persons within one's own group with whom one is in opposition. Kwakiutl shamans could use sorcery against enemy groups. Among the Trobrianders, as noted in Chapter 9, the people of a district feared that their chief would use sorcery against them if they went against his commands. Sorcery here, as in other societies, was being used as a means of social control.

In many societies, when a person in the prime of life becomes sick or dies, it is necessary to ascertain what caused the illness or death. This means going beyond the immediate cause of, say, a death, such as the tree that fell or the lightning that struck, to the more important underlying reason this particular person died. There is often a belief in such societies that the illness was caused by witchcraft or sorcery. British social anthropologists working in Africa, especially E. E. Evans-Pritchard and Max Gluckman, adopted an approach in which they saw such sorcery and witchcraft accusations as the product of tensions and conflict within the community. When a person in the prime of life dies, investigators try to divine through supernatural means who caused the death. Like the detective in a "who-dunit" in our own society, the diviner asks who has the most to gain to determine who is the most likely suspect.

Claims of witchcraft are usually made in such a way that they reveal the cleavages in a society. According to Douglas, who analyzed witchcraft accusations, such as the witch trials of sixteenth-century England and the accusations of witchcraft among Yao villagers from Malawi in the 1950s, the witch is someone on the opposite side of a power conflict. He or she is accused of antisocial behavior or libeled by his or her accuser (1991). The person accused of antisocial behavior may be charged with eating food that is repellent to the accuser, even human bodies; aberrant sexual behavior, such as sex with the devil; or the murder of children for occult ritual purpose.

MAGICIANS

Magic is another kind of religious specialization, as noted above. Magic, witchcraft, and sorcery all involve the manipulation of the supernatural. Magic is directed toward a positive goal—to help individuals or the whole community. In parts of Melanesia one frequently finds societies in which there are several part-time religious specialists who carry out magical rites to bring rain, promote fertility in the gardens, and ensure successful fishing. The garden magician among the Trobrianders is one of the most important people in the village. He recites his magical spells and performs his rituals at every stage of the process of growing yams, and what he does is seen as being as essential to the growth and maturation of crops as weeding and hoeing. He officiates at a large-scale ceremony involving all the men of the village that takes place before any gardening begins. He carries out specific rites at the planting and weeding and in assisting the plants to sprout, bud, grow, climb, and produce the yams. Since the garden magician must perform his rites before each stage of production, through his spells he acts, in effect, to coordinate and regulate the stages of work throughout the entire village (Malinowski, 1935). Each village has its own special system of garden magic, which is passed on by matrilineal inheritance, so a sister's son succeeds his mother's brother as garden magician.

Magical practices have always coexisted with universal religions such as Christianity, Islam, and Judaism in many Old World societies. The institution of the evil eye operates in the same way as witchcraft. If misfortune occurs, it is assumed to have happened because of the use of the evil eye by some enemy. People believe that it is dangerous to praise a child as beautiful, strong, or healthy, since this will create jealousy on the part of others and cause them to invoke the evil eye. Various kinds of magic, including protective devices and verbal ritual formulas, are used to ward off the evil eye. Among the Basseri, a nomadic pastoral society of Iran, a mirror is placed on the back of the horse on which the bride is taken to her groom, since a joyous occasion like a wedding is likely to promote envy on the part of some onlookers. The mirror is used to reflect the evil eye back to its sender. Communities of believers from Cairo to New York City recite magical spells to ward off the evil eye, wear charms and religious medals to bring good fortune, and nail religious symbols to walls and doorways to serve as magical charms to protect households. These are all forms of magic practiced today. The religious objects whose commodification and sale in Cairo we discussed in Chapter 8 all represent magical ideas set within the context of Islam (Starrett, 1995). The refracting vinyl stickers of raised hands and unopened copies of the Qur'an displayed in automobiles are intended to ward off the evil eye. Islamic religious leaders consider these practices as running counter to the basic teachings of Islam, for the Qur'an is to be read, not to be used as a charm for protection.

PRIESTS

With the evolution of more complex forms of society, in earlier and later states, religion became more elaborated and more differentiated as a separate institution. In contrast to the shaman and the magician, who operate as individual practitioners and part-time specialists, priests function in concert, carrying out a more codified and elaborated series of rituals, and their activities are associated with a shrine or temple. The body of ritual knowledge, which is the priest's method of contacting the supernatural, must be learned over a lengthy period of time. Archaeological data on Mesopotamia reveal that in societies that were the forerunners of full-fledged states, there was a single figure who was both the political and religious head of the community, and there was a priestly class. Subsequently, as the state evolved, there was a separation of political and religious positions. In Chapter 9, we noted that formal legal codes evolved out of religious codes in early states. These religious codes comprised moral statements that have remained an integral part of the universal religions, such as the Judeo-Christian tradition, Islam, and Buddhism. The class of religious specialists was but one of a number of stratified classes in an increasingly more hierarchically organized society.

Priests were intimately associated with development and control of the calendar in the early civilizations of the Maya and the Aztecs, and in Egypt and Mesopotamia. It is not known whether priests invented the calendar, but it was used for determining when communal religious rites should take place. In these early civilizations the priesthood seems also to have been associated with scientific observations of the heavens. In ancient Egypt, the flooding of the Nile was absolutely regular; its onset could be dated 365 days from the last onset. The development of a solar calendar, in place of the more widespread lunar calendar, enabled the flooding to be predicted. The development of this solar calendar depended on a certain amount of astronomical knowledge. The ability to predict natural phenomena, such as the yearly flooding, was connected, in the eyes of the people, to priestly proximity to the supernatural. This in turn gave the leader of the theocracy—the priest-king—great power over the ordinary agriculturalists.

RELIGIOUS SYNCRETISM

Earlier, we noted the existence of witchcraft side by side with Christianity in England and the United States. The term *syncretism* refers to this integration of older cultural traits into newly adopted cultural practices. In these same societies, some people still wear amulets to ward off the evil eye, seek advice from fortune-tellers, and go to faith healers to be cured by the laying on of hands. Various earlier pre-Christian beliefs including local spirits were incorporated into Christianity as it spread through Europe. This also occurred as Islam moved through the Middle East and parts of Africa. When Christian missionaries carried Christianity throughout the world, the same process was also operative. This missionary activity, which continues today, did not result in the eradication of earlier traditional beliefs and activities. We will discuss this in greater detail in Chapter 13.

We have pointed out that religious institutions respond to changing conditions and are influenced by other belief systems. In America, this process has produced new forms of Christianity and Islam, for example, Mormonism (Church of Jesus Christ of Latter-Day Saints), Christian Science (Church of Christ, Scientist), and the Nation of Islam. Sometimes entirely new religions, such as Scientology, emerge. These religious groups represent responses to the distinctly American scene. Although the forms of religious expression may change, the functions they fulfill remain constant.

OLD RELIGIONS IN NEW GUISES

All religions believe that their rituals have been practiced since time immemorial. The rituals that we discussed earlier were all created at some point in time. Thanksgiving was only declared a holiday in the twentieth century. In this section, we will describe major changes that have taken place in entire religions.

The imposition of colonialism and independence and the events of the post-colonial period have transformed the nature of sorcery in many places. For example, among the Kaliai of West New Britain there has been a syncretism of traditional Kaliai forms of sorcery with European culture (Lattas, 1993). Men who have traveled widely while working for Europeans and serving in the constabulary have the reputation of being sorcerers. Their great power derives from their connection to Europeans and from the sorcery knowledge they have had the opportunity to acquire while working in other areas. In fact, the nation-state, conceptualized as a white institution, is itself seen as imbued with the powers of sorcery.

Shamanism has taken on a modern appearance in Westernizing societies in Asia. Before Korea began its rapid industrialization 30 years ago, shamanic rituals were held in response to life-threatening illnesses and to promote the health, harmony, and prosperity of the small farming families. These families were primarily rural in outlook, though they were tied to commercial markets (Kendall, 1996: 522). In the 1970s, Korea embarked on a course toward modernity. In the clash between modernity and superstition, between rationality and magic, shamanism was considered to be superstition. Government policy stressed that shamanism "deluded the people" and fostered "irrational" beliefs (Kendall, 2001: 29). Shamanic rituals aimed at "reconciliations between the living members of the household and their gods and ancestors who appear . . . in the person of costumed shamans." As time went by, these rituals were increasingly accepted as part of "national culture" because they are considered ancient Korean traditions.

Today these same shamanic rituals, or *kut,* have spread from the rural farmers to a new class of small-businesspeople and entrepreneurs living in the cities, who are holding *kut* ceremonies to ensure success in their business enterprises as well as to cure their illnesses. For those engaged in high-risk enterprises, business is precarious and success or failure seems arbitrary and beyond their control. Thus, "doing well by the spirits" is important. Since financial distress and worry can often lead to illness, it is understandable that the *kut* ceremony has dual functions (Kendall, 1996: 516–518).

In the United States, we have also had a period of religious transformation and innovation, which began in the 1970s following the demise of the counterculture movements of the "flower children" of the 1960s (Bromley, 1998: 328). At first, the development of these alternative religious movements, sometimes referred to as New Age movements or New Religious Movements, was paralleled by an erosion of the "major" religions—Judaism, Catholicism, Protestantism. However, in the most recent past, the growth of Christian Fundamentalism and the resurgence of Orthodox Judaism have marked a turnaround for these dominant faiths. Nontraditional religious movements have a long history in the United States. Some of these groups, for example, the Shakers, are only minimally present today, while others, the Mormons (Church of Jesus Christ of Latter-Day Saints), for example, continue stronger than ever. In recent years, the immigration of many non-Westerners, Buddhists, Muslims, Hindus, and others into our now multicultural, pluralistic society have introduced still other religion belief systems into the mix. Many of the New Religious movements are cultural transplants representing groups of Asian origin, such as the Hare Krishna movement (International Society for Krishna Consciousness). These New Religious Movements are seen as "different responses to the failure of mainline religious traditions to provide a meaningful moral context for everyday life" (Bromley, 1998: 330).

For the same reasons that New Religious Movements have become popular, shamanism has also grown in importance in America and Europe. Spurred by an interest in the writings of Carlos Casteneda and the work of Michael Harner, an anthropologist who is an authority on shamanism, Westerners disillusioned with their own religious institutions have turned to "neoshamanism." As Atkinson notes: "It [shamanism] presents in the 1980s and 1990s what Buddhism and Hinduism provided in the preceding decades, namely a spiritual alternative for Westerners estranged from Western religious traditions" (1992: 322). Harner holds seminars in shamanism. Participants attend these seminars, which are in reality shamanic rituals, either to be cured of illness, the traditional function of the shamanic ritual, or to enable them to make the journey into another world simply to undergo the shamanic experience (Drury, 1989: 93ff.). Neoshamanism is nonhierarchical in comparison with traditional Western religions, emphasizes self-help, and links participants to nature. Consequently, it is appealing to seekers of alternative religious experiences.

Witchcraft has existed in America, in one form or another, from the seventeenth century on (Melton, 1982). There have been periodic infusions from Europe, as its popularity waxed and waned. Douglas, as noted earlier, sees basic similarities between Malawi witchcraft and sixteenth-century witchcraft. In both instances, accusations of witchcraft reflect cleavages within the community and are, in effect, methods of social control. However, though witches today see themselves as the reborn victims of witch-hunts in past centuries, in fact, there have been no accusations of witchcraft paralleling those in sixteenth-century England and seventeenth-century Salem (Orion, 1995: 52). The flowering of what has come to be known as the neopagan religion, or Wicca, began in the 1960s. In 1954, shortly after the repeal of antiwitchcraft laws in Britain, Gerald Gardner published an account of witchcraft that stimulated its revival. While in Gardner's version of Wicca, covens, the minimal religious unit, were characterized by levels of initiation, a hierarchical organization, and a more codified set of traditions and rituals, Wicca in America is democratized, individualized, highly creative, and inventive. Its major focus has been to disown, by lifestyle, word, and philosophy, the religious and political ideas that dominate the rest of American society. Christian conservatives and fundamentalists understandably see this opposition to American society and to Christianity as a direct threat. Interestingly, those who identify themselves as members of Wicca come primarily from Protestant and Catholic backgrounds (Orion, 1995: 63). Wicca is therefore a pointed rejection of Christianity—it is both pre-Christian and the object of Christian persecution.

The Wiccan belief system is widely diverse in the interpretation of fundamental beliefs; there is great variation in organization and practice and constant creativity in the development of the ritual structure. However, there are certain ideas that are held in common. Wicca and neopaganism partake of a new vision of the witch as the healer, the champion of alternative therapies, such as massage therapy, spiritual healing, crystal healing, and homeopathy, distrusting of and in opposition to the omnipotent physicians in the prevailing medical establishment. They also support midwifery and the use of herbs in healing. Their approach to their own health care usually involves healers and medical doctors as supplements to, rather than substitutes for, one another (Orion, 1995: 165). People also look to Wicca as a way of regaining control over their lives. Nature and human beings are seen as one, and worship of nature is important. Human action and sacred forces are counterparts of one another and can influence one another; hence ritual action involves using human action to enlist the assistance of the sacred. The world is seen as constantly in motion, vibrating with energy as a life force intrinsic to all things, infusing, creating, and sustaining humans and all other life. Energy is thereby empowering, and most rituals have been created to concentrate and channel energy to where it can do the most good, whether healing an individual or supporting those who oppose the despoiling of the environment by the building of a nuclear power plant (Orion, 1995: 111).

Wiccan rituals usually involve the sacred circle, formed of individuals whose constant circular movement generates a cone of energy directed to specific tasks to better the earth. This is also seen as a form of therapeutic "healing magic," releasing and dissipating "maladaptive emotional states" for the individual as well as for the earth by creative energy. Wiccan celebrations mark the solstices, equinoxes, and key occasions of the agricultural year, as well as biweekly sabbaths. They also have come to include rite-of-passage ceremonies; such as Wiccaning—the blessing and presenting of infants to the pagan spirits; girls' and boys' puberty rites or initiation; handfasting, the tying together of the hands of the couple at a ceremony to signify trial or permanent marriage, heterosexual or homosexual; and ritual preparation for death. The *New York Times* even included a description of a Wiccan ceremony of handfasting in its wedding section of June 30, 1996, in which the bride's and groom's hands were bound together with ribbon by all the guests. A high priest-ess, licensed by the state, pronounced them man and wife, and the June wedding ended in the traditional Wiccan way, with the couple jumping over a broomstick.

The Wiccan pantheon has the Mother Goddess, giver of life and incarnate love; the Sun; and the Moon at the core. In addition, magical beliefs from ancient Egypt, Greece, Babylonia, and the Jewish Kabbalah, as well as Celtic, Druid, Norse, and Welsh pagan beliefs, have been eclectically included (Melton, 1982). Women enjoy a special status, and the person of the high priestess is venerated.

Wicca in America has all the organizational characteristics of a religion. In fact, a federal appeals court in 1986 ruled that Wicca was a religion protected by the Constitution. As a consequence, believers in Wicca are today trying to change the public view of their belief system. Its practitioners feel that Wicca should be pro-tected by the same laws that protect the practice of other religions against the at-tacks of Christian fundamentalists. In an article in the *New York Times* on October 31, 1999, entitled "Witches Cast as the Neo-Pagans Next Door," Wicca worshipers were quoted as saying, "We will change the future through tolerance, education and through love" and "I'm probably going to have a sign that says, 'I'm Wiccan and I vote [on the Nebraska Capital steps].' " In addition, some Wiccan rituals are advertised as "open rituals," which the public can attend. Pagan Pride Days have been organized by witches in various cities. Fundamentalist Christians, however, still associate witches and Wicca with satanism. When some soldiers at Fort Hood, Texas, conducted Wiccan rituals near the base, local ministers and Representative Bob Barr of Georgia objected to these "sinister rites." In the same manner, the op-ponents of Santeria in Hialeah, Florida, discussed in the last chapter, objected to the practice of animal sacrifice, characterizing it as "devil worship."

An emphasis on feminist spirituality, which developed as an offshoot of radi-cal feminism in the 1970s, was influenced by Wicca and the American neopagan movement, giving rise to the "American Goddess movement." It is an eclectic movement with "beliefs and practices which are becoming increasingly idiosyn-cratic . . . dynamic, [with an] increasingly diverse form of popular religiosity that has emerged among women" (Gottschall, 2000: 60). However, worship of the God-dess and Goddess spirituality are primary. In southern California, for example, Goddess believers gather to celebrate summer and winter solstices, and pagan hol-idays like Hallomas and Lammas as large public rituals with belly dancers, drum-mers, poets, and vocalists (Gottschall, 2000: 61–62). Several men came to one ritual studied by Gottschall, but by and large most Goddess events like the first Interna-tional Goddess Festival, are for "women only." Goddess worshipers are feminist separatists interested in reducing in importance the patriarchal religious framework that characterizes the major Western religions. This schism, represented by the Goddess movement, is most interesting since women already have a central leadership role in American Wiccan covens, though there are High Priests as well as High Priestesses (Berger, 2000). Though both male and female deities are worshipped by neopagans, the Goddess is a more central figure.

CYBERSPACE AND RELIGION: "GIVE ME THAT ONLINE RELIGION"

One can go on the Internet, into cyberspace today, click on the Digital Avatar site, and the cyber version of a Kali temple welcomes you with the image of the god Shiva and a menu of worship experiences from the mystical utterance of Vedic praise, which affirms the totality of creation, to mediation while watching a mystical, rapid alteration of Shiva images. In 2001, there were more than 1 million online religious websites in operation, and the number is increasing daily (Brasher, 2001: 6). All of the major religions in the world, as well as newer religious groups, recognize the vast audience they can reach in cyberspace, far beyond the churches, synagogues, ashrams, and temples to which religions were formerly confined, and they are intent on exploring the global arena.

Online religion is a new form of religious experience that has the capacity to transform the nature of earlier religious practices, resulting, in the near future, in "sermons Emailed to your home account, virtual baptism and a simulcast *bris*" (Brasher, 2001: 23). For example, Jewish websites provide online Torah education, "Ask the Rabbi" interactive sites, Hebrew instruction, a Cyber-Seder, and even a site that offers to transcribe any message desired to be placed on the Western Wall, a sacred place for Jews where the messages are messages to God. The Chabad-Lubbavitch movement sites were set up to deal not with those within the group but with outsiders. The aim is proselytization among Jews who might return to the fold of Orthodoxy (Zaleski, 1997: 15), and there are Chabad sites all over the world, linked together by the teachings of their Rebbe.

The Cyber-Seder has been in operation for several years. The Seder is the meal eaten during Pesach, which celebrates the tradition of the Jews exodus from Egypt where they had been held as slaves. A physical Seder is held at Lincoln Center and with the necessary software, virtual participants from around the world log into the chat-room of the Seder, discuss the Seder, and then see and hear the physical Seder as it progresses. The Seder content includes not only the traditional reading of the Haggadah, the story of the exodus, but an interreligious flavor is also created by showing the Martin Luther King "I have a Dream" speech (Brasher, 2001: 75–76).

Other mainstream religions have also become active in cyberspace. Their websites include "an introduction to their beliefs, a directory of congregation locations, a calendar explaining upcoming religious events, and a prayer room" (Brasher, 2001: 70). About 80 percent of the websites of the major religions—Judaism, Islam, Buddhism, Hinduism, and Christianity—were for Christianity, though one must remember that the computer and the Net are dominated by the United States, Canada and Western Europe, where Christianity dominates. Beside the official

Vatican site, there are both lay and official Roman Catholic sites—for example, the Christ in the Desert site of the Benedictine Monastic Order, which is unofficial. This site included such options as "Today's Martyrology," the monastery gift shop, online monastic chants, how to request prayers, the week's homily, and how to learn more about the order's retreat house. The majority of all religious sites online are Protestant, such as those belonging to the Church of Christ, which attempts to use its 300 sites in cyberspace to bring converts to the physical church. Most Protestant denominations have their own websites. The Christian Fundamentalists part of evangelical Christianity in America, which has a long tradition of preaching their beliefs, first in churches, then on the radio and now on television, have a large variety of websites.

Muslims use the website to announce prayer times in a host of cities. However, there is limited access to the Internet in most Muslim countries, though there are some Islamic chat rooms and sites devoted to Sufism (Zaleski, 1997: 55, 68). Buddhist sects also use the Web but it is American Buddhist who have developed the sites. Tibetan Buddhism and Zen Buddhism are well represented. Hinduism is also represented in that yoga, Hare Krishna, and gurus like Sri Sathya Sai Baba also have their sites.

Even the Amish, in Pennsylvania, who do not use cars but ride in horse-drawn carriages, have a website, as do neopagans who are "revising customary neopagan rituals for a virtual environment . . . and designing new ones for cyperspace" (Brasher, 2001: 87, 88). There is even a cyberheaven where one can memorialize one's deceased relative with a picture and brief tribute to that relative. The producers of the site see it as analogous to heaven; hence angels against a background of clouds are presented as the introduction to the site. This site is part of a category of sites not connected to any religious group where an individual can create a site as a virtual sacred place and preach his or her own religious ideas and include music and created rituals (Brasher, 2001: 69). Cyperspace has also become the location for Apocalyptic websites, as well as those devoted to religious satire.

Though traditional religions have used cyberspace to convey their messages and broaden their religious base, they are, in the main, conveying the same spiritual messages. By and large they have not dealt with the implications of the technological revolution that computers and cyberspace represent and the implications of the human-technology interface for religious belief systems. The messages of the major religions have not been adapted to possibilities of the creation of new forms or life, like cloning, or the qualities of lifelike robots and cyborgs. Cyberspace instead is used as a new technology to reach out to those who have strayed from the community and bring them home again. Americans cling to a belief that one should always return home, as we observed earlier about the game of baseball.

POLITICS AND RELIGIOUS FUNDAMENTALISM

In today's world, religion seems to play an extremely important role in politics. In a sense, we have come full circle. When states and civilization began in the Middle East, they were theocracies, and politics and religion were intertwined. This connection between politics and religion has been widespread throughout history and in different societies. For example, today, political parties in Europe often have religious labels, such as the Christian Democratic party in Germany.

In the past 20 years, Islamic fundamentalism has become a very significant dimension in Middle Eastern and Central Asian politics. Recently, Islamic fundamentalism has had a worldwide effect, in the form of Al Queda. Throughout their history, Islamic peoples have responded to the call of religious leaders like the Mahdi, "the rightly guided one," who, in the Sudan in the late nineteenth century, called for a renunciation of corruption and a return to the true moral values of Islam. Present-day fundamentalists are merely following earlier examples. Reza Shah Pahlevi, the Shah of Iran, had embarked on a program of Westernization and modernization after World War II. Women were no longer required to wear veils and were encouraged to attend schools and colleges. Western clothing, Western music, and Western ideas were emphasized. In the late 1970s, the Ayatollah Khomeini, with his fundamentalist ideas involving a strict interpretation of Shi'ite Islam, succeeded in overthrowing the Shah. This Shi'ite fundamentalism of Iran has been influential in many parts of the Muslim world, reverberating as far as northern Nigeria, where Shi'ite and Sunni Muslims have, very recently, been fighting one another. This contrasts with the long-standing conflict between the Muslims in the north and the Yoruba and Ibo Christians of the south. The Muslim Brothers, a Shi'ite movement centered in the Hausa city of Zaria, are calling for an Iranian-style Islamic revolution in Nigeria, and the imposition of *sharia*—Islamic law. This call has resonated with unemployed, angry young men, who see little hope for the future under a corrupt and repressive military dictatorship.

In widely separated Muslim countries like Algeria, Egypt, and Turkey, fundamentalist groups have launched political movements, attempting to take over the governments of these countries and govern strictly according to the Qur'an. Afghanistan, a monarchy attempting to modernize, turned communist in 1978 under Soviet pressure, resulting in a civil war. The Taliban movement was originally formed by students from rural areas, studying in Islamic religious schools (*madrassahs*) in the Kandahar region of Afghanistan. Their number was swelled by young men eager to end the factionalism and fighting. The Taliban movement drove out the Soviets, won the civil war, and took control of most of the country until the autumn of 2001 when they, in turn, were driven out by the United States. While they ruled, the Taliban instituted decrees banning women from attending school or working, permitting them to leave their houses only when completely veiled. Men had to give up wearing Western clothing and had to wear wear full beards. Children were forced to abandon music, dancing, kite flying, and playing marbles. The United States, in the search for Osama bin Laden, took control of the country and installed Hamid Kharzai to lead Afghanistan until a democratic government is elected.

Islamic fundamentalism had expanded from Afghanistan to threaten Turkmenistan, Uzbekistan, Tajikistan, and Kyrgyzstan, now independent republics, formerly part of the Soviet Union. Armed Islamic fundamentalist fighters seek to undermine the governments of these republics by taking hostages and conducting guerrilla warfare. Though the population of these countries is almost exclusively

Muslim, they are not doctrinaire like the Taliban had been. But living standards have plummeted since the collapse of the Soviet Union, making people easy targets for radical fundamentalism. The fighting in Dagestan and Chechnya, republics farther to the west and also Muslim, has also been stirred up by Muslim fundamentalists.

In an interesting way, Islamic fundamentalists have their parallel in Christian fundamentalists in America today, who are calling for a return to Christian values and a strict interpretation of Biblical text. This is similar to Islamic fundamentalists who want a strict interpretation of the Koran. Christians mobilize their followers to help bring this about at the ballot box by electing individuals who support their aims. Many of these Christian fundamentalists were formerly mainline Protestants who joined evangelical denominations, which were practicing an unambiguous, stricter morality. Members of such religious groups may teach their children at home instead of sending them to school, thereby controlling the content of their education and fostering ideas about creationism, discussed earlier in this chapter. They seek to keep the interactions of the members of their families within their own religious community. They listen to their own kind of music on Christian radio stations, read books written for Christians and purchased in Christian bookstores, and watch Christian television. As members of the new Christian Right political movement, they have tried to shape elections from local school boards to presidential politics by being active in the Christian Coalition. There are also Orthodox Jews who are religious fundamentalists in that they adhere to a very strict interpretation of Jewish tenets to guide their lives. Fundamentalism, wherever it is found, has certain features in common. Fundamentalists "know" that they are right in their beliefs and practices and that the watered-down varieties of their religions are wrong.

WHY RELIGION?

Much of religious behavior has an instrumental goal; that is, the individual has some particular goal in mind when the religious ritual is performed. Those who carry out the rites and perform the spells desire to produce results, such as stopping a storm, bringing rain, or ensuring fertility for their crops. The Inuit shaman contacts his spirits to find out where the hunter should go to find his prey. The Trobriand garden magician recites the particular spells that will make the yams grow. The Kachin sacrificed to the *nats* to ensure that their crops would successfully grow to maturity. In many cultures, women perform religious rites to help them become pregnant. For example, in Poland, Catholic women went to the tombs of Catholic saints and Jewish rabbis to recite prayers to enable them to become pregnant. Orthodox Jewish women in Israel go to the tomb of Rachael, in Hebron, with the same goal. The motives and goals in all these cases are to bring about quite specific results to make natural forces and natural processes respond to human need.

Some religious behavior is directed toward guiding human action and enabling people to make decisions about how to act. Oracles and fortune-tellers are consulted to determine which course of action to take when faced with a choice.

Whenever individuals are uncertain about what they should do, what course of action to take now or in the future, they may enlist the assistance of the supernatural to enable them to make a decision. What are the motives of the individual in doing this? When filled with doubts about making the right decision, one is provided with a reassuring means for obtaining an answer.

In many societies religious behavior is directed toward curing illness. In shamanism, the cause of the illness must be ascertained from the supernatural. Illness is often seen to be the result of the manipulation of the supernatural by evil people for evil purposes. The cure, of necessity, will also involve supernatural means. In our own society, believers in Christian Science (members of the Church of Christ, Scientist) believe that prayer alone will cure illness and refuse to accept medical care for themselves and their children.

Sometimes, worshipers and religious practitioners may say that the purposes of the religious rite are to emphasize communal values and to inculcate these values in the young. At this point the conscious purposes are close to the latent functions of reinforcing the communal bonds of society. Rites of passage specifically have this purpose. Such rituals serve not only to teach those involved the specifications of their new roles, but also to reinforce the structure of the society, as people are moved from one social position to another. Rites of intensification tied to the yearly calendar also provide order, structure, and meaning for the organization of society, as well as for the life of each individual. Religious ritual is a dramatization that acts to reinforce and standardize a world view among the members of a congregation.

Sometimes religious action has particular effects that the individual may not be aware of. These are different from the conscious goals and purposes of the participants themselves. American baseball players use magic rituals and formulas in areas of the game most fraught with uncertainty—hitting and pitching (Gmelch, 1971). Reducing anxiety for the pitcher or the hitter and giving the individual a sense of confidence, even if it is false confidence, improves performance. Anxiety is reduced for the Korean businessman after he goes through the performance of a shamanic ritual. He feels more confident as a consequence. One could argue that anxiety itself has important functions in dangerous situations. Under such circumstances adrenaline should be flowing and all one's senses should be alerted to potential danger. In terms of this argument, performing magical rites just before such situations produces anxiety, which is advantageous, since it makes people alert. To resolve these two seemingly irreconcilable positions, one could say that excessive anxiety may be paralyzing, but overconfidence may also lead to bad performance. When a person is faced with uncertainty in possibly dangerous situations, alertness to the real dangers and confidence in one's ability to cope with the situation are the most desirable mix and can be brought about by performing some magical or religious ritual.

In addition to the many purposes of religion we have discussed above, religion provides a model for how individuals should behave and interact with one another. Morality and good behavior are supported by religious tenets and if one does not behave, religious sanctions are the result.

SUMMARY

• Religion is defined as the cultural means by which humans deal with the supernatural, but many humans also believe that the reverse is true—that the supernatural deals with humans.

• Religion fulfills certain universal functions, such as the allaying of anxiety; explanatory functions, which answer such questions as why humans came to be on earth and the meaning of life; and expiatory function, in which individuals are assisted in dealing with guilt and misfortune.

• Humans attempt to understand and at least influence or control through a belief in the supernatural what is otherwise uncontrollable and unexplainable, and by doing this, they alleviate their anxieties about their helplessness in the situation.

• The forms that religious practices take vary from society to society.

• Today, we would say that many aspects of the natural world, which were formerly explained by religion, are now explained by means of science.

• In terms of its explanatory function, religion is to be distinguished from science in that the latter is based on empirical observations and the former on belief.

• Magic and religion differ from science in that what is unexplained by science in the natural world is explained in magic and religion by recourse to the concept of the supernatural.

• Societies have a variety of ways of conceiving of the supernatural. These conceptualizations are directly related to the ways in which their societies are organized.

• The population of gods and deities recognized by a society is referred to as a pantheon. The relationships between the gods of a pantheon are frequently conceived of in human terms.

• In some societies, like the American Indians who lived on the Plains, individuals go out alone to seek a vision of an animal spirit, who then becomes their protector and guardian spirit throughout life.

• Often people believe in a monotheistic religion such as Judaism, Christianity, and Islam, and still maintain beliefs in ghosts, witches, and spirits of nature as parallel systems. Indeed, as we have observed, this occurs in our own society.

• Generally speaking, human beings approach the supernatural by carrying out ritual acts, usually involving a combination of speech and patterned behavior that alters the emotional state of the participants.

• A variety of techniques are used to approach the supernatural, such as prayer, sacrifice, and different kinds of rituals, including rites of passage and of intensification.

• Rites of passage are communal ceremonies held to publicly mark the changes in status an individual goes through as he or she progresses through the life cycle.

• The other major category of ritual—rites of intensification—is celebrated communally either at various points in the yearly cycle, such as spring, fall, or the winter and summer solstices, or at times when the society is exposed to some kind of threat, like the threat that terrorists pose to the United States today

• Religious specialists, with special abilities that connect them to the supernatural, exist in all societies to assist members of their societies in approaching the supernatural.

• Shamans deal with two dilemmas. One of them is the loss of self, and the other is that something, perhaps a tumor or cancer cells, is growing in a person's body. These concerns are universal, found in all societies.

• Diviners are part-time religious specialists who use the supernatural to enable people to make decisions concerning how they should act in order to have success.

• Sorcery is defined by anthropology as something that is learned, whereas witchcraft is something people are born with a propensity toward.

• In contrast to the shaman and the magician, who operate as individual practitioners and part-time specialists, priests function in concert, carrying out a more codified and elaborated series of rituals, and their activities are associated with a shrine or temple.

• The term *syncretism* refers to the integration of older cultural traits into newly adopted cultural practices.

• Frequently, older religious ideas, such as shamanism and Wicca, are resurrected in new guises. Shamanism has taken on a modern appearance in Westernizing societies in Asia.

• Wicca, or neopaganism, in America is democratized, individualized, highly creative, and inventive. Its major focus has been to disown, by lifestyle, word, and philosophy, the religious and political ideas that dominate the rest of American society.

• Online religion is very popular, and in 2001 there were more than 1 million online religious websites in operation, and the number is increasing daily.

• In today's world, religion seems to play an extremely important role in politics.

• Islamic fundamentalists have their parallel in Christian fundamentalists in America today, who are calling for a return to Christian values and a strict interpretation of Biblical text. This is similar to Islamic fundamentalists, who want a strict interpretation of the Koran, and Orthodox Jews, who strictly interpret the Talmud and other texts.

SUGGESTED READINGS

Antoun, Richard. *Understanding Fundamentalism, Christian, Islamic and Jewish Movements.* Walnut Creek, CA: Altimira Press, 2001. An analysis of religious fundamentalist movements, examining scripture, myth, colonial and postcolonial history, and the roles of both women and men.

Becker, Penny E., and Nancy L. Eiesland (eds.). *Contemporary American Religion: An Ethnographic Reader.* Walnut Creek, CA: Altimira Press, 1997. A series of ethnographic studies illustrating some of the new directions that religious beliefs and practices have taken in the United States.

Billings, Dorothy K. *Cargo Cult as Theater: Political Performance in the Pacific.* Walnut Creek, CA: Altimira Press, 2002. A study of "The Johnson Cult," a recent cargo cult centered around President Lyndon B. Johnson, which developed on New Hanover Island, Papua New Guinea.

Klass, Morton, and Maxine K. Weisgrau (eds.). *Across the Boundaries of Belief: Contemporary Issues in the Anthropology of Religion.* Boulder: Westview Press, 1999. A book of readings covering contemporary issues and major topics in the anthropology of religion.

Lambek, Michael (ed.). *A Reader in the Anthropology of Religion.* Malden, MA: Blackwell Publishers, 2002. A series of essays dealing with the history of the anthropological study of religion, covering all the major figures up to the contemporary period.

Lewis, I. M. *Religion in Context: Cults and Charisma.* 2nd ed. Cambridge, England: Cambridge University Press, 1996. Examines various cultural contexts of manifestations of religious power such as spirit possession, witchcraft, cannibalism, and shamanism.

Mason, Michael Anwood. *Living Santeria: Rituals and Experiences in an Afro-Cuban Religion.* Washington, DC: Smithsonian Institution Press, 2002. An exploration of Santeria as a contemporary phenomenon by a researcher who is also a priest of Santeria.

Saler, Benson. *Conceptualizing Religion: Eminent Anthropologists, Transcendent Natives, and Unbounded Categories.* Leiden, Holland: B. J. Brill, 1993. A work considering religion as a universal category of culture.

   SUGGESTED WEBSITES

http://www.indiana.edu/~wanthro/religion.htm#web A site discussing the anthropology of religion, including a selective bibliography on the subject.

http://www.deoxy.org/shaman.htm A general overview of shamanism, defining terms and concepts and describing shamanic practices in various parts of the world, such as South America.

http://paganwiccan.about.com A site put out by the Wiccan Church to attract possible followers. It includes Wiccan texts, rituals, and spells.

11

Myths, Legends, and Folktales
Past, Present, and Future

People attempt to explain the unknowable by constructing a supernatural world; they also talk about that world. They tell folktales about supernatural creatures. They relate legends about the distant past of unrecorded history in which knights slew dragons. They tell myths about the origins of the world and of people and their social groups. They tell the myths of how God gave them the very land on which they dwell. They tell stories about the exploits of supernatural animals that talk; about big bad wolves that swallow grandmothers; about the brother of the wolf, the coyote, who acts as a trickster. They tell stories about fairies, elves, and the Little People. These different types of stories all deal with certain universal themes, such as birth, growing up, male-female relations, and death. In America, today, the media for such stories, for the most part about universal themes, include television, films, and other modern modes of mass communication.

Myths, *legends*, and *folktales* represent a continuum. These terms derive from our own categories, but they provide a useful framework for organizing this material. Myths deal with the remote past, often with the time of the origin of things both natural and cultural—how the world and its people were created, how fire was discovered, and how crops were domesticated. Myths are associated with the sacred, especially in ancient and small-scale societies (Von Hendy, 2002: 77). As the time period becomes less remote, myths fade into legends, which are sometimes thought to have a basis in historical fact. Folktales deal with an indeterminate time, which, in European folktales, is indicated by the standard opening, "Once upon a time . . ." To the tellers as well as the audience of these stories, they constitute accounts of real people and real events.

MYTHS

The people of Wogeo, whose cosmology was described in the preceding chapter, have a myth that tells how the flutes that represent the *nibek* spirits came to be. As is typical, this myth takes place in the distant past when the culture heroes, discussed in Chapter 10, who created everything in the world lived. Two female heroes dreamed the idea of making flutes. They cut two sticks of bamboo and bored a hole in each, forming flutes that immediately began to play. They were overjoyed with the self-playing flutes. When they went to work in the gardens, they stoppered the holes to make the flutes stop playing. An adolescent boy stole the flutes from the two women and tried to blow them, causing the women to return. On seeing that the boy had stolen the flutes, the women told him that the flutes would never again play by themselves. Since a male had stolen them, no female could ever look at the flutes again. The women told him that it would be hard to learn to blow the flutes, but if boys did not make the effort, they would never grow up to be men. The two women then set off, leaving the island of Wogeo in disgust. The two islands where they eventually settled, Kadovar and Blupblup, and the mainland of New Guinea, where they passed some time, are the only places where bamboo for flutes can currently be found.

There are various theoretical approaches that have been proposed to explain the existence of myth. One approach interprets myths as literal history. People who use this approach view the myths about great floods that inundated the world as the retelling of stories about actual floods. In such an approach, the Wogeo myth would be interpreted as signifying that there really was an earlier period of matriarchy, when women controlled those aspects of society which men now control. Nineteenth-century evolutionists, such as Lewis Henry Morgan and Johann Jakob Bachofen, would have interpreted this myth as demonstrating an earlier stage of matrilineal social organization and matriarchy. They hypothesized that all societies went through such a stage as they developed. This stage was followed by patrilineal social organization and patriarchy. Along with the unilineal theory of the evolution of societies through a fixed succession of stages, this method of interpreting myths as literal history was discredited by anthropologists.

Twentieth-century approaches to the interpretation of myths include, among others, the Freudian approach, which has been adopted by people interested in psychoanalysis, including anthropologist Alan Dundes. The Wogeo myth lends itself readily to a Freudian interpretation. The flutes are masculine objects, associated only with males, and are obvious phallic symbols. What happens to the flutes in the myth seems to involve penis envy on the part of the women and anxiety about castration on the part of the men. Just as individuals express unconscious fears and anxieties in symbolic form through dreams, myths are seen as reflecting the collective anxieties of a society. Myths in this approach are seen as giving cultural expression to these anxieties. Freud considered certain repressed anxieties and frustrations to be universal—that is, connected to panspecies characteristics related to growth and development.

Another approach to myths was provided by Malinowski, who was antievolutionist and anti-Freudian. He insisted on the necessity of analyzing a myth in relation to its social and cultural context. Myth to Malinowski was a charter for how and what people should believe, act, and feel. Just as our Declaration of Independence states that "all men are created equal," a body of myths lays out the ideals that members of a culture use to guide their behavior. The Malinowski approach

Wogeo flutes, which can be seen only by men, are played by initiated men and represent the voices of the nibek spirits.

to myth as charter requires that the Wogeo myth be examined in the context of Wogeo culture. One needs the following additional cultural facts. There is a men's cult that revolves around the men's house where the sacred flutes are kept. At adolescence, boys go through a rite of passage and are initiated into this cult. The initiation involves scarification of the tongue so that the boys can be rid of the effects of their mother's milk. Only after this is done can they learn to play the flutes. Boys are also taught to incise their penises with a sharpened clamshell while standing in the ocean. The blood flows into the ocean and not on his body, which would be dangerous and polluting to the boy. Men do this periodically to rid themselves of the pollution resulting from sexual intercourse with women. Both men and women are seen as polluted by sexual intercourse. Women get rid of this pollution naturally through menstruation. Women are kept away from the men's house and are never allowed to see the sacred flutes. The people of Wogeo say, "Men play flutes, women bear infants." Malinowski's approach to myth would interpret the Wogeo myth as providing the justification and rationale for men's performing certain ritual and ceremonial roles from which women are excluded.

The American anthropologist Clyde Kluckhohn stressed the interdependence of myth and ritual (see also Von Hendy, 2002: 178ff.). This approach has its antecedents in the nineteenth-century work of William Robertson Smith, who saw the two connected, with ritual antedating myth, which is an explanation of it (Segal,

1999: 37ff.). In many instances, according to Kluckhohn, myths provide statements about the origins of rituals, as well as details of how they are to be performed. However, Kluckhohn saw ritual and myth as fulfilling the same societal needs. The same kinds of emotional feelings are aroused in the telling of the myth and in the performing of the ritual. He also saw myth and ritual as serving the psychological function of alleviating various forms of anxiety. There is a direct connection between the myth and the ritual in Wogeo. The flutes have a central role in ritual activity, being the voices of the *nibek* spirits. The initiation ritual of boys, which involves their learning how to play the flutes, is directly connected to the mythic statement about a boy's not growing up until he learns to play the flute.

Lévi-Strauss has pursued a large-scale, detailed analysis of myths from North and South American Indian societies (Lévi-Strauss, 1963, 1971). According to Lévi-Strauss, myths provide explanations for contradictions that are present in a culture and that cannot be resolved. The Wogeo myth emphasizes the separation of women from men, after men obtained possession of the flutes. In Lévi-Strauss's terms, the myth attempts to resolve the contradiction between the ideal of keeping males and females apart and the need for them to come together in order to reproduce society. Like all other myths, this myth, too, fails to provide a permanent solution to this contradiction.

Most anthropologists analyzing myths today would agree that myths must always be understood in connection with other cultural facts. In Wogeo, the aphorism "Men play flutes, women bear infants" is very important. Male and female are seen as separate but complementary. Women bear children as part of a natural biological process. Flutes are cultural objects manufactured by men. Women are associated with natural things and men with cultural things. When men play the flutes, they are associating with the *nibek* spirits, whose voices are the flutes, and they must practice sexual abstinence. Women get rid of the bad blood of sexual intercourse naturally, through menstruation. But men must do this through culturally learned behavior—the incising of their penises. Ideally, each sex should lead its life separately, but in order for women to bear children, as the aphorism says they should, the sexes must come together. This is the only way that society can reproduce itself.

Boys' initiation consists of a series of ceremonies during which the boys are symbolically separated from women and are reborn from the *nibek* spirits as men. The myth deals with a time when women dreamed and then made the flutes, which played by themselves. No cultural learning was involved. At this time men and women were not separate. After the boy stole the flutes, men had to learn to play them because the flutes would no longer play by themselves. At this point, men separate themselves from women. The same pattern of the aphorism "Men play flutes, women bear infants" is repeated in the initiation ceremonies and in the myth. That is, men, representing culture, are separated from women, representing nature. Boys, who are associated with their mothers and have not yet learned the secrets of their culture, learn those secrets at initiation and acquire culture in the process. But the myth says more than that. It says that, at one time, women were superior to men. They bore the children and had the flutes as well. The present domination of men rests upon their having stolen what was once women's. Women by nature are superior because they can bear children, and cleanse themselves naturally through menstruation. They were superior in the past because for them, the flutes played by themselves. Men have to do everything the hard way—by means of cultural practices that must be learned. But according to the Wogeo myth, when men took control of culture, they were able to dominate women. Ultimately, the myth is about the origins of culture and the tension inherent in male-female relations.

This theme of the tension in male-female relations is universal in human societies and, as such, is often expressed in their mythologies. On the other side of the world, the Mundurucu of the Amazon forest of Brazil have a myth that is strikingly similar to the Wogeo myth (Murphy and Murphy, 1985). The Mundurucu have sacred trumpets that are kept from the women. In the myth, the trumpets were discovered by the women, who then owned them. At that time, men performed all the women's tasks, such as getting firewood and water and making manioc cakes, and women were dominant over them. The trumpets had to be fed meat, which only the men could provide through hunting. Finally, the men took over the trumpets, as well as control of the men's house. The women were no longer allowed to see the trumpets, were no longer permitted into the men's house, and were henceforth subordinate to the men. Like the Wogeo myth, the Mundurucu myth is a justification for male domination over females. As in Wogeo, the myth begins with a reversal of roles and the attribution of superiority to females in mythic times. Tension in the relationship between males and females in Mundurucu and in Wogeo, and male insecurity about domination over females, leads to the common occurrence of such a myth.

There are echoes of the same theme in ancient Greek mythology, which is an integral part of our Western civilization. Both the Amazons, superhuman women who controlled their society, and the Fates, women who, through their weaving, determined the destiny of all humanity, are taken to be evidence in the myths for a matriarchal stage of society. In his introduction to *The Greek Myths*, Robert Graves (1955) linked the myths to what he believed to be an earlier matriarchal stage in the development of European society. But the Greek myths certainly cannot be taken as evidence of literal history any more than the Wogeo or Mundurucu myths can. These Greek myths tell us about contradictions and tensions in ancient Greek society. As we can see, the universal theme of male-female relations is handled in similar ways in very different societies.

LEGENDS

Myths treat the ancient past and the origins of things, while legends deal with the less remote past, just beyond "the fringe of history." Legends are about heroes who overcome obstacles, slay dragons, and defeat conquering armies to establish the independence of their homelands. Such legends are retold to justify the claim of a people to their land and their integrity as a people. The traditions of Polynesian societies, as they have been retold over the generations, illustrate the way myths fade into legends. For example, the Maori, the Polynesian population that first settled New Zealand, have a myth of how Maui fished up the island of New Zealand from the ocean depths and later became a culture hero who obtained fire. Kupe, another culture hero, subsequently rediscovered the island while chasing a supernatural octopus and reported back to the other Maori living in their legendary homeland. The first settlers set sail and reached the island now called New Zealand by following Kupe's directions. Maori genealogies are remembered and repeated down through the generations. These genealogies, which go back as far as 40 generations, link the present population to the first settlers and to Kupe. The legends of the Maori are concerned with the several migrations to New Zealand and the manner in which each tribe and kin group successively occupied its land. Maori legends, which were recorded by English missionaries and scholars in the nineteenth century, are now being used in various political contexts in which the Maori, as the indigenous people of New Zealand, are not only asserting their ethnic identity but demanding restitution for lost land.

The traditions of the native Hawaiians, who are also Polynesian speakers, are similar to those of the Maori. Like the Maori, the Hawaiians are great genealogists, with a tradition of migrations by canoe from Tahiti to the islands of Hawaii. The genealogy of the Hawaiian royal family, the Kumulipo, is a prayer chant that traces descent directly back to the gods. The gods appear to be like men in their form and actions, and it is hard to separate them from chiefs who lived and were later deified. Thus the world of myth imperceptibly becomes the world of legend and finally, the known world of history.

LEGEND BECOMES HISTORY: KING ARTHUR AND THE KNIGHTS OF THE ROUND TABLE

King Arthur and his Knights of the Round Table have been considered in the category of legend for many centuries, with people in each century recreating his story in their own fashion. In fact, some, who place him in the category of culture hero, argue that "the story of his life and death has been the principal myth of the island of Britain" (Castleden, 2000: 1; see also Higham 2002: 1). He was surrounded by such mystery that it was believed that he never lived. However, recently there has been a reexamination of various historical documents, such as the *Historia Brittonum,* written in 830 by the monk Nennius. It is based on sources, some going back to the sixth century, the one in which Arthur lived, which now attest to the actual existence of Arthur. Archeological materials support this. There is dispute as to whether he was actually a king, though in one source from around 1100, (500 years later) he is described as "Chief of the Kings of Britain" (Higham, 2002: Chapter 2, Chapter 3, 110). He was a Celtic king, the commander and chief, during a portion of the sixth century. However, unfortunately he was mortally wounded by the Saxon armies who eventual conquered the southwest part of Britain, which had been the Celtic domain. It is interesting to note the continued influence of Roman culture in Britain despite their earlier defeat. According to Higham, "Arthur

Early portrayal of King Arthur and the round table.

sounds like the very best post-Roman British aristocracy" (2002: 113) The story of King Arthur is an important example of how historical reality was distorted and overlaid by medieval romances and later literary treatments until his very existence was doubted. He had been transformed into a legendary, even mythic, figure who became identified with the nation.

FOLKTALES

Folktales are set within a timeless framework. They are concerned with imparting moral values and usually take the form of demonstrating what happens to individuals who violate the moral code of the society. Often animals freely interact with humans as heroes or villains; at other times tales may be about animals who talk, act, and think like human beings. Fairy tales are also included within the category of folktales. One of the most common folktale motifs is that of the trickster. Among many North American Indian societies, the trickster takes the form of the coyote, though among the Kwakiutl, the trickster is a raven. There are many sides to the character of Coyote. Sometimes he is depicted as being very cunning—he feigns death in order to catch game; he cheats at races and wins. At other times he is singularly stupid. In some tales he is a glutton, and in others he is involved in amorous and ribald adventures.

Typical of the Coyote tales is "Coyote and Bullhead," which was told by the Wintu of northern California (Pitkin, 1977). Coyote, while traveling north, encounters a swarm of small, black bullhead fishes and is able to roast and eat all but one by tricking them into swarming onto hot stones over a fire. Subsequently, he meets a rotten tree stump creaking in the wind who refuses to respond to him. Thinking himself teased, Coyote punches at the stump until he is stuck fast. Some people come along and free him. Later, Coyote again encounters the sole surviving bullhead, whom he provokes, insulting him by implying that his relatives are all dead, until the fish eats Coyote. The fish then rolls into the water under a big rock. The people come looking for Coyote and see the fish. They spear the fish after they get a magical sky-spear, slit open its belly, and out pops Coyote. On emerging, he pretends that he has dozed off and does not know how he came to be in the fish's belly. The people then sew up the bullhead and return him to the water.

In this Wintu tale about Coyote, he is revealed as a strange combination—the clever deceiver and teaser, as well as the dupe and victim of his own actions. The people refer to him as "uncle," though he is really more like a child. He must be extricated from his difficulties by the grown-ups—the people in the story, who lecture him not to behave in this way anymore. Like a mischievous child, he of course does the same thing again. This sequence of events has a twofold function—it amuses the listeners while at the same time imparting the moral that insulting, provoking, and teasing are wrong.

A structural analysis of this Coyote tale will enable us to understand its message more clearly. It can be broken down into three distinct episodes: (A) Coyote eats the little bullheads, (B) Coyote fights with the stump, and (C) the last bullhead eats Coyote. Arranging the three episodes in columns allows us to see the relationships among the episodes more clearly:

Episode	I	II	III
A	Coyote tricks bullheads.	Coyote eats bullheads.	One bullhead escapes.
B	Coyote is provoked by the stump.	Coyote is stuck to the stump.	Coyote escapes with the people's help.
C	Coyote teases the last bullhead.	Bullhead eats Coyote.	Coyote escapes with the people's help.

When lined up in this way, the three episodes are seen to be very similar. However, episode B is diametrically opposed to episode A. In A, Coyote successfully tricks the bullheads, while in B he himself is tricked as a result of his own stupidity. In A, he wins and eats all but one of the bullheads; in B, he loses and is trapped, though he ultimately escapes. Episode C reconciles and unites the seemingly unrelated episodes A and B into a single story. Episode C refers back to episode A in that the bullhead has his revenge on Coyote for eating his relatives. Episode C is a reversal of episode A, since the bullhead eats Coyote in C, while Coyote eats the bullheads in A. Episode C is very similar to episode B in that Coyote's teasing leads to his entrapment in both episodes.

What is the meaning of this Coyote story? What message does it convey? The structural analysis reveals the message of the tale. In Wintu culture Coyote represents the child. This story is an attempt to teach Coyote the rules of the society, though Coyote will never really learn. Though Coyote succeeds as a trickster in the first episode, he fails in the second and third episodes and must be extricated by the people, the larger community. The message conveyed is that, though a trickster may seem at first to be successful, one must ultimately conform to the rules in order to be a successful member of the group. The Wintu rules that Coyote violates are striking out on one's own, teasing, and insultingly referring to the dead. The gathering of food was a communal activity; striking out on one's own, as Coyote did, violated this. Teasing and allowing oneself to be provoked by teasing were not considered proper adult behavior by the Wintu. But worst of all, Coyote broke the Wintu taboo against referring to the dead by teasing the last surviving bullhead. The message to the listeners was that if you violate these rules, you will end up like Coyote, a child who can survive only if he is constantly rescued by adults from dilemmas. In the Wintu tale, humor and teasing are emphasized. In contrast, among the Okanagan of the Plateau, Coyote is portrayed as a culture hero who named the tribes and taught them the essential cultural practices, though he also played tricks and did many foolish things (Teit, cited in Baillargeon and Tepper, 1998: 74). As John Fire Lame Deer, a traditional Sioux holy man, was quoted as saying, "Coyote, Iktomi, and all their kind [tricksters] are sacred. A people that have so much to weep about as we Indians need their laughter to survive" (quoted in Erdoes and Ortiz, 1998: xxi).

The trickster figure seems to be a universal folklore figure that represents the incongruous combination of monster, loutish liar, braggart, creator and destroyer, and duper, as well as the one who is always duped himself (Goldman, 1998). According to Peck, "European immigrants brought to North America tales in which a *human* trickster outwits other people, and such stories have never waned in popularity" (1998: 203). In European tales, the trickster is almost always a human male, while in Native American tales he is usually personified as an animal, though he may sometimes assume a human shape (Erdoes and Ortiz, 1998: xiii). Goldman identifies two main strands of "trickster scholarship" among those who have studied the trickster motif. In the first, the trickster enables breaches of the accepted order to occur within the realm of the imagination, allowing adults and children to be amused by behavior categorized as antisocial while at the same time being socialized. The Wintu tale about Coyote does this. The second deals with the marginal, liminal status of the trickster who is a mediating being, resolving dilemmas of human existence. It is a way of talking about ourselves in a satiric, ironic, and comedic fashion (Goldman, 1998: 90).

With the expansion of cultural studies, the concept of the trickster, which originated as coyote or raven in Native American tales, has been applied in analyzing the literary works of Mark Twain, Herman Melville, and Jack London, as well as to the analysis of many aspects of popular culture like Bugs Bunny and Roadrunner

(Reesman, 2001). In the writings of Mark Twain, especially in *Huckleberry Finn*, the trickster is the deadpan storyteller, Mark Twain himself. Melville, however, uses John-the-slave, a well-known trickster in African-American folklore, as a character in his classic novella *Benito Cereno*. John-the-slave can be either a trusted slave or a black slave driver who deceives and manipulates his master. While appearing to be the trusted slave, John-the-slave really is the master. In *Benito Cereno*, an American ship comes upon a seemingly deserted slave ship. In fact, the ship is under the complete control of the slaves after a slave revolt. Baba, leader of the revolt, and his son Mure appear to be the groveling retainers of the Spanish captain; however, like John-the-slave, they really are totally in control (Bickley, 2001).

FAIRY TALES

Just as Coyote tales taught morality to children, fairy tales, according to Bruno Bettelheim, teach children about what it means to grow up. While myths are about extraordinary, superhuman heroes or gods, the characters in fairy tales are ordinary mortals. "Whatever strange events the fairy tale hero experiences, they do not make him superhuman, as is true for the mythical hero. This real humanity suggests to the child that, whatever the content of the fairy tale it is but fanciful elaborations and exaggerations of the tasks he has to meet, and of his hopes and fears" (Bettelheim, 1977: 40). Fairy tales were transmitted orally, tales told around the fire after the work of the day, and consequently changed as the centuries went by, as all oral literature does, until they began to be recorded, first by Charles Perrault in the late seventeenth century, and then by the brothers Grimm during the nineteenth century. Fairy tales perform an important function in that they are "among our most powerful socializing narratives. They contain enduring rules for understand who we are and how we should behave" (Orenstein, 2002: 10). One might say that they convey universal and timeless truths.

Fairy tales like "Red Riding Hood," up until the nineteenth century, were "a bawdy morality tale, quite different from the story we know today" (Orenstein, 2002: 3). There have been changes in the meanings of the characters, and although the wolf has always signified evil, in the earlier adult version Red Riding Hood was the unchaste woman. Most fairy tales are stories that are familiar throughout Europe and North American. However, fairies and their stories in Ireland seem to be particular to Irish culture. Irish fairies are an intimate part of Irish culture even today. For example, Purkiss notes that "on Internet newsgroups, a troll is a person who haunts Usenet in an attempt to stir up controversy by posting inflammatory statements" (2000: 306)

PERFORMANCE

Originally, myths, legends, and folktales were transmitted orally, and each telling was a *performance*. They were retold from generation to generation, to the awe and amusement of successive audiences. Each time a story was retold, it came out slightly differently. Variations were introduced, different episodes were included, and, eventually, different versions of the same story developed. Stories usually diffused from one society to another over a wide area, and in each of these societies a somewhat different version of the story could be found. Anthropologists collect as many versions of a single story told in a particular society as they can. By comparing these different versions, they are better able to ascertain the meaning of the story. In similar fashion, the same and related stories in different societies over a wide area are collected and compared by anthropologists. Lévi-Strauss analyzed different versions of the same myth and related myths in different South American Indian societies (Lévi-Strauss, 1971). His analysis revealed the presence of the same themes and contradictions in mythologies throughout this large area.

When we shift to an examination of the performance aspects of myths, legends, and tales—which are, in effect, oral narratives—the factor of creativity enters the picture. Huntsman points out that the different presentations of the same story move from a veneration of "tradition" to a celebration of "creativity" (1995: 124). Tokelau tales, or *kakai*, which are fictitious tales told as entertainment, must contain the episodes, chants, songs, and key phrases that the audience expects. But the tellers of these tales have a wide latitude to elaborate and embellish a story as long as they include what their listeners expect (Huntsman, 1995: 125). In contrast, Tokelau *tala*, which are myths, legends, historical narratives, or accounts of the pre-Christian past, have as their primary purpose to inform, though they may also be entertaining. Specific geographic place-names "'ground' the narrative as an account of events that happened at known, named places" (Huntsman, 1995: 154). These place-names must be narrated accurately. Huntsman also makes the point, made by many others, that storytellers and raconteurs "tailor" their narrative performances to their audiences (1995: 154). It should be noted that tellers of stories and tales also vary in their storytelling abilities.

Consideration of the performance aspects of oral narratives places them within a temporal framework, which brings up the question of the continuities and changes of such accounts. The ghost narratives of the Cook Islands, or *tupapaku*, recount stories about spirits in animal form, which are deeply rooted in Polynesian history. Recently, they have come to include stories about cows, pigs, dogs, goats, horses, and cats—introduced domesticates—as spirit vehicles. As Clerk notes, *tupapaku* accounts "have never been separated from the life of the community as a whole. They have adapted consistently to new circumstances, incorporating new experience, yet maintaining a continuity with traditions of great antiquity" (1995: 173). Continuity and change also characterize all other aspects of culture. As we noted for the potlatch in previous chapters, although people now give away power boats and tea sets instead of elk skins, the organization of the potlatch remains the same. The contents of myths, tales, and potlatches change much more rapidly than does structure.

When myths, folktales, and legends are written down, an oral narrative becomes written literature. The stories may form the basis for the literary tradition of the society. The legends of King Arthur and the Knights of the Round Table ceased to be stories told by bards, or professional storytellers, and became English literature, as we noted above. The fact that the story is now written down does not mean that it will not continue to change. It may be rewritten by poor writers or by good writers and may change with each retelling. The characters, motifs, and central themes of these stories may often be used by poets, novelists, and dramatists in their own works. For example, in Mary McCarthy's novel *The Group* (1963), the knights have been transformed into female students at Vassar in the 1950s. The American musical *Camelot* also retells the legend of King Arthur and the Knights of the Round Table. Camelot later became the referent for the Kennedy presidency.

LEGENDS AND FOLKTALES IN AMERICAN CULTURE

One may pose the question, Does our culture have myths, legends, or folktales? Myths deal with the remote past and with superhumans who created the world, the people in it, and all their material objects and cultural institutions. American culture does not include these kinds of myths. However, stories about how American culture was forged and about its origins are our American myths. Legendary figures abound. Some were historical people, such as Billy the Kid, Davy Crockett, Daniel Boone, Kit Carson, Annie Oakley, and Buffalo Bill. Stories about their lives became legends, but other legends about them had no basis in fact. Other heroes, who are the subjects of folktales, such as Pecos Bill, John Henry, and Paul Bunyan, probably never lived. The setting for all these legends was the expanding American frontier. The stories demonstrated how these people conquered natural obstacles and made the frontier livable. They were scouts who led the wagon trains across the dangerous and endless Plains. They were rivermen who opened up the rivers to settlement and commerce. They were railroad builders who laid the steel track across an expanding nation. They were the sheriffs and marshals who made the frontier safe. In American legends, the theme is a characteristically American one—the conquest of the frontier and the settlement of the land. As occurs in legends in general, American heroes, by their bravery, their ingenuity, and their labor, assert the claim of a people to their land. This, of course, totally ignored and overrode the claim of the Native American population who were on the land first.

Sometimes the heroes of the legends, like Paul Bunyan, assumed superhuman proportions. He was a legendary lumberjack and logger. As the lumber industry moved across America from Maine to Michigan and Minnesota, and then later to Washington and Oregon, the Bunyan stories moved with it, and Paul Bunyan, at first a regional hero, became a national hero. Bunyan, his ax, and his blue ox Babe are of enormous and superhuman size. Bunyan's feats are distinctive because of both his cleverness and his great strength, and many of the stories are humorous (Peck, 1998: 131ff.). In some of the stories he creates natural landmarks, like Puget Sound. Many stories demonstrate his ability to conquer nature. In one story he makes a river run backward in order to break up a log jam. Paul Bunyan stories are also told in the oil fields of Texas and Oklahoma. Here, Bunyan is an oil man who is even given credit for inventing the tools and methods of drilling for oil. The Bunyan stories began in the tales told in the lumber camps of northeastern Michigan and reached a maximum popularity and audience when they became the subject of newspaper columns and advertising copy in the second decade of the twentieth century. Newspaper advertisements turned Paul Bunyan from a folkloric hero into a popular superhero of that time. It is interesting to note that today the work of press agents and publicists is to turn their clients, ordinary human beings, into mythic figures, like Arnold Schwartzenegger.

While the legends of Paul Bunyan and other tall tales are indigenously American, many folktales and fairy tales told in America are largely derivative, having come with immigrants from other countries. Joel Chandler Harris was a journalist and also a writer of short stores and the Uncle Remus tales, but it was "his studies into folklore, and his writing of the tales told to him by American Blacks . . . that made him one of the nation's leading folklorists" (Brasch, 2000: xxii). Though a white man, his Uncle Remus stories are said to be a relatively accurate translation of American Black English, which we discussed in Chapter 4. As a young man, Harris worked for a publisher who owned a plantation and slaves. It was while sitting in the cabins of the slaves on that plantation that he learned about their culture and heard the language and the stories, which he later transformed into the Uncle Remus stories. Brer Rabbit, a central character in the stories, is clearly a trickster figure, with his trickery, deceit, and deviousness. He and the other animals in the stories represent transformations of the animals with which the slaves, who came from West Africa, were familiar. Portraits of the rabbit as a trickster also appear in the tales of the Creek, Natchez, and other southeastern Native American groups. Scholarly analysis has shown that the tales were borrowed by the Native Americans from the slaves. Harris considered himself merely a "compiler" of the stories. It is interesting to note that in a recent collection, *From My People: 400 Years of African American Folklore*, edited by Daryl Cumber Dance, Harris is nowhere mentioned. The volume includes folktales—a number about Brer Rabbit and Brer Fox, folk music, soul food, and proverbs, among other categories.

AMERICAN FILMS AS LEGENDS AND MYTHS

Legends and tales are rarely told by storytellers in present-day America. Parents may read stories to small children, and perhaps these stories may be read in required literature courses. The major themes of such stories, however, continue to be repeated, but now in the media of mass communications. It is in films and television that these same themes from legends and tales reappear. One has only to think of the Western film to understand this point, since Westerns have become inextricably linked to the American identity. The hero of the classic Western, like the heroes of American legends, is a rugged individualist who tames the frontier. But Americans have an ambivalent attitude about taming the frontier. They look back with fondness to the time when the frontier represented escape from the constraints of society—a time when individuals took the law into their own hands. The cattlemen who used the open range for cattle grazing represent the beginning of law and order. But they fought the farmers who wanted to fence in the range and who represented a further step in the process of control over nature.

In the classic film *The Man Who Shot Liberty Valence*, director John Ford captures the ambivalence between the wilderness of the frontier, represented by the outlaw Liberty Valence; civilization, represented by Senator Ransom Stoddard; and Donovan, the real hero, who straddles both worlds. The tension in the film is between Liberty, the outlaw, and Ransom, the civilized man. The story of the killing of Valence, the villain, is told in a series of flashbacks from a civilized present time to an earlier frontier time. But a sense of loss and nostalgia for that earlier period pervades the film. Despite the changes in emphasis of the 1960s and 1970s, "the Western's overall thrust sanctified territorial expansion, justified dispossession of the Indians, fueled nostalgia for a largely mythicized past, exalted self-reliance and posited violence as the main solution to personal and societal problems" (Coyne, 1997: 3). However, the usual representation of American identity in the Western was white and male. This picture was to some extent transformed in the late 1970s, when the TV miniseries *Centennial,* based on a novel by James Michener, presented the history of a Colorado town, emphasizing the multicultural composition of the frontier and condemning the mass slaughter of the Indians by a racist army officer (Coyne, 1997: 184). More recently, *Dances with Wolves,* which many might not call a Western, clearly presents a different picture of Native Americans than do classic Westerns such as *Stagecoach.* Even today, in 2003, the themes of the Western are recapitualitated in the images that our president has chosen to use in his portrayal of our country in international affairs. Osama Bin Laden is wanted "Dead or Alive." We have assumed a "go it alone stance" in our relations with other countries, a "cowboy" stance. We are in a struggle of good and evil and you are "either with us or against us." This is the rhetoric of the classic Westerns.

The legend of Billy the Kid has been told and retold in films, plays, novels, and ballets. How did Billy the Kid, who was a real person, turn into a legend, and what are the characteristics that differentiate the legendary Billy from the real Billy? Billy the Kid was shot and killed by Pat Garrett (himself a legendary figure), the sheriff of Lincoln County, New Mexico, in July 1881. He had been arrested for murder and sentenced to hang seven months earlier, but he shot and killed his two guards and escaped from prison. Garrett and his posse tracked him down to Fort Sumner, an abandoned army fort, where they killed him. Shortly thereafter, Garrett, with the help of a former newspaperman, wrote the book *The Authentic Life of Billy the Kid,* and the myth was launched. Since so many false stories were being told about Billy at that time, Garrett wanted to set the record straight. According to Garrett, Billy committed his first murder at the age of 12 to defend his mother's honor. Billy carried out later murders in Lincoln County after the execution of his friend John Tunstall, becoming an avenging angel until Sheriff Garrett, with a heavy heart, ended his life. Much of the information in Garrett's account was either mistaken (including Billy's real name) or invented.

Years later, a researcher collecting folklore as part of an oral-history project in New Mexico interviewed a Hispanic member of Sheriff Pat Garrett's posse. The Billy that he recalled was very generous, spoke fluent Spanish, and wore moc-

The only known photograph of Billy the Kid, whose life became an American legend.

casins. "Everybody liked Billy the Kid." He claimed that Garrett's account of Billy's death was all wrong and that Billy was much too smart to be caught in the room where Garrett said he shot him. Though for two weeks the posse surrounded the house where the shooting took place, they never caught sight of Billy or recovered his body.

Each teller of the Billy the Kid story expands a different aspect of the "myth." What do we know about the real person who was Billy the Kid? Above is the one photograph extant of the man who was known as Billy the Kid. He was born Henry McCarty, probably in New York City, of Irish Catholic ancestry. While he was still young, his mother took him and his brother out West, ending up in Silver City, New Mexico. Before he came to Lincoln County, New Mexico, Henry McCarty, at the age of 18, seems to have killed a man in a gunfight in Arizona in 1877. After that, he assumed the name William Bonney. The Lincoln County "war" into which Henry McCarty was drawn was, in reality, a battle between two factions of the county for political control. One faction consisted of a group of Irish Catholics. The other faction consisted of Protestants led by John Tunstall, the Englishman who was killed. The Lincoln County war has been interpreted as a continuation of the ethnic-religious conflict that was taking place in Northern Ireland (O'Toole, 1999). McCarty, born a Catholic, was on the opposite side of the

Irish-Catholic faction in this war. Since Henry's mother remarried when he was 13 to a Scotch-Irish Protestant man, it appears that Henry and his mother converted. Therefore Henry, now Billy, became a member of a group of gunfighters for the Protestant faction, which ended in his capture and trial for murder and his killing by Pat Garrett after he escaped from jail.

What are the elements in the myth of Billy the Kid that resonate and touch the emotions of so many Americans? From the very beginning, even in Pat Garrett's story, which has as its primary purpose to glorify Garrett, the sheriff, we see the figure of Billy as the avenging angel and the fighter for justice. Though an outlaw, he is no wanton killer. Garrett sees the first murder that Billy committed as justified, because he was defending his mother's honor. Billy was driven to commit this crime. He is an outsider, yet he understands and obeys a code of honor. He honors friendship and loyalty. He is generous to the poor, and consequently, they help him escape from the authorities, who are evil. Like the wind, Billy cannot be captured. He lives on somewhere. The characteristics attributed to Billy were those of legendary outlaws and heroes such as Jessie James and, much earlier, Robin Hood. Finally, Billy the Kid is only 21 when he is killed. His youth itself is an important part of the myth. These features may not, in fact, describe Henry McCarty, but they are all characteristics of the myth of Billy the Kid. They explain why his story has been and will continue to be retold in films, with Robert Taylor, Paul Newman, Val Kilmer, Kris Kristofferson, or some unknown young actor playing the role of Billy.

In addition to seeing Western films as contemporary versions of American legends, some analysts have examined American films as myths whose meanings encode somewhat different symbolic patterns characterizing American society. Nathanson, for example, has analyzed the film *The Wizard of Oz* in terms of the way its specific mythic properties relate to the important problems of human existence (1991). This film has become a classic. As Nathanson notes, "*The Wizard of Oz* may be called a 'secular myth' because, though not overtly religious, it functions in a modern ostensibly secular society, to some extent, the way myths function in traditional and religious societies" (1991: 312). The use of fantastic imagery, the inclusion of supernatural forces and beings, and the fact that it relates to basic human questions, such as where we have come from, where we are going, where we belong, and who we are in relation to others, situate *The Wizard of Oz* in the realm of myth. *The Wizard of Oz* is about coming of age and building new relationships and also about going home. Though the Wizard himself initially appears to be a fraud, he is the source of important folk wisdom: The qualities Dorothy and her companions are searching for—a heart for the Tin Man, courage for the Cowardly Lion, a brain for the Scarecrow, and the capacity to be grown-up for Dorothy—are to be found within oneself. The heroine, Dorothy, comes of age in the Emerald City where she is transformed from a child into an adult, after which she is transported back to Kansas. The film was made during the Depression, a very unsettled time, and films from this period often depict explicitly going home and implicitly growing up. Various American symbolic landscapes can be identified in the film, including

Munchkin City—a small midwestern city; the Emerald City—the eastern metropolis; the Haunted Forest—the wilderness, threatening and hostile untamed nature; the Yellow Brick Road—a path that pierces the wilderness and represents the unification of America, as well as the freedom and hope of the open highway; and, finally, the Frontier Farm—home, order, and civilization. The Wizard also communicates the notion of the progressive urban setting as set against the traditional rural countryside of the populist world view, the ultimate resolution of the two being technological agriculture in a bucolic paradise (Nathanson, 1991: 173). Kansas is the beginning, the paradise; Oz is the world in which Dorothy searches for order in chaos (the Haunted Forest). At the end of the film, she repeats the mantra, "There's no place like home," and she's back in her bedroom in Kansas (Mackey-Kallis, 2001: 137). This represents one of the most important themes of the film, the need to return home, having grown up. The fear of losing one's home was a particularly poignant theme in the 1930s when the film was made.

The film gives mythic expression to what are seen as the deepest feelings of the American people, a nostalgia for the past combined with a hope for the future. The myth of Dorothy in Oz has been more recently recycled in the film *Tootsie*. Michael Dorsey, an out-of-work actor, a failure whom nobody will hire, becomes Dorothy Michaels. In the course of life as Dorothy, he learns about himself. He observes, at the end, "I was a better man as a woman than I ever was as a man." Like Dorothy in *The Wizard of Oz*, Michael Dorsey grows up by finding the truth inside himself. *The Wizard of Oz* is one of the 50 most popular movies ever televised (Mackey-Kallis, 2001: 129).

The *Star Wars* trilogy, to which a fourth film has recently been added, has been said to represent "one of the great myths of our time," combining the theme of a heroic journey with that of the eternal battle between good and evil (Henderson, 1997: 3). As noted above, Westerns as a film genre popular from the end of World War I to the early 1970s were no longer very significant in either films or television after that point. *Star Wars* is the "quintessential hero quest" (Mackey-Kallis, 2001: 202, 214ff.). However, in the *Star Wars* series, George Lucas, the filmmaker, recycled some Western themes that resonate with more general American conceptualizations. At the beginning of the first film, *Star Wars: Episode IV, A New Hope*, Luke Skywalker is living with his foster parents on the remote desert planet Tatooine, the frontier of civilization, which is also occupied by the Sand People, the equivalent of the Native Americans, as the uncivilized Other. Luke starts on his heroic journey of revenge after his foster parents are killed and his home destroyed. This parallels the destruction by Native Americans of frontier settlements established on Indian territory by American pioneers, who saw the area as a wilderness to be occupied and tamed, and the survivors who sought revenge. Some of the characters in the film recapitulate prototypical figures from Westerns, for example, Han Solo (the loner), the quick-on-the-draw gunfighter, and Greedo, the bounty hunter. This first film in the series is climaxed by a classic Western-style shoot-out with the Death Star, with the Evil Empire as the O.K. Corral (Henderson, 1997: 129). In *Return of the Jedi*, Luke, representing the force for good, returns to his home planet, now overrun by a powerful criminal and his gang, and turns out the villains. This theme in *Return of the Jedi* is a recapitulation of the themes of *Dodge City* and *My Darling Clementine.*

Since the beginning of the twentieth century, Americans have been captivated by technology and its great potential; this is a also a significant theme in the *Star Wars* series. Science and technology transformed our lives. To Americans, science not only has the potential to solve the world's problems but also can eventually provide knowledge about all aspects of nature. Science fiction, in the form of literature, comic books, and film, was the setting in which this category of themes was explored. In the *Star Wars* films, intergalactic travel is an everyday occurrence, and the level of technological development is accelerated to a degree far beyond what today's humans experience or can even imagine. American faith in the future of technology began to be undermined, to some extent beginning in the 1970s, when Rachel Carson in *Silent Spring* and Charles Reich in *The Greening of America,* among others, depicted how technology run wild was despoiling our environment and threatening the future of the earth. Both sides of the dilemma, of how humans maintain their humanity in relating to technology, are depicted in *Star Wars.* In the Empire, technology is supreme and the aim is to turn human beings into machinelike servants to technology, suppressing their humanity. The Empire becomes a dystopia, the opposite of a utopia, a place where totalitarian power and violence reign supreme (Henderson, 1997: 152–153). Luke Skywalker must use his interior strength and fortitude to fight the system, not to oppose machines as the Luddites of the last century did, but to put humans and their feelings and emotions in control of the machines, instead of having the machines control humans. Another theme is the fear of the Evil Empire, which could be interpreted as a fear of aliens or Others. In this battle between good and evil, Luke takes on heroic characteristics. In the Republican primary contest of 2000, John McCain referred to himself as Luke Skywalker because, like Skywalker, he fought against the system. The *Star Wars* series also echoes the King Arthur stories, in that Luke grows up in "relative obscurity" and finds Obi-Wan Kanobi, his Merlin (Mackey-Kallis, 2001: 206ff., 226).

Cultural studies specialists are beginning to talk about the "American monomyth," seeing the heroes we have discussed as "mythic heroes" and the midwestern small town as a "monomythic Eden" (Lawrence and Jewett, 2002: 21ff.). *Monomyth* is a term used by Joseph Campbell to refer to the hero who ventures into a supernatural world in which he ultimately attains victory and returns home. This is exactly like the journey of the shaman into the supernatural world, which we described in the previous chapter; however, the curing aspect of the shaman is not present. *Star Wars, Star Trek,* and the TV program *Touched by an Angel* are seen as aspects of American mythic consciousness (Lawrence and Jewett, 2002: 6)

THE SOPRANOS: AN AMERICAN MYTH

The Sopranos, the spectacularly popular television series, has also been analyzed in terms of its mythic qualities. Why have the Mafia characters of *The Sopranos* and *The Godfather* films risen to become mythic figures like Jesse James and Billy the Kid? What do they tell us about American culture? *The Sopranos* operates at three levels: a representation of the real world, the underworld of the Mafia, and the world of fantasy that is told to therapists. The title immediately reveals two things. Sopranos are women who have high voices, and to use Soprano as the family's last name means that Tony is likened to a woman. The implication is that his manhood is threatened, perhaps by castration. Tony himself says, "This whole war could have been averted. Cunnilingus and psychiatry brought us to this" (Barreca, 2002: 7). The title of the series also tells us that we are dealing with soap opera, with the emphasis on opera.

Tony Soprano, pondering over the collapse of Western civilization, is Everyman (Barreca, 2002: 3). He is also the Hamlet of New Jersey. Tony and Hamlet are both "profoundly introspective and prone to self-doubt, intimidated by formidable mothers, worried about public roles, concerned about treacherous uncles, and irresolute about matters of the heart. . . . The worlds inhabited by Tony and Hamlet appear to them as stale, flat, and unprofitable (or, as Tony puts it, 'I'm losing my mind here')" (Barreca, 2002: 3). Tony is like the rest of us and deals with real-life problems. He is a husband, a father, a brother, and a son. In these roles, he interacts with forceful and determined women. Livia, his mother, pretending to be the suffering woman, knows and effectively uses her emotional power over Tony. Carmela, equally forceful, confronts Tony about all the problems at home, like financial security and Tony's lack of a pension. Tony worries about his daughter Meadow getting into a good college. When she gets into Columbia, she scornfully throws it up to him that he doesn't even know the canon of dead, white males, which she is forced to read at Columbia! But Meadow admits that Tony is no different from other fathers, or other husbands or other sons (Barreca, 2002: 38).

The myth of the Mafia, told in *The Godfather* and reiterated in *The Sopranos,* is that the underworld and the real world operate according to the same basic values. In both worlds, factions compete and war with one another. When they "waste" an opposing member, they go out of their way to point out that its nothing personal. When asked by Dr. Melfi if he will go to hell for his actions, Tony replies, "Soldiers don't go to hell. It's business, we're soldiers, we follow codes, orders" (Barreca, 2002: 31). Tony's creed is "You gotta do what you gotta do." There are bad guys, like Ralph, like there are bad guys everywhere—in the movie business, in accounting, in academia, and so on, as there are good guys. Tony is different from Ralph because Tony is a good guy. There is a Mafia code: you act forcefully when you have to, meaning you murder someone or have some one murdered. The other side of the code is strong loyalty to superiors and inferiors. Tony strictly observes this Mafia code. In this respect Tony is no different from the average "good soldier" in the everyday world.

The level of therapy, or psychiatry, constitutes still a third level. What people tell their therapist reflects something other than reality. It reflects their distortions, their desires, and sometimes their fantasies. Dr, Melfi is a therapist whose interaction with Tony Soprano represents one of the most popular themes in the *Sopranos.* Real-life patients even discuss her with their therapists. The idea of a Mafia killer bearing his breast to his female therapist is a brilliant device, because it reveals Tony's rationalizations about his actions. We quoted Tony as saying, "I'm losing my mind here," meaning he recognizes that he needs help, since he is ambivalent and indecisive. If anyone in his organization were to find out about this, it would be disastrous for Tony. He must always appear to be totally in control (like Vito Coreleone). This action of going to a therapist could never happen to real Mafiosi because it would undermine their power. Like all therapists, Dr. Melfi, has a serious problem of countertransference. One literary critic, in her analysis of the series, is very taken with the character of Dr. Melfi. She says, "*Dr. Melfi is (or might be) me— me* watching with concern, distaste . . . and eventually a kind of fascination" (Barreca, 2002: 25).

Americans are fascinated by gangsters, especially Mafia gangsters. Programs like *The Sopranos* and films like *The Godfather* show the way in which the Mafia represent a dialectic between beloved American values, like family, home, loyalty and roots, and the murder and rapaciousness of the underworld. Interestingly, rapaciousness itself has been and continues to be an aspect of American capitalism, making some corporate executives resemble Mafia kingpins. It is the leadership ability of these dons as depicted in film that Rudolph Guiliani admires when he holds Don Coreleone up as a model leader (Giuliani, 2002: 36, 312). Inculcating obedience in followers is one of the principles of leadership, and Tony Soprano is a good soldier who follows orders. For him this is the justification for his violent acts. Yet, in doing so, he often suffers pain and experiences panic. That is what makes *The Sopranos* so appealing.

URBAN LEGENDS

What are urban legends and how do they reflect modern life? An urban or contemporary legend can be defined as "a story in a contemporary setting (not necessarily a city), reported as a true individual experience, with traditional variants that indicate its legendary character . . . [and the stories] typically have three good reasons for their popularity: a suspenseful or humorous story line, an element of actual belief, and a warning or moral that is either stated or implied" (Brunvand, 2000: 6). There is a very broad range of such legends and clearly some drop out as others begin to be told.

Fine analyzes the "Kentucky Fried Rat" stories, whose basic theme involves rat meat being served as chicken at Kentucky Fried Chicken fast-food stores (1992). He shows how this and other similar "food legends," which had earlier involved Italian and Chinese restaurants, represent fear of outsiders—in one case, foreigners; in the other, giant multinational corporations, both outside the community. Food earlier came from family, church, and community, constituting nourishment from known individuals. Now food is provided by unknown persons in corporations, whose only reason for existing is to make a profit. Though the public has eagerly accepted fast foods as part of a transforming environment with its increased emphasis on leisure time and the changing roles of women, it is not completely reconciled to the structural changes entailed. In this as well as other cases, new values continue to exist with and often in contradiction to the traditional values (Fine, 1992: 132–133). The "Kentucky Fried Rat" story is told and retold as the tellers themselves stop at the nearest fast-food chain for burgers. It is similar to the story about the mouse tail found in a soda bottle. Such stories are recounted as true stories, though witnesses to the event can never be found. You may have heard the tale that Brunvand calls "The Elevator Incident," in which a large man, who "happens to be black," enters an elevator occupied by three elderly ladies, with his Doberman pinscher dog. The man says, "Sit, Lady," and the three women slowly drop to the elevator floor. Urban legends like this are told over and over, with slight variations.

There is now a whole group of legends concerning the "heroic hacker." Legends abound of the programming feats and exploits of particular individuals and these circulate throughout the Internet community, which includes e-mail, chat rooms, World Wide Web, and newsgroups. They are based on the real-life exploits of particular hackers. (Brunvand, 2000: 170 ff.).

The mass media often play a key role in the dissemination of urban legends, which lends a further aura of truth to the story. Brunvand points out that "the stories do tell one kind of truth. They are a unique, unselfconscious reflection of major concerns of individuals in the societies in which the [urban] legends circulate" (1998: 146). In this sense, urban legends in our culture are no different from the myths we discussed earlier, which also deal with such major concerns.

SUMMARY

• Myths, legends, and folktales represent a continuum.

• Myths deal with the remote past, often with the time of the origin of things both natural and cultural—how the world and its people were created, how fire was discovered, and how crops were domesticated. Myths are associated with the sacred.

• There are various theoretical approaches that have been proposed to explain the existence of myth. One approach interprets myths as literal history.

• Twentieth-century approaches to the interpretation of myths include, among others, the Freudian approach.

• Malinowski insisted on the necessity of analyzing a myth in relation to its social and cultural context. It was a charter for how and what people should believe, act, and feel.

• Clyde Kluckhohn stressed the interdependence of myth and ritual.

• According to Lévi-Strauss, myths provide explanations for contradictions that are present in a culture and that cannot be resolved.

• Myths fade into legends, which are sometimes thought to have a basis in historical fact.

• The story of King Arthur is an important example of how historical reality was distorted and overlaid by medieval romances and later literary treatments until his very existence was doubted. He had been transformed into a legendary, even mythic, figure who became identified with the nation.

• Folktales deal with an indeterminate time, which, in European folktales, is indicated by the standard opening, "Once upon a time . . ."

• One of the most common folktale motifs is that of the trickster, who often takes the form of the coyote, although he may sometimes be a raven.

• The trickster figure seems to be a universal folklore figure that represents the incongruous combination of monster, loutish liar, braggart, creator and destroyer, and duper, as well as the one who is always duped himself.

• Just as Coyote tales taught morality to children, fairy tales teach children about what it means to grow up.

• Originally, myths, legends, and folktales were transmitted orally, and each telling was a performance.

• When myths, folktales, and legends are written down, an oral narrative becomes written literature.

• It is in American films and television that the themes from legends and tales reappear. Western films can be seen as contemporary versions of American legends.

• Americans are fascinated by gangsters, especially Mafia gangsters. Programs like *The Sopranos* and films like *The Godfather* show the way in which Mafia life represents a dialectic between beloved American values like family, home, loyalty and roots, and the murder and rapaciousness of the underworld.

• An urban or contemporary legend is a story in a contemporary setting, reported as a true individual experience, which has an element of actual belief and a warning or moral.

  SUGGESTED READINGS

Dance, Daryl Cumber. *From My People: Four Hundred Years of African American Folklore.* New York: Norton, 2002. A collection of many African American folktales that have survived and been adapted through the centuries. Some of the tales are shown to contain motifs and characters which are of African derivation.

Drummond, Lee. *American Dreamtime: A Cultural Analysis of Movies and Their Implications for a Science of Humanity.* Lanham, MD: Rowman and Littlefield, 1996. A general consideration of themes in contemporary American films and their relationship to American culture.

Lavery, David. *This Thing of Ours: Investigating the Sopranos.* New York: Columbia University Press, 2002. A series of critical essays examining and evaluating *The Sopranos* from a cultural studies point of view. Topics such as Americans' love of gangster films and the connection between food and violence are considered.

Lévi-Strauss, Claude. *The Savage Mind.* Chicago: University of Chicago Press, 1966. An exposition of Lévi-Strauss's structuralist theoretical framework for the analysis of myth, symbols, and systems of classification.

Orenstein, Catherine. *Little Red Riding Hood Uncloaked: Sex, Morality, and the Evolution of a Fairy Tale.* New York: Basic Books, 2002. An exploration of the sexual politics of "Little Red Riding Hood," including a consideration of the meaning of the cross-dressing wolf.

Von Hendy, Andrew. *The Modern Construction of Myth.* Bloomington, IN: Indiana University Press, 2002. A consideration of the anthropological theories about the invention and evolution of myth.

 SUGGESTED WEBSITES

<u>http://www/mythweb.com</u> The heroes, gods, and monsters of Greek mythology are discussed in an amusing manner.

<u>http://www.albany.edu/scj/jcjpc/vol3is5/myths.html</u> A discussion of myths about America as the "gunfighter" nation.

<u>http://www.britannia.com/historyh12/html</u> The sites associated with King Arthur are discussed along with the historical evidence for his existence.

12

The Artistic Dimension

Every culture, universally, produces what we of the Western world label art. Objects are not only shaped and formed to meet utilitarian needs, but also frequently embellished and decorated. Such embellished objects are referred to in the West as the decorative arts. Other objects have no utilitarian purpose, but are created solely for aesthetic reasons. Everyday language communicates information, thought, and emotion. However, poetry and song are heightened and more expressive, embellished ways of communicating the same things.

Like language, art is a mode of communication. While art conveys messages, it does more than communicate. Anthropologists like Anthony Forge and Nancy Munn see art as a system of visual communication. Forge (1973) also includes dance and gesture, along with painting, sculpture, and architecture, as part of this system of visual communication. Munn (1973) has analyzed the art of the Walbiri of Australia in terms of the fundamental graphic elements of which it is composed. Each element has a range of meanings, and the elements combine in regular ways according to rules. In this approach, art has rules of combination, similar to rules of grammar in language. The artistic products of the Walbiri, such as sand drawings or decorated objects used in ceremonials, contain representations of totemic myths, known as dreamings. These are stories about the mythical totemic ancestors of the Walbiri and their travels.

On the Northwest Coast, masks, totem poles, sculpted house posts, painted house fronts, decorated ceremonial bowls, and other utilitarian objects include designs that represent particular clans. (A totem pole is illustrated in Chapter 5.) These designs depict the mythological ancestors of the clan, such as the wolf, the grizzly bear, the sea bear, the raven, the eagle, and the killer whale. The message conveyed here is that the art object represents the kin group. The kin group and its representation are conceptually one. Art objects may be used at rituals, as are, for example, the masks worn by individual chiefs at the Kwakiutl wedding potlatch (described in Chapter 2). During such rituals, myths recounting the adventures of the mythological ancestor will be told, or the dance or song associated with that myth will be performed. Forge (1973) points out that in Arnhem Land, in Australia, art, myth, and ritual are completely interlocked and interdependent. They are three different ways of expressing the same thing—in words, in actions, and in visual form. The interconnection among art, myth, and ritual on the Northwest Coast illustrates the same point.

Art also communicates emotion. The emotion may be awe, as is the case when statues represent powerful supernatural spirits. It may be terror, as when the Poro masks, which we will discuss later in this chapter, are invoked. It may be mirth and pleasure, as when masked dancers carry out their antics or when satirical art caricatures pomposity. Is it possible to talk about a universal aesthetic impulse? Are masterpieces of art produced in one culture recognized as such by people in all cultures? Or does the aesthetic appreciation of art objects extend only to the members of the society within which they were made? Each society has particular standards by which it judges its art. However, there are masterpieces that are appreciated aesthetically by people of very different cultures. In some instances, the emotional impact of the object appeals to some universal sense and does not require particular cultural knowledge in order to be appreciated. In an experiment carried out by Irvin Child, a psychologist, and Leon Siroto, an anthropologist (1965), photographs of BaKwele masks from Central Africa were shown to BaKwele elders, including carvers, all of whom were knowledgeable about masks. These men ranked the masks in terms of their aesthetic value, from the best mask to the worst. The same photographs of the masks were then shown to a group of art history students at Yale University, and they too ranked the masks according to their opinions of the aesthetic value of each mask. There was significant agreement between the two groups of judges. Though the American students knew nothing about the masks or about BaKwele culture, they tended to agree with the BaKwele experts about which masks were aesthetically superior and which masks were mediocre. This is an area in which investigation is just beginning. However, research seems to indicate that there is some universal aesthetic sense manifested in all cultures in what we call the arts.

Beyond this universal aesthetic impulse, which enables us to identify cross-culturally a category called art, cultures differ from one another with regard to the form of their artistic expression. The Tikopia stress poetry but have little in the way of visual arts. The Chimbu of Highland Papua New Guinea decorate their bodies, while the Kwakiutl used to decorate their houses. This kind of concentration on one or another of the arts is also found in many societies in the Western world if one examines them over a long span of time. In German culture, the highest achievement among all the arts is to be found in music; English culture excels in literature; painting finds its highest expression in Holland and in Italy. Still others seem to stress each of the arts equally. The reasons a culture emphasizes one art and not another are unclear. Art is to be found in all societies, but Gell argued that there is no universal aesthetic separate from the artwork itself (1999: 20). The aesthetic sensibility, which deals with judgments about beauty, is intrinsically connected to artworks (Gell, 1999: 335). For Gell, it is not the art work that is important; rather, importance lies in the agency of the artist who has produced the work and the social network within which it is embedded.

The interpretation of the meaning of a work of art in a culture can be made only in terms of its symbolic system. Witherspoon, in his work on the Navajo, shows the nature of the relationship among the categories of the beautiful, the good, and the evil, and the ways these are reflected in Navajo rug design and sandpainting. However, as we noted in our discussion of the BaKwele experiment, people from other cultures can appreciate a work of art in terms of its aesthetic qualities, without understanding its meaning in the culture that produced it. Art embodies the style with which a particular culture expresses its symbols. Each culture has its own distinctive style, in the same way that a tapestry does.

Up until recently, only in the Western world was art produced for art's sake, to be hung in museums, galleries, and homes or to be performed in concerts before large audiences. This was also the case in complex societies like China and Japan, which had Chinese opera and Kabuki performances. In the kinds of small-scale societies that anthropologists first studied, art was embedded in the culture. Ritual performances employed art, and the meanings that the art communicated related to the meaning of the ritual and the mythology associated with it. Today, for example, Australian aboriginal artists and artists from the Northwest Coast produce art in Western genres (silkscreen prints or acrylic paints) embodying traditional styles that are exhibited in sophisticated urban art galleries.

In our own culture, much of what is labeled art is created solely to give aesthetic pleasure, to be admired. This point has so influenced the definition of art in our society that we make a distinction between that which is useful, or utilitarian, and that which is art and has no practical use. Utilitarian objects are often recognized as art at a later time, when they are valued for their aesthetic beauty and referred to as decorative arts. Furniture and other objects made by the Shakers and quilts made by the Amish are examples of this type of art. Today, the term *decorative arts* has come to include objects in current use that are admired for their aesthetic qualities. In small-scale societies there was no such thing as pure art; therefore, in those societies this distinction has no relevance.

STYLE

Art can be examined in terms of style, beyond its communicative function. If the function of art is the role it plays in society, its use in rituals, and the information and the aesthetic pleasure that it communicates through its content, then its structure is the component parts. **Style** refers to a consideration of the component elements of art and how the elements are put together. For example, the art of the Northwest Coast is characterized by a particular style, as is apparent from illustrations. What are the characteristics of that style that make it easy to identify art from that area? The art of the Northwest Coast area is primarily three-dimensional carving in wood. This undoubtedly relates to the fact that the societies of the Northwest Coast are located in the northern coastal rain forest, where massive trees like cedar and spruce provided excellent raw material for the carver. The colors used in Northwest Coast art were predominantly yellow,

 *Painting from a Tsimshian house front representing a bear.*

black, red, and green-blue, with the unpainted natural wood as a background color. The pigments used were made from natural materials—fungus, berries, ochre, moss, charcoal. The distinctive green-blue used was produced by allowing native copper to corrode in urine.

Because of the emphasis on sculpture, round, oblong, oval, circular, and curvilinear forms predominate, even on flat surfaces. The interlocking of animal and sometimes human forms, such as that found on totem poles, is typical. Franz Boas noted that the depiction of animals in Northwest Coast art is characterized by the emphasis of certain features—eyes, mouths, ears, fins, feathers, and tails. Each animal species, from killer whale to dragonfly, can be identified by the representation of the features unique to that species. Thus, the curved beak is the distinctive feature of the eagle, and the snout, the distinctive feature of the wolf. The same techniques for carving wood were adapted for use in other media, such as stone, bone, and metal. Besides carving in the round, Northwest Coast artists also worked on two-dimensional surfaces. The change from three dimensions to two dimensions required a transformation of design. The technique adopted on the Northwest Coast for two-dimensional designs is called split representation. The painting on a Tsimshian house front on the illustration above depicts this technique. The bear has been sliced in half and the two sides placed next to each other to make up the house front. This represents a bear—the two sides in profile—but together they form a bear looking frontward.

Two other features of Northwest Coast art style are also important. Design elements cover an entire surface, leaving no blank spaces, and eyelike shapes are used as fillers and in place of joints. The portrayal of eyes in masks indicates the great importance of eyes in Northwest Coast society. All these features, taken together, form the distinctive style of the art of the Northwest Coast.

There is a hierarchical aspect to the concept of style. One can speak of the style of the individual artist, that is, the features that are characteristic of the work of a particular artist. Sometimes the art style of a village, city, or region can be identified. It is more frequent to refer to the art style of a single society, such as Kwakiutl. Certain general features delineate the art style of a larger area, made up of a number of societies, as we have shown above for the Northwest Coast. Contem-

Detail from sculpture by Haida artist Bill Reid, which stands in front of the Canadia Embassy in Washington, DC.

porary Northwest Coast artists, such as the remarkable Haida carver Bill Reid, use the traditional content and the distinctive style of Northwest Coast art but add their own individual quality to it. The style of each artist is therefore different, as is the case for European and American contemporary artists. The sculpture in bronze, patinated to look like argillite, by Bill Reid (above), entitled "The Spirit of Haida Gwaii" ("The Spirit of the Haida Islands"), exemplifies the combination of traditional themes from Haida mythology and the genius of a creative artist.

The same hierarchical concept of style applies to the art of complex societies. One can speak of the style of Renaissance art, of the Italian Renaissance in particular, of the schools of Venice or of Florence, and of the particular style of Raphael. The concept of style is applicable at each level. It is also applicable to music and literature, where it has the same hierarchical structure.

THE ARTIST

In the past, scholars questioned whether one could speak of the style of the individual artist in small-scale societies, as comparable to the style of Raphael in terms of its uniqueness. As we have noted, art in such societies was embedded in social, ritual, and ceremonial contexts, and it therefore had to be produced within a set of

A contemporary malanggan carver from New Ireland, holding his carving adze, beside an unfinished carving.

constraints, since it had to convey certain messages. The artist who carves a Poro Society mask or a Kwakiutl potlatch mask operates under such a set of constraints, but beyond that he can show some degree of inspiration and individualism. After all, he does not merely copy a previously existing mask. He carves a representation of a known spirit in terms of his conceptualization of that spirit. He gets his inspiration in dreams. Accounts from other societies indicate that there, too, inspirations are said to come from dreams. As we will show in our discussion of *malanggan* carvers on New Ireland, the carver dreams the image he will carve. Dreams are the sources of individual creativity since each person's dreams differ. William Davenport (1968) reports that wood-carvers in the Solomon Islands receive their inspiration from the supernatural, which comes to them in dreams. Creativity or genius in some people and not in others is a difficult phenomenon to explain, and people the world over resort to external factors, such as divine inspiration from the supernatural or the Muses, to account for it. In addition to inspiration, the artist must also have the technical skills to translate a vision or a dream into a work of art. Thus craftsmanship is also a part of creativity. Not all carvers and artists are the same. Some are better than others and some are worse. People in all societies distinguish between good and bad art. They do this by applying a set of aesthetic standards.

Seeing the art of small-scale society as the product of an anonymous artist working within a communal tradition and the art of our society as the product of the creativity of the individual artist is an erroneous construct of Western society (Price, 1989). Within the cultural context and in the community in which the art is produced, the creativity of the individual artist in small-scale societies is recognized and rewarded, and the names of superior artists are known far and wide. Such art is made anonymous when it is extracted from its original cultural context by Westerners and transformed into objects in their museums representing "other" or "primitive" art.

The fame of Yoruba artists and carvers was known well beyond the towns in which they lived (see Walker, cited in Abiodun et al., 1994: 91). However, when King Tezifon of the Yoruba kingdom of Alada sent a carved divination board to King Felipe IV of Spain in 1659, the carver's name was not included. Like almost all examples of art from small-scale societies that wound up in European museums, the artist who carved it became "Anonymous." The carved divination board now resides in a German museum. In response to this gift, Felipe IV sent 12 Capuchin missionaries bringing with them a translation of Christian doctrine into the language of Alada. We can therefore assume that the Alada divination tray was, in a sense, equal in Christian eyes to the text on Christian doctrine brought by the missionaries. As Yai, a Yoruba scholar, explains it today, "The king of Alada, in an attempt to establish an equal cultural and political exchange must have thought of sending to European kings a divination tray that he perceived as a perfect equivalent of the text European missionaries carried with them along the West African coast. . . . It was a carved text par excellence. Tezifon was therefore engaging the contemporary European elite in a cultural dialogue, an exchange of texts or discourses" (1994: 111). The tray was used by an oracle or diviner and was meant to hold the blood of sacrifices. As Bassani points out, the carving on the tray portrays the Yoruba cosmos that the diviner employs in his ritual performances (1994: 81–82). The Yoruba artist's task is to translate this cosmos or text into another form—into artistic, visual expression.

Like the New Ireland carver, who translates a myth into a *malanggan*, the Yoruba carver translates one medium into another; he translates words into visual art. How well he does this is a measure of his creativity. Though the identity of the carver of this divination tray can probably never be recovered, anthropologists today attempt to find out who the artists were who carved many of the masterpieces to be found in museums. They are very often successful, as in the case of Olowe, a carver who died in 1938, considered by many the most important Yoruba artist of the twentieth century. Although he was famous in Nigeria, ethnographers of the time paid no attention to the identity of this outstanding carver (Walker, 1994: 91).

THE VISUAL ARTS

The visual arts include such modes of representation as painting, sculpture, body decoration, and house decoration. Masks are a special kind of sculpture, found in a number of societies around the world, but certainly not universally. We have chosen to examine masks as an exemplification of art in culture because they have certain intrinsic features, yet their meaning and use differ from one culture to the next. The two stone masks pictured on page 326 have been acclaimed as works of art. What makes them works of art? What do we know about their place in the culture that made them? These two masks were collected from the Tsimshian of British Columbia in the late nineteenth century. They were found in two different locales by two different individuals and ended up in two different museums, one in Ottawa and the other in Paris. An anthropologist, Wilson Duff, thought they matched. In 1975 he brought them together for an exhibit at Victoria, British Columbia, and found that the sighted mask fit snugly into the back of the unsighted one, the two forming a single entity. The inner mask had holes drilled in it for the wooden harness with which it was attached to a human head. We know, therefore, that they

Tsimshian stone masks, one with eyes open and another with eyes closed, fit together as a set.

were used as masks, but this is the only direct information that we have on their use. The two masks form a set, and their meaning must be interpreted in that light. The alternation of sighted and unsighted has a particular meaning for us, but what did the masks mean in Tsimshian culture?

We do know a good deal about the meaning of masks and how and when they were used in ritual and ceremonial life among the Kwakiutl, southern neighbors of the Tsimshian. Using these data, in addition to what we know about Tsimshian culture, we gain some insights into their uses among the Tsimshian. In the Kwakiutl wedding potlatch, described in Chapter 2, chiefs wear masks and costumes that depict the supernatural ancestors who are the mythological founders of their *numayms*. Each chief makes a speech in which he relates how his privileges, including the right to wear a particular mask, have descended to him from mythological times. Two different masks are described in Chapter 2. One is called The Devourer of Tribes and represents a sea bear, a mythological monster combining characteristics of the bear and the killer whale. The father of the bride is able to call forth this supernatural creature because his *numaym* is descended from it, and only that *numaym* has the right to make a mask representation of it and personify it in a ritual.

Similarly, another chief, Made-to-Be-Tied, wears the great wolf mask of Walking-Body, the chief of the wolves. This chief is descended from the original mythological owner of the wolf mask and owns the great wolf ceremonial. The Kwakiutl masks, which now hang inertly on museum walls, were used in dramatic ritual performances to enact the myths of the spirits they represented.

The Tsimshian, carvers of the twin stone masks, used masks in a way similar to that among the Kwakiutl. Tsimshian masks represent supernatural spirits. They were used at potlatches and at supernatural dance society rituals. Contact with supernatural spirits operated along lineage lines, and at initiation, power from the supernatural spirits, associated with a boy's own lineage, was "thrown" into him. Somewhat later he was initiated into a secret society. He then had the right to sing the song of his spirit and wear its mask at ceremonies. When a chief wore his mask, the supernatural spirit was in him. Its presence was also indicated by the sound of a whistle, which represented the voice of the spirit. Among the Tsimshian, carvers of masks, artists, song composers, and dramatists were all men who had received supernatural power. Returning to the stone masks, we can imagine these masks, now in museum cases, being used in a Tsimshian ceremony. It is dead of winter in a village on the Skeena River, and the *halaíit*, the sacred dance of the Tsimshian, is being held. Whistles announce the approaching spirit, and before the entranced audience the chief appears with the face of the sightless stone mask. As he slowly dances, the stone mask miraculously opens its eyes. The great power of the spirit residing in the chief has caused this miracle.

The two stone masks represent a single face, which opens and closes its eyes. What does this mean? Wilson Duff (1975) suggests that the sighted/sightless states represent looking outward and looking inward or self-recognition, sight and memory, seeing and imagining, looking ahead and seeing the past.

MASKS

Let us now look at the use of masks in another part of the world, West Africa, an area where masks also play a central role in the art of societies. These masks, one of which is pictured on page 328, are associated with the Poro, the secret society found among a group of tribes in Liberia and adjacent Sierra Leone. George Harley, a missionary doctor, amassed a great deal of information in the early twentieth century on the **Poro Society** among the Mano of Liberia to enable him to better understand the significance of the masks he collected during the many years of his medical practice there.

All the Poro Society masks represent some kind of spirit. In fact, the same word, *ge,* is used for both "spirit" and "mask" in Mano. When a person dons a mask, the spirit is said to be present in him. Among the Mano, as among the Tsimshian, whistles and horns symbolize the voice of the spirit. As we noted in the previous chapter, the people of Wogeo believed that the flutes were the voices of the *nibek* spirits. Mano women and uninitiated boys are not permitted to see masks or anything else associated with the Poro Society spirits, except for special masked dancers who perform on stilts and entertain a general audience at certain occasions. There are basically two

A Poro Society mask from the Gio of Sierra Leone.

kinds of masks. The first are portrait masks, the repositories for the spirits of important deceased leaders and more ancient tribal heroes, who are also ancestor spirits.
The spirit of the mythical founder of the Poro Society is also embodied in a sacred
portrait mask. The other kind of mask is a grotesque half-animal, half-human associated with the spirits of nature and other spiritual beings, such as the god of the
dance, the god of fertility, and the god of war. Ritual sacrifices of chickens or sheep
were made to the masks on a regular basis in order to enable them to sustain their
power. The masks were smeared with the blood of the sacrificed animal like the
Yoruba Alada divination tray discussed earlier.

The Poro Society, with which these masks were associated, was a secret male
cult with several initiatory grades. Men wishing to gain access to the higher grades
had to pay large sums of money in order to go through the rites that earned them
these high positions. At the top of the hierarchy were the old men who, through a
combination of inheritance and payments to the Poro Society, achieved the right to
wear the most powerful masks. Among the activities of the Poro Society was the
ritual for determining whether an individual accused of a crime was innocent or
guilty. After discussion by the powerful elders, the masks were said to make the
judgment. Since the wearer of the mask assumed its spirit when he put it on, as was
also the case with the Tsimshian, the Mano would say that the mask punished or
even executed someone when the wearer carried out the mask's decision. The
masks and their wearers also stopped village quarrels, controlled fighting warriors, promoted fertility of the fields, presided at various public functions and life
crisis rituals, and taught young initiates the proper ways to behave in the bush
schools of the Poro. People conformed to societal rules because they feared the
power of the spirits, which were contained in the wooden masks of the Poro Society. Here spirits, which are physically represented by artistic means in masks, were
used as a means of social control.

For the Mano people, how the masks came to exist poses an interesting problem in view of their role in the Poro Society. Warren d'Azevedo (1973) has studied
wood-carvers among the Gola and Vai peoples, neighbors of the Mano in Liberia
who also have the Poro Society. In these societies, the link between the carvers and
the masks that they manufacture is denied. Young children are punished if they ask
who made a particular mask. Adults, if questioned, simply say that the masks must
have been made long ago and were passed on by the ancestors. But there are always carvers who continue to make masks. D'Azevedo found that parents try to
dissuade their children from becoming wood-carvers. Carvers of Poro Society
masks, like professional singers, dancers, and musicians, as we shall note below,
are regarded by the community as irresponsible and concerned more with their
own creativity than with communal well-being. Boys intent on becoming carvers
frequently run away and apprentice themselves to master carvers. Many carvers
have a direct relationship with a particular spirit, and inspiration for masks comes
to them from that spirit through dreams.

Since they carve masks for the Sande Society, the secret women's society, as
well as for the Poro Society, carvers are the only younger men who have direct contact with women in the Sande and know the secrets of their society. Because he is

a man with access to women's secrets, the carver is in an ambiguous position. In his negotiations with the Sande Society, the carver shows reluctance to take on the task, and the women try to induce him to make the mask by offering him sexual favors. The carver of the mask and the women of the Sande Society, who own the mask, never fully terminate their relationship. He has special access to the group, and they jokingly use the term meaning "lovers" for one another. The carver in these West African societies is someone who, through his creativity and artistic skill, produces an object with supernatural power. But the relationship between the carver and his artwork is not even formally recognized. Like his work—the mask, which is a combination of the natural and the supernatural—the artist who creates this thing is himself somewhat outside society. Artists in a great many societies, including our own, are frequently considered marginal people who are not bound by the norms of usual behavior.

Masks have some special characteristics that differentiate them from other forms of art. A mask is worn by a person and is always a face. It can represent the face of a human being, the face of an animal, or the face of an imaginary creature, such as a monster or a supernatural being, in which human and animal features are combined in the face portrayed on the mask. In Bali, Indonesia, the face itself is considered a mask. While the Balinese do wear masks in ritual performances, donning a mask and leaving the face bare are symbolically equivalent. The masks in Kwakiutl, Tsimshian, and Mano societies represent statements about the nature of the individual in each of these societies. Each society has a particular view of the individual—what his or her relation is to others in the society, where he or she came from, how he or she came to be, what his or her place is in the natural world. Thus, Tsimshian clan masks make a statement about the connection between the individual human wearer and the mythical clan ancestor, often an animal, that the mask portrays.

Lévi-Strauss has pointed out that the Kwakiutl Dzonokwa and Xwexwe masks used in the Winter Ceremonial are stylistically reversals of one another (1979). The eyes in both are emphasized. In the Dzonokwa mask they either are deeply recessed or are deep holes, while in the Xwexwe they protrude extraordinarily, as can be seen in the illustrations on page 331. This emphasis on eyes runs throughout Kwakiutl art, as well as through the art of other societies of the Northwest Coast, including the Tsimshian. Lévi-Strauss has suggested that the protruding eyes of Xwexwe indicate extraordinary visual abilities, such as clairvoyance—the ability to see the future. The sighted stone mask has normal vision; the Xwexwe mask has the capacity to see the future; the sightless stone mask has the capacity to see the past. In these societies, eyes as a recurrent theme in the art seem to relate to the great importance placed on shaming. When an important man tripped and fell or accidentally overturned his canoe, he was shamed and had to give a potlatch in order to wipe out the shame. As we noted above, eyes, used as fillers or joints, are an important part of Northwest Coast art style. It may be said that eyes are constantly watching and observing everyone's behavior. Kwakiutl individuals believe that their behavior is always in public view, and they must avoid actions that will shame them. The theme of eyes in the art, especially in the masks, reflects this view

 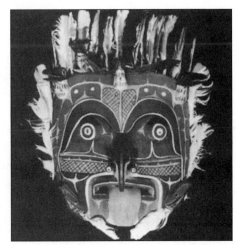

A Kwakiutl Dzonokwa mask (left) and a Kwakiutl Xwexwe mask (right).

of the individual. If an American painter constantly used eyes in his or her art, we would say that the paintings reflect a slight paranoia.

Among the Kwakiutl, summer and winter were clearly separated as the secular and sacred periods, and the art objects employed in the different rituals in summer and winter contrasted in style (Rosman and Rubel, 1990). Summer was the time for potlatching, such as the wedding potlatch discussed earlier in this chapter, and on these occasions claims to rank were demonstrated. Chiefs wore masks illustrating their mythological ancestors, such as the wolf mask of Walking-Body, the chief of the wolves, in order to show their ancestry and high rank. The wolf in this mask, as shown in the illustrations on page 332, is portrayed in the secular art style. Between the secular world of summer and the sacred world of winter, there was a ritual period of transition when the spirits came into the village and the Winter Ceremonial was held. The Kwakiutl Winter Ceremonial dances, which lasted several months, parallel the *halaíit*, the sacred dance of the Tsimshian discussed earlier. Young people who were seized and devoured by the spirits were initiated into secret societies and then subsequently emerged during a ceremony. The spirits were portrayed by individuals wearing masks that represented particular spirits. The initiated members of the secret society were considered shamans, since they crossed the border from the natural world into that of the supernatural and became dangerous cannibal spirits. The art style used in these Winter Ceremonial masks was an exaggerated and distorted style, in contrast to that used in the masks of secular summer rituals. It was a style appropriate to the supernatural world of the shaman. As can be seen in the illustrations, the strongly curved beak of the eagle in the secular potlatch mask becomes the greatly distorted beak of the Crooked

On the top are the masks of wolf and eagle worn during secular potlatches. The eagle is a transformation mask that opens up to reveal another mask, representing the face of the man (middle). These masks contrast in style with the wolf and Crooked Beak (eagle) of the sacred Winter Ceremonial (bottom).

Beak of Heaven. The pronounced snout of the wolf in the secular potlatch mask becomes the exaggerated mask worn in the Winter Ceremonial.

   Masks are embedded in culture and play a significant role in the performance of religious rituals. The masks along with the dances and songs performed by the wearer usually symbolize central ideas in the culture and convey important information relevant to kinship, social relationships, myths, and political activities, as in the Kwakiutl Winter Ceremonial. In contrast, once the masks are removed from the society they assume a completely different character as inert art objects displayed in museums.

Contemporary malanggan carvings, which utilize traditional designs, displayed at mortuary rites held at Tabar Island, off Ireland.

NEW IRELAND MALANGGANS, YESTERDAY AND TODAY

Malanggan mortuary sculptures from northern New Ireland, now part of Papua New Guinea, are striking examples of visual art. The carvings were used in the religious ritual held to commemorate the deaths of several individuals of a single clan and simultaneously to initiate the boys of that clan. European explorers of the early nineteenth century, who spent only a short time on the island, were sufficiently captivated by the sculptures to bring back examples to Europe and America. When missionaries brought Christianity to the people of New Ireland in the late nineteenth century, they tried to suppress the *malanggan* ceremony and the carvings associated with it, since these represented earlier pagan beliefs. However, the *malanggan* ceremony did not die and continues to be celebrated today. The Catholic Church no longer sees a conflict between the *malanggan* rite and Catholicism and has even incorporated *malanggan* sculpture into church architecture.

The designs for *malanggans* are still owned and sold by one clan to another. When a *malanggan* sculpture is ordered for an upcoming ritual, the owner of the design tells the carver the myth embodying the design and what the carving should look like. The carver then translates the words into a visual image. Sometimes the process of translation for the carver involves dreaming the image, which he will then carve. Like the carver of masks for the Poro Society, the carver of a *malanggan* works within a set of constraints such that the design can immediately be recognized as a member of a particular named category of images. Further, the owner of the design must be able to recognize it as his particular design. Since the carver does not use a sculpture from a previous *malanggan* ceremony as a model, a degree of artistic creativity is also involved. Carvers are evaluated in terms of how well they express the design, and several have islandwide reputations.

Before contact, after the *malanggans* were used in a ceremony, they were burned or left to rot. After European colonization, *malanggans,* since they were no longer valued after the ceremony, were given or sold to Europeans, and many wound up in museums all over the world. Today, in New Ireland, after they are used in ceremonies, *malanggans* may sometimes be sold to tourists and collectors. One contemporary carver has carved a *malanggan* on a post for the National Museum in Port

Moresby. Modern carvers use steel chisels and commercial paints. When shown pictures of *malanggan* carvings 100 years old and now in the Australian Museum, they admired the workmanship of the earlier carvers, particularly since the earlier carvers had only stone tools to use. However, the present-day carvers felt their own carvings were superior. The three-dimensional *malanggan* art of New Ireland has also provided the inspiration for the New Ireland printmaker David Lasisi.

ETHNIC IDENTITY AND TORAJA ART

The architecturally based carvings of the Toraja have graced museum walls over the world for a hundred years. Heretofore, art has been treated as a minor and passive aspect of ethnic identity marking, but it can be "an active ingredient in identity politics . . . as well as a critique of established ethnic, colonial, or political hierarchies" (Adams, 1998: 328–329). The Sa'dan Toraja of highland Sulawesi, a province of Indonesia, have been marginalized in the multiethnic Indonesian state not only by their small numbers and geographic isolation, but also because they are Christians in a predominantly Muslim country. The Toraja area has recently become a mecca for international tourists who travel seven hours by bus to see the interesting architecture and elaborate carving of the houses and the slaughter of bulls that accompanies what seems to be a never-ending series of funeral rituals. The carving on the Toraja house, or *tongkonan,* is the visual embodiment of the ancestry and elite rank of the family that occupies it. It is a key symbol of an individual's identity. The motifs represent mythic designs, emblems of the status and solidarity of the family, and the activities of peasants and slaves toward whom the "nobles" had a range of responsibilities. Nowadays, nonnoble Toraja tourist guides often introduce newer explanations of motifs, such as the cross motif used long before Toraja conversion, which is said to represent "evidence of their ancestors' intuitive proximity to Christianity" (Adams, 1998: 333). A few carvings include sequences, which represent the ambivalent Toraja relationship with the Dutch, their former colonial masters. For example, a soldier is seen beating a Toraja child who flees to his mother's arms. The postindependence period of upheaval is represented on one carved panel by troops of the Darul Islam movement of lowland Sulawesi. They sought to establish a separate Muslim state and are represented as shooting a Toraja man. In the 1960s, the Indonesian government and the Protestant Toraja church encouraged the abandonment of this type of house, with its elaborate carvings, because it represented a visible sign of Toraja "backwardness," and the Toraja were encouraged to move into houses built of cinder block (Adams, 1998: 337).

However, in the 1970s and 1980s, both the government, which began to celebrate regional diversity as a cornerstone of Indonesian national identity, and the church, where Dutch clergy moved out of positions of power, reversed their positions. Churches began to be embellished with Toraja motifs, and new churches were built that resembled *tongkonans* in their architecture, like the New Ireland churches that were embellished with *malanggan* sculpture. Tourism had become more and more important, and the house architecture that had formerly represented elite power now came to represent Toraja ethnic identity. *Tongkonan* images began to be seen decorating pubs and intersections in Rantepo, the Toraja capital, on T-shirts, on model houses, and on silver jewelry. More recently, Toraja carvers have begun to produce finely carved wall plaques, or carved paintings, which the carvers themselves see not as ornaments or handicrafts but as art (Adams, 1998: 341). This new medium of expression is frequently used to portray the symbols of political dissent. Toraja carvings and motifs have also begun to appear in Ujung Pandang, the south Sulewesi port city occupied by Bugis and Makassarese people, rival ethnic groups. The growth of tourism has led to the increase in the use of this type of "exotic" motif. As a consequence, there have been changes in ethnic conceptualizations and relationships. Whereas the Toraja were formerly seen as the victims of Bugis-Makassarese raiders, the relationship is being renegotiated. The Toraja see this use of their traditional motifs and house architecture as a minor ethnic triumph, while the Bugis and Makassarese have misgivings about this and feel vague ethnic malaise. Even the Indonesian government has co-opted the image of the *tongkonan*, featuring it on the 5,000 rupia banknote.

DECORATING THE BODY

A rather special kind of visual art involves the decoration of the human body. People all over the world "use the skin as a surface for artistic expression and embellish themselves with decorations which carry a wide variety of meanings" (Reichel-Dolmatoff, 1998: 12). The messages conveyed by body decoration range from statements about social, economic, or political status or class or the different phases of a life to ones referring to the sacred and profane. Body decorations must always be examined within a particular context in order to decode their meanings. Of course, the nature of body decoration often changes as the culture changes. For example, Maori tattooing, performed with a chisel-like implement by a revered and highly paid expert over a period of years, was a very significant aspect of Maori culture up to the nineteenth century. Today, Maoris use the same tattoo designs for ceremonial purposes, but they are applied with pigment.

Among the peoples of the central highlands of New Guinea, body decoration is the most important type of art, since these people do little carving, painting, or mask making. The decorations people wear and the painting of the body at ritual performances and exchange ceremonies, like the *kaiko* of the Maring (discussed in Chapter 8), convey messages about the social and religious values of the people and also demonstrate the relationship of the people to their clan ancestral spirits. Certain ideals and emotions are evoked for audience and participants by the wearing of the decorations. The use of particular colors in body painting and certain combinations of colors in feathers, shells, and beads, taken together, convey abstract qualities like health and vitality among the Melpa of highland New Guinea (Strathern and Strathern, 1971). Similarly, darkness and brightness relate to the opposition between men and women. The Wahgi of highland New Guinea, who live not very far from the Melpa, also express their aesthetic impulses entirely through the decoration and adornment of the human body. These displays of feather adornments and

Facial tattooing, or the art of moko *was characteristic of the Maori of New Zealand. Haora Tipa Koinaki, depicted here, was a Maori chief prominent in the tribal wars of the early nineteenth century.*

painting of the face and body during dances carried out at the Wahgi pig festivals serve to communicate the strength and health of the clan hosting the festival. But the most important part of the message conveyed is the moral strength of the host group. This derives from the absence of sorcery accusations or of friction within the group and from its sense of security in having fully fulfilled its obligations to others. The moral strength or weakness of the host group directly affects the brightness and quality of their adornment and the success of their performance during the ceremony (O'Hanlon, 1989).

Body decoration, or body modification as it is sometimes called, also occurs in modern American society. Tattooing and piercing are popular ways of embellishing the body. Hewitt sees a parallel between the transformation of the body and religious conversion since such self-alterations are, in effect, acts of self-transformation, ways of creating a new identity, or expressing one's individuality or affiliation with a particular alternative subcultural group (1997: 3, 4). For example, the punk look, which developed first in England in the late 1970s as a reaction to the conservative Thatcher regime and then spread to America, is a distinctive, provocative demonstration of a counterculture (Groning, 1998: 234–235). The spiked and brightly colored hair, the black metal-studded leather clothing, and the face piercing and makeup clearly set this group apart, representing their rejection of middle-class subculture.

Body tattooing with a hot needle, originally associated with the exoticism of the circus in America, became popular with lower-class and blue-collar workers at the beginning of the twentieth century (Hewitt, 1997: 71). In the 1950s, there was a tattoo renaissance as a new, safer technology was introduced and the new interest in Asian cultures, which revere tattooing, made it into "more of a fine art" (Hewitt, 1997: 71, 73). Clients with more income and better education often design their own tattoos, making the tattoo into an aspect of self-expression and self-identification. Various types of body piercing have also recently become popular, especially among Generation X females. Piercing has moved from a countercultural sign of identity to become a trend and a fashion, represented in mainstream magazines. Americans have transformed a marginal practice into a trendy one (Hewitt, 1997: 84). Over time noncomformity has become conformity.

COLLECTING "ARTIFICIAL CURIOSITIES"

The removal of artifacts from exotic places began with the Age of Exploration. Captain Cook brought back many specimens that people in Europe saw as representative of the way of life of the people he encountered. He also brought back a living specimen—Omai, the Tahitian—"artificial curiosities" as well as "natural curiosities" such as fossils, rocks, and shells. These found homes in the collectors' cabinets of royalty and the aristocracy. Such collections were the nuclei around which museums like the British Museum were later formed during the nineteenth century. In the heyday of colonialism, the latter part of the nineteenth century, large quantities of such objects were taken by traders, missionaries, and government officials from small-scale societies that had become parts of colonial empires and sent to museums in all the capitals of Europe, as well as to America. In the course of this process, the ethnographic objects that now hang on museum walls were removed from the cultural context in which they were created and used; and their creators were reduced to anonymity. These objects now in the museums of the capitals of colonial empires represent the success of colonialism, the conquest of pagan gods, and the transformation of the indigenous people who represented a "primitive" stage of existence into producers of cash crops. For example, the objects of Native Americans began to be collected by European explorers, ending up in Cabinets of Curiosity, and this practice was continued by explorers like Lewis and Clark, whose objects are to be found at the Peabody Museum at Harvard.

At the turn of the twentieth century, European artists such as Vlaminck, Matisse, and Picasso began to appreciate and to collect what Westerners then called "primitive" art. These artists, who created modern art, were seeking new ways to depict the world about them, in particular, the human form. Much of the art they collected came from the French colonies in Africa. In these carvings and sculptures, the Western artists saw what was for them a completely new way of conceiving of and depicting the human figure, and they used these conceptualizations in their own sculpture and paintings.

Just as Western artists borrowed artistic ideas from the peoples of colonized areas, so did the artists of colonized areas borrow from Western societies, this time of content but not of style. Numerous examples from all over the world showing how the art of subject peoples reflected their views of their colonial masters were provided in Julius Lips's book *The Savage Hits Back* (1937). This art makes pointed political comments and is both humorous and satirical in nature.

ART MARKETS TODAY

The translation of a sculptural style into modern graphics has occurred not only on New Ireland, but on the Northwest Coast as well. For example, the Kwakiutl artist Tony Hunt is a printmaker as well as a sculptor. Traditional styles of what were small-scale societies like those of New Ireland and the Northwest Coast continue today, vibrant and alive, translated into new media. In these new forms, the art has become part of a commercial art market, exhibited in elegant galleries and sold to buyers from all over the world. Australian artists exhibit their unique paintings in art galleries from Sydney to Santa Fe and New York. Northwest Coast designs have also been incorporated into glassmaking, another medium not traditional for this area, by Preston Singletary (*Native Peoples*, 1999).

When tourism develops in an area, simplified versions of traditional art objects and objects embodying traditional motifs in new media frequently begin to be manufactured as **tourist art**. In the mid-nineteenth century, the Haida of British Columbia began to carve miniature totem poles, platters, and boxes out of argillite, a soft, black, easily carved form of coal, using traditional designs. This is a medium that the Haida had not used before European contact. These items were all carved for sale to tourists. Some argillite carvings portrayed Europeans, such as ship captains and their wives. What has been called airport art can be found from Nairobi to Port Moresby. When style and content are dictated by what tourists buy, and Navajos make crosses and Stars of David out of silver and turquoise to be sold in Albuquerque, traditional art styles no longer completely retain the characteristics of an earlier period. Silver jewelry is itself an introduced art form. Sometimes, the designs of tourist art become so popular that miniature ivory totem poles, symbols of the Northwest Coast, are made in Japan and sold in Vancouver, and Navajo silver and turquoise jewelry, mass-produced in Hong Kong, is sold in Santa Fe. This tourist art is clearly distinct from creative translations of traditional forms by artists like Reid, Singletary, and Lasisi.

THE ART WORLD

When cultural anthropology began to investigate modern urban society, it turned its gaze upon new kinds of communities. The New York art world is the core of one such community, composed of commercial, communicative, and social networks that spread from there all over the world (Sullivan, 1995). This art world includes the artists, dealers, art critics and theorists, collectors, curators of corporate collections, curators and directors of museums, and auction house personnel who decide what will be the important images to be illustrated in international art magazines and shown at museum shows, and who formulate what will become the posterity of Western art. The community is defined not only in terms of a shared identity, common interests, and a network of social relations, but also in terms of politics and economics.

Sullivan focuses on this community and the changes that have transformed it over the past 30 years (1995). At the beginning of the 1960s, a communications explosion took place that changed the way people encountered art by expanding the number and the types of settings—studios, new museums, and public collections—within which such an encounter could take place. There was also a concomitant growth in the number of art publications devoted to reviewing and critiquing contemporary art. Artists perceived themselves as increasingly alienated from their art and losing control over it. They felt that they were not benefiting sufficiently from their art and demanded legal agreements from purchasers to ensure some remuneration to them in resales, which were becoming increasingly frequent. Art was being treated as a commodity, especially by artists, to be purchased and resold, most often at auction. The 1970s found many artists, whose works were increasing in value, becoming economically successful and entering the leisure class, with more affinities to middle- and upper-class collectors and dealers. This was in contrast to the peripheral position artists had earlier held in American society and in other societies as well, as we have noted above.

Curators' decisions on what to exhibit and critics' decisions whether or not to praise the art determined the aesthetic value of the artwork. Their decisions crucially determined who was creating art and who was not. Art dealers and gallery owners were in a parallel position, deciding whose work to include in a show and whose work to advise collectors to purchase. At the apex of this structure were the world-famous artists, collectors and dealers, and museum directors. In the 1970s this world began to change as contemporary art moved into the auction galleries and price was determined publicly rather than by means of the backroom negotiations that dealers and clients had formerly engaged in. Collectors began to shop at auctions, paying astronomical prices for works by world-famous artists. New money was entering the scene, and financiers of many nationalities, interested in art as an investment, were bidding up prices. Van Gogh's painting *Irises* sold for $53 million in 1987, and his portrait of Dr. Gachet sold in 1990 for $82.5 million, the highest price ever paid for a painting. Even museums moved into the auction market to reconstitute their collections, deaccessioning works "not of museum quality" in favor of what their directors thought represented important trends, to broaden their collections. Museum directors learned "the art of the deal" in sales as well as exchanges. This process also occurred in the area of ethnographic art. Sotheby's auctioned off a Maori house post, whose sale price was over a million dollars, and Navajo blankets, which sold for hundreds of thousands of dollars.

By focusing on the art "community," which represents the type of unit anthropologists have always studied, one can see the ways in which the roles and positions of people in the art world have changed. Art, like the religious artifacts in Cairo discussed in Chapters 8 and 10 on economics and religion, has become a commodity, purchased by the wealthy as an investment and to show their good taste. Both the art market and the meanings of the art have been transformed in the process. This illustrates a point made in the chapter on economics, that art like anything else can become a commodity.

The Native American Graves Protection and Repatriation Act, passed in 1990, acts to transform art objects that have become commodities back into objects that have religious and cultural significance. All museums are required to survey their collections and repatriate any objects that belong to tribes "and are essential to the continuance of that tribe's traditions" (Dubin, 2001: 23). The act also "bans trade" in funerary and sacred objects. At a Sotheby's auction some years ago a figure of a Zuni war god was purchased by an anonymous donor and then returned to the Zuni where it was placed back into its outdoor religious setting. Objects from various museums have also been repatriated and undergone this same transformation.

MUSIC AND DANCE

Like painting and sculpture, music and dance are considered arts because they evoke emotion and can be evaluated in terms of aesthetic qualities. However, music and dance differ from painting and sculpture in a number of ways. Music and dance are like spoken language in several important respects. All three unfold through time. Every sentence, every musical composition, every dance has a beginning, a middle, and an end. This is not true of a painting or a carving, which has no beginning or ending and for which the dimension of time is irrelevant. Once made, it continues to exist. Musical compositions and dances are ephemeral. They find expression in performances, but once the performance is over, they no longer exist. The musical instrument upon which the composition was performed is still there, and an idea of how the piece should be performed persists; however, the performance of the piece dies away unless it has been recorded on tape or film, a modern phenomenon. Like the tale or legend told by a bard, the musical piece exists as a concept in people's minds, and each performance is a slightly different manifestation of that idea. In this conceptualization of a piece of music, it is like the mental template a potter uses to make and decorate a certain kind of pot. Only in Western societies were musical compositions written down, using some form of musical notation. Until recently, dances were performed and only memory guided the next performance. Now there are systems of dance notation that are analogous to written language. Ethnomusicologists and anthropologists, when they studied music and dance in small-scale societies, were studying a tradition, transmitted orally and by performance. In these societies, music and dance, like oral literature and folktales, were taught and learned without benefit of written notational systems.

The anthropological emphasis has always been on the relationship between music and dance and other aspects of culture. In our discussion of the visual arts in small-scale societies, we saw that art was not produced simply to be admired but was integrated with other aspects of culture. The same is true of music and dance. In fact, when anthropologists first began to study dance, they were more interested in the cultural context of the dance than in the dance itself. There is a great range of ritual and ceremonial settings in which music and dance play important roles. Birth, initiation, weddings, and funerals are typically occasions for music and dance. The Kwakiutl and American weddings described in Chapter 2 both included music and dancing. These two examples illustrate the contrasting ways in which music and dance function in the two societies. The dances and songs performed at the Kwakiutl wedding were owned by the *numayms* of the chiefs who performed them, as were the crests on the masks worn by the performers, in contrast to the dance music played at the American wedding by a hired band. The ancestral myths recount how the mythical ancestor spirit gave these songs and dances to the ancestor of the *numaym* to be transmitted down through the generations. In Kwakiutl culture, music and dance are forms of communication that convey messages. In addition to the message of ownership, the songs and dances of the groom's side convey the power, based on supernatural contacts, that is intended to move the bride. We must also consider who has the right to perform a piece of music or dance and who owns it. There is a great range of variation regarding the degree of specialization involved in the performance of music and dance, even within societies. Sometimes, as is the case among the Kwakiutl, songs and dances are privately owned and may be performed only by their owners. There are dances that may be performed only at a particular stage in life, such as dances for a male initiation. Within all societies, there are always some songs or dances that everyone, regardless of age or sex, may perform.

Ethnomusicologists and anthropologists also investigate music in complex societies, from Iran, Japan, and Bali to the urban barrios of New York and Los Angeles. Adelaida Reyes (1999) has analyzed the way certain aspects of the music and dance of recent Vietnamese immigrants to New Jersey persist, while new elements from the American scene have been introduced. The maintenance of ethnic identity by the New Jersey Vietnamese centers on the celebration of Tet, the Vietnamese New Year. At the event that Reyes describes, a piece by a well-known émigré Vietnamese composer was performed, which incorporated many regional Vietnamese folk songs within an overall symbolic theme of Vietnamese unity. In the social dancing that followed, the dance forms were Western (tango, rumba, bebop, and twist), while the lyrics were sung in Vietnamese and the music was considered Vietnamese. The performance of music and dance is a sensitive indicator of the dialectic between continuity and the adaptation of immigrant groups in America. The Vietnamese are only one of many immigrant groups whose music and dance demonstrate this dialectic.

MUSIC

While the function of music and dance is similar to that of the visual arts, each is characterized by a different kind of structure. The elements of music are sounds and their characteristics, such as pitch and duration. Sounds produced consecutively form what is called a melody. Sounds produced simultaneously form harmony. Melody, harmony, and rhythm, which is a steady succession of beats marked by regular accents, represent the basic concepts for analyzing the structure of music. The music of different cultures varies in terms of its structure. For example, most of the music of our society is based upon a system of eight tones, an octave—usually taught as do, re, mi, fa, sol, la, ti, do. However, from time to time, other structures have also been used, such as Debussy's use of a whole-tone scale and Schoenberg's use of a 12-tone scale. Many other societies in the world base their music on a scale in which there are only five tones. This is called a pentatonic scale and, in fact, it is more common in the world than our octave, or eight-tone scale. Rhythm is also subject to cultural variation. In our own society, each musical composition is usually characterized by a single, regular rhythmic impulse. A waltz has one kind of rhythm, and a march another kind of rhythm. Recent music in Western culture may shift rhythms throughout the piece. This is in contrast with other societies, such as those in Zaire in Africa, where a single musical composition can have two different rhythms carried on simultaneously. These and other marked variations make the music of other cultures sometimes sound strange to our ears. In addition, the instruments created to produce musical sounds are enormously varied.

Music is a form of communication. The music at an American wedding conveys a message. When the organ plays as the bride, dressed in white, marches down the aisle, the audience silently repeats the words, "Here comes the bride, all dressed in white." The message conveyed is the ideal of the purity and virginity of the bride. This message is carried by the whiteness of the bride's gown, by the words of the song, and even by the melody of the music. Music also plays a role in funerals. In this instance, music can convey the emotions of grief and sadness better perhaps than any other medium. Because music is a powerful vehicle for expressing emotions as well as ideas, it can be a central mechanism for symbolizing culture and cultural differences. Vietnamese music is a means for maintaining ethnic distinctiveness.

The style of playing panpipes (a group of pipes bound together, each one emitting a different note) among the Aymara, the indigenous people of highland Peru, was equally distinctive of their culture. From the 1920s on, it has had an interesting **diffusion**, which reveals the nature of asymmetrical power relations in Peru (Turino, 1991). This musical style among the Aymara, who were the clients of mestizo patrons living in the town of Conima, was characterized by ad hoc musical ensembles organized in an egalitarian fashion playing music in several different traditions at various kinds of fiestas. This was in keeping with the emphasis on equality and on group solidarity in Aymara communities. Any man could play in an Aymara panpipe ensemble. The mestizo rural elites held the Aymara in disdain until the 1920s, when a movement, *indigenismo,* made people begin to take an interest in the local indigenous culture. Aspects of Aymara culture, such as the panpipe tradition, began to be selected as symbols to stand for Peruvian national identity. In this process, however, the panpipe tradition of the Aymara was transformed into one with fixed membership, regular rehearsals, the maintenance of performance quality, and change in the nature of the harmony. This transformation took place in the town of Conima, and the changed musical form was later brought to Lima and other cities when the newly organized group traveled there to perform. During the 1970s, by which time Lima was swollen with rural migrants from the highlands, the panpipe tradition from Conima began to be performed by migrants who had heretofore been ashamed to perform their music in the city because of social prejudice against Aymara Indian culture. Radicalized middle-class students in the city also began to perform the panpipe music and subsequently brought it back to the rural towns from which these students came. Young Aymara people in the villages, increasingly influenced by national culture, now ignore the majority of indigenous musical instruments and community traditions in favor of the urban panpipe movement. This example illustrates the way in which an indigenous musical tradition is altered in form and comes to symbolize Peruvian national culture, and then is brought back to the countryside where it displaces earlier musical forms.

In many societies, men and women have two rather differentiated spheres of expressive activity. Concurrently with the increased interest in gender roles, researchers have begun to more systematically explore women's musical practices (Koskoff, 1987). Since a woman's identity is believed to be embedded in her sexuality, women's role in music frequently expresses this. Musical performance is seen as enhancing sexuality, and female court musicians in the past in India, Indonesia, and Tunisia were associated with sexuality and profane pleasures. In many societies, the genre (or type) of music performed, the style of the performance, and the location of the performance are different for males and for females.

MUSICIANS

As societies become more complex, musicians as well as dancers often become full-time specialists. For example, Kanuri musicians are a highly trained and specialized group who occupy a particular position in the social structure. The performers play as a group, which includes a vocalist, drummers, and a player of an oboelike reed instrument. The musicians are male, but the vocalist may be female. They are referred to as praise-singers. They frequently are attached to a patron, an aristocrat, who supports them in exchange for singing his praises on ceremonial occasions. They can also travel and perform as a group, living on the money they receive from their audiences. They are generally considered to be of low status by the rest of the Kanuri populace, since the way they earn their living is considered to be begging by the Kanuri. Nevertheless, virtuoso performers are greatly admired by everyone. Though the performers are aware of what other people think of them, they consider themselves artists. They value their own talents and thrive on the admiration of the audience. Thus the musician in Kanuri society is ambiguous in a way similar to that of the carver in Mano society. In general, artists are in a vague and enigmatic position in most societies, including our own. Artists' talents are admired, yet the creativity that makes them different from

An ensemble of Kanuri praise-singers and musicians in Geidam, Nigeria.

other people also makes them suspect. The Kanuri musician wears an earring in one ear, unlike ordinary Kanuri males.

The praise-singers of Mali, called *jeli* but also known by the French term *griots,* were, like Kanuri praise-singers, a separate, endogamous group in the social structure. However, their position has undergone a transformation (Schulz, 1998). In the past, praise-singers were attached to freeborn upper-class families in a patron-client relationship. In exchange for citing the illustrious genealogies and extolling the virtues of their patrons, praise-singers were provided with food and housing for life. With increasing modernization and urbanization, praise-singers began to appear who were not *jeli,* and who would sing anyone's praises for money. A still further transformation of praise-singers was brought about when radio and television came to Mali in 1958 and 1985, respectively. Praise-singers became media stars, but they were considered "inauthentic" because they performed for financial payments. They would sing the praises of the ancestors of people they didn't even know, those newly rich people who gloried in these praises. Praise-singing had become a commodity, to be bought and sold. Nevertheless, praise-singers on TV were thought to be carrying on an important tradition of the culture. These new "media stars" on TV and in urban theaters would sing about the evil and corrupting effect of money, and people would rush to the stage to shower them with money.

Sometimes performers are of a different ethnic group from the rest of the people in the society. Gypsies of Afghanistan and Pakistan are traveling performers and musicians who differ from the rest of the population and are considered a low-status group, completely outside the existing social structure. The Gypsies of Romania, distant relatives of those in Afghanistan, are also professional musicians who play the Gypsy violin, which is so closely associated with Romania.

DANCE

Dance has been defined as those cultural practices that "formalize human movement into structured systems in much the same way that poetry formalizes language" (Kaeppler, 1985: 92). There may or may not be an indigenous conceptualization that translates into the category of dance. Kaeppler has proposed that the anthropological consideration of dance focus upon the movement dimensions of particular cultural activities and the messages such movements are conveying, to develop a cultural conceptualization of dance for a particular society (1985). The basic elements used to analyze the structure of dance are body movements. A formal description of dance would include the steps, spatial patterns, relationships to music, and postural positioning. Beyond the description, the focus of an anthropological analysis of dance is on its cultural setting and its meaning. Dances, like all other forms of art, encode particular cultural messages. They may be visual manifestations of social relations, as we shall see in examples below, or they may be part of a visual aesthetic system. Westerners frequently isolated the formal-movement aspects of rituals and ceremonials as dance, neglecting the role such movements played in the total social phenomena within which they were performed. In doing this, they were utilizing a Western categorization, since in our society, dance, for the most part, has become entertainment, disassociated from ritual and ceremonial.

The culture of the Swahili, a Muslim people living in East Africa, represents a syncretism of Islamic cultural codes and indigenous Swahili culture. The Swahili have a category, *ngoma*, that means "drum," or "dance," or "music," illustrating the interrelationship—indeed, in Swahili, the inextricable connection—between music and dance. Among the Swahili, *waungwana*, or high status, was marked by the possession of tall white-washed stone houses with enclosed courtyards, within which women were completely secluded, in keeping with the custom of *purdah*. They were the settings for rituals and ceremonials, poetry and dance competitions, held in the public rooms and the courtyard (Franken, 1992). Two *ngoma* performed in these houses were exclusive to the Swahili high-status class. One was the *ngoma la hazua*, a men's dance performed in spotlessly white prayer robes and richly embroidered prayer caps at weddings and circumcisions. It was a line dance performed with music and accompanied by a singer recounting the heroic deeds and distinguished ancestors of the family. The men held swords, moving them as they moved their bodies. Today this dance is held outdoors at weddings during the week celebrating the birth of the Prophet. The *lelemama* was performed by married women as a rite

Dancers at a Mae Enga funeral.

of passage. It was also a line dance in which the dancers wore special costumes and finger cymbals and danced to the accompaniment of music and poetry.

The movements in the *ngoma* or dances of lower-class Swahili contrasted with the dance movements of the high-class *waungwana*. Lower-class people are the recent arrivals to town, economically poor, lacking important ancestors, and not very religiously observant. The men's dance, the *uta,* or the "coconut-cutters' dance," is held outdoors, during the birthday week of the Prophet on a sandlot between houses (Franken, 1992: 206). The dancers, wearing typical Swahili men's work clothing and leg rattles, dance in a circle, leaning on canes and stamping their feet in unison to the rhythm of *uta.* The second lower-class dance, the *mwaribe,* used to be performed together by men and women to a drum accompaniment. It is also performed outdoors during the week of the Prophet's birthday. The participants, wearing Western street clothes, invite partners to dance, then hop forward and backward in unison to the music. Today, this dance is performed by young men. Its lower-class character was demonstrated by the fact that it brought men and women together in violation of the rules of *purdah,* or female seclusion, and because it was also associated with non-Muslim believers. It is clear that the movements in these dances communicate contrasts about status. But they also demonstrate the inextricable connection between music and dance.

SUMMARY

• Art is a mode of communication, communicating ideas as well as emotions.

• Art is more than communication since it involves an aesthetic impulse—what constitutes beauty.

• There seems to be a universal aesthetic impulse, though cultures may express aesthetics in many different ways using different art forms.

• One culture may emphasize visual arts like carving while another places greater emphasis on music and dance.

• Art can be analyzed structurally in terms of what is known as art style. Style characterizes the art of all societies and can also be used to characterize the art of an individual or a particular historical period.

• The various arts operate within a set of traditional constraints. Yet every carver, painter, musician, and dancer adds his or her individual conceptualization, his or her own interpretation to the final product. It is in this aspect of art that creativity is to be found, and this creativity forms the basis for the audience's judgment of the aesthetic worth of the art produced.

• Masks, which are to be found in a variety of societies, illustrate the range of meanings that can be attached to what is a single form of art.

• Masks also make statements about a culture's view of the self.

• Various forms of art may be used to express ethnic identity, as illustrated by Toraja carving and Vietnamese dance and music.

• In the nineteenth century, the collecting of the artifacts of the small-scale societies that anthropologists were to later study was referred to as the collection of "artificial curiosities."

• Global tourism has resulted in the production of tourist art, the manufacture of objects by local artists to meet the demands of consumers, that is, tourists, who want a remembrance of the places they visited.

• The art world has become a community of buyers and sellers as a consequence of the commodification of art and the development of a worldwide auction market.

SUGGESTED READINGS

Boas, Franz. *Primitive Art.* New York: Dover Publications, 1955. Reprint of 1927 volume. A classic work by a pioneer in the field of ethnographic art, with emphasis on the art of the Pacific Northwest where Boas did fieldwork and collected artifacts for the American Museum of Natural History.

Hatcher, Evalyn. *Art as Culture: An Introduction to the Anthropology of Art.* 2nd ed. Westport: Bergin and Garvey, 1999. A general introduction to the anthropological study of art.

Jacknis, Ira. *The Storage Box of Tradition: Kwakiutl Art, Anthropologists and Museums, 1881–1981.* Washington, D.C.: Smithsonian Institution Press, 2002. Deals with the history of the collecting of Kwakiutl art by anthropologists and museum curators and the image of Kwakiutl culture created by the collectors.

Jessup, Linda, and Shannon Bagg (eds.). *On Aboriginal Representation in the Gallery.* Hull, Quebec: Canadian Museum of Civilization, 2002. Collection of essays using the aboriginal art of native population of Australia as a take-off point for a discussion of native art and culture in North America as well as Australia.

Meyers, Helen. *Music of Hindu Trinidad: Songs from the Indian Diaspora.* Chicago: University of Chicago Press, 1998. An ethnomusicological study of Felicity, a town in the East Indian enclave of Trinidad, which deals not only with its musical culture, but also with the music brought by nineteenth century North Indians, when they came to Trinidad as indentured laborers.

Nettl, Bruno. *The Study of Ethnomusicology: Twenty-Nine Issues and Concepts.* Urbana, IL: University of Illinois Press, 1983. A general work by the foremost American authority in the field of ethnomusicology.

O'Hanlon, Michael. *Paradise: Portraying the New Guinea Highlands.* London: British Museum Press, 1993. A study of a Highland New Guinea people whose aesthetic is expressed in the decoration of their shields currently being used in warfare.

Philips, Ruth B., and Christopher B. Steiner (eds.). *Unpacking Culture: Art and Commodity in Colonial and Postcolonial Worlds.* Berkeley: University of California Press, 1998. A series of essays providing a comparative perspective on the history, character, and impact of tourist art in colonized societies in Africa, Oceania, and North America. The global phenomenon of tourist art production is recognized as a significant and authentic expression of visual traditions.

 SUGGESTED WEBSITES

http://www.inuit.com/index.html The Inuit Gallery of Vancouver shows the range of Inuit and Northwest Coast sculpture and graphics being done by contemporary artists.

http://www.fmnh.org/exhibits_sites/javamak/Javamask.htm The Javanese mask collection of the Field Museum, Chicago, which contains many of the oldest and most beautiful Indonesian masks in the United States, is illustrated here.

http://www.susanlerer.com/methodology.htm An ethnographic art dealer discusses how market values vary today for different ethnographic pieces.

http://www.art-pacific.com/artifacts/nuguinea/malagan/htm A discussion of different types of malanggan sculptures from New Ireland and the ritual settings in which they are used.

13

The Colonial and Postcolonial Worlds

Globalization and the Role Anthropologists Have Played in Directed Culture Change

In the first part of the last century, anthropologists, for the purposes of analysis, looked at cultures as if they were static, unchanging entities. Malinowski, who carried out several years of fieldwork among the Trobriand Islanders between the years 1912 and 1917, recorded his observations without paying attention to the changes taking place before his very eyes. In reality, cultures are constantly undergoing change, but in today's world change occurs at a very rapid rate. If we conceptualize cultures as having an overall design as a tapestry does, then in situations of change we see either a part of the design beginning to unravel or sometimes a transformation taking place in the overall design itself. Under extreme or traumatic circumstances the tapestry of culture survives only in shreds.

In the 1930s, American anthropologists finally recognized that the American Indian cultures they were studying had been and were continuing to be drastically transformed. They turned their analytical attention to the topic of culture change, publishing a memo in the *American Anthropologist* outlining the topics that were important to consider. They were particularly concerned with the drastic effects that the American government's policy toward Indians had had on their lives over the centuries. British social anthropologists, including Malinowski, also began to be concerned with the effects of culture contact and the effects of the British colonial administration on the small-scale societies they had been studying.

The forces for change in the world today are numerous and powerful. Colonialism, which was one of the strongest forces for change, is all but gone, and in its place is a series of new nation-states based on the geography of colonial empires rather than on sameness of culture. These new nations form a large part of what is known as the Third World. Within most of these Third World nations are the tribal people, who constitute the **Fourth World peoples**. Fourth World peoples are brought to public attention when they put up heroic struggles to preserve their autonomy and culture, such as the Kurds of Turkey, Iran, and Iraq and the Nagas of India did and are still doing. The Yanomamo constitute a Fourth World people and news of the invasion of their territory by miners and settlers has been reported in the *New York Times*. The new postcolonial nation-states are building national cultures in their attempt to supplant and suppress the various indigenous cultures within their nation-state, in the same way that, in the past, the nation-states of Europe attempted to forge national cultures with varying degrees of success. Despite political independence, the continued economic reliance of one-time colonies on their former colonial masters, in many places, constitutes neocolonialism. Over several centuries, changes have greatly altered earlier economic institutions. These changes include the introduction of cash crops, the desire for modern manufactured goods, foreign exploitation of native resources, and the need for labor. The enormous expansion of cities in these new nations presented economic and cultural inducements that attracted many migrants from rural areas. When they returned to their villages, they brought urban culture with them, introducing changes into village culture. Even those remaining in remote villages are now familiar with urban ideas as a consequence of mass communications. Transistor radios, tapes, and video bring new images, sounds, and ideas to the countryside. The Fourth World peoples mentioned above are the people with whom anthropologists have always been concerned. At the present time, it is the anthropologists who are studying the effects of economic expansion and transformation, mass communication, rural-urban migration, and the other consequences of globalization upon the lives of Fourth World peoples.

Colonialism and postcolonialism can be examined at several different levels. The unit that anthropologists usually isolate for study in the field is at the microanalytic level. However, they do not study it alone, but in relation to like units and to the more inclusive political levels. The next more inclusive level of analysis is that of the nation-state, where the focus of the anthropologist has been on the construction of a national culture and the creation of national identity. Since nation-states operate as independent, politically autonomous units, political decisions and economic planning take place at this level. Consequently, the unit of analysis of economic development is also the nation-state. At a still higher, more inclusive level of analysis is the world system, the level of globalization. This concept, developed by Immanuel Wallerstein (1974), refers to the historic emergence of the economic interrelationship of most of the world in a single market system, in which the concept of the division of labor, usually seen as operative in a single society, is projected onto the world. Wallerstein sees the system developing after the breakdown of feudalism and the rise of capitalism and entrepreneurship and the succeeding Industrial Revolution.

During and after the Age of Exploration, Europeans vastly expanded their search for sources of raw materials and mineral resources, as well as for markets for their manufactured goods. These European countries formed the core of a world system, and the colonies and protectorates that they dominated formed the periphery. The world system operates according to capitalist market principles, with profits constantly reverting to the investors of capital, who are located, for the most part, in the core. Anthropologists have been particularly concerned with the effects of the penetration of the world system on tribal, or Fourth World, peoples all over the

Two Iranian women examining a Sara doll. Iran has rejected American Barbie dolls and created their own versions—Sara and Dara.

world and their active responses to this penetration. Eric Wolf (1982), in *Europe and the People without History*, has explored this topic, focusing, for example, on how the Kwakiutl and other native people of North America responded to the fur trade network set up by the Hudson's Bay Company in the eighteenth century.

Within recent years, another concept, **globalization,** has come to the fore. World systems theory focused primarily on the existence of structures, like core and periphery, with anthropological research directed toward the examination of the dynamics of the relationship between the smaller, local parts of the system in the periphery and the larger parts of the core. In contrast, globalization is a process that has been marked by rapid transformations in the lives of people in most parts of the world (Orlove, 1999: 195–196). For example, despite the fact that the Iranian government does not favor the adoption of cultural ideas coming from the West, Barbie dolls, which have been designated as un-Islamic by the government, have found their way there. Iranian toymakers have begun to make Sara, a doll wearing the traditional chador or a folk costume, and Dara, her twin brother, a more conservative doll than Barbie's boyfriend, Ken (*New York Times,* May 23, 2002). The American magazine *Cosmopolitan* now has some 40 international versions, such as Chinese, Indonesian, Russian, Polish, and French versions. The "Fun, Fearless Female to whom Romance is very important needs to be made over to resonate with local populations" (*New York Times,* May 26, 2002). Covers picture local beauties; sex is not mentioned in the Chinese version since it is not allowed. Apparently things American are not viewed as negatively as it would appear.

Globalization has been brought about by the development of a worldwide network of finance and capital. This has occurred on a greater scale than ever before, and at an increasingly rapid rate as a result of enormous advances in telecommunications and computer technology. International institutions like the World Bank, the World Trade Organization, and the International Monetary Fund represent attempts to integrate states into a global economy. At the World Trade Organization meeting held in 2002, American citizens demonstrated their dissatisfaction with what this organization stands for. Some demonstrators were concerned about ecological devastation and global environmental threats. Labor unionists were dissatisfied with changes in tariffs, which in turn would threaten workers' jobs. Others expressed a general unhappiness that Americans may no longer have complete control of their economy. The latter speaks to the issue that nation-states no longer have the ability to make fundamental decisions regarding exchange rates, tariffs, taxation, and the like, having lost this power to global institutions.

As transnational or multinational corporations expand and "globalize," they move beyond the scope of nation-states, and the latter lose the power to regulate and control them. These corporations have also expanded into the former Communist countries, participating in the privatization of state enterprises. Within various parts of the industrializing world, globalization has resulted in great economic successes, for example, in South Korea and Malaysia, while other parts of the world, like the Central American countries, have fallen behind, no longer being seen as targets of global investment.

Transnational migration, which we will discuss in detail in the next chapter, has been brought about by the disappearance of the kinds of jobs people formerly had. New positions become available as a consequence of the new global economy, but they are positions for which these people do not have the skills. Though globalization seems to be similar to and represent historical continuities with colonialism and the neocolonialism of the latter part of the twentieth century, in reality it represents a quantum leap in the reach, penetration, and power of global capitalism (Loker, 1999: 13–14). Capital, goods, communications, pollutants, knowledge, images, cultural information, fashions, belief systems, crime, and drugs all flow very freely across national borders. The anthropologist's role in the study of the phenomenon of globalization is to focus as they always have on the people in different communities, in order to "put human faces on what would otherwise would be anonymous, impersonal statistics" (Orlove, 1999: 196). They pose questions such as these: How have local institutions adapted to the challenge of manufacturing new products and exploring different markets? What has been the consequence of the establishment of a factory by the Nike corporation in a Vietnamese urban area? In Chapter 8 we documented economic changes of this type. Clearly, globalization affects economic institutions and political organization. Ideologies and value systems are being

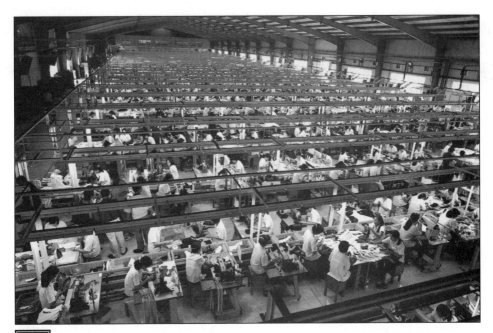

 *Vietnamese workers assembling shoes in a Nike factory on the outskirts of Ho Chi Minh City. Nike, an American company, is Vietnam's single largest private employer.*

changed, and these changes have also been the focus of anthropological research. Let us now go back in time to examine the colonial period, where one might say that globalization had its beginnings.

THE HISTORIC BACKGROUND TO GLOBALIZATION: THE COLONIAL PERIOD

Colonialism over the course of history has taken many forms, with different effects on the peoples colonized. It is important to grasp colonial history to understand what is happening today in the globalizing world. There were various reasons for the establishment of colonies. Sometimes it was the search for raw materials and markets. At other times, colonies were established because of the need to protect the boundaries of an empire from marauding peoples or other empires. Sometimes, only colonial administrators and people involved in the extraction of resources lived in the colony. In other instances, many people came to the colony as settlers. At the beginning of the colonization of North America, the only contacts that Native American societies had were with explorers and governmental representatives of the British and French colonial empires. Over time, a large and more powerful immigrant population engulfed these societies and often completely destroyed them. This situation soon became one marked by grossly unequal power and coercion.

In Australia, the kinds of changes affecting the indigenous peoples, the Australian Aborigines, were similar to those found in the United States. A small native population was soon overwhelmed by the much larger settler population. In New Zealand, the indigenous Maori population was proportionately larger than its counterparts in Australia and the United States, and the greater political influence of the Maori today is probably a result of this proportional difference. In Kenya and Zimbabwe, the settler population remained a minority in relation to the larger indigenous population, whom the settlers used as a labor force to exploit the natural resources of the area. In most of Africa, South and Southeast Asia, and Oceania, European colonial empires were established without large numbers of European settlers. Instead of a small indigenous society confronting waves of technologically advanced settlers, as was the case in America, in these colonial situations, usually, a large indigenous population was conquered and placed under the domination of a small colonial administration, backed by armed forces. These colonies endured in some cases from the sixteenth century to the end of World War II.

The initial motivation for the establishment of colonies was economic gain, which frequently took the form of exploiting raw materials as well as providing markets for the goods of the mother country. The Industrial Revolution led to shortages of resources locally and the need to find them farther afield. Often, a single large trading company, such as the British East India Company, the Hudson's Bay Company, or the Dutch East India Company, held a monopoly on trade and was sometimes given political control as well.

There were differences in the ways colonial powers, established after the Industrial Revolution, governed. The British developed the policy of indirect rule, which was then applied throughout the British Empire. This model was first used in India, where a handful of Englishmen controlled a subcontinent of Indians by means of indigenous governments—the princely states. In contrast, the French ruled directly, establishing military garrisons and large administrative staffs throughout their empire. The French had a policy of accepting an educated individual from their colonies, who was then referred to as an *évolue*, as a citizen of France. The British never had such a policy and refused to accept the best-educated Indian, Pakistani, or African as their equal. Though the indigenous population was usually much larger than the foreign population, power and wealth were all in the hands of the representatives of the colonial power. The nature of these contacts was in every respect an unequal one.

Recent writings by anthropologists on colonialism indicate how complex were the dimensions of colonial life (Cooper and Stoler, 1989). The colonizers felt that it was constantly necessary to define the boundary between themselves and the colonized, whose "otherness" was perpetually being redefined. European colonizers had a variety of intentions toward the indigenous populations. Methodist missionaries hoped to turn the tribes of southern Africa into yeoman farmers modeled on the yeomanry of eighteenth-century England (Comaroff and Comaroff, 1986). Other colonizers attempted to transform the existing social organization to provide laborers who would work in the mines. The boundary between the European colonizers and the local population was sometimes eroded by sexual relations between European men and local women, which produced an intermediate population with an ambiguous identity in the European racial system of classification.

It should be clear from the preceding discussion that the complexities of the colonial period are relevant to anthropological research in the present day and need to be understood. Each example of Western colonial expansion may appear to be different from any other case. Nevertheless, the establishment of the colony and the course of events that followed can be described in terms of a number of variables. These include land policy, resource exploitation, type of labor recruitment, and intensity and type of missionary activity.

The nature of initial contact varied from colony to colony. Colonial control was sometimes set up in the form of patrol posts in the native territory. This method was used by the Australian government to achieve control over the tribal peoples of highland New Guinea, who were frequently hostile to the colonizers. First contact was often peaceful, as illustrated in the picture of the mutually beneficial exchange between the Maori of New Zealand and a member of Captain Cook's crew on his first voyage on the *Endeavour* (1768–1771). Military resistance usually occurred later, as in the case of the Maori, when people realized that they were losing their independence, autonomy, cultural distinctiveness, and ability to determine their own destiny. The fighting between British and Maori ended with the Treaty of Waitangi in 1840. The Maori were treated as a sovereign state with which treaties were made. Under the terms of the treaty, the British Crown received all rights and powers of sovereignty over Maori territory, though the Maori chiefs thought they were giving up only partial rights. In 1996, an official report found that an entire province in New Zealand had been illegally taken from the Taranaki Maori tribes by the Treaty of Waitangi. The report recommended that the Maori be given back the land surrounding Mount Taranaki, or equivalent financial compensation.

Different colonial empires had somewhat different policies with respect to the rights of native peoples over their land. Furthermore, these native peoples themselves had a variety of different conceptualizations about land rights. In the Australian case, the colonial government understood the native pattern of land utilization and the claims of various Australian bands to ancestral homelands, but it chose to ignore them and claim the entire continent as unoccupied wasteland, recognizing neither the land rights nor the sovereignty of the natives.

In America, both the British colonial government and the American government, in the Ordinance of 1787, recognized Native Americans' rights to land and these relationships were maintained with Native American tribes through the nineteenth century. As the immigrant population of the United States grew and with it the demand for land, the Indian land base began to be reduced by successive treaties that the Indians were forced to conclude with the United States

An unknown artist's depiction of the first exchange of a crayfish for a piece of cloth between Maori of New Zealand and a sailor from Captain Cook's crew.

government. The fight over land continues today, but the positions are reversed. Tribes like the Passamaquoddy of Maine have gone to court to lay claim to their traditional land, on the basis of their contention that the United States government broke treaties made with the tribes in centuries past.

Exploitation of resources other than land was critical in defining the nature of the colonial experience and is profitably examined at the level of the world system. The demand for rubber has had an interesting history. It illustrates the way the economic fates of people on three different continents were linked. The natural stands of rubber trees in the Amazon and Congo river basins were exploited during the wild rubber boom of 1895 to 1910. In both places, tribal peoples, who had been subsistence agriculturalists, provided the source of labor for the tapping of latex from the rubber trees in the tropical forest.

British entrepreneurs took wild rubber plant seedlings from the Congo and Amazon basins and transported them to the British colony of Malaya, where they established rubber plantations to provide a steady source of this raw material. Rubber from these plantations captured the world market, bringing to an end the boom in wild rubber from the Congo and Amazon basins. Subsequently, rubber plantations were developed in Liberia by the Firestone Rubber Company of America, and this rubber also gained a share of the world market. Since rubber was the dominant cash crop, the entire economy of Liberia at that time was controlled by Firestone. The shift to synthetic rubber, developed during World War II, signaled the great reduction in importance of plantation-grown rubber. The exploitation of mineral resources was also significant in the African colonial experience as well as in the relationship between American Indians and the United States government.

Exploitation of resources in colonial areas and their successor nation-states required labor. This need for labor was met in a variety of ways, which had profound effects on the indigenous peoples, dislocating their economies and their traditional forms of family and social organization in varying degrees. In the earliest period of the colonization of the New World, the demand by the colonizers for a large-scale labor force to exploit resources was satisfied by the enslavement of native tribal peoples like the Tupi-speaking coastal peoples of Brazil. They were enslaved by the Portuguese and their population was decimated as a result of disease and the conditions of slavery. From the sixteenth century to the beginning of the nineteenth century, some 8 to 10 million Africans were brought to the New World as slaves to furnish labor for the plantations there. As Africans from different cultures speaking different languages were forced to adapt to the new conditions of slavery and to the cultures and languages of their plantation masters, new cultures were forged.

Plantation labor was also obtained by means of indenture. This was the case for indentured laborers from India who went to Trinidad, British Guiana, Fiji, and South Africa. Local corvee labor was the method of the colonial government used in the Congo to force people to work as rubber tappers. In the Pacific, blackbirding, as the kidnapping of Melanesians was referred to, was used to fulfill the labor requirement of the sugar plantations on Fiji and in Australia. These forms of labor recruitment eventually gave way to contract labor, which was used to exploit the mineral resources of southern Africa. Men migrate from the tribal areas to the mines for a period of nine to eighteen months. In the past, the South African government controlled the flow of workers through Pass Laws, preventing those without a contract from leaving tribal areas for the towns and cities. This migration left the tribal areas bereft of men, children without fathers, and wives without husbands. The earlier organization of the family was undercut and weakened, and women alone raised the children. During the time they worked in the mines, the men became increasingly familiar with urban life and new associations such as unions developed. Leadership based on skill and on education superseded tribal leadership in most situations.

When a colonial administration was set up in a tribal area, concerted efforts were made to abolish those practices that violated the colonizers' moral code, a

Missionaries taught Christianity to the people of New Guinea in the early 1900s.

product of their own Western European cultures. Missionaries were the most zealous enforcers of these kinds of changes. For the Methodists, the goal was to establish churches that would be led by local, indigenous leaders. Catholic missionaries
instead established mission stations totally staffed by Europeans, and only much
later did local Catholics become involved on the lower level in the activities of the
church. Head-hunting and cannibalism, where they occurred, were actively suppressed by the missionaries. Sexual practices that differed from Western custom
and that missionaries considered abhorrent were also forbidden.

Sometimes an entire ritual or ceremonial complex was outlawed on the insis-
tence of the missionaries. Anglican and Methodist missionaries among the Haida
considered the potlatch a heathen custom, since it was a significant native religious
rite that they felt impeded the spread of Christianity among these people. The missionaries also objected to the economics of the potlatch. The amassing of material
goods was a good thing, but the practice of inviting guests and giving away the
goods to them at a potlatch seemed irrational since it violated Western ideas of capitalist economic behavior.

NEW IRELAND: AN EXAMPLE OF INCREASING INCORPORATION INTO THE GLOBAL SYSTEM

It is useful to examine the ways in which the variables we have just discussed operate in a particular case, New Ireland, now part of the nation-state of Papua New Guinea. New Ireland is located in the Bismarck Archipelago, close to the equator and east of the much larger island of New Guinea. The first Western explorer known to have made contact with New Irelanders, in 1619, was the Dutchman Schouten. He was searching for trading opportunities in the Pacific outside the geographic area over which the Dutch East India Company had established a monopoly. Schouten tried to exchange beads with the New Irelanders for needed supplies, but the exchange could not be transacted because, as one would expect, neither side understood the other. When the New Irelanders attacked Schouten's men with their slings and clubs, he responded with cannon fire, killing 10 or 12 of them. This initial contact with the West was certainly a violent one, not easily forgotten by the New Irelanders. Over the next two centuries some seven European expeditions sought to replenish their supplies on New Ireland. They offered trade goods, such as beads and cloth, which did not seem to interest the New Irelanders, and consequently they were given little in the way of supplies in return.

During the first decades of the nineteenth century, ships began to put in more and more frequently at New Ireland locations. By this time, the New Irelanders knew that the European ships anchoring in their harbors wanted to reprovision with coconuts, tubers, and pigs, and the Europeans had become aware of the New Irelanders' desire for iron. Iron hoops, used to hold casks of whale oil together, were cut into three- or four-inch segments, and given in exchange for supplies. They were greatly prized by the New Irelanders since they were used to make adzes and axes, which made gardening much easier. The process of carving *malanggan* sculptures, mentioned in Chapter 12, also became much easier. In the early nineteenth century, English whalers and American whalers from New Bedford and Nantucket put in to the bays of New Ireland for fresh water and supplies, giving in exchange hoop iron, along with buttons, bottles, strips of cloth, and, later, tobacco. A number of seamen became castaways on New Ireland at this time. In 1825, Thomas Manners, an English whaler, asked to be put ashore, where he subsequently lived with the villagers, took wives, and fathered children. As a result of Manners's presence, the Big Man of his village seemed to have had more political power. For men such as Manners, the islands of the Pacific were a romantic escape from the alienation of industrializing society.

During this period, the island was, for the first time, enmeshed in the world system when traders came seeking tortoise shell to be sent to Europe for the manufacture of combs and other decorative items, which became the rage of fashionable Europe. Bêche-de-mer (sea cucumbers) were also collected and then dried and sold to the Chinese as a food delicacy. By this point, a mutually agreed-upon barter system had been established, and some New Irelanders were able to communicate in Pidgin English. The New Irelanders, without being aware of it, had thus become part of the global system of trade.

The first trading post was set up on New Ireland in 1880 by the German trader Eduard Hernsheim to purchase coconuts. From his base on Matupi Island in New Britain, Hernsheim set up a network of trading stations, including a number on New Ireland. His agents at these stations—Englishmen, Scandinavians, and, later, mostly Chinese—bought unhusked coconuts (later, only the nuts) from the New Ireland villagers in exchange for tobacco, beads, and ironware from Europe. The price the villagers received for coconuts varied, depending on the price of copra on the world market, the price of beads in Europe, and the number of competing traders in the area. These were factors from the world economic system of which villagers on the local level were completely unaware. In the indigenous system of exchange, shell valuables and pigs did not fluctuate in value. Hernsheim transported the dried copra on his own ship to be sold in Hamburg, where he was raised and where he sent his profits. The success of his business enterprise depended on the world price of copra. Hernsheim had competitors in the area, among them some colorful South Sea Island adventurers such as His Majesty O'Keefe, Bully Hayes, and the notorious Queen Emma, the daughter of a Samoan mother and the American consul to Samoa.

Relying on villagers to bring in their coconuts did not produce a steady supply of copra. As Hernsheim notes in his memoirs, "It was impossible to make long-term agreements with these savages; there were no chiefs and no large villages" (1983). Because the New Irelanders had Big Men, rather than chiefs, there was no one in a position of central political authority with whom traders and later political administrators could make binding agreements and sign treaties. There was no single indigenous political structure that unified the whole island, only villages. The alternative to the unpredictable supply of copra provided through trading stations was the establishment of a plantation system, which began on New Ireland at the beginning of the twentieth century. Land for plantations had to be purchased by Europeans from New Irelanders. Since land on New Ireland was owned by matrilineal clans, only clan representatives could negotiate such sales.

Labor recruiters began in the 1880s to call at locations in New Ireland to recruit workers for plantations in Fiji and, later, Australia, often resorting to "blackbirding," mentioned above. Captain Wawn, one of the first labor recruiters, or blackbirders, in the area, recruited for the sugar plantations in Queensland, Australia. Despite the fact that some of the men changed their minds and jumped overboard, the remainder were forcibly taken to Queensland to work as laborers. When they returned home three years later, the recruits brought back boxes filled with Western goods, which they used to maximize their positions in the political arenas of their own villages, becoming leaders and Big Men. Many came back to New Ireland speaking Pidgin English, and this enabled them to deal more successfully with the European traders on the island. The sugar produced in Queensland and the copra from Fiji and Samoa where the New Irelanders worked were destined for sale on the world market.

Missionary activity began in New Ireland in 1875 when the Methodist Reverend George Brown, an Englishman, stationed two Fijian religious teachers there, where no colonial administration existed. Fijian teachers were important to the Methodist missionary enterprise because they were like New Irelanders and could more effectively spread the message of Christianity. The Methodist missionaries voiced their strong opposition to local habits and tried to eliminate the New Irelanders' customs such as wearing no clothing, ritual dancing—which the missionaries considered lewd—and cannibalism. The progress of missionizing was impeded by the absence of authoritative leadership and the many languages spoken on the island. When a chief converts, as in Fiji, an entire chiefdom converts with him; Big Men do not have the same kind of authority over their followers. Catholic missionaries visited New Ireland in 1882. The Catholic approach to missionizing differed from that of the Reverend Brown. It involved setting up mission stations run by Europeans to which the local people would come for religious instruction and schooling.

There was one attempt at European settlement on New Ireland, sponsored by the Marquis de Ray, a French aristocrat who had never been in the Pacific. Four ships, with 700 settlers, left Europe for New Ireland, which they called New France, between 1880 and 1882. Unfortunately, the area chosen was the least suitable for the settlement envisioned. Completely unprepared for what they had to face in New Ireland, within two years most of the settlers died of tropical diseases and the survivors were eventually taken off the island to Australia. The Marquis de Ray was later tried in France and found guilty of fraud.

Although traders of several nationalities were operating in the Bismarck Archipelago after 1880, German companies dominated the area economically. Australia, then a British colony, was concerned about German influence on the island of New Guinea and proceeded to annex the southern half of that island. Within a year an agreement was signed in which Germany took control over northern New Guinea and the Bismarcks and the English were to control the remainder of New Guinea. The German flag was raised over New Ireland in November 1884. While it had already been tied to the rest of the world economically for several decades, New Ireland now politically became part of the German colonial empire.

It was not until 1900 that a government station was established at Kavieng, the present provincial capital, with Franz Boluminski as district commissioner. For the first time in its history, the whole island constituted a single political entity, a district within the colony of German New Guinea, instead of many autonomous villages. Former employees of the large German trading companies began to apply for land to establish plantations in such numbers that shortly thereafter the colonial government had to enact regulations to prevent the New Irelanders from losing all their land. The monument Boluminski left in New Ireland was the coastal road, stretching for over 100 miles from Kavieng, built by means of corvée labor extracted from the villages along its path.

During the German administration, great efforts were made by the colonial government to end the state of perpetual feuding between local communities and to end raiding and looting of European trade stations by the New Irelanders. Beyond the retaliatory raids against offending communities by the local native police organized and led by the Germans, pacification took the form of moving villages to the coast, where they could be more easily supervised. This movement of inland villagers to the coast tore whole communities away from their ancestral clan lands, bringing them into the coastal villages as intruders. This left the interior of New Ireland relatively deserted. Headmen, called *luluais*, not always the traditional leaders, were appointed for each village by the German administration. Sometimes the men who had worked in plantations overseas, learned Pidgin English, and had become Big Men were appointed *luluais*.

In contrast to most of the earlier European traders, like Hernsheim, who went to Australia or returned to Europe after they had made their fortunes, Chinese traders, who came somewhat later, stayed on in New Ireland, intermarried with the local people, and eventually took control of the trade stores. The Chinese, who had come as traders, did not feel the same way as Europeans did about maintaining sharp boundaries between colonizers and colonized.

The Germans were stripped of their colonies, including New Ireland, after they lost World War I, and Australia took over the administration of New Ireland under a mandate from the League of Nations. The Australians expropriated German-owned plantations and sold them at low rates to Australian ex-servicemen, who employed local New Irelanders from nearby villages. In other respects, life for the New Irelanders did not change much when colonial control passed from the Germans to the Australians. When the price of copra rose on the world market in the 1920s, Australian plantation owners became quite successful, but when it fell during the Depression, they lost money. Villagers had to sell coconuts from their own trees to raise cash to purchase trade goods and to pay the head tax. Patrol officers encouraged the villagers to cut and dry the meat of the coconut kernels themselves so that they could sell it as processed copra and receive a higher price for it than for the kernels.

The Australians established patrol posts at various locations over the island and continued to use the *luluai* system put in place by the Germans. Patrol officers periodically visited almost every village to collect the head tax; adjudicate disputes, particularly over land; examine health conditions; see that labor recruitment rules were adhered to; and conduct censuses. In this way, the colonial masters increasingly penetrated many aspects of the daily life of the New Irelanders. By this time, Pidgin English had developed as the lingua franca for New Ireland, as well as many other areas of the southwest Pacific. The Europeans used it to communicate with the local people. New Irelanders from different parts of the island, who spoke different languages, used it to converse across linguistic boundaries.

New Ireland was occupied by the Japanese during World War II and the primary hardship of the indigenous population arose from Japanese confiscation of pigs and foodstuffs. The Australians returned after World War II to administer Papua New Guinea as a United Nations Trusteeship Territory, with independence as the eventual aim. The Australian plantation owners reopened their plantations, and the economy continued much as it had before the war, though new crops, such as cocoa, began to be grown alongside the coconut palms. In the 1950s, as a first step toward independence, the Australians introduced a system of elected local government councils, which took over some of the functions that had been carried out by patrol officers. A House of Assembly was established in Port Moresby, with representation from districts all over Papua New Guinea. In 1975 the independent nation of Papua New Guinea was established. New Ireland was set up as a province, with its own elected provincial assembly and a provincial government headed by a prime minister.

Since independence, Australian expatriates have been withdrawing from the economic system of New Ireland, though they still own some of the plantations. Some of the plantation laborers are New Irelanders, while others have been brought in from the Sepik River area of New Guinea. The world price for copra has been very low in recent years, and many of the plantations are run at a minimal level since the owners do not wish to take a loss. As plantations are abandoned, they revert to the local villages, which still basically have a subsistence economy, supporting themselves through gardening, raising pigs, and fishing. In addition, the local villagers have moved into cash cropping, producing copra and cocoa to sell to government marketing boards, which then sell these products on the world market. Sometimes villagers have organized themselves into cooperatives to buy and operate a truck or a boat. In recent years, Malaysian and Japanese companies have exploited the timber resources in the interior part of the island. Though fixed royalties are paid to national and provincial governments and to local people, no thought is being given to the replenishing of this resource through reforestation.

The legacy of the Reverend George Brown is the many Methodist congregations all over the island led by indigenous religious leaders. The Catholic mission stations of the island are now run by expatriate American priests of the Order of the Sacred Heart, while the diocese of New Ireland is headed by a German bishop.

The significant unit for most New Irelanders continues to be their village. Villages had been politically independent before New Ireland became a colony. Today, though there are still Big Men and matrilineal clans, every village is part of an electoral district. In contrast to people elsewhere who have become wage laborers or who depend exclusively on cash crops, New Ireland villagers have resisted being completely absorbed into a market economy. Many prefer to sell products only when they need cash. However, for more than a hundred years, New Irelanders have not been able to think of themselves solely in terms of their clan or village membership. They are increasingly forced to view themselves in regional terms, as New Irelanders, and in national terms, as Papuan New Guineans. Changes at the world level affect them economically and politically, and they see themselves as necessarily part of the world system.

APPLIED ANTHROPOLOGY: WHAT IS THE ANTHROPOLOGIST'S ROLE IN DIRECTED CULTURE CHANGE?

Anthropology can be seen as having two aspects. One is concerned with the investigation of different cultures for the knowledge it brings to us about how other people live their lives, for the production of intercultural understanding, and for the general theoretical information gained concerning similarities and differences between cultures and societies. The other is *applied anthropology,* which is concerned with the production and application of anthropological knowledge to the solution of practical problems, initiating direct action or contributing to the formation of a broad range of policies.

Even before the development of anthropology as a discipline, missionaries and government officials were involved in gathering anthropological information to implement their policies of conquest and conversion. During the colonial period, ethnographic studies were always included in the training of government administrators destined to work in colonies all over the world, who instituted many changes in all aspects of life of the people they controlled, as we have documented earlier. They saw these changes as bringing "progress" to peoples, doing away with "savage" practices like nakedness and cannibalism, helping to make them "modern"—that is, civilized and Westernized. Even the Bureau of American Ethnology, founded in the 1850s, "an early manifestation of anthropology in the United States . . . was created as a policy research arm of the federal government" (Willigen, 2002: 23). Most of the changes that were instituted were not desired by the peoples themselves, but their opinions were never sought. Because anthropologists assisted colonial governments to achieve their goals, they are now frequently considered to have been the tools of colonialism.

The passage of the Indian Reorganization Act by the United States Congress, which was to aid American Indians tribes to develop self-governance, was the occasion for the development of the Applied Anthropology Unit in the Office of Indian Affairs in 1934. The government also introduced a stock-reduction program among the Navajo during the mid-1930s based on a study of all the rangeland on the Navajo reservation, which concluded that overgrazing had caused soil erosion. The Navajo had their own way of managing their herds of sheep, goats, and horses, and, therefore, the government policy of stock reduction caused great consternation. Their livestock represented their wealth and was a source of great prestige. Because of this program, Navajo resentment toward the government simmered for many years after.

In addition, anthropologists gathered ethnographic information in the form of policy-focused basic research for the government during the thirties on the subject of rural life (Goldschmidt, 1947). Later during the war years anthropologists put together ethnographic handbooks used to prepare administrators for areas being recaptured from the Japanese, to provide intelligence on the Japanese and other adversaries, and to give the government advice on how to improve national morale (Willingen, 2002: 25–29). Many of those involved, like Margaret Mead, Gregory Bateson, and Ruth Benedict, straddled the academic and applied fields during that time.

During the Vietnam War, governmental policies sealed the fate of tribal Montagnard peoples, requiring them to move from their traditional homelands. Ethical questions began to be raised when some anthropologists were involved in providing ethnographic information that suggested the most efficient ways of carrying out the policy of resettling villagers. Many in the discipline began to recognize that there was no such thing as "value-free research." Earlier, during the colonial period, anthropologists had tried to "increase the fairness and humaneness of various domestic and international colonial systems" (Willingen, 2002: 31). However, it became quite clear that that was impossible. Value-explicit research meant that anthropologists thenceforth had to clearly define their goals and values for the communities within which they wished to work. Ethical issues became important, and the American Anthropological Association, after much discussion, established a code of ethical conduct in which issues such as privacy, the need for informed consent, and confidentiality are spelled out. A commission was also established to deal with ethical problems as these arose. A primary question for researchers became, Does the research serve the needs of the people?

In the 1950s, the Fox project was developed, which involved anthropologists from the University of Chicago, particularly Sol Tax, working with Fox Indians. The project became known as "action anthropology" and involved a new role for anthropologists. Community self-determination was emphasized, with the anthropologist as a resource person who explores, in a continuing interactive fashion, the possibilities for the changes that the people envision, the possible problems that might develop, and future prospects for the group. Self-determination is the key concept in this endeavor. This kind of collaborative work in support of community development goes back several decades to that period. Another role that anthropologists assumed was that of culture broker. This role parallels the patron-client relationship that we discussed earlier, only in this context, it is the anthropologist who acts as culture broker, sometimes as expert witness in a whole variety of cases from those concerning fishing rights to those regarding tribal recognition.

The shrinking market for academic positions in the late 1980s and early 1990s, coupled with the demand for more involvement of anthropologists in policy research, resulted in the development of full-time applied anthropologists, individuals who were no longer academics but rather full-time practicing anthropologists. (They now have their own association—the National Association for the Practice of Anthropology.) The areas of their research include overseas projects as well as research in the United States on topics ranging from homeless people to radioactive waste storage siting. This research is usually collaborative in every sense of the word. The special skills of the anthropologist are shared with the community, in that the anthropologist is the resource person acting, at all times, in a participatory role. However, the applied anthropologist is often hired by an agency, government or otherwise, to do a rapid assessment of a particular situation and come to some conclusions regarding a policy that might be implemented. In that type of situation, the degree of "collaboration" varies.

After World War II, as we have noted above, the development of revolutionary movements led to the establishment of many new states in Africa and Asia. Though the colonial yoke had been thrown off, modernization, industrialization, urbanization, and "development"—the processes based on the success of technology that had made Europe, the Western world, or "the North" so successful—were seen as the key to success in what came to be known as the "underdeveloped world." In the 60s, development—the growth of the economy—was seen in terms of stages through which countries had to go. Later, Andre Gunther Frank saw underdevelopment in a different way. It is a state that is produced by the process under which the developed countries extracted resources and raw materials from the underdeveloped countries. The underdeveloped countries constituted the markets to which developed countries sent their finished products to be sold. Development, "the imposition of the West as the model of the 'developed' . . . has come under increasing attack . . . [since] it continues the culture of colonialism" (Kamat, 2002: 2)

Those underdeveloped countries, in what came to be known as the South, needed help in order to overcome problems of poverty and backwardness, and assistance to overcome their "underdeveloped state." In the West this help was seen as evidence of our altruistic nature, helping those in need. Interestingly, the history of development, with aid and assistance coming from the West, is viewed by others not as altruistic but rather as geopolitical. Development is connected to the "domino theory," which was provided by the United States as the excuse for their military activity in Southeast Asia in the 1970s to prevent Russia and China from taking over the area (Weisgrau, personal communication). The theme was clear: Send in development experts and you will help a country modernize and prevent it from going communist.

Development is also seen as replacing "local and rational technologies" with capitalist forms, ignoring local knowledge. Today local knowledge is seen as crucial, and one must pay attention to it in suggesting any forms of change. Local knowledge means "the culture, values, and social institutions of the place," which are and always have been, in effect, the principal foci for anthropologists. This has also been referred to as "indigenous knowledge" (Sillitoe, 2002: 8). There has been a shift in emphasis from " 'top-down' intervention to a 'grassroots' participatory perspective" (Sillitoe, 2002: 2). People at the local level want to share in technological advances with the West but on their own terms. An excellent example of this is the interaction of First Nations (Canadian Indians) with the Canadian government regarding the resources on First Nations lands. Each Nation has worked out its own agreement. "Various mixtures of this indigenous knowledge with Euro-American approaches have produced some spectacular successes, greatly improving some communities in 25 years" (Croal and Darou, 2002: 83).

Over several decades, nongovernmental organizations (NGOs) have arisen in many countries, and they have become important vehicles for development at the local level as a consequence of the failure of "bureaucratically driven inflexible governmental development programs" (Weisgrau, 1997: 1). These programs tend to be small-scale, individually organized programs at the village level, aimed at reaching the rural poor in remote areas. The NGOs try to involve villagers in both planning and execution, addressing locally identified priorities. This is also known as "participatory development" (Sillitoe, 2002: 6). The NGO budgets are usually small, often with some money coming from outside organizations. Problems have sometimes arisen with NGOs that are parts of international organizations. Their village representatives are often members of the elite from the city, of a different social class from the villagers. What these NGOs introduce are plans and proposals suggested and often imposed from the outside, and related to international programs or programs from state bodies. The NGO, rather than the local group, sets

Local village women of Rajastan, India, meet with the representative of an NGO to discuss political mobilization relating to voting and women's issues.

the agenda and the priorities, and these often fail. Anthropologists are sometimes called in to provide a perspective on the activities of NGOs in villages and evaluate their strategies and successes (Weisgrau, 1997; Loizos, 1991)

Among the technological changes that development programs sponsored by the government and by NGOs have addressed is the introduction of new crops and improved varieties of older crops. New food crops have been successfully introduced to tribal peoples all over the world. However, sometimes an improved variety of an old crop is introduced that has a taste somewhat different from the old one and is not accepted. Sometimes a new method of processing food is introduced as a labor-saving device, but if the taste of the food changes, the new method may be unsuccessful. Traditionally, Kanuri women grind sorghum, the staple crop, by hand between two stones to make the basic food dish of the Kanuri. Mechanization of the grinding process was attempted by setting up a mill to grind the grain, which would have saved enormous amounts of daily labor, but the mill-ground sorghum did not have the gritty taste that the Kanuri liked, and they would not use sorghum ground in that way.

Modern veterinary science has been successfully introduced to nomadic herdsmen. Nomadic pastoralists like the Bakhtiari in Iran readily worm their herds with pills distributed by the veterinary services of the national government. In general, changes in veterinary practices that the people themselves see as increasing the productivity and fertility of herds are readily accepted. However, government attempts to reduce herd size among pastoral cattle-keeping peoples of East Africa have run into the same problems that herd reduction programs instituted by the United States government encountered when introduced to the Navajo because of the cultural importance of herds.

Another and more drastic form of directed culture change involving nomadic pastoralists was the programs to sedentarize them. Nomadic pastoralists lived in many countries in the Middle East. Since they were highly mobile, it was difficult for national governments to control them. Their emphasis on tribal identity above national loyalties also constituted a political threat. As a result of this, governments throughout the area have attempted to settle the nomadic pastoralists in villages. These plans have invariably been resisted. As noted in Chapter 8, a policy of forced sedentarization of nomadic tribes was instituted by the government of Iran during the period 1925 to 1941. Among the Basseri, for example, most families were prevented from migrating. Since their herds of sheep and goats were adapted to the migratory cycle, large percentages of the herds died because the enforced sedentarization subjected the animals to extremes of temperature to which they were not accustomed. After 1941, most of these nomadic pastoral tribes resumed migration. Attempts at sedentarization or partial sedentarization in other countries, as in the case of the Bedouins of the Israeli Negev, have been more successful.

Earlier in our discussion of law and social control, we pointed out that anthropologists, because of their expertise in customary law, have been called in as consultants by newly established nations who were in the process of developing new legal codes. The Customary Law Project in Papua New Guinea had the task of assembling information on the legal systems of different cultural groups to develop a Papua New Guinea common law that would be in accord with customary law. Legislators and policymakers in the national government are attempting to reconcile the customary form of managing the resolution of conflicts with the demands of modern life. Many of the societies that constitute the nation of Papua New Guinea pay homicide compensation after a killing. The size of the compensation varies with the severity of the act and the magnitude of the dispute, but payment of compensation acknowledges acceptance of responsibility and the termination of conflict. In recent times, demands for homicide compensation have been extended to deaths due to automobile accidents. The Papua New Guinea government is attempting to construct a legal code that will incorporate indigenous ways of resolving conflict (by the payment of compensation), define the limits of applying them, and determine what aspects of homicide compensation will be standardized.

Other development programs have involved the introduction of tourism. From Highland New Guinea to Bali, tourist dollars have become an importance source of extra income. Mt. Hagen "Sing-Sings" are a "must" stop on tours of Highland Paua New Guinea. Special dances, utilizing local myths and costumes from a variety of rituals, have been created by the Chimbu in the Highlands further east to perform before tourists who come on special tours. The anthropology of tourism focuses upon the ways in which people in a wide variety of societies connected themselves to the developed world through the mechanism of tourism.

 ## SUMMARY

- Cultures are constantly undergoing change at a very rapid rate in today's world.

- Colonialism, which was one of the strongest forces for change, is all but gone, and in its place is a series of new nation-states based on the geography of colonial empires rather than on sameness of culture. These new nations form what is known as the Third World., within which are the tribal people, who constitute the Fourth World peoples.

- The new postcolonial nation-states are building national cultures in their attempt to supplant and suppress the various indigenous cultures within their nation-state.

- Colonialism and postcolonialism can be examined at several different levels. The unit that anthropologists usually isolate for study in the field is at the microanalytic level.

- Globalization has been brought about by the development of a worldwide network of finance and capital.

- The anthropologist's role in the study of the phenomenon of globalization is to focus on the people in different communities in order to put human faces on what would otherwise would be anonymous, impersonal statistics.

- Though globalization seems to be similar to and represent historical continuities with colonialism and the neocolonialism of the latter part of the twentieth century, in reality it represents a quantum leap in the reach, penetration, and power of global capitalism.

- Colonialism has taken many forms, with different effects on the peoples colonized. It is important to grasp colonial history to understand what is happening today in the globalizing world.

- The initial motivation for the establishment of colonies was economic gain, which took the form of exploiting raw materials as well as providing markets for the goods of the mother country.

- The British developed the policy of indirect rule using the indigenous political structure, which was then applied throughout the British Empire. In contrast, the French ruled directly, establishing military garrisons and large administrative staffs throughout their empire.

• The establishment of a colony and the course of events that followed can be described in terms of a number of variables. These include land policy, resource exploitation, type of labor recruitment, and intensity and type of missionary activity.

• Different colonial empires had somewhat different policies with respect to the rights of native peoples over their land. Furthermore, these native peoples themselves had a variety of different conceptualizations about land rights.

• In Australia, the rights of the Aborigines to land was not recognized, while in America, both the British colonial government and the American government, in the Ordinance of 1787, recognized Native Americans' rights to land.

• British entrepreneurs took wild rubber plant seedlings from the Congo and Amazon basins, and they transported them to rubber plantations in the British colony of Malaya where they captured the world market, bringing to an end the boom in wild rubber.

• Exploitation of resources in colonial areas and their successor nation-states required labor, which was met in a variety of ways. Labor recruitment dislocated the economies and the traditional forms of family and social organization of colonized populations.

• Millions of Africans were brought to the New World as slaves to furnish labor for the plantations. Plantation labor was also obtained by means of indenture.

• Missionaries were the most zealous enforcers of changes in the cultural practices that offended them, such as the potlatch and cannibalism.

• Applied anthropology is concerned with the production and application of anthropological knowledge to the solution of practical problems.

• Missionaries and government officials were involved in gathering anthropological information to implement their policies of conquest and conversion, in effect, practicing applied anthropology before the discipline of anthropology existed.

• During the colonial period, ethnographic studies were always included in the training of government administrators destined to work in the colonies. Most of the changes that were instituted were not desired by the peoples themselves, but their opinions were never sought.

• The passage of the Indian Reorganization Act by the United States Congress, which was to aid American Indian tribes to develop self-governance, was the occasion for the development of the Applied Anthropology Unit in the Office of Indian Affairs in 1934.

• As a consequence of the research done by some anthropologists, who made recommendations to the government during the Vietnam War about resettlement of villagers moved because of government war objectives, many in the discipline began to recognize that there was no such thing as "value-free research."

- Value-explicit research meant that anthropologists thenceforth had to clearly define their goals and values for the communities within which they wished to work.

- Ethical issues became important and the American Anthropological Association, after much discussion, established a code of ethical conduct in which issues such as privacy, the need for informed consent, and confidentiality are spelled out.

- In action anthropology, which developed in the fifties, the anthropologist became a resource person who explores in a continuing interactive fashion the possibilities for the changes which the people envision, the possible problems that might develop, and future prospects for the group. Self-determination is the key concept in this endeavor.

- The shrinking market for academic positions in the late 1980s and early 1990s coupled with the demand for more involvement of anthropologists in policy research resulted in the development of full-time applied anthropologists, individuals who were no longer academics but rather full-time practicing anthropologists.

- After the establishment of many new states in Africa and Asia, modernization, industrialization, urbanization, and "development" were seen as the key to success in what came to be known as the "underdeveloped world."

- Citing altruistic motives, people in the West offered help to underdeveloped nations. However, the history of development, with aid and assistance coming from the West, is viewed by others not as altruistic but rather as geopolitical, an attempt to prevent these countries from becoming communist.

- Over several decades, nongovernmental organizations (NGOs) have arisen in many countries and have become important vehicles for development at the local level as a consequence of the failure of bureaucratically driven inflexible governmental development programs.

- Development programs sponsored by the government as well as by NGOs have introduced new crops and improved varieties of older crops, and modern veterinary science has been successfully introduced to nomadic herdsmen.

 SUGGESTED READINGS

Appadurai, Arjun. *Modernity at Large: Cultural Dimensions of Globalization.* Minneapolis: University of Minnesota Press, 1996. Modernization and globalization presented from a postmodern viewpoint.

Chambers, Erve (ed.). *Tourism and Culture: An Applied Perspective.* Albany: State University of New York Press, 1997. A series of detailed case studies that explore the complexity of modern tourism relationships between "hosts" and "guests." The book focuses on applied anthropology, with many contributors describing their direct involvement in the development or assessment of tourism in different parts of the world.

Cooper, Frederic, and Anne Laura Stoller (eds.). *Tensions of Empire: Colonial Cultures in a Bourgeois World.* Berkeley: University of California Press, 1997. A series of essays that focus upon colonial encounters in various parts of the world and how they shaped ideas about imperialism in Europe and the politics of inclusion and exclusion in the colonies.

Dirks, Nicholas. *Colonialism and Culture.* Ann Arbor: University of Michigan Press, 1992. Essays dealing with the culture of colonialism and its multifaceted nature.

Friedman, Jonathan (ed.). *Globalization, the State, and Violence.* Walnut Creek, CA: Altimira Press, 2002. A discussion, by a distinguished group of contributors, of how transnational capital represents a truly global force with increasing hegemony in some areas and declining hegemony in others. Conflict and violence due to ethnic rivalries and the formation of transnational criminal networks are also considered.

Inda, Jonathan Xavier. *The Anthropology of Globalization: A Reader.* Malden, MA: Blackwell Publishers, 2002. A series of essays concerning topics ranging from corporate discipline in the pink-collar sector in Barbados, global traffic in human organs, globalization and localization, and the marriage of feminism and Islamism in Egypt.

 SUGGESTED WEBSITES

http://www.pscw.uva.nl/gm/articles/pp1997.htm A history of anthropology's engagement with colonialism.

http://www.artsci.wustl.edu/~anthro/courses/306/RedRubber/html The story of rubber collection and rubber plantations in the Belgian Congo, now known as Zaire, compared with rubber collection in other parts of the world like Brazil and Malaysia.

http://www.oakland.edu/~dow/anthop.htm A website for applied anthropology that describes what applied anthropologists do and the employment opportunities for applied anthropologists.

14

Migration, Diasporas, and Cultural Identity Reasserted

Migration, or the movement of populations, has characterized the evolving human species from the beginning. The most recent information from physical anthropologists tells us that our ancestors moved out from Africa in wave after wave to populate Asia, Europe, and finally the New World and the Pacific Islands. Humans have always been on the move, as we have seen in the last chapter. There are different kinds of migration, which we shall consider in this chapter. We will also deal with situations in which groups have transformed themselves while remaining in the same general area, as well as groups who have reasserted their identity, overcoming forces for cultural change.

INTERNAL MIGRATION

Internal migration refers to population movements within a nation-state. Such migrations have been taking place in our own country since its settlement almost 500 years ago. The expansion of our country from the original 13 colonies represents a form of internal migration. The nineteenth-century movement of population ever westward to the Pacific Ocean continued this pattern. At the beginning of the twentieth century, large numbers of African-Americans, dissatisfied with life in the segregated rural South, began their movement to the northern urban cities where they hoped to find work and freedom from the segregated culture of the South. This movement continued for many years. During the twentieth century, migration from rural areas to cities represented another significant movement of population. Whereas in the nineteenth century most of the population of the United States lived in the rural areas of the country, increasingly, in the twentieth century, the urban and suburban populations have come to dominate. The mechanization of farming and farm consolidation forced many farming families to seek their fortunes in the cities of the nation. Labor migration, the movement of people to where jobs are available, is also a form of internal migration. After World War II, many people sought their fortunes in "sunny California," where they saw new employment opportunities. People have also moved from the urban Northeast to seek employment elsewhere, since the industries of that area were moving to other parts of the country or even overseas. Senior citizens, referred to as "snow-birds," whose retirement communities we discussed in a previous chapter, move from northern states, with their cold winters, to Florida, California, and the Southwest, where the climate is more to their liking. One might even consider professors as exemplifying internal migration, since, during the course of their careers, they may teach at different colleges and universities in different parts of the country.

TRANSMIGRATION

Transmigration refers to populations who migrate far from their homelands to many different parts of the world. These people may be completely assimilated into the culture of their new country. Assimilation means that they adopt the language and culture of their new country. Many people who were persecuted in their homelands or who were dissatisfied with their lives in the countries of their birth came to America and desired to be completely assimilated.

Historians like Sobel (2002) have examined the process of migration from Europe and Africa to America during the eighteenth century by looking at autobiographical statements the migrants wrote. While many of them looked forward to the advantages offered by living in the New World, especially religious and political freedom, migration meant giving up a culture and a social structure that they were comfortable with, and it sometimes meant learning a new language as well. The autobiographical narratives reveal that the migrants underwent significant changes in their personal identity as they adapted to life in colonial America and became Americans. Often they underwent important religious changes such as conversion to new Christian denominations like the Moravian Church, or they became Baptists or Quaker. The migrants first encountered these religious denominations in America. The new sense of self felt by the migrant was also frequently accompanied by a newly discovered sense of "otherness" (This is what I am. It is completely different from those deceitful others). For example, Venture Smith was brought to America as a slave at the age of six. From that point on, he saw whites as the enemy, who valued lying and deception, and blacks as valuing truth and integrity (Sobel, 2002: 189). "Freedom," said Venture Smith, "is a privilege which nothing else can equal" (Sobel, 2002: 189).

The phenomenon of "being born again" occurs often in the narratives (Sobel, 2002: 199). We have drawn attention to the way in which the initiation rites of boys involve being born again, this time through men rather than through women. The process of migration to a new land, to a new culture, involves remaking one's self and creating new identity for one's self. It is as though one were "born again" in the New World. After the American Revolution, a collective identity was consciously being constructed. The importance of the concept of the "not-me" in

American culture and the construction of American identity are reflected in the continued racism directed at African-Americans and Indians (Sobel, 2002: 202).

DIASPORAS

Some migrants maintain their original ethnic identity for centuries and today are known as *diaspora populations*. In recent years, the overseas migration of groups like the Chinese and Indians just described have come to be known as **diasporas.** This term is now applied to populations who have moved to other parts of the world and retained some connection to their homelands. The word *diaspora* was originally a Greek term that meant "dispersion." It came to be applied to the uprooting of the Jewish people after the destruction of the Second Temple in A.D. 70, their exile from the Holy Land and subsequent dispersion throughout the Old World and, later, the New World. They kept alive their memories of Jerusalem and of the land of Israel, and a belief in a Messiah who would deliver them. At every Passover ceremony, Jews around the world express the hope that next year will mark their return to Jerusalem. Jews in the diaspora have also begun to investigate their ancestral roots in Europe.

The term *diaspora* is now applied to diverse migrant groups that settled in countries away from their homelands for a whole variety of reasons. Some analysts have argued "that the term should be reserved for groups forced to disperse, and whose members conscientiously strive to keep past memories, maintain their heritage and are involved in a survival struggle" (Tatla, 1999: 3). Such diaspora groups have faced ethnocide—forced cultural integration—or even genocide in the effort to eliminate or exterminate them. Cohen (1997) has suggested a number of specific features that all diasporas have in common. First, they all represent a dispersal from a homeland. Members of the diaspora always maintain a collective memory about their homeland, including its location, history, and achievements, idealizing their ancestral home. They have a collective commitment to its maintenance, restoration, safety, and prosperity, and to its re-creation if it no longer exists as a separate political entity. Frequently, a movement to return to the homeland among members of the diaspora becomes important to the group. Diasporas also sustain strong ethnic group consciousness over a long period of time, based on a sense of distinctiveness compared to their neighbors, a common history, and the belief in a common fate. They may have a troubled relationship with the host society, which does not accept them, and in such situations there is always the possibility that another calamity, a wave of persecution or perhaps another dispersal, will befall the group. In contrast, in some situations, where the host country constitutes a plural society, members of a diaspora may continue to have a distinctive creative life. Diaspora populations also have a strong sense of empathy and solidarity with co-ethnic members residing in other countries (Cohen, 1997: 26).

The reasons for the dispersal of a diaspora population may vary. Armenians, Africans, and Jews represent "victim diasporas." That is, their movement was a consequence of forced removal, as was the case for the Africans who were brought to the New World, or persecution and threats of death, which forced the Armenians to flee from Turkey and the Jews to flee from the pogroms in Poland and the Ukraine. The Armenian diaspora population of London represents individuals from a number of different countries, such as Cyprus, Lebanon, and Iran, who speak either the eastern Armenian dialect, and trace their ancestry to Iran or Armenia, or western Armenian, which was spoken in eastern Turkey before the genocide of the Armenians of Turkey in 1915. This distinction was often the basis for diviseness in the London Armenian diaspora. The mostly first-generation immigrants belong to "a shifting set of voluntary organizations which sponsored a small cultural centre, two churches . . . , a Sunday school and wide variety of less regular activities from lectures to movies to musical recitals to teas or fund-raising dances" (Amit, 2002: 268). Since this Armenian population interacts with non-Armenians, especially those born in Britain, their ethnicity was only a "part-time" ethnicity. Since the Armenians were not residentially organized, their Armenian identity and its reproduction in the next generation required effort and self-conscious recognition of their ethnic background. Families maintained extensive personal networks and contact with relatives in Lebanon and the United States in the manner of the transnational families we will describe below (Amit, 2002: 272). As Amit notes, "The transcendent unity of the 'diasporic' divided Armenians was established through the proclamation and narrative reiteration of a primordial connection" (2002: 275). The primordial connection, "relationship through blood," was reinforced by an interest in archeological or linguistic data that supported the Armenians as the indigenous inhabitants of Asia Minor as an Armenian Nation in antiquity, regardless of their present location. This is why they constitute a true diaspora, with a collective memory of their homeland that holds them together.

Sometimes, like the Indians or the Turks, men had to leave families and their homelands, in which employment was scarce, and go in search of work abroad. The Chinese and Lebanese represent the movement of people to other countries in search of trade opportunities (Cohen, 1997).

We have already noted the way Indian populations retained their Indian identity long after their periods of indenture in Fiji were over. "Overseas Indians" are to be found in other places in the world, including countries in East Africa and in Trinidad. "Overseas Chinese" have lived for generations in many countries in Southeast Asia, Indonesia, Papua New Guinea, Cuba, and elsewhere. These populations also constitute diasporas. They are well established in these countries and are frequently very successful economically. Their ethnic identity still remains Chinese or Indian. These "overseas" populations have been studied extensively by anthropologists, who have been concerned with the **adaptations** that the Chinese and Indians have made in different cultural settings and the means by which they have maintained their ethnic identities.

The overseas Chinese were originally viewed as "sojourners," that is, individuals who migrated because of economic opportunities, sending a portion of their wages home, with the intention of returning. They were identified in terms of the provinces or areas from which they came, like Canton, Hong Kong, or Shangtung, perhaps because the dynasty was Manchu, not Chinese. After the formation of the

An Indian spice seller living overseas in South Africa. The signs in his shop are in Afrikaans and English.

Chinese Republic their identity was shifted to a Chinese national identity. In the latter part of the twentieth century, after the Communist Revolution, the Chinese shed their sojourner status, but even though they emigrated with the intention of setting up permanent residences, they were still identified as overseas Chinese. The ethnic Chinese played an important role in economic development in East and Southeast Asia. Many of these overseas Chinese continue to identify with Chinese culture and language. There are also Chinese who have been identified as transnationals, in that they are interested in economic gain and opportunity wherever it can be found. Chinese transnational families exist in which siblings may be citizens of the different countries where their families have invested and established businesses. Kinship, culture, and commerce keep these families together. Many Chinese families have assimilated, since they have lived in the countries to which their ancestors moved for several generations. However, even these individuals are identified as Chinese, though they may not be culturally or linguistically Chinese. This is where what is identified as the "race" factor comes into play. Identity is "forced" on an individual as a consequence of appearance. Chinese who are remote from their culture may visit China, their ancestral home. Such encounters, "diasporic encounters," have begun to occur with some frequency, as we noted earlier.

More recently, the process of globalization has had an effect on diasporas. Air transportation has made international migration much easier. People migrate more frequently and, rather than permanently settle in another country, remain in continuous contact with their homelands, to which they often return upon retirement. Cities have become more international, more cosmopolitan in their acceptance of cultural differences. Notions of plural societies and multiculturalism in many places have coexisted with or replaced the idea of a national culture. Complete assimilation and the idea of the "melting pot" no longer characterize only our country but others as well.

The diaspora population of Germans in Russia, who were known as Volga Germans, retained their ethnic identity over centuries and recently were able to return to their homeland. In the eighteenth century, Germans were invited to settle in Russia to introduce their agricultural and organizational skills to a Russia that had just been opened up to Western ideas. When they first arrived, they lived in an area around the Volga River. Many were moved to Siberia during World War II, ending up in Kazakhstan, still remaining ethnically German. When Kazakhstan recently became independent from Russia, the nationalist hostility against Germans increased, as it did against European Russians. German laws guaranteed ethnic Germans full citizenship and automatic access to the liberal welfare system, while children of Turkish workers who were born in Germany did not have such rights until very recently. More than a million ethnic Germans have moved back to Germany since the end of the Cold War, only to encounter hostility because of the strain on economic resources, the lack of employment for them, and especially, their cultural differences. They have trouble with the German language, which is no longer their native language. Though encouraged by the German government to return, in their former homeland, the Volga Germans now constitute a separate ethnic group.

TRANSNATIONALISM

Transnationalism refers to family members who migrate from their homes to another country, such as the United States, and continue to maintain close contact with those left behind, thus forming new kinds of families (Kearney, 1995). Other relatives may follow them, in a pattern of chain migration. These family members now in the United States maintain a kind of dual existence. They live and work in our country, sometimes even in different cities, but remain members of their families back home, sending money, owning property, and even voting. They may become United States citizens and still maintain these close connections. In Chapter 6 we referred to this type of transnational family, which uses the mails, the telephone, and the airlines as ways of maintaining close contact.

In a recent Dominican election, individuals living in New York, the "absent Dominicans," were seen as playing an absolutely vital role in terms of not only their votes but also their financing of one candidate or another. Turkish people who migrated to Germany or the Netherlands as "guest workers" (sometimes referred to as "international commuters") also operate in this manner. Often, they may remain for many years, completely separate from the members of the host nations, without the possibility of citizenship. They bring over spouses for their children born in European countries, and they return to their homelands when they are pensioned off. German people have reacted negatively toward the Turkish people who have lived in their country for decades. The Turks are always seen as outsiders. One may expect that second- and third-generation Turks born in the Netherlands and in Germany will probably have a gradually weakening connection with their homeland. However, it is most likely that they will not be assimilated and, like other diaspora populations, will remain Turkish in identity, as have the overseas Indians and Chinese.

Terms such as *internal migration, transmigration, diasporas,* and *transnationalism* represent relatively new concepts in the anthropological vocabulary. However, anthropologists for decades have been studying ways of life of, among others, Haitian migrants in New York City, Turkish guest workers in Germany, Kalmyk Mongol immigrants in New Jersey, African-Americans in New York and Philadelphia neighborhoods, and Chinese in San Francisco. These new concepts are of assistance analytically, enabling anthropologists and others to have a better understanding of what is happening. For example, they permit us to describe more accurately a new type of family, the transnational family. By using the concept *diaspora populations,* we can more readily recognize the necessity of looking at African-Americans, African-Cubans, and African-Brazilians in terms of what they have in common.

CULTURAL IDENTITY REASSERTED AND TRANSFORMED

Most tribal people recognize that the introduction of changes from the industrialized world, which is itself constantly undergoing change, has had and will continue to have a profound effect on their cultures. Frequently, people are ready and willing to accept those changes that they perceive as immediately useful, such as steel axes. Sometimes change is forced upon them, and sometimes they forcibly resist change. One form of resistance is to run away, as the Kreen-akore of the tropical forest of Brazil ran from attempts to contact and pacify them. But you can only run so far and for so long, and eventually, even the Kreen-akore stopped running. Other tribal groups retain their identity and uniqueness by conscious efforts to preserve the traditional and customary and to reject the new. As the Menomini man defiantly said to the former Commissioner of Indian Affairs, "You can make the Menomini reservation into Menomini County but you can't make a white man out of me!"

It has been recently pointed out that predictions made in the first half of the twentieth century about what would happen to small-scale tribal societies have turned out to be incorrect (Sahlins, 1999). An earlier generation of anthropologists, typified by Boas and Malinowski, assumed that such societies could not withstand the onslaught of industrialization and Westernization, that they would either become like "us" or would disappear entirely. Throughout the northern areas of the globe, peoples who formerly practiced hunting and gathering have accepted modern technology to carry out the same subsistence practices. They use rifles, snowmobiles, and modern traps. They have transformed their technology without giving up many other aspects of their culture. The distribution of results of the hunt is carried out as it was done in the past. As we noted at several junctures, structure, like the pattern of distribution after the hunt, changes more slowly than content—the use of snowmobiles to hunt for the animals. For example, the relationship to animals of the Yup'ik-speaking people of Alaska has continued in the same manner used in the past. As one Yup'ik informant puts it, "When we bring animals into our houses, we treat them as guests" (Hensel, cited in Sahlins, 1999: xvi). Despite their long and intensive interaction with the global market economy, northern hunters like the Yup'ik "have not fundamentally altered their customary organization of production, modes of ownership and resource control, division of labor, or patterns of distribution and consumption; nor have their extended kinship and community bonds been dissolved or the economic and social obligations thereof fallen off; neither have social (cum 'spiritual') relations to nature disappeared; and they have not lost their cultural identities, not even when they live in white folks' towns" (Sahlins, 1999: xvii). The last point is a particularly important one. It is precisely when they live in "white folks' towns" and cities that there is a need to assert their cultural identity as different. The manner in which cultural identity is asserted differs according to the social context, for example, multicultural America versus ethnonationalistic European nations. As Sahlins states it, "I am simply making the point that the Eskimo are still there—and still Eskimo" (1999: vii). So are the Kwakiutl; so are the Trobrianders.

When a national identity is being built, political pressure is applied to suppress cultural differences, as noted in Chapter 9. Frequently, this pressure has the opposite effect from what was intended. In response to such pressure, cultural identity is often reasserted. Malaysia has been dominated by Moslem Malay speakers since it gained its independence, after World War II. The non-Moslem Iban, who live in Sarawak, that part of Malaysia on the island of Borneo, have recently begun to reassert their cultural identity. In the past, the Iban had been headhunters and pirates in the South China Sea. Today, when Iban boys leave home to go to school, search for work, or join the military or the police, that is seen as symbolically equivalent to the traditional journey into the unknown that an Iban boy made as part of his initiation into manhood. The Iban rite of passage from boyhood to manhood is being maintained, but in a new form. Iban politicians talk about preserving their traditional lifestyle while at the same time fighting for a larger share of civil service and other employment in the Malaysian government for their people.

People develop various ways to assert their continued cultural identity. The ways they separate themselves from the dominant society are known as **boundary maintenance mechanisms.** For example, the Rio Grande Pueblos of New Mexico—Tewa and Keres—who were in contact with the Spanish missionaries and explorers in the seventeenth century, have divided their religious life into two sep-

 *A sign can mark a social boundary between groups as well as between areas of land.*

arate domains: the indigenous one with its *katchinas* (religious figurines), priests, and *kivas* (underground religious chambers), which is operated in secret, closed off from the outside world and the eyes of the white man; and the village structure of the Catholic Church, which is part of the outside world. By preserving their language and much of their ritual structure, the Rio Grande Pueblos have been able to maintain their culture and their identity for more than 300 years, despite their nominal conversion to Catholicism and their integration into the U.S. economy. In contrast, the Navajo living in the same general area have been more receptive to changes, from their acceptance of livestock raising, silver working, and rug weaving from the Spaniards, to their embrace of new ideas brought back by Navajo veterans who served in World War II.

REVITALIZATION MOVEMENTS

Often, after changes have taken place in significant aspects of their culture, people recognize that they are in the process of being stripped of their own culture but have not been assimilated into the hegemonic culture. The uncertainty of their position makes them ready to follow a religious innovator, who has a more concrete vision of a better future. Out of these conditions, religious cults are born, which have been termed **nativistic movements** or **revitalization movements**.

These religious movements synthesize many traditional cultural elements with elements introduced from the dominant society.

An example of such a movement is the Handsome Lake religion of the Seneca, one of the six tribes that constituted the League of the Iroquois. By the end of the American Revolution, the Seneca had suffered partial devastation of their villages, decimation of their population, and the general dislocation of many aspects of their culture. In the 1780s, Handsome Lake, who was a sachem, or tribal leader, of the Seneca, had a series of visions, during which he had contact with the various Iroquois deities and foresaw what the life of the Seneca should be like in the future. What he envisioned was an amalgam of older Iroquois traditions and new ideas derived from the Quakers and other missionaries. The social organization of the Seneca had been based on matrilineal descent and uxorilocal postmarital residence. In contrast, Handsome Lake stressed the importance of the nuclear family and de-emphasized the matrilineage. The Quakers had come as missionaries to the Seneca, and many of their economic values, such as thrift, were adopted by Handsome Lake. At the same time, much traditional Seneca ceremonialism was also maintained. Handsome Lake had many adherents during his lifetime, although there were other political leaders who opposed and competed with him. After his death, his doctrines were written down and formed the Code of Handsome Lake. Though it was revolutionary when it first appeared, over the centuries the Handsome Lake religion, as it came to be called, became a conservative force as more and more changes were accepted by the Seneca. Today the supporters of the Handsome Lake religion are among the more conservative members of the Seneca tribe living on their reservation in upstate New York. What began as a vision of Seneca accommodation to the culture of the white population was transformed over time into a bulwark resisting change.

Cargo Cults

A particular type of revitalization movement that has occurred repeatedly in Melanesia is the **cargo cult.** Cargo cults made their appearance early in the twentieth century. However, they proliferated after World War II, which was a period of more intensive contact with outsiders, particularly with the American soldiers who drove out the Japanese and used the islands of Melanesia as a staging base. The Melanesians were astonished by the technological might of the Western world, as represented by the American armed forces. Like all revitalization movements, these cargo cults revolved about a charismatic leader or prophet who had a vision. This vision usually involved conversations with the spirits of deceased ancestors, and the prophet foretold that the ancestors would rise from the dead. At that time, black Melanesians would get white skins, and white people either would become black or would be driven into the seas. The ancestors would arrive in a big ship or plane, bringing with them an inexhaustible cargo of steel axes, razor blades, tobacco, tinned beef, rice, and rifles. More recently, the expected cargoes include transistor radios, wristwatches, and motorcycles. People built piers into the sea, erected huge warehouses, and even prepared landing strips when planes were expected. They neglected their gardening and often killed off their pigs, since the expectation was that no one would have to work anymore after the cargo arrived. Sometimes elements of Christianity were included in the visions of the prophet, so that Jesus Christ was expected to arrive along with the cargo.

Like all other revitalization movements, cargo cults are a synthesis of the old and the new. In a situation of culture contact where tribal peoples find themselves helpless and overwhelmed by the power of the dominant society, a prophet appears who preaches turning to the ancestors to seek their help in acquiring the very things that make the dominant society so powerful. The cargo is seen as the secret of the white people's power. Like all forms of religion that attempt to explain the inexplicable, cargo cults attempt to offer a supernatural explanation of what it is that makes white people so powerful. Converts to the cargo cult have faith that the secret of white people's power, the cargo, will come to them as a result of supernatural forces. Cargo cults are religious movements, though many of them are short-lived. At the same time, however, they make statements about power relations; for when the cargo comes, the present situation will be reverse—black will become white, and the powerless will become powerful. Cargo cults exemplify how the force and emotive power of religious belief can add great strength to a political movement. In the past, such religious cults in East and West Africa were dreaded by colonial powers. Nativistic movements, revitalization movements, and cargo cults represent responses to colonialism that combine cultural continuity as well as cultural change. The particular forms they take not only represent responses to colonialism but also reveal a great deal about the cultures in which they are found.

REBUILDING CULTURAL IDENTITY

Sometimes, a group loses everything except its sense of its own cultural identity. The Mashantucket Pequot Tribal Nation of Connecticut is such a group. The Pequot were nearly obliterated as a people in the Pequot War of 1637 and stripped of most of their land. However, they were able to demonstrate to the Department of the Interior that their tribal existence never ceased, enabling them to receive recognition as a tribe from the American government on October 18, 1983. The introduction of high-stakes gambling in 1992 has made the tribe wealthy and influential and has enabled members to fund events that are part of a conscious attempt to "recreate" their culture. They have approached the task of cultural building or rebuilding on two different fronts. First, they have sponsored Mashantucket Pequot historical conferences, which bring together scholars to discuss topics such as the history of the Indians of New England and the current state of knowledge about native peoples of New England and their adjustment to the encounter with Euro-Americans. They have established their own museum, which focuses on Native American culture in general and on Pequot culture in particular. Second, they have sponsored a powwow, or *schemitzun*, translated as "Feast of Green Corn and Dance," which brings together American Indian performers from many tribes all over the country. The performers were attracted by the $200,000 purse, the richest

The Mashantucket Pequot Tribal Nation dancers at a tribal powwow, or schemitzun.

purse offered on the competitive powwow circuit. After almost 300 years, the traditions of the Pequot are almost forgotten, along with their language and ceremonial songs and dances. The Pequots are endeavoring to re-create their own culture by borrowing and adapting what they can from other tribes. The process the Pequot are now going through, as they attempt to construct a tribal or cultural identity, is identical to that involved in the fashioning of ethnic identity that is now going on in multicultural America.

BLOOD, CULTURE, AND RACE

The Cherokee of Oklahoma illustrate the way identity can be "socially and politically constructed and how that process is embedded in ideas of blood, color and race" (Sturm, 2002: 2). The federal government requires that Native Americans must have one-quarter or more of Indian blood, meaning that one of their grandparents had to be Indian, in order for them to obtain social services such as health care, housing, and food commodities. They need to present a certificate in which the Bureau of Indian Affairs and their tribe have authenticated the fact that they are Indians. Despite this "racial" restriction, the Cherokee nation has a multiracial population of more than 175,000 members of which as many as 87,000 have less than 1/16 Cherokee blood. Cherokee tribal law merely requires that an individual be a lineal descendant of a tribal member, with no blood requirement at all (Sturm, 2002: 2). Informants see blood as the most important thing about Cherokee identity. One may ask why blood is significant in this situation, since the range in the population is from full-blood to 1/2,048 (Sturm, 2002: 201).

Before the arrival of Europeans, the Cherokee had had a class of slaves who were captives taken during intertribal warfare. If they were adopted, then they became full members of the tribe; otherwise, they were individuals in bondage. After the arrival of the Europeans, a large-scale Indian slave trade developed, whereby individuals captured from other communities were exchanged for European goods. By the middle of the eighteenth century with the African slave trade at its height, the Cherokee shifted to a trade in runaway African slaves. In fact, the Cherokee themselves had African slaves up until 1863. Euro-American conceptualizations about race were adopted despite the fact that sexual relations and intermarriage between Africans and Cherokee had begun to take place. The council of the Cherokee nation passed an act forbidding such intermarriages as well as intermarriage with whites.

Today, tribal membership is claimed by multiracial individuals, some of whom are "black" and the descendants of "freedmen" and former slaves, and others who are "white." Though they may be able to document the necessary descent by blood, they may still be rejected by some Cherokee and other Native Americans. The question of who is to be counted as Cherokee is an important one. To Native Americans like the Cherokee, blood is the "measure of racial, cultural, social and national belonging . . . [and] Federal Indian Policy and Cherokee national policy both have fetishized and objectified Native-American blood" (Sturm, 2002: 203). Cherokee have conflated blood, race, color, and culture, with blood becoming a "particularly potent substance for Cherokee identity" (Sturm, 2002: 203).

ETHNOGENESIS

Contact and colonialism can produce a process by which a people assert a new ethnic identity and take on a new name. This is known as **ethnogenesis.** William Sturtevant first used the term to refer to the process through which the Seminole historically differentiated and separated themselves from the Creek, the larger group of which they were a part. Nancy Hickerson (1996) has noted that the historic record reveals the disappearance, often quite abruptly, of certain peoples (like the Mayan Empire) and the sudden appearance of others (like the Scythians), likening this process to the three-stage sequence that Van Gennup proposed for rites of passage, discussed in Chapter 10. The first phase is separation, the severing of a group's previous loyalties; the second is a liminal phase during which surviving ties wither away and new ones are initiated; the third is the birth of a new identity, which is affirmed through the adoption of new rituals and a new mythology to validate them. This last phase "may obscure all traces of the earlier history (or histories) of the population and even promote a belief in a miraculous origin or special creation" (Hickerson, 1996: 70). Manipulation of the historical past is one of the distinctive characteristics of the process of ethnogenesis. As Hill observes, "Ethnogenesis is not merely a label for the historical emergence of culturally distinct peoples but a concept encompassing peoples' simultaneously cultural and political struggles to create enduring identities in general contexts of radical change and discontinuity" (1996: 1).

In the ebb and flow of populations after the arrival of the Europeans in the New World, ethnogenesis occurred many times as groups were physically dislocated from the areas they had traditionally exploited. During the sixteenth and seventeenth centuries, Tanoan-speaking people known as the Jumano, who were bison hunters and traders, were exploiting an area east of the Rio Grande in the southern Plains. As a consequence of unsuccessful warfare with the Apache over trade routes and access to trade centers, they appear to have dispersed, many moving north. The use of the name Jumano then declined, but subgroups with their own names continued. The term Kiowa later appeared as the label for these groups, now in their new homeland in the Platte-Arkansas River area. Today, the people of the modern Kiowa nation have an origin myth that begins with their ancestors' emergence from the underworld in a cold land far north—thought to be in the Yellowstone River Valley. The ancestors subsequently moved south and east to their historic territory (Hickerson, 1996: 83). Here we see a sequence in which the Jumano disappear and "die" and a new people, the Kiowa nation, are born, following the rites-of-passage pattern described above. In several instances earlier we have referred to the metaphor of "being born again" and this is an example of a people being born again.

ETHNONATIONALISM

The process of ethnogenesis not only is applicable to the tribal or ethnic groups in the New World but also parallels the development of **ethnonationalism** in Europe. When European ethnonationalists are able to take control of the state, they co-opt the state's use of force, which they now turn to their own nationalistic purposes. Ethnogenesis in Europe has a long history. The French Revolution may be seen as "the expression of emerging French national self-identity" (Pickett, 1996: 12). Under the banner of "Liberty, Equality, and Fraternity," Napoleon brutally brought France's "civilizing principles" to the rest of Europe. Though pretending to spread universal principles, he was actually expanding the scope of French nationalism and hegemony. As often happened throughout history, one group's ethnogenic awakening produced a reaction among that group's neighbors. German ethnogenesis and the movement toward German unification in the latter half of the nineteenth century was a reaction to what was happening in France. This led Germany to develop a sense of its own special destiny.

One may argue that nationalism's goals are diametrically opposed to the universalistic ideals of Christianity and more recently of socialism, which apply equally to all humanity. As Pickett points out, "Ethnogenesis is hostile to knowledge" (1996: 16). Ethnogenesis ignores science in favor of its newly created myths; it denies history in order to distort it and control it. French hegemony under Napoleon—that is, nationalism under the guise of universal principles—proved ephemeral. In the same way, Soviet Russian hegemony—Russian nationalism under the guise of universal socialist principles—has also disappeared. In the next chapter, we will examine the various nations and ethnonational movements that have taken place, as well as the ways ethnicity and nationalism have become battlegrounds all over the world.

SUMMARY

- Internal migration refers to population movements within a nation-state.

- Transmigration refers to populations who migrate far from their homelands to many different parts of the world. Assimilation means that they completely adopt the language and culture of their new country.

- The process of migration to a new land, to a new culture, often involves remaking one's self and creating a new identity for one's self.

- Some migrants may maintain their original ethnic identity for centuries and today they are known as diaspora populations.

- Transnationalism refers to family members' migrating from their homes to another country, such as the United States, and continuing to maintain close contact with those left behind, thus forming new kinds of families which cross-national boundaries.

- Many small-scale societies that have become part of nation-states have transformed their technology without giving up other aspects of their culture. It is precisely when they live in "white folks' towns" and cities that there is a need to assert their cultural identity—that which makes them different.

- People develop various ways to assert their continued cultural identity. The ways they separate themselves from the dominant society are known as boundary maintenance mechanisms.

- After changes have taken place in significant aspects of their culture, people recognize that they are in the process of being stripped of their own culture but have not been assimilated into the hegemonic culture. In their uncertainty they turn to a religious innovator who has a more concrete vision of a better future. In this way are born religious cults, which have been termed nativistic movements or revitalization movements. These religious movements synthesize many traditional cultural elements with elements introduced from the dominant society.

• Cargo cults, one type of nativistic movement, are a synthesis of the old and the new in which a prophet appears who preaches turning to the ancestors to seek their help in acquiring the very things that make the dominant society so powerful. The cargo is seen as the secret of the white people's power.

• Contact and colonialism can produce a process by which a people assert a new ethnic identity and take on a new name. This is known as ethnogenesis.

• Ethnonationalism is like ethnogensis in that new forms of national identity are created in Europe by peoples using history or sometimes bogus historical myths, and in this way attempt to become a nation-state.

 SUGGESTED READINGS

Benedict, Jeff. *Without Reservation: The Making of America's Most Powerful Indian Tribe and the World's Largest Casino.* New York: Harper Collins, 2000. The history of how the Mashantucket Pequot became the world's richest American Indian tribe.

Cardero-Guzman, Hector R., Robert Smith, and Ramon Grosfoguel. *Migration, Transnationalization, and Race in a Changing New York.* Philadelphia: Temple University Press, 2001. A series of essays describing the way in which New York has been changing as a consequence of migration and changing ethnic and racial dynamics.

Chirot, Daniel, and Anthony Reed (eds.). *Chinese and Jews in the Modern Transformation of Southeast Asia and Central Europe.* Seattle: University of Washington Press, 1997. A series of essays on the Chinese and Jewish diaspora populations and their entrepreneurial success, as well as the scapegoating and violence these groups have encountered.

Ebaugh, Helen, and Janet Chafetz (eds.). *Religion across Borders: Transnational Immigrant Networks.* Walnut Creek, CA: AltaMira Press, 2002 A series of case studies dealing with the role religion plays in creating transnational networks that cross international borders.

Kennedy, Paul, and Victor Roudometof (eds.). *Communities across Borders: New Immigrants and Transnational Cultures.* New York: Routledge, 2002. How present-day migrants create new forms of ethnic communities that are transnational. A series of case studies looks at immigrants in various parts of the world, including Mexico, the Netherlands, and the United States.

Rumbaut, Rubin, and Alejandro Portes (eds.). *Ethnicities: Children of Immigrants in America.* Berkeley: University of California Press, 2001. A series of papers considering the way in which second-generation immigrants adapt in the United States and deal with the question of assimilation.

Sturm, Circe. *Blood Politics: Race, Culture, and Identity in the Cherokee Nation of Oklahoma.* Berkeley: University of California Press, 2002. How the use of blood defined who was and was not a Cherokee.

Werbner, Pnina. *Imagined Diasporas among Manchester Muslims: The Public Performance of Pakistani Transnational Identity Politics.* Santa Fe, NM: School of American Research Press, 2002. Concerns the ways in which Pakistani immigrants in Britain have maintained more or less separate communities from the British and the role that their Islamic religion has played in their adaptation.

http://www.foxwoods.com/pequots/mptn_home.html The home page of the Mashan-tucket Pequots, which has links to Mashantucket Pequot history, their museum, and details regarding the annual Schemitzun ceremony.

http://users.erols.com/guerig An online journal to enable the dispersed members of the worldwide Armenian community to meet, share information, and discuss matters of mutual interest.

http://hindustan.net/exchange This website provides a dating service for overseas Indians in order to ensure ethnic endogamy.

http://www.iconscreen.de/cargobox/sites/cargocult2.html Discusses contemporary mining activities in Papua New Guinea as a source of the origin of new cargo cults.

15

Ethnicity, Ethnic Conflict, Race, and Nationalism

Abroad and at Home

Independent nation-states are the successors of colonies in the contemporary world, as we noted earlier. The goal of these new nations has been to create a national culture that supersedes or incorporates "tribal peoples," who then are transformed into ethnic groups within the new nation-state. We have pointed out that culture is the integrating concept in anthropology, and cultural identity was the means by which individuals identified themselves. In today's pluralistic, multicultural world, the terms *ethnic* and *ethnic identity*, as a way of identifying oneself, are frequently used as alternatives to *culture* and *cultural identity*.

For example, in the previous chapter we saw the way the German colonial government established a single political entity, like New Ireland, where previously there had been independent, autonomous villages speaking different languages. The word **tribe** was originally used by anthropologists to refer to cultural groupings, each of which spoke its own language. Anthropologists now understand that tribes were, in effect, created by colonial governments to enable them to deal more efficiently with groups with a common culture and language but whose most complex political groupings were villages or bands (Fried, 1975). In the new nation-states, identity can be framed in terms of a hierarchy in which the tribal identity, now ethnic identity, becomes less inclusive and national identity, more inclusive.

The terms *ethnic identity, ethnic group, ethnogenesis, ethnonationalism, nationalism, multiculturalism,* and *race* are not only conceptual tools used by anthropologists and other social scientists but also part of the language of television news programs and newspaper headlines—they are themes for our times. Ethnic groups share common cultural norms, values, identities, patterns of behavior, and language. Their members recognize themselves as a separate group and are so recognized by others. They may or may not be politicized. Ethnic identity, or ethnicity, is seen by some analysts as based on primordial sentiments, that is, sentiments that are conceptualized as going back to ancient times and that tie group members to one another emotionally, despite persistent attempts to assimilate them. To others, ethnic identity is entirely situational, utilized in some contexts but not in others. In Europe, ethnic groups were often also territorially defined. Influenced by ideas of ethnonationalism, they frequently sought political autonomy and even the freedom to form their own nation-states. Czechoslovakia was originally part of the Austro-Hungarian Empire, but became independent after World War I. It remained a separate nation-state until recently, when the Slovakian people decided that they wanted to be an independent nation. Today there is the Czech Republic and Slovakia—two separate nation-states.

Religion is one of the important factors serving to distinguish one ethnic group from another. In a number of examples discussed below, we will see that in addition to ethnic differences, meaning cultural differences, there are also religious differences. When religious differences are present, the ethnic conflict is heightened and intensified. Fighting the other ethnic group, the "infidel," becomes a sacred mission. Each side finds support in the moral authority of its own religion for continuing the conflict and for using violent action against those whom it characterizes as heretics. The former Yugoslavia illustrates this very well. The dominant Serbs are an Orthodox population, who view themselves historically as Christian martyrs who suffered under the Muslim Ottoman Empire. Bosnians and Albanians, in Kosovo, are Muslims. Croatians, on the other hand, are Roman Catholics. Despite similarities in language and culture among these ethnic groups, their religious differences have exacerbated the ethnic conflict and are sometimes used today to justify even the raping of women of the other ethnic group.

Ethnic differences may also parallel class differences. In some societies, the underclass is a separate ethnic or racial group. Under those conditions, ethnic conflict may be characterized as class conflict. In addition, race and racial classifications often are a basis for making distinctions between ethnic groups. Many people tend to think of race as a scientific concept based on biological systems of classification. In reality the definition and form of the concept of race differs from one society to another. This means that race is socially constructed. For example, in Brazil, color of complexion, which is one aspect of the concept of race, forms an element in the conceptualization of status and group. The lighter the complexion, the higher the class status of the individual. In the United States, an individual, on the basis of complexion color, is categorized as either white or African-American. Genealogy is also involved in the assignment of people to these two categories. A person with African-American ancestry whose complexion is indistinguishable from a white person's may decide to pass as a white person. If the African-American ancestors of such a person are then revealed, he or she can no longer pass as white and will be categorized by others as African-American. The social construction of race is illustrated by the fact that while in Brazil race is a continuum, in the United States it is clearly a bipolar category. Forces of racism work to keep the two categories of white and African-American separate. As anthropologist John Gwaltney's African-American informants in *Drylongso* expressed it, oppressed by the white majority, they were one of two "nations" in the United States (Gwaltney, 1993). Social scientists have echoed this point, from Gunnar Myrdal, who called America's treatment of African-Americans *An American Dilemma*, to Andrew Hacker's view of *Two Na-*

tions: Black and White, Separate, Hostile, Unequal. Later in this chapter we will see how African-Americans, since the 1960s, have been creatively constructing cultural aspects of their identity.

NATION-BUILDING

The previous chapter ended with a discussion of ethnogenesis and ethnonationalism. The idea of *nation-building* began in Europe, the **nation** being defined as a sovereign political state with a single national culture (Gellner, 1983; Hobsbawm, 1992). France, Italy, and England began to develop their nation-states before other European countries. The development of national cultures involved conscious culture-building on the part of the hegemonic group in political control of the state—the goal being the elimination of regional ethnic cultures in favor of a national culture. Anthropological research has revealed the way this process of conscious, national culture-building, in Africa, for example, takes place in various media such as radio, TV, and newspapers.

Even archaeology is utilized in the service of creating national identity, as is the case in Pakistan and Israel. States choose to emphasize one aspect of their archeological past rather than another, in keeping with the messages about the past, which the archaeological results are meant to support. Each state tells its own myth about its past. In Israel, archaeology has always served the function of conveying the Israeli myth about the rights of the Israelis to the land. Israel chooses to emphasize archaeological research related to religious rather than secular sites. It concentrates on the periods of the First and Second Temples, that is, the Iron Age through early Roman times, ignoring earlier sites such as the Mount Carmel caves where Neanderthal skeletal material was found. Archaeological sites, like that of Masada, are used as the locations for national ceremonies to imbue Israeli national values. Emphasis on this particular archaeological information builds a mythic cultural past for Israel. In Pakistan, during the colonial period, Buddhist sites such as Taxila were important locations for archaeological investigation. When the Islamic state of Pakistan was established, there was no longer any scientific interest in these sites by the Pakistani state, which emphasized only its Muslim historical roots. As Kohl points out, "Control of the past provides a source of legitimization for control of the present" (1999: 236).

The imposed national culture was usually that of the hegemonic group. In Great Britain, that meant that the language and culture of the English, the politically dominant group, were to supersede the Celtic cultures and languages of Wales, Scotland, and Ireland. Regional differences between the people of Cornwall and Yorkshire should disappear in favor of standard English language and culture. The same process occurred in France and somewhat later in Germany and in Eastern Europe. Despite attempts to impose a national culture emanating from the capital, London or Paris, regional cultural and dialect differences persisted and national identity never really fully penetrated the countryside, especially the more remote areas. More recently, in Great Britain, the Scottish people have moved beyond the assertion of their ethnic identity. The establishment of the Scottish Parliament is an expression of their movement to ethnonationalism. Wales now has its own national assembly, and the Welsh language is taught to youngsters in public schools and can be heard in radio broadcasts.

Sometimes the process of nation-building involves the breakup of older empires. For example, in the nineteenth century the intellectual elites in the Czech area of the Austro-Hungarian Empire sought the freedom to have their own nation-state. Through the process of ethnogenesis, they set out to rediscover and re-create a national cultural repertoire, consciously selecting cultural items, often from rural folk culture, that they identified as Czech. Some people went to the trouble of inventing a Czech ancestry using bogus early records, such as medieval manuscripts supposedly discovered in Bohemia in 1817 and 1818 (Lass, 1988). The French philosopher Renan has sarcastically defined the nation as a group of people held together by an erroneous view of the past and a shared hatred of neighbors surrounding them. Renan's remarks also relate to the idea of ethnocentrism, introduced in Chapter 1, the notion that one's own language and culture are superior to all others. Both nations and ethnic groups can be ethnocentric with regard to their neighbors. In the language of ethnocentrism, the people in the next valley are seen as practicing bizarre rituals, stealing babies, and copulating like animals. It is often said that superstition is the religion of the people in the next valley.

The process of nation-building accelerated in Europe after World War I with the creation of several nations out of both the old Ottoman Turkish and Austro-Hungarian Empires. However, the new nations that resulted, such as Czechoslovakia, Poland, Romania, and Yugoslavia, ended up being multiethnic states, like the new states in Africa. These states included one dominant ethnic group and several minority groups. For example, Poland included Germans, Ruthenians, Kashubians, and Jews as minority groups. In Czechoslovakia, the Czechs were the dominant group. Recently, they and the Slovaks decided that they wanted to be separate nation-states. Czechoslovakia was peacefully divided into the Czech and Slovak nations. However, even within the Czech Republic there are Moravian and Silesian people who demand a measure of autonomy and self-government (Bugajski, 1994: 306–310). Gypsies, present in considerable numbers in the former Czechoslovakia, are not welcome in either the Czech Republic or Slovakia. The mayor of the Slovakian town of Usti nad Labem in northern Bohemia had a wall built to separate the Gypsies from ethnic Slovaks. Yugoslavia was another nation-state created after World War I; its borders encompassed a congeries of ethnic groups lumped together at that time on the basis of the ethnogenesis of a South Slavic identity. The nation was under the hegemony of the Serbs. It was a union of several different ethnic groups speaking very closely related languages (Serbo-Croatian) but divided by religious and cultural differences. They never surrendered their distinct ethnic identities. The Yugoslavian communist state, based on universal principles, began to fall apart after the death of Tito, the communist head of state. Croatia, Slovenia, and Bosnia, asserting their ethnonationalism, became separate states, with Serbian minorities. Only Serbia and Montenegro remain as Yugoslavia.

Both the process of nation-building and its obverse—in which nation-states, once created, then collapse—are to be found not only in Europe but also in Africa and Asia (Fox, 1990). These nation-states include the tribes, or Fourth World Peoples, whom anthropologists have been studying since the beginning of the discipline; but now the focus is on the adjustment of these societies to the penetration of the newly developed national culture. Nations are composed of one politically autonomous ethnic group, while **state** is the term used to refer to any politically autonomous entity, whether it is composed of one or many different ethnic groups. The term **nation-state** is used when nation and state are coterminous.

A multicultural state is composed of several ethnic groups, none of which is dominant. Instead, all are ideologically considered equal. In the nineteenth century, when the United States welcomed large numbers of immigrants seeking refuge from persecution, they became Americans, part of what was referred to as the "melting pot." American, as a national identity, was being constructed, and an American culture was developing. However, since the 1960s we have come to think of ourselves differently. Most of us now view ourselves as a multicultural society. This means a recognition of diversity, highlighting "neglected aspects of our social history, particularly the histories of women and minorities" (Trotman, 2002: ix). Other nations, for example, Great Britain, are reflecting on whether they have become multicultural states. In contrast, the French state has officially rejected multiculturalism. However, as noted in Chapter 9, the French legal system has accepted Islamic law in cases involving family law. The Muslims from North Africa who have settled in France are challenging the official suppression of ethnically based identity. While Germany does not consider itself a multicultural state, it is, in effect, beginning to move in that direction in an interesting manner. The Turkish migrant workers brought their cuisine to Germany when they migrated. Donner kebab, which consists of thin cuts of lamb laid on pita flat bread and steeped in *tsatsiki* sauce, a favorite Turkish dish, has now become a German fast food. The factories that mass-produce the German version of this dish for stalls and restaurants in many German cities surpass the sales of McDonald's and Burger King combined. For many Germans, eating donner kebab represents their first contact with Turkish culture. However, it does not seem to have moved the Germans to think about their country in multicultural terms. Multiculturalism is distinctly different from the characteristically European situation in which one ethnic group is the national core. In that case, the values of the dominant group constitute the national culture, politically and religiously, and that group dominates smaller minorities, creating two classes of citizenship.

As noted above, in Great Britain today, political power and linguistic recognition have now been given to the Scottish and Welsh people. However, those people who migrated to Great Britain from other parts of the commonwealth have been dealt with in a different way. Earlier waves of people coming to England as conquerors, like the French, left marks of their culture and language, as described in Chapter 3. Other migrants, in later centuries, have been assimilated into mainstream English culture and life, so that by the middle of the twentieth

Muslim women wearing the traditional head scarf walk to the mosque, located in a former brake parts factory, in Avlnay-sous-Bois, just northeast of Paris. Though 5 million Muslims live in France today, it does not consider itself a multicultural nation.

century there was a widespread belief that British culture was homogeneous, though, in reality, it was dominated by English culture.

After World II, large numbers of migrants from the Caribbean and, more particularly, from India and Pakistan came to Great Britain to better themselves economically, accepting work that the English no longer wished to do. Though it was originally thought that they would return to their homelands, instead, they sent for their families and settled permanently. Language and religious differences set apart the South Asians, especially, from the rest of the population. Islam provides its adherents with a communal way of life with separate religious institutions—mosques, separate schools, the right to wear their type of clothing and eat *halal* meat—all of which challenges assimilation. As we noted in Chapter 5, Islamic Sufi adherents in Manchester periodically parade to demonstrate the way they have "conquered" new territory as well as their right of religious expression. Further, in terms of the ideas of Edward Said, "orientalist" concepts of the West have defined Muslims as perpetually the "other" in opposition to and inferior to the Christian white West—Europe and America. Though the British authorities have made concessions in the direction of multiculturalism, British Muslim activists have been challenging the Islamophobia, which has not diminished with time (Ellis and

Khan, 1999: 45). In fact, since 9/11 Islamophobia in Britain has increased. State support for separate Muslim schools has been an especially thorny issue. Multiculturalism, as currently practiced in Britain, still does not allow for full participation in the society if one chooses a public Muslim identity rather than an accommodation that confines one's Muslim identity to the domestic and local community environments. Though the dialogue of multiculturalism is voiced, Britain has remained essentially a homogeneous, Western, Christian society rather than a pluralist society accepting of people who are significantly different in religion or race. Anthropological research has revealed that Muslims and immigrants from the Caribbean wish to retain a separate, hyphenated identity while participating fully in the institutions of the society. This is what multiculturalism is all about. "The British government has emphasized equality of opportunity while respecting and even celebrating cultural differences . . . [while at the same time it] has made taking on a common sense of British nationhood by the immigrant population a critical measure of progress in its push for racial integration and assimilation " (*New York Times*, April 4, 2002). Economic advancement is not the same for the "ethnic population" as it is for British whites, since a racial barrier exists, and non-whites with PhDs find it hard to find work suitable to their education level. The British white population and British ethnic minorities still lead mostly separate lives and the hyphenated Britons do not feel that they are a part of Britain. The education system is sometimes the only arena that is multiethnic. Links with those "back home" is still maintained by sending remittances and by frequent visits.

Northern Ireland is politically part of Great Britain, though the Catholics would like it to be part of Ireland. Every year, Protestant men march during the summer on a holiday that marks a military triumph over the Catholics. Much as the Muslims march to mark their space (as we noted in Chapter 5), the Protestants march, or attempt to march, through an Irish neighborhood to mark their space.

ETHNICITY AND NATIONALISM AFTER COMMUNISM

After the Russian Revolution in 1917, the Union of Soviet Socialist Republics was created out of the Russian Empire. This empire had been based on the conquest of many non-Russian peoples, just as the Ottoman Empire had included many non-Turkish people and the Austro-Hungarian Empire had incorporated peoples who were neither Austrians nor Hungarians. This example reveals the dialectic between hegemonic state culture and different ethnic cultures who desire to have their own nation-states. The Marxist Soviet government tried to construct a Soviet culture as the national culture of the Union of Soviet Socialist Republics. This Soviet culture included the idea that workers of the world should unite as a class and rise above national sentiments. The government's attitude toward the different "nationalities" vacillated between the celebration of ethnic differences and the suppression of ethnic national identity, which was seen as challenging Soviet identity. Under the freedom of Gorbachov's glasnost, ethnic identity and nationalist sentiment could be expressed.

When the Soviet Union crumbled at the end of the 1980s, its 15 constituent re-publics—Lithuania, Armenia, Georgia, Uzbekistan, and the others, including Rus-sia itself—became independent sovereign states. Ethnic minorities, who formerly had had their own autonomous republics or autonomous oblasts (districts) con-tained within the newly established independent states, now demanded self-determination in the form of cultural and political autonomy or independence. Such ethnic minorities exemplify ethnonationalism as they strive to establish in-dependent sovereign states.

These identities, which had been suppressed during the Communist era, are what propel politics in all the areas of the former Soviet Union today. The newly independent republics must cope with the legacy of 70 years of Soviet rule. This means that they must deal with larger or smaller numbers of individuals who are culturally Russian or members of other ethnic groups who migrated there or were moved there by the Soviet government. They must also contend with territorial borders that were drawn by the Soviet state. Within the Russian state itself, eth-nonationalism has emerged and is being dealt with.

The Chechens present an unusual sort of problem involving ethnonationalism and ethnic violence, which has long historical roots. The Chechens are a Muslim people, speaking a Caucasian language totally unrelated to Russian, who were conquered by the czarist empire in the nineteenth century. They resisted Russian domination and control. During World War II the Chechens sided with Nazi Ger-many and fought against their enemy Russia. In response to their traitorous ac-tions, Joseph Stalin deported many of them to Siberia and few lived to return home. The eve of the post-Soviet Russia found the Chechens, an ethic minority fighting for self-determination, facing the majority Russians who considered them gangsters and traitors. The Russian government is determined not to give them their independence—in contrast to what they did with Tajiks, Uzbeks, Kirgyz, Turkomen, and others. The Chechens have turned to fighting for their freedom and independence. Terror is one of the weapons they use. After the occurrences of 9/11, the American government grouped Chechen revolutionaries with other Islamic terrorists like Al Queda, to the delight of the Russian government. We send Special Forces to aid Georgia in its fight against rebellious Muslim groups, which spread from Chechnya into Georgia. At the same time, as we shall see, the Georgians are fighting another Muslim people within the state of Georgia, the Abkhasians.

Joseph Stalin—who ruled the Soviet Union as a dictator from the mid-1920s to 1953, when he died—had borders drawn between Armenia and Azerbaijan in such a way as to prevent the emergence of a Transcaucasian Federation. The area has had a complicated history, having been under the Muslim rule of either the Ot-toman or Persian Empires for centuries. The enclave of Nagorno-Karabakh, within the territory of Azerbaijan, had long been occupied by Armenians. The Azerbaija-nis not only prevented the Armenians of Nagorno-Karabakh from culturally ex-pressing themselves, but also discriminated against them because they were different in culture and in religion. Armenians speak an Indo-European language, are Christians, and are intellectually oriented toward the West, while Azerbaijanis, or Azeris, as they are also called, speak a Turkic language and are Muslims. Here, religious differences exacerbated ethnic differences. With glasnost and the lifting of Soviet repression, the Armenians of Nagorno-Karabakh began a campaign for the transfer of their territory to Armenia (Dudwick, 1992). There was also strong support for this in Armenia as part of a national movement expressing resentment at what was seen as the Russification of Armenian culture. The fact that Nagorno-Karabakh was the location of ancient Armenian shrines made it particularly significant in what became a resurgence of Armenian nationalism. Demonstrations by Armenians in Nagorno-Karabakh were met with anti-Armenian violence on the part of Azerbaijanis, and conflict between the two groups escalated. Armenia and Azerbaijan became independent states when the Soviet Union fell apart. Open warfare broke out between the armies of the two states over the fate of Nagorno-Karabakh. The assassination of the prime minister of Armenia has set back the delicate negotiations that have been taking place between Armenia and Azerbaijan over the future of Nagorno-Karabakh. Members of the Armenian-American diaspora support a nonviolent settlement, and recently, the Armenian government has enlisted their support to this end. This ethnic conflict, which began in 1988, has not yet been settled.

The new nation-state of Georgia, in the Caucasus Mountains south of Russia, contains several non-Georgian ethnic groups with sizable populations, such as the South Ossetians and the Abkhazians. In addition, Georgia has ethnic Russians, Armenians, and Azerbaijanis. Meskhetians originally lived in Georgia but were expelled by Stalin after World War II and sent to live in Uzbekistan. Under Soviet rule, the Abkhazians and Ossetians had some degree of political and cultural autonomy, though the Georgians were politically dominant in the Republic. The Abkhazians are linguistically and culturally distinct from the Georgians, though they are physically similar to West Georgians (Benet, 1974). Their mythic history stresses their distinctiveness. However, they have historically been oriented toward the Mediterranean since Abkhazia is on the Black Sea. Christianity entered Abkhazia in the sixth century, and Islam much later, in the fifteenth and sixteenth centuries. While most Abkhazians are nominally Muslim, a small minority have remained Christian. Abkhazians retain their cultural distinctiveness through their style of dress, dance, folklore, legends, kinship system, and other cultural items. Their exceedingly difficult language, which Russians, Georgians, and Armenians rarely learn, also serves to set them apart. Within the Abkhazian Autonomous Republic, the Abkhazians form only a quarter of the population; the other three-quarters are Russians, Georgians, Greeks, Turks, and Armenians.

The forces of ethnonationalism propelled the Georgian Republic to independence. However, the attempts of the Abkhazians and South Ossetians, with their own ethnonationalistic feelings, to gain their independence or autonomy were seen as threats to the Georgian state and Georgian political hegemony. Though political leadership at the local level was in the hands of Abkhazians and South Ossetians, they were overrepresented in low-class manual and rural occupations (Jones, 1992). The Georgians considered these people ethnic groups not entitled to their own sovereignty. In fact, all those who were not ethnic Georgians were seen as having no rights, as foreigners in Georgia. South Ossetians and others, such as

Fighters for Abkhazian independence preparing for attack by Georgian forces who will reincorporate them into the Georgian state.

Russians, were viewed as invaders who should return to where they came from. Government policy favored Georgian expansion into non-Georgian areas. The aim of the educational system was to indoctrinate all students in Georgian language and culture, regardless of their ethnic background. The Abkhazians and Ossetians declared their independence, resulting in fighting on all sides. The Abkhazian fight for independence has become a subject for the international media, as shown by the accompanying photograph. The South Ossetians of Georgia would like to unite with the North Ossetians, who live in Russia, which is now a separate country. The Abkhazians have succeeded in gaining control over their territory. In fact, some 200,000 Georgians who fled Abkhazia claim that they have been subjected to a policy of ethnic cleansing. Russia had continued to maintain several military bases in Georgia. The Gudauta base was situated in Abkhazia, and the Georgians had suspected that the Russians were aiding the Abkhazian separatists. Georgian officials negotiated for the closure of this base and have recently been successful. Despite this the Russian government has still periodically sent soldiers in Abkhazia ostensibly to fight guerrillas from Chechnia who have occupied a gorge on the edge of Abkhazian territory. The Georgian government has protested and these "uninvited soldiers" have pulled out (*New York Times,* April 12 and 14, 2002). The Georgian case exemplifies a situation in which a politically dominant group's attempts to homogenize a population of different ethnic groups result in demands by those groups not merely for cultural autonomy but for complete political independence.

Like Georgia, the newly independent nation of Uzbekistan in Central Asia is ethnically diverse. The Uzbeks themselves, two-thirds of the population, are Muslims who speak a Turkic language. They are in the process of making decisions about which part of their historic past constitutes their true Uzbek heritage. This would then be used as a rallying point for building Uzbek national culture and developing an Uzbek national identity. Is the focus of Uzbek nation-building to be the heritage represented by Turkic Runic script and the Chaghatai Turkic language (Menges, 1967) or the Islamic tradition with its Arabic script, which the Arabs brought into the area when they overran the Turks in the seventh and eighth centuries? The question of whether to shift from Cyrillic, introduced by the Russians, to Arabic or Turkic Runic script represents the dilemma of whether Uzbek heritage is to be Islamic or pre-Islamic. The building of national identity is always a creative as well as a political process. This often involves choosing to emphasize one aspect rather than another from a very complicated multiethnic history. The choice of one script over another, as in this case, becomes an important political decision.

Most recently, the state institutions of Uzbekistan have been under attack by an Islamic fundamentalist insurgency, known as the Islamic Movement of Uzbekistan, which desires to purge the current government of corruption. It has set car bombs and in one incident killed 16 people in Tashkent, Uzbekistan's capital. The government has closed 900 mosques and arrested people suspected of antigovernment sentiments after the slaying of several policemen. The resurgence of Islam in Central Asia as a whole has led some people in this area to talk about an Islamic state—a revival of an earlier idea of a grand Turkestan, or, in more modern terms, a United States of Asia, which would join Uzbekistan with Kyrgyzstan, Kazakhstan, Tadzhikistan, and Turkmenia, all nations with Islamic backgrounds (Hall, 1992). The Uzbek Islamic fundamentalist movement has sent fighters from its bases in northern Tajikistan into Kyrgyzstan to use villages in an Uzbek enclave in that country as bases from which to attack Uzbekistan. Russia and Uzbekistan sent support to the Kyrgyzstan government to repel this attack. There are Uzbeks also living in Afghanistan where they are a minority population (see photograph on page 249). We will discuss their relationship with the American-supported Afghan government below.

The Pan-Islamic movement has created turmoil in the newly independent states of Central Asia. The comparative perspective in anthropology involves examining Islamic fundamentalism as it is developing from Nigeria to Central Asia to look for what these movements have in common and the ways the particular local setting of each results in differences.

ETHNIC DIFFERENCES, ETHNIC VIOLENCE, AND THE NEW NATION OF AFGHANISTAN

Afghanistan provides us with an excellent example of why it is so important to understand the culture, the social structure, and the political system of other regions of the world today, particularly regions with which the United States is directly involved. After 9/11, American forces went into Afghanistan to seek out and destroy Al Queda and the Taliban, who were governing Afghanistan and providing protection for the Al Queda forces. After the Taliban were no longer in control of Afghanistan, our troops moved in and we became involved in nation-building in a country with a shallow tradition of "nationhood" and with a mix of many ethnic groups. The Afghanistan situation was very different, for example, from the ethnonationalism of the former Yugoslavia, which was found in part of Kosovo, Bosnia, Serbia, and Croatia, where people speaking a common language (Serbo-Croatian) were each demanding their own nation-states.

In our discussion of Afghanistan we will focus on the Pushtuns, the largest ethnic group in the country. They number perhaps 10–12 million people and straddle the border between Afghanistan and Pakistan. Perhaps 7 million Pushtuns are in Afghanistan (Magnus and Naby, 2002: 93). The remainder are in Pakistan. It is a result of colonial history that Pushtuns are found on both sides of the Afghanistan/Pakistan border. As czarist Russia extended its empire southward, it came into contact with British India. During the nineteenth and early twentieth centuries, Britain and Russia waged the "Great Game," which was a war over the land of the Pushtuns (also known as "Pathans" in the writings of Rudyard Kipling and others). The Durand line marks the present boundary between Pakistan and Afghanistan. After colonial England fought and lost three Afghan wars trying to conquer Kabul, Afghanistan's capital, the buffer nation of Afghanistan was created with Russia's approval, which separated Russia from India, with an eastern "tail," the Wakhan Corridor, which served to further separate China from India and Russia.

As a consequence, the nation of Afghanistan includes a large number of ethnic groups. To the north are Tajiks, Uzbeks, Turkomen, and Mountain Khirgiz, each of which at the present time also has its independent nation-state outside of Afghanistan as a result of the breakup of the Soviet Union. Other ethnic groups are the Hazaras, Baluch, Aimaqs, and Nuristanis who were non-Muslims in the nineteenth century but were conquered and converted at the end of that century. The Pushtuns, the largest ethnic group, had ruled Afghanistan through a monarchy until 1978. Though the Pushtuns dominated the political system and exercised hegemony over Tajiks, Uzbeks, and all the others, they did not try to make them into Pushtuns. The pattern had been set more than 200 years ago by the great Afghan ruler Ahmed Shah Durrani (1747–1773), who conquered and ruled over an empire than extended from Persia to Delhi in northern India. Over his own people, the Afghans, he ruled as an "elected tribal chief," but over conquered peoples he exacted tribute (Magnus and Naby, 2002: 30).

The border between Afghanistan and Pakistan is sometimes referred to as a lawless area, but it is not lawless at all. It is simply beyond the control of the governments of Afghanistan or Pakistan. The law that governs this tribal area is the customary law of the Pushtuns. Various Pushtun tribes are found on both sides of the border. Many are nomadic pastoral peoples. Earlier we noted that pastoralists move with their herds to rich summer pastures high in the mountains, and back down to lowland areas when autumn comes. Pushtun nomads move their herds into the Sulayman mountains of Afghanistan in summer, and back down to the Indus valley in Pakistan in winter. When they moved with their herds, Pushtun men were always armed—Enfield rifles in the past, Kalashnikovs more recently. This has always been one of the world's most porous borders. When American military forces tried to pin down Al Queda forces along this border in Operation Anaconda, they found that the Al Queda (and probably Osama bin Laden as well) simply crossed into Pakistan. A recent article in the *New York Times* stated that the new Afghan government, with little tax revenue to depend on, would try to collect customs taxes more diligently along this border (November 21, 2002). However, Pushtuns living there have depended on smuggling from time immemorial. In fact, their definition of "freedom" is not to be under the yoke of a central government, which collects taxes from them.

In an earlier chapter, we discussed the use of the term *warlord* as used in newspaper accounts. Control of the drug trade, in the Afridi tribe for example, has created a number of warlords in this area. As the *Times* article notes, "American customs officials assessing border crossings will find a completely unregulated system, much of it controlled by regional warlords who bypass the central government" (*New York Times,* November 21, 2002: A15). These warlords operate much like Big Men or Mafia dons do. Their access to resources (arms, smuggling, the drug trade) enables them to act as centers of redistribution of resources to their followers, who are predominantly from the same tribe. Barth, who studied Pushtuns of the Yusufzai tribe in Swat, Pakistan, observes that every Yusufzai "chief" had his men's house. Allegiance to a particular chief is expressed by visiting his men's house and eating the food he provides. Barth observes that "only through his hospitality, through the device of gift-giving, does he create the wider obligations and dependence which he can then draw upon in the form of personal political support—in the final resort, military support" (1959: 12). Chiefs in Afghanistan are acting as warlords. These leaders are now also being referred to as "field commanders." They head armed militias, bound to their leader by Pushtun concepts of loyalty. During conflict, however, the leader may ally himself with one faction or another.

The customary code of the Pushtuns is known as Pushtunwali. "Equality of all adult members of the group is, at least in theory, one of the key principles of Pushtun life" (Vogelsang, 2002: 24). Another principle is hospitality. Hospitality is obligatory to outsiders, and Pushtun leaders show their generosity by feeding strangers, along with their followers, in their guest houses. In return, one has obligations of loyalty. However, the Pushtun concept of loyalty is to a personal leader, not to a principle or to an ideology (Caroe, 1958: 256). An extension of hospitality is the obligation to offer sanctuary. Someone fleeing the law may request sanctuary. To refuse the request would stain one's honor (Caroe, 1958: 351). Finally, revenge against someone who has killed a member of one's clan is an obligation (Barth, 1959: 83–86). This type of customary law, which bases carrying out criminal punishment on the kinship system rather than on central government, is an anachronism in many ways. Yet it prevails among Pushtuns in the tribal areas of Pakistan and in large parts of Afghanistan. This is not simply the absence of law. This very different customary legal system is in effect in the Pushtun tribal area.

The social structure of the Pushtuns is one that we have encountered before. It is the segmentary lineage system described for the Cyrenaican Bedouin (on page 133), and for the Somali. All Pushtun believe that they are descended from a common ancestor, named Qays (Caroe, 1958: 11). At present, Pushtuns are subdivided into a number of tribes, perhaps 30 or 40, stretching from Quetta and Kandahar northeast into Swat, in Pakistan. The tribes, in turn, are divided into clans and subclans. The Pushtuns are patrilineal, and practice patrilocal postmarital residence, as do all their neighbors in Afghanistan, the central Asia peoples to their north, and the Persian-speaking peoples to their west. The central feature of segmentary lineage systems is to foster a balance of power. If one lineage, clan, or tribe grows more powerful, another opposing lineage, clan, or tribe will rise up to challenge the first. When there is an external threat from a common enemy, like the British in colonial times or the Soviets recently, Pushtuns will unite to meet the threat. According to the saying, "The Afghans are at peace among themselves only when they are at war" (Institute of Regional Studies, 1997: 98). This has happened throughout Pushtun history.

The early history is dominated by Ahmed Shah Durrani, of the Abdali tribe. He took the name Durrani, meaning "pearl of pearls," for the group of tribes centering in Kandahar. They constitute the Durrani major section of the segmentary lineage system. Opposing him and his successors were the leaders of the Ghalji (or Ghilzai) tribes, another major section, centered in Ghazni, many of whom were nomadic pastoralists. In the wars during the eighteenth and nineteenth centuries over control of parts of northern India, the Durrani and Ghalji vied with one another, though the Durrani managed to maintain control during this whole period until Mohamad Zahir Shah, a Durrani of the Populzai tribe, abdicated in 1973. Da'ud Khan, his cousin and of Durrani descent as well, led a military coup and established a republic. In 1978, Nur Mohammad Taraki, of the opposing Ghalji faction, came to power and established a communist state. He carried out a purge of all Durrani elements in the government, and Da'ud and his family were killed. The opposing segments of the segmentary structure had regained control from the Durranis.

The present government of Hamid Kharzai, a Durrani from the Populzai tribe, established after the overthrow of the Taliban regime and supported by the "nation-builders" from America, rests on a very precarious balance. Pushtuns in general are not accustomed to a strong central government, and the balance of power inherent in their segmentary lineage structure favors a decentralized structure. Military commanders (sometimes called warlords) are traditionally found dispersed in various clans and tribes. For example, Gulbuddin Hekmatyar, a Pushtun, who fought against the communist takeover and is a well-known field commander, "is a Kharoti Ghalji and his group is primarily composed of his own tribe" (Yusufzai, 1997: 112). In the past, Hekmatyar, a member of the Kharoti tribe, which belongs to the Ghalji faction, was part of the government. Today, he is considered a powerful warlord who is not included in the Kharzai government. In addition to balancing the forces within the Pushtun political system, it is also necessary to balance political leaders of the various different ethnic groups in the country—especially Tajiks and Uzbeks, with their own array of field commanders and warlords. This is the culture and the underlying social structure that American policy in the area must cope with.

ETHNIC PROCESSES IN SRI LANKA

The ethnic conflict that has continued in Sri Lanka for decades exemplifies the way ethnic identity is heightened and transformed under certain conditions: the role played by differences in religion and language, the operative economic factors, and the ways majority-minority relations can worsen to the point of civil war (see Tambiah, 1986, 1988). The conflict is between two ethnic groups: the Sinhalese, who speak an Indo-European language, and the Tamils, who speak a Dravidian language. Both languages have borrowed significantly from one another over the centuries. Since 74 percent of the population is Sinhalese, that language became the official language when Sri Lanka gained its independence from Britain. However, public education continued to be provided in parallel Tamil and Sinhalese tracks. The majority of the Sinhalese are Buddhist, with some Christians, mostly Roman Catholics; the Tamil are primarily Hindu, also with a Roman Catholic minority. There is, in addition, a small Muslim population descended from Arab, Persian, and Malay seafarers and people from the Malabar coast of India. There are many cultural similarities between the Sinhala and Tamil groups and no perceived racial differences, despite these differences in language and religion and different mythic charters.

The Tamils consider the northern part of the island of Sri Lanka their traditional homeland, though much of the Tamil population is scattered among the Sinhalese in the rest of the island. The two were separate ethnic communities until the advent of British colonial rule in 1796. The British developed a colonial economy on the island that was based on tea plantations. It was then known as Ceylon. A small English-speaking elite, educated in English-style schools run by missionaries, included both Tamils and Sinhalese. However, for some time the Sinhalese have resented what they see as a Tamil monopoly of the white-collar and professional positions that were the rewards of such an education.

Sri Lanka became independent in 1948. During the postwar period, Sri Lanka went through the uneven economic development that characterized many developing countries. It tried to organize a welfare state to improve the educational and health systems for its people, but its economy did not improve. The plantation economy declined, attempts to develop exports failed, living standards fell, and rising expectations went unfulfilled as young people left school educated but with no employment prospects. The underclass began to suffer, but protests were organized in terms of ethnic differences rather than along class lines. Earlier in this chapter, we described the way class differences may be expressed as ethnic differences. Animosity was directed by the Sinhalese majority, who saw themselves as the original population, against the Tamils, whom they characterized as outsiders.

From the beginning of the colonial period, a revival of Buddhism was spearheaded by Buddhist monks who borrowed the evangelical techniques of the

Saffron-robed Buddhist sinhalese monks staged a protest in Colombo, Sri Lanka's capital, in 1996, to condemn Tamil attacks on innocent civilians.

Christian missionaries who had come to Ceylon under the colonial umbrella. Their role became a more secular one involving social service and eventually politics (Seneviratne, 2001: 15) While the urban, English-speaking elite had political power, a group of Sinhalese-speaking rural leaders, schoolteachers, indigenous medical practitioners, traders, and merchants began to see themselves as the conservators of Sinhalese language, culture, and religion. They joined forces with the monks in the 1950s in a Sinhala revival, which emphasized not only the Sinhalese language and Buddhism, but also a view of the Sinhalese as an Aryan race who were claimed to be different from the allegedly dark-skinned, Dravidian-speaking Tamils. This use of "Aryan" raised the "bogey of racist claims" (Tambiah, 1986: 5). It represented the imposition of a conceptualization from India, where "fair-skinned Aryans" were the invaders from the north who conquered the "dark-skinned" people of the south. The Sinhalese looked to a mythic history that saw their destiny as conquerors and rulers over the whole island for the glory of Buddhism and the expulsion of the Tamil invaders in the north.

The strength of this mythic history is seen as the reason the Sinhalese majority still persist in exploiting the Tamil minority, despite the fact that the alleged Tamil overrepresentation in education and employment was corrected. In recent years the consequence has been Tamil reprisals and violence, and the Sinhalese have responded in kind. The Tamil now demand self-determination, recognition as a nationality, and a guarantee that they will be able to continue to live in their traditional homeland. The government of India became involved when Prime Minister Rajiv Ghandi, who had originally sided with the Tamil separatists, tried in 1985 to broker a peace settlement between the Sri Lankan government and the Tamil rebels. When he sent Indian troops into Sri Lanka in 1987 as peacemakers, they clashed with Tamil guerrillas and the relationship soured. In 1991 Ghandi was assassinated, reputedly by a Tamil rebel group. For some time the Tamil have been using "suicide bombers" and as a consequence have been labeled terrorists by the United States and Britain. During the summer of 1999, a distinguished Tamil legal scholar, who advocated negotiation, compromise, and a legislated settlement of the strife with the Sinhalese, was murdered by members of his own ethnic group, Tamil Tiger extremists who will settle for nothing less than independence. In 2001, Norwegian diplomats negotiated a cease-fire to be followed by direct talks between the warring parties themselves. The prospects for a lasting peace are not great since this is the fifth cease-fire since the war began (*New York Times*, April 11, 2002). The Tamils still saw an independent country as their objective, with the cities held by the Tamils constituting the territory of the Tamil state, Eelam. This is the familiar pattern we encountered between the Georgians and Abkhazians. One of the potential problems is the position of the Muslim minority in the eastern part of Tamil territory. Mistrust between the Muslims and the Tamil Tigers could injure prospects for a settlement. The legendary Tamil leader Velupillai Prabhakaran, who is notorious because he sent forth more than 220 suicide bombers during the period of fighting, held a news conference in Tamil-held territory where he refused to renounce the Tamil objective of complete independence in April. By November 2002, the Tamils had changed their minds and were willing to settle for autonomy and self-government (*New York Times*, November 26, 2002). The Tamils are interested in taking part in the democratic government of Sri Lanka and would allow other political parties to operate in Tamil territory. If negotiations fail, the Tamils will settle for nothing less than independence and their own country.

The Tamil Tigers are currently on the United States list of foreign terrorist organizations and are banned in Australia, Canada, Britain, and India, as well as in the United States. Despite this the Tamil rebel movement "maintains itself through an international network with offices in London and Paris and through the financial contributions of expatriate Tamils all around the world" (Eller, 1999: 139–140). Once again we have members of a diaspora supporting an ethnonationalist movement.

Anthropological comparison of the Tamil-Sinhalese conflict in Sri Lanka with similar conflicts in other parts of the world reveals the same militant, rampant ethnonationalism related to religious differences. In Sri Lanka, a resurgent Sinhalese Buddhism felt itself threatened by Tamil Hinduism from the north. Once again, class intersected with ethnicity, as resentment was expressed against Tamils, who were seen as educated and successful in greater numbers than they should have been. Although there were indeed real differences between Sinhalese and Tamils in Sri Lanka, their ethnic identities were invented and constructed, based on both mythic histories and differing views of recent history, as well as in oppositional terms—"we are the opposite of them." Each side defined itself in terms of its opponent. Another moral to this story is that troops sent in as peacekeepers do not always succeed in keeping combatants apart. In this case, Indians ended up fighting the Tamil insurgents. Both sides are always the losers in such fierce ethnic conflicts, and the militarily weaker side often faces genocide, whether it the Tamils in Sri Lanka or the Kosavars who faced genocide at Serbian hands.

FROM MELTING POT TO MULTICULTURALISM IN THE UNITED STATES

According to archaeologists, the first settlers of North America were the ancestors of the American Indians, as they now want to be called, who started coming across the Bering Strait perhaps as early as 25,000 or 30,000 years ago. The Indians, in their construction of their cultural past, as we have seen with the Kiowa in the previous chapter, view their mythic ancestors as having emerged from places in their native areas. Hence, they have always been in America, which is what their mythology tells them, tying them to the landmarks of their territories from time immemorial. They see the "story," told in American history books, of their crossing the Bering Strait as the white people's attempt to turn them into immigrants in America, like the white population itself. Today, members of American Indian tribes, with all that this category implies legally, as described earlier, may remain on the reservation as tribal members, move into urban areas and turn their tribal identity into ethnic identity, or lose themselves through assimilation in the general population.

The Europeans who came to North America in the 1600s as colonists called themselves English, Irish, Scottish, Dutch, Swedish, German, French, Spanish, and Russian. Slaves who were brought from Africa were imported by the colonists to work the plantations that had been established. An American culture began to develop from an English-Continental base, and earlier national identities merged to become an American identity. In the 1840s, American culture was portrayed by Alexis de Toqueville as emphasizing entrepreneurship, the "self-made man," personal advancement, individualism, restlessness, and the upholding of a biblical tradition. The British had a social structure based on an inherited aristocracy, a monarchy, an official religion headed by the monarch, king or queen, and a class structure. This was clearly different from the American culture, religious organization, and social structure.

As immigration swelled in the late nineteenth and early twentieth centuries, the idea was that all who came to the United States would be assimilated into the emerging American culture. Ethnic differences were to eventually disappear, certainly after the immigrant generation passed on. This idea is similar to the process of nation-building described above. The picture the United States had of itself was that of a "melting pot," a receiver of people from many different cultures and societies who would learn the language of the country—English—and its culture, and assimilate into the developing American culture and society. Immigrants had chosen to come here because they saw it as a land of opportunity, and they were welcomed by the new society with open arms. America was industrializing. There was a great need for labor, and jobs were plentiful.

Many of the immigrants who came from Eastern Europe in the middle of the nineteenth century used ethnic terms, rather than terms referring to a nation-state, to identify themselves, demonstrating the weakness of national identity in some places in Europe like the Austro-Hungarian Empire at this time. They did not consider themselves Poles, but Silesians or Kashubians, since there was no independent Poland during the nineteenth century. These ethnic identities continued to be maintained in the domestic realm and within the community, despite the ideology of the melting pot. In the communities they established in Pennsylvania, for example, they retained much of their Silesian and Kashubian language and culture, as well as their religious affiliation. The Scotch-Irish have also maintained their ethnic identity, but their past is generally misunderstood. This group is commonly thought to be the result of intermarriage between Scottish and Irish peoples. In fact, they are descendants of a Protestant group from Scotland, moved by the conquering English into Ulster County in Northern Ireland, who subsequently emigrated to America in the eighteenth and nineteenth centuries. Many Scotch-Irish immigrants came from economically poor areas and moved into equally marginal frontier areas in the United States. The Scotch-Irish retained their ethnic identity in the economically less desirable border areas of Appalachia, providing us with the feuding Hatfields and McCoys, but they also gave us such self-made entrepreneurs as Andrew Mellon, patriots such as Patrick Henry, and five presidents of the United States—Polk, Buchanan, Jackson, Arthur, and Wilson.

THE MEXICAN-AMERICAN TRANSFORMATION IN TEXAS

We may consider the history of the Mexican-Americans in one Texas town as an example of what happens to an immigrant group over a period of 150 years (Foley, 1988). It is a history of the way Mexican-Americans, who first came to the area as sharecroppers, become politically empowered to the point where they elected one of their own as mayor. This section of Texas was owned by Mexico but became part of the United States after the Mexican-American War, ended in 1848. Anglos, who were Civil War veterans, received land grants and established large cattle ranches, squeezing out the original Mexican landowners. By 1890 some of the large ranches were divided into smaller farms settled by Germans from central Texas, cotton farmers from the southeast, and others who practiced small-scale commercial farming. The town of North Town (the town studied by Foley) was established during this period. A number of Mexicans had been cowboys and wage laborers earlier, but larger numbers of Mexicans began to migrate to Texas to earn money because of the turmoil created by the Mexican Revolution at the beginning of the twentieth century.

Some of these immigrants lived in *Las Colonias* on one side of the town while more lived in small hamlets with several Anglo families in cotton-growing areas. The hamlets were organized around a cotton gin and a store, owned by the Anglo rancher, plus a church and a school. Still other Mexican immigrants lived on individual farms and ranches, serving as clients of an Anglo *patron*. Many were sharecroppers who raised cotton and, later, corn. The landlord provided the land and sometimes also animals, a plow, tools, and seed. The Anglo *patrones* took care of their Mexican workers in a paternalistic fashion, giving them credit, food, and tools in return for services such as labor on roads, domestic child care, and chores around the *patron's* house. Despite a superficial amiability between Anglo *patron* and Mexican client, the Mexicans were considered the "donkeys of the land," economically exploited and socially unequal. The Anglos had the churches and schools as their centers of social life from which Mexicans were excluded. Mexicans set up their own churches and schools. The Anglos considered schooling for Mexicans to be useless, since they were destined to be only the underclass, the labor force.

The Mexican community maintained a strong cultural tradition, conducting a yearly round of ritual celebrations, fiestas, and dances completely segregated from Anglos. Large extended families were favored, with a strict division of labor in which women worked mostly at home. While Anglos could invade Mexican space, the reverse was not possible. Public buildings were considered Anglo space. Until 1920, the county government, the significant level of government, was run by an Anglo political machine. Though there were ethnic, religious, occupational, and political differences among the Anglos, as a group they saw themselves as racially superior to the Mexicans and devoted much energy to maintaining that separation and forcing the Mexicans to accept an inferior position. Mexicans had to assume a deferential posture and a respectful tone of voice in talking to Anglos, while Anglos could be familiar and derogatory. There was no pretense at a melting-pot ideology in this corner of Texas.

After 1930, the economic structure of the area began to change with the decline of cotton and spinach production as well as with the erosion of the patron-client sharecropper relationship. The structure of farming changed with mechanization, the introduction of irrigation techniques, and the beginning of farm leasing. The paternalistic system in south Texas broke down, to be replaced by absentee landlords and the use of seasonal "wetback" labor coming in from Mexico at harvest time. The Mexican families, who had been living in the area for many years, began to be recruited as families to work seasonally for growers in west Texas and in the north. Mexican entrepreneurs organized these labor relations, becoming cultural brokers who earned enough money to become farmers in their own right, merchants, or even moneylenders. The experience of the Mexicans who periodically went north was broadening and economically productive, providing them with money to send their children to school or to buy and run retail stores. This enabled them to become socially mobile.

In the 1950s and 1960s, while the civil rights movement was gaining force in other parts of the country, the Mexicans were also beginning to push against the invisible wall of social segregation. The number of Mexicans voting greatly increased as a result of the penetration of new ideas about civil rights, political activism, and a more public recognition of the injustices that had been suffered at the hands of the Anglos. A cadre of new Mexican leaders began to create ethnic political organizations, such as the League of United Latin American Citizens and the G.I. Forum, a veterans' group for whom the war had been a learning experience, to challenge the earlier patterns of economic exploitation and social segregation. Mexicans then began to move into the political bureaucracy at the lower levels. Though schools were not fully desegregated until 1969, the general level of town schools improved as Mexicans pushed for educational opportunities for their children, since education was clearly the road for the socially mobile. School board elections became a political arena for Mexican-Americans, and by 1960 political participation had increased to the point where there was a Mexican candidate for the city council. More moderate Anglo groups were recruiting Mexicans and attempting to form coalitions, though some of this activity represented tokenism.

As Mexican-Americans moved into the modern Anglo world, there were greater aspirations, but also greater frustrations and resentment against Anglo society. Men begrudged the need for their wives to work as domestics in Anglo houses in order to have enough money to sustain a decent standard of life. They took to drinking in cantinas. The extended families in which Mexicans lived in the earlier period began breaking up when nuclear families moved into American-style homes and started to raise their children "the American way." Compadre relationships within the Mexican-American community were no longer important. Weddings and other rite-of-passage celebrations ceased being communal affairs; instead, they were now held in restaurants and clubs, with fewer guests invited. Musical tastes changed from mariachi music to popular American forms. While they retained their identity as Mexican-Americans, the content of their culture was becoming Americanized.

By the end of the 1960s, the Mexicans were ready for public political confrontation with Anglos, complaining openly about the poor schools and the lack of streets and proper drainage facilities. The Mexican-Americans had broken down the walls of their ethnic enclave and forced the adoption of a different set of rules for Mexican-American–Anglo dialogue, seeking to control more of their destiny than they had before. However, the Mexican-American community was not unified in its political aspirations. The threat to the development of Mexican-American ethnic unity and political power came in the form of factions that developed at the very time that Mexican-Americans sought to make a common political front against the Anglos.

In 1964, the first city council and the first school board were elected that included both Mexican-Americans and Anglos. A new, more liberal group of Anglo political leaders had emerged who were interested in cooperating with the local Mexican-American middle-class businesspeople, community leaders, and professionals. As a consequence of the national civil rights movement, students and other younger Mexican-Americans also formed a group, the Raza Unita party, which was dedicated to the complete overthrow of Anglo rule. They considered Mexican culture to be at least as good as, if not superior to, the Anglo way of life. They were like the Black Panthers and other black-power groups of the time—aggressive and confrontational in demanding their rights. In reality, they were the college-educated sons and daughters of middle-class Mexican-American businesspeople and were critical of their elders for not being sufficiently active politically and for not militantly opposing the Anglos. Their candidate had already been elected to the city council. Though these Mexican-American groups were alienated from one another for a time, by 1973 they had joined forces and elected Mexican-Americans to a majority of the city council seats. With Mexican-Americans speaking out and in control, the Anglos began to feel threatened, resulting in frequent confrontations. However, many Mexican-Americans stayed neutral, afraid of the economic consequences of taking sides.

The formation of a biracial Better Government League was an attempt to counter both extremist Anglos and Mexican-American radicals. After a period of further polarization and conflict, a strengthened Better Government League, now 50 percent Anglo and 50 percent Mexican-American, and the election of a Mexican-American mayor marked a subsequent period of ethnic accommodation. A new generation of Mexican-Americans now demand to be recognized as full citizens, with economic, political, and social equality with Anglos while being able to maintain their Mexican-American identity. The content of their culture today, however, is more American than Mexican.

CULTURE UNASSIMILATED, REITERATED, AND RENEWED IN AMERICA

As we noted above, in retrospect, the idea of the melting pot was a myth for all Americans. The ideal, when the Founding Fathers wrote the Declaration of Independence, the Constitution, and the Bill of Rights, was to have no single dominant ethnic group. In contrast, in other countries, such as Great Britain, France, and Germany, one religion was the state religion and the culture of one group was dominant. However, we must note that in the United States what was written on paper was not the case in reality. Immigrants who came here learned English, and Christmas was a legal holiday, but not Hanukkah or the Prophet's Birthday. Though people conformed to majority norms in the public spheres of work, school, government, and so on, ethnic cultural practices were often retained in the private spheres of life. While assimilation was being emphasized, the persistence of ethnic practices in any form was officially ignored and even denied, being revealed only in scholarly articles. Over the past 30 years the United States has recast its image and replaced the melting-pot symbol with that of a multiethnic, multicultural, pluralistic society. Americans are now enjoined to become more aware of and to respect the differing cultural backgrounds of ethnic groups other than their own. All the groups, taken together, are seen to constitute American culture today. The implications of this shift in our image of ourselves from assimilation to multiculturalism continue to reverberate in school curricula, in urban politics, on television, and in the other media, as well as in many other aspects of our lives. For example, the film *My Big Fat Greek Wedding* has been a runaway success, with its appeal to people of many ethnic groups. It attests to the multicultural nature of our society. Now that multiculturalism and multiethnic images occupy center stage, we are also paying more attention to cultural continuities with the past and to ethnic practices that continue from yesterday, in a reworked form.

African-Americans and Their Heritage

The defiant reiteration, strengthening, and redefinition of ethnic identity by various ethnic groups in recent years was in response to the civil rights movement in the 1960s, which gave birth to the idea of black power—the empowerment of African-Americans—and the conscious construction of African-American culture. In the mid-1960s, African-Americans proclaimed that "black is beautiful" and strengthened their African-American identity by reiterating their African traditions and constructing their African-American heritage anew.

Some had argued that the devastating effects of slavery had stripped African-Americans of any of the elements of the African cultures of their ancestors (Frazier, 1963). Others saw African cultural practices perpetuated in the culture of African-Americans (Herskovits, 1941; Turner, 1949). With today's emphasis on different ethnic traditions, scholars of African-American culture are again investigating continuities with African cultures. For example, rural African-Americans in southern states such as Georgia, Alabama, and South Carolina had a tradition of cooking, washing, and sharing gossip in swept yards surrounding their houses. This custom is now found only among members of the older generation. Swept yards were the center of family activity during the slave period and after. This use of space has been linked by Westmacott to West African village practices (1992). Cultural continuities with both West African and Central African cultures have been traced in a number of other areas. African-American speech, discussed in Chapter 3, shows African retentions in verb tense usage (Asante, 1990) and the use of many lexical items from African languages (Herskovits, 1941; Turner, 1949). Some of these African words, like the terms *gumbo* and *goober*, have been borrowed by white speakers of English. Africanisms also survived in the various musical traditions that developed among African-Americans, including the gospel tradition, jazz, and the blues (Maultsby, 1990).

Quilt-making is an African-American tradition that has its origin in America. Gee's Bend, Alabama was, up until recently, a rather isolated place, with a population today of 300 families, half of them with incomes of less then $10,000 per year. Yet quilt-making in the autumn was an annual tradition for the women of Gee's Bend, handed down from grandmothers to granddaughters. The bold rhythms, strong color, and artistic quality of these quilts have finally been recognized by collectors, antique dealers, and museum curators. A show of a selection of these quilts opened at the Museum of Fine Art in Houston and then moved to the Whitney Museum in New York. The quilts, which were made for events like the graduation of a grandchild from school, are now being recognized as masterpieces of the quilting art (*New York Times*, November 21, 2002).

The strengthening of African-American identity involved cultural creativity. Alex Haley's television miniseries *Roots*, first aired in the 1970s, graphically depicted the epic history of his family as he reconstructed it, beginning with his West African ancestor who was enslaved and transported to America. All America watched *Roots*, but it had an especially powerful impact on African-Americans and their sense of ethnic identity. *Roots* served to directly connect African-American culture to West African culture. Learning Swahili, wearing Kente cloth, using African greetings, and learning to cook African foods were tied to a cognizance of a Pan-African heritage of historic accomplishments and greatness.

The holiday of Kwanzaa is an example of cultural creativity that incorporates a number of African practices. It was developed in 1966 by a professor of black studies at California State University at Long Beach and is widely celebrated today all over the country with the sending of Kwanzaa cards and gift-giving. The seven-day cultural festival, held from December 26 to New Year's Day, is observed by African-Americans of all faiths. The photograph on page 415 shows one of the ceremonies of Kwanzaa. Like Kwanzaa, most holidays, religious and secular, were conscious cultural inventions, constructed at some point in the past. Christmas, which celebrates the birth of Christ, was originally a pagan rite celebrating the winter solstice, and the Christmas tree and Santa Claus are more recent inventions.

Kwanzaa is particularly associated with the purchase of goods associated with African identity, though these objects are purchased at other times of the year as well. A market has been created, and Africans from West Africa have begun to bring goods from Africa for sale to African-Americans. During Kwanzaa, the Metropolitan New York Kwanzaa Exposition attracts many African sellers of goods like kente cloth. These Africans are strict Muslims who come from various countries in West Africa. They leave their families behind, but while here try to be observant of Islamic rules, like praying five times a day. As we have noted earlier some of them set up shop outside museums in Manhattan to sell masks and statues. These African entrepreneurs also sell in street markets in various locations in Harlem and elsewhere in Manhattan where buyers are likely to be. In addition, they have expanded to other cities with sizable African-American populations. African-American businessmen have also found a niche in this Afrocentric market. Afrocentrism refers to pride in things African or quasi-African. Objects that represent Africa include ersatz kente cloth, scarves, combs, trade beads, and leather goods (Stoller, 2002: 82). In addition to material from West Africa, they also sell American-made material with an Afrocentric theme. Objects related to Malcolm X, including T shirts, baseball hats, and sweatshirts marked with X, are also big sellers. This marketing of Afrocentrism represents an attempt to replicate the signs and symbols of Africa through a series of objects which serve to tie African-Americans to their heritage.

From the beginning, the one-drop rule held that "offspring of interracial unions were defined racially as African-American, regardless of the racial identity of their other parent" (Daniel, 2002: x). The grandchildren, great-grandchildren, and so on, down the generations were also thus categorized. Recently, those of multiracial background have begun to feel that all of the backgrounds of their ancestry are important and should be recognized—European, American Indian, and

An African-American family light the candles to celebrate Kwanzaa.

so forth. Unfortunately, this new multiracial identity is seen as contrary to the goal of unifying African-Americans into a strong political force. However, as Daniels notes, "The new multiracial identity, rather than imploding African-American identity, can potentially forge more inclusive constructions of blackness and whiteness" (2002: 175). Cultural and racial diversities as well as commonalities should be celebrated. "Integrative pluralism" is the key word.

African-Americans on the Sea Islands of Georgia: The Gullah The African-Americans who live on the coastal islands of Georgia were more or less isolated until the beginning of this century. Few bridges connected their island homes, separated from the mainland by coastal marsh lands, to the mainland. The effects of the construction of Interstate 95 in 1974, which transformed the coastal zones of other states, were slow to affect this area. As Blount notes, "They represent the most distinctive, best-known case of African and African-American linkages. Not only are there genealogical connections, there are cultural retentions that collectively can be referred to as 'Africanisms' " (2002: 160). These included forms of music, words from African languages, and basketry. Their ties to their African heritage are seen as more direct than that of other African-Americans. Fishing and agriculture had been the primary economic activities of the Africans, who came to this area as slaves in the eighteenth century to work on the plantations whose primary product was rice. Slaves were allowed to fish in order to supplement the diet. They made their own boats. Fish became an important source of food. After the abolition of slavery, families established small farms to engage in subsistence farming and cash cropping, but this mode of subsistence has almost disappeared. Fishing continued to be important and fish were sold in markets and even peddled in the streets of Savannah at the turn of the century. The political system was still strongly segregationist, keeping African-Americans out of positions of political power.

African-Americans had a strong sense of community. The local community was close-knit; neighbors were likely to be relatives, particularly patrilineal, but affinal kin were also important. Relatives provided social and economic support (Blount, 2002: 164). Large support groups and reciprocity were important. Family, kin, neighborhood, and church provided the foci for individuals. Many communities remain this way today. However, politically, with the passage of civil rights legislation in the 1960s, there is less direct discrimination, but racial tensions remain. African-Americans have been elected to local offices like sheriff, but not above the level of the county. Communities could now demand improvements in roads and parks. Community elders who are greatly respected lead the community by example. Respected elders serve as deacons in the local church, usually Baptist, which gives them the religious authority to back up their political standing (Blount, 2002: 165). The church is an important focus not only for religious affairs, but also more broadly for community political activity. The respect accorded older men and women is a distinctively African trait.

Economically, the Gullah African-Americans have not fared so well. Several generations ago, Italian immigrants moved to this area and took over and mechanized the oyster industry. African-Americans had been harvesting oysters for subsistence and sale for several generations, but within a short time most of them became wage laborers in oyster fisheries and canneries. The same thing happened when the Portuguese came in and began to monopolize the shrimp industry. They soon acquired power boats that could pull nets through the water, far superior to the wooden boats of the African-American fishermen. Only a few of the latter had the capital to acquire the bigger boats. The beginning of the pine tree industry also represented an intrusion, though it did provide wage labor. With the interstate highway came tourism, causing a rise in land prices that represented another threat to the stability of the African-American community. Movement to urban areas has also begun. How long these communities will be able to maintain some semblance of cultural life as it has been over a long period of time is a good question. For this reason, the ethnographer Blount refers to them as an "endangered people" (Blount, 2002: 159–176).

HYPHENATED CULTURES

We used to view ethnicity as a perpetuation of cultural traditions from the past. We now understand that the utilization of symbols of ethnic identity has always involved creativity and inventiveness (Sollars, 1989; Stern and Cicala, 1991). The question of authenticity of customs is frequently raised when they have been invented recently, but customs invented a century ago are accepted as authentic. However, the age of a custom or the number of years an event has been celebrated has nothing to do with its authenticity.

Other ethnic groups, following African-Americans, began reasserting and reiterating their own ethnic identity and group solidarity and building their own hyphenated cultures in an increasingly public manner. Italians formed the Italian Anti-Defamation League, sponsoring a huge rally at Columbus Circle in New York City on Columbus Day. Soon, instead of only a single Columbus Day parade dominated by Italian-Americans, two parades were held in New York City on different days around Columbus Day, one sponsored by Italian organizations and the other by Hispanic organizations. The latter had contingents of hyphenated Americans from all the Latin American countries who marched in alphabetical order of their countries' names. Parades along Fifth Avenue in New York, occurring on many weekends, reflect the kaleidoscope of groups publicly displaying and reiterating their ethnic identity with floats, bands, costumes, and dignitaries. While ethnic parades of the Irish and the Pakistanis in Great Britain symbolize each ethnic group's claim to certain spaces, ethnic parades in New York make a different symbolic statement. Most of the ethnic groups use the same space—Fifth Avenue in New York City. They are proclaiming and celebrating their ethnic identity as hyphenated Americans. Among the ethnic parades on Fifth Avenue during the year are the Irish, Greek, Indian (from India), Puerto Rican, Scottish, Polish, German, and Turkish Day parade, as depicted in the photo on page 418. The largest ethnic parade of all is that of the West Indians, who march in Brooklyn on one of the days of the West Indian Labor Day celebration.

Whether it is Slovenians who settled in Cleveland several generations ago, or Somalis who have recently settled in Lewiston, Maine, or those of Nordic descent who are recapturing the culture of their ancestors, we are becoming more and more aware of the diversity of cultural background of new and old Americans. New minorities, like the Hispanic Muslims in California, constantly proclaim their existence (*New York Times*, December 27, 2001). We are made aware of those who celebrate the Persian New Year—Nowruz, the ancient beginning of the spring equinox (*New York Times*, March 21, 2002) or the Jews from India, the Bene Israel, who have a distinctive thanksgiving ritual dedicated to the Prophet Elijah, which is celebrated at weddings (*New York Times*, December 9, 2001). The city of New York, and its ever-changing immigrant population, is a testimony to the growing cultural diversity of our country.

Recent immigrants from places such as Korea, Japan, Vietnam, India, and Haiti place great emphasis on their ethnic identity and the maintenance of their cultural traditions in the food they eat, the music they play, the dances they perform, and the celebrations they commemorate. We described the nature of Vietnamese music in America in an earlier chapter, and the way in which it combined traditional Vietnamese elements with American elements. At the same time these recent immigrants are also adapting in many ways to American culture. Prejudice and discrimination against racially distinct groups—like Mexican-Americans, as we have seen above, Chinese-Americans, and Japanese-Americans—have also prevented them from being absorbed into the larger society.

This float in the annual Turkish Day parade in New York City emphasizes the unity of all Turkish-speaking peoples, including the Uzbeks.

America is a nation based on religious freedom, and from the beginning, it attracted religious believers persecuted in their European homelands. Despite this, there is a strong streak of religious intolerance in the country, sometimes coupled with racism. The majority's intolerance of African-American Muslims, or Native American churches that practice the peyote "cult," or Caribbean "sects" like Santeria, discussed earlier, seeking to carry out animal sacrifice, exemplifies this streak. The rituals of these religious groups offend the Christian majority, which legally tries to eliminate these practices.

How do third- and fourth-generation individuals with mixed ethnic heritages deal with ethnic identity today? Such Americans are now making choices regarding which of several ancestries they want to stress and which they will omit through selective forgetting (Waters, 1990). More and more of these people choose to be ethnic, though their ethnicity may be only situationally expressed. Those claiming Irish ancestry may demonstrate it on Saint Patrick's Day. In similar fashion, people of multiracial backgrounds are celebrating their identity by marching in Washington, D.C., under the banner of the Multi-Racial Solidarity March. Though immigrants from Asia and their descendants still feel a strong sense of their ethnic identities as Chinese-Americans, Filipino-Americans, and Korean-Americans, the racial attitudes of some Americans seem to be forcing them into an Asian-American racial category.

 This is Flushing, New York, where Chinese, Pakistanis and Indians live and shop in close contact with one another.

The United States is now a multicultural, multiethnic, pluralist society. The ongoing debates regarding how to implement multicultural curricula in colleges, high schools, and elementary schools reflect our groping for new ways to symbolize and express the multiple aspects of our cultural traditions. The significance of these debates is that they have almost eclipsed the consideration of what remains of a shared American culture and value system, which includes religious tolerance and the principles embodied in the Bill of Rights and the Constitution.

SUMMARY

• In today's pluralistic, multicultural world, the terms *ethnic* and *ethnic identity*, as a way of identifying oneself, are frequently used as alternatives to culture and cultural identity.

• Ethnic groups share common cultural norms, values, identities, patterns of behavior, and language. Their members recognize themselves as a separate group and are so recognized by others.

• Religion is one of the important factors serving to distinguish one ethnic group from another. When religious differences are present, ethnic conflict is heightened and intensified.

• Ethnic differences may also parallel class or racial differences. Under those conditions, ethnic conflict may be characterized as class or racial conflict.

• When nation-building occurred, the imposed national culture was usually that of the dominant, group, as occurred in England and France.

• Nations are composed of one politically autonomous ethnic group, while the term *state* refers to any politically autonomous entity, whether it is composed of one or many different ethnic groups. Nation-state is used when nation and state are coterminous.

• The Georgian/Abkhazian case exemplifies a situation in which a politically dominant group's attempts to homogenize a population of different ethnic groups result in demands by those groups not merely for cultural autonomy but for complete political independence.

• The building of national identity is always a creative as well as a political process. The question of whether to shift from Cyrillic, introduced by the Russians, to Arabic or Turkic Runic script represents the dilemma of whether Uzbek heritage is to be Islamic or pre-Islamic, and it becomes an important political decision in Uzbekistan.

• The example of Afghanistan illustrates why it is so important to understand the culture, the social structure, and the political system of other regions of the world today, particularly regions with which the United States is directly involved.

• The social structure of the Pushtuns is a segmentary lineage system, and all Pushtun believe that they are descended from a common ancestor.

• Warlords in Afghanistan operate much like Big Men or Mafia dons do. Their access to resources (arms, smuggling, the drug trade) enables them to act as centers of redistribution of resources to their followers, who are predominantly from the same tribe.

• The ethnic conflict that has continued in Sri Lanka for decades exemplifies the way in which ethnic identity is heightened and transformed under certain conditions. These include the role played by differences in religion and language, the operative economic factors, and the ways majority-minority relations can worsen to the point of ethnic violence and civil war.

• The Europeans who came to North America in the 1600s as colonists called themselves English, Irish, Scottish, Dutch, Swedish, German, French, Spanish, and Russian. American culture began to develop from an English-Continental base, and earlier national identities merged to become an American identity.

• Mexican-Americans first came to Texas as sharecroppers over 150 years ago, dominated economically and politically by the Anglo population. Over the years they became politically empowered to the point where they elected one of their own as mayor.

• While the idea of the melting pot was dominant in the United States, and assimilation was being emphasized, the persistence of ethnic practices in any form was officially ignored and even denied. However, over the past 30 years the United States has recast its image and replaced the melting-pot symbol with that of a multiethnic, multicultural, pluralistic society.

• The defiant reiteration, strengthening, and redefinition of ethnic identity by various ethnic groups in recent years was in response to the civil rights movement in the 1960s, which gave birth to the idea of black power—the empowerment of African-Americans—and the conscious construction of African-American culture.

• The holiday of Kwanzaa is an example of African-American cultural creativity that incorporates a number of African practices.

• We now understand that the utilization of symbols of ethnic identity has always involved creativity and inventiveness.

• Other ethnic groups, following African-Americans, began reasserting and reiterating their own ethnic identity and group solidarity and building their own hyphenated cultures in an increasingly public manner.

• Whether it is Slovenians who settled in Cleveland several generations ago, or Somalis who have recently settled in Lewiston, Maine, or those of Nordic descent who are recapturing the culture of their ancestors, we are becoming more and more aware of the diversity of cultural background of new and old Americans.

• How do third- and fourth-generation individuals with mixed ethnic heritages deal with ethnic identity today? Such Americans are now making choices regarding which of several ancestries they want to stress and which they will omit through selective forgetting.

SUGGESTED READINGS

Beissinger, Mark, and Crawford Young (eds.). *Beyond State Crisis? Postcolonial Africa and Post-Soviet Eurasia in Comparative Perspective.* Washington, DC: Woodrow Wilson Center Press, 2002. Articles on the crises, such as contested boundaries, mafias, and warlords, facing contemporary states in Africa and post-Soviet Eurasia.

Cornwell, Grant, and Eve Walsh Stoddard (eds.). *Global Multiculturalism: Comparative Perspectives on Ethnicity, Race, and Nation.* Lanham, MD: Rowman and Littlefield, 2000. Essays concerning the widespread multiculturalism brought about by contemporary migration and globalization.

Daniel, E. Valentine. *Charred Lullabies: Chapters in an Anthropography of Violence.* Princeton, NJ: Princeton University Press, 1996. An examination of ethnic conflict and violence and the problems anthropologists have in conveying the experience of brutality in ethnographic texts.

Dominguez, Virgina, and David Y. H. Wu (eds.). *From Beijing to Port Moresby: The Politics of National Identity in Cultural Policies.* New York: Routledge, 1998. The contributors to this volume illustrate the way in which "culture" and cultural construction operate in debates about national identity and national integration, and the way in which politics and cultural policy fashion a nation's heritage. Nationhood in transition has been part of the modernization process in these newly independent nations. The articles in this volume deal with the way in which these trends have operated in countries such as Papua New Guinea, Vanuatu, Samoa, and the Cook Islands.

Gregory, Steven, and Roger Sanjek (eds.). *Race.* New Brunswick, NJ: Rutgers University Press, 1994. Explores the way racial ideologies intersect with gender, class, nation, and sexuality in the formation of social identities and hierarchies.

Hinton, Alexander (ed.). *Annihilating Difference: The Anthropology of Genocide.* Berkeley: University of California Press, 2002. Anthropologists examine ethnocide and genocide as the dark side of modernity, detailing the experiences of groups such as Mayans, Cambodians, and Rwandans.

Magnus, Ralph, and Eden Naby. *Afghanistan: Mullah, Marx, and Mujahad.* Boulder, CO: Westview Press, 2002. An examination of the contemporary situation in Afghanistan, the history that brought it about, and the course of history from nineteenth-century rulers to rule by the Marxists and then the Taliban.

Min, Pyong Gap (ed.). *The Second Generation: Ethnic Identity among Asian-Americans.* Walnut Creek, CA: AltaMira Press, 2002. Deals with the subtle play between the racial categorization of the larger society and the identity choices made by minority individuals that will ultimately determine how today's Asian immigrant groups will fit into the larger American society.

Otto, Tom, and Nicholas Thomas. *Narratives of Nations in the South Pacific.* Harwood Academic, 1997. Nationhood in the Pacific Islands is rather new and tenuous. Efforts to develop national identity, and national narratives, are depicted.

 ## SUGGESTED WEBSITES

http://www.geocities.com/athens/5180/tamil.html An extensive discussion of the Tamils and their religious history.

http://www.pipeline.com/~rgibson/warlords.html Describes ethnic conflict between Pushtuns and other ethnic groups in Afghanistan, and the role played by warlords.

http://www.immi.gov.au/multicultural A website advertising the multiculturalism of Australia and its advantages.

EPILOGUE

The goal of anthropology is to demonstrate that there are many cultures in the world and that our culture is but one of them. The mission of the anthropologist is to explore cultural differences to see the ways in which cultures are similar and the ways they differ. By gaining insight into other cultures, one is able to gain insight into one's own culture. Today, many people emphasize cultural relativism—that all cultures have uniquely different cultural traits and that cultural comparison will reveal only differences. We have shown in the various chapters of this book that cultural comparison reveals similarities as well as differences.

The fledgling anthropologist journeys to a culture very different from his or her own—to the Yanomamo or Kwakiutl—to gain an understanding of a way of life different from his or her own. This apprenticeship is a period during which the anthropologist learns how another culture works, and the different conceptualizations and ideas that guide its people. Today, many anthropologists study complex cultures in Europe and Asia or use archeological methods to study the Aztecs. They may also study groups in their own culture that are usually different from themselves in ethnic background and class membership. However, studying one's own culture often raises problems of its own—a tendency to justify one's own culture.

In earlier chapters, we talked about globalization as a process that is having a significant impact on our world. Anthropology and its associated methodology is particularly well suited to explore the ways this global process affects the local communities. Anthropologists have always focused upon small-scale entities (the microanalytic unit), concerned with the way they operate and the impact upon them of outside forces, such as the penetration of external markets and national governmental agencies. As we have shown in many of the examples we have discussed, the anthropological perspective is able to reveal the ways people "on the ground" are reacting to the larger forces beyond their communities, which have greatly affected their villages and their lives. It can show the ways peoples' lives have been changed in response to the building of new factories locally, which are owned by multinational companies; or as a consequence of the introduction of new ways of growing crops, which have been developed in the laboratories of Western nations; or as a result of the availability of new products manufactured beyond the borders of their countries. This focus on the local level, where people live their lives, is central to the anthropological approach.

Anthropology as a discipline is a product of Western culture. It is an outgrowth from the earlier Age of Exploration and a product of Enlightenment thinking and of European encounters with non-European peoples, their languages and cultures. To appreciate what anthropology is all about is to understand and respect cultural diversity. When we quoted Samuel Johnson, the English sage, as saying, "One set of savages is like another," we were citing the voice of ethnocentrism and of ignorance. To Johnson, the Yanomamo, the Tahitians, and even the Scots in the mountains bordering England were all the same—savages—in contrast to the civilized English like himself. But many philosophers of that time did read Cook's *Voyages* and Bougainville's *Voyages* and came to conclusions very different from those of Johnson. Montaigne and Diderot pointed out that a Tahitian might very well look at France and conclude that being drawn and quartered, as a punishment, was a barbarous custom indeed.

Respect for cultural diversity is one of the central messages of anthropology and of this book. It leads one to conclude that our cultural practices are but one possible way of doing things, and that our way is not the "right way," the God-given way, the only way. Our form of the family is organized in a particular way for historical and functional reasons. The narrow, ethnocentric view of European settlers who came to America is exemplified by their idea that Native Americans should live in nuclear families like the Europeans, instead of in their own clans and extended families, and that each family should live on the property that it owned. Even today many Americans think ethnocentrically that our ideas about property and our legal system are superior to all others. They wince when informed that under other legal codes present in the world today, a thief might have his right hand severed, which they consider barbaric. Yet America and Japan are the only advanced, industrialized nations with the death penalty. Other industrialized nations consider the execution of criminals barbaric.

Cultural diversity and cultural differences are linked to the central concept in anthropology, that of *culture.* The culture concept is a holistic idea, which forces one to consider the many aspects of culture as they relate to one other. Anthropologists do not examine the family structure or the legal system of society in isolation from the other aspects of culture. The focus is always on the way the family or the legal system is related to the economy, to religion, to morality, to ritual, to performance, and so on. The Trobriand family has a particular structure because it is part of the Trobriand economic system, political system, and religious system in particular ways.

The metaphor of the tapestry of culture, which we have used as the framework for this book, relates to the interrelationship, or interweaving, of these various aspects of culture or cultural institutions. Like the colors and designs of an enormous tapestry, every thread—meaning people's activities and individual behaviors as they live out their lives, observed by the anthropologist in the field—contributes to the pattern. However, not even the most elaborate medieval tapestry can approach the splendor and complexity of any single culture. However, this is only a metaphor. Culture is not really a tapestry, it is an abstraction about how people lead their lives according to cultural rules. It is an abstraction about good and evil, rules and transgressions. Members of a community are themselves often in vigorous disagreement about the underlying values of their own culture. Today, the metaphor of the tapestry must be seen in the light of the disjunctions that have occurred as a consequence of colonialism, post-colonialism, and globalization.

In this ever-changing world, decisions are constantly being made concerning the future direction of particular societies and ethnic groups. These decisions should be made by the people of these groups, and they should be informed decisions. This is where anthropology, in the form of applied anthropology or the practice of anthropology, comes in. Basic anthropological knowledge can be provided by anthropologists from other places coming in to work with the members of the society, or it can be provided by trained anthropologists from that culture who have an understanding of culture change. The latter group themselves can act as policymakers. The late Jomo Kenyatta, who was president of Kenya, was such an individual with training in anthropology as well as great political skills. In this manner, anthropology works in the service of mankind, in addition to gathering basic knowledge that contributes to cultural understanding worldwide.

CITED REFERENCES

Abiodun, Rowland, Henry Drewal, John Pemberton, and Museum Rietberg. *The Yoruba Artist: new theoretical perspectives on African Arts*. Washington, D.C. Smithsonian Institution Press, 1994.

Abotchie, Chris. *Social Control in Traditional Southern Eweland of Ghana: Relevance for Modern Crime Prevention*. Accra: Ghana Universities Press, 1997.

Abu-Lughod, Lila. "Shifting Politics in Bedouin Love Poetry." In *Language and the Politics of Emotion*, edited by Lila Abu-Lughod and Catherine A. Lutz. Cambridge, England: Cambridge University Press, 1990.

Adams, Kathleen M. "More Than an Ethnic Marker: Toraja Art as Identity Negotiator." *American Ethnologist 25*: 327–351, 1998.

Ahearn, Laura. "Language and Agency. In *Annual Review of Anthropology:* 30: 109–137, 2001.

Alexander, Jennifer. "Women Traders in Javanese Marketplaces." In *Market Cultures: Society and Morality in the New Asian Capitalisms*, edited by Robert W. Hefner. Boulder, Colo.: Westview Press, 1998.

Al-Issa, Ihsan. "Culture and Mental Illness in Algeria". In *Al-Junun: Mental Illness in the Islamic World*, edited by Ihsan Al-Issa. Madison, Connecticut: International Universities Press, 2000, pp. 101–120.

Amit, Vered. "Armenian and Other Diasporas: Trying to Reconcile the Irreconcilable". In *British Subjects: An Anthropology of Britain*, edited by Nigel Rapport. New York: Berg Press, 2002. pp. 263–280.

Andresen, Jensine, "Introduction: towards a cognitive science of religion". In *Religion in Mind; Cognitive Perspectives on Religious Beliefs, Ritual, and Experience*. Cambridge: Cambridge University Press, 2001.

Anthony, David W. "Shards of Speech." *The Sciences*, January/February 1996, pp. 34–39.

Appadurai, Arjun (ed.). *The Social Life of Things: Commodities in Cultural Perspective*. Cambridge, England: Cambridge University Press, 1986.

Arnold, Jeanne E. "Transportation Innovation and Social Complexity among Maritime Hunter-Gatherer Societies." *American Anthropologist 97* (1995): 733–747.

Aronson, Meredith and David Bell, Dan Vermeer. "Coordination of Technological Practice and Representation at the Boundaries". In *Anthropological Perspectives on Technology*, edited by Michael Bryan Schiffer. Albuquerque: University of New Mexico Press 2001.

Asante, Molefi Kete. "African Elements in African-American English." In *Africanisms in American Culture*, edited by Joseph E. Holloway. Bloomington: Indiana University Press, 1990.

Ashwell, Sylvia L. "Some Suggestions for a (Relatively) New Model of Conversation Analysis" In *Hearing Many Voices*, edited by M. J. Hardman and Anita Taylor. Cresskill, New Jersey: Hampton Press, 2000.

Atkinson, Jane Monnig. "How Gender Makes a Difference in Wana Society." In *Power and Difference: Gender in Island Southeast Asia*, edited by Jane Fishburne Collier and Sylvia Junko Yanagisako. Stanford, Calif.: Stanford University Press, 1990.

_____. "Shamanisms Today." *Annual Review of Anthropology 21* (1992): 307–330.

Azhar, M. Z. and S. L. Varma. "Mental Illness and Its Treatment in Malaysia". pp. 163–186. In *Al-Junun: Mental Illness in the Islamic World*, edited by Ihsan Al-Issa. Madison, Connecticut. International Universities Press, 2000.

Baillargeon, Morgan, and Leslie Tepper. *Legends of Our Times: Native Cowboy Life.* Seattle: University of Washington Press, 1998.

Barclay-McLaughlin, Gina. "Communal Isolation: Narrowing the Pathways to Goal Attainment and Work". In *Coping With Poverty: The Social Context of Neighborhood, Work, and Family in the African American Community,* edited by Sheldon Danziger and Ann Chih Lin. Ann Arbor: University of Michigan Press, 2000.

Barnes, Robert H. "Alliance, Exchange, and the Organization of Boat Corporations in Lamalera (E. Indonesia)." In *Kinship, Networks, and Exchange,* edited by Thomas Schweizer and Douglas R. White. New York: Cambridge University Press, 1998.

Barreca, Regina, editor. "Introduction". In A Sitdown with the Sopranos: Watching Italian-American Culture on TV's Most Talked-About Series. New York" Palgrave-Macmillan, 2002.

Barrett, Frank J. "The Organizational Construction of Hegemonic Masculinity: The Case of the US Navy. In *The Masculinities Reader,* edited by Stephen M. Whitehead and Frank J. Barrett. Cambridge: Polity Press, 2001.

Barth, Fredrik. *Political Leadership among Swat Pathans.* London: Athlone Press, 1959.

Beal, E. Ann. "Consuming Women, Producing Men: The Gendered Construction of Elite Jordanian Shoppers." *Research in Economic Anthropology 19* (1998): 153–178.

Beattie, John. *Bunyoro: An African Kingdom.* New York: Henry Holt, 1960.

Benedict, Ruth. *Patterns of Culture.* Boston: Houghton Mifflin, 1934.

Benet, Sula. *Abkhasians: The Long-living People of the Caucasus.* New York: Holt, Rinehart and Winston, 1974.

Berger, Helen A. "High Priestess, Mother, Leader, Teacher". In *Daughters of the Goddess: Studies of Healing, Identity, and Empowerment.* Walnut Creek, CA: AltaMira Press, 2000.

Berlin, Brent, and Paul Kay. *Basic Color Terms: Their Universality and Evolution.* Berkeley: University of California Press, 1969.

Berman, Judith, "The Production of the Boas-Hunt Kwaw'ala Texts." In *Working Papers for the 26th International Conference on Salish and Neighboring Languages.* Vancouver, B.C.: University of British Columbia, 1991.

Bettelheim, Bruno. *The Uses of Enchantment: The Meaning and Importance of Fairy Tales,* 1977. Reprint. New York: Vintage Press, 1989.

Bhatt, Rakesh M. "World Englishes", *Annual Review of Anthropology* 30: 526–550, 2001.

Bickerton, Derek. "Creole Languages, the Language Biogram Hypothesis and Language Acquisition." In *Handbook of Child Language Acquisition,* edited by William C. Ritchie and Tej K. Bhatia. New York: Academic Press, 1999.

Bird-David, Nurit. "Beyond 'the Hunting and Gathering Mode of Subsistence': Culture-Sensitive Observations on the Nayaka and Other Modern Hunters and Gatherers." *Man 27* (1992): 19–44.

Blok, Anton. *Honour and Violence.* Malden, MA: Blackwell Publishers, 2001.

Blount, Ben G. "African-Americans in the Coastal Zone of Georgia". In *Endangered Peoples of North America: Struggles to Survive and Thrive,* edited by Tom Greaves. Westport: The Greenwood Press, 2002, pp. 159–176

Boas, Franz. Introduction to *Handbook of American Indian Languages,* 1911. Reprint. Lincoln: University of Nebraska Press, 1966.

_____. *Kwakiutl Ethnography,* edited by Helen Codere. Chicago: University of Chicago Press, 1966.

Botiveau, Bernard. "Islamic Family Law in the French Legal Context." *Cambridge Anthropology 16* (1992/1993): 85–96.

Bourdieu, Pierre. *Outline of a Theory of Practice.* Cambridge, England: Cambridge University Press, 1977.

Brandon, George. "Sacrificial Practices in Santeria, an African-Cuban Religion in the United States." In *Africanisms in American Culture,* edited by Joseph E. Holloway. Bloomington: Indiana University Press, 1990.

Brasch, Walter M. *Brer Rabbit, Uncle Remus and the 'Cornfield' Journalist': The Tale of Joel Chandler Harris.* Macon: Mercer University Press, 2000.

Brasher, Brenda. *Give Men That ONLINE RELIGION.* San Francisco: Jossey-Bass, 2001.

Briggs, Jean L. "Conflict Management in a Modern Inuit Community". In *Hunters and Gatherers in the Modern World: Conflict, Resistance, and Self-Determination*, edited by Peter P. Schweiter, Megan Biesele and Robert K. Hitchcock. New York: Berghan Books, 2000.

Brittan, Arthur. "Masculinities and Masculinism" In *The Masculinities Reader*, edited by Stephen M. Whitehead and Frank J. Barrett. Cambridge: Polity Press, pp. 51–55.

Brown, Donald E. *Human Universals.* Philadelphia: Temple University Press, 1991.

Brown, Penelope. "Everyone Has to Lie in Tzeltal". In *Talking to Adults: The Contribution of Multiparty Discourse to Language Acquisition.* Mahwah, N.J.: Lawrence Erlbaum Associates, 2002, pp. 241–276.

Brown, Roger. "The Language of Social Relationship." In *Social Interaction, Social Contest, and Language*, edited by Dan Slobin, Jule Gerhardt, Amy Kyratzis, and Jiansheng Guo. Mahwah, N.J.: Lawrence Erlbaum, 1996.

Brunvand, Jan Harold. "Urban Legends." In *What's So Funny: Humor in American Culture*, edited by Nancy A. Walker. Wilmington, Del.: Scholarly Resources Books, 1998, pp. 145–154.

_____. *The Truth Never Stands in the Way of A Good Story.* Urbana: University of Illinois Press, 2000.

Buckley, Thomas, and Alma Gottlieb (editors). *Blood Magic: The Anthropology of Menstruation.* Berkeley: University of California Press, 1988.

Bucko, Raymond. *The Lakota Ritual of the Sweat Lodge: History and Contemporary Practice.* Lincoln: University of Nebraska Press, 1998.

Bugajski, Janusz. *Ethnic Politics in Eastern Europe.* Armonk, N.Y.: M. E. Sharpe, 1994.

Cai Hua. *A Society without Fathers or Husbands: the Na of China.* New York: Zone Books, 2001.

Caroe, Olaf. *The Pathans: 550 B.C. – A.D. 1957.* New York: Macmillan & Co., 1962.

Carrillo, Jo (ed.). *Readings in American Indian Law: Recalling the Rhythm of Survival.* Philadelphia: Temple University Press, 1998.

Casique, Irene. *Power, Autonomy and Division of Labor In Mexican Dual-Earner Families.* New York: University Press of America, 2001.

Castleden, Rodney. *King Arthur: The truth behind the legend.* New York: Routledge Press, 2000.

Cavalli-Sforza, Luigi Luca. *Genes, Peoples, and Languages.* New York: North Point Press, 2000.

Chagnon, Napoleon. *Yanomamo*, 4th ed. New York: Harcourt Brace Jovanovich, 1997.

Child, Irvin, and Leon Siroto. "BaKwele and American Aesthetic Evaluations Compared." *Ethnology 4* (1965): 349–360.

Chomsky, Noam. "On the Nature, Use, and Acquisition of Language." In *Handbook of Child Language Acquisition*, edited by William C. Ritchie and Tej K. Bhatia. New York: Academic Press, 1999.

Clerk, Christian. " 'That Isn't Really a Pig': Spirit Traditions in the Southern Cook Islands." In *South Pacific Oral Traditions*, edited by Ruth Finnegan and Margaret Orbell. Bloomington: Indiana University Press, 1995, pp. 161–176.

Coates, Jennifer. *Women, Men and Language: A Sociolinguistic Account of Gender Differences in Language*, 2d ed. New York: Longman, 1993.

Coates, Jennifer. *Women Talk: Conversation Between Women Friends.* Cambridge, Mass: Blackwell, 1996.

Cohen, Robin. *Global Diasporas: an Introduction.* Seattle: University of Washington Press, 1997.

Colloredo-Mansfield, Rudi. "The Handicraft Archipelago: Consumption, Migration, and the Social Organization of a Transnational Andean Ethnic Group." *Research in Economic Anthropology 19*: 31–68, 1998.

Comaroff, Jean, and John L. Comaroff. "Christianity and Colonialism in South Africa." *American Ethnologist 13* (1986): 1–19.

Cooper, Frederick, and Ann L. Stoler. "Introduction: Tensions of Empire: Colonial Control and Visions of Rule." *American Ethnologist 16* (1989): 609–621.

Coulihan, Carol. *The Anthropology of Food and Body: Gender, Meaning and Power.* New York: Routledge, 1999.

Coyne, Michael. *The Crowded Prairie: American National Identity in the Hollywood Western.* New York: I. B. Tauris Publishers, 1997.

Croal, Peter and Wes Darou. "Canadian First Nations' experiences with international development". In *Participating in Development: Approaches to indigenous knowledge,* edited by Paula Sillitoe, Allan Bicker and Johan Pottier. London: Routledge, 2002.

Dance, Daryl Cumber, ed. *From My People: 400 Years of African American Folklore.* London: W. W. Norton & Company, 2002.

Daniel, G. Reginald. *More Than Black? Multiracial Identity and the New Racial Order.* Philadelphia: Temple University Press, 2002.

Davenport, William. "Sculpture of the Eastern Solomons." *Expedition 10* (1968): 4–25.

d'Azevedo, Warren. "Mask Makers and Myth in Western Liberia." In *Primitive Art and Society,* edited by Anthony Forge. London: Oxford University Press, 1973, pp. 126–150.

De Boek, Filip. "Of Trees and Kings: Politics and Metaphor among the Aluund of Southwestern Zaire." *American Ethnologist 21* (1994): 451–473.

Degh, Linda. *American Folklore and the Mass Media.* Bloomington: Indiana University Press, 1994.

Dietz, 1977 (in Pader, 1993: 18).

Donald, Leland. *Aboriginal Slavery on the Northwest Coast of North America.* Berkeley: University of California Press, 1997.

Donham, Donald L. "Thinking Temporally or Modernizing Anthropology". *American Anthropologist* (2001) 103: 134–149.

Douglas, Mary. *Natural Symbols: Explorations in Cosmology.* New York: Pantheon Books, 1970.

_____. "Deciphering a Meal." In "Myth, Symbol and Culture." *Daedalus* (Winter 1972): 61–81.

_____. "Witchcraft and Leprosy: Two Strategies of Exclusion." *Man 26* (1991): 723–726.

Draguns, Juris. "Psychological Disorders of Clinical Severity." In *Handbook of Cross-Cultural Psychology,* vol. 6, Psychopathology. Boston: Allyn and Bacon, 1980, p. 174.

Drummond, Lee. *American Dreamtime: A Cultural Analysis of Popular Movies, and Their Implications for a Science of Humanity.* Lanham, England: Rowman and Littlefield, 1996.

Drury, Nevill. *The Elements of Shamanism.* Longmead, England: Element Books, 1989.

Dubin, Margaret. *Native America Collected: The Culture of An Art World.* Albuquerque: University of New Mexico Press, 2001.

Dudwick, Nora. "The Quest for Identity." *Cultural Survival 16,* no. 1 (1992): 26–29.

Duff, Wilson. *Images: Stone: B. C.* Seattle: University of Washington Press, 1975.

Dundes, Alan. "Into the Endzone for a Touchdown: A Psychoanalytic Consideration of American Football." *Western Folklore 37* (1978): 75–88.

Durkheim, Émile. *The Elementary Forms of the Religious Life,* 1915. Reprint. Translated by Joseph W. Swain. New York: Free Press, 1965.

Edwards, Jeanette, Sarah Franklin, Eric Hirsch, Francis Price, and Marilyn Strathern. *Technologies of Procreation: Kinship in the Age of Assisted Conception.* Manchester, England: Manchester University Press, 1993.

El Guindi, Fadwa. *Veil: Modesty, Privacy and Resistance.* Oxford: Berg Publishers, 1999.

Eller, Jack David. *From Culture to Ethnicity to Conflict: An Anthropological Perspective On International Ethnic Conflict.* Ann Arbor: University of Michigan Press, 1999.

Engels, Frederick. *The Origin of the Family, Private Property, and the State,* 1884. Reprint. New York: International Publishers, 1942.

Erdoes, Richard, and Alfonso Ortiz. *American Indian Trickster Tales.* New York: Viking, 1998.

Erera, Pauline Irit. *Family Diversity: Continuity and Change in the Contemporary Family.* Thousand Oaks, California: Sage Publications, 2002.

Erikson, Erik H. *Childhood and Society*, 2d ed. New York: W. W. Norton, 1963.

_____. *Gandhi's Truth: On the Origins of Militant Nonviolence*. New York: W. W. Norton, 1969.

Errington, Shelly. "Recasting Sex, Gender and Power: A Theoretical and Regional Overview." In *Power and Difference: Gender in Island Southeast Asia*, edited by Jane Monnig Atkinson and Shelly Errington. Stanford, Calif.: Stanford University Press, 1990.

Ewing, Katherine. "Consciousness of the state and the experience of the self: the runaway Daughter of a Turkish guest worker". In Power and the Self, edited by Jeannette Marie Mageo. New York: Cambridge University Press, 2000.

Fedorova, Elena G. "Mansi female culture: rules of behavior". In *Identity and Gender in Hunting and Gathering Societies*. Osaka, National Museum of Ethnology, 2001, pp. 227–235.

Feld, Steven. "Dialogic Editing: Interpreting How Kaluli Read Sound and Sentiment." *Cultural Anthropology 2* (1987): 193–210.

Ferguson, R. Brian. *Yanomami Warfare: A Political History*. Santa Fe, N. Mex.: School of American Research Press, 1995.

Finckenauer, James O., and Elin J. Waring. *Russian Mafia in America: Immigration, Culture and Crime*. Boston: Northeastern University Press, 1998.

Fine, Gary Alan. *Manufacturing Tales: Sex and Money in Contemporary Legends*. Knoxville: University of Tennessee Press, 1992.

Finkler, Kaja. *Experiencing the New Genetics: Family and Kinship on the Medical Frontier*. Philadelphia: University of Pennsylvania Press, 2000.

Firth, Raymond. *Elements of Social Organization*. London: Watts, 1951.

Foley, Douglas E. *From Peones to Politicos: Class and Ethnicity in a South Texas Town, 1900–1987*. Austin: University of Texas Press, 1988.

Forge, Anthony (ed.). *Primitive Art and Society*. London: Oxford University Press, 1973.

Foster, Robert. "Commoditization and the emergence of *Kastom* as a Cultural Category: A New Ireland Case in Comparative Perspective." *Oceania 62* (1992): 284–293.

Foucault, Michel. *The History of Sexuality*. Vol. 1, *An Introduction*. Translated by Robert Hurley. New York: Vintage-Random, 1990.

Fox, Richard G. (ed.). *Nationalist Ideologies and the Production of National Cultures*. American Ethnological Society Monograph Series, no. 2, 1990.

Frazier, E. Franklin. *The Negro Church in America*. New York: Schocken Books, 1963.

Freud, Sigmund. *The Future of an Illusion*. London: Hogarth Press, 1928.

Fried, Morton. *The Notion of Tribe*. Menlo Park, Calif.: Cummings Publishing, 1975.

Friedman, Robert L. *Red Mafiya: How the Russian Mob Has Invaded America*. Boston: Little, Brown, 2000.

Fromm, Erich. "Individual and Social Origins of Neurosis." *American Sociological Review 9* (1944): 38–44.

Fuller, Chris. "Legal Anthropology, Legal Pluralism and Legal Thought." *Anthropology Today* no. 31 (1994): 9–12.

Gaffin, Dennis. "Production of Emotion and Social Control: Taunting, Anger and the Rukka in the Faroe Islands. *Ethos* 23 (2): 134–172, 1995.

Gaidzanwa, Rudo. "Indigenisation as Empowerment? Gender and Race in the Empowerment Discourse in Zimbabwe." In *The Anthropology of Power: Empowerment and Disempowerment in Changing Structures*, edited by Angela Cheater. New York: Routledge, 1999.

Gampel, Violent. "Reflections on the prevalence of the uncanny in social violence". In *Cultures under Siege: Collective Violence and Trauma*. Cambridge: Cambridge University Press, 2000.

Geertz, Clifford. "Deep Play: Notes on the Balinese Cockfight." *Daedalus 101* (1972): 1–37.

_____. *The Interpretation of Cultures*. New York: Basic Books, 1973.

_____. "From the Native's Point of View—On the Understanding of Anthropological Understanding." *Bulletin of the American Academy of Arts and Sciences 28*, no. 1 (1974).

Gell, Alfred. *The Art of Anthropology.* New Brunswick: The Athlone Press, 1999

Gellner, Ernest. *Nations and Nationalism.* Ithaca, N.Y.: Cornell University Press, 1983.

Gerschlager, Carline. "Introduction". In *Expanding the Economic Concept of Exchange: Deception, Self–Deception and Illusions,* edited by Caroline Gerschlager. Boston: Kluwer Academic Publishers, 2001.

Ginsburg, Faye D. *Contested Lives: The Abortion Debate in an American Community.* Berkeley: University of California Press, 1989.

Gmelch, George. "Baseball Magic." *Trans-Action 8* (1971).

Goldman, L. R. "A Trickster for All Seasons: The Huli *Iba Tiri.*" In *Fluid Ontologies: Myth, Ritual and Philosophy in the Highlands of Papua New Guinea,* edited by L. R. Goldman and C. Ballard. Westport, Conn.: Bergin and Garvey, 1998, pp. 87–124.

Goldschmidt, Walter. *As you Sow: three Studies in the Social Consequences of Agribusiness.* Glencoe, Ill.: Free Press, 1947

Good, Byron J. "Culture and Psychopathology: Directions for Psychiatric Anthropology." In *New Directions in Psychological Anthropology,* edited by T. Schwartz, G. White, and C. Lutz. Cambridge, England: Cambridge University Press, 1992.

Goodenough, Ward. *Description and Comparison in Cultural Anthropology.* Chicago: Aldine Publishing Co., 1970.

Gottschall, Marilyn. "The Mutable Goddess: Particularity and Eclectism within the Goddess Public. In *Daughters of the Goddess: Studies of Healing, Identity and Empowerment.* Walnut Creek, CA: AltaMira Press, 2000.

Graves, Robert. *The Greek Myths.* New York: George Braziller, 1955.

Greenberg, Joseph. *Language Universals.* The Hague: Mouton, 1966.

Gregor, Thomas. *Anxious Pleasures: The Sexual Lives of an Amazonian People.* Chicago: University of Chicago Press, 1985.

Groning, Karl. *Body Decoration: A World Survey of Body Art.* New York: Vendome Press, 1998.

Grossman, Lawrence S. "Women and Export Agriculture: The Case of Banana Production on St. Vincent in the Eastern Caribbean". In *Women Farmers and Commercial Ventures: Increasing Food Security in Developing Countries,* edited by Anita Spring. Boulder, Lynne Rienner, 2000.

Gudeman, Stephen. *Economics as Culture: Models and Metaphors of Livelihood.* London: Routledge and Kegan Paul, 1986.

Guiliani, Rudolph. *Leadership.* New York: Hyperion, 2002.

Gusterson, Hugh. *Nuclear Rites: A Weapons Laboratory at the End of the Cold War,* 1996.

Guttman, Mathew C. "A (Short) Cultural History of Mexican Machos" In *Gender Matters: Rereading Michelle C. Rosaldo,* edited by Alejandro Lugo and Bill Mauer. Ann Arbor: University of Michigan Press, 2000.

Gutterman, David W. "Postmodernism and the Interrogation of Masculinity". In *The Masculinities Reader,* edited by Stephen M. Whitehead and Frank J. Barrett. Cambridge: Polity Press, 2001, pp. 56–72.

Gwaltney, John Langston. *Drylongso: A Self-Portrait of Black America.* New York: New Press, 1993.

Hall, Michael. "From Marx to Muhammad." *Cultural Survival 16,* no. 1 (1992): 41–44.

Halpern, Joel M., and Barbara K. Halpern. *A Serbian Village in Historic Perspective.* New York: Holt, Rinehart and Winston, 1972.

Hamilton, Gary G. "Culture and Organization in Taiwan's Market Economy." In *Market Cultures: Society and Morality in the New Asian Capitalisms,* edited by Robert W. Hefner. Boulder, Colo.: Westview Press, 1998.

Hammel, Eugene. *Alternative Social Structures and Ritual Relations in the Balkans.* Englewood Cliffs, N.J.: Prentice-Hall, 1968.

Hansen, Karen Tranberg. "Commodity Chains and the International Secondhand Clothing Trade: *Salaula* and the Work of Consumption in Zambia". In *Theory in Economic Anthropology,* edited by Jean Ensminger. Walnut Creek: Altamira Press, 2002.

Hansen, Thomas and Finn Steppputat. *States of Imagination: Ethnographic explorations of the postcolonial state.* Durham, N.C.: Duke University Press.

Harley, George W. *Notes on the Poro in Liberia.* Papers of the Peabody Museum of American Archaeology and Ethnology, Harvard University, vol. 19, no. 2. Cambridge, Mass., 1941.

Harrison, Simon. "The past altered by the present: A Melanesian village after twenty years". *Anthropology Today* 17 (5): 3–9, 2001.

Hawley, C. John. *Postcolonial, Queer: Theoretical Intersections.* Albany: State University of New York Press, 2001.

Headland, Thomas N., and Lawrence A. Reid. "Hunter-Gatherers and Their Neighbors from Prehistory to the Present." *Current Anthropology 30* (1989): 43–66.

Hefner, Robert W. "Introduction: Society and Morality in the New Asian Capitalisms." In *Market Cultures: Society and Morality in the New Asian Capitalisms,* edited by Robert W. Hefner. Boulder, Colo.: Westview Press, 1998.

Henderson, Mary. *Star Wars: The Magic of Myth.* New York: Bantam Books, 1997.

Hernsheim, Eduard. *South Sea Merchant.* Port Moresby: Institute of Papua New Guinea Studies, 1983.

Herskovits, Melville J. *The Myth of the Negro Past,* 1941. Reprint. Boston: Beacon Press, 1951.

Herzfeld, Michael. *A Place in History: Social and Monumental Time in a Cretan Village.* Princeton: Princeton University Press, 1991.

Hewitt, Kim. *Mutilating the Body: Identity in Blood and Ink.* Bowling Green, Ohio: Bowling Green State University Popular Press, 1997.

Hickerson, Nancy P. "Ethnogenesis in the South Plains: Jumano to Kiowa." In *History, Power, and Identity: Ethnogenesis in the Americas, 1492–1992,* edited by Jonathan D. Hill. Iowa City: University of Iowa Press, 1996.

Hicks-Bartlett, Sharon. "Between a Rock and a Hard Place: The Labyrinth of Working and Parenting in a Poor Community. In *Coping with Poverty: The Social Contexts of Neighborhood, Work, and Family in the African-American Community,* edited by Sheldon Danziger and Ann Chih Lin. Ann Arbor: University of Michigan Press, 2000.

Higham, N. J. *King Arthur: Myth Making and History.* London, Routledge, 2002.

Hill, Jonathan D. "Introduction: Ethnogenesis in the Americas, 1492–1992." In *History, Power, and Identity: Ethnogenesis in the Americas, 1492–1992,* edited by Jonathan D. Hill. Iowa City: University of Iowa Press, 1996.

Hirchcock, Robert K. and Megan Biesele. "Introduction". In *Hunters and Gatherers in the Modern World: Conflict, Resistance and Self-Determination,* edited by Peter P. Schweitzer, Megan Biesele and Robert K. Hitchcock. New York: Berghan Books, 2000.

Hobsbawm, E. J. *Nations and Nationalism since 1780: Programme, Myth, Reality,* 2d ed. Cambridge, England: Cambridge University Press, 1992.

Hogbin, Ian. *The Island of Menstruating Men: Religion in Wogeo, New Guinea.* Prospect Heights, Ill.: Waveland Press, 1996.

Hovelsrud-Broda, Greta K. "Arctic Seal-Hunting Households and the Anti-sealing Controversy." *Research in Economic Anthropology 18* (1997): 17–34.

Humphrey, Caroline. *The Unmaking of Soviet Life: Everyday Economies After Socialism.* Ithaca: Cornell University Press, 2002.

Humphrey, Caroline, and Stephen Hugh-Jones (editors). *Barter, Exchange and Value: An Anthropological Approach.* Cambridge, England: Cambridge University Press, 1992.

Humphrey, Caroline and David Sneath. *The End of Nomadism? Society, State and the Environment in Inner Asia.* Durham: Duke University Press, 1999.

Huntingford, G. W. B. *The Nandi of Kenya.* London: Routledge and Kegan Paul, 1953.

Huntsman, Judith. "Fact, Fiction and Imagination: A Tokelau Narrative." In *South Pacific Oral Traditions,* edited by Ruth Finnegan and Margaret Orbell. Bloomington: Indiana University Press, 1995, pp. 124–160.

Ichikawa, Mitsuo. "'Interests in the Present' in the Nationwide Monetary Economy: the Case of the Mbuti Hunters in Zaire". In *Hunters and Gatherers in the Modern World: Conflict, Resistance, and Self-Determination*, edited by Peter P. Schweitzer, Megan Biesele, and Robert K. Hitchcock. New York: Berghahn Books, 2000.

Ingold, Tim. *Evolution and Social Life*. Cambridge, England: Cambridge University Press, 1986.

Jacobs, Sue Ellen, Wesley Thomas, and Sabine Lang. *Two-Spirit People: Native American Gender Identity, Sexuality and Spirituality*. Urbana: University of Illinois Press, 1997.

Jenike, Mark R. "Nutritional ecology: diet, physical activity and body size". In *Hunters and gatherers: an interdisciplinary perspective*, edited by Catherine Panter-Brick, Robert H. Layton and Peter Rowley-Conway. Cambridge: Cambridge University Press, 2001.

Jones, Stephen F. "Indigenes and Settlers." *Cultural Survival 16*, no. 1 (1992): 30–32.

Juillerat, Bernard. *Children of the Blood: Society, Reproduction and Cosmology in New Guinea*. New York: Berg, 1996.

Jules-Rosette, Bennetta. *Black Paris: The African Writers' Landscape*. Urbana: University of Illinois Press, 1998.

Kaberry, Phyllis. "The Abelam Tribe, Sepik District, New Guinea." *Oceania 21* (1940): 233–258, 345–367.

Kaeppler, Adrienne. "Structure Movements in Tonga." In *Society and the Dance*, edited by P. Spencer. Cambridge, England: Cambridge University Press, 1985.

Kamat, Sangeeta. *Development Hegemony: NGOs and the State in India*. New Delhi: Oxford University Press, 2002.

Karmiloff, Kyra and Annette Karmiloff-Smith. *Pathways to Language: From Fetus to Adolescent*. Cambridge: Harvard University Press, 2001.

Kearney, M. "The Local and the Global: The Anthropology of Globalization and Transnationalism." *Annual Review of Anthropology 24* (1995): 547–565.

Keenan, Elinor. "Norm-makers, Norm-breakers: Uses of Speech by Men and Women in a Malagasy Community." In *Explorations in the Ethnography of Speaking*, edited by Richard Bauman and Joel Sherzer. Cambridge, England: Cambridge University Press, 1974.

Keesing, Roger M. "New Lessons from Old: Changing Perspectives on the *Kula*." *Finnish Anthropological Society Transactions 27* (1990): 139–163.

Kelly, Raymond C. *Warless Societies and the Origin of War*. Ann Arbor: University of Michigan Press, 2000.

Kendall, Laurel. "Korean Shamans and the Spirits of Capitalism." *American Anthropologist 98* (1996): 512–527.

———. "The Cultural Politics of 'Superstition' in the Korean Shaman World: Modernity Constructs its Other" In *Healing Powers and Modernity—Traditional Medicine, Shamanism and Science in Asian Societies* edited by Linda H. Connor and Geoffrey Samuel Westport, Conn., 2001, pp. 25–41.

Kenin-Lopsan, M. B. *Shamanic Songs and Myths of Tuva*. Los Angeles: International Society for Trans-Oceanic Research, 1997.

Kent, Susan. "Cultural diversity among African foragers: causes and implications". In *Cultural diversity among twentieth century foragers*, edited by Susan Kent Cambridge: Cambridge University Press, 1996.

Kimmel, Michael S. "Masculinity as Homophobia: Fear, Shame, and Silence in the Construction of Gender Identity". In *The Masculinities Reader*. pp. 266–287, edited by Stephen M. Whitehead and Frank J. Barrett. pp. 266–287. Cambridge: Polity Press, 2001.

Kinoshita, Yasuhito, and Christie W. Kiefer. *Refuge of the Honored: Social Organization in a Japanese Retirement Community*. Berkeley: University of California Press, 1992.

Kipnis, Andrew B. *Producing Guanxi: Sentiment, Self and Subculture in a North China Village*. Durham, N.C.: Duke University Press, 1997.

Kleinman, Arthur, and Byron Good (editors). *Culture and Depression: Studies in the Anthropology and Cross-Cultural Psychiatry of Affect and Disorder*. Berkeley: University of California Press, 1985.

Kluckhohn, Clyde. "Myths and Rituals: A General Theory." *Harvard Theological Review 35* (1942): 45–79.

Kluckholn, Clyde. "Universal Categories of Culture." In *Anthropology Today: an Encyclopedic Inventory,* edited by A. L. Kroeber. Chicago: University of Chicago Press, 1953.

Kochanek, Stanley A. *Patron-Client Politics and Business in Bangladesh.* Newbury Park, Calif.: Sage Publications, 1993.

Kohl, Philip. "Nationalism and Archeology: On the Construction of Nations and the Reconstructions of the Remote Past." *Annual Review of Anthropology 27* (1998): 223–246.

Koskoff, Ellen (ed.). *Women and Music in Cross-Cultural Perspective.* New York: Greenwood Press, 1987.

Kuhn, Steven L. and Mary C. Stiner. "The antiquity of hunter-gatherers". In *Hunter-gatherers: an interdisciplinary perspective,* edited by Catherine Panter-Brick, Robert H. Layton and Peter Rowley-Conwy. Cambridge, Cambridge University Press, 2001.

Kurtz, Donald. *Political anthropology: Power and Paradigms.* Boulder: Westview Press, 2001.

Labov, William. "Co-existent Systems in African-American Vernacular English." In *African-American English: Structure, History and Use,* edited by Salikoko S. Mufwene, John R. Rickford, Guy Bailey, and John Baugh. New York: Routledge, 1998.

Lass, Andrew. "Romantic Documents and Political Monuments: The Meaning—Fulfillment of History in 19th-century Czech Nationalism." *American Ethnologist 15* (1988): 456–471.

Lattas, Andrew. "Sorcery and Colonialism: Illness, Dreams and Death as Political Languages in West New Britain." *Man 28* (1993): 51–78.

Lawrence, John Shelton and Robert Jewett. *The Myth of the American Superhero.* Grand Rapids: William B. Erdmans Publishing Company, 2002.

Layton, Robert H. "Hunter-gatherers, their neighbours and the nation-state". In *Hunter-gatherers": an interdisciplinary perspective,* edited by Catherine Panter-Brick, Robert H. Layton and Peter Rowley-Conwy. Cambridge: Cambridge University Press, 2001.

Leach, Edmund. *Political Systems of Highland Burma: A Study of Kachin Social Structure,* 1954. Reprint. Boston: Beacon Press, 1965.

_____. "Magical Hair." *Journal of the Royal Anthropological Institute of Great Britain and Ireland 88* (1958): 147–164.

_____. "Anthropological Aspects of Language: Animal Categories and Verbal Abuse." In *New Directions in the Study of Language,* edited by Eric Lenneberg. Cambridge, Mass.: MIT Press, 1964, pp. 23–64.

Ledeneva, Alena. "Shadow barter: economic necessity or economic crime?". In *The Vanishing Rouble: Barter Networks and Non-Monetary Transactions in Post-Soviet Societies,* edited by Paul Seabright. Cambridge: Cambridge University Press.

Lee, Mee Sook. "Kinship Structure and Behaviors of Kin-Relatives in Modern Korea." In *Till Death Do Us Part: A Multicultural Anthology on Marriage,* edited by Sandra Lee Browning and R. Robin Miller. Stamford, Conn.: JA Press 1999.

Lepowsky, Maria. "Big Men, Big Women and Cultural Autonomy." *Ethnology 29* (1990): 35–50.

Lett, James W. *Science, Reason and Anthropology: the Principles of Rational Inquiry.* Lanham, Md: Rauman and Littlefield, 1997.

Lévi-Strauss, Claude. *Tristes Tropiques,* 1955. Reprint. Translated by John Russell. New York: Atheneum, 1961.

_____. "The Structural Theory of Myth." Chapter 11 of his *Structural Anthropology.* New York: Basic Books, 1963, pp. 206–231.

_____. *L'Homme Nu: Mythologique 4.* Paris: Plon, 1971.

_____. *La Voie des Masques.* Paris: Plon, 1979.

Levine, Nancy E. "Fathers and Sons: Kinship Value and Validation in Tibetan Polyandry." *Man 22* (1987): 267–286.

LeVine, Robert A. and Karin Norman. "The Infant's Acquisition of Culture: Early Attachment Reexamined in Anthropological Perspective". In *The Psychology Of Cultural Experience*. pp. 83–104, edited by Carmella C. Moore and Holly F. Mathews. Cambridge, England: Cambridge University Press, 2001.

Lewin, Ellen "Weddings Without Marriage: Making Sense of Lesbian and Gay Commitment Rituals". In *Queer Families, Queer Politics: Challenging Culture and the State*, edited by Mary Berstein and Renate Reimann, New York: Columbia University Press, 2001.

Lewis, I. M. *Arguments with Ethnography: Comparative Approaches to History, Politics and Religion.* New Brunswick, N.J.: Athalone Press, 1999.

Lieberman, Philip. *Eve Spoke: Human Language and Human Evolution.* New York: W. W. Norton & Company, 1998.

Lips, Julius. *The Savage Hits Back,* 1937. Reprint. New Hyde Park, N.Y.: University Books, 1966.

LiPuma, Edward. *Encompassing Others: The Magic of Modernity in Melanesia.* Ann Arbor: University of Michigan Press, 2000.

Lizot, Jacques. "Words in the Night: the Ceremonial Dialogue—One Expression of Peaceful Relationships among the Yanomami." In *The Anthropology of Peace and Non-Violence,* edited by Leslie E. Sponsel and Thomas Gregor. Boulder, Colo.: Lynne Rienner, 1994.

Loizos, Peter. "Disenchanting Developers." *Anthropology Today 7,* no. 5 (1991): 1–2.

Loker, William M. "Grit in the Prosperity Machine: Globalization and the Rural Poor In Latin America." In *Globalization and the Rural Poor in Latin America,* edited by William M. Loker. Boulder, Colo.: Lynne Reinner Publishers, 1999.

Louwe, Heleen. "Police-Reformers: 'Big Men' Failing Their Followers." In *Private Politics: A Multi-Disciplinary Approach to "Big Man" Systems,* edited by Martin A. Van Bakel, Renee R. Hogesteijm, and Pieter von de Velde, vol. 1, Studies in Human Society.

Leiden, Holland: Brill, 1986, pp. 174–181.

Lowdin, Per. *Food, Ritual and Society: A Study of Social Structure and Food Symbolism Among the Newars.* Kathmandu, Nepal: Mandala Book Point, 1998.

Lowe, Kathy. "Gendermaps." In *Gender in Early Childhood,* edited by Nicola Yelland. New York: Routledge, 1998.

Lukanuski, Mary. "A Place at the Counter: The Onus of Oneness." In *Eating Culture,* edited by Ron Scapp and Brian Seitz. Albany: State University of New York Press, 1998.

Lutz, Catherine, and Lila Abu-Lughod (editors). *Language and the Politics of Emotion.* Cambridge, England: Cambridge University Press, 1990.

Lynch, John. *Pacific Languages: An Introduction.* Honolulu: University of Hawaii Press, 1998.

Mackey-Kallis, Susan. *The Hero and the Perennial Journey Home in American Film.* Philadelphia: University of Pennsylvania Press. 2001.

Mackie, Jamie. "Business Success among Southeast Asian Chinese." In *Market Cultures: Society and Morality in the New Asian Capitalisms,* edited by Robert W. Hefner. Boulder, Colo.: Westview Press, 1998.

Mageo, Jeannette Marie. "Male Transvestism and Culture Change in Samoa." *American Ethnologist 19* (1992): 443–459.

Mageo, Jeannette Marie. *Theorizing Self in Samoa: Emotions, Genders and Sexualities.* Ann Arbor: University of Michigan Press, 1998.

Magnus, Ralph H. and Eden Naby. *Afghanistan: Mullah, Marx and Mujahid.* Boulder: Westview Press, 2002.

Malinowski, Bronislaw. *Argonauts of the Western Pacific,* 1922. Reprint. New York: E. P. Dutton and Co., 1961.

_____. *The Sexual Life of Savages in Northwestern Melanesia.* New York: Harcourt, Brace and World, 1929.

_____. *Coral Gardens and Their Magic: A Study of the Methods of Tilling the Soil and of Agricultural Rites in the Trobriand Islands.* New York: American Book Co., 1935.

Manganaro, Marc (editor). *Modernist Anthropology: From Fieldwork to Text.* Princeton, N.J.: Princeton University Press, 1990.

Marin, Dalia and Monika Schnitzer. *Contracts in Trade and Transition: The Resurgence of Barter.* Cambridge: The MIT Press, 2002.

Marshall, Yvonne. "Transformations of Nuu-chah-nulth Houses." In *Beyond Kinship: Social and Material Reproduction in House Societies,* edited by Rosemary A. Joyce and Susan D. Gillespie. Philadelphia: University of Pennsylvania Press, 2000.

Mason, Mary Ann. "The Modern Step Family: Problems and Possibilities." In *All Our Families: New Policies for a New Century,* edited by Mary Ann Mason, Arlene Skolnick, and Stephen D. Sugarman. New York: Oxford University Press, 1998.

Maultsby, Portia K. "Africanisms in African-American Music." In *Africanisms in American Culture,* edited by Joseph E. Holloway. Bloomington: Indiana University Press, 1990.

Mauss, Marcel. *The Gift,* 1925. Reprint. Translated by Ian Cunnison. London: Cohen and West, 1954.

McCarthy, Mary. *The Group.* New York: Harcourt, Brace and World. 1963.

McCauley, Martin. *Bandits, Gangsters and The Mafias: Russian, The Baltic States and the CIS since 1992.* New York: Longman, 2001.

McClennon, James. *Wondrous Healing: Shamanism, Human Evolution and the Origin Of Religion.* DeKalb, IL: Northern Illinois University Press, 2002.

McDonough, Christian. "Breaking the Rules: Changes in Food Acceptability among Tharu of Nepal." In *Food Preferences and Taste: Continuity and Change,* edited by Helen Macbeth. Providence, R.I.: Berghahn Books, 1997.

McGrew, W. C. "The intelligent use of tools: Twenty propositions". In *Tools, language, And cognition in human evolution,* edited by K. R. Gibson and T. Ingold, pp. 151–170. Cambridge: Cambridge University Press, 1993.

McKnight, David. *People, Countries, and the Rainbow Serpent: Systems of Classification among the Lardil of Mornington Island.* New York: Oxford University Press, 1999.

Mead, Margaret. *Sex and Temperament in Three Primitive Societies,* 1935. Reprint. New York: Mentor Books, 1950.

Meggitt, Mervyn. " 'Pigs Are Our Hearts!' The Te Exchange Cycle among the Mae Enga." *Human Ecology 1,* no. 2. (1974).

_____. *Blood Is Their Argument: Warfare among the Mae Enga Tribesmen of the New Guinea Highlands.* Palo Alto, Calif.: Mayfield Publishing, 1977.

Meigs, Anna S. "Food Rules and the Traditional Sexual Ideology." In *Cooking, Eating, Thinking: Transformative Philosophies of Food,* edited by Deane W. Curtin and Lisa M. Heldke. Bloomington: Indiana University Press, 1992, pp. 109–118.

Meisch, Lynn A. "The Reconquest of Otavalo, Ecuador: Indigenous Economic Gains and New Power Relations." *Research in Economic Anthropology 19* (1998): 11–30.

Melton, J. Gordon. *Magic, Witchcraft, and Paganism in America: A Bibliography.* New York: Garland Publishing, 1982.

Menges, Karl H. "People, Languages, and Migrations." In *Central Asia: A Century of Russian Rule,* edited by Edward Allworth. New York: Columbia University Press, 1967.

Mertz, Elizabeth. "Legal Language: Pragmatics, Poetics, and Social Power." *Annual Review of Anthropology 23* (1994): 435–455.

Meshorer, Hank. "The Scared Trail to Zuni Heaven: A Study in the Law of Prescriptive Easements." In *Readings in American Indian Law: Recalling the Rhythm of Survival,* edited by Jo Carrillo. Philadelphia: Temple University Press, 1998, pp. 318–323.

Meyer, Stephen. "Work, Play and Power: Masculine Culture on the Automotive Shop Floor, 1930–1960." pp. 13–32. In *Boys and Their Toys: Masculinity, Technology and Class in America,* edited by Roger Horowitz. New York: Routledge, 2001.

Miles, Steven, Kevin Meethan and Alison Anderson. "Introduction: the meaning of consumption: the meaning of change?. In *The Changing Consumer: Markets and Meanings.* New York: Routledge, 2002.

Morgan, David. "Family Gender and Masculinities". In *The Masculinities Reader,* edited by Stephen M. Whitehead and Frank J. Barrett. Cambridge: Polity Press, 2001.

Morgan, Lewis Henry. *Ancient Society,* 1877. Reprint. New York: World Publishing, 1963.

Morgan, Marcyliena. "Theories and Politics in African American English." *Annual Review of Anthropology* 23: 325–345, 1994.

Mufwene, Salikoko S., John R. Rickford, Guy Bailey, and John Baugh (editors.). *African-American English: Structure, History and Use.* New York: Routledge, 1998.

Muhlhausler, Peter. *Linguistic Ecology: Language Change and Linguistic Imperialism in the Pacific Region.* New York: Routledge, 1996.

Munn, Nancy. "The Spatial Presentation of Cosmic Order in Walbiri Iconography." In *Primitive Art and Society,* edited by Anthony Forge. London: Oxford University Press, 1973.

Munroe, Ruth H., and Robert L. Munroe. "Child Development." *In Encyclopedia of Child Development,* edited by David Levinson and Melvin Ember. New York: Henry Holt and Company, 1996.

Murphy, Robert F. "Social Distance and the Veil". *American Anthropologist* 66 (1964): 1257–1274.

Murphy, Yolanda, and Robert F. Murphy. *Women of the Forest,* 2d ed. New York: Columbia University Press, 1985.

Nakamura, Keiko. "The Use of Polite Language by Japanese Preschool Children." In *Social Interaction, Social Context, and Language: Essays in Honor of Susan Ervin-Tripp,* edited by Dan Slobin. Mahwah, N.J.: Lawrence Erlbaum, 1996.

Nakanishi, Hisae. "Power Ideology and Women's Consciousness in Post-Revolutionary Iran." In *Women in Muslim Societies: Diversity within Unity,* edited by Herbert L. Bodman and Nayereh Tohidi. Boulder, Colo.: Lynne Rienner Publishers, 1998.

Nathanson, Paul. *Over the Rainbow: The Wizard of Oz as a Secular Myth of America.* Albany: State University of New York Press, 1991.

Nelson, Katherine and Lea Kessler Shaw. "Developing a Socially Shared Symbolic System". pp. 27–58. In *Language, Literacy and Cognitive Development: The Development And Consequences of Symbolic Communication,* edited by Eric Amsel and James P. Burns. Mawah, N.J.: Lawrence Erlbaum Associates, 2001.

Nettle, Daniel and Suzanne Romaine. *Vanishing Voices: the Extinction of the World's Voices.* New York: Oxford University Press, 2000.

Neville, Gwen Kennedy. *Kinship and Pilgrimage: Rituals of Reunion in American Protestant Culture.* London: Oxford University Press, 1987.

New York Times Magazine Section, August 25th, 2002.

New York Times February 23, 2002. "Truce Accord in Sri Lanka Could Herald Peace Talks".

New York Times April 8, 2002. "After Fierce Fighting, Sri Lanka Struggles with Peace".

New York Times October 10th, 2002. "An Intrusion of Soldiers Threatens Amazon Tribe.

Obeyesekere, Gananath. *The Apotheosis of Captain Cook: European Mythmaking in the Pacific.* Princeton, N.J.: Princeton University Press, 1992.

O'Brien, Kevin A. "Privatizing Security, Privatizing War? The New Warrior Class and Regional Security". In *Warlords in International Relations.* London: MacMillan Press, 1999.

Ochs, Elinor. "From Feelings to Grammar: A Samoan Case Study." In *Language Socialization across Cultures,* edited by Bambi Schieffelin and Elinor Ochs. Cambridge, England: Cambridge University Press, 1986.

O'Connor, Carla. "Dreamkeeping in the Inner City: Diminishing the Divide Between Aspirations and Expectations" In *Coping with Poverty: The Social Context of Neighborhood, Work and Family in the African American Community,* edited by Sheldon Danziger and Ann Chih Lin. Ann Arbor: University of Michigan Press, 2000.

Ogawa, Naoko. "Age, Sex, and Linguistic Judgements". In *Hearing Many Voices,* edited by M. J. Hardman and Anita Taylor. Cresskill, New Jersey: Hampton Press, 2000.

O'Hanlon, Michael. *Reading the Skin: Adornment, Display and Society among the Wahgi.* London: British Museum Publications, 1989.

Orenstein, Catherine. *Little Red Riding Hood Uncloaked: Sex, Morality and the Evolution of a Fairy Tale.* New York: Basic Books, 2002.

Orion, Loretta. *Never Again the Burning Times: Paganism Revived.* Prospect Heights, Ill.: Waveland Press, 1995.

Orlove, Benjamin. "Working in the Field: Perspectives on Globalization in Latin America." In *Globalization and the Rural Poor in Latin America,* edited by William M. Loker. Boulder, Colo.: Lynne Reinner Publishers, 1999.

Ortner, Sherry B. "Theory in Anthropology since the Sixties." *Comparative Studies in Society and History* 26 (1984): 126–165.

O'Toole, Fintan. "The Many Stories of Billy the Kid." *The New Yorker,* vol. 74, no. 10, December 28, 1998—January 4, 1999, pp. 86–98.

Otterbein, Keith F. "The Doves Have Been Heard from, Where are the Hawks". *American Anthropologist* 102 (4): 841–844, 1999.

Pader, Ellen J. "Spatiality and Social Change: Domestic Space Use in Mexico and the United States." *American Ethnologist* 20 (1993): 114–137.

Palmie, Stephan. "Which Centre, Whose Margin? Notes Towards an Archaeology of U.S. Supreme Court Case 91-948, 1993 (*Church of the Lukumi vs. City of Hialeah, South Florida*)." In *Inside and Outside the Law: Anthropological Studies of Authority and Ambiguity,* edited by Olivia Harris. New York: Routledge, 1996, pp. 184–209.

Panter-Brick, Catherine, Robert H. Layton and Peter Rowley-Conwy, editors. *Hunter-Gatherers: An Interdisciplinary Perspective.* Cambridge: Cambridge University Press, 2001.

Parkin, Robert. *Kinship: An Introduction to Basic Concepts.* Malden, Mass.: Blackwell Publishers, 1997.

Patillo-McCoy, Mary. "Negotiating Adolescence in a Black Middle-Class Neighborhood". In *Coping with Poverty: The Social Context of Neighborhood, Work, and Family in the African-American Community,* edited by Sheldon Danziger and Ann Chih Lin. Ann Arbor: University of Michigan Press, 2000.

Peck, Catherine (compiler and annotator). *A Treasury of North American Folk-Tales.* New York: W. W. Norton, 1998.

Pemberton, John III, *Art and oracle: African Art and Rituals of Divination.* New York: Metropolitan Museum of Art, 2000.

Pennycook, Alastair. *Critical Applied Linguistics: A Critical Introduction.* Mahwah, New Jersey, 2001.

Peters, Emrys. "The Proliferation of Segments in the Lineage of the Bedouin of Cyrenaica." *Journal of the Royal Anthropological Institute of Great Britain and Ireland* 90 (1960): 29–53.

Peters, John F. *Life Among the Yanomai: the story of change among the Xilxana on the Mucajai River in Brazil.* Peterborough, Ont.: Broadview Press, 1998.

Pinker, Steve. *The Language Instinct.* New York: Harper Perennial, 1994.

Pitkin, Harvey. "Coyote and Bullhead: A Wintu Text." Native American Text Series. *International Journal of American Linguistics* 2.2. Chicago: University of Chicago Press, 1977, pp. 82–104.

Platt, Katherine. "Cognitive Development and Sex Roles on the Kerkennah Islands of Tunisia." In *Acquiring Culture: Cross-Cultural Studies in Child Development,* edited by Gustav Johada and I. M. Lewis. London: Croom Helm, 1988.

Powdermaker, Hortense. *Life in Lesu,* 1933. Reprint. New York: W. W. Norton, 1971.

Poynton, Cate. *Language and Gender: Making the Difference.* London: Oxford University Press, 1989.

Price, Lisa Leimar. "The Fields Are Filled of Gold: Women's Marketing of Wild Foods from Rice Fields in Southeast Asia and the Impacts of Pesticides and Integrated Pest Management". In *Women Farmers and Commercial Ventures: Increasing Food Security in Developing Countries,* edited by Anita Spring. Boulder: Lynne Rienner, 2000.

Price, Richard. *First Time: The Historical Vision of an Afro-American People.* Baltimore: Johns Hopkins University Press, 1983.

Price, Sally. *Primitive Art in Civilized Places.* Chicago: University of Chicago Press, 1989.

Purkiss, Diane. *Troublesome Things: A History of Fairies and Fairy Stories.* London: Allen Lane, The Penguin Press, 2000.

Radcliffe-Brown, A. R. *Structure and Function in Primitive Society.* Glencoe, Ill.: Free Press, 1952.

_____, and Daryll Forde (editors). *African Systems of Kinship and Marriage.* London: Oxford University Press, 1950.

Ramirez, Rafael L. *What It Means to Be a Man: Reflections on Puerto Rican Masculinity.* New Brunswick: Rutgers University Press, 1999.

Rapp, Rayna. "Reproduction and Gender Hierarchy: Amniocentesis in America." In *Sex and Gender Hierarchies,* edited by Barbara Diane Miller. Cambridge, England: Cambridge University Press, 1993, pp. 108–126.

Rappaport, Roy A. *Pigs for the Ancestors: Ritual in the Ecology of a New Guinea People,* 2d ed. New Haven, Conn.: Yale University Press, 1984.

Reesman, Jeanne Campbell. *Trickster Lives: Culture and Myth in American Fiction.* Athens: The University of Georgia Press, 2001.

Reichel-Dolmatoff, Elizabeth. "Foreword." In *Body Decoration: A World Survey of Body Art,* edited by Karl Groning. New York: Vendome Press, 1998.

Reyes, Adelaida. *Songs of the Caged, Songs of the Free: Music and the Vietnamese Refugee Experience.* Philadelphia: Temple University Press, 1999.

Rich, Paul B. "Introduction". In *Warlords in International Relations,* edited by Paula B. Rich. London: Macmillan Press, Ltd. 1999a.

_____. "The Emergence and Significance of Warlordism in International Politics". In *Warlords in International Relations,* edited by Paul B. Rich. London: Macmillan Press, Ltd. 1999b.

Richards, Audrey. *Land, Labour and Diet in Northern Rhodesia: An Economic Study of the Bemba Tribe.* London: Oxford University Press, 1961.

Rickford, John R. "The Creole Origins of African-American Vernacular English: Evidence from Copula Absence." In *African-American English: Structure, History and Use,* edited by Salikoko S. Mufwene, John R. Rickford, Guy Bailey, and John Baugh. New York: Routledge, 1998.

Riekse, Robert J., and Henry Holstege. *Growing Older in America.* New York: McGraw-Hill, 1996.

Ritchie, William C. "Child Language Acquisition: Introduction, Foundations, and Overview." In *Handbook of Child Language Acquisition,* edited by William C. Ritchie and Tej K. Bhatia. New York: Academic Press, 1999.

Roscoe, Will. *Changing Ones: Third and Fourth Genders in Native North America.* New York: St. Martin's Press, 1998.

Rosman, Abraham, and Paula G. Rubel. "Structural Patterning in Kwakiutl Art and Ritual." *Man 25* (1990): 620–640.

_____. "Colonialism and the Efflorescence of Warfare". In *War and Society,* edited by Stephen P. Reyna and R. E. Downs. London: Gordon and Breach, Publishers .

Rowley-Coney, Peter. "Time, change and the archaeology of hunter-gathers: how original is the 'Original Affluent Society"? In *Hunter-gathers: an interdisciplinary perspective",* edited by Catherine Panter-Brick, Robert H. Layton and Peter Rowley-Conwy. Cambridge, Cambridge University Press, 2001.

Rubel, Paula G. *The Kalmyk Mongols: A Study in Continuity and Change.* Indiana University Publications, Uralic and Altaic Series, Vol.64. Bloomington: Indiana University Press, 1967.

Rubel, Paula G., and Abraham Rosman. *Your Own Pigs You May Not Eat.* Chicago: University of Chicago Press, 1978.

Sahlins, Marshall. *Islands of History.* Chicago: University of Chicago Press, 1985.

_____. "What Is Anthropological Enlightenment? Some Lessons of the Twentieth Century." *Annual Review of Anthropology 28* (1999): i–xxiii.

Salaff, Janet W. *Working Daughters of Hong Kong: Filial Piety or Power in the Family?* New York: Columbia University Press, 1995.

Saler, Benson. *Conceptualizing Religion: Eminent Anthropologists, Transcendent Natives, and Unbounded Categories.* Leiden, Holland: E. J. Brill, 1993.

Salter, Frank K. "From Mafia to freedom fighters: Questions raised by ethology and sociobiology". In *Risky Transactions: Trust, Kinship and Ethnicity,* edited by Frank K. Salter. New York: Berghan Books, 2002.

Saussure, Ferdinand de. *Course in General Linguistics,* 1915. Reprint. New York: McGraw-Hill, 1966.

Sax, William S. *Dancing the Self: Personhood and Performance in the Pandav Lila Of Garwal.* New York: Oxford University Press, 2000.

Scaglion, Richard. "Customary Law Development in Papua New Guinea." In *Anthropological Praxis—Translating Knowledge into Action,* edited by Robert M. Wulff and Shirley J. Fiske. Boulder, Colo.: Westview Press, 1987.

Schiefenhovel, Wulf, and Ingrid Bell-Krannhals. "Of Harvests and Hierarchies: Securing Staple Food and Social Position in the Trobriand Islands." In *Food and the Status Quest: An Interdisciplinary Perspective,* edited by Polly Wiessner and Wulf Schiefenhovel. Providence, R.I.: Berghahn Books, 1996.

Schieffelin, Bambi. "Teasing and Shaming in Kaluli Children's Interactions." In *Language Socialization across Cultures,* edited by Bambi Schieffelin and Elinor Ochs. Cambridge, England: Cambridge University Press, 1986.

Schieffelin, Bambi B., and Elinor Ochs. "The Microgenesis of Competence: Methodology in Language Socialization." In *Social Interaction, Social Context, and Language,* edited by Dan I. Slobin, Julie Gerhardt, Amy Kyratzis, and Jiansheng Guo. Mahwah, N.J.: Lawrence Erlbaum, 1996.

Schneider, David M. *American Kinship,* 2d ed. Chicago: University of Chicago Press, 1980.

————. *A Critique of the Study of Kinship.* Ann Arbor: University of Michigan Press, 1984.

Schrauwers, Albert. "'It's Not Economical': The Market Roots of a Moral Economy in Highland Sulawesi". In *Transforming the Indonesian Uplands: Marginality, Power and Production,* edited by Tania Murray Li. New York: Harwood Academic Publishers, 1999.

Schroeder, Ingo W. and Bettina E. Schmidt. "Introduction: Violent imaginaries and violent practices" In *Anthropology of Violence and Conflict,* New York: Routledge, 2001.

Schulz, Dorothea E. "Morals of Praise: Broadcast Media and the Commoditization of Jeli Praise Performances in Mali." *Research in Economic Anthropology 19* (1998): 117–132.

Seabright, Paul. *The Vanishing Rouble.* Cambridge: Cambridge University Press, 2000.

Sebba, Mark. *Contact Languages: Pidgins and Creoles.* New York: St. Martin's Press, 1997.

Segal, Robert A. *Theorizing about Myth.* Amherst: University of Massachusetts Press, 1999.

Seligmann, Linda J, editor. *Women Traders in Cross-Cultural Perspective: Mediating identities, Marketing Wares.* Stanford: Stanford University Press, 2001.

Seneviratne, H. L. "Buddhist monks and ethnic politics". *Anthropology Today* 17:15–21, 2001.

Sharp, Leslie A. "Commodified Kin: Death, mourning, and competing claims on the bodies of organ donors in the United States. *American Anthropologist* 103(2001): 112–133.

Sherman, Suzanne (ed.). *Lesbian and Gay Marriage: Private Commitments, Public Ceremonies.* Philadelphia: Temple University Press, 1992.

Shott, Michael J. "On Recent Trends in the Anthropology of Foragers: Kalahari Revisionism and Its Archaeological Implications." *Man* 27 (1992): 843–871.

Shweder, Richard A. "Rethinking the Object of Anthropology and Ending Up Where Kroeber and Kluckhohn Began" *American Anthropologist* 103:437–440, 2001.

Shweder, Richard, Manamohan Mahapatra, and Joan G. Miller. "Culture and Moral Development." In *Cultural Psychology: Essays on Comparative Human Development,* edited by James Stigler, Richard Shweder, and Gilbert Herdt. Cambridge, England: Cambridge University Press, 1990.

Sillitoe, Paul. "Participant observation to participatory development: making anthropology work. In *Participating Development: Approaches to indigenous knowledge,* edited by Paul Sillitoe, Alan Bicker and John Pottier. London: Routledge, 2002.

Skolnick, Arlene. "Solomon's Children: Psychological Parenthood, Attachment Theory, and the Best Interests Standard." In *All Our Families: New Policies for a New Century,* edited by Mary Ann Mason, Arlene Skolnick, and Stephan D. Sugarman. New York: Oxford University Press, 1998.

Smith, W. Robertson. *Lectures on the Religion of the Semites.* New York: D. Appleton, 1889.

Smitherman, Geneva. "Word from the Hood: The Lexicon of African-American Vernacular English." In *African-American English: Structure, History and Use,* edited by Salikoko S. Mufwene, John R. Rickford, Guy Bailey, and John Baugh. New York: Routledge, 1998.

Sollars, Werner (ed.). *The Invention of Ethnicity.* New York: Oxford University Press, 1989.

Spiro, Melford E. "Religion: Problems of Definition and Explanation." In *Anthropological Approaches to the Study of Religion,* edited by Michael Banton. A. S. A. Monograph, no. 3. London: Tavistock Publications, 1966, pp. 85–126.

Sponsel, Leslie. "Response to Otterbein". *American Anthropologist* 102 (4): 837–841, 2000.

Ssorin-Chaikov, Nickolai. "Bear skins and macaroni: the social life of things at the margins of a Siberian state collective". In *The Vanishing Rouble": Barter Networks and Non-Monetary Transactions in Post-Soviet Societies,* edited by Paul Seabright. Cambridge: Cambridge University Press, 2000.

Stacey, Judith. "Gay and Lesbian Families: Queer Like Us." In *All Our Families: New Policies for a New Century,* edited by Mary Ann Mason, Arlene Skolnick, and Stephan D. Sugarman. New York: Oxford University Press, 1998.

Stack, Carol B. *All Our Kin: Strategies for Survival in a Black Community.* New York: Harper and Row, 1974.

Starrett, Gregory. "The Political Economy of Religious Commodities in Cairo." *American Anthropologist* 97 (1995): 51–68.

Stern, Stephen, and John Allan Cicala (editors). *Creative Ethnicity: Symbols and Strategies of Contemporary Ethnic Life.* Logan, Utah: Utah State University Press, 1991.

Steward, Julian. *Theory of Culture Change.* Urbana: University of Illinois Press, 1955.

Stoller, Eleanor P. "Informal Exchanges with Non-Kin among Retired Sunbelt Migrants: A Case Study of a Finnish American Retirement Community." *Journal of Gerontology: Social Sciences 53B* (1998): S287–S298.

Stoller, Paul. "Ethnographers as Texts/Ethnographers as *griots.*" *American Ethnologist 21* (1994): 353–366.

_____. *Money Has No Smell: the Africanization of New York City.* Chicago: University of Chicago Press, 2002.

Strathern, Andrew, and Marilyn Strathern. *Self-Decoration in Mount Hagen.* London: Gerald Duckworth, 1971.

Strathern, Marilyn. *Reproducing the Future: Essays on Anthropology, Kinship and the New Reproductive Technologies.* New York: Routledge, 1992.

Sturm, Circe. *Blood Politics: Race, Culture, and Identity in the Cherokee Nation of Oklahoma.* Berkeley: University of California Press, 2002.

Suarez-Orozo, Marcelo M. and Antonius C. G. M. Robben. "Interdisciplinary perspectives on violence and trauma". In *Cultures under Siege; Collective Violence and Trauma.* Cambridge: Cambridge University Press, 2000.

Suchman, Lucy A. "Building Bridges: Practice-Based Ethnographies of Contemporary Technology" In *Anthropological Perspectives on Technology,* edited by Michael Brian Schiffer. Albuquerque: New Mexico Press, 2001.

Sullivan, Nancy. "Inside Trading: Postmodernism and the Social Drama of *Sunflowers* in the 1980s Art World." In *The Traffic in Culture: Refiguring Art and Anthropology,* edited by George E. Marcus and Fred R. Myers. Berkeley: University of California Press, 1995.

Suryana, Krisnawati, "From Home Gardens: Resource Stabilization and Rural Differentiation in Upland Java". In *Transforming the Indonesian Uplands: Marginality, Power and Production,* edited by Tania Murray Li. New York: Harwood Academic Publishers, 1999.

Sutherland, Anne. *Gypsies—The Hidden Americans.* Prospect Heights, Ill.: Waveland Press, 1986.

Tambiah, S. J. "Animals Are Good to Think about the Good to Prohibit." *Ethnology 8* (1969): 423–459.

_____. *Sri Lanka: Ethnic Fratricide and the Dismantling of Democracy.* Chicago: University of Chicago Press, 1986.

_____. "Ethnic Fratricide in Sri Lanka: An Update." In *Ethnicities and Nations: Processes of Interethnic Relations in Latin America, Southeast Asia, and the Pacific,* edited by Remo Guidieri, Francesco Pellizzi, and Stanley J. Tambiah. Austin: University of Texas Press, 1988.

Tatla, Darshan Singh. *The Sikh Diaspora: The Search for Statehood.* London: UCL Press, 1999.

Tattersall, Ian. *Becoming Human: Evolution and Human Uniqueness.* New York: Harcourt Brace, 1998.

Tausig, Michael. *"Culture of Terror-Space of Death: Roger Casement's Putumayo Report and the Explanation of Torture".* In *The Anthropology of Politics: A Reader in Ethnography, Theory, and Critique.* Oxford, UK: Blackwell Publishers, 2002 (1984)

Thomas, Wesley. *Two-spirit People: Native American Gender Identity, Sexuality, and Spirituality.* Urbana: University of Illinois Press, 1997.

Thomason, Sarah G. *Contact Languages: A Wider Perspective.* Philadelphia: John Benjamins Publishing, 1997.

Tomasello, Michael and Elizabeth Bates. "Introduction". In *Language Development: The Essential Readings,* edited by Michael Tomasello and Elizabeth Bates. Malden: Blackwells, 2001, pp. 1–11.

Townsend, Joan B. "Shamanism". In *Anthropology of Religion: a handbook.* Westport, Conn.: Greenwood Press, 1997.

Trotman, C. James. "Introduction: *Multiculturalism: Roots and Realities".* In *Multiculturalism: Roots and Realities,* edited by C. James Trotman. Bloomington: Indiana University Press, 2002.

Turino, Thomas. "The History of a Peruvian Panpipe Style and the Politics of Interpretation." In *Ethnomusicology and Modern Music History,* edited by S. Blum, P. Bohlman, and D. Neuman. Urbana: University of Illinois Press, 1991.

Turner, Jonathan H. *On the Origins of Human Emotions: A Sociological Inquiry into the Evolution of Human Affect.* Stanford: Stanford University Press, 2000.

Turner, Lorenzo. *Africanisms in the Gullah Dialect,* 1949. Reprint. New York: Arno Press, 1968.

Turner, Victor. "Betwixt and Between: The Liminal Period in Rites de Passage." In his *The Forest of Symbols: Aspects of Ndembu Ritual.* Ithaca, N.Y.: Cornell University Press, 1967, pp. 93–111.

Tylor, Edward B. *Primitive Culture: Researches into the Development of Mythology, Philosophy, Religion, Language, Art and Custom,* 2 vols. London: John Murray, 1874.

Van Gennep, Arnold. *The Rites of Passage,* 1909. Reprint. Translated by Monika B. Vizedom and Gabrielle Caffee. Chicago: University of Chicago Press, 1960.

Verkaaik, Oskar. "The Captive State: Corruption, Intelligence Agencies and Ethnicity in Pakistan. In *States of the Imagination: Ethnographic Explorations of the Postcolonial State,* edited by Thomas Blom Hansen and Finn Stepputat. Durham: Duke University Press, 2001.

Vogelsang, Willem. *The Afghans.* Malden: Blackwell Press, 2002.

Von Bremen, Volker. Dynamics of Adaptation to Market Economy among the Ayoreode of Northwest Paraguay". In *Hunters and Gatherers in the Modern World: Conflict, Resistance and Self-Determination,* edited by Peter P. Schweitzer, Megan Biesele and Robert K. Hitchcock. New York: Berghan Books, 2000.

Von Hendy, Andrew. *The Modern Construction of Myth.* Bloomington: Indiana University Press, 2002.

Wallerstein, Immanuel M. *The Modern World System: Capitalist Agriculture and the Origins of the European World Economy in the Sixteenth Century.* New York: Academic Press, 1974.

Waterbury, Ronald. " 'Lo Que Dice el Mercado": Development Without Developers in a Oaxacan Peasant Community". In *Globalization and the Rural Poor in Latin America,* edited by William M. Loker. Boulder" Lynn Rienner Publishers, 1999.

Waters, Mary C. *Ethnic Options: Choosing Identities in America.* Berkeley: University of California Press, 1990.

Weber, Max. *The Protestant Ethic and the Spirit of Capitalism.* London: Allen and Unwin, 1930.

Weiner, Annette B. *Women of Value, Men of Renown: New Perspectives in Trobriand Exchange.* Austin: University of Texas Press, 1976.

Weisgrau, Maxine K. *Interpreting Development: Local Histories, Local Strategies.* Lanham, Md.: University Press of America, 1997.

Werbner, Pnina. "Stamping the Earth With the Name of Allah: Zikr and the Sacralizing of Space among British Muslims." *Cultural Anthropology 11* (1996): 309–338.

Westmacott, Richard. *African-American Gardens and Yards in the Rural South.* Nashville: University of Tennessee Press, 1992.

Weston, Kath. *Families We Choose: Lesbians, Gays, Kinship.* New York: Columbia University Press, 1991.

Whalley, Lucy A. "Urban Minangkabau Muslim Women: Modern Choices, Traditional Choices in Indonesia." In *Women in Muslim Societies: Diversity within Unity,* edited by Herbert L. Bodman and Nayereh Tohidi. Boulder, Colo.: Lynne Reiner Publishers, 1998.

White, Leslie. *The Science of Culture.* New York: Farrar, Straus and Giroux, 1949.

_____. *The Evolution of Culture.* New York: McGraw-Hill, 1959.

Whitehead, Stephen M. and Frank J. Barrett. *The Masculinities Reader.* Cambridge: Polity Press, 2001.

Whitehead, Stephen M. and Frank J. Barrett. "The Sociology of Masculinity". In *The Masculinities Reader,* edited by Stephen M. Whitehead and Frank J. Barrett. Cambridge: Polity Press, 2001.

Wierzbiecka, Anna. *Emotions across Languages and Cultures: Diversity and Universals.* Paris: Cambridge University Press, 1999.

Willigen, John Van. *Applied Anthropology: An Introduction.* 3rd Edition. Wesport: Bergin and Garvey, 2002.

Wilson, Monica. *Good Company,* 1951. Reprint. Boston: Beacon Press, 1964.

_____. *For Men and Elders: Change in the Relations of Generations and of Men and Women among the Nyakyusa-Ngonde People 1875–1971.* New York: Africana Publishing, International African Institute, 1977.

Winkelman, Michael. *Shamanism: The Neural Ecology of Consciousness and Healing.* Westport: Bergin and Garvey, 2000.

Wolf, Eric R. *Europe and the People without History.* Berkeley: University of California Press, 1982.

Woodbury, Anthony C. "A Defense of the Proposition, 'When a Language Dies, A Culture Dies.' " *Texas Linguistic Forum 33* (1993): 1–15.

Wrangham, Richard W., James Holland Jones, Greg Laden, David Pillbeam and Nancy Lou Conklin-Brittain. "The Ran and the Stolen: Cooking, and the ecology of human origins, *Current Anthropology* 103(2001): 112–133.

Yai, Olabiyi Babalola. "In Praise of Metonymy: The Concepts of 'Tradition' and 'Creativity' in the Transmission of Yoruba Artistry over Time and Space." In *The Yoruba Artist: New Theoretical Perspectives on African Arts,* edited by Rowland Abiodun, Henry J. Drewal, and John Pemberton III. Washington, D.C.: Smithsonian Institution Press, 1994.

Young, Alfred Jr. "On the Outside Looking In: Low-Income Black Men's Conceptions of Work Opportunity and the Good Job". In *Coping with Poverty: The Social Context Neighborhood, Work and Family in the African-American Community,* edited by Sheldon Danziger and Ann Chih Lin. Ann Arbor: University of Michigan Press, 2000.

Yusufzai, Rahimullah. "The Influence of Durrani-Ghalji Rivalry on Afghan Politics". In *Afghanistan: Past, Present and Future.* Islamabad: Institute of Regional Studies, 1997 pp. 76–124.

Zaleski, Jeff. *The Soul of Cyberspace; How New Technology is Changing Our Spiritual Lives.* San Francisco: Harper Edge, 1997.

Zicker, John P. "Kinship and Exchange among the Dolgan and Nganasan of Northern Siberia." *Research in Economic Anthropology 19* (1998): 191–238.

GLOSSARY

acculturation   the process of culture change resulting from the contact between two cultures.

achieved status   position in a social structure dependent upon personal qualifications and individual ability.

adaptation   the process in which a population or society alters its culture to better succeed in its total environment.

affinal link   connections between kin groups established by marriage.

age grade   categories of individuals of the same age that are recognized by being given a name and that crosscut an entire society.

age set   a group of individuals of the same age that moves as a unit through successive age grades.

agency   refers to the fact that individuals are active responders to their culture.

alliance   a linkage between kin groups established through marriage for the mutual benefit of the two groups.

allomorph   a variant form of a morpheme.

allophone   a variant form of a phoneme.

ancestor-oriented group   a social unit that traces kin relationships back to a common ancestor.

animism   a belief in the spiritual or noncorporeal counterparts of human beings.

ascribed status   an inherited position in the social structure.

authority   an institutionalized position of power.

avunculocal residence   a form of postmarital residence in which the bride goes to live with her husband after he has moved to live with his mother's brother.

band organization   a type of social group with a fixed membership that comes together annually for a period to carry out joint ritual and economic activities.

barter   an immediate exchange of unlike objects, which may involve bargaining.

berdache   Native American term for a man who assumes a woman's role and dresses as a woman.

Big Man structure   an achieved position of leadership in which the group is defined as the Big Man and his followers.

bilateral cross cousin   cross cousins through both the mother's and father's side.

bilateral societies   societies with kindreds but without unilineal descent groups.

bilocal residence a form of postmarital residence in which husband and wife alternate between living with the husband's relatives for a period of time and then with the wife's relatives.

boundary maintenance the ways in which a social group maintains its individual identity by separating itself from the dominant society.

bride service a custom whereby the groom works for the bride's family before marriage.

bridewealth payments payments made by the groom's family to the family of the bride.

cargo cult a particular type of revitalization movement that first appeared in the early twentieth century in Melanesia and represents a synthesis of old and new religious beliefs.

caste system a grouping of economically specialized, hierarchically organized, endogamous social units.

chieftainship a type of political organization in which fixed positions of leadership are present along with a method for succession to those positions.

clan a social group based on common descent but not necessarily common residence.

clan totem an animal from which members of a clan believe themselves descended and with whom they have a special relationship that may prohibit the eating of that animal.

cognate a relative traced through either the mother's or the father's line.

cognate (linguistic definition) words in two different languages that resemble one another and demonstrate that the two languages are related to one another.

cognatic rule of descent a rule of descent in which group membership may be traced through either the father or the mother.

collateral relative a relative not in the direct line of descent.

community a naturally bounded social unit.

compadrazgo ritual godparenthood found in Mediterranean Europe and Latin America.

comparative approach comparing societies to uncover similarities and reveal differences.

components the criteria used to characterize and differentiate any kind of category.

consumption the process by which products are used by humans.

corporate descent group a social group based upon common descent that owns property in common and extends beyond the lifetime of any one individual.

creole a pidgin language acquired by children as their native language.

cross cousins children of one's mother's brother or one's father's sister.

cultural evolution the anthropological theory that refers to the development of culture into ever more complex forms.

cultural relativism the emphasis on the unique aspects of each culture, without judgments or categories based on one's own culture.

cultural rules internalized rules of behavior covering all aspects of life.

cultural universals cultural features that are to be found in all societies.

culture the way of life of a people, including their behavior, the things they make, and their ideas.

dala the Trobriand matrilineal subclan.

delayed exchange the return of goods or of women a generation after their giving; associated with preference for marriage with father's sister's daughter.

demonstrated descent   descent in which kinship can be traced by means of written or oral genealogies back to a founding ancestor.

dialects   variations within a single language between one speech community and another.

diaspora   a population spread from its original homeland to other countries, which continues to maintain contact with that homeland.

diffusion   the process by means of which a culture trait that originates in one society spreads to another.

direct reciprocal exchange   a continuing exchange of like for like between two parties.

distinctive features   see *components*.

distribution   the manner in which products circulate through a society.

double descent   the presence of matrilineal and patrilineal descent rules in a single society.

dowry   goods that are given by the bride's family to the groom's family at marriage.

duolocal residence   a postmarital rule of residence in which husband and wife live with their respective kinsmen, apart from one another.

ebene   hallucinogenic substance used by the Yanomamo.

ego-oriented group   a kinship unit defined in terms of a particular ego.

enculturation   the process by which culture is learned and acquired by particular individuals.

endogamy   a rule requiring group members to marry within their own group.

ethnic groups   distinctive groups within a state who preserve cultural items from their past.

ethnocentrism   the idea that what is present in one's own culture represents the natural and best way to do things.

ethnogenesis   the creation of a new ethnic group.

ethnonationalism   the desire of ethnic groups within a state to have their own nation-state.

ethnosemantics   the anthropological investigation of native systems of classification.

exogamy   a rule requiring group members to marry outside their own social group.

extended family   several related nuclear families living together in a single household.

Fourth World peoples   oppressed tribal peoples living in Third World nations.

fraternal polyandry   a form of marriage in which a woman is simultaneously married to several brothers.

function   the way a particular unit or structure operates and what it does.

generalized exchange   a form of marriage in which women move from wife-givers to wife-takers but never in the opposite direction.

globalization   the worldwide connection between societies based upon the existence of global market connections and the spread of cultural items everywhere.

godparenthood   see *compadrazgo*.

government   the process by which those in office make and implement decisions on behalf of an entire group in order to carry out commonly held goals.

grammar   the complete description of a language, including phonology, morphology, and syntax.

guardian spirit   among North American native peoples, an animal spirit that becomes the protector of an individual as a result of his quest for a vision.

gumlao   the egalitarian form of the Kachin political organization.

gumsa   the chieftainship form of the Kachin political organization, in which wife-givers are higher in rank than wife-takers.

hekura   small, humanlike supernatural creatures that are part of the Yanomamo religious belief system.

hortatory ritual   an exhortation to the supernatural to perform some act.

horticulture   a form of cultivation in which crops are grown in gardens without the use of a plow.

idiolect   the distinctive linguistic features or cultural features characteristic of an individual.

incest taboo   prohibition on sexual relations between certain categories of close relatives.

Informal leadership   a type of political organization in which there is no single political leader but rather leadership is manifested intermittently.

influence   the ability to persuade others to follow one's lead when one lacks the authority to command them.

innovation   the process of bringing about cultural change through the recombination of existing ideas into creative new forms.

joint family   a type of extended family in which married brothers and their families remain together after the death of their parents.

kaiko   a lengthy Maring religious ceremony.

kayasa   a competitive period of feasting, including a competitive giving of yams to the chief, and games like cricket among the Trobrianders.

kindred   a kin group oriented in terms of a particular individual.

kinship terminology   a set of terms used to refer to relatives.

kula   an exchange system involving one kind of shell valuables moving in a clockwise direction and another kind moving in a counterclockwise direction that links the Trobriand Islanders to a circle of neighboring islands.

langue   refers to language and its grammatical rules in contrast to parole which refers to individual speech.

levirate   a rule whereby the widow of a deceased man must marry his brother.

lewa   Wogeo spirits represented by masks.

liminal period   the in-between stage in a rite-of-passage ceremony when the individual has not yet been reincorporated into society.

lineages   unilineal descent groups in which descent is demonstrated.

lineal relative   a relative in the direct line of descent.

linguistic imperialism   the imposition by a dominant group of its language on minority speakers of other languages.

linguistic relativity   a point of view that emphasizes the uniqueness of each language and the need to examine it in its own terms.

malanggan   a term referring to New Ireland mortuary ritual, as well as the carvings displayed at such a ritual.

mana   belief in an impersonal supernatural force or power that is found in all aspects of nature.

manau   a Kachin religious ceremony consisting of a feast and sacrifice to the spirits.

markedness   the process whereby a category (the marked category) is distinguished from a larger, more inclusive category (the unmarked category) by the presence of a single attribute.

matrilineal rule of descent   a rule stating that a child belongs to his or her mother's group.

maximizing   the concept in economic anthropology whereby individuals are seen as interpreting economic rules to their own advantage.

mayu/dama   Kachin lineage categories; wife-giving lineages are *mayu*, and wife-taking lineages are *dama*.

metaphor   an analytical concept in which one idea stands for another because of some similarity they are seen to share.

metonym   the symbolic substitution of one of the constituent parts for the whole.

moieties   a grouping based upon descent in which the entire society is divided into halves.

monogamy   marriage with only one spouse at a time.

morpheme   the smallest unit of a language conveying meaning.

nat   spirits of the Kachin supernatural world.

nation   a sovereign political state with a single national culture.

nation-state   see *nation.*

nativistic movements   religious cults that develop in periods of drastic cultural change and synthesize traditional cultural elements with newly introduced ones.

neolocal residence   a rule of postmarital residence in which the newly married couple forms an independent household.

nibek   Wogeo spirits represented by flutes.

nomadic pastoralists   societies completely, or almost completely, dependent upon herds of domesticated animals.

nuclear family   a family consisting of husband, wife, and their unmarried children.

numaym   cognatic descent group of the Kwakiutl.

office   a recognized political position.

parallel cousins   the children of two brothers or of two sisters.

parole   see *langue.*

participant observation   the anthropological method of collecting data by living with other people, learning their language, and understanding their culture.

patrilineal rule of descent   a rule stating that a child belongs to his or her father's group.

patron-client relationship   a hierarchical relationship in which the superior (the patron) acts as an intermediary and protector of the inferior (the client) vis-à-vis the national government.

phonemes   the minimal sound units that make up a language.

pidgin   a lingua franca that developed when people speaking different languages but no common language needed to communicate with one another.

political economy   the interpretation of politics and economy.

politics   the competition for political positions and for power.

polyandry   marriage in which one woman has several husbands at one time.

polygamy   marriage with plural spouses, either husbands or wives.

polygyny   marriage in which one man has several wives at one time.

Poro Society   secret society associated with the use of masks, found in Liberia and Sierra Leone.

postmarital residence rule   a rule that states where a couple should live after marriage.

postmodernism   refers to a contemporary point of view that is antiscientific and opposed to making generalizations in anthropological thinking.

potlatch   a large-scale ceremonial distribution of goods found among the indigenous peoples of the Northwest Coast of North America.

power   the ability to command others to do certain things and get compliance from them.

primogeniture   a rule of inheritance of property or office by the firstborn child.

private symbols   symbols that individuals create out of their own experience and that they do not share with other members of their society.

production   the process whereby a society uses the tools and energy sources at its disposal and its own people's labor to create the goods necessary for supplying itself.

proto-language   ancestral form of a language arrived at by reconstruction.

public symbols   symbols used and understood by the members of a society.

reciprocal exchange   a type of exchange system in egalitarian societies in which women or material goods of equal value continue to be exchanged over generations.

revitalization movements   see *nativistic movements.*

rites of intensification   communal rituals celebrated at various points in the yearly cycle.

rites of passage   communal rituals held to mark changes in status as individuals progress through the life cycle.

sagali   a large-scale ceremonial distribution among the Trobriand Islanders.

segmentary lineage system   a descent system, typically patrilineal, in which the largest segments are successively divided into smaller segments, like branches of a tree.

serial monogamy   the practice of marrying a series of spouses, one after the other.

shaman   a ritual specialist whose primary function is to cure illness.

shifting cultivation   a type of horticulture in which new gardens are made every few years, when the soil is exhausted.

sister exchange   a marriage pattern in which two men marry each other's sisters.

social organization   behavioral choices that individuals make in connection with the social structure.

social role   the behavior associated with a particular social status in a society.

social status   the position an individual occupies in a society.

social structure   the pattern of social relationships that characterizes a society.

society   a social grouping characterizing humans and other social animals, differentiated by age and sex.

sociolinguistics   the study of that aspect of language that deals with status and class differences.

sorcery   the learned practice of evil magic.

sororal polygamy   the marriage of a man to several sisters.

sororate   the custom whereby a widower marries his deceased wife's sister.

state   a type of political organization that is organized on a territorial basis and integrated through social stratification rather than through kinship.

status personality   the characteristic personality associated with a social position.

stem family   a two-generation extended family consisting of parents and only one married son and his family.

stipulated descent   a social unit, such as a clan, in which all members consider themselves to be related though they cannot actually trace the genealogical relationship.

structure   a description of parts or elements in relationship to one another.

style   a characterization of the component elements of art and the way those elements are put together.

suaboya   the single kinship term that the Yanomamo use for both female cross cousin and wife.

subcultural variation   cultural differences between communities within a single society.

swidden   see *shifting cultivation.*

syncretism   the integration of older cultural traits into newly adopted cultural practices.

syntax   that part of grammar that deals with the rules of combination of morphemes.

Te   the ceremonial distribution of pigs and pork among the Mae Enga of Papua New Guinea.

technology   that part of culture by means of which people directly exploit their environment.

total social phenomena   large-scale rituals that integrate all aspects of society—economic, political, kinship, religion, art, etc.

tribe   a unit used by colonial powers to refer to groups with a common language and culture.

tschambura   among the Abelam, partners who exchange long yams with one another.

ultimogeniture   a rule of inheritance of property or office by the last-born child.

unilineal descent group   a kin group, such as a clan, in which membership is based on either matrilineal or patrilineal descent.

urigubu   a Trobriand harvest gift given yearly by a man to his sister's husband.

uxorilocal residence   a rule of postmarital residence whereby the newly married couple resides with the relatives of the bride.

virilocal residence   a rule of postmarital residence whereby the newly married couple resides with the relatives of the groom.

vision quest   the search for a protective supernatural spirit through starvation and deprivation.

warabwa   large-scale ceremonial distribution in Wogeo.

warlord   a militarized big man. He and his followers are structurally similar to a faction.

witchcraft   a form of magic practiced by individuals born with this ability.

PHOTO CREDITS

INDEX